The Last Will and Testament of Alexander the Great

An Empire Left to the Strongest

The Last Will and Testament of Alexander the Great

An Empire Left to the Strongest

The Truth Behind the Death and Succession that Changed the Graeco-Persian World Forever

David Grant

PEN & SWORD HISTORY

AN IMPRINT OF PEN & SWORD BOOKS LTD.
YORKSHIRE - PHILADELPHIA

First published in Great Britain in 2021 by
Pen & Sword History
An imprint of
Pen & Sword Books Ltd
Yorkshire – Philadelphia

Copyright © David Grant 2021

ISBN 978 1 52677 126 1

The right of David Grant to be identified as Author
of this work has been asserted by him in accordance
with the Copyright, Designs and Patents Act 1988.

A CIP catalogue record for this book is
available from the British Library.

All rights reserved. No part of this book may be reproduced or transmitted in
any form or by any means, electronic or mechanical including photocopying,
recording or by any information storage and retrieval system, without
permission from the Publisher in writing.

Typeset in 10.5/13 Ehrhardt by Vman Infotech Pvt. Ltd.
Printed and bound in the UK by CPI Group (UK) Ltd, Croydon, CR0 4YY.

Pen & Sword Books Limited incorporates the imprints of Atlas, Archaeology,
Aviation, Discovery, Family History, Fiction, History, Maritime, Military,
Military Classics, Politics, Select, Transport, True Crime, Air World,
Frontline Publishing, Leo Cooper, Remember When, Seaforth Publishing,
The Praetorian Press, Wharncliffe Local History, Wharncliffe Transport,
Wharncliffe True Crime and White Owl.

For a complete list of Pen & Sword titles please contact

PEN & SWORD BOOKS LIMITED
47 Church Street, Barnsley, South Yorkshire, S70 2AS, England
E-mail: enquiries@pen-and-sword.co.uk
Website: www.pen-and-sword.co.uk

Or
PEN AND SWORD BOOKS
1950 Lawrence Rd, Havertown, PA 19083, USA
E-mail: Uspen-and-sword@casematepublishers.com
Website: www.penandswordbooks.com

Contents

Author's Foreword vii
Publisher's Note ix
A Reader's Resource xi

Chapter 1:   Introducing Three Warring Witnesses 1
Chapter 2:   The Portentous Prelude To Death 7
Chapter 3:   The Assassins' Assembly; Path To Civil War 23
Chapter 4:   Wills And Testaments In Classical Greece 65
Chapter 5:   Death And Poison: The Toxic Cup 81
Chapter 6:   Hunting The Architects Of Deceipt 89
Chapter 7:   Royal Secretary, Royal Seal, Royal Charade 125
Chapter 8:   How, Why And When The Will Emerged 153
Chapter 9:   The Overlooked Evidence 197
Chapter 10: Epitaph In Rome, Obituary Today 225

Reference Notes 239
Bibliography 319
Index 331

AUTHOR'S FOREWORD

When I commenced my Masters degree in ancient history in 2009 I had no idea where it would lead. My thesis was titled 'The Lost Last Will and Testament of Alexander the Great'. With the encouragement of a Greek anthropologist who read an early draft, over the next eight years I refashioned the manuscript into a book. In that process, and through a constant aggregation of ideas, I became more convinced of my original theory, one that challenged the 'standard model' of Alexander's death and the chaos it led to.

In 2017, *In Search of the Lost Testament of Alexander the Great* went to print. It was written foremost as an academic book, with chapters arranged thematically, like my original thesis, and it came in 917 pages long with 4,000 footnotes and a thirty-page bibliography. I could never have guessed that *The Daily Mail Online* would run an article featuring its central contention: Alexander's will, which appears in the popular book of fables we know as *Greek Alexander Romance*, was based on a genuine, lost and deliberately hidden original succession document.

Despite that coverage, due to its 'unacceptable' length as well as my controversial reinterpretation of events (so I was informed by traditional book publishers), the title had to be self-published, and so it remained generally inaccessible and unknown, languishing deep in the recesses of website search engines.

In Search of the Lost Testament of Alexander the Great was, however, read by Greek researchers, who invited me to meet and discuss a possible collaboration with many historical parallels as well as identity conundrums. From mid-2017, I spent considerable time with them, either in person at archaeological sites or corresponding, as part of a team of archaeologists and material scientists dedicated to unravelling the mysteries and controversies behind the royal tombs of Macedon.

Alexander's family was buried at the ancient city of Aegae, which was discovered in ruins in the late 1970s beside the modern town of Vergina in northern Greece, and I centred my research there. That collaboration resulted in my 2019 title *Unearthing the Family of Alexander the Great: the Remarkable Discovery of the Royal Tombs of Macedon*, published by the Pen & Sword History imprint. What I learned in the process of investigating each book is that nothing related to the members of the royal Argead line of Macedon is straightforward or what it seems.

Their deaths in Aegae, the spiritual state capital and burial ground of its kings, were just as inexplicable and suspiciously documented as Alexander's in Babylon.

In the case of Alexander's demise in the former Persian Great King's bed, the principal forensic curiosity has revolved around whether he was poisoned, who may have been the culprit and what type of poison suited the symptoms. Much scientific curiosity has gone into determining the exact time or date of death, whether 10 or 11 June using the Babylonian astronomical diaries. Little energy has been directed towards the possible existence of a written succession instruction, which I more simply term a 'will'. Consequently, every biography of Alexander, old or new, has accepted one of the three 'intestate' endings which appear in the mainstream ancient texts.

My own long-standing fascination with Alexander's succession instructions – or suspicious lack thereof – was sparked by a 1988 academic paper from a pre-eminent expert on the people who feature in our sources, and it was promisingly titled *The Last Days and Testament of Alexander the Great: a Prosopography Study*.[1] A 'prosopography' focuses on the 'who's who' of the day, and was in this case by a renowned expert on the period. But only the reissued fake will was dissected for clues as to the author of the political document I have come to term the '*Pamphlet*'; no original succession document was ever pondered. With some justification, then, we could say that a 'genuine' will has never been the subject of an investigation; only an assumed fabrication has come under scrutiny.

This new book, *The Last Will and Testament of Alexander the Great: an Empire Left to the Strongest*, was written with the encouragement of my current publisher. It focuses on the period from 323 BC to the end of 316 BC, from events immediately preceding Alexander's final entry into Babylon down to the conclusion of what is known as the 'Second Successor War', and it extracts much of the material and core contention from my 2017 title. I present it as a forensic dissection and reinterpretation of interrelated events, rather than a straightforward history of the period. Nothing, I stress once more, was 'straightforward' reporting.

I have presented the facts as clearly as possible (from decidedly conflicted accounts) to enable as wide an audience as possible to delve into the mysterious end of Alexander's tale and the covert forces which kept this momentous episode of history such a dark secret. Alexander's death in Babylon, recorded by the mainstream histories as a wholesale failure to nominate a successor, remains, I believe, nothing short of the greatest succession cover-up of all time, and as misunderstand as any event in the ancient world. Some would say, like Alexander himself.

David Grant, August 2020

PUBLISHER'S NOTE

A useful companion to this book is David Grant's profiling of the historians featured in this book, to help readers better understand the agenda, bias and influences at work on the ancient contemporary reporting of events. It is titled *Alexander the Great: A Battle for Truth and Fiction, the ancient sources and why they can't be trusted*. Due to appear in spring 2022 under the Pen & Sword History imprint, it also extracts much of the research from Grant's 2017 title.

A READER'S RESOURCE

Readers are encouraged to satisfy themselves on what the ancient sources said and not to take my (or anyone's) word for it. I would encourage anyone to read the five surviving biographies or campaign accounts by the Roman-era authors Diodorus, Plutarch, Curtius, Justin and Arrian – plus the collected fragments from the corpus of lost historians – ahead of consuming any modern interpretation.[1] To be forewarned is to be forearmed.

The fragments from lost sources and an explanation to their backgrounds are most readily accessible in L. Pearson's *The Lost Historians of Alexander the Great* (1960) and C.A. Robinson's *The History of Alexander the Great; a Translation of the Extant and Fragments and the Ephemerides of Alexander's Expedition* (1953); see bibliography.

To assist with the deciphering of this ancient testimony, I have provided extensive footnotes here to enable backtracking to the sources and modern commentary, so that a wide swathe of opinion is covered. For those without the classical texts covering the events either side of Alexander's death, I would have reproduced them here in their entirety. However, their length makes this impractical, though key extracts are reproduced in relevant chapters. The increasing availability of texts online provides a solution.

The relevant extracts directly related to Alexander's death are numbered (T1) to (T25) and are referred to at pertinent points in the chapters, with links to them provided below. Here I have used their popular English titles.

SECTION 1: THE '*PAMPHLET*'

(T1) The content of the '*Pamphlet*' as preserved at the end of the *Metz Epitome*.
Unfortunately, there is no current online translation.

A recommended comparison is the translation in W. Heckel and J.C. Yardley, *Alexander the Great: Historical Sources in Translation* (Blackwell Publishing), pp.281–89. This publication appears in the bibliography as Heckel-Yardley (2004).

xii   The Last Will and Testament of Alexander the Great

(T2) The content of the '*Pamphlet*' as it appears in Recension A of the *Greek Alexander Romance*.
The relevant section is 3.30–3.34; translation at:
www.attalus.org/translate/alexander3d.html

The full *Greek Alexander Romance* can be accessed at:
www.attalus.org/info/alexander.html

A recommended comparison is the *Greek Alexander Romance* translation and commentary by R. Stoneman (Penguin Books, 1991), pp.148–56. This publication appears in the bibliography as Stoneman (1991).

SECTION 2: THE '*JOURNAL*'

(T3) The '*Journal*' detail as it appears in Arrian's *The Campaigns of Alexander*.
The relevant section is 7.25.1–7.26.1; translation at: https://en.wikisource.org/wiki/The_Anabasis_of_Alexander/Book_VII/Chapter_XXV

(T4) The parallel '*Journal*' detail as it appears in Plutarch's *Life of Alexander*.
The relevant section is 76.1–77.1; translation at: https://penelope.uchicago.edu/Thayer/E/Roman/Texts/Plutarch/Lives/Alexander*/10.html

(T5) Additional '*Journal*' detail appears in Aelian's *Historical Miscellany*.
The relevant section is 3.23; translation at:
http://penelope.uchicago.edu/aelian/varhist3.xhtml

SECTION 3: ALEXANDER'S DEATH ACCORDING TO THE VULGATE GENRE

(T6) Diodorus, *Library of World History*.
The relevant section is 17.116.1–118.4; translation at: https://penelope.uchicago.edu/Thayer/E/Roman/Texts/Diodorus_Siculus/17F*.html

(T7) Curtius, *History of Alexander the Great of Macedon*.
The relevant section is 10.5.1–10.5.7; translation at:
https://babel.hathitrust.org/cgi/pt?id=mdp.39015008158407&view=1up&seq=525

(T8) Justin, epitome of Gnaeus Pompeius Trogus' *Philippic History*.
The relevant section is 12.13–12.15; translations at: www.forumromanum.org/literature/justin/english/trans12.html www.attalus.org/translate/justin11.html#12.1
The Vulgate detail was also briefly (and dismissively) mentioned by Plutarch and Arrian, though their biographies were not Vulgate-genre accounts.

(T9) Arrian, *The Campaigns of Alexander.*
The relevant section is 7.27–7.28; translation at: https://en.wikisource.org/wiki/The_Anabasis_of_Alexander/Book_VII/Chapter_XXVII

(T10) Plutarch, *Life of Alexander.*
The relevant section is 77.2–77.5; translation at: https://penelope.uchicago.edu/Thayer/E/Roman/Texts/Plutarch/Lives/Alexander*/10.html

SECTION 4: THE INFIGHTING AT BABYLON FOLLOWING ALEXANDER'S DEATH THAT LED UP TO THE BABYLONIAN SETTLEMENT AND THE FORMAL DISTRIBUTION OF THE EMPIRE

(T11) Curtius, *History of Alexander the Great of Macedon.*
The relevant section is 10.5.7–10.10.20; translations at: https://babel.hathitrust.org/cgi/pt?id=mdp.39015008158407&view=1up&seq=527

(T12) Justin, epitome of Gnaeus Pompeius Trogus' *Philippic History.*
The relevant section is 13.1–13.4; translations at: www.forumromanum.org/literature/justin/english/trans13.html www.attalus.org/translate/justin1.html

(T13) Diodorus, *Library of World History.*
The relevant section is 18.2–18.4; translation at: https://penelope.uchicago.edu/Thayer/E/Roman/Texts/Diodorus_Siculus/18A*.html

(T14) Arrian, *Events After Alexander* **as précised in Photius'** *Library of History* **– (*Myriobiblion* or *Bibliotheke*), Codex 92.**
A translation at:
https://www.livius.org/sources/content/arrian/arrians-events-after-alexander-photius-excerpt/

(T15) Photius, précis of Dexippus' epitome of Arrian's *Events After Alexander***, Codex 82.**
A translation at:
www.tertullian.org/fathers/photius_03bibliotheca.htm#81

SECTION 5: THE DIVISION OF THE EMPIRE FOLLOWING THE SETTLEMENT AT BABYLON

(T16) Diodorus, *Library of World History.*
The relevant section is 18.2.1–18.5; translation at: https://penelope.uchicago.edu/Thayer/E/Roman/Texts/Diodorus_Siculus/18A*.html

(T17) Arrian, *Events After Alexander*, as précised in Photius' *Library of History* (*Myriobiblion* or *Bibliotheke*), Codex 92.
Translation at:
https://www.livius.org/sources/content/arrian/arrians-events-after-alexander-photius-excerpt/

(T18) Photius, précis of Dexippus' epitome of Arrian's *Events After Alexander*, Codex 82.
Translation at:
www.tertullian.org/fathers/photius_03bibliotheca.htm#81

(T19) Curtius, *History of Alexander the Great of Macedon*.
The relevant section is 10.6.1–10.9.21; translation at: https://babel.hathitrust.org/cgi/pt?id=mdp.39015008158407&view=1up&seq=563

(T20) Justin, epitome of Gnaeus Pompeius Trogus' *Philippic History*.
The relevant section is 13.4–13.24; translations at: www.forumromanum.org/literature/justin/english/trans13.html www.attalus.org/translate/justin1.html

SECTION 6: PRE-DEATH PORTENTS

(T21) Plutarch, *Life of Alexander*.
The relevant section is 73–75; translation at: https://penelope.uchicago.edu/Thayer/E/Roman/Texts/Plutarch/Lives/Alexander*/10.html

(T22) Diodorus, *Library of World History*.
The relevant section is 17.112.1–17.116.7; translation at: https://penelope.uchicago.edu/Thayer/E/Roman/Texts/Diodorus_Siculus/17F*.html

(T23) Arrian, *The Campaigns of Alexander*.
The relevant section is 7.16.5–7.24.4; translation at: https://en.wikisource.org/wiki/The_Anabasis_of_Alexander/Book_VII/Chapter_XXIV

(T24) Justin, epitome of Gnaeus Pompeius Trogus' *Philippic History*.
The relevant section is 12.13.1–12.13.6; translations at: www.forumromanum.org/literature/justin/english/trans12.html www.attalus.org/translate/justin11.html#12.1

SECTION 7: ALEXANDER'S 'LAST PLANS'

(T25) Diodorus, *Library of World History.*
The relevant section is 18.4.1–18.4.6; translation at: https://penelope.uchicago.edu/Thayer/E/Roman/Texts/Diodorus_Siculus/18A*.html

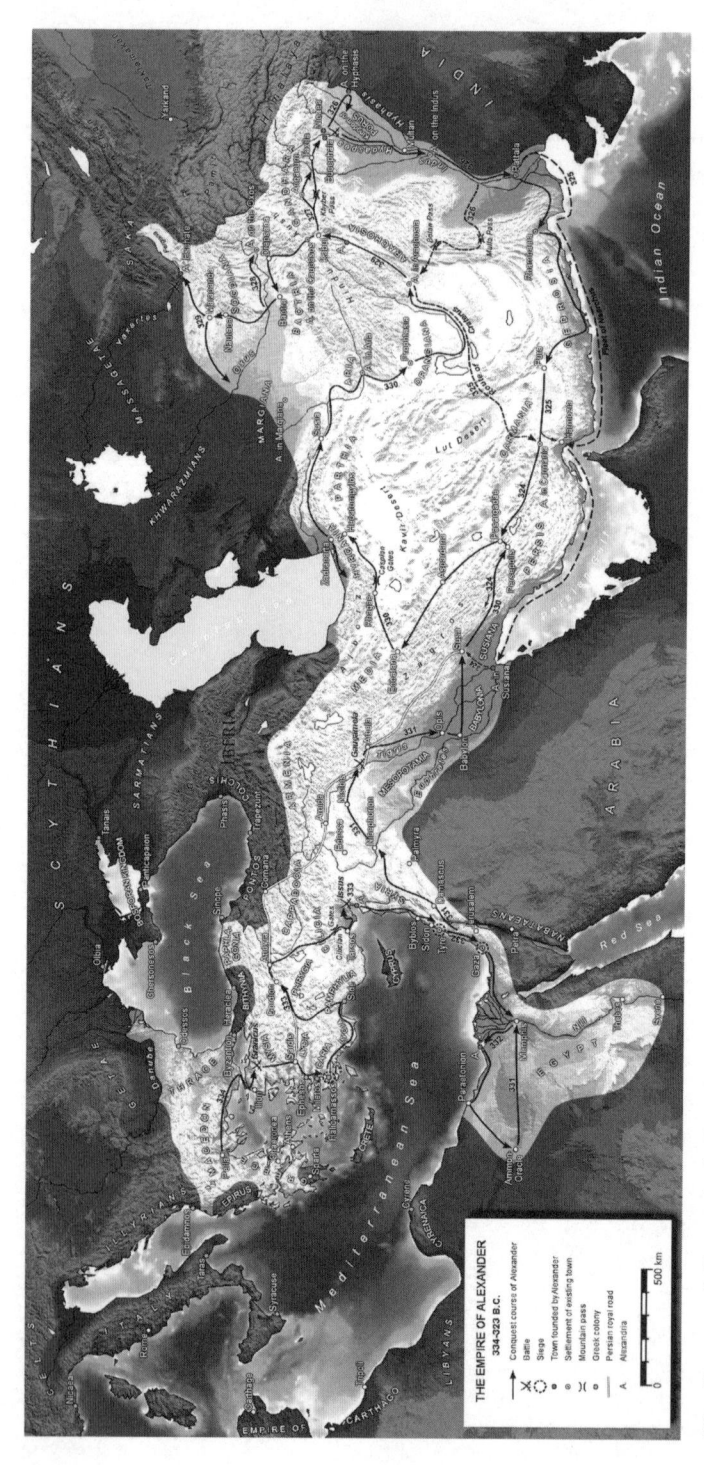

The Extent of Alexander's Empire and the provinces of the former Achaemenid Empire. (Wikimedia. CC BY-SA 3.0)

1

INTRODUCING THREE WARRING WITNESSES

Who reported on Alexander's death?

The ancient texts describe Alexander dying in three distinct ways, each of them contradicting the other. Here I review what the surviving accounts provide us with and where this gender-ridden reporting originated.

2 The Last Will and Testament of Alexander the Great

> ...the uncomfortable fact remains that the *Alexander Romance* provides us, on occasion, with apparently genuine materials found nowhere else, while our better-authenticated sources, *per contra*, are all too often riddled with bias, propaganda, rhetorical special pleading or patent falsification and suppression of evidence.[1]
>
> Peter Green, *Alexander of Macedon*

When Alexander III of Macedon took the throne at age 20 in 336 BC, no one – perhaps with the exception of Alexander himself – could have foreseen the magnitude of change he would bring to the Graeco–Persian World. That shift in power and in his cultural surrounds inevitably caused his own personality to evolve, as well as the mindset of his men and their command structure. Alexander's reign spanned almost thirteen years, eleven of which were spent marching through the Asian provinces of the former Persian Empire. His Macedonian-led army, supported by grudging Greek mercenaries from the garrisoned Hellenic world and auxiliaries from subjugated Balkan states and tribes, toppled 220 years of Achaemenid rule, only to face the prospect of the new world order imploding at Alexander's death in Babylon in June 323 BC. He was aged 32.

Today, some 2,343 years on, a few barely intact accounts survive to tell the almost coherent story. While at times in close agreement on certain campaign episodes, they are more frequently at odds with one another. What remains of a once-more-extensive library that narrated Alexander's final days concludes with a contradictory and suspicious set of claims and death-scene rehashes. One portrayed him dying silent and intestate, he was Homeric and vocal in the next, whilst a third detailed Alexander's last will and testament, though it is now attached to the end of a book of fables: a 'romance'. Which account can we trust?

It has long been recognized that the surviving sources are riddled with disinformation. 'Know your enemy', military historians advise. This is never a more sound tenet than when applied to the men who campaigned with Alexander and wrote their eyewitness pages: these are referred to as 'primary sources', and the resulting testimony from them was nothing short of 'civil war' being waged on papyrus.

To make sense of all this, I had to drill down through the fabric of personal agenda of these primary sources and then strip away the rhetoric from interested onlookers, as well as keeping on the lookout for the dramatical garnishes added by later historians trying to make a name for themselves. Determining how Alexander truly died was akin to deconstructing and deciphering an ancient code within a paradigm. From the knotted evidence, I was able to conclude that the time-worn manuscripts have brought us three distinct and competing witnesses all the way from Babylon in June 323 BC, as the testimony they contain likely originated with the very men who were standing beside Alexander's deathbed.

The first of the three comes in the form of what I will refer to as the '*Journal*', which documented Alexander's final twelve-day decline.[2] The *Journal* detail was allegedly extracted from an impeccable contemporary source – the official campaign 'royal diaries' (*Ephemerides* in Greek) – and it is found most lucidly in the final pages of the Roman-era historians Arrian (*ca.* AD 86–160) and Plutarch (*ca.* AD 46–120), as well as in the *Historical Miscellany* of the Roman antiquarian Aelian (AD 175–235 AD) (see T3, T4, T5).

The *Journal*'s dry, laconic and deadpan prose sits in stark contrast to the vivid portrayals of pre-death portents appearing elsewhere in the biographers' previous pages, and it makes no reference at all to a transfer of power; Alexander, it claimed, was comatose and speechless through his final two days and nights. Known for his attention to detail and meticulous military planning, the *Journal* implied the dying king used none of these famous faculties, leaving neither a will nor any succession instructions for either the home kingdom or his newly conquered Asian empire. It was this state of affairs, historians have since assumed, that led to infighting immediately after, and soon to Macedonian 'civil war'.[3]

It was left to what I have termed the '*Pamphlet*' to provide a more detailed and colourful account of Alexander's death (T1, T2). This apparently partisan political document is thought to have originated in the first decade of the Successor Wars waged by Alexander's generals for their share of the divided empire. The *Pamphlet* alleged there was nothing natural or even supernatural (as other sources imply) to Alexander's death, for it revealed a conspiracy to poison him at an impromptu banquet in Babylon thrown by a prominent court friend. Many attendees were implicated, including the king's royal Bodyguards corps (in ancient Greek the *Somatophylakes*, traditionally seven in number; the top echelon of power) and his closest Companions (high-ranking officers and other court notables, military and political), whilst six of the guests were cited as innocent and ignorant of the plot.[4]

The *Pamphlet* explained the motives behind the assassination and the poison used. It detailed the drafting and then the reading of a lucid last will and testament in which Alexander distributed the empire to the most prominent men at court as his end approached. This was not a formal 'partitioning' or breaking up of the newly conquered lands, but rather the regional governance of an intact empire on behalf of his son (or sons).[5] The will bequests were listed beside commemoratives and donations to leading cities and religious sites, and Alexander paired the surviving royal women with carefully chosen generals to secure the safety of the princes, born or still *in utero*, for they were the future of the Macedonian Argead royal line.[6] In fact, the will stands as a voice of reason

4 The Last Will and Testament of Alexander the Great

against the backdrop of competing narratives in which anarchy and treasonous power plays dominated the scene in other versions of his death.

Some indeterminate years later, this *Pamphlet*-originating detail appears to have been absorbed by the quasi-historical, highly rhetorical and eulogistic template of Alexander's deeds once erroneously credited to the official campaign historian Callisthenes; hence it was once referred to as a 'Pseudo-Callisthenes' production. In circulation, the colourful tale soon absorbed the wonders that were attaching themselves to Alexander, and in quick time it metamorphosed into something of a book of fables popularly referred to today as the *Greek Alexander Romance* (T2).[7]

Confined to this literary coffin, Alexander's death was not immune to the encroachment of these fabulous elements, and the *Romance* texts we read today conclude with him addressing his warhorse Bucephalus, which was standing obediently by his death bed. So once the *Pamphlet* version of Alexander's last days and the attached conspiracy had been wholly absorbed by the *Romance*, Alexander's last will and testament became, unsurprisingly, a pariah to scholars and historians, something unworthy of further consideration. As a result, the biographies, monographs, universal histories and academic studies over the past two millennia have concurred on one key issue: Alexander the Great died intestate and never made a will. The irony – a positive one for my contention – is that these fanciful multi-cultural romance versions (known as 'recensions'), so welcomed in the Middle Ages and translated into myriad languages, significantly outsold them all.

Unlike his rejected will, the plot to poison Alexander was too alluring to be exiled by other eager writers keen on attaching controversy to his death. So this conspiratorial section of the *Pamphlet* was swept up by 'mainstream' history, and it became a colourful adornment to the closing pages of the Roman-era Vulgate accounts (T6, T7, T8), the third witness thread we have. The use of the term 'Vulgate' here suggests the 'popular' or the 'widely-accepted' genre, and is represented by the surviving texts of Curtius Rufus (likely published mid-first century AD), Diodorus Siculus (published between 60 and 30 BC) and Gnaeus Pompeius Trogus (late first century BC), whose lost work is preserved in an epitome (a highly compressed précis) by an otherwise unknown Roman writer named Justin (likely third century AD). Their textual similarities and style points to a common, if not exclusive, earlier source for campaign information, and many scholars conclude that was the Alexandria-based historian Cleitarchus, a likely contemporary of Alexander's veterans or their sons.[8]

According to the Vulgate tradition, Alexander's final words left his kingdom (not specifically the 'empire') to 'the strongest' or 'most worthy' of his men.[9] The dying king was still sufficiently lucid to add that he foresaw the 'funeral games' which would follow.[10] Here, rather than referring to the posthumous Homeric contests honouring the fallen heroes – like those games Achilles had held for Patroclus at Troy in the *Iliad*, for example – it seems Alexander was cynically referencing the power struggle that would inevitably follow.[11] The highly rhetorical epitome of Justin was more lucid on the import of these 'games': '[Alexander] could foretell, and almost saw with his eyes, how much blood Macedon would shed in the disputes that would follow his death, and with what slaughters, and what quantities of gore, she would perform his obsequies.' The account of Curtius went on to paint a picture of Persian mourning and dissent amongst the assembled generals, whereas Justin went as far as suggesting the Macedonians were glad to see Alexander go.[12]

The rumours of the conspiracy to poison Alexander at Babylon reverberated far and wide; even Arrian and Plutarch, adherents to the *Journal*'s silence on a will and dismissive of these more-sensational Vulgate claims, nevertheless felt duty-bound to report the detail of his poisoning (T9, T10). Plutarch was even more specific, adding that some five years after Alexander had been embalmed, his mother Olympias exacted revenge on the architects of the assassination by 'putting many men to death'.[13]

Diodorus and Curtius believed that contemporary historians had dared not write of the plot while the men at the heart of the conspiracy were still fighting to become first among equals in their bid for the Macedonian throne or control of the Asian empire (or both), and 'whatever credence such stories gained, they were soon suppressed by the power of the people implicated by the rumour'. More specific was the claim (possibly in the original *Pamphlet* itself) that the court philosopher and late-campaign historian Onesicritus deliberately avoided naming the banquet guests for fear of reprisals. The *Pamphlet* was clearly virulent, and one of our aims is to identify its still-anonymous author in our bid to navigate back to Alexander's original will.[14]

Then we need to factor into the unsolved equation the mindset of Alexander himself; the mortal man, not a god in the making, as he was popularly portrayed in antiquity. In my earlier treatise, I summed him up with a paragraph which, paradoxically, makes it clear he cannot be summed up at all:

> Alexander was an elusive equation: a calculable axiom of Aristotle's empirical and categorising present, and an indefinable irrational number from the Homeric past. He was a mythopoeic conqueror who at once lived by the tenets of the strategically sound and the proportionally outrageous; a tribal leader recalling heroic deeds, and a mortal seeking apotheosis through his progression from Macedonian king to commander-in-chief of the Greeks, de facto pharaoh of Egypt and a Persian King of Kings. Indeed, his was the blood of a mortal and an immortal essence (ichor) mixed in one, and I suggest the content of his testament would have been no less ambitious.[15]

What becomes clear from reading any biography or campaign account, whether penned in the ancient world or by modern historians overlaying their own interpretations on events, is that the prince who came to power at the age of 20 was not the same man who re-entered Babylon aged 32. There were too many scars – mental and physical – too many losses despite the gains, too many rejections beside successes and too many who wanted him dead despite his loyal support, for Alexander not to have been irrevocably changed.

Regardless of whoever he had become, my contention is that Alexander was *never* a person to let fate decide an outcome; not in lineage, memory nor battle, and certainly not in death. Death is an episode most easily manipulated; the protagonist is, after all, deceased and cannot plead his case. In reply to those historians today who still accuse Alexander of unforgivably dying intestate and failing to name a successor, guilt can only be established when the supporting evidence is beyond reasonable doubt. So here, like a judge presiding over a long-closed case, I bring the subject of historical fraud, duplicity and political manipulation into the vortex of my argument. Following a decade studying the evidence, I believe that one unavoidable verdict emerged: after these 2,340 years, the last will and testament of Alexander III of Macedon needs to be extracted from 'romance' and reinstated to its rightful place in mainstream history.

2

THE PORTENTOUS PRELUDE TO DEATH

Do the final chapters in Alexander's biographies look convincing, or were supposedly divine and 'supernatural' agendas at work?

Summarizing what Alexander 'did' in his reign has always been easier than approximating 'what he was'. 'Who he had become' by the time he returned to Babylon ten years after leaving Macedon is even more of a riddle, not least because sources are remarkably light on detail for this final period and chronologically uncertain on either side, so the exact order of events is difficult to determine.

Here I summarize the state of affairs, as sources present them, in Alexander's final year. The eyewitness historians either genuinely believed the gods had abandoned him, or – more insidiously – they preferred their readers to reach this conclusion to divert any forensic curiosity in what really occurred.

> Alexander, then, since he had now become sensitive to indications of the divine will and perturbed and apprehensive in his mind, converted every unusual and strange occurrence, were it never so insignificant, into a prodigy and portent; and sacrificers, purifiers, and diviners filled his palace ... [he] began to be low-spirited and was distrustful now of the favour of Heaven and suspicious of his friends.[1]
>
> Plutarch, *Life of Alexander*

> The Royal Journals say that Peithon, Attalus, Demophon, and Peucestas, with Cleomenes, Menidas, and Seleucus too, slept the night in the temple of Serapis, to solicit the god's answer to their question whether it would be better and right for Alexander to be brought into the temple and given into the god's care as a supplicant. The divine response communicated to them was that he should not be brought into the temple, but it was right for him to remain where he was. The Companions made this response public, and shortly afterwards Alexander died. This, then, was what was now 'right' for him.[2]
>
> Arrian, *Campaigns of Alexander*

Alexander and the Macedonian war machine prepared for its return to Babylon in spring 323 BC, a city he had first entered some seven-and-a-half years before on his way to becoming de facto 'Great King' of the Achaemenid empire. He was perhaps the wealthiest man the world had, or has, ever seen, with control of the treasuries and income across a newly integrated Graeco–Persian world. The surviving campaign accounts read as an exhilarating roller-coaster ride of successes against the odds, with uplifting feats of conquest and a generosity of spirit to those Alexander conquered, only matched by the depth of despair attached to the darker episodes of personal loss and the tragedy of mass slaughter.

What remains clear, however, is that all was not well in the brave new world forged by Alexander's imagination and by his legendary yearnings to exceed all that came before, made possible by the unmatched army he commanded. Troops were cynical, friends had been executed and close Companions were dead. Moreover, the absolute chain of command was not as 'absolute' as it first appears. There had been mutinies – two or three – mass executions of dissenters, a treasurer-come-boyhood friend absconding (twice) with waggons loads of gold and silver, and generals who answered back, only to be skewered by Alexander with a blade. Yet Persian royals thrived and even entered court life through marriage in what looked like the beginnings of a hybrid dynasty.

The spear-won empire by now was under the command of the top-tier generals, some of them veterans of the reign of Alexander's father Philip II with the authority of regions vaster than the much-expanded kingdom of Macedon itself. Alexander's own Bodyguards corps – 'autocrats within their own armies long before the assumption of royal title' – along with the most prominent of his pan-provincial governors and the generals under them, were hugely influential, both regionally and amongst their own brigades of men.[3] The hallowed band of personal Bodyguards who survived the campaign purges, politics and passions of their mercurial king now included Perdiccas, Leonnatus, Seleucus, Ptolemy, Peithon, Lysimachus and Aristonus, with other court favourites snapping at their heels should any falter in their duty or lose favour.

By now, Antigonus the One-Eyed had governed much of Anatolia (commonly referred to as 'Asia Minor', modern Turkey, from late Antiquity onwards) for over a decade, with capable satraps and officers about him. Parmenio, the most talented of Philip's generals, had been vested with a pivotal administrative and military overseer role at Ecbatana in Media, guarding the royal treasury and keeping communication and supply routes open between Anatolia and the Near East – until Alexander had him executed. And if he had survived the banquet at which Alexander ran him through with a spear, the vocally dissenting Cleitus 'the Black' might have assumed a similar role from Bactra (the capital of Bactria, modern Balkh) to govern the vast 'upper satrapies' (principally encompassing Bactria and Sogdia; broadly covering today's northern Afghanistan, Pakistan, Tajikistan and Uzbekistan).

In Alexander's vanguard, the voice of Craterus resounded loudly with the veterans. These influential commanders, along with the long-serving rank and filers and their popular infantry officers, remained the conservative face of a Macedonian authority which, for many of the troops, represented a far more coherent and attractive order than Alexander's increasingly indecipherable behaviour and favour shown to – and marriage with – those whom he had conquered.

Perhaps above them all in authority, as the long-time Macedonian regent based in the state capital at Pella, Antipater had ably governed a subdued Greece, Thessaly, Illyria, Epirus, the cantons of Upper Macedon and neighbouring tribes for more than a decade in Alexander's absence, and far longer if we consider his role under Philip. His 'home army' may well have preserved a nationalist spirit that Alexander's troops in Asia were to lose, for in Macedon it was still the state-expanding achievements of Philip II that the army nostalgically recalled.[4] His consolidation of the state and military success was, after all, the platform that allowed Alexander to campaign abroad, until Philip was assassinated in suspicious circumstances at Aegae in 336 BC.

The Economics of Upheaval

The theme of the late campaign years leading up to 323 BC was instability and uncertainty, both in the Greek world and in Asia. The Persian Empire at its height had enjoyed an annual income of 30,000 talents (talents were often ambiguously referred to – when specifying weight, a talent equalled approximately 26kg, and in value 6,000 drachmas; 30,000 talents was equivalent to almost 25 years' total income of the city-state of Athens and all its vassal wealth), and sources suggest Alexander and his new order spent over 50,000 talents in his extravagant last two years.[5] Some 10,000 had repaid soldiers' personal debts, gold crowns were handed out to top commanders at Susa (though surely not the 15,000 talents-worth claimed by a fragment we have from the royal chamberlain Chares) and a further 10,000 talents paid off veterans' debts, with a similar sum destined for temple restoration in Greece. Presents, wedding dowries to the senior staff he convinced to marry Persian nobility and a research grant of 800 talents to Aristotle added to the bill, as well as payments to orphaned children in Asia and their promised education.[6]

The compliant Indian rajah of Taxila had even been given 1,000 talents, and Alexander's treasurer-friend Harpalus had fled to Athens with a further 5,000 from the treasury, equating to some 140 tons in silver or 14 tons of gold, which alone (if in gold) would have required a minimum of thirty ships to transport it.[7] In the months preceding Alexander's death, major projects that had been underway included gargantuan Babylonian dockyards and the construction of 700 warships.[8] We read of opulent dinners being hosted with 600 to 700 Companions at extraordinary cost.[9] Some 180,000 talents had reportedly been captured from Persian treasuries (estimated at some 7,290 tons of gold and silver) during Alexander's campaign, possibly the equivalent of $100 billion dollars today; it would have been sufficient to run Athens and the Aegean for two centuries. By 323 BC, Justin suggested, some 50,000 talents remained, and they were being fast depleted.[10]

Alexander had recently appointed a Rhodian, Antimenes, to upkeep the roads in the region and he had already imposed a previously unenforced ancient duty of 10 per cent on imported goods, a levy that must have been hugely unpopular; the edict was no doubt required to fund these heady projects in the face of a waning treasury.[11] This points to the collapse of the Achaemenid tax-raising network which saw serfs paying great landowners, who in turn paid satraps who collected for the Great King; it was clear that the treasuries across the empire would soon be bled dry.[12]

The regional military overseers and the king's Bodyguards above them, who were impatient to administer a chunk of the new empire, knew it, and a confrontation was inevitable, though whether that was resolved with a poisoned cup remains one of the many mysteries attached to Alexander's reign. Evidence suggests the common Macedonian would have considered the state treasury as a wealth safeguarded by the kings for the people, and that their tax revenues were similarly the property of the state, if administered under the feudal landlord–tenant system we envisage existed in Macedon. They supposedly had a voice in its management through their representative landlords and nobles at what was known as the Common Assembly of Macedones. If this was true, Alexander's continued extravagance would have increased the resentment at Babylon from the men who had not yet been provided with bonuses or anything more than a soldier's basic remuneration, when the uncertainty of keeping waggons of hoarded plunder had risen after the disastrous journey back from India and the remaining distance from home.[13]

Alexander struck enormous quantities of what was expected to become the new reference currency in the late campaign. It is estimated that from 330 BC onwards, after raiding the Persian treasuries, Alexander minted some 4,680 tons of silver in the form of the king's coinage; this was an enormous circulation increase, with some coins remaining in use for up to a century. Unsurprisingly, an unusually large issue was minted in 324–323 BC for Alexander's grandiose plans.[14] The result would be hugely inflationary over the decades to come.

A more obvious cause of upheaval in Macedon itself was the ongoing recruitment campaigns that saw some 33,800 or more men-at-arms shipped to Asia, besides the 14,000 Macedonians Alexander had originally departed with; in total, this may have equated to something like one in eight of every adult eligible for military service.[15]

Meanwhile, Alexander's mother had returned to her native Molossian kingdom in Epirus after a well-documented feud with the regent Antipater. It was a civil strife that led to frequent corresponding pleading her case to her son. The home Argead dynasty was far from content, whittled down as it had been by Alexander before he departed for Asia, with no acceptable male heirs now remaining. What Olympias made of her son's marriages to Asiatic women we can only speculate, but judging by the campaign troop mutinies, which were in part caused by local recruits entering the elite Macedonian squadrons, Alexander's wedding to 'conquered' women was not popular anywhere, except in the Achaemenid royal family itself, whose survival depended upon the new blood ties.

In contrast to the earlier widespread appointments of 'domestic' Asian governors, by the time Alexander returned to Babylon, tellingly, only three Persians still held office.[16] The new administration was never the Graeco–Oriental harmony many believe he attempted to bring about. Within this new administrative model, Alexander relied on resettled mercenaries, principally Greeks, to keep peace across the empire. Curtius reported that 'Alexander ... was thinking that Asia could be held by an army of modest size because he had distributed garrisons in many places and filled his new cities with settlers eager to preserve the status quo.'[17] The policy was a huge overestimate of their enthusiasm and stability; some 3,000 of these military settlers in new mud-brick 'cities' eponymously named 'Alexandria' had earlier revolted upon false rumour of Alexander's death in India. Other far-flung mercenaries in Macedonian employ had murdered the satrap of the expanded Indian-bordering provinces east of the Indus.[18]

Trouble was brewing both in the Asian provinces and in southern Greece. Despite the previous success of the Macedonian army, his men were now stretched precariously thinly across the empire, in garrison posts from Sogdia (broadly modern Kazakhstan) to the Indus Delta, and west across the Mediterranean coast. Greek mercenary numbers had swelled to dangerous levels, and many had been dismissed from service by Alexander to populate the new 'Alexandrias' he founded in distant lands.

Alexander had issued an edict to his Asian satraps in 326 BC ordering them to disband their own hired armies in anticipation of trouble, for by now over 100,000 mercenaries (if cited numbers can be believed) had seen service with the Macedonians and were stationed across the empire; many of them had once been in the pay of Darius III.[19] Partly motivated by the need to repatriate these itinerant soldiers and to gain a core of support in the Greek cities, Alexander issued the Exiles Decree, which was read aloud at the 324 BC Olympic Games (held that year from 31 July to 4 August) and which must have broadly coincided with the trouble with execution of army mutineers and wayward satraps at Opis (or Susa, the chronology is ambiguous).[20]

The subsequent re-emergence of up to 20,000 political outcasts in Greece, many experienced fighters, was to cause huge property conflict, though Antipater was instructed to act against any resisting city. In this he was precariously placed, for the decree undermined his own political architecture; perhaps Alexander was aiming to achieve just that, because Craterus was already journeying home through Asia with 10,000 veterans with orders to take over the regency. Olympias' correspondence and pleading with her son may have finally taken their toll.

The Athenian commander Leosthenes, ironically the son of an exile once given sanctuary by Philip II in Macedon, was singled out for the sacred duty of leading the Greek forces against Macedon. He was encouraged by a newly vocal and ever-hostile Hyperides, another of the so-called Athenian 'Ten Attic Orators', and offered wandering mercenaries a home at Taenarum in the former Spartan-controlled region of the Peloponnese. Here, the seeds of the Lamian (originally 'Hellenic') War against Macedon were already furtively being irrigated by covert Athenian sponsorship in a broader multi-state alliance, using fifty of the talents from the Athenian treasury, and thanks to the earlier arrival of Alexander's defecting treasurer, Harpalus, a further 700 talents guarded on the Acropolis.[21] Alexander must have been aware of the gathering of what would soon be 22,000 soldiers of fortune, some 8,000 of whom were formerly employed in Asia.[22]

Alexander's well-documented requests for deification as a new god had accompanied the Exiles Decree which was delivered at Olympia by Alexander's general, Nicanor of Stagira (possibly Aristotle's nephew and soon-to-be son-in-law), along with a demand for the return of Harpalus, stolen money and a threat of repercussions. Possibly to undermine Antipater's regency role and deprive him of the funds, Olympias demanded the same. The equally vocal Athenian orator-statesman Demosthenes, surely heeding those warnings from Nicanor, declared: 'Alexander can claim to be the son of Zeus and Poseidon as well for all we care.'[23] Listening on, the pragmatic pro-Macedonian statesman Demades warned the arguing Athenians that they were so concerned with the gods above that they would lose the earth below.[24]

Ecbatana to Babylon

Things were no-less unstable at the temporary campaign headquarters of Ecbatana, the former summer residence of the Persian Great Kings (modern Hamadan). Alexander's closest companion (many also assume his lover) and de facto second-in-command, Hephaestion, died in mysterious circumstances and poisoning must have been suspected, although excessive drinking at a series of rowdy banquets was recorded as the likely culprit. The attending absent-without-leave doctor was executed; as events had already shown on more than one occasion, it was the seers and doctors, fearful of providing inaccurate divinations or ineffective prognoses, who had the most to lose: their lives.[25] 'To lighten his sorrow', after reportedly destroying the temple of the unheeding healing god Asclepius at Ecbatana and shearing the manes of his horses and mules in a Homeric mourning, Alexander next embarked on a 'blood-soaked hunt' of the Cossean mountain tribes, murdering everyone from the youths upwards. Plutarch termed it a 'sacrifice to the shades of his dead friend'.[26]

It was against this darker backdrop and excessive mourning that Alexander set off for Babylon with the royal army in early 323 BC. With Hephaestion dead, the most senior of the Bodyguards, Perdiccas, was elevated to commander of the elite First Companion Cavalry brigade and charged with escorting Hephaestion's body to Babylon.[27]

Each Royal Bodyguard had received gifts of gold crowns at Susa for their loyalty, with, of course, an Asiatic royal wife to further handcuff them at the famous mass weddings to Alexander's new vision of hybrid governance.[28] This compulsory 'honour' was the first real sign of the new order after the carnage of India and recent mutinies, and it represented a real integration of Persian royalty into the future model via the promise of a mixed blood generation. And it was here that Alexander probably promised each of these seven Royal Bodyguards (eight if we include Peucestas, who was now governing the Persian homeland provinces) a chunk of the empire to govern.

Also in Alexander's entourage was Eumenes of Cardia, who headed the campaign secretariat, but who had already displayed his skill in cavalry command in India. And now, with Hephaestion dead, Eumenes was entrusted with Perdiccas' cavalry command once he, in turn, took control of the elite cavalry brigade still carrying Hephaestion's name in posthumous respect.[29]

Of course, there were the court 'friends' who had made their fame and fortune from association with the king: doctors and seers, fawning poets, performers, flatterers and philosophers, as well as strategically important guest friends, who may or may not have seen action on campaign. Among them was Medius of Larissa, of noble Thessalian birth and allegedly the lover of the regent's son, Iollas, who had become Alexander's cupbearer.[30] Enrolling the sons of barons, generals and absent governors was both an honour and an informal hostage guarantee of the good behaviour of their influential fathers.

Then there was Onesicritus, the new campaign historian who had replaced the executed Callisthenes some four years or so before. A former pupil of the cynical school of thought, Onesicritus had cut his teeth in India interviewing the naked wise men or philosophers known as 'gymnosophists', and he also seems to have had some nautical experience as he clashed with the prominent admiral and boyhood court friend of Alexander, Nearchus, on naval authority.[31]

Before the Bitumen Walls

The returning army – now more of a metropolis on the move – must have been a grand sight as it approached Babylon's bitumen-sealed walls, and news of its re-emergence from the East had clearly spread afar. As Justin described it: 'On Alexander's return, he was acquainted with embassies from the Carthaginians and other states of Africa, as well as from the Spains, Sicily, Gaul, and Sardinia, and some also from Italy. So powerfully had the terror of his name diffused itself through the world, that all nations were ready to bow to him as their destined monarch.'[32] Modern scholars question the geography of this expansive tribute, labelling it as a back-construct of the Roman era, like much else, I believe.[33]

But the end was fast approaching, and the prelude to Alexander's death soon became a chapter sympathetic to mysterious portents, prophecies, diviners, superstition and the inevitability of deity-sanctioned death. If the healing god Asclepius had abandoned Hephaestion at Ecbatana, fate and the new hybrid god Serapis seem to have simultaneously turned their backs on Alexander. The conqueror's entourage, which had been warmly welcomed by the city in October 331 BC as liberating heroes, was this time met by its resident Chaldean priests, who must have been fearful of Alexander's return (like many others, they most likely never expected him to survive the Eastern campaigns) as it undermined their unquestioned power over the populous. Consequently, they played upon their exulted positions and the well-known superstition of the Macedonian soldier (T21, T22, T23, T24).[34] A recent oracle from the god Marduk, they claimed, warned of the danger of entering the city at that time, unless Alexander diverted to the east side, where it turned out be swampy and impossible to cross. Then, exploiting a promise Alexander had previously made to restore their sacred Esagila Temple – which had been destroyed by Xerxes upon his hasty return from Greece following defeat at Plataea a century-and-a-half before – Diodorus tells us the Chaldeans predicted safe passage if Alexander immediately set about its repair. It seems the Chaldeans had enjoyed the temple revenues for the intervening years of Alexander's absence without contributing to its rebuilding themselves.[35]

Arrian recorded that Nearchus cautioned Alexander to heed the warning (Nearchus possibly claimed this in his own book, which Arrian used), but Alexander's Greek seer, Anaxarchus, in danger of being subordinated to the older Chaldean mysticism of Asia, advised his king to ignore it.[36] And disregard it he did, after an unsuccessful detour past the uninhabited city of Borsippa on the opposite side of the Euphrates. Yet 'when he arrived at the walls, he saw many ravens flying about and clawing one another, and some of them fell dead at his feet.'[37] Alongside the dark Chaldean prophesy, the sources reported other dire divinations from seers and similar sinister signs from animal sacrifices which warned of grave dangers to come.[38]

Once installed in the city, Alexander's fleet captains began returning from the Persian Gulf and reconnaissance of the Arabian Peninsula, while trees were being distantly felled for a new fleet that would head that way and hopefully convince the Arabs to install him as a third god in their pantheon of deities, so grand were his achievements.[39]

On his own voyage of discovery, Alexander sailed some 90 miles down the Euphrates to the seasonal flood lands to inspect the sluices built by the silted-up run-offs into the region's marshes and lakes. Here he built a fortified city and settled more mercenaries and disabled veterans unfit for further service. Upon his return, ominously, part of his fleet was temporarily lost in the marshlands where the tombs of the old Assyrian kings lay. A gust of wind blew Alexander's royal diadem off his hat, which snagged on reeds by an ancient tomb. This too was considered inauspicious, as was the fate of the sailor who swam out to retrieve it; attempting to keep it dry, he sacrilegiously put the diadem on his own head. Some sources say he was rewarded and others that he was flogged. Later propaganda attached the story of the Royal Bodyguard Seleucus, signifying the coming rise of his own Seleucid Empire.[40]

New embassies arrived from Greece offering golden crowns as if 'on a pilgrimage to honour a god', surely to deflect any suspicion that a tinder box of dissent had accumulated south of Athens; but Alexander's requests for divination must have seemed close to bearing fruition. There also arrived significant Asian-recruited reinforcements.[41] The army's ranks were thus even more diluted with Asiatic troops. As few as 13,000 Macedonian infantry and 2,000 cavalry are thought to have remained in the royal army, though newly arrived recruit numbers make calculations uncertain.[42]

By mid-summer 323 BC, warships, grain ships, pack animals, cavalry mounts and Indian elephants were being prepared for the new Arabian expedition, while the citadel – guarding wealth the Greeks had never imagined – was being mined for funds to pay what was clearly a multinational army.

Spanning both banks of the Euphrates, Babylon housed not only a vast native population of indeterminate numbers, but once again an occupying army. Credits and debts and chits of payment evidenced the growing divide between the now-fabulously wealthy aristocrats who represented Alexander's inner sanctum of power, and the levied state infantrymen whose wages were spent on the army auxiliaries and camp traders providing the necessaries of roving army life. This often led to debt. The relatively few infantry veterans remaining in Babylon were fractious and resented their lot. Many had married along the way and sired children with campaign mistresses, and were torn between pending instructions to return to Macedon or a permanent life in the newly conquered provinces of Asia.

Amongst all this activity, the outstanding issue of Hephaestion's funeral still had to be addressed. Each of Alexander's most prominent courtiers was obliged to provide gold and ivory likenesses of Hephaestion in preparation for the grand funeral pyre planned for him, as was the custom, surely in part to appease the wrath of a by-now unstable Alexander.[43] When debating the permanence of the extraordinary memorial, we should recall that other monuments to the far-from-universally liked Hephaestion were planned in Alexandria. In a letter to Cleomenes, Alexander had allegedly warned his wayward financial administrator in Egypt that Hephaestion's two 'shrines', the first on the island of Pharos and the second in the heart of the new city, needed to be splendid to exonerate him from the repercussions of his financial mismanagement.[44]

The impossibly grand pyre designed for Hephaestion at Babylon supposedly cost 12,000 talents. Diodorus described the spectacular funeral commemorative, with its thirty compartments forming furlong-length sides and foundations formed from the golden prows of 240 quinqueremes (galleys known as 'fives', which must have depleted the fleet) supporting seven ornate tiers soaring to 140 cubits (approximately 210ft).[45] Debate continues on whether this elaborate, gargantuan structure was to be burned as part of a ritualized funeral ceremony which 'not only surpassed all those previously celebrated on earth but also left no possibility for anything greater in later ages', or whether it was built as a permanent monument or hero shrine.[46]

A reconstruction of the funeral pyre of Hephaestion based upon the description given by Diodorus. (A woodcut by Franz Jaffe ca. 1900)

Hephaestion's commemorative appears to have remained incomplete, possibly because Alexander 'longed for' the Rhodian architect Deinocrates (elsewhere named Stasicrates), responsible for the building of Alexandria, to construct it and he was not immediately available.[47] Yet, typifying the great holes in the fabric of reporting of the events leading up to Alexander's death, Diodorus suggested the funeral took place before the king 'turned to amusements and festivals' following Hephaestion's elevation to god (or 'associate god') after consulting the oracle at Siwa in Egypt on the deification request. Other sources tell us the reply was 'not as a god, but a hero', following which a so-named cult emerged.[48]

The Baleful Banquet

It is at this point that Alexander's frame of mind was called into question by the surviving sources. Plutarch claimed the king soon became excessively paranoid, assuaging his fears with drinking and sacrifices, and with 'foolish misgivings' concerning his court friends: 'Since he had now become sensitive to indications of the divine will and perturbed and apprehensive in his mind, he converted every unusual and strange occurrence, were it never so insignificant, into a prodigy and portent.'[49] Alexander filled the palace at Babylon with soothsayers of every description, and 'now distrustful of the favour of Heaven and suspicious of his friends', he became a 'slave to his fears'. We have, it seems, been passed the description of a man losing his sanity, and some claimed this was due to mind-altering drugs he was administered in the lead-up to his assassination.[50]

This also marks the point where corroborating sources highlight the string of banquets and drinking bouts that heralded Alexander's end, details allegedly from the so-called 'Royal Diaries' from which the *Journal* entry was allegedly extracted. The final banquet took place at the house of Medius, who apparently intercepted Alexander as he was returning to bed from earlier carousing, promising the king that 'he would enjoy it'.[51] The end was nigh.

If Athenaeus' testimony is accurate, Alexander was launching himself into an animated recital from Euripides' tragedy *Andromeda* and toasting his guests with unmixed wine; an otherwise-unknown author of court scandal named Ephippus claimed his usual banquet cup held twelve pints. This fits the description of the great cup of Nestor which features in the *Iliad*, so large it was a challenge to lift. It appears Alexander remained true to his Homeric roots even in inebriation.[52]

Here marks the parting of ways of our sources for good, which evidences the literary 'war' originating with eyewitness testimony of the final events at Babylon: the scandal in the *Pamphlet* – which pointed to poison and conspiracy, with a will which was supressed – and the diametrically opposed *Journal*, which was silent on both intrigue and succession instructions from an even more tight-lipped Alexander. The later Vulgate-genre authors, inspired by earlier writers who had incorporated the *Pamphlet* claims, tell us Alexander suddenly shrieked in pain and collapsed as if he had been stabbed.[53] Justin and Diodorus were quite specific about what happened next:

> . . . being carried half dead from the table, he was excruciated with such torture that he called for a sword to put an end to it, and felt pain at the touch of his attendants as if he were wounded all over. His friends reported that the cause of his disease was excess in drinking, but in reality it was a conspiracy, the infamy of which the power of his successors threw into the shade.[54]

A gap in Curtius' text (known as a 'lacuna') deprives us of his version, but the compatibility of what Justin and Diodorus reported suggests his text would have corroborated their accounts. Here is Justin's narrative:

> The author of this conspiracy was Antipater, who, seeing that his dearest friends were put to death, that Alexander Lyncestes, his son-in-law, was cut off, and that he himself, after his important services

in Greece, was not so much liked by the king as envied by him, and was also persecuted with various charges by his mother Olympias; reflecting, too, on the severe penalties inflicted, a few days before, on the governors of the conquered nations, and hence imagining that he was sent for from Macedon, not to share in the war, but to suffer punishment, secretly, in order to be beforehand with Alexander, furnished his son Cassander with poison, who, with his brothers Philip and Iollas, was accustomed to attend on the king at table. The strength of this poison was so great, that it could be contained neither in brass, nor iron, nor shell, nor could it be conveyed in any other way than in the hoof of a horse. Cassander had been warned to trust nobody but the Thessalian and his brothers; and hence it was that the banquet was prepared and renewed in the house of the Thessalian. Philip and Iollas, who used to taste and mix the king's drink, had the poison ready in cold water, which they put into the drink after it had been tasted.[55]

Diodorus was more brief:

They say that Antipater, who had been left by Alexander as viceroy in Europe, was at variance with the king's mother Olympias. At first he did not take her seriously because Alexander did not heed her complaints against him, but later, as their enmity kept growing and the king showed an anxiety to gratify his mother in everything out of piety, Antipater gave many indications of his disaffection. This was bad enough, but the murder of Parmenion and Philotas struck terror into Antipater as into all of Alexander's Friends, so by the hand of his own son, who was the king's wine-pourer, he administered poison to the king. After Alexander's death, Antipater held the supreme authority in Europe and then his son Cassander took over the kingdom, so that many historians did not dare write about the drug. Cassander, however, is plainly disclosed by his own actions as a bitter enemy to Alexander's policies. He murdered Olympias and threw out her body without burial, and with great enthusiasm restored Thebes, which had been destroyed by Alexander.

The Vulgate authors were also clear on what happened next at Alexander's death. After providing a rather florid and rhetorical account of the mourning of Alexander's troops and their kissing the hand of the dying king, Justin gave this account:

When the soldiers were gone, he asked his friends that stood about him, 'whether they thought they should find a king like him?' All continuing silent, he said that, 'although he did not know that, he

knew, and could foretell, and almost saw with his eyes, how much blood
Macedon would shed in the disputes that would follow his death, and
with what slaughters, and what quantities of gore, she would perform
his obsequies.' At last he ordered his body to be buried in the temple
of Jupiter Ammon [at Siwa in Egypt]. When his friends saw him
dying, they asked him 'whom he would appoint as the successor to his
throne?' He replied, 'The most worthy.'[56]

Justin was also quite clear on the length of Alexander's illness:

> On the sixth day from the commencement of his illness, being unable to
> speak, he took his ring from his finger, and gave it to Perdiccas, an act
> which tranquillized the growing dissension among his friends; for though
> Perdiccas was not expressly named his successor, he seemed intended to
> be so in Alexander's judgment.[57]

The conclusion to Diodorus' book is again more abbreviated:

> When he, at length, despaired of life, he took off his ring and handed
> it to Perdiccas. His friends asked: 'To whom do you leave the kingdom?'
> and he replied: 'To the strongest.' He added, and these were his last
> words, that all of his leading Friends would stage a vast contest in honour
> of his funeral.

Arrian and Plutarch, adherents to the *Journal* entry, which was supposedly
extracted from the Royal Diaries, rejected this testimony with the claim that
Alexander was in fact silent and comatose leading up to his death. Nevertheless,
they provided a similar overview of the rumours of poison and conspiracy
which closely confirmed to the above.[58] Plutarch made his scepticism clear:
'This [illness] did not come upon him after he had quaffed a "bowl of Heracles",
nor after he had been seized with a sudden pain in the back as though smitten
with a spear; these particulars certain writers felt obliged to give, and so, as it
were, invented in tragic fashion a moving finale for a great action.'[59]

Arrian added that upon leaving Medius' party, Alexander took a bath and ate
a little before falling asleep on the spot and developing a fever.[60] Both Arrian and
Plutarch then cited, almost word for word, what they read in the final pages of
the books of Ptolemy and Aristobulus, where this *Journal* entry was to be found
(see Chapter 6 for full *Journal* texts).

These five Roman-period biographers – Diodorus, Curtius, Justin, Plutarch
and Arrian – could not help but enter into digressions next on Alexander's
virtues, vices and his comparative legacy to close their biographical pages, as was

the common practice of the time. But whatever their view on his achievements and the highs and lows of his conquests, with Alexander's passing, 'the civilised world, which had never before known only one master, now found itself in a novel situation, that of knowing no master at all'.[61]

Momentum was immediately lost and Alexander's fragile statecraft began to implode. The vacuum united everyone who had suffered his policies in quiet dissent, including the infantry who had walked beside their king for some 20,000 miles.[62] Civil war between the rudderless common soldier and the aristocratic Royal Bodyguards set to inherit great swathes of empire was only days away.

3

THE ASSASSIN'S ASSEMBLY: THE PATH TO CIVIL WAR

What truly happened at Alexander's death in Babylon, and can events be reinterpreted in the presence of a will?

The conflicting reports of what came to pass in the days following Alexander's death raise more questions than they answer; Babylon was itself a city shrouded in myth.

The circumstances embodied in the claims of the Vulgate, the *Journal* and the *Pamphlet* texts were born here, and so was a mysterious list of projects known as the king's 'last plans'. What was really said at the gathering of men-at-arms, by whom and to what end? And could the dialogues have been related to a will? Crucially, how were events at Babylon portrayed by the eyewitness writers who had a vested interest in the outcome?

I return to June 323 BC and to the infighting that was a precursor to Macedonian civil war, and I overlay the testament on the confused narratives.

> Diogenes to Alexander: 'But now, whom did you leave your great empire to?'
> Alexander to Diogenes: 'Diogenes, I cannot tell you. I had no time to leave any directions about it, beyond just giving Perdiccas my ring as I died. Why are you laughing?'[1]
>
> Lucian, *Dialogues of the Dead*

> [At Babylon] the chiefs, moreover, were looking to sovereignty and offices of command; the common soldiers to the treasury and heaps of gold, as a prize unexpectedly presented to their grasp; the one meditating on the possibility of seizing the throne, the other on the means of securing wealth and plenty.[2]
> (T12)
>
> Justin, *Epitome of the Philippic History of Pompeius Trogus*

In early June 323 BC in Babylon, the 'gateway of the gods', prostrated in the Summer Palace of Nebuchadnezzar II on the east bank of the Euphrates, wracked by fever and having barely survived another night, King Alexander III, the ruler of Macedon for twelve years and seven months, had his senior officers congregate at his bedside. Abandoned by Tyche, who governed fortune, and the healing god Asclepius, he finally acknowledged he was dying.

Growing fear and uncertainty filled the portent-laden air. Priests interpreted omens, livers and entrails as whispered intrigues and newly divulged ambitions filled heavy sweat-soaked nights. Life signs were tenuous; the king's breathing was almost imperceptible. Finally, Alexander was publicly pronounced dead and the haunting prophecy of the Chaldean seers came to pass.

The ancient city founded over 1,000 years before the legendary fall of Troy was a fitting stage for the death of the king who had conquered the empire of the Persian Great Kings and vanquished their progeny, for Alexander had married daughters of both Darius III and Artaxerxes III Ochus. The backdrop was no mud-brick town in the eastern regions the Greeks loosely termed 'India', or windswept pass in the upper satrapy of Bactria, but the greatest opulence the world had to offer. It was appropriately theatrical and it was uniquely 'Alexander', and yet the reporting is wholly unconvincing as a conclusion to his story.

Alexander's final days should have provided us with the rich and colourful imagery we read in the campaign accounts. Gossiping eunuchs, concubines and wives frequented the Summer Palace of Nebuchadnezzar II. Bodyguards, physicians, slaves, scribes, cooks, tasters and royal pages filed through anterooms filled with waiting ambassadors who brought dispatches from distant lands at the borders of the known world. We are told the palace was now full of soothsayers, seers, sacrificers, purifiers and prognosticators, their presence a by-product of the king's late obsession with death-harbouring portents. No doubt spells and incantations had been covertly cast as complex fears and political intrigues manifested themselves in dark corridors while Alexander's health continued to deteriorate.

Propped up on the Great King's bed, Alexander had about him all that was required to formalize his succession and articulate instructions for the empire, along with a prolonged illness that provided sufficient time. But according to the surviving mainstream accounts, he failed in every respect even when he was being pressed by his generals to announce a successor.

The Source Fracture

Unravelling the events that took place between Alexander's death on 10 or 11 June 323 BC and the fragile accord that was reached after the infighting at Babylon some indeterminate days later, becomes essential if we are to understand how, and why, the will was whitewashed from the mainstream accounts. In the process, I reveal an unsung hero, Eumenes, who helped make the settlement possible.

Two early narratives of the conflict that followed Alexander's death survived to the Roman period; these were produced by historians who were not themselves present at Babylon, but who had eyewitness accounts. Yet they were not free from personal agenda or obligation. The first version was from Cleitarchus, who had access to campaign veterans who settled in Egypt in the decades following Alexander's death. His narrative of events at Babylon in the aftermath of Alexander's death is thought to survive today most closely in the closing pages of the Roman writer Curtius (T11). He also had access to the scrolls of Ptolemy and Aristobulus (though their respective publication dates are open to question), as well as other court sources (from Nearchus, Onesicritus and the royal chamberlain Chares, for example), though we are not sure of their content or whether they covered Alexander's final days in any detail.[3]

The second formative historian with access to eyewitness testimony was Hieronymus, a Greek from Cardia, and it formed the opening pages of his now-lost history which commenced at Alexander's death and covered the fifty-odd years that followed (titled the *History of the Diadochi* or *Epigoni* – meaning 'successors', or more literally 'offspring' or 'sons of'). For some years after Alexander's death, Hieronymus served fellow Cardian Eumenes (who may have been his uncle), who was certainly at Alexander's deathbed. Hieronymus' initial testimony is preserved today most completely in the eighteenth book of Diodorus' *Library of World History*, which picked up the narrative of the post-Alexander world. Further isolated pixels from the infighting at Babylon are visible in the epitomized fragments of Arrian's *Events After Alexander*, which, once again, drew from Hieronymus' account (T14, T15).[4] Alongside them we have Justin's thirteenth book, in which précised elements of both Cleitarchus' and Hieronymus' accounts appear to be bound together (T12).

The accounts of the two formative historians, Cleitarchus and Hieronymus – who were broadly contemporaries – unsurprisingly conflict, as they lived and worked under opposing political regimes: Cleitarchus in Alexandria under the Ptolemies (thus he could not write anything hostile to the Ptolemaic regime), and Hieronymus at the Antigonid court (after first serving Eumenes) which was at war with Ptolemaic Egypt.

Cleitarchus provided the pre-packaged drama that templated the final chapter of the Roman-period Vulgate biographies (Curtius, Diodorus and Justin used it to wind up their accounts of Alexander's life), whilst Hieronymus' coverage was attractive to any writer extending their work into the Successor Wars, for it set the scene for the follow-on events (Diodorus, Arrian and Justin drew from it for the years after Alexander's death, while Plutarch extracted from it for his biographies of Greek statesmen who survived into the Hellenistic period).

Judging from Diodorus' text, Hieronymus commenced his book of the Successor War years with a summary of the fallout from the Macedonian king's death and a description of the shape and extent of the provinces of the former Persian Empire to help readers understand geographic landscape (as was common practice).[5] He listed the 'chief and most influential commanders', and went on to describe the embassies sent to the rival factions at Babylon, then the compromise reached, the punishment of the dissenters and the crowning of Alexander's half-brother, Arrhidaeus. He detailed Perdiccas' precarious retention of overall command, which was aided by Eumenes, who remained inside the city walls to broker a compromise.[6] All this detail, from the truce between the army factions to the allocation of provinces to the top-tier generals for the new governorship of the empire, is preserved well enough in the Hieronymus-derived summaries, though compressed to varying degrees and with gaps in the text.

In this environment, Perdiccas, the king's former acting 'chiliarch' (likened to a grand vizier in status), now represented something of an uncomfortable hybrid authority that arguably encompassed the regency of a kingdom, the guardianship of new kings and a mandate to oversee the management of the empire, under one – or all – of a number of contentious titles denoting overarching and not-to-be-contested power vested in him. Therein lay the dilemma and the source of the hostility towards Alexander's former senior Bodyguard, for whatever authority Macedonian tradition attached to these titles, here – emerging from a series of unique events at Babylon – their boundaries were being self-determined.[7]

The account of Curtius, who was most probably a professional Roman rhetorician with the political clout of a senator, is the most detailed extant narrative of the infighting that led up to that final settlement of men-at-arms and is punctuated by vivid dialogues (T11). As a result, we are left with an uncomfortable melee of anti-barbarian voices that rejected both of Alexander's sons (one *in utero*, as Rhoxane was still pregnant), highly treasonous accusations hurled at Perdiccas, a suddenly articulate halfwit royal, Arrhidaeus, and the contentious suggestion of group rule by other Bodyguards.[8]

Curtius' recounting of events at Babylon may have reconstructed 'constitutional procedures' on the basis of the few previous examples he saw of the army's intervention into 'state' affairs: the earlier tragic trial and execution of Parmenio's son Philotas, for example, an episode he most likely heavily embellished as well.[9] Nevertheless, the original deeper Cleitarchean currents can still be felt beneath the rhetorical eddies and riptides which pushed Curtius' pen along. For there remains clarity to the emotions emanating from the Assembly gathering that was convened to hear the fate of the empire: the ambition, distrust, uncertainty, divided loyalty and outright jealousy of the gathered generals, 'lightened only by adventurous hopes and shadowy ambition'. This was all neatly summed up by Justin in the chapter-heading text.[10]

After Alexander's death, the Athenian statesman and orator Demades compared the remnants of the Macedonian army in Asia 'to the Cyclops after his one eye was out, seeing their many disorderly and unsteady motions'.[11] Much work has been done attempting to unravel those 'unsteady motions', using the prevailing 'standard intestate model' of what occurred at Babylon when Alexander failed to appoint a successor. But a reinterpretation of the events, most fully captured in Curtius' final pages, can explain equally well, or in fact better, the reading of a contentious will. Here I explain how and why, with the following reinterpretation.

The claims originating in the *Pamphlet*, which are preserved in the *Romance* and also in a late-Roman period précis (of a fragment of only a small portion of the campaigns) known as the *Metz Epitome* (T1, T2), stated that a will was drafted, or more logically revised, through the day and night when Alexander's hopes of recovery were fading, though he was still sufficiently lucid to dictate his wishes to his most trusted men.[12]

Although the content of the testament would have held no big surprises for the top echelon of power, no one could have been completely satisfied with the result. As we might expect, the first reading was a private Bodyguard affair, but inevitably word got out. This explains what happened next in the accounts of Plutarch and Arrian, who never considered a will and so suggested that it was the rumour of Alexander's death which squeezed under the door. But what spread to the army was probably the rumour of a posthumous will recital, which suggested the same, at which point the excluded higher-ranking infantry officers – those already told to wait outside the bedchamber doors – forced their way in, 'suspecting intrigue', believing that their king was dead or at death's door.[13] This was the prelude to full-blown fighting and is lucidly detailed in the *Metz Epitome* manuscript:[14]

> Meanwhile, a rebellious clamour arose among the troops, who threatened to kill Alexander's entourage unless his body was brought before them. For they thought that his death was being concealed from them. So they converged rowdily and in large numbers on the palace, and, Alexander hearing the noise, asked what it was. Perdiccas then told him of the soldiers' suspicion and their rush to the palace, whereupon Alexander issued orders that he be taken from the bedroom and set in an elevated place so that they could be admitted despite their numbers and set out by another door. The men now visited him company by company, admitted wearing only a single tunic. After saluting him tearfully they then went out by the other door. Since he was already in the very throes of death and unable to speak, Alexander returned the salute in silence to all of them with a movement of the hand or a nod.

Their right of entry could not be denied under Macedonian court custom; the soldiers were acknowledged by a barely conscious Alexander and withdrew to brood on the implications of what the testament might contain and ponder whether his wishes would be accurately transmitted, or respected, by those who were destined to inherit power. Though constitutional, the intrusion breached Macedonian military protocol, under which the Bodyguards and royal pages restricted entry to the king; it was an episode that foreshadowed the divided loyalties that would manifest themselves so clearly in the troubled days ahead.

Alexander then passed into a deep coma according to the *Journal*, though there is no mention of this in the Vulgate, where he was vocal to the end. A coma is more credible, or at least a period of silence as life ebbed away. Once life signs were beyond detection, Perdiccas summoned the Companions and the most eminent infantry officers and publicly pronounced the king 'dead'. At this point, Curtius provided a two-and-a-half-page digression on the mourning that followed, when 'conqueror and conquered were indistinguishable' in their grief. He detailed the regrets of the army at denying their king the divine honours he sought (the troops derided his attachments to his new 'father' Zeus-Ammon at the gathering at Opis, just as Alexander's request for deification were mocked in Athens), and listed Alexander's qualities and their attachments to fate and fortune.[15] Justin's précis follows a similar rhetorical template, but here the Macedonians 'rejoiced at his death as at that of an enemy, execrating his excessive severity and the perpetual hardships of war to which he exposed them'.[16] This appears to be more obvious Roman-period rhetoric.

While these sentiments appear polarized, both the feelings of grief and relief *were* doubtlessly present at Babylon, and a complex conjoining of both emotions likely existed in many of those then present. But to understand the framework of the severe discord, we need to unravel the mechanism that drew together those colliding parts – the infantry officers, cavalry command, Bodyguards and chiliarch – and then summarily sundered them. An insightful comment in a study on the legacy of the Asian campaign captures the challenge of analyzing what we have on what is termed the 'Babylonian Settlement', by which the affairs of state were finally agreed:

> ...the situation then was constitutionally unique and politically complex. In that light, it comes as quite a shock to read much of the traditional literature on the Settlement. It presupposes that there was something akin to statute law, with fixed positions and procedures for a regency, and deals with a single definitive settlement, which was reached at Babylon and agreed by all the diverse players in the dynastic game.[17]

Of course, a will would have provided those missing ingredients: a form of statute law, fixed positions and procedures; a defined mandate yet open to ambiguity, abuse and, inevitably, to challenge. For here in foreign lands, 'the king's power was not institutional but situational', and so too was the Common Assembly of Macedones.[18]

The Common Assembly of Macedones

The origins of the Common Assembly are obscure, as is the extent of its constitutional authority at home and even more so overseas in Babylon in 323 BC; arguments on Macedonian constitutionalism have, as one scholar noted, generated a 'cottage industry'.[19] On one extreme, commentators see the Assembly representing formalized state law, while on the other it was nothing but a social tradition that enabled traditional freedom of speech in the presence of a dominant warlord. The debate on whether the Macedonians had even formalized the national title 'king' remains just as vigorous, though Herodotus and Thucydides believed that they had.[20] But 'king', *basileus* in ancient Greek, was never minted on Philip's coins, which suggests that in Macedon the warlord status may have eclipsed any regal recognition. Only towards the end of Alexander's reign were coins struck with '*basileus*'.[21] Again, this suggests the unique army-commander bond was not supplanted by the formalities of regnum until the campaign was well advanced; symbolically, this correlates with Alexander's character metamorphosis in the Vulgate biographies.

With probable roots in a conclave that supported the sovereign power of a warrior-elected leader, the Assembly continued to evolve as equestrian aristocratic landowners emerged in the military state; they acted as a balance, or conduit of authority, between the king and the growing power of the nobility on whom mineral extraction, harbour levies, timber felling and other commercial leases had been bestowed. The king was deemed to control all the state assets, the judicious distribution and gifting of which assured him their support, although this does not undermine the notion that the 'people' considered that the treasury was to be used for their wellbeing and protection.

In turn, the Assembly guarded against the tyranny of the nobility, who, for their privileged positions, were doubtless expected to furnish troops on demand and organize local defence. While in the reign of Philip II 'hardly more than a hundred chiefs of aristocratic families formed the King's Companions', he could have easily become a hostage if he abused their support, which is perhaps why Philip instituted his own private royal guards brigade.[22] Under Alexander's father, the northern and western cantons, which had previously enjoyed a degree of autonomy, were eventually folded into a more centralized state; their nobles and their sons were enrolled into the elite Companion Cavalry.

It was probably at this point that a more formalized Assembly was convened to represent wider national interests.[23] This public forum of expression would have provided the veneer of checks, balances and regional representation, even if the Macedonian 'king' could ultimately sway its vote, whether by charm or execution, or by the threat of his personal pike battalions.[24] But when it came to voting on matters of state during a military campaign, inevitably the common 'people' were the Macedonian 'army'. More often than not, under these circumstances – war – the Assembly was hastily convened, for the army was in fact a far easier body to congregate. It was also easier to manipulate and manage (and more predictable) than scattered peasants and the landlord nobility of peacetime.

Alexander would have read the treatises of the Athenian-born (but pro-Spartan) general Xenophon, who emphasized the importance of having the army's support through assembly decisions where morale could be boosted, and leadership clearly demonstrated. The army, both aristocratic cavalry and the peasant-stocked infantry, was represented by senior battalion commanders. If the idea of some quasi-democratic process is suggested by such a conclave, it remains unlikely that representation ever saw uneducated tenant farmers in the king's hall; but then again, they would not have been seen in Athenian democratic gatherings either, where the Assembly was backed by a Council of tribal representatives meeting on statutory dates. It may have been only military men, perhaps one-tenth of the national male population, who were ever enfranchised in any way.

The Assembly was, in effect, an extension of the king's own personality in what may still have been the absence of wider constitutional laws in Macedon. When the court gatherings ended in traditional drinking parties with their distinct Homeric origins, bonds were galvanized between officers and their commander-in-chief, whose office now represented the foremost religious official, a role in which he became their intermediary with the national gods.[25] It was a relationship that permitted the nobles and army officers access without the formalities of rank, ceremony and formalized obeisance, and though they were still subjects of a monarchy, this explains the Macedonian abhorrence of Achaemenid-style prostration.[26]

The principal functions of the Common Assembly appear clearer than its origins. The gathering retained the ability to elect a new state leader, and it became judge and jury in cases of treason. Although it had been invoked, for example, at the trial of Philotas (and his father, Parmenio, *in absentia*) and at Cassander's revenge-fuelled trial of Olympias some eight years after Alexander's death, quicker executions appear to have taken place on the king's direct command. Alexander did not wait for common opinion to execute the thirteen ringleaders of the dissent at Opis.[27] But to what extent, as king, he could act independent of the Assembly, remains conjecture. Curtius stated that in capital cases, 'the position of the king counted for nothing unless his influence had been substantiated before the trial.'

If, on the other hand, the king's power was absolute (as some scholars see it), how far that could extend probably depended, once again, on his personal charisma, his diplomatic skills, the weight of support he enjoyed from his nobles (as a result) and the nature of the immediate danger being faced. A popular leader would get his way with a minimum of formality, whereas an unpopular figurehead (or a popular king making an unpopular decision) would need formal Common Assembly approval to avoid revolt.[28]

The Assembly also had to deal with the rules of succession, which are not wholly clear. Primogeniture (power to the first born) was not the absolute *requirement* in Macedon, although elder brothers (or uncles) often prevailed for purely practical reasons, often on the pretext of guardianship of the young. Philip II's authority in place of his brother's young son, Amyntas Perdicca, is just one example. But as suggested in a speech recorded by Livy, primogeniture was an established tradition.[29]

Alexander's ancestors had often produced several male heirs who were proclaimed joint kings. In practice, the conflicts engendered by this 'oversupply of kings' often led to pretenders to the throne (often backed by interested neighbouring states) and, inevitably, to fratricide, a result the Successor Wars were to amplify.[30] At other times, kings were elected *in utero* or brothers shared the rule, and if still immature, more formalized guardians would be appointed; here again, the Assembly could play its part, though whether this represented a succession requirement is again unclear.[31]

Considered against the background of the Assembly's traditional function, the situation in Babylon in 323 BC was unique, and it would inevitably challenge the judicial boundaries and the authority of those presiding. Alexander's early 'security measures' – the execution of conspirators, pretenders and their relatives upon his own accession (including Amyntas Perdicca and Philip's new wife and their child) – 'had ensured the Argead house was virtually extinct', and of course that had suited his immediate cause.[32] But Alexander had filled the void by unsatisfactory means as far as the rank and file picking up the pieces at Babylon were concerned.

The Macedonian army was, I propose, now being subordinated in a king's will to what were deemed defective options: an as yet unborn half-Asiatic child by Rhoxane; a further juvenile half-Asiatic son, Heracles, born to Alexander's mistress Barsine; and a mentally defective Argead, Arrhidaeus, Alexander's half-brother. Meanwhile, the distrusted chiliarch Perdiccas was acting as *de facto* head of state. Moreover, the endowments of the will failed to recognize, or even mention, the common foot soldiers who had played a vital part in transforming a kingdom into an empire.

If we assume that the attendance by the infantry officers was a requisite part of the Assembly vote, at Babylon they were hamstrung, for they lacked the voice of the influential generals they had served: Craterus, who was in Cilicia with 10,00 veterans; Antigonus, who controlled much of Anatolia; and the regent in Macedon, Antipater. These were the men who commanded their true respect and who could have challenged the presiding and now hugely wealthy Persian nobility-married Bodyguards.

Cleitarchus and his audience might have envisioned a gathering in the great throne room of the palace, and though it is tempting to visualize a sea of men, the Bodyguards most likely orchestrated a quarantined affair; three courtyards are thought to have led to the throne room of the Summer Palace of Nebuchadnezzar II in Babylon, and they presented a practical means of separation.[33] Indeed, a herald called the officers by name; although 'many were unable to enter the royal quarters', the select summons was widely disregarded and others squeezed through the cordon. Wherever the gathering took place, waiting outside of the palace grounds *was* surely a sea of anxious and impatient men.[34]

Perdiccas chaired the meeting and the salient points of the king's will were read aloud. Curtius claimed that reports of a will were unfounded:

> Some have believed that the distribution of the provinces was prescribed by Alexander's Will, but I have ascertained that this report, though transmitted by our sources, is without foundation.[35]

Curtius nevertheless described how 'a crowd of the rank and file was anxious to know to whom the fortune of Alexander would pass'.[36] This seems paradoxical. But before we jump into the disquiet that followed, we should take a look at Perdiccas' first course of action, on which the parties were all agreed: the cancelling of the ruinously costly and unrealistically ambitious 'last plans'. For embedded within them may be the remains of the bequests from an equally extravagant and ruinous will.

Hidden Last Plans

> For when Perdiccas found in the memoranda of the king orders for the completion of the pyre of Hephaestion, which required a great deal of money, and also for the other designs of Alexander, which were many and great and called for an unprecedented outlay, he decided that it was inexpedient to carry them out. But that he might not appear to be arbitrarily detracting anything from the glory of Alexander, he laid these matters before the common assembly of the Macedonians for consideration.[37] (T25)

Historians appear to accept that although Alexander declined to write a will, he had kept personal royal records (*hypomnemata* in ancient Greek) in which his grandiose plans were outlined in detail. Immediately after his death, Perdiccas apparently 'found' in the king's memoranda (we might suppose in the Eumenes-managed secretariat) a number of incomplete projects and wishes. The most prominent of them included a funeral pyre for Hephaestion, fleet building on an unheard-of scale, harbour constructions that could dock 1,000 warships, population transfers and racial population conglomerates through the establishment of new mixed cities, as well as plans to campaign in Arabia and the West, supported by an ambitious new network of roads.

Some are credible as part of the projects that featured in the main narrative of ongoing military preparations with the associated harbours, canals and dredging improvements at Babylon, though the reported scale, if anywhere near accurate, is extraordinary.[38] As for the remainder, reaction amongst scholars ranges from wholehearted acceptance to wholesale disbelief,[39] but obvious Hellenistic and Roman embroidery has been spotlighted and some non-authentic-looking embassies appeared from far-off supplicants (as already noted) seeking Macedonian 'friendship' at the same time.[40]

What remain notably out of tune in Diodorus' list of scuppered projects were the king's requests for tombs, temples and monuments, for these have a distinctly 'testamental' aroma:

> ... to erect six most costly temples, each at an expense of 1,500 talents ...
> The temples mentioned were to be built at Delos, Delphi, and Dodona, and in Macedonia a temple to Zeus at Dion, to Artemis Tauropolus at Amphipolis, and to Athena at Cyrnus. Likewise at Ilium in honour of

this goddess there was to be built a temple that could never be surpassed by any other. A tomb for his father Philip was to be constructed to match the greatest pyramids of Egypt.[41] (T25).

This detail should be compared with the donatives and memorials demanded in the *Metz Epitome* and *Romance* Wills (T1, T2), in which we read of a tomb for Philip to 'rival the pyramids'. This was, more credibly, to be a great earthwork tumulus in the established Macedonian tradition which followed Platonic guidelines; the 'Great Tumulus' at ancient Aegae, modern Vergina, is a fine example, with a similar structure at Agios Athanasios between Ancient Aegae and Pella.[42] The label 'royal records', *hypomnemata*, could also credibly have accompanied a lifetime covenant or a written testament, and it can be equally translated as 'drafts', 'accompanying notes' or even 'inventories', such as the list of names, deeds and events that once featured in Strabo's *Historica hypomnemata* and the *Hypomnemata* of the Greek philosopher Aristoxenus of Tarentum, and the historian of the Successor War period, Hegesander, which we do now refer to as 'memoirs' or 'commentaries'.[43]

Texts are ambiguous on whether these so-called 'last plans' were discussed at the first, or possibly a second, Assembly. It seems the degeneration of the initial gathering required a further conclave once the infighting at Alexander's death had died down, and it was here that decisions were finally ratified. Claims that Alexander's body was left untreated for some three, six or even (an impossible) thirty days, before the seer Aristander addressed the Assembly, add to the confusion.[44]

When he did finally broach the issue of the 'last plans', Perdiccas' arguments would have focused on treasury limitations and the impracticalities of implementing such heady schemes. He would surely have used the opportunity, now that the will had been broadcast aloud, to solicit the cancelling of both the ongoing campaign plans and the will-demanded monuments in a single breath, thus they were fused together in the recounting of the session.

Making the will contents public, as a Greek scholar has recently pointed out, would have reflected contemporary Macedonian practice (as detailed in Chapter 4).[45] And here at Babylon, rather than sounding controversial, the project abandonments proposed by Perdiccas likely brought a sense of relief to the soldiers, who must have been thinking of heading home with booty and any outstanding back-pay (as had frequently been the case on campaign). They would have been additionally supported by the Bodyguards, who planned to journey to their new satrapies with the treasuries still intact.

Also annulled was the pending change of command in Macedon, in which Antipater was supposed to step down in favour of the returning Craterus, who would have then enjoyed the support of the 10,000 veterans discharged at Opis.[46] On this issue, Perdiccas may have disguised his true intent by arguing for a 'respectful' status quo – in terms of both Craterus' location (Cilicia) and

Antipater's regency – as he was unlikely to have relished the prospect of such a sizeable and experienced force congregating in Macedon under a potentially hostile regent. Perdiccas would have wanted to assimilate Craterus' veterans into his own ranks, considering that as few as 13,000 Macedonian infantry and 2,000 cavalry are thought to have remained at Babylon in the royal army; the rest were Asiatic troops, though newly arrived recruits make calculations uncertain. This annulment *may* have been contentious because Craterus had supporters in Babylon. Many infantry officers present would have served under him, including the vocal battalion commander, Meleager, the most important infantry officer then present and the man at the centre of what would next take place.[47]

Craterus and his veterans (including the prominent commanders White Cleitus, Polyperchon, Antigenes and Gorgias) were still camped in Cilicia when Alexander died, though why they had delayed there remains unexplained. News of the king's death could conceivably have reached Cilicia in ten to twelve days by royal relay, and faster by crier, yet there is no record of Craterus immediately stirring to action. He may well have been watching events at Babylon unfold, and might even have considered making a bid for Perdiccas' post if the winds blew favourably, possibly soliciting reaction first from Antigonus in Phrygia; he, in turn, was no doubt in contact with Antipater in Pella. Craterus and Antigonus might between them have discussed a united front against Perdiccas in Anatolia on the expectation of defections, as they did later.[48] Even when news of the Lamian War in Greece reached them, they may have contemplated letting Antipater embroil himself in trouble in Greece. Having dealt with Perdiccas, they would then cross the Hellespont to save the day and re-administer Hellas and Asia on their own terms.

Many were the permutations (and unhatched schemes we may never know of) and many were the risks. In the end, both Craterus and Antigonus decided to cross to Macedon, but not until clear threats on both sides of the Aegean had emerged.[49] As it turned out, the Lamian War, which commenced soon after news of Alexander's death reached Athens, initially benefited Perdiccas (it is not beyond reason that he was in touch with the Greek uprising) – as it prevented any concerted action being taken against him for a year or more (and it temporarily vacated satrapies in Anatolia) – but it ultimately played a major part in uniting the veteran generals against him.

The textual positioning of the 'last plans' in the extant manuscripts of Diodorus' *Library of World History* has led historians to link Craterus to certain other of these cancelled projects, for the entry credited to the royal records (*hypomnemata*) began (immediately after the allocation of satrapies):

> It happened that Craterus, who was one of the most prominent men, had previously been sent away by Alexander to Cilicia with those men who had been discharged from the army, 10,000 in number. At the

same time, he had received written instructions that the king had given him for execution; nevertheless, after the death of Alexander, it seemed best to the successors not to carry out these plans.[50] (T25)

A description of each project followed. Quite credibly, Craterus could have been given a shipbuilding task by Alexander, for Cilicia was rich in timber from the Taurus ranges and in high-grade iron. Pitch, tow, copper, cloth, shipwrights, carpenters, sawyers and smiths would have been additionally required. Meanwhile, canvas, goat hair, flax and papyrus for ropes and sailcloth, bitumen, bailing buckets, anchors, anchor chains and other tools and accessories needed procuring, and that would have taken time. We are told that copper, hemp and sails had been requisitioned from Cyprus, and cedar wood from Mount Lebanon, whose forests were made famous by the Epic of Gilgamesh and eulogized by Diodorus. Sailors and pilots from all parts of the world were already collecting at nearby Thapsacus on the Upper Euphrates, some 700km from Babylon, for Alexander's planned Arabian–African circumnavigation.[51]

As part of this grand expedition, Cilicia might have been a recruiting point for deck soldiers, oarsmen under a rowing master and helmsman, with the navy operating under fleet trierarchs (those who oversaw the funding and fitting out of a ship).[52] The royal treasury in the fortress of Cyinda high in the Cilican Taurus Mountains would have been called upon to finance the work, assuming the Eastern treasury hauls had already been transferred there. It is possible that the movement of gold and silver was a part of Craterus' brief, aided by the Silver Shields brigade – the *Argyraspides* in ancient Greek – on their journey westward from Opis, and that would explain their slow progress as well as their continued presence in Cilicia.[53]

Craterus' brief may have additionally tasked him with transporting his veterans in part of the new fleet back to Macedon, and then sending Antipater back with new recruits, that is if claims that the aged regent had been summoned are genuine; certainly, Alexander would not have left Macedon devoid of a regent and an army.[54] 'White' Cleitus did construct (or inherit) a navy in Cilicia that was to clear the path for Craterus' re-crossing of the Hellespont two years on. Using part of a 240-strong Macedonian fleet, Cleitus successfully engaged the Athenians in two battles in the Lamian War.[55] A sea voyage home by Craterus could have even included a punitive action against Athens, for Alexander must have been aware of the mercenary concentrations at Cape Taenarum and the polemical noises filtering out of Greece in the months before his death. Antipater would certainly have had a network of spies in Athens.[56]

But the overriding instruction to Craterus was clearly to relieve Antipater of his regency, and the link-line in Diodorus' paragraphs dealing with the conglomerated plans – 'at the same time, he had received written instructions' – could equally have referred to Alexander's orders to Perdiccas.[57] Moreover, Diodorus' previous paragraph closed with an account of the preparations for Alexander's sarcophagus and its journey to Egypt: 'The transportation of the body of the deceased king and the preparation of the vehicle that was to carry the body to Ammon they assigned to Arrhidaeus [another so-named officer, not the halfwit co-king].'[58] The whole passage is badly constructed and the true division of the historian's original intent has been lost. This may have been due to Diodorus' own confusion over a will that appeared nowhere in Cleitarchus' account of Babylon, but which might have featured in Hieronymus' summation of events in which the testament wishes were, nevertheless, ambiguously distinguished from expedition royal records (*hypomnemata*) – cloudy water made murkier by Diodorus' own précising. Or it may be that we are reading incompetent transmissions by monastery-based scribes in the intervening centuries who were themselves unclear on the separation.

This is what Diodorus claimed in a later chapter of his book dealing with events some years after Alexander's death:

> ...honouring Rhodes above all cities [Alexander] both deposited there the testament disposing of his whole realm and in other ways showed admiration.[59]

We know that in classical Greece the word *diatheke* would have most commonly been used when referencing a will, yet it was more specifically a covenant in the legal sense of a contract. Derived from *diatithesthai* – 'putting aside' – the ancient Greek structure *katalipein diatithemenon* – 'to leave by testament' or by 'covenant' – may indeed have been used by Hieronymus somewhere in this narrative.[60] Unless the immediate text was accompanied by clear will-invoking dialogue (Aristotle's will, for example, quoted in full by Diogenes Laertius with all its bequests), the 'contract' was easily shadowed in ambiguity for later historians. If Hieronymus had simply stated 'as the king had covenanted' against these projects, there was little to support a will further in the context of Perdiccas' speech. This would explain the military nature of some of the 'last plans' and the commemorative nature of others.

As a result, the references to Craterus were sandwiched confusingly between the division of the empire and Perdiccas' dilemma with the 'last plans', potentially with the will bequests within them.[61] But the final instruction, which concerned Alexander's funeral hearse, would have been one will-demanded project that Perdiccas and the Assembly dared not reject; they may simply have acquiesced to it as posthumous compensation to their king, despite its ruinous cost. A grand tomb at Aegae, in Macedonian royal tradition, would have probably cost no less – Tomb II at Vergina, probably belonging to Philip, is a fine example.[62]

What Diodorus did make clear was that he was openly excerpting from a fuller list – 'the following were the largest and most remarkable items of the memoranda' – while he added that others 'were many and great' (T25).[63] We would imagine that the list included journal entries from the Eumenes-supervised Royal Diaries that detailed still more demands and projects with their scheduling and costs.[64] It takes no great leap of faith to appreciate how 'diaries'– generically *ephemerides* to Plutarch and Arrian – became 'royal records', *hypomnemata*. Neither is it difficult to appreciate how a reference to 'last wishes', a term often associated with a will, became part of 'last plans' by a historian merging detail from conflicting sources.

Hieronymus was not looking to delve into the campaign past too deeply, as his own forty-plus years of active service were begging their space on parchment. He may not have been fully dispassionate, but neither was he a sensationalist; his book was later described as 'longwinded and boring'.[65] Judging from Arrian's précis of it in his *Events After Alexander*, Hieronymus' summation of Babylon appears to have been 'matter of fact', not plumped up with rhetoric. Moreover, he would not have spent time dissecting a will whose boundaries and bequests were challenged by his patrons from the outset (as I explain in later chapters), and his narrative was dull testate ash when compared to Cleitarchus' intestate flames and the famous words 'to the strongest' Alexander is said to have uttered in answer to the question: 'to whom do you leave your kingdom?' Hieronymus' entry could have conceivably looked something like this:

> Perdiccas dispensed the regional governorships as the king had covenanted and arrangements were made for the transport of the king's body to its final resting place; the task of preparing the funeral bier given to Arrhidaeus. Perdiccas brought before the Assembly the king's list [*hypomnemata*] of last wishes which included … [here followed the list that Diodorus précised] … At the same time he cancelled the other projects found listed in the royal diaries [*Ephemerides*] for the completion of a funeral pyre for Hephaestion, and the plans Craterus had been given for the repatriation of 10,000 veterans to Macedon, as well as for his construction of 1,000 warships larger than triremes for a campaign West, and a road to run through Libya to support the campaign; the construction of new cities with population transfers between them were also cancelled due to the financial situation and uncertainties that faced them … All these final plans were then presented before the Assembly.

But did the overt grandeur of the projects originate with Hieronymus? General scholarly opinion holds that their descriptions are more in keeping with Cleitarchus' sensational style and thus more Vulgate exaggeration that approached 'wonderment' in their scale.[66] If so, how did the detail end up in Diodorus' follow-on book, which leaned principally on Hieronymus? The answer is straightforward enough: Curtius made it clear that Alexander had already announced many of the projects, along with his desire to campaign westwards, the previous year, and they remained at the planning stage, or were at least incomplete, with Arrian providing corroborating detail.[67] When switching sources at the point of Alexander's death, Diodorus embellished what he found presented blandly by Hieronymus with this earlier material that was already painted in Cleitarchean colour (as Diodorus had used Cleitarchus as principal source for his books on Alexander's life, before switching source to Hieronymus when Cleitarchus' book ended). As one historian has commented: 'The more austere history of Hieronymus was enriched by supplements from the Alexander Vulgate.'[68] Hellenistic and then Roman imaginations may have later inflated the scale of the projects. 'Fascinated by the King's personality, historians have failed to see that the story of the *hypomnemata* belongs not to the history of Alexander, but to the history of the Successors' – so concluded one scholar, and so I partially conclude as well.[69]

First Signs of Dissent

When addressing the Assembly, it comes as no surprise to read that Perdiccas broached the succession issue by placing Alexander's ring, crown and robes in front of him for the crowd to see.[70] If the king's will was known to have been drafted and first read in the presence of the Bodyguards, then Perdiccas was re-emphasizing the authority that stemmed from the bequests within the testament. Yet this brought with it the suspicion that he might have unduly influenced the king or the shape of the document itself.

What we consider as an ongoing second-in-command role (a *chiliarchia*) implied Perdiccas' authority filtered down through the king's seven (possibly by now, eight) personal Bodyguards to the cavalry officers, then to the infantry commanders and to the troops below them. Perdiccas was himself of royal stock, from the house of Orestis, the westernmost Upper Macedon canton that lay closest to Epirus, as was Leonnatus, possibly the second-most-influential of them. By now, however, the common infantrymen and the veterans amongst them found the true source of authority in their immediate commander.[71] A later parallel would be the Roman army, whose legionnaires put faith in their centurion ahead of the politically appointed tribunes or legates – the equestrian classes above. For rather than galvanizing an army far from home into a homogenous national unit, Alexander's campaign had seen the social, political and even the financial gaps widen.

The untested authority of the Assembly on foreign soil was being stretched further by an army behaving ever more like a mercenary unit than an imperial force.[72] Since the mutinies in India and at Opis, their willingness to be swayed by their king – the single tenuous thread that had held the authority chain together – had been tested too.

In Curtius' portrayal, Perdiccas handed back the ring of authority he had received from Alexander and then invited the Assembly to choose a new leader, adding that he hoped Rhoxane's child, due within three months (or sooner), would be a boy (T11).[73] Though the Macedonian army had rallied behind royal infants before – the cradled King Aeropus I, for example, who was once carried into battle two-and-a-half-centuries before[74] – here, in contrast to Perdiccas' seeming humility, this final wish appeared to broadcast several tendentious messages. The first was his own vested interest in that outcome, and thus his personal ambition, for he had either been given Rhoxane's hand in marriage (as the *Pamphlet* will claimed) or he had become Rhoxane's *de facto* protector, which amounted to much the same thing.

Perdiccas' words further implied that the claims of other contenders – Alexander's existing son Heracles, and even the king's half-brother Arrhidaeus – might be undermined by his supremacy, despite any wishes in their direction Alexander had articulated in the will. The chiliarch is reported to have rounded-off his speech with, 'meanwhile, nominate those you want as your leaders'.[75]

Perdiccas would not have handed back the emblem of power, when, as events were to show, he did all he could to wrest that power from those who would oppose him. The conclusion to Perdiccas' speech has the hallmark of a Cleitarchean device, and one that legitimized Ptolemy's role in the power play that followed – that is, if it was not Curtius' own theatrical overlay.[76]

The will's demands themselves were sufficiently contentious to cause Assembly uproar. In the thick of the clamour, we hear that Nearchus upheld the claims of both of Alexander's potential sons to the throne, but with a sensible reminder that Rhoxane may give birth to a girl; that would be a situation demanding the recognition of the absent 3- or 4-year-old Heracles.[77] Nearchus had married into the family of the boy's mother at Susa, a fact that has encouraged speculation that it was his written history which brought Heracles out of obscurity as a prelude to his promotion.[78] But at Babylon, Nearchus was pushing his case a little too vigorously, and the crowd saw through another nepotistic promotion that was summarily rejected. If Nearchus did subsequently advance the boy's claim through the medium of his book, it is unlikely he would have mentioned that humiliating Assembly rejection.

At this juncture, Ptolemy was introduced in a pivotal role: he gave a speech that amounted to a total rejection of both of the 'half-barbarian' princes mothered by a 'conquered race'.[79] Mirroring this sentiment, Curtius had previously commented that Alexander's 'friends had been shamed' when he chose to marry Rhoxane, a girl from the 'subject people'.[80] Of course, none could have voiced this in Bactria or at the Susa weddings. Cleitus, who headed the king's own elite cavalry Bodyguard corps, was run through for his straight talking, and the executions at Opis provided an instructive example of what befell dissenters. But here in Babylon, with Alexander dead, these sentiments were emerging at last.

In a sense, Ptolemy's alleged words were also a rejection of Nearchus. Already famous for his sea voyage, Nearchus did indeed steadfastly oppose the Ptolemaic regime in his service under Antigonus in the years to come. But the clearly treasonous words credited to Ptolemy could never have been publicly delivered by a Bodyguard or one of the king's high-ranking Companions so soon after the king's death, intestate or otherwise.[81]

No doubt private utterances proffered exactly this view, especially amongst the infantry for whom the Persians were still the 'enemy'; the notion of a half-Asiatic on the Macedonian throne was, at that time, wholly abhorrent. However, the moral message emanating from this rework, if a product of Cleitarchus, would have suited the tone of the day some thirty-plus years on in Ptolemaic Alexandria (when and from where Cleitarchus published), in which even Egyptians recalled the heavy hand of the Persian yoke. Ptolemy, who declined to cover the Babylonian aftermath in his own book (its last page featured the *Journal* entry with Alexander dying silent), notably never took a wife of Asiatic or Egyptian stock, marrying and fathering children with sisters and daughters of the Macedonian Diadochi.[82] Curtius' own idea of Roman superiority, if overlaid on Cleitarchus' words, would have permitted the reinforcing of such a prejudice against the conquered races.

What followed from Ptolemy appears couched in the suggestion of a working together for a 'common interest' – in this case 'group rule' – because this undermined Perdiccas' absolute supremacy.[83] Arrian, who used Ptolemy as his principal source on Alexander life, had indeed earlier stated that Alexander 'made no fresh appointment to the command of the Companion cavalry' after Hephaestion's death. This sounds like a regurgitation of Ptolemy's attempt to suggest that the chiliarch post – here meant to imply the second-in-command – had disappeared,[84] a statement which contradicts Arrian's *Events After Alexander* (which took its details from Hieronymus) in which Perdiccas *had* clearly assumed Hephaestion's role. Regardless of 'official' titles held at this point, Cleitarchus (with a necessary pro-Ptolemaic slant) appears to have prudently made it clear that whereas 'some agreed with Ptolemy, fewer followed Perdiccas' (T11).[85]

This recommendation might have had legitimate origins. Group rule, by what would be akin to a privy council, would have been credible and workable on the basis that a Bodyguard-dominated group of a few 'super-governors' had been selected by Alexander to bind the empire together cohesively. While I propose his

42   The Last Will and Testament of Alexander the Great

will implemented just that, it also required them to operate under a centralized authority: Perdiccas, who retained control of the royal army in the name of the king(s).[86]

Watching the rising hostility towards the chiliarch with some satisfaction, the Bodyguards had thought it the right moment to tender their own claim for that power without central handcuffing. This proposal was nevertheless rejected by the throng of men, which now firmly inclined away from the aristocratic cabal in favour of more traditional roots in the heat of the indignant moment. Additionally, group rule implied the Assembly itself was being subordinated to this aristocratic collective, which had indeed constituted the highest commands on campaign.

As a countermeasure to that dissent, Aristonus, another Bodyguard who featured less frequently in the surviving texts, reminded the assembly that the will vested power in Perdiccas above all others, a position confirmed by Alexander's emblematically passing to him of the royal seal or ring (T11).[87] This endorsement is indeed consistent with Aristonus' later Perdiccan support, and whilst it is counterintuitive to accept that the pro-Ptolemy Cleitarchus would have wished to reinforce knowledge of Perdiccas' primacy (which could hardly be hidden against the background of his actions in the next three years), the greater message that emerged in the narrative is the flaw in the man, and thus the flaw in Alexander's choice.[88] Aristonus' timely reminder could not be denied, but Perdiccas 'wavered between inclination and shame, and believed that the more modestly he sought what he coveted the more persistently they would press it upon him. So, after delaying and being for a time uncertain what to do, he finally retired to the back part of the Assembly and stood behind those who were nearest to the throne.' (T11)[89]

This troubling paragraph has long been discussed, and is viewed by some scholars as Curtius' own re-rendering of the 'Tiberian farce', because the Roman emperor Tiberius had initially declined the emperorship, 'a wretched and burdensome slavery' that held what he had termed a 'wolf by the ears'.[90] It is noteworthy, too, that Tiberius' hesitation followed the reading of Augustus' will, which reportedly began with 'since a cruel fate has bereft me of my sons',[91] Curtius was possibly embellishing Cleitarchus' portrayal of a devious chiliarch milking the moment at the expense of the other Bodyguards, and presenting it as a familiar episode his Roman audience could readily relate to, though here without any attachment to a will, which Cleitarchus had already removed from events.

There followed a contentious voice from the infantry which was credited to the infantry brigade commander Meleager, here portrayed as a demagogue articulating a common resentment (Curtius implied 'hatred') of the haughty Perdiccas, who had probably failed to integrate with the common soldier on campaign. Yet it might have been that very aloofness and distance from any faction that had made him effective as Alexander's second-in-command; Hephaestion may well have represented this dispassionate authority before him. It appears Cleitarchus was conveniently using Meleager to frame the negative portrayal of the chiliarch, and his accusation was clear: Perdiccas would use Alexander's wife and son, the future king of Macedon, to exploit his own position.[92]

The theme of unchecked ambition captured the dark mood of the Assembly. In contrast to Curtius' narrative, which was derived from Cleitarchus' original and then suitably embellished in Rome, we have Justin's alternative précis: Meleager argued that their proceedings should not be suspended for the result of an uncertain birth, for residing at Pergamum was Alexander's son Heracles – as Nearchus had already reminded them – and better still, already at Babylon was Arrhidaeus, Alexander's half-brother; both of whom, I will argue, surely were recognised in the will.

Alexander's appointing of his mentally deficient half-brother as a figurehead king, in the absence of other options, was a logical move to provide Argead continuity until his sons came of age, and potentially after the 'strongest' or 'most worthy of them' – *toi kratistoi* in Greek (here transmitted as *qui esset optimus* or *dignissimus* in Latin by Curtius and later Justin) – was chosen to wear the crown.[93] To reinforce his case, Meleager reminded the Assembly that Arrhidaeus was begotten by Philip and so was part of his royal line.[94]

Yet what follows suggests Justin conflated the previous sentiment of Nearchus and Ptolemy with Meleager's own dissent into a senseless contradiction; for here again, Rhoxane's Asian origins were rejected with: 'It was unlawful that kings should be chosen for the Macedonians from the blood of those whose kingdoms they had overthrown.' This is senseless if it came from Meleager (rather than Ptolemy, but Justin's text is garbled at this point) because Heracles was also half-Asiatic. Justin was apt to confuse names, and so his accuracy can hardly be relied upon.[95] Justin finished by incorporating the claim that Alexander made no mention of Rhoxane's issue; we may presume that this, once again, alluded to the brevity of his last words in the Vulgate genre texts.

Meleager was a notable infantry commander (a taxiarch) with prominent military posts stretching back twelve years, and he had been amongst the six elite phalanx leaders at the Darius-toppling final battle at Gaugamela alongside Craterus, Perdiccas, Coenus, Amyntas and Polyperchon.[96] Although he was the highest-ranking infantry officer in Babylon, and the only one mentioned in Arrian's list of the most important men, other recorded incidents on campaign suggest Meleager was indeed opinionated, with a voice that at times had bordered on insubordination.[97] At the Babylon Assembly, and understandably angry if he had been passed over in the will – possibly for exactly that reason – Meleager next proposed that Alexander's half-brother, Arrhidaeus, carry the name 'King Philip III' (commonly he was referred to as 'Philip III Arrhidaeus') for political poignancy. It was effective; as Justin put it, he was exploiting an 'indignant infantry' that had been given no share in deliberations.[98]

How incendiary Meleager's speech at the Assembly really was (assuming it came from him) remains conjecture. If Alexander's will did recognise Arrhidaeus in some ceremonial and figurehead role, the speech was not treasonous at all. If properly managed under a formal court guardianship, Arrhidaeus was, in fact, the perfect 'safe' and manageable choice as an interim Argead figurehead, as Alexander may have reasoned, and Meleager could have been reminding the Assembly of just that.[99]

Yet the speech also captured a significant reality: although the Macedonians were prepared to maintain their loyalty to the Argead house, Alexander's sons – born, unborn and bred of Asiatic wives – were simply *not* acceptable as immediate choices, and neither were the highborn Companions and Bodyguards to whom the empire was being conspicuously distributed.

Intriguingly, a fragment of the cuneiform tablet diary known as the *Babylonian Chronicle* recorded the reign of Arrhidaeus (titled 'King Philip III' in it) as eight years long, whereas Diodorus claimed six years and four months (Justin simply stated six years). If the *Chronicle* is accurate, it suggests Alexander had elevated his half-brother to 'ceremonial king' (in Babylon at least) in 324 BC, as some scholars have proposed. This possibility may also be implied by the next Assembly speech, in which 'a man unknown to most of the Macedonians' and apparently of lowly birth claimed Arrhidaeus was recently made the king's 'associate in sacrifices and ceremonies'.[100]

A bond may have been established between the simpleton and his half-brother Alexander, who conspicuously exempted Arrhidaeus from the extended family executions at Philip's murder some thirteen years before, when we imagine Alexander's mother Olympias must have pushed for his immediate death.[101] Arrhidaeus could well have been capable of basic regal functions despite his impaired condition, caused by, it was claimed, Olympias giving him mind-destroying drugs as a boy.[102] He was possibly epileptic (as a manuscript known as the *Heidelberg Epitome* stated), or perhaps more plausibly autistic, for epilepsy did not stop Socrates, Caesar or Caligula from making their indelible marks on history.[103]

Historians old and new are generally in agreement that the speech which followed from the prominent Bodyguard, Peithon son of Crateuas, was a further show of support for Perdiccas, for in 'plain language' he gave an assessment of Arrhidaeus (though this opinion was attached to Ptolemy in Justin's précis); from that we may assume Peithon highlighted his mental limitations. 'Peithon began to follow the plan of Perdiccas, and named Perdiccas and Leonnatus, both of royal birth, as guardians of the son to be born to Rhoxane'; in fact, Macedonian tradition held that only a member of the royal house could in fact be regent.

Rhoxane's potential son was now co-king alongside Arrhidaeus.[104] But Peithon added that the absent Craterus and Antipater should direct affairs in Europe, with Justin reiterating this expanded line-up of guardians. Hidden below the Cleitarchus-originating intestate drama, it appears Peithon was presenting a credible counter-suggestion that maintained the basic fabric of the will.[105]

Here the debate thickens, because to conclude that Peithon was upholding Perdiccas' position is not consistent with their relations immediately after the settlement: Peithon was one of his assassins in Egypt some three years on.[106] If the will had indeed granted Perdiccas overall command, Peithon's speech was anything but supportive. Rather, it was designed to neutralize his sole possession of the boy and made to counter Aristonus' speech. In line with the mood of the gathering, Peithon sweetened the suggestion by bringing the popular but absent Craterus and Antipater into the frame.

What becomes apparent here is Leonnatus' high standing amidst the Macedones. Previously described by Curtius as 'from the purple' (denoting royal or noble birth), he was clearly now the 'second man' then present beside the chiliarch Perdiccas, perhaps due to those regal roots (T11, T12).[107] Peithon's proposal held; the ageing regent, Antipater, was reconfirmed in his role and the popular Craterus, arguably the most senior infantry commander still in Asia, and who had been given supreme control of the entire army when campaigning in the eastern satrapies, was given a protector's role (*prostasia*) alongside him and 'charge of royal property'. The exact division between his military and civil duties remains speculation, but for Craterus it was something of a compensation for his own regency that was now on hold. But whether this would emerge as an 'honorific without power', or arguably the top role in the empire that eclipsed even a chiliarch, only time would tell.[108]

We might speculate that not all of the infantry officers present cared who governed the lands outside Macedon, or perhaps the lands east of the Greek coastal cities of Anatolia, for the army had seen its fill of India and the upper satrapies. They *did*, however, care about the fate of the Macedonian throne and their right to participate in its destiny. Moreover, the Assembly in Babylon was a unique and perhaps once-in-a-lifetime opportunity to decide on something truly hard-earned and of real value to returning veterans. Antipater's regime in Pella had already been instructed by Alexander to endow the repatriated campaigners with garlands and the privilege of front-row seats at public performances.[109] But those picking up the pieces at Alexander's death – the men who were forced to remain in Asia – had not yet enjoyed the fruits of their labour, and now, under the new regime unfolding before them, they wondered if they ever would.

So there were likely to have been quite different mindsets coalescing within the infantry ranks, that now included men intent on getting home, those ambivalent as they had little to return to and those who could not return. Within these last two groups were genuine settlers with wives, concubines, children and waggons laden with booty, and career fighters looking for the next chance to plunder or obtain a land grant as a reward. Finally, there were auxiliary mercenaries and exiles, principally Greeks.

Arrian claimed 10,000 Macedones were registered at Susa as having married Asiatic wives, and though the figure is more than suspiciously high, it is likely that a good number of those then in Babylon had more reason to stay than return to Macedon.[110] For them, the future was in the 'empire' under the wing of the generals who controlled the wealth and vast resources of the newly opened lands they had seen first-hand. As far as these soldiers were concerned, the stature of the immediate commander or satrap of the provinces *did* matter. Some 90 per cent or more of the governors appointed by the prominent Diadochi remained Macedonian or Greek. Opportunity abounded for a talented officer; moreover, evidence suggests a further 15,000–20,000 settlers arrived in the next two decades, when new towns named 'Pella' after the capital of Macedon were founded in Asia.[111]

With this in mind, the surviving texts most likely provide an oversimplified interpretation of the position of the Macedonian soldiers who remained in Babylon, for they are treated as 'state conscripts' billeted where directed. If this was an accurate picture when Alexander was alive, then judging by the tone of the Assembly, it was hardly the case now. Many veterans surely attempted to attach themselves to a province and a new patron under the cleruch (land grant) system that most suited their situation, if not immediately and upon departing Babylon, then over the next several years once the outcome of the early conflict and Lamian War had been decided. So the most prominent Bodyguards – Ptolemy, Peucestas, Lysimachus, Seleucus and Peithon, once free from central command (and probably even before) – would each have been making financial offers, pledges for the future and offers of land grants to secure a solid core of Macedonians and Greeks in their own provincial armies. Indeed, Justin claimed that Alexander's 'friends' had already been secretly paying court to the common soldier to win the favour of the army before the king had died.[112]

Although the infantry officers at the Assembly were arguing the fate of the old kingdom – excluded as they were from wider decisions and from will bequests – the aristocratic Bodyguards were gathered in the spirit of 'empire' and for their will-inherited chunk. So we might surmise that without the confrontational overlaps – Perdiccas' role that would oversee both kingdom and empire, the future of Alexander's half-caste sons and the fate of the Asian treasuries (and its impact on back-pay and any promised bonuses) – the Assembly could have separated the Macedonian cake from its new Asian icing rather less contentiously.

Up to this point, the immediate demands of Alexander's will superficially remained intact, if stretched a little at the edges by wider guardianships. Perdiccas' position was not specifically cancelled, Rhoxane's unborn son remained a potential king and the most prominent Bodyguards now had a hand in his protection as well as the management of Arrhidaeus' temporary kingship. Craterus had been finally recognized in office and the Bodyguards would get their testament-confirmed regional rewards and ceremoniously erect a statue or two to Alexander, as the will demanded.

Additionally, Alexander would be buried with suitable splendour, and at this stage, no will-demanded marriage match to Argead women (those visible, for example, in the *Romance* and *Metz Epitome* testaments) had been openly repudiated. But just when further conflict looked to have been avoided, Meleager dragged the unwitting halfwit Arrhidaeus into the thick of the confrontation. If theatrical, it is not impossible that he was physically presented, and the crowd once again began to slide towards the wholesale rejection of Alexander's sons in favour of a more permanent elevation of a purer Argead heir – an elevation beyond the will's design.[112] It was at this point that the subtle dividing line between tradition and treason was being tested.

To quote Curtius, who was clearly recalling (and adding to) lines from Homer's *Iliad*: 'No deep sea, no vast and storm-swept ocean rouses such great billows as the emotions of a multitude, especially if it is exulting in a liberty which is new and destined to be short-lived.'[114] The 'funeral games' predicted by the dying king in the Vulgate texts now began. Donning arms and cuirass, and adorning Arrhidaeus with Alexander's robes, Meleager led a rebellious procession out to claim the dead king's body, with a phalanx 'ready to glut themselves with the blood of those who had aspired to a throne to which they had no claim'.[115]

Assemblies did, we believe, gather 'under arms' and so soldiers were permitted to attend with their weapons, though tradition required them to remove their helmets when addressing the king.[116] Curtius' account continued: 'In terror, Perdiccas ordered the locking of the chamber in which Alexander's body lay. With him were 600 men of proven valour; he had also been joined by Ptolemy and the company of the Royal Pages.'[117] There followed a skirmish – in which the excited Arrhidaeus was featured – over the possession of Alexander's corpse, which had become a prize and an emblem of authority; this was hardly the action of men who had been abandoned by Alexander with a quip about the bloodshed he knew would soon follow. Whether this took place exactly as we read it, or whether it is another Homeric comparison to the *Iliad*, is open to speculation, but Aelian recognized that the struggle was 'in some ways akin to the one over the phantom at Troy, which Homer celebrates in his tale, where Apollo laid it down among the heroes to protect Aeneas'.[118]

A valiant defence reportedly ensued, though Perdiccas is not specifically credited with any heroics, but rather with early submission: 'After many had been wounded, the older soldiers ... began to beg the men with Perdiccas to stop fighting and to surrender to the king and his superior numbers. Perdiccas was the first to lay down his arms, and the others followed his example.'[119] Actually, the text more convincingly placed Ptolemy as one of the more effective 'protectors'. If I reiterate here that Curtius, writing as he was some three-and-a-half centuries after events, had no obvious political pretensions towards the Diadochi except to add sizzle to an already well-seasoned biographical steak, then Cleitarchus remained consistent in his overall treatment of both Perdiccas and Ptolemy. We may assume he took his lead from the Egyptian dynast's own hostile treatment of the chiliarch which had been published some years before.[120]

The outnumbered senior command was forced to retire, though Perdiccas did initially attempt to remain in the city to keep the veneer of unity intact. Meleager warned that Perdiccas' 'undisciplined spirit' would result in a coup, and he urged 'king' Arrhidaeus to call for his death. He added that 'Perdiccas well remembered how he had treated the king', and 'no one could be truly loyal to someone he feared'; this clearly called into question Perdiccas' earlier behaviour.[121] The half-witted Arrhidaeus acquiesced and Perdiccas was summoned. According to Justin, the prominent phalanx commander, Attalus, dispatched some of his men to assassinate the chiliarch.

The plan failed. Protected by sixteen royal pages, the chiliarch faced-off the would-be assassins, 'Meleager's lackeys', who summarily fled in terror, whereupon Perdiccas joined Leonnatus with the cavalry on the plains outside the city. Justin (who was again clearly blending the narratives of Cleitarchus and Hieronymus where they joined) credited Perdiccas with delivering an effective speech calling for national unity, with 'eloquence particular to himself' (T12). This sounds Hieronymus-derived, for his first patron, Eumenes, was a Perdiccas supporter.[122] A blockade was initiated and this led to a famine inside the walls after only a few days, though this was possibly a rhetorical device inserted to heighten the tension. Curtius himself had already stated that significant tracts of land remained under cultivation in Babylon to feed the population in case of such a siege, unless Xerxes' earlier diversion of the Euphrates had ruined the initiative.[123]

When considering Macedonian army numbers at Babylon in the summer of 323 BC, and with the addition of Asiatic auxiliaries, it is possible that the main body of the cavalry, with their mounts and equipment, were already billeted along the river outside the city, which is estimated to have contained no fewer than 300,000–400,000 inhabitants.[124] The elephant corps, at least, would have been more safely attended outside the inner wall, and keeping Macedonians and Asian levies billeted apart was probably a prudent move. Some 20,000 Persian troops had recently arrived under the command of Peucestas, along with 'a good number of Cossaeans and Tapurians', beside recruits from Caria and Lydia under Philoxenus and Menander.

We do not know how many of the armed Asiatic cadets (*epigonoi*) from Susa were present, or what percentage remained of the 30,000 Greek mercenary infantry and 6,000 cavalry that had survived the march through the Gedrosian desert and forced settlement and garrison duty along the way.[125] Although the Summer or Outer Palace of Nebuchadnezzar II in the Babil suburb of Babylon was constructed with defence in mind and as a military headquarters (as were the structures referred to as either the Northern and Southern Fortresses or Palaces, close to the Ishtar Gate), it could not have accommodated anywhere near these numbers.[126] And recalling that new campaigning in the West was being planned, the city would have swelled significantly if housing the whole army inside its eight fortified gates, or perhaps its inner wall.

With food reputedly short, plus significant hostile cavalry now amassed on the surrounding plains, and when reflecting further upon their insubordination to both the higher command and the demands of Alexander's will, the infantry officers began to contemplate their fate. Sources drawing from Hieronymus' summation cited Meleager as one of the emissaries sent from the cavalry command to the infantry to negotiate a truce, whereupon he defected to their cause and became their *de facto* leader; if so, Perdiccas clearly misread where Meleager's true allegiances lay (T13, T14). But this was an unlikely appointment if he had already attacked Perdiccas so vehemently at the Assembly, so we must treat the vitriol within that Curtian dialogue with care.[127] The envoy role (possibly after he was promised a share of command) is, however, sound if we consider his campaign career, in which he served under both Perdiccas and Craterus and which spanned the authority of both infantry phalanx and Companion Cavalry command, though this appointment does upset Curtius' chronology of events.[128] Whether royal traitor or peoples' hero we may never know, but at some point Meleager crossed the line.

Curtius next narrated what appears to be a rather genuine and unadorned picture of the state of affairs in the palace: 'In fact, the royal quarters still looked as they had before: ambassadors of the nations came to seek audiences with the king, generals presented themselves and armed men and attendants filled the vestibule.' Envoys were arriving from across the known world with new pledges of fealty to the new Great King, and this was undoubtedly to avert the Macedonian war machine from landing on their shores. This short and rhetoric-free digression paints a poignant picture of the confusion that must have terrified both Macedonian and foreign statesman alike, when 'mutual suspicion' prevailed so they 'dared not converse with anyone but turned over secret thoughts each in their own minds'.[129]

Following Meleager's defection, the infantry faction now formally proclaimed Arrhidaeus 'King Philip III of Macedon' (perhaps enacted through a hastily convened infantry-only Assembly, more akin to a war council), and to quote Plutarch more fully: 'A mute diadem, so to speak, passed across the inhabited world.'[130] In response, Perdiccas sent the infantry officers his new terms: a truce would require them handing over the troublemakers. Meleager, sensing a backing wind, had already spent three days 'brooding over plans he kept changing'. The trapped infantry now fully appreciated the gravity of their position, for they had now been branded 'traitors'. Many surely reflected on the vast distance home and on Arrhidaeus' capacity to lead them there, for they were 'in the midst of foes dissatisfied with the new rule', which rather summed up the state of the Macedonian-governed empire. When the terms of the truce were announced, uproar ensued and soldiers armed themselves once more.[131]

The clamour brought the newly crowned Arrhidaeus out of his tent. The halfwit king was not so mute after all, and although up to this point he had been 'cowed by the authority of the generals', he made an impassioned plea for peace and reconciliation and for a funeral that had as yet been denied Alexander.[132] He reportedly ended with: 'So far as I am concerned, I prefer to relinquish this authority of mine rather than to see the blood of fellow citizens flow because of it, and if there is no other hope of accord, I beg and entreat you to choose a better man.'[133]

If Cleitarchus had heard reports that Arrhidaeus had been associated with performing sacrifices and ceremonies at Babylon, he could have drawn a number of conclusions, as could we.[134] The first: Alexander *did* indeed have plans for him, perhaps as a figurehead in Pella, when Alexander headed to Arabia and to the West along the southern Mediterranean shores; Craterus' installation at Pella might have been to facilitate and oversee just that. New mention of his name in the ceremonial role could also suggest that Arrhidaeus may have recently arrived from Macedon, for he was never previously mentioned in any campaign account (he could have arrived with Cassander). So as far as Cleitarchus and Curtius after him were concerned, Arrhidaeus *was* capable of some articulation; it was that perception which led to the construction of the impossibly noble speech from the half-witted Assembly pawn who apparently never uttered a coherent word again until his death some six years or so later.[135]

Arrhidaeus' speech appears, once again, to be sautéed in Roman seasoning, here capturing elements of the cowed Claudius who was found hiding behind curtains upon the assassination of Caligula, for Claudius also surprised Rome later with his own (though genuine) eloquence and political savvy, as well as with his military and infrastructure projects.[136] As has been noted, Arrhidaeus' olive branch captured something of the Roman struggle between aristocrats and the plebiscite in its attempt to please the 'people'.[137]

Accepting that the manipulative hand of Curtius was undoubtedly at work, it seems unlikely he would have placed such vocal articulation upon an otherwise completely dumb character unless Cleitarchus had already recorded some communication, as Curtius would have been risking his credibility at a crucial juncture in his book. Ultimately, the voice provided to Arrhidaeus was one that reinforced his inability, or refusal, to govern the state, let alone the empire, and this provides further justification to Ptolemy's proposal of group rule by those who could, which is more suggestive of Cleitarchus' agenda. The infantry commanders had made fools of themselves by elevating Arrhidaeus beyond the will's design, and they were about to atone in blood.

The envoys sent by Perdiccas from the cavalry camp now returned. Those chosen had been Greeks, including mercenaries – not Macedonians – and it seems they provided him with a list of troublemakers.[138] Eumenes may well have had an active hand in that, for he 'remained behind in the city and mollified many of the men at war and made them more disposed towards a settlement of the quarrel'. Plutarch suggested that Eumenes sided with Alexander's 'principal officers, or Companions, in his opinions', but he added that Eumenes had remained silent in the Assembly as he 'was a kind of common friend to both and held himself aloof from the quarrel, on the ground that it was no business of his, since he was a stranger, to meddle in disputes of Macedonians'.[139] Moreover, if in his position as royal secretary Eumenes had been instrumental in drafting Alexander's will, he needed to maintain the veneer of neutrality lest any suspicion of manipulation fall on him. The statement of Eumenes' useful neutrality was surely sourced by Plutarch from Hieronymus.

A brief calm with a fragile concord emerged, and one that superficially accepted Meleager as a 'third' general (*hyparchos*) alongside Perdiccas himself (and, we assume, Leonnatus, if absentees were not being referred to). Justin interpreted the outcome as follows: 'Such an arrangement being made, Antipater was appointed governor of Macedon and Greece; the charge of the royal treasury was given to Craterus; the management of the camp, the army, and the war, to Meleager and Perdiccas.' (T20) Both armies exchanged salutations and were finally reconciled. Or so they thought.

The Revenge of the Chiliarch

With the complicity of an unwitting Meleager, Perdiccas (probably with the help of the previously hostile Attalus, now promised the hand of Perdiccas' sister) called for a lustration of the 'united' army.[140] This was a ritual of purification linked to pastoral migration and the springtime cleansing of armed men, and it was usually held in the Macedonian month of Xanthikos, shortly before the vernal equinox in March. The religious observance should have signified reconciliation, and it may have been invoked ceremonially at the accession of new kings.[141] Protocol called for a bitch to be cut in two (the fore part of the dog placed to the right, the hind part and entrails to the left) and for the army to march between the disembowelled flesh, with royal insignia and the king's weapons carried before it. Possibly because the infighting at Babylon had commenced in the last days of Daisios (the moon of May month, traditionally harvest gathering), when superstition held that no battle should take place, the importance of the delayed ceremony was heightened.[142]

The cavalry and war elephants were arranged opposite the phalanx, and the infantry soon sensed a trap. Perdiccas 'in his treachery' had the new king call for the execution of the dissenters. The infantrymen were 'stunned', the insurgents singled out and the elephants urged forward by their Indian mahouts. Some 300 men (thirty according to Diodorus) were trampled at the foot of the city walls and an outmanoeuvred Meleager took refuge in a nearby shrine, where he was hunted down and 'not even protected by the sanctuary of the temple', a further slur on Perdiccas' impiety (T11, T14, T20).[143] Despite the inference that Perdiccas was operating alone, which may again serve to illustrate his manipulation of affairs, the Bodyguards and influential Companions, now acting as a kingless war council, were probably united in the action to protect their combined inheritances. If so, it was the only unity they would ever know, and the 'first flush of freedom' was indeed short-lived. Compromise is never sweet, but as Aristotle's *Politics* reasoned, 'a common danger unites even the bitterest of enemies'.[144]

The sedition had been quelled, yet a dilemma remained: the distant Heracles in Pergamum (in western Anatolia) had been vocally rejected, and the pregnant Rhoxane could still bear a girl. The half-witted Philip Arrhidaeus III had to be recognized as the new king simply to avoid further bloodshed. So the Babylonian settlement was concluded; like the will itself, it was an uneasy and unworkable state of affairs that fully satisfied no one, whilst disappointing many.

It was at this point, I propose, that Perdiccas allotted the satrapies as Alexander had detailed in his testament, and not in accordance with his own machinations, as has always been unanimously believed (T16, T17, T18, T20). The most influential generals must have had their say in 'who fitted where', for it would be naive in the extreme to assume no discussions had ever taken place between Alexander and his Bodyguards about empire 'administration'.[145] The appetite and territorial ambition of each manifested itself throughout the Successor Wars, and was unlikely to have been absent before. Perhaps at Susa, when gold crowns were bestowed on the court favourites, requests were tendered, promises made and a broad shape of 'who would govern where' was in place long before the return to Babylon, if not even before that, following Alexander's earlier brushes with death.

Even if the king had survived his last illness, the new planned campaigns westward would have necessitated the installation of loyal satraps behind him. Plutarch was specific that the already feverish king 'conversed with his officers about the vacant posts in the army, and how they might be filled with experienced men'. This shortfall is most readily explained by the appointment of Bodyguards and other prominent officers as governors in Asia.[146] If Alexander's will did reflect these pre-agreed divisions, it did not preclude last-minute amendments, explaining the overnight drafting we read of in the *Pamphlet*-derived texts. If the principal men were to become regional overlords, Perdiccas may, nevertheless, have been influential in selecting their under-governors and perhaps in surrounding his own provincial base of operations with men loyal to him.

Curtius made it clear that Perdiccas 'exposed the royal throne to public view' at each Assembly gathering (T11).[147] Justin, who reported that a second conclave took place after the lustration, corroborated that: 'These proceedings they conducted with the body of Alexander placed in the midst of them, that his majesty might be witness to their resolutions.' (T20)[148] The opening section of Arrian's *Events After Alexander* added: 'nevertheless, he [Perdiccas] proclaimed for the satrapies those who were suspected [to receive them], as if under the orders of Arrhidaeus.' (T14)[149] But here the reference to 'Arrhidaeus' could be interpreted differently if Arrian, or his epitomiser Photius (Arrian's original is lost), misconstrued the phrase 'in the presence of the king' or 'as the king had wished'.

I suggest that each text preserved a key ingredient. Perdiccas, and surely the Bodyguards, when considering the audience they faced, were making it absolutely clear that the regional distribution of power being made came from Alexander, which was hardly possible if he had refused to nominate them to govern across the empire. Perdiccas may have even read aloud something approximating the final lines we see in the *Metz Epitome* will, 'Should any of these named act in contravention of my Testament, I beseech the Olympian Gods to see that he not go unpunished',[150] not an unlikely insertion by a suspicious dying king. Thereafter, Perdiccas took steps to ensure all formal proceedings continued in the same manner – with the king's insignia – making it quite clear whence his own, and inconveniently King Philip Arrhidaeus III's, elevations stemmed from. As one scholar put it, 'Alexander was never so revered as when he was newly dead.'[151]

When constructing the biographical detail of Alexander, Plutarch mined for information outside the texts of Cleitarchus, Hieronymus and the eyewitness historians, and so he alone tantalized his audience with a unique and politically explosive snippet: following his own claim that 'nobody had any suspicions [of conspiracy] at the time' (thus adhering to the *Journal*), he concluded his Babylon narrative by alleging that Rhoxane conspired to kill Stateira, Alexander's Persian wife, and her sister Drypetis, the widow of Hephaestion. Both were daughters of the deposed Great King, Darius III; captured after the Battle of Issus in 333 BC, they were later installed at Susa. Plutarch further claimed that the sisters had been lured to Babylon with a forged royal letter, whereupon they were murdered and their bodies were concealed down a backfilled well.[152]

Apparently, Rhoxane had Perdiccas' consent. If the episode has any substance, we might again implicate the royal secretary, Eumenes, a clear Perdiccan, for his secretarial seal would have rendered the correspondence genuine.[153] The royal women were, alas, more collateral damage of yet more cancelled plans. Hephaestion's heroic legacy was already in trouble, and so were the members of Alexander's Persian family.

The Badly Veiled Accords

What finally emerged at Babylon was an army held together by resented compromises and badly veiled accords. Even Eumenes' role in brokering peace has been described as a necessary deal at Perdiccas' expense, though the intent must have been otherwise.[154] Essentially, three factions had coalesced: firstly the Perdiccans, the most prominent of whom were Aristonus and Eumenes, along with Alcetas (Perdiccas' younger brother), Attalus the son of Andromenes (soon to be Perdiccas' brother-in-law) and his brother Polemon, alongside the resourceful Docimus, whose future allegiances with Antigonus and finally with Lysimachus (at least to the conclusion of the battle at Ipsus twenty-two years later) were punctuated by reported acts of treachery. The soon-to-be-infamous Medius of Larissa briefly joined Perdiccas' ranks.[155] Apart from a reference by Justin to his command of the guards (again possibly confusing his future position in the post-Perdiccas world), there was no mention of Cassander, who had recently arrived in Babylon and who may, indeed, have departed rather quickly following Alexander's death to inform his father Antipater in Pella – and potentially other generals on the way – a state of affairs the *Pamphlet* author later capitalized on when claiming Cassander and his brother poisoned Alexander.

Opposing them there coalesced an anti-Perdiccan Bodyguard faction which had proposed group rule on empire matters to undermine his chiliarch command, at the heart of which were Peithon, Ptolemy and Seleucus (neither Peucestas nor Lysimachus were mentioned at the Assembly gathering).

The third group, the throng of men-at-arms and their infantry officers, had now empowered themselves under 'their' King Philip Arrhidaeus III, and they called for the voices of the state regent Antipater and popular veteran Craterus to protect their interests. The rejected Heracles featured no more and his backers had to fall in line elsewhere; Nearchus, who likely inherited a satrapy himself and who disappeared from texts for the next few years, appears to have kept his head low.[156]

The Bodyguards, now regional governors of vast provinces, were dispatched to their satrapies and Eumenes finalized his own plans to pacify Cappadocia, as, I argue, his will grant required (as stated in the *Romance* and *Metz Epitome* wills, T1, T2). It is unlikely that Perdiccas could have departed Babylon until after

Rhoxane had given birth; a boy was born and the result underpinned Perdiccas' primacy through his immediate guardianship and, not impossibly, through his marriage to Rhoxane, the very terms of the will which gave Meleager his suspicions.

But this was not a time for reflection, it was a time for moving on before any further challenges emerged. Events that followed indicate the anti-Perdiccan league did communicate with Antipater in Macedon, and its members probably pledged their support for his ongoing regency. Antipater, meanwhile, was offering his daughter, Nicaea, to Perdiccas to leverage his own position (or buy time), an arrangement Perdiccas also milked while developing further options of his own.[157]

To counter the regent's long-established influence in Greece, Perdiccas is said to have opened a dialogue with Demades, the Athenian demagogue, who invited him 'to cross over swiftly into Europe to oppose the oligarchs of Antipater', whom he likened to a 'rotten thread'. Perdiccas was likely bartering with promises of Athenian 'freedom' to undermine Antipater's regime (the ultimate aim of Greek forces in the Lamian War), and he secretly planned to reject Nicaea in favour of marriage to Cleopatra, Alexander's full-sister, which suggests further correspondence was taking place with Olympias, likely brokered through Eumenes.[158] Perdiccas next installed Docimus in Babylon, removing the previous governor, Archon, who might have assisted Ptolemy's preparations for capturing Alexander's funeral hearse, and Perdiccas additionally supported Cleomenes in his ongoing administrative role in Egypt, thus undermining Ptolemy's administrative control.[159]

Perdiccas (or rather, I suggest, Alexander in his will) had already ordered Leonnatus and Antigonus to assist Eumenes in the invasion of Cappadocia; both refused, and ended up crossing over to Greece and Macedon and linking up with Antipater.[160] The first 'domestic' clash of arms (outside of the trouble at Babylon) came about with Ptolemy's hijacking (or 'rescuing') of Alexander's funeral hearse, following which Medius and Aristonus were put to use by Perdiccas in an invasion of Cyprus, whose kings were now supporting the Ptolemaic regime. The responses were inevitable, and so commenced the 'greatest armed conflict between fellow Macedonians in more than a generation'.[161]

Peithon, along with Antigenes who commanded the crack Silver Shields brigade, grudgingly operated under Perdiccas until his (officially, King Philip III Arrhidaeus') failed retaliatory invasion of Ptolemy-held Egypt, whereupon they (and possibly Seleucus with them) murdered Perdiccas in his tent in May/June 320 BC.[162] Perdiccas' disastrous attempts at canal dredging when attempting to cross the Nile, and his failed attacks at the Fort of Camels at Pelusium and above the delta near Heliopolis on the route to Memphis, may well have been in part due to the lack of army enthusiasm and this treachery in the planning.

Perdiccas had been forced to grant gifts and promises just to keep the officers from defecting to Ptolemy.[163]

Photius' epitome of Arrian's *Events After Alexander* (uniquely) recorded that Perdiccas aired in front of the army (thus at an impromptu Assembly) 'many charges' against Ptolemy, who successfully defended himself. It is hardly credible that Ptolemy attended a 'show trial' in person. Any speech at this point was simply Perdiccas attempting to prop up morale with accusations before the attack, and, as Diodorus recorded, Ptolemy defended his actions in person when he crossed the Nile to greet the Macedonians the day *after* Perdiccas' death.[164]

Disinterested in Perdiccas' authority, the highborn Leonnatus had earlier departed for Greece with his own plans for power in Macedon (he died in the Lamian War), and Peucestas must have been content in being safely installed in Persis (broadly today's Fars Province of Iran centred at Shiraz), away from the crisis. Lysimachus would have been equally relieved to be governing a satrapy across the Hellespont, removed from the initial strife, though King Seuthes III, who married a Macedonian bride and tried to re-establish the Odrysian Kingdom, gave him a run for his money in Thrace. Neither Lysimachus, nor Peucestas, had anything to lose from watching those embroiled in the emerging factions begin to self-destruct. 'Centrifugal forces were at work', and the fabric of the will was not resilient enough to hold them together.[165] The Babylonian settlement, finalized on the plains outside the city walls, had simply been the early sparks of the pyrotechnics of the Successor Wars.

Origins of the Bias in Curtius' Account

Throughout his portrayal of the Babylon settlement, Cleitarchus appears to have endowed Ptolemy with a 'patriotic' anti-barbarian voice, and to have burdened Perdiccas with a treacherous usurper's role. Ptolemy was, in addition, presented as the rational, legitimate and even 'democratic' voice of the Bodyguards with his proposal of group rule. But Cleitarchus' reshaping of events fulfilled further aims: Alexander's leaving of an empire 'to the strongest' (T6, T7, T8, T9) nullified the significance of Perdiccas receiving the king's ring, while the will was neatly removed from the centre of events, because that concurred with what the *Journal* claimed, and thus with Ptolemy's final pages. It was a literary triumph, capitalized on by Curtius, for its influence on later interpretations and for its challenging of the boundaries established by the *Pamphlet* and the *Journal* without calling out either as a liar.

So where did Cleitarchus end his book? Well, as far back as 1874 a German scholar noted the pro-Ptolemaic slant in the post-Babylon narratives of Diodorus (and Justin's epitome of Trogus), whose detail ought to have been sourced from Hieronymus.[166] But that slant makes little sense when considering

The Assassin's Assembly: The Path to Civil War 57

that the Cardian-born historian served first under the pro-Perdiccas Eumenes and then the Antigonid dynasty, both demonstrably hostile to the Ptolemaic regime. And it seems doubtful that Diodorus, based in Romanized Sicily, had such personal inclinations in favour of Ptolemy I Soter, unless it was to highlight Rome's recent crime of annexing Egypt.[167]

The first of Diodorus' uncharacteristic laudations dealt with the transport of Alexander's body: 'Ptolemy, moreover, doing honour to Alexander, went to meet it with an army as far as Syria, and, receiving the body, deemed it worthy of the greatest consideration.'[168] Diodorus followed with a description of Alexandria 'lacking little of being the most renowned of the cities of the inhabited earth', which neatly supported an earlier flattering reference to the city. This statement *may* include some personal admiration, as Diodorus had himself spent time researching in Alexandria and Strabo certainly lauded the city following his stay a few years on (perhaps from 25/24–20 BC).[169] After describing the tomb Ptolemy had prepared for the sarcophagus, along with sacrifices and magnificent games he threw, Diodorus continued:

> For men, because of his graciousness and nobility of heart, came together eagerly from all sides of Alexandria and gladly enrolled for the campaign ... all of them willingly took upon themselves at their personal risk the preservation of Ptolemy's safety. The gods also saved him unexpectedly from the greatest dangers on account of his courage and his honest treatment of all his friends.[170]

Diodorus' eulogistic tone dovetailed with Curtius' concluding paragraph, which is backed up by the Parian Chronicle: '...but Ptolemy, under whose control Egypt had come, transported the king's body to Memphis, and from there a few years later to Alexandria, where every honour was paid to his memory and his name.'[171] Further, we have Diodorus' polemic against Perdiccas' Egyptian invasion, which framed Ptolemy's higher qualities: 'Perdiccas, indeed, was a man of blood, one who usurped the authority of the other commanders, and in general, wished to rule by force; but Ptolemy, on the contrary, was generous and fair and granted to all commanders the right to speak frankly.'[172]

The overtly favourable treatment of Ptolemy does look Cleitarchean, and yet that would indicate his account extended past Alexander's death and even some two or more years into the Successor Wars. What seems more likely is that Cleitarchus summed up his book with forward-looking laudations but only extended his main narrative to the logical conclusion for an Alexandrian historian: Alexander's burial in Egypt.[173] Within this wrap-up, Cleitarchus constructed his account of the funeral hearse arriving along the lines: 'Alexander's body remains in Egypt where Ptolemy paid it the greatest of respect, despite the hostile attempts of Perdiccas, a man of blood and violence, to cross the Nile and acquire it for his own glory'; this was a sentiment that was dragged into the Successor War accounts by the Vulgate authors writing follow-on books, thus by Diodorus and Justin. Perdiccas' failed invasion of Egypt must still have been a vivid memory in Cleitarchus' day. Of course, it is not impossible that Cleitarchus was regurgitating Ptolemy's own self-promoting ending, though neither Arrian nor Plutarch captured any hint of that; they stated that neither Ptolemy nor Aristobulus had any more to say when winding up their books on Alexander than what had been stated in the *Journal*.[174]

Diodorus followed with: 'Egypt was now held as if a prize of war.' A prize it was, 'due to Ptolemy's prowess', and the city of Alexandria thrived, uniquely, in the Successor Wars and beyond. Ptolemy had initially, and expediently, interred Alexander's body out of harm's way at Memphis, possibly in the Imensthotieion – the Temple of Ammon and Thoth – or in the necropolis of Nectanebo II at Saqqara. The sources that claimed Alexander wished to be buried in Egypt do look to be Hieronymus-derived, and this lends them authenticity.[175] Here the sarcophagus may have originally been surrounded by the life-sized semi-circle of statues of the Greek poets and philosophers most influential to Alexander and found by excavations in the Avenue of Sphinxes in 1850/51.[176]

So Diodorus' stating that 'he [Ptolemy] decided for the present not to send it [the body] to Ammon, but to entomb it in the city that had been founded by Alexander himself' appears contradictory, though it was probably the result of his usual compression. It seems that Ptolemy I Soter, or his son Ptolemy II Philadelphus (or according to Zenobius, Ptolemy IV Philopater even later), finally transferred Alexander's corpse to the Sema at Alexandria sometime after the battle at Ipsus in 301 BC, when borders were under less of a threat.[177] The Alexandrian Sema resonated with the heroic connotations found in the *Iliad* and *Odyssey*, and the bodies of the Ptolemies were now inseparable from that of Alexander.[178] The arrival of his corpse may have coincided with Cleitarchus' own residence in the city, thus again explaining why it featured prominently in his closing paragraphs.

With its origins in Egypt, it was somewhat inevitable that the relocation was foretold by portents in the *Romance* texts: contrary to earlier predictions of Alexander's seers, the chief priest of Memphis foretold that wherever the body rested would be 'constantly troubled and shaken with wars and battles'.[179] A myth emerged which held that the empty green breccia (granite) sarcophagus of Pharaoh Nectanebo II, never used by him and so ferried to Alexandria from Memphis, was his embalmed corpse's initial resting place. If Alexander's mummified body was placed in Nectanebo's coffin, it would help explain why the latter featured so prominently in the *Romance*, which claimed that he, the last Egyptian-born pharaoh, had impregnated Olympias.[180] In a later age, this stone sarcophagus was used as a ritual bath in the Attarin Mosque, as suggested by the twelve drainage holes drilled around the base. Ptolemy's alleged reuse of the pharaonic granite casket, which now resides in the British Museum, does paradoxically support Aelian's contention that the hearse with the original gilded sarcophagus was just a decoy, while Alexander's casketless remains were sped to Egypt by a secret route. There is scant evidence, however, to support these alluring ideas.[181]

What was an original sarcophagus of gold did become a tempting prize. Strabo reported that it was plundered by Ptolemy 'the Usurper' (of Syria), alternatively known as 'the Scarlet' and possibly identifiable with Ptolemy XI, installed by the Roman dictator Sulla (*ca*. 80 BC). Strabo added that by his day, however, Alexander's body resided in another coffin of alabaster (some translations say 'glass').[182] How or when it lost its illustrious inhabitant remains one of history's great mysteries. But as

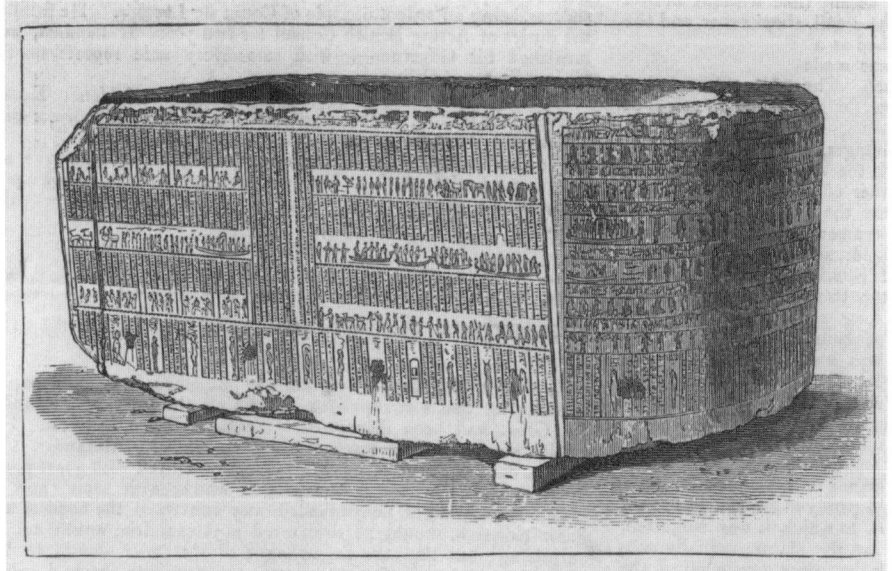

SARCOPHAGUS IN WHICH THE EMBALMED BODY OF ALEXANDER THE GREAT WAS SUPPOSED TO HAVE BEEN DEPOSITED BY PTOLEMY—FROM THE RUINS OF THE SOMA IN ALEXANDRIA

A drawing of the sarcophagus of Nectanebo II found in the Attarin Mosque at Alexandria. The idea that it once contained the body of Alexander is still widely propagated; an engraving, for example, by Thomas Medland and William Alexander was featured on the cover of 'The Tomb of Alexander the Great', a dissertation on the sarcophagus brought from Alexandria and now in the British Museum by E.D. Clarke, published in 1805. The decorative carving on the sides, however, narrates the Egyptian Book of the Underworld without reference to Alexander. The sarcophagus was obtained by Napoleon's expedition to Egypt, and arrived in the British Museum in 1802 under the Treaty of Alexandria.

A mid-nineteenth-century artist's impression of Alexander's funeral hearse pulled by sixty-four mules, after the description by Diodorus.

a scholar has pointed out, one way or another, Alexander had travelled further after his death than most Greeks travelled in a lifetime.

Diodorus provided an extremely detailed description of the funeral cortège and the hearse that departed Babylon, most likely in late spring 321 BC, in which Alexander travelled many of those posthumous miles. Some historians believe this detail could be of Cleitarchean origin too, despite Athenaeus' statement that it came from Hieronymus.[183] If Cleitarchean, we would have expected the Vulgate wrap-ups to have been lured a page or two further to capture the fulsome colour of the remarkable 'Ionic temple on wheels'.[184] The description of its friezes, carvings and adornments is long, precise and rhetoric-free, in line with Hieronymus' style. It has been insightfully noted that 'not a single image of peace was included among these awesome tableaux of Macedonian military might', and further, that the description failed to feature the regular phalanx at all, a punishment perhaps for the infantry dissent at Babylon.[185] But the clue to the original source of the description comes from Diodorus' concluding words, 'and it appeared more magnificent when seen than when described', because 'seen' is the regurgitation of a statement that could have only been made by an eyewitness historian.

The construction of the bier required almost two years.[186] Hieronymus may have returned to Babylon with Eumenes following the unsuccessful Cappadocian invasion, or more likely, he witnessed the bier on its journey to, or in, Syria (where I believe Perdiccas was based) before it was seized by Ptolemy.[187] An intimate description would have reinforced Hieronymus' credentials and acted as the perfect badge of authenticity for the opening of his book. For similar reasons, we should not discount the Cardian historian as the source of the lengthy detail on Hephaestion's funeral pyre; he was after all campaigning with Eumenes in the six-and-a-half years of war that followed Alexander's death, when much information would have been passed between them. So the last pages of Diodorus' seventeenth book, and the early pages of his eighteenth, were indeed a 'patchwork' of the interweaving of Cleitarchus and Hieronymus, with confusing repercussions.[188]

How the Empire was Divided

There remains some uncertainty as to the identity of the archetypal source behind the lists of governors and satrapies in the division of the empire at Babylon (T16, T17, T18, T19, T20). Yet, again, there really is no need to look any further than Hieronymus; many of the governorships were short-lived, providing a tight temporal triangulation.[189] But what might once have been Hieronymus' vibrant excursion into the origins and ethnicities of the Persian Empire in his geographical digression has since (possibly) crumpled to a 'tired, perfunctory catalogue of satrapies' in the condensing.[190]

62 The Last Will and Testament of Alexander the Great

As Diodorus and Trogus were writing continuous world histories, and not simply monographs on Alexander, their rundown of the satrapal list sat in the logical position: at the opening of their books heralding the Successor Wars, consistent, I suggest, with its position in Hieronymus' own account. As expected, their texts, alongside Photius' epitomes and other précised fragments of Arrian's *Events After Alexander*, are remarkably similar in content, pace and non-florid style, with the inevitable compression scars epitomisers leave.

Curtius, on the other hand, did not have the luxury of extended spacing, for he was not writing a follow-on account. So to retrieve the detail he needed, he alone delved into Hieronymus' first chapter to retrieve the satrapal list for his biographical summation. This is exactly where he may have seen Hieronymus' reference to the will he so vocally rejected. In that interpolating process, Curtius shunted Cleitarchus' conspiracy detail back to his final page to give it the dramatic Vulgate wrap-up position.

Curtius wound up his book with a reference to Cassander's murder of the remaining Argead line some thirteen years later in 310/309 BC.[191] Doubting Cleitarchus' book reached forward this far, it once more backs up our contention that Curtius extracted detail from Hieronymus' follow-on books. Plutarch also extracted his own concluding lines on Olympias' revenge (and much detail for his other *Parallel Lives*) from Hieronymus, and for similar reasons: biographies required suitably rounded-off epitaphs, whereas ongoing universal histories did not. Of course, Curtius could have extracted this detail on Cassander's retribution 'second-hand' from an earlier Hieronymus-derived source, thus from Diodorus or even Trogus, but this would still leave the origin of his polemic on the will unexplained (unless he was referring to Diodorus' later reference to it); but as has been pointed out, no Latin author seems to have respected Diodorus or used him extensively.[192]

Could Cleitarchus have detailed the divisions of the empire? The positioning of this tight and specific detail in the follow-on histories (including that of Arrian, who was not a Cleitarchean adherent) argues against that. Moreover, the list dovetails too neatly with the direction of Hieronymus' geographical treatise and the detail does suggest a single source. With some minor discrepancies aside (which can largely be blamed on gaps in text and brevity), the surviving satrapal lists agree on the core territorial claims, or roles of, Ptolemy, Peithon, Lysimachus, Peucestas, Eumenes, Antigonus, Leonnatus, Laomedon, Antipater and Craterus.[193] The first three named Bodyguards, and the order of their names, remain identical in all accounts, as broadly do the divisions of Anatolia.[194] It seems these historians appreciated the logical geographical progression being made through Asia, from south to north (Egypt to Thrace), in the first part of the list, and perhaps this formative detail was simply too unique to be adorned with rhetoric, even if some original background colour (satrapal history, for example) was stripped away in the process.

If the lists appearing in all surviving sources are linked by what cannot be casual coincidences, then the conclusion that each of them extracted from the same original source, or later derivatives of that, appears undeniable.[195]

So what is the significance of establishing Hieronymus as the historian behind this detail? In short, it helps to explain the will's disappearance, as he alone could have referred to it when recounting events at Babylon and linked it to the handing out of satrapies, and yet the following circumstances would have combined to circumnavigate that claim. Firstly, we have the possible ambiguity of Hieronymus' reference to a 'covenant' (*diatheke*). Additionally, though Arrian used Hieronymus for his *Events After Alexander*, he and Plutarch were ultimately adherents to the intestate *Journal*. If Arrian sidestepped the testament in his Babylon summation, then those who used his Successor War history would not have used it either. As Diodorus and Trogus were drawing from Cleitarchus for detail of Alexander's death, a will could hardly feature in their account of the settlement at Babylon, where Alexander's last words left the empire 'to the strongest' in the absence of a succession document.

And so the will was crowded out – of accounts we know about, at least – leaving Curtius to remind us that it once existed in an unnamed source (or sources) he was reading. If that did not include Hieronymus, or an early less embellished copy of the *Pamphlet*, and if he was not making reference to a more sober forerunner of the *Romance* (still reputationally unlikely), then the will had found new friends elsewhere. The late-Roman era *Metz Epitome* indicates that the detail that we now call the 'Book of Death and Last Will and Testament of Alexander' was independently – and still anonymously, it seems – floating around the Roman literary world for centuries thereafter, for when Arrian and Plutarch dismissively summarised the conspiracy rumours, neither mentioned the author's name (T9, T10).[196]

In summary, what we read today of events at Babylon is an episodic amalgam of settlements within settlements, by both men-at-arms and by historians in conflict, and it remains as misunderstood as any momentous juncture in history. The tectonic plates of Ptolemy's *Journal*, Cleitarchus' syncretic theatre, Hieronymus' possibly will-derived list of governors, and the enigmatic *Pamphlet* collided at the point of Alexander's death and left an untidy fault line.

The result was that Alexander's final wishes at Babylon were eventually manipulated away from him by his men and by historians in a flanking manoeuvre he had never witnessed on the battlefield. Dried in embalmer's natron and bound in linen, following the Eastern practice, his body was finally mummified to preserve his corpse from the summer heat. But before Alexander's organs were replaced and protected by Canopic jars, the truth behind his death was being ignominiously buried elsewhere. He had no choice in the matter, for despite the giants of the age it empowered, Alexander's will was just a frail document after all, and one not destined for the Alexandrian archives. The testament was as vulnerable as the material on which it was penned, and as flammable as its own short-lived content. Alexander 'died untimely', and like the truth behind events at Babylon, his will was soon hidden under the ink of his agenda-laden biographers.

4

WILLS AND TESTAMENTS IN CLASSICAL GREECE

Did Wills Truly Exist in Alexander's Day?

Did kings, dictators and statesmen use wills in Classical Greece and the Hellenistic world to ensure successions, pass down estates and document their last wishes? And is the claim that Alexander made a will at Babylon supportable in the context of the social practice, succession precedents and legislation of the time?

I review the development of what is now referred to as the 'Last Will and Testament', and look at infamous examples of their manipulations, implementations and the world-changing repercussions in the classical world of the time.

Extracts from the prelude to the reading of Alexander's will from the Metz Epitome manuscript.[1]

This is the most lucid text containing Alexander's will and the lead up to its reading at Babylon. It was appended later and was not part of the original *Metz Epitome* text, and is presented without the obvious embellishment that has attached itself to the later versions of the *Greek Alexander Romance*. Like the Romance texts, the *Metz Epitome* is corrupted in places with textual gaps and indecipherable infill, here denoted as [ ], and punctuated with references to the poison conspiracy and a second poisoning by Alexander's cup bearer Iollas (Antipater's son) just before the will is read out. For brevity, I have omitted this and focused on the testament.

The obvious faulty transmission of names has been corrected and Romanized references (to the names of gods, for example) reverted to Greek. Alexander pluralizes to 'we' and 'our' when referring to his own decisions, which was not an uncommon practice by writers of the period when re-rendering a speech or even their own opinions.

> When dawn arrived, Alexander summoned Perdiccas, Holcias, Lysimachus and Ptolemy and bade them not to grant anyone access to him, until he had finished what he needed to do. Then they left, but two young boys he kept with him, named Hermogenes and Cambaphes, one to take down his testament and the other to tend the lamp. And so he spent a day and a night penning his testament ...
>
> ... After all the men had filed past and he was back in his bedroom, he called in Perdiccas and the others. He handed to Holcias his testament to be read aloud to him, but he first ordered that a letter he had written to the Rhodians be read out clearly. The letter went as follows:
>
> 'King Alexander to the senate and people of Rhodes: Greetings! We, beyond the pillars of our ancestral god, Heracles [ ] from the territory, leaving our enemies [ ] we have divided our realm and our wealth. We consider you to be the most suitable executors and guardians; because we have come to know your exceptional reliability and integrity, and that is why we have always kept your city in the highest regard. We have therefore sent written instructions to [Cebes] to remove the garrison from your town, and I have made sure that you will know from my will – a copy of which I have sent you – that I am also attentive to your other interests.
>
> 'Basing our assessment on relevant merit and rank, we have made an allotment of territories and we have directed their governors to ensure that each be given an amount from the royal treasury which we decreed. This includes 300 talents in gold coin for you to enhance the beauty of

your city, 40,000 bushels of wheat per year and forty warships. We have also provided instructions that our body be transported to Egypt and the resident priests attend to the burial. Because of your integrity and authority you have a moral duty to make especially sure that this is done and to be meticulous in carrying out my instructions. Farewell.'

Once this was written in the letter, Alexander ordered his will to be read back to him closely. Attaching numerous seals, he passed the document to Holcias, instructing him to find a loyal person to courier the letter to Rhodes as soon as possible with a copy of the will. Holcias brought in a Theban named Ismenias, gave him the letter and pointed out to him the favourable manner with which the king dealt with the Thebans in the will. Delighted at the benefits afforded to his homeland, Ismenias was now more attentive and faster in bringing the letter to Rhodes.

... I have outlined in my will what I wish done after my death. Perdiccas, you and Antipater take care of affairs in the meantime and see to it that the terms of my will are followed.

At this point, Holcias took his hat off his head, covered his streaming eyes and departed. Then Alexander summoned Lysimachus and said, 'Depart for Thrace', following which Lysimachus left the room in tears. Alexander then said to Ptolemy: 'You also depart, for Egypt, and ensure my body is well looked after.' There were other instructions he then whispered in his ear. When Ptolemy heard them he could not hold back his tears; with his face covered, he left the gathering.

... With an effort Alexander barely managed to groan the words: 'Take me Divine Heracles and Athena; and to you my friends, farewell!', after which he removed his ring from his finger and handed it to Perdiccas. The king, grinding his teeth as he realised he was uttering his last breath, took her [Rhoxane] in his arms and started kissing her. He held her right hand and he put it in Perdiccas' right hand and nodded his approval ...

So Alexander the Great departed this life at the age of thirty-three and following a reign of thirteen years. Next, even though the army was still unaware of their king's death, terror and panic broke out suddenly, seemingly for no reason. The men all rushed to arms with a clamour, yet no man really knew what the issue was. Meanwhile, Perdiccas with those in the palace put the dead king in a coffin, dressed him in a tunic and purple cloak and laid a crown on his head. Many perfumes were added and mixed with honey before they covered the coffin with a purple shawl over which they set a Babylonian tapestry.

Then, with covered heads and eyes focused on the ground, they made their way to the raised platform to face the soldiers. After the herald had called for silence, Perdiccas addressed a large gathering. 'Macedonians', he said, 'know that your king, Alexander, has joined the gods. You must therefore speak among yourselves in words of good omen and avoid language of ill portent.' Then, the herald had again called for silence, he instructed Holcias to read out the Will, which was as follows:

'The testament made by King Alexander, son of Ammon and Olympias. If my child by my wife, Rhoxane, is a son, he above all others is to be King of Macedon, and in the interim Arrhidaeus, son of Philip, should lead the Macedonians. If my wife, Rhoxane, births a daughter, may the Macedonians ensure she is raised and married in the style befitting their loyalty to me and my prestige, and then let them choose as their king the man they think worthy. The man once elected [should be] king of Macedon.

'To my mother, Olympias, I bestow the right to live in Rhodes or anywhere else she wishes and the king of Macedon is to see that she is given each year all the things she enjoyed during my lifetime. Until the Macedonians choose a king, King Alexander, son of Ammon and Olympias, nominates Craterus as overseer of his entire kingdom of Macedon, and [gives] him in marriage Cynnane the daughter of Philip, the former King of Macedon. Lysimachus is put in charge of Thrace and [gives] as in marriage to him Thessalonice, daughter of Philip, the former King of Macedon. To Leonnatus I bestow the satrapy of the Hellespont and the hand in marriage of Holcias' sister, Cleonice. I appoint Eumenes, my former secretary, as ruler of Cappadocia and Paphlagonia. I declare the islands free; let them keep their former possessions and be self-governing.

'I appoint Antigonus as governor of Pamphylia, Lycia and Greater Phrygia, and I place Asander in authority over Caria [and the territory which lies beyond] the river called the Halys; over this region I appoint Antipater as governor. I make Nicanor governor of Cilicia, and Peithon governor of Syria as far as the so-called Mesopotamian Line. Babylon and Babylonian territory which borders it I place under the command of Seleucus who was my shield bearer. I assign Phoenicia and Coele-Syria to Meleager. The kingdom of Egypt I bequeath to Ptolemy, with the hand in marriage to my sister, Cleopatra.

'As for the regions lying between the borders of Babylonia and Bactria, the satraps should retain what they already govern, and as commander-in-chief over them I appoint Perdiccas, to whom I bestow in marriage, Rhoxane, who was my wife, the Bactrian daughter of Oxyartes. The Rhodians are to be granted 300 talents of gold from the royal treasury for enhancing the beauty of their city; they are also to be given 40 triremes and a gratis yearly subsidy of 20,[000] medimni of Egyptian grain and, also gratis on a yearly basis, 20,[000] medimni of wheat from the Asian territories adjacent to Rhodes. I also order the removal from the town of the resident garrison I put there.[2]

'The priests in Egypt are to be granted 2,000 talents in gold coin from public treasury, and Ptolemy is to arrange the transportation [to Egypt] of my body, which the priests of Egypt are to carry out as they think best. The sarcophagus in which the body is to rest is to be made from 200 talents of gold.

'To the Thebans of Boeotia I give 300 talents of coined gold for the rebuilding of their city, and to the exiles who were refugees from there [because] of the war, I restore to them all the property they were deprived of. I consider they have been sufficiently punished for their foolish opposition to me. The Athenians are to be given a golden throne for the Temple of Athena and also a robe of gold. My arms and insignia plus 1,000 talents of silver are to go to the temple of Hera at Argos, while Apollo at Delphi is to be given all the elephant tusks and [two] snake skins plus 100 golden libation bowls. The Milesians are granted 150 talents of silver as are the Cnidians to be given 150.

'Taxiles is to become governor of those regions of India which border the Indus river, Porus of those regions between the river Hydaspes and the Indus. I appoint the Bactrian Oxyartes, father of my wife, Rhoxane, governor of Paropanisadae, and Sibyrtius is to rule over the Arachosians and Cedrosians. I give authority over the Areians and Drangians to Stasanor of Soli.

'Philip is to rule the Bactrians. Parthia and what borders Hyrcania I give to Phratapherenes, Carmania to Tlepolemus. Peucestas is to maintain overall command over all the Persians. From all [these] governorships Oxydates is to be replaced and Peithon son of Crateuas is to take over his governance of the Medes. Argaeus is also to be removed from Susiana, where Coenus will govern in his place.[3]

'Over all the Illyrians I appoint Holcias governor and I grant him a squadron of 500 requisitioned horses and 3,000 talents of silver coin, which he is to use to construct statues of Alexander, Ammon, Athena, Heracles, Olympias and my father, Philip. These are to be set up by him in the shrine at Olympia. The men to whom I have given these overall commands are to set up gilded statues of Alexander in Delphi, Athens, [hiolce]. Ptolemy is to set up in Egypt gilded statues of Alexander, Ammon, Athena, Heracles, Olympias and my father, Philip.

'Witness to all this be Olympian Zeus, Heracles our nation's god, Athena, Ares, Ammon the Sun, and King Alexander's Fortune.

'Should any of these named breech of the terms of my testament, I call upon Zeus and the Olympian gods to see that he not go unpunished for it, and that he be held guilty of mendacity before gods and men.'

Thus it is an error of men who are not strictly upright to seize upon something that seems to be expedient and straightaway to dissociate that from the question of moral right. To this error the assassin's dagger, the poisoned cup, the forged Wills owe their origins.[4]

Cicero, *On Duties*

'All will be well but in case anything should happen, I make these dispositions'; so began typical Greek wills in the age of Alexander, and so opened the wills of both Aristotle and his successor Theophrastus, legends of the Lyceum school in Athens and contemporaries of the campaigning king.[5]

These documents were not the hastily penned bequests of men dying unexpectedly, but highlighted a judicious respect for mortality in a legal system that recognized trusts, inheritances and estate planning. Aristotle's will was substantial enough to provide one modern legal scholar with sufficient detail for a treatise on Greek estate law.[6] A product of the Peripatetic School, Aristotle's last written wishes – a *diatheke* in ancient Greek, and more literally a 'covenant' denoting a formal and legally binding declaration of benefits given by one party to another – did not have room for rhetoric; the testament was precise, practical and provided for multiple scenarios.

We have many other examples that demonstrate the intricacy, ceremony and sophistication that wills had attained by the fourth century BC, along with the challenges and frauds that accompanied them.

Hipponax, an Athenian doctor, noted the arrangements of his patient, Lycophron, as his death approached: 'He made his will and called in his friends to witness it, and one must hope there can be no doubt about the validity, the signets attached etc, for otherwise the heirs may find themselves in a pretty lawsuit.'[7] Lycophron's will pledged his young wife and the guardianship of his daughter to a trusted bachelor friend, and it included instructions for his tomb with financial legacies to other named associates. Lastly, three reliable friends were appointed as the executors.

The full title of the testator – the person making the will – was Lycophron the Marathonian, for Athenian legal documents recorded the residential district of the interested parties (the *demos*, each deme having its own sanctuary and founding deity) alongside the personal name (*onoma*) and the father's name (*patronymikon*).[8] In the case of a foreign resident known as a 'metic', the place of birth was required.

The description of Lycophron's funeral rites made it clear that the formalities demanded were part of a highly ritualized event. The will was replete with litigious connotations, suggesting an attention to detail in accordance with the demands of (the still not fully deciphered) Athenian legislation.[9] By the time the Athenian Constitution had been drafted, the mechanism of passing an estate had been formalized into what we term today the last will and testament, derived from the Roman *testamentum*. Although not every Greek state permitted the individual such latitude, the use of wills was undeniably widespread in the developing Hellenic world.

But would the type of will that survives in the various versions (known as 'redactions') of Alexander's *Romance* and in the *Metz Epitome* (recreated in full at the beginning of this chapter), which originated with the *Pamphlet*, have truly been the mechanism Alexander would have used to assure a clean succession and one respected by the army? The answer lies in part in our analysis of the Macedonian king and in our interpretation of the authority a will could have carried in the unique position Alexander found himself at Babylon in June 323 BC. But how much of his original testament was transmitted faithfully by the author of the *Pamphlet* is another question altogether.

How Wills Emerged

Wills did not originate in Classical Greece. Bronze Age texts preserve the death-covenants of northern Mesopotamia preceding the neo-Babylonian period (626–539 BC), where tablets and other inscriptions reveal the double estate share due to the eldest sons.[10] Older still are the written testaments of Egypt. Sir Flinders Petrie, the 'father of Egyptology', discovered their oldest recorded forerunners dating back 4,500 years; they have been described as 'so curiously modern in form that it might almost be granted probate today'.[11] The Greeks adopted much from Egypt, and that may well include the architecture of legal inheritance, and its development in Greece is evidenced.

Hesiod composed his highly valued *Works and Days* sometime around 700 BC (dating is still speculative). This was an instructional poem that captured a dispute with his brother, Perses, over his squandering of a disproportionate share of their father's estate that had avowedly been left to them equally in his will, and the bribed judges who ruled against Hesiod were attacked through the poem.[12]

According to Plutarch, a Spartan ephor, Epitadeus, proposed that the Lycurgan law (legend dates it to 885 BC) of leaving all possessions to one's son were outdated, so new will bequests were needed as well as lifetime gifts. Spartan inheritance in Lacedaemon was further complicated by land lots that could not be bought or sold in life or passed from father to son, but which could be bequeathed at death to anyone; so claimed Aristotle in a hostile appraisal of its constitution, which also claimed that two-fifths of the state was owned by women as a result.[13]

In Athens, Solon began the articulation of estate planning in his set of laws enacted in 594/593 BC once he had been appointed archon and arbiter on social issues.[14] Although Solon was praised for introducing wills, the law under what is known as the Draconian Statutes still firmly favoured the Athenian nobility, a class that dominated in Attica longer than in other regions of Greece. Solon's own father had 'impaired his estate in sundry benevolent charities', prompting him to apparently declare: 'Wealth I desire to have; but wrongfully to get it, I do not wish. Justice, even if slow, is sure.'[15] However, by 500 BC, in line with Cleisthenes' transformation of the Areopagus – the aristocratic judicial court – into a more citizen-represented council (*boule*), laws on intestacy evolved: inheritance rules relating to orphans and heiresses, property settlement, donations and adoption were debated, refined and, inevitably, contested.[16]

Here, most relevantly, there is plentiful evidence that testators were fearful their wills could be hidden, manipulated or subverted in some way, and this was illustrated by the efforts they made to have them recorded and authenticated. One example is the Athenian politician Callias, who, returning from his questionably successful mission to Susa to broker a peace with Persia (sometime in the 440s BC) and fearing he would be cut off by a 'wicked conspiracy' in his absence, is said to have made an open declaration of his will before the popular Assembly at Athens.[17]

Subversions were facilitated when the testator declared a will before witnesses as a 'memorium', a verbal recitation without committing it into writing. This required something of an honour-based code, like the timeworn tradition of the later vocal or auricular living covenants and the nuncupative testaments (such as last words relating to assets uttered by a dying soldier) of the Roman period. Confusingly, as we have noted, in Greece a commercial covenant, assignment or contract was referred to under the same name as what we now term a will.

The latitude for challenging estate-related bequests narrowed when Solon introduced documented testaments that would be pronounced before several judges and jurors of the popular court. According to Diogenes Laertius, Solon's own will requested that his ashes be scattered around his birthplace at Salamis.[18] In Athens, the practice of authentication involved depositing wills at public offices, signed and sealed in the presence of magistrates, who were very often at their original drafting. The procedures epitomize Athens' more general shift from orality to the increasing use of writing, which had disappeared after the fall of Mycenaean Greece, only to gradually re-emerge after the so-called 'Dark Ages' in the form of a more versatile alphabet adapted from the Phoenicians.[19]

This development unfortunately also locked in Solon's less attractive legislation, some of it termed 'peculiar' by Plutarch, for example a procedure that oversaw the law of Athenian heiresses. These were the daughters of fathers with no male heirs and they were required to marry their father's closest male relative to keep property within the family, with sex provided to her thrice per month as a show of esteem. The ruling often led to the daughter residing in a household with an existing wife, and led to further conflict where the heiress daughter was already married herself.[20] Married daughters had no claims against an estate if not named in the will. In the event of the father's intestacy, unmarried daughters had no immediate estate rights except for dowry and maintenance until they wed, at which point their estate went with them to the new male husband. If a daughter subsequently gave birth to a son by the male relative, he would ultimately acquire that part of the estate.[21] It's worth noting that women could take no part in the politics of Greece and were not considered full citizens at this time.

Diogenes Laertius stated that it was Ariston of Kea who penned the wills of the Peripatetic Scholars (those of Aristotle's school), testaments whose legal structure was motivated by the desire to maintain the private ownership of the philosophical school itself, including its all-important library. It is likely that all surviving versions of the Peripatetics' wills come from this collection. Apart from those of Aristotle and Theophrastus, the list included the testaments of their successors Strato of Lampsacus (*ca.* 335–269 BC), Arcesilaus (*ca.* 316/315–241 BC), Lyco (*ca.* 299–225 BC) and Epicurus (*ca.* 341–270 BC).[22]

Epicurus was born just fifteen years after Alexander and he founded the eponymously named philosophical movement (the Epicureans) following the Macedonian king's death. Although only a few fragments of his treatises survive, we know his family was dislodged by the Successor Wars and moved from Samos to Colophon, a city eventually destroyed by Alexander's former Bodyguard Lysimachus, who became ruler of Thrace and beyond. Epicurus, for whom 'pleasure was the beginning and end of a blessed life', finally died in Athens aged 72 and his sophisticated will is another lesson in estate planning: he set up a Lifetime Trust and included a Deed of Gift within it so that his Epicurean school and its iconic 'Garden' would continue to flourish. The will provided for the future funeral costs of his family and it contained annuities and marriage directions for children of the prominent members of his school.[23]

Arcesilaus, a former pupil of Aristotle's follower Theophrastus and founder of the Middle Academy which brought scepticism into philosophical debate, attacked the doctrine of the Stoics which claimed that truth is defined by perception alone. In pure Sceptic fashion, Arcesilaus claimed 'to know nothing, not even his own ignorance', and yet he knew how to prepare for death.[24] Three copies of his will were prepared; one was deposited at Athens with friends, another at Eretria and a third was sent home to a relative, Thaumasias, with a covering letter explaining his rationale:

> I have given Diogenes a copy of my will to convey to you. For, because I am frequently unwell and have become very infirm, I have thought it right to make a will, that if anything should happen to me I might not depart with feelings of having done you any injury, who have been so constantly in affection to me.[25]

Evidence of the use of Wills in Ancient Macedon

The ubiquity of wills in Greece and later in Rome – where emperors refined, codified, contested, manipulated and hid estate documents in their attempts to change the course of history – clearly illustrated that such written succession documents were the legal mechanism for transferring power before, during and after the time of Alexander. But we need to ask whether Macedon adopted the same tradition. On the one hand, it may be irrelevant, as Alexander was more Greek in education, 'Homeric' in spirit and Macedonian in arms alone. Yet we do have examples of noteworthy testaments attached to men who featured in Alexander's story, and evidence that Macedonian law recognized their structure.

Alexander's own tutor Aristotle prepared for his own death by appointing Antipater, the Macedonian regent, as the general executor of his will, and this is significant to us for several reasons. Firstly, it confirms that a bond and a trust existed between the two men, a fact exploited by a tradition which linked them, working in unison, to the plot to murder Alexander which first appeared in the *Pamphlet* poison conspiracy; Aristotle supposedly provided the poison ferried to Babylon by Antipater's sons, which became a garnish to the claims made in the Vulgate genre (T9, T10).[26] Diogenes Laertius knew of nine letters sent from Aristotle to the regent (compared with four to Alexander), and if a tight relationship between them does not necessarily point to covert regicide, it does suggest mutual interests, and 'ample traces' of correspondence between them still exist.[27]

A soldier named Nicanor was named as the garrison commander of Antipater's son Cassander at Athens in the Successor Wars. If, as many commentators believe, Nicanor was Aristotle's nephew (who married Aristotle's daughter under the terms of his aforementioned will), we have further evidence of those close relations between the scholar and house of Antipater.[28] But above all, Aristotle's testament indicates that the Macedonian nobles, at any rate, were familiar with the will as a mechanism of estate planning, for it is hardly likely that Antipater would have been enrolled in such a pivotal role if not willing to recognize and uphold its legality. Aristotle may himself have been granted full Macedonian citizenship by the time he died, either for his services to the monarchy or simply because Stagira where he was born was now part of the greater Macedon forged by Alexander's father Philip as he annexed border lands.

The appointment of Antipater as the executor may additionally suggest Aristotle was seeking the regent's protection, for it appears Aristotle fled Athens after Alexander's death, fearing reprisals for his long career supporting (and supported by) the Macedonian monarchy. Yet the city-state of Chalcis on Euboea was not significantly safer or much further from an assassin's reach. As we know, a well-documented enmity had existed between Olympias, the queen mother, and Antipater.[29] If the hostile Athenian orator Hyperides had indeed already lost his tongue for proposing honours to Iollas for his part in the Babylonian plot (as we read, and even if not), we wonder if Aristotle feared the agents of Olympias rather more than those of Athens.[30] A few years on, Olympias did wreak vengeance on Antipater's sons, no doubt guided by, or at least legitimized by, the plot 'revealed' in the *Pamphlet*, which, I argue, she co-authored with Eumenes.[31]

In his own will, Aristotle, notably, asked that life-size stone statues to Zeus and Athena the Saviour be erected, just as Alexander's surviving will, as we read it in the *Romance* and *Metz Epitome*, requested statues of himself, the gods and his parents to be set up in the most noteworthy of cities.[32] As neither Alexander nor Athens was mentioned in Aristotle's will, it has been suggested that it was probably penned in Chalcis in 322 BC after the king's death (his birthplace, Stagira, may have formerly been a colony of Chalcis).[33] For Aristotle was a metic, a guest-resident of Athens who would usually pay the non-resident tax of one drachma per month for males (half for women), and as such, the will would traditionally have carried no authority in the city, though as a possible former colony of Athens and member of the Delian League, Athenian law may have been observed in Chalcis.[34] Obtaining Athenian citizenship was not a formality; we read of just fifty grants of citizenship between 368 and 322 BC, and as a resident alien, Aristotle would have been banned from owning property in the city-state and across wider Attica.[35]

If Peripatetic-era wills were business-like and rhetoric-free, they were not necessarily safe *from* rhetoric. Referring to another contemporary of Alexander, Demosthenes' father's will had been exploited by his guardians, which prompted his first judicial speech at the age of 20 to reclaim what was left of the estate, thus setting in motion his oratorical career. His inheritance included over thirty sword-making slaves and twenty slaves engaged in the manufacture of furniture, bringing in a total of 4,200 drachmas annually. There were also interest-bearing loans out at 12 per cent, besides property and chattels.[36]

We do have one later example that clearly testifies more directly to the existence of Macedonian royal wills: that of Antigonus III Doson (*ca.* 263–221 BC), the grandson of Demetrius the Besieger (and great-grandson of Ptolemy I Soter). He notably appointed a secretary in charge of the royal archives, which surely paralleled the role of Alexander's own personal secretary, Eumenes. The Greek historian Polybius (*ca.* 200–118 BC) knew the details and stated that Doson nominated to power a loyal top echelon 'in order to avoid conflicts'. The testament further demanded that its content be read in public, though whether that meant to a convened Assembly of Macedones (the *Pamphlet* claimed Alexander's will had been similarly read out at such a gathering) or to a wider audience is not clear.[37]

When making a case for the legitimacy of Alexander's will, I am not proposing that the typical tribesmen who made up the Macedonian infantry ranks would have been adept in the subtleties of inheritance. Nevertheless, Alexander's veteran campaigners had possessions, booty and possibly land grants too, with relatives still at home and now in Asia by virtue of wives and sons accumulated over the years. Death on campaign was only ever a spear point away, and mobile bank deposits took a primitive form: pursers in charge of heavily guarded waggons. Some form of written covenant must have existed to ensure the wealth was distributed as the campaigners would have wished, should they perish in the phalanx or from a snakebite in India.[38] Further, I contend that the Macedonian monarchs required more than the Common Assembly's traditional beating of spear on shield to show approval and shepherd through the intricacies behind succession. The 'back office' of regal power, and the secretariat which we know recorded state affairs, would have also required that the dissemination of inheritances, appointments and bequests be documented and honoured.

More specifically, I contend that Alexander, in the never-before-witnessed position as Great King of Persia, ruler (if not the formalized pharaoh) of Egypt, 'King of Lands' in Babylonia (an ancient title the Great Kings carried), head of the royal line and thus tribal king of Macedon, would have needed a particularly well-constructed and clear legal document to pass on the expanded reins of power in a meaningful way. For the territory now nominally under Argead rule was immense, and at the point of Alexander's death there still existed his own sons and wives in Asia, his mother and sisters (and half-sisters) in Epirus and Pella who could maintain the Macedonian royal line.

Alexander's Mindset at the Campaign Court

There can be no doubt, then, that Alexander, along with those of his higher echelons at the Macedonian court in Pella and at the roving campaign 'court', would have been well acquainted with the construction and legal basis of the will, a far surer mandate for influencing the future than fate, fortune, ambitious friends and the fickle will of the gods.

But Alexander was also attached to Homer and the heroic past, as sources convincingly suggest, so he would have been familiar with the pre-suicide speech of Ajax in Sophocles' tragedy that takes the form of an oral testament in which – against the norms of a warrior protocol which requested burial with armour – Ajax left his 'vast sev'nfold shield' to his son, Eursaces.[39] The *Iliad* additionally made references to the oral disposition of estates linked to Agamemnon and Hector, whilst Sophocles' play *Women of Trachis* described the hero Heracles uttering an oral will in the madness of dying.[40]

As for Alexander's generals, they would have demanded clarity upon succession long before their eventual return to Babylon in 323 BC, and probably before the Macedonian war machine headed into Asia. Alexander may indeed have satisfied their early demands by penning a fulsome testament that dedicated his own panoply to temples and shrines, as we read in the *Pamphlet*.[41] We must not forget that Alexander had borrowed handsomely from his nobles to fund the crossing to Asia, no doubt on the promise of land grants and commercial concessions, repayments that would have needed documenting and underwriting in some way should he die.[42]

Perhaps a will was first drafted when Antipater and Parmenio pleaded with their king to take a wife and produce an heir before the voyage to Anatolia.[43] It may have been updated at various stages as influential generals and governors were killed, executed or elevated; following the murder of Parmenio, for example, or the running through of Black Cleitus, or perhaps after Alexander's near-death experience in India when Craterus and Ptolemy echoed the common fear that 'He should set a limit to the pursuit of glory and have regard for his safety, that is, the safety of the state.'[44]

We could imagine that the new marriages at Susa would have prompted the discussion of a succession document when a new military and administrative order was clearly emerging. Surely additional provisions would have been added when his wife fell pregnant and his closest friend and first chiliarch, Hephaestion, died at Ecbatana in 324 BC. If the future of empire administration had been planned and documented by Alexander in some form of covenant, with contingency plans for a world without him, then his senior command and Bodyguards would have surely been privy to its content, as well as the royal secretary Eumenes. In which case we should not visualize a last-minute, hastily drafted succession document or oral whisper as Alexander approached death, for that could have come at any time on the decade-long campaign. Wills are about planning ahead, and about catering for all possible scenarios. They can, however, be updated and revised at the last moment, in line with current events.

Aristotle had already written his treatise *Nicomachean Ethics* when Alexander was a child. In it, he had proposed 'we should as far as possible immortalise ourselves'.[45] In life and deeds, Alexander followed his advice. Yet historians believe he failed to prolong and immortalize all he had achieved on his deathbed by tossing everything to 'the strongest'. Why, having seen the Mausoleum at Halicarnassus, having admired and repaired the humble tomb of Cyrus, marched past the Pharaonic pyramids at Cheops and after demanding a funeral pyre of Babylonian proportion for Hephaestion, would Alexander have not planned or requested such a monument for himself?[46] I suggest the rejected so-called last plans found at Babylon are the missing piece of this intestate puzzle (T25).

Who in Alexander's retinue would have been the likely candidate to draft the king's will? I believe the answer is rather straightforward: the royal secretary, Eumenes of Cardia, whose curriculum vitae needed no explanation then and needs none today; Hieronymus, Plutarch and Cornelius Nepos saw to that with their biographies of him. Eumenes knew the intimacies of the treasury, the politics in Pella and the administrative shape of the empire, and this neatly leads us to one significant piece of evidence that points towards the use of wills on campaign: the testament of Eumenes himself.

Plutarch tells us that Eumenes wrote, or amended, his own will on the eve of his final battle at Gabiene at the close of 316 BC. Learning of the coming treachery of his men, Eumenes retired to his tent and drafted his last wishes, in the process tearing up and destroying his papers so that none of the secrets they contained would be known.[47]

Banqueting with the Gods

While the infighting raged at Babylon after the Assembly of men-at-arms had gathered, before Eumenes himself helped broker the fragile accord, and while elephants trampled the leaders of the discord to a pulp, Alexander's body remained untreated. Unsurprisingly, the time of neglect varies. Plutarch claimed that three days after Alexander had been pronounced dead, his body, which had been left untreated in the stifling June heat, remained in perfect condition. Curtius incorporated typical Vulgate sensationalism and suggested the king kept his vital look for a full six days, to the extent that the embalmers dared not touch him, fearing he may still be alive. Aelian mentioned an even more discreditable thirty days, unless this is a later manuscript corruption.[48] Even so, Alexander's body is said to have looked so fresh that it was hardly creditable he was dead. That inevitably led to speculation about his god-like status.

The tradition of the late kings in Macedon was to cremate the dead on a funeral pyre of Homeric proportions, like that Achilles raised for Patroclus at Troy, following which the bones would be collected from the pyre debris, washed and wrapped in a fabric of gold thread and purple, before being incarcerated in a larnax or ossuary of some kind. The recent discoveries at Vergina in northern Greece, the site of the royal burial ground of ancient Aegae where Alexander's father was buried, support this, besides providing evidence of other ritualized practices such as dressing the dead in funeral masks.

The remains would then be entombed with the finest accessories of royalty after a highly ritualized funeral ceremony. Once the heavy marble doors were closed, his body would have begun its journey, escorted by the god Hermes, to Hades' Underworld across the banks of the River Styx, whence the ferryman Charon, for payment of an obol, would have rowed him on his further journey to banquet with the gods and heroes in Elysium.[49]

Alexander, however, was never destined to follow the Argead path to the ancient family necropolis. By now, the greater part of his adult life had been spent outside Macedon. Babylonian Chaldeans, Indian gymnosophists, Phoenician sailors and traders, as well as embalmers from Egypt, complemented the Graeco–Macedonian entourage. The inner circle at the court symposia included Thessalians, Cretans, Cypriots and Persian royalty. His wives were just as exotic, and he had attachments to Carian and Persian 'mothers', adopted by one and adopting the other. Alexander was not a man longing to return to the provincial pastures of Pella in life or death, and his final wishes enshrined in his will were surely greater than the ceremonies of the home kingdom. Alexander was demonstrably lost to the West and consumed by the East.[50] And with him went his monogamous adherence to the classical gods of the Greek world.

Alexander was now a hybrid legend of East and West, like the archaic beginnings of Greek religion itself, though the Egyptian embalmers on hand in Babylon offered him a more enduring path to the afterlife. But first came the journey to his final resting place. The very existence of Alexander's lavish funeral hearse and its unchallenged construction at Babylon over two full years is evidence enough that he requested burial somewhere else.[51] The fact that Alexander had arranged two shrines to be built for Hephaestion in his new metropolis of Alexandria supports a case for interment there in Egypt, although the oracle of Zeus-Ammon at Siwa, where his own immortality was said to begin, was an attractive alternative, as some sources confirmed. Here, the resident priest's earlier allegorical slip of the tongue from '*O, Paidion*' ('O, my son') to '*O, pai Dios*' ('O, son of God', thus Zeus) had been all Alexander needed.[52] Callisthenes, the first officinal campaign historian, must have spread the word for and wide, and Olympias began, it seems, spreading the propaganda of her son's divinity as he headed deep into Persia, before he became the de facto Great King and Pharaoh.

But as events were to prove, Alexander was altogether mortal. Aside from his professed silence in the *Journal* and his succession failure in the Vulgate accounts, what did Alexander truly contemplate in the fevered days before he died? He must have recalled the Chaldean warning not to enter the city, or, perhaps he regretted heeding his own seer Anaxarchus, who advised him to ignore it. Reflecting that most of the Argead line had died before the age of 30, said Justin, did the first Macedonian 'Great King' – now with one young son, a pregnant wife, an illustrious family and the wealth of Croesus – complain that the goddess of fortune Tyche and the healing god Asclepius had treated him unkindly?[53]

Through Alexander's final hours, when fever-wracked and sweat-soaked in Nebuchadnezzar's bedchamber, did he think of the warriors he, like Achilles, had cast into the Underworld, or had he conveniently become a believer in the Pythagorean immortal soul? What did the Egyptian embalmers in Babylon promise the dying king? Perhaps he simply considered the words of the dispossessed Greek hero Themistocles, that 'the gods and heroes begrudge that a single man in his godless pride should be king of Hellas and Asia, too'.[54]

The eyewitness authors would have us believe that none of these introspections, regrets, the blood guilt and the pleas to the gods of Olympus, Egypt and Esagila made their way to Alexander's fever-cracked lips as his men gathered around him. Was the king who had been quoting Euripides about to acquiesce to another silent tragedy, leaving the last lines of his own play unwritten, or to be penned by those about him?

I propose not, for Alexander was a manipulator of men, Pythia, diviners and their gods; he exploited imagery of the past and he attempted to change the present. And whether truly the first 'citizen of the world', as some have proposed, or whether this was a purely practical initiative, the mass weddings at Susa made it clear that Alexander was setting out to manipulate the future as well. The only mechanism left to him was the established practice of writing succession instructions into a king's will.

Death does not belong to the deceased but to the biographers who frame it. It was never a part of life's true portrait, but rather suited to their cause, whether by a philosopher looking to accessorize his metaphysical stance, a historian seeking fame from edifying his audience, a general with a pen justifying an expansionist policy, or by a king who served the deceased and was looking to magnify his part.

Alexander's long-lost will, suppressed at Babylon I venture, had essentially been an imperial edict; it was the legal mandate that was to indelibly stamp his ambition, vision and bloodline across the face of his now vast empire. It was supposed to beckon in what later historians have termed a 'Hellenistic era', in which Alexander's hybrid dynasty would have ruled the Graeco–Persian world.

Instead, it was Alexander's Bodyguards and most ambitious generals who eventually proclaimed themselves kings in place of the royal line, and when they did, the independence of autonomous city-states and island federations, the status of vassal kingdoms in Asia and semi-autonomous satraps acting as 'royal landlords', disappeared in an instant, along with Alexander's will-empowered half-Asiatic sons, who were still blocking their path to power.

5

DEATH AND POISON: THE TOXIC CUP

Would the allegations of poison have been a credible foundation?

How widespread was the use of poisons in the ancient world, and could Alexander truly have been poisoned at Babylon? Or was the *Pamphlet* cleverly crafted to play upon court tensions and suspicions?

I investigate the 'toxic technology' associated with the Graeco–Persian world, and in particular, Alexander's contemporaries who were executed or assassinated using lethal drugs.

> I, who crossed all the inhabited earth,
> And the uninhabited places, and the places of darkness,
> Was unable to evade fate.
> A small cup can yield a man to death,
> And send him down among the dead with a drop of poison.[1]
>
> *Greek Alexander Romance*

> I shall make just as pretty a cupbearer as you – and not drink the wine myself. For it is the fact that the king's butler when he offers the wine is bound to dip a ladle in the cup first, and pour a little in the hollow of his hand and sip it, so that if he has mixed poison in the bowl it will do him no good himself.[2]
>
> Xenophon, *On the Education of Cyrus*

The biographies of the giants of the Classical age of Greece are full of untimely deaths, many by covert toxic hands or state-sanctioned deadly potions. The sacred medical oath of Hippocrates of Kos commenced with: 'I swear by Apollo the physician, and Asclepius, and Hygeia, and Panacea, and all the gods and goddesses ... I will neither give a deadly drug to anybody if asked for it, nor will I make a suggestion to this effect.' The deities must have been mortified, for Persia and Greece saw the oath abandoned to aconite, arsenic and antimony, the toxic arsenal of emperors, tyrants and kings – and allegedly, King Alexander III of Macedon.

There can equally be no doubt that assassination was an integral part of Macedonian machinations. One scholar has noted: 'Only two of Alexander's predecessors in the fourth century BC had not died by assassination ... and only three among all the successors of Darius I.'[3] Alexander and his father, Philip II, had contributed generously to the death toll of candidates (and their supporters) for the throne, and Pausanias alleged that Cassander used poison when murdering both of Alexander's sons, Alexander IV and Heracles.[4]

Poison Arrows and Poison Pens

Like mythology itself, poison allegedly had beginnings in the murky mists of time. Ovid dated the use of aconite (also named wolfsbane) back to the Bronze Age, terming the plant the 'stepmother's favourite brew'. Medea attempted to poison mythological Theseus, the founder-hero of Athens, with an aconite mix.[5] However, we need to go back to the Heroic Age to evidence the first use of nature's toxic gifts on heroes and men. In the *Odyssey*, Homer related that

Odysseus made a special voyage to obtain supplies of a deadly poison to coat the bronze tips of his arrows, and he further described the 'drugs mixed together, many good and many harmful' that were used when Helen spiked the drinks of Telemachus and Menelaus.[6] Heracles also famously dipped his arrows in the poison of the slain Lernean Hydra.

So the craft of toxicology was truly ancient. Spears and arrowheads are a good place to start. Deadly nightshade (possibly Pliny's *strychnos*) is one candidate for the ingredient in the Latin *dorycnium*, 'spear poison', suggesting a widespread use of the sap that would have been smeared on a blade.[7] The Greek word for bow was *toxon*, the arrow was *toxeuma* (besides *oistos*) and poison was *pharmakon*, thus arrow poison was known as *toxikon pharmakon*. The Roman derivative was *toxicum* when referring to poison alone, though it still originally implied an archer's toxin.[8] The weapons wielded by *toxotai*, the formidable horseback archers, were renowned for their poison tips in Scythia; the viper-extracted *scythicon* they used on arrowheads was lethal. Toxic plants would have been collected by skilled 'root-cutters', who used knives to dig out what they dared not touch themselves.[9]

Ancient Persian texts described additional toxins and their methods of fabrication. The Great Kings took precautions and kept a calculus – the stone from the kidney or gall bladder of the mountain goat – at the bottom of their wine cups, for the nobility regularly dished out poisons at dinner. The chapter heading extract above from Xenophon's *On the Education of Cyrus* confirmed the ubiquity of the crime. The porous structure of the calculus was credited with counteractive powers and was called a *padzahr*, which broadly translates as 'against poison'.[10] Diodorus related how Darius III thwarted the assassination attempt by the grand vizier, Bagoas the 'kingmaker', finally forcing the captured eunuch to drink his own deadly brew.[11]

Plutarch and Ctesias reported that Queen Parysatis, mother of Artaxerxes II, fatally intoxicated her daughter-in-law by means of a carefully prepared knife. Venom was administered by her maidservant to the side of a blade used to cut a bird in half. Taking the untainted meat, Parysatis chewed in pleasure while her daughter-in-law choked on her inheritance. Hesiod's advice was never more relevant: 'Invite your friend to supper, not your enemy.' Revenge can, however, be a double-edged sword, for Plutarch went on to explain: 'The legal mode of death for poisoners in Persia is as follows. There is a broad stone, and on this the head of the culprit is placed; and then with another stone they smite and pound until they crush the face and head to pulp.' That was the fate of the maidservant, while Parysatis was packed off to Babylon in shame.[12]

Diodorus described the snakes behind the various venoms used on blades, along with the Indian custom of burning wives on the dead husband's funeral pyre, supposedly to discourage them from poisoning their spouses:

The country, indeed, furnished no few means for this, since it produced many and varied deadly poisons, some of which when merely spread upon the food or the wine cups cause death. But when this evil became fashionable and many were murdered in this way, the Indians, although they punished those guilty of the crime, since they were not able to deter the others from wrongdoing, established a law that wives, except such as were pregnant or had children, should be cremated along with their deceased husbands.[13]

Alexander's troops were to suffer the consequences of malevolent archery in India when both the enemy arrows and sword blades were coated with viper and cobra venom. This was in contravention of the Hindu *Laws of Manu*, for Brahmins and the higher castes prohibited their use. Local Indian physicians had to be employed by the Macedonians to neutralize the effects, and in the Vulgate texts Ptolemy almost succumbed before Alexander reportedly found an antidote, though this sounds suspiciously like Cleitarchean propaganda to raise Ptolemy's profile and favour with his king.[14]

State-Banned Toxicity, State-Sanctioned Death

The use of hemlock and more-locally available toxins was widespread in Greece by the end of the Archaic Age. When laying out the basis of his ideal state, Plato had divided magic (the Greek were extremely superstitious) into two categories, and the first focused on harm to the body caused by food, drinks and unguents by poisons.[15] A fifth-century BC Athenian law prohibited their use, as did the Tean Curses, a decree read each year by city officials and banning production of harmful drugs.[16] Hippocrates had reported on the use of arsenics for skin ulcers and the methods to control the absorption of poisons a century-and-a-half before Alexander's day.

Despite earlier Athenian legislation and the ban of the Tean Curses, poison became a favourite tool of the state in times of famine or, worse, philosophical challenge. The Roman period geographer Strabo claimed that more than sixty citizens of the Aegean island of Kea were ordered to take the poison in the fourth century BC during a food shortage to ensure the survival of others.[17]

In Athens, Socrates was found guilty of impiety and corrupting the city's youth with his politics-challenging philosophical questions. As a result, he was sentenced to a lethal dose of hemlock by the jurors of 'democracy', though he allegedly managed to debate with his friends as the poison took hold. Aristotle's protégé and successor at the Lyceum-based school, Theophrastus, helps us out with his suggestion that a cocktail of hemlock, poppy and herbs would render death more peaceful.[18]

Then we have contemporary examples in the reigns of Philip and Alexander. Phocion, a former pupil of Plato who had been elected city military leader (*stategos*) forty-five times (during which he turned down a 100-talent gift from Alexander), was to suffer for his pro-Macedonian policy. Condemned to die on the day of the Athenian festival of Olympia, he had to pay 12 drachmas to his executioner for more hemlock to be bruised (pulped ready for use).[19]

The Athenian orator Demosthenes, so vocally opposed to Philip and Alexander, was eventually hunted down by Archias, an assassin in the employ of the Macedonian regent Antipater. Once Demosthenes was surrounded in the supposedly sacred Temple of Poseidon on the island of Calauria (Poros), he sucked poison from his reed pen before quoting tragic lines.[20]

Alexander's teacher Aristotle was to follow Demosthenes to the Underworld soon after: 'Eurymedon, the priest of Deo's mysteries in Athens, was once about to indict Aristotle in the charge of impiety, but he, by a draught of poison [possibly hemlock] escaped prosecution. This then was an easy way of vanquishing unjust calumnies.' The charge of impiety was always difficult to counter; in another version, Aristotle ended his life by taking aconite at the age of 70 at Chalcis on Euboea in 322 BC.[21]

Still closer to home, and rather more relevant to the claims of the *Pamphlet*, Aristotle's successor Theophrastus went on to describe the skills behind aconite poisoning, along with masking techniques, recommending strychnine for practical purposes since the poison's taste could be disguised in wine.[22]

Today's Evaluation

Analysing the cause of Alexander's death, by assassins or otherwise, is not my central aim, but it is worth taking a look at recent autopsies of the claims, because they showcase the ongoing uncertainties attached to the final chapter of his life.

One formative portrayal of Alexander reminds us that 'our ancient sources all record a tradition that Alexander was poisoned', recalling that even Arrian and Plutarch referenced the conspiracy adjacent to their *Journal* extracts (T9, T10).[23] This influential portrait, written in 1970, concluded: 'this, rather, suggests poison, of a king who was unbearable and murderous.' And yet the author added: 'The illness had been long. On this one fact alone, all stories of poison founder ... If, on the other hand, the King was not poisoned, the chances are that he was suffering from either raging pleurisy or, more probably, malaria.'[24]

These apparent volte-faces re-emphasize the lack of evidence, or rather an investigative fog. Others too have argued for natural causes of death, with typhoid fever, West Nile encephalitis, methanol toxicity, acute pancreatitis and perforated peptic ulcers being promoted. One admirer quite plausibly suggested that a water-borne disease, acquired from drinking the contaminated and excrement-filled Euphrates, had developed into pneumonia and then to pleurisy.[25]

Plutarch and Arrian knew of a tradition – an offshoot of the *Pamphlet*'s finger pointing (T1, T2) – which claimed Aristotle gathered the poison from the River Styx by the cliffs of Nonacris (in the northern central Peloponnese) and had it ferried to Babylon in a mule's hoof, for this was the only vessel capable of holding the ferment.[26] When describing the source of the drug that professedly felled Alexander, it appears that the obviously educated originator of this story (which now implicated Aristotle) was exploiting a well-known legend.

In Greek mythology, the gods swore their oaths upon the dark waters of the Styx (possibly the modern Mavroneri River) at Nonacris; if their word was broken, Zeus forced them to drink a cup of the icy cold flow, causing coma and loss of speech.[27] Pliny, Aelian and Strabo all report the tradition of deadly sulphurous streams trickling from the mountains, while Pausanias commented that the 'lethal power' of the Styx, 'seemingly invented for the destruction of human beings', was first recognized after goats drank from the watercourse and subsequently perished.[28] Through time, the locals renamed it the 'Black Waters' or 'Terrible Waters' in support of its deleterious effects on metals and clay containers.[29] If there is any truth to this, there must have been many who would have suffered the consequences.

Plutarch claimed that three days after Alexander had been pronounced dead, his body, which had been left untreated in the stifling June heat, remained in perfect condition.[30] Curtius incorporated typical Vulgate exaggeration – the king kept his vital look for a full six days, to the extent that the embalmers dared not touch him, fearing he may still be alive. Aelian mentioned an even more discreditable thirty days, unless this is a later manuscript corruption.[31]

This condition, as many toxicologists would confirm, is an argument *for*, not *against*, the presence of chemical poison (if not methanol toxicity): 'a remarkable preservation of the body is commonly, but not constantly, observed', concluded one authoritative publication on arsenic use.[32] One scholar has argued for strychnine use at Babylon, though another proposed malaria to explain the preservation; both conditions, when resulting in either cyanosis or deep coma, could have led to the delayed putrefaction of the body.[33]

However, a recent study of the episode in New Zealand by the National Poisons Centre in the Department of Preventive and Social Medicine at the University of Otago – perhaps the most detailed literary autopsy since the 1996 clinicopathological report prepared for the *New England Journal of Medicine* – argues against the above conclusions. It states that 'lethal doses of strychnine' would 'typically cause death within 3–5 hours', not longer. Moreover, in cases of arsenic poisoning, 'death occurs within 24h to 4 days'; 'these symptoms do not match those displayed' by Alexander 'and can therefore also be discarded'.[34] Although the Greeks would have had access to a wide range of attested toxic plants such as aconite, hemlock, wormwood, henbane and autumn crocus, a better fit to Alexander's relatively long decline would be the alkaloids present in white hellebore.

Plutarch stated that Alexander had earlier written to Pausanias, the physician treating Craterus, to remind his veteran general to be vigilant in his use of hellebore, widely used as a self-induced purge, as was antimony.[35] The study quoted above continued: 'Its emetic properties were well known to the Hellenes and it was readily available from Alpine pastures of Europe and Asia.'[36] A key symptom of hellebore poisoning is the onset of epigastric pain, that may also be accompanied by nausea and vomiting, and though victims can become completely incapacitated and even unable to move or speak, they do remain conscious. The National Poisons Centre report concluded that hellebore 'alkaloids are readily extracted into alcohol by fermentation, and it is therefore possible' that Iollas (Alexander's cup bearer, the son of Antipater and brother of Cassander) spiked Alexander's wine 'with a volume of fermented [hellebore] extract'.[37]

There can be no doubt that the production of poison and its use was highly developed by Alexander's reign. So attaching the accusation of poisoning at Babylon to the *Pamphlet* with its strategically targeted conspiracy charges would not have been dismissed out of hand, and is even given credence today. That, alongside the natural superstition of the common soldier and the well-documented suspicion that Alexander's Bodyguards were withholding information from the army officers as he approached death at Babylon, made the *Pamphlet* a truly formidable and sophisticated weapon of the Successor Wars. It's now time to hunt down the architects of the deceit.

Source Stemma for the Surviving Accounts of Alexander's Death

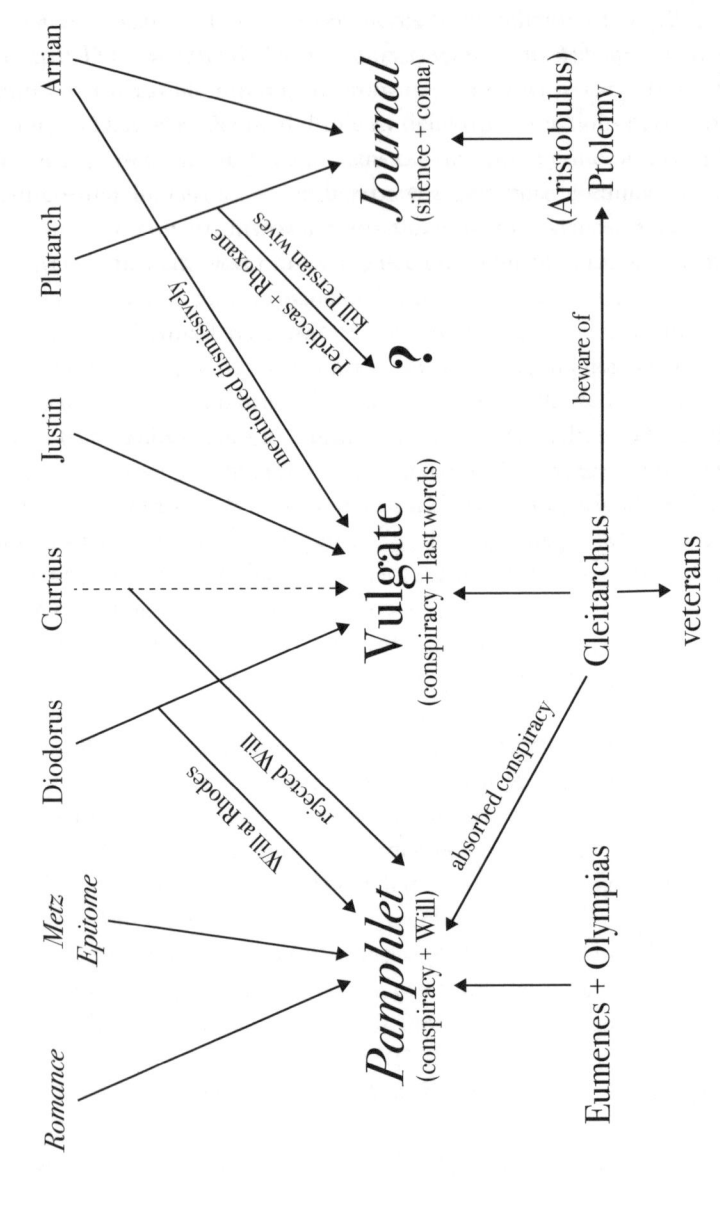

(The dotted line to Curtius denoted the loss of his text which would almost certainly have followed the Vulgate template.)

6

HUNTING THE ARCHITECTS OF DECEIPT

Can we more positively identity the authors of the *Journal*, *Pamphlet* and the Vulgate accounts?

Alexander's last days in Babylon resulted in three differently reported outcomes, stemming from at least three early influential sources. Two of them are potentially linked to the official court diaries from which the *Journal* entry was extracted, or to their supposed author, with the third inspired by them both.

I take a closer look at the messages that underlie each and at the possible identities of the authors, to reveal the architects of an early literary war that took place in the aftermath of Alexander's death.

> He [Alexander] recognised his officers when they entered his room but could no longer speak to them. From that moment until the end he uttered no word. That night and the following day, and for the next twenty-four hours, he remained in a high fever. These details are all to be found in the Diaries.[1] (T3)
>
> Arrian, *The Campaigns of Alexander*, extract from the *Journal*

> When they asked him to whom he left his kingdom, he [Alexander] replied, "to him who was the best man", but that he already foresaw that because of that contest great funeral games were in preparation for him. Again when Perdiccas asked when he wished divine honours to be paid to him, he said he wished it at the time when they themselves were happy. These were the king's last words, and shortly afterwards he died.[2] (T7)
>
> Curtius, *The History of Alexander*

We have pinpointed where the evidence lies, and we now have a sense of the deceptions and agendas embedded within it. We also know that written succession instructions existed in Alexander's day and that they were used by Macedonian royals and regents. It is also clear that poison was a widespread means of exacting quick regime change, so any such rumours would have carried currency if an atmosphere of suspicion, dissatisfaction and paranoia truly permeated the court at Babylon, as sources would have us believe. It is also abundantly clear that the death as an episode was demonstrably embellished, manipulated and subverted to the agendas of the writers who recorded it.

Taking all this into account, here I cross-examine the three witnesses more ruthlessly (*Journal*, *Pamphlet* and Vulgate genre) in a quest to identify the architect of each, while explaining how and why Alexander's original testament reappeared in the midst of those who wanted it buried.

One of the few absolutes we are presented with is that our central witnesses, perhaps better termed our 'prime suspects', incriminate one another in their recounting of Alexander's death. Simply put, the *Journal* and the *Pamphlet* cannot exist together in history as fact: if a will was read as the *Pamphlet* claimed, the *Journal* hid the detail, and if the *Journal* extract is genuine, the *Pamphlet*'s fulsome testament, absorbed later by the *Romance*, was a complete fabrication. And if either contained the truth, then Alexander's last words leaving power 'to the strongest' and his prediction of 'funeral games' as portrayed in the Vulgate texts cannot have been said in the context attached to them.

If we review the 'primary source' historians who accompanied Alexander and those writing in the generation that followed, and then the later 'secondary' and 'tertiary' source Roman-era authors who built their own interpretations from these accounts, it becomes clear that each historian did adopt one – or elements of more than one – of Alexander's three epitaphs. However, we also know that all of the mainstream accounts rejected the reading of Alexander's last will and testament in the unanimous belief that he failed to organize his estate and declined to nominate a successor, or successors, to govern the greatest empire the Graeco–Persian world had ever seen.

The archetypal documents behind these opposing endings have been reviewed only in isolation. But the full extent of their deceit becomes apparent when they are considered together, for the *Journal* and the *Pamphlet* bear witness to an ancient literary war. They were not the products of hair-splitting wordsmiths; the *Journal* – despite its benign exterior – and the *Pamphlet* were launched into the histories armed to the teeth with accusation, insinuation, strategic omission and, more dangerous still, a convincing reinsertion of detail. What becomes clear, when they are reviewed side by side, is that the one was born to kill off the allegations of the other. Their historic relationship was misunderstood and awkwardly dealt with by the classical historians, who may have suspected, yet could not pinpoint, a subterfuge somewhere between Babylon and Alexandria some decades on when (I argue) the first influential accounts appeared and monopolized the debate.[3]

Each production has at least one enigmatic individual attached to its story. Thanks to a reference in Athenaeus' *Dinner Philosophers* relating to the *Journal* extract (T3, T4), we have Diodotus of Erythrae who was cited as one of the compilers of the official court diaries (the *Ephemerides*), working – we assume – under Alexander's chief clerk, Eumenes of Cardia, who was also clearly cited as its compiler.[4] Diodotus' name appears once and is never mentioned again (a fate shared with Evagoras, who was named as secretary of the huge Indus–Hydaspes fleet). It seems the histories bypassed intelligence, surveying and clerical staff unless they appeared in a military capacity.[5]

In support of the existence of the *Pamphlet* and its circulation in the Successor Wars – a scholar-backed theory born of its clear political designs and dissimilarity to the rest of the fabulously inclined *Romance* – Plutarch refers to a man named Hagnothemis who apparently first heard of the *Pamphlet* detail and Aristotle's alleged involvement in the conspiracy to poison Alexander (T9, T10).[6] Additionally, we have Holcias who allegedly read the will aloud to the most powerful generals by Alexander's bedside on the morning of his death. Never previously mentioned in the campaign histories, Holcias was sufficiently important to the author of the *Pamphlet* to be cited as inheriting the governorship of Illyria (T1, T2).[7]

The obscurity of these individuals has cast doubts over the authenticity of both productions, for surely these notable men, here briefly illuminated in crucial affairs, ought to have appeared more frequently in the campaign accounts. But we must remember the pernicious power of the pen: able to ink in an ally to the pantheon of history, or whiteout an opponent to the exile of anonymity.

A Book of Death: the Partisan *Pamphlet*

The content of the enigmatic will-citing *Pamphlet* is believed to be best preserved in what is referred to as 'Recension A' (the oldest) of the *Greek Alexander Romance* (T2) (in the final chapter of Book Three), as well as its later redactions, but it is also fulsomely detailed at the conclusion to the *Metz Epitome* (T1).[8] A later corrupted and even briefer reference to the will remains in a poor eighth-century Latin translation of an earlier anonymous fifth-century work known as the *Kronika Alexandrina*, which stated: 'When he was close to death, Alexander left a testament, that each of his officers should rule in their individual provinces, as Alexander had instructed, as follows …'[9]

We do not know when the first edition of what is otherwise known as a Pseudo-Callisthenes production entered circulation; this more historical and less fabulous parent of the original *Romance* archetype, which scholars label 'α', was possibly written between fifty and 100 years after Alexander's death when all the necessary ingredients had been established (i.e. when the first wave of campaign histories had been published and then embellished with more colour, rumour and exaggeration).[10] Neither do we know exactly when the detail from the *Pamphlet*, which was issued early during the Successor Wars, first entered the *Romance*, whether soon after its genesis or if it was swept up much later, as it was into the third-century *Metz Epitome*.[11] A possible clue is a papyrus dating to the Ptolemaic period (*ca*. 100 BC) which houses a further fragment of the will without any *Romance* attachments.[12] But once the *Romance* did absorb the earlier political document, much 'didactic' (rhetorically instructive) filler was inevitably built around its original content. Yet the key elements comprising the original weaponised *Pamphlet* are not difficult to pinpoint, for any obvious marvels and overtly supernatural content would have hamstrung its focused political and military aims in the Successor Wars.

However, one 'marvel' attached to the description of Alexander's death in the *Romance* texts just may have existed in the original political *Pamphlet*. Taking the form of a gruesome prodigy – which may have served to represent the imminent treachery of Alexander's men – a half-child, half-beast was brought to the king. Its description recalls the monstrous sea-goddess Scylla from Greek mythology, a composite animal resonant of the cheetah-serpent-eagle-like *sirrush* symbolizing the Babylonian god Marduk. In the *Romance*, the top human part of the body was dead, but the limbs of the animals were still alive, thus it was potentially meant to imply that Alexander's men had killed their host.[13] And though this detail looks more convincingly like a later intruder, superstition and the portentous played a significant role in the psyche of the time, and soldiers were particularly susceptible.[14]

Whether original or not, what comes next formed the central intent of the *Pamphlet* author, or authors: a description of the plot to poison Alexander in Babylon, with an outline of the political background as well as the means and the motive. It was Alexander's chief cupbearer Iollas, the son of the presiding Macedonian regent Antipater, who handed him the poisoned wine at the impromptu party, held in typical Macedonian rowdy banqueting style (known as a 'symposium', or *komos* in ancient Greek), hosted by the aristocratic court frequenter, Medius of Larissa. There were twenty-or-so guests and the *Pamphlet* named those complicit in the regicide. The list varies slightly in surviving texts, but the following individuals were clearly 'in the know': Medius himself, three of the Royal Bodyguards corps – Leonnatus, Peithon and Peucestas – as well as Meleager, the most senior infantry officer at Babylon, the fleet commander Nearchus and the high-ranking court Companion Menander, alongside other less prominent officers and notables mentioned on campaign.[15] While complicit in the assassination, the central architects of the crime remain the Macedonian regent and his sons.

This was a heavyweight line-up that was afforded a modicum of credibility by Antipater's alleged summons to Babylon by Alexander; he was, it is said, fearful that Alexander was planning to execute him, and so he took the initiative.[16] As significant as those cited as guilty were the few guests named as ignorant of the plot: Perdiccas, Ptolemy, Lysimachus, Eumenes, Asander and Holcias (T1, T2).

Following a description of the king's sudden pain after drinking from the cup and his worsening condition, as well as Rhoxane's tender intervention when Alexander attempted to throw himself into the Euphrates River, the surviving texts (in the *Romance* and *Metz Epitome*) detailed a private reading of the testament by Holcias to a small, select group of the king's most trusted men. Besides Holcias, three more of the 'innocent' group were listed as present when Alexander drafted his will, and we are no doubt expected to imagine that Eumenes, royal secretary and keeper of the Royal Diaries, would have overseen the scribes who recorded Alexander's wishes in the form of a testament.

The *Romance* and *Metz Epitome* texts, assuming they are reasonable transmissions of the original political document, make it clear that the *Pamphlet* author(s) slanted it to be strikingly favourable to the island of Rhodes, both within the main will narrative and in Alexander's so-called 'Letter to the Rhodians' which preceded the will bequests. The Rhodians are praised for good behaviour and loyalty, appointed guardians of Alexander's will and his body on its way to

Egypt, the Macedonian garrison is removed and financial gifts (plus food and warships) are bestowed on the island state.[17]

The *Metz Epitome* preserved additional detail of Alexander's final utterances, in which he pledged his friends to recognize the will and urged the new acting chiliarch, Perdiccas, along with his old regent in Macedon, Antipater (we are to assume that Alexander was unaware of his part in the plot), to see that its terms were carried out.[18] Finally, as Alexander's energy was spent, he beseeched the gods to accept him and passed his ring to Perdiccas, to whom he had pledged his wife in marriage, and placed his and Rhoxane's hands together in public affirmation. As in the Vulgate accounts of Curtius, Diodorus and Justin (T6, T7, T8) which preserve Alexander's final utterances on 'funeral games' and an invite to fight for power, the king remained vocal to the end, but here giving instruction to his men about his estate and burial wishes.

Also uniting the claims of the *Pamphlet* and the Vulgate genre is the common agreement that Alexander was finally proclaimed dead perhaps five days after the first dose of poison, after which Perdiccas had the body laid in a coffin and dressed in his regal robes, whereupon he announced the king's passing and then read Alexander's will to the larger gathering of men.[19] This lucid and coherent reporting does contrast in every way to the general tone of the rest of the 'fabulous' *Romance* which houses it; even Rhoxane, for example, is correctly referred to as Alexander's Bactrian wife, whereas she is incorrectly referred to as the daughter of Darius III in the preceding *Romance* text.[20]

The whole construction – the gruesome animal prodigy, the background to the conspiracy, the writing and then reading of the will with Alexander's final instructions – was dubbed the *The Book of the Death and Testament of Alexander the Great* (often cited in Latin as *Liber de Morte Testamentumque Alexandri Magni*), though the simplicity of the title *Pamphlet* seems to better suit the original political origins.[21]

The *Pamphlet* has been dubbed 'neither romance, nor history, but rather a political propaganda', a conclusion not too distant from the verdict on the *Journal* (explained below).[22] Whilst the identity of its authorship divides the community of scholars, the *Pamphlet*, which (prodigy aside) provided a more rational conclusion to Alexander's final days than any 'serious' account, still sits in a rejected corner, whereas the *Journal* still enjoys more legitimate attachments in the final pages of the biographies of Arrian and Plutarch (T3, T4).

We recall that scholars are broadly united in the belief that the *Pamphlet* was circulated for political effect in the first decade (or so) of the Successor Wars following Alexander's death.[23] Their studies have focused on the identification of its publisher, with the divining rod being the political slant of the will along with the guilt, or exoneration, attached to those at Medius' banquet. The unchanging conclusion by modern historians that the *Pamphlet* will is pure propaganda is perplexing, for historians have never satisfactorily questioned why Alexander 'decided' to die intestate, the nature of his death being far from sudden. His decline incontrovertibly took place over a number of days in all surviving accounts, providing him an opportunity to designate heirs and successors and to disseminate the power in a manner that would have truly prolonged his legacy as well as the survival of his family.

So, what of the *Pamphlet*'s authorship? Since early critique separated it from the clearly unhistoric elements of the *Romance*, thereby providing the credibility for its political birth in the Successor War years, a number of studies have summarized the conflicting dates of its origin.[24] What *is* unanimously agreed upon is that the *Pamphlet* was partisan in its construction: 'It is replete with details, tendentious and misleading, anchored to historical personages.'[25] In which case we may conclude that its construction and design coincided with the political agenda of at least one of those cited as 'innocent': Eumenes, Perdiccas, Ptolemy, Lysimachus, Asander and Holcias.[26]

The conspicuous salvation of Ptolemy and Perdiccas led to deductions that one or the other was the author; wholly logical proposals at first glance. Perdiccas died three years after Alexander, and yet hostility between him and Ptolemy was evident from the settlement at Babylon onwards, and perhaps even at Babylon, eventually culminating in war.[27] This is troubling, for it would have been 'remarkably counter-productive' for Perdiccas to extricate Ptolemy from guilt if the chiliarch was the author.[28] This alone ought to rule out Perdiccas, who was killed in the summer of 320 BC when attacking Ptolemy-controlled Egypt (according to what is referred to as the 'low' chronology, which we follow).[29]

Other scholars argue for Ptolemaic origins of the *Pamphlet* and for a publication period following the so-called Peace of the Dynasts of 311 BC. Military successes in Anatolia and Greece saw Ptolemy facing his rivals with a new confidence that led him to intrigue for the hand of Cleopatra, Alexander's sister. It has been argued that in this context, and courting Rhodian naval power, the *Pamphlet* was issued at the expense of Ptolemy's rivals. The will does indeed pair Ptolemy with Cleopatra. But the same reasoning that discounts Perdiccan authorship can be applied here: there was no logic in Ptolemy absolving his arch-rival Perdiccas, or his chief supporter, Eumenes, from conspiratorial guilt. Both had been dead some years by 311 BC and Ptolemy could have easily slandered them, despite their former affiliations to Cleopatra.[30] But above all other arguments, we know from Arrian's statement that the conclusion to Ptolemy's book either corroborated, or itself invented, the *Journal* entry, with its speechless and intestate conspiracy-free death, and this was the absolute opposite of what was claimed by the author of the *Pamphlet*.[31] So Ptolemy must be ruled out.

An alternative publication date has been proposed in a more recent study of Alexander's mother Olympias, in which the *Pamphlet* is referred to as a 'scrap of partisan literature'. Its origins are pinned on the decade after her death in 315 BC, when Olympias' 'airbrushed' image fitted the sentiment of that time as nostalgia for the murdered queen mother newly surfaced.[32] Yet the term 'scrap' may understate its virulence; its survival through the wars of the Diadochi, and in one form or another through the 2,300 years since, speaks for its historical stamina. Nevertheless, Olympias may well have been involved in the *Pamphlet*'s provenance, as I aim to argue.[33]

Another prominent expert on the 'who's who' in the age of Alexander recently built on earlier theories that positioned the *Pamphlet* as a product of Polyperchon and his regency *ca*. 317 BC (Polyperchon, a campaign veteran, held the regency until around late 316 or early 315 BC, when Cassander attained power).[34] The seeming flaw is that Polyperchon was never himself mentioned in the document, when he had every chance to grant himself will-sanctioned authority; that was hardly an effective strategy if he sought legitimacy from its circulation. When developing his case for this argument, in which it was proposed that Holcias worked in league with Polyperchon, this was seen as 'subtle and ingenious'. But that subtlety verges on self-incrimination. As has been elsewhere pointed out, Polyperchon owed his own regency to the dying wish of Antipater, and to damn the former regent with regicide was to call into question his association and the resulting appointment.[35]

Polyperchon finally came to terms with Cassander in 309 BC and received grants and troops in return for the murder of Heracles, Alexander's eldest son.[36] Bearing in mind the vitriol with which the *Pamphlet* treated Cassander and his family, it seems implausible that he would have entertained any strategic alliance (which lasted almost a decade) with the by-then vulnerable Polyperchon if he was known to be, or suspected as, the author. Moreover, it is unlikely that Polyperchon would have promoted a son he had written out of the *Pamphlet*, for Heracles was never recognized in the reissued will.

Alternatively, it has been suggested that Antigonus the One-Eyed, not present at Babylon and so not on Medius' guest list, may have been behind the design of the conspiracy theory. But he is not a good fit either, because of all the major coalition players, Antigonus had no significant immediate role.[37] What is more, he fought against those named innocent in the Successor Wars. I propose, nevertheless, that Antigonus did have an *influence* on the birth of the *Pamphlet*, though its delivery and the midwife were not what he had in mind.

The shifting sands of proposed authorship clearly illustrate that none of the aforementioned proposed authors is a comfortable match to its content, and for each candidate there remains an indigestible logic and a very 'nasty conundrum'.[38]

Having ruled out the more prominent candidates, the innocent list is whittled down to the king's Bodyguard Lysimachus, the governor of Cardia named Asander, the king's secretary Eumenes and the elusive Holcias. Lysimachus' initial participation in the Successor Wars fell in line with Antigonus, as did the early actions of Ptolemy, each related to one another by marriage through daughters of Antipater, and both were to demand their just rewards for their part in Antigonus' eventual victory over Eumenes. So Lysimachus would have had no reason to salvage the former royal secretary from guilt either when naming the innocents.[39] Asander was most likely a relative of Antigonus the One-Eyed; he appears to have defected from Perdiccas in 321/320 BC and we believe he supported Antigonus until 315 BC, after which he switched allegiance to Ptolemy.[40] Asander would have harboured no desire to put the former chiliarch he betrayed on the innocent list, and neither his supporter Eumenes, nor the opposition rebel Holcias who was eventually captured by Antigonus. So they too can be discounted as credible *Pamphlet* authors.[41]

Putting Holcias aside for the time being, this leaves us with Eumenes of Cardia, who *did* enjoy the support and trust of both Olympias and Polyperchon, from late 319–316 BC. Just as influential to Eumenes' place in history was the fact that one of his most trusted staff and loyal followers was his fellow Cardian, Hieronymus, who was, in fact, likely Eumenes' own nephew. Hieronymus went on to write the formative eyewitness account of the Successor Wars. Following Perdiccas' defeat in Egypt, at a strategic reconvening of generals at Triparadeisus later in 320 BC, Eumenes (with Hieronymus already in his entourage) was declared an outlaw and proscribed (a death sentence was laid on him), along with the surviving Perdiccan remnants.[42]

History has never handed Eumenes the *Pamphlet* pen because Lysimachus, Ptolemy and Asander, also named innocent of guilt, appear to have opposed him through the First and Second Successor Wars. However, as will become clear, there were two, or possibly three, periods between his release from a siege at the mountain fortress of Nora in 319 BC, and his execution at the end of 316 BC (or early 315 BC) by Antigonus, when the line-up in the *Pamphlet* would have suited his, and significantly Olympias', desperate position – and by association, Polyperchon's too. For Eumenes needed Ptolemy and Lysimachus in a coalition against the by-then powerful Antigonus, although as events were to show, they believed they did not need him; and in that they were quite mistaken, as the next fifteen years would prove.

Scholars are correct in stating that the *Pamphlet* will – in the form we inherited it today in the *Romance* and *Metz Epitome* – has been contaminated to some degree. Unsurprisingly, in the Latin *Metz Epitome* it is the Roman gods who are called to witness the content of the will: Jupiter, Hercules, Minerva and Mars, rather than the Olympian Zeus, Heracles, Athena and Ares (corrected in the translation in Chapter 4), the deities beseeched to punish any who acted in contravention of the will's dictates. Obviously, the use of the term 'senate' (rather than its Greek equivalent, Council, Assembly, *boule*, etc) at Rhodes is

Roman overlay too.⁴³ In the *Romance*, there appear to be later textual additions and even some omissions, again possibly politically motivated. It has, for example, been proposed that the first Latin translation of the original Greek *Romance* text (by Julius Valerius) deliberately omitted the prediction – reportedly emanating from Serapis, the new deity conceived in Ptolemaic Egypt – that Alexandria would surpass 'the more ancient cities', for Rome had by then supplanted the Egyptian city as the universal metropolis.⁴⁴

Of course, wills could be updated and amended during the testator's life. Alexander is portrayed as penning – or, I suggest, *revising* – his will throughout the night, when a slave boy Hermogenes recorded the words, and another, Combaphes, held a lamp. Those named as present with them were Ptolemy, Lysimachus and Perdiccas, while Holcias read out the finished document.⁴⁵ Along with Eumenes, not specifically mentioned in this scene (his presence as royal secretary may have been implied), these comprised five of the six innocents, and so there can be no doubt that the allegations of conspiracy, and the setting of the will, were penned by the same hand as a cohesive packaged product.

If Eumenes was behind the authorship of the *Pamphlet*, why did he absent himself from his description of the will's drafting? Was that not as self-defeating as Polyperchon's absence if he had written it? Well, as a jealous Molossian royal named Neoptolemus once reminded the men gathered in post-Alexander Babylon, Eumenes' fame with the royal pen was well known empire-wide; it would have naturally been assumed that it was he who turned the papyrus draft into an officially sealed vellum testament, in the same way the Roman Aelian assumed Eumenes had prepared the *Ephemerides* (T5).⁴⁶ By citing himself (and Perdiccas, whose orders he followed) as 'innocent', as well as rebroadcasting his own significant territorial inheritance (Cappadocia and Paphlagonia), under the will, Eumenes achieved all he needed to without the suggestion of overt manipulation. This is exactly why, it seems logical to believe, Ptolemy did not include himself more prominently in the *Journal* entry I propose he crafted.

Holcias and Hagnothemis the Obscure

So, who was Holcias, the man who features so prominently in the *Pamphlet* and who read Alexander's will at the initial private gathering? Did he perhaps have some significance to the pamphleteer(s)? The answer is 'yes', if Eumenes, in league with Olympias, was its author. Courtesy of a passage in Polyaenus' military treatise titled *Stratagems of War*, we find Holcias who was apparently sympathetic to the Perdiccan cause, and so to Eumenes. He defected, or escaped, from the army of Antigonus. Holcias and his 3,000 heavy-armed Macedonian renegades were finally rounded up when Eumenes was under siege at the fortress of Nora in late 319 BC.⁴⁷ So it appears he was a prominent and trusted commander.⁴⁸

Curiously, Holcias was offered a pardon and paroled to Macedon on the promise of inactivity. His subsequent disappearance suggests he was either disposed of in Macedon when Cassander came to power, or that contemporary historians decided to 'write him out of Hellenistic history', in the same way, it has been suggested, he may have written himself in.[49]

The same identity questions may be asked of the otherwise unreferenced Hagnothemis (elsewhere spelled Agnothemis); so could this be a corruption of 'Hagnon (or Agnon) of Teos', as both characters appear in Plutarch's *Life of Alexander*?[50] Hagnon was a flamboyant flatterer and influential figure at the campaign court, and he was apparently hostile to the royal historian–philosopher Callisthenes.[51] An extract from Plutarch's treatise *How One May Discern a Flatterer from a Friend* suggested Hagnon managed to deceive Alexander with his fawning.[52] Arrian's *Indica* captured his role as a trierarch selected to fund and equip a barge in the mammoth Hydaspes–Indus fleet, a clear indicator of his wealth.[53] Further, Plutarch and Athenaeus claimed a Companion named Agnon wore golden studs in his sandals (or boots) at the court banquets, and this is surely the same man (Arrian appears to have named him Andron, or more likely, a later manuscript corruption did).[54]

A surviving Greek inscription suggests that at some point in the Successor Wars Hagnon joined Antigonus, possibly upon the death of Craterus, for we find Hagnon operating in Caria in the region of Ephesus in the period 320–315 BC (he was granted citizenship of the city in 321/320 BC), an understandable location if he hailed from nearby Teos. Plutarch claimed that 'Hagnothemis' was the first to hear and rebroadcast Aristotle's part in the *Pamphlet* allegations; he in turn had garnered the detail from Antigonus at a time when, I suggest, the one-eyed general was on his way to becoming the most powerful man in Asia, a position he achieved with his eventual defeat and execution of Eumenes at the close of 316 BC.[55]

Origins of the Competing *Journal*

We know that everything claimed by the *Pamphlet* was thoroughly undermined by the content of the *Journal*. Cited by Plutarch and Arrian at the close of their books (T3, T4), this was presented as a genuine extract from the king's official campaign diaries, the *Ephemerides*. Arrian's statement made it clear that both Aristobulus and Ptolemy either ended their books at this point, or they had no more detail to add on Alexander's death other than that claimed in this *Ephemerides* extract.[56]

It is tempting to visualize this supposedly single surviving entry as part of a log of the king's daily orders and movements, as Arrian and Plutarch probably did. More likely there existed, for a time, a vast corpus of campaign correspondence covering ordinances, requisitions and ledgers that comprised a record of the camp and army activity, and the king's movements would have been an integral section. Some commentators argue the Macedonian kings had enjoyed a long tradition of journal keeping, and certainly the satirist Lucian later referenced the Macedonian Royal Archives which covered the movements of the regent Antipater through the years 322–319 BC. Although this may be no more genuine than the suspicious corpus of letters which Plutarch used as a resource in his biography of Alexander (which supposedly emanated from the Macedonian court), it was, nevertheless, conceived from a well-known practice, and one that was continued by the Antigonid kings.[57] Polybius referenced the letters of the kings or imperial letters (*basilika grammata*) that the Antigonids tried to keep from Roman hands, and Hieronymus would later extract from Pyrrhus' own official memoirs (*hypomnemata*, which can additionally be translated as 'drafts', 'accompanying notes' or even 'inventories').[58]

According to some commentators, the practice of maintaining court journals commenced with Alexander himself, following the Persian archive tradition.[59] If the tradition went back further, we could imagine Eumenes had maintained records for Alexander's father Philip II in Pella when employed at the royal court from aged 20. If the former conclusion is correct, Eumenes maintained a similar role as the campaign advanced through Asia.[60] Lucian did refer (perhaps tongue in cheek) to a letter sent from Eumenes to the Macedonian regent Antipater detailing Hephaestion's embarrassing slip of the tongue before the Battle of Issus in 333 BC, a probable by-product of Eumenes' secretarial role.[61]

Adding to the breadth of arguments is the idea that the *Ephemerides* actually existed as cuneiform ('those inscribed with a wedge-shaped stroke', describing the shape of the incisions) clay tablets at Babylon and only concerned Alexander when he was in residence.[62] But such tablets only had room for the briefest of detail, and we actually have the inscription relating to the very day that Alexander expired – it simply relates: 'The king died, clouds made it impossible to observe the skies.'[63]

The Babylonians were hoarders of inscribed cuneiform tablets.[64] Callisthenes encountered thousands of years of astronomical diaries (said to date back 31,000 years) in this format, and he set about sending them back to Greece. The oldest extant diary we know of, however, dates to 651 BC, though records for the eighth century BC are referenced elsewhere: Berossus, the resident Chaldean priest of Bel-Marduk in Babylon, claimed they dated back further into antiquity, but any explanation of events or causal links we might have hoped to find in them was, it seems, subordinated to timekeeping by celestial observation.[65] As one scholar points out, clay is far more durable than papyrus; a city set ablaze only hardens the material, so the surviving corpus of Babylonian and Assyrian clay inscriptions exceeds the entire library of extant Latin texts, on a word count basis.[66]

Whatever were the origins of the king's *Ephemerides*, by the time the army finally returned to Babylon from the eastern satrapies, and when considering the logistical challenge of running a vast empire, Eumenes – who by now had a cavalry command of his own – would have required a whole secretariat to deal with court records, and that would have been the information nerve centre of the expanded Macedonian-governed world.[67] The aforementioned Diodotus (or Diognetus) may well have been involved in its management, no doubt supported by others; Myllenas, for example, was additionally referenced by Curtius as a royal secretary (*scriba regis* in Latin), who, like Eumenes, saw active military service.[68]

I have already challenged assumptions that these official records survived the Successor Wars,[69] for the conflicts within the extant accounts clearly suggest otherwise. Suspiciously, the only alleged survivor of the once-vast *Ephemerides* is the single *Journal* entry cited by Plutarch and Arrian dealing with Alexander's death. Their two versions are remarkably similar, and the divergences are easily explained. Plutarch claimed to be reciting the *Journal* entries almost 'word for word', and yet he précised his source material more aggressively than Arrian. Nevertheless, what was cited by him was almost verbatim. The style, pace and daily references undeniably parallel one another, so we cannot doubt Plutarch and Arrian were virtually metaphrasing (reproducing word for word) a single source.[70]

This is Arrian's *Journal* extract:

> The Royal Diary gives the following account, to the effect that he revelled and drank at the dwelling of Medius; then rose up, took a bath, and slept; then again supped at the house of Medius and again drank till far into the night. After retiring from the drinking party he took a bath; after which he took a little food and slept there, because he already felt feverish. He was carried out upon a couch to the sacrifices, in order that he might offer them according to his daily custom. After performing the sacred rites he lay down in the banqueting hall until dusk. In the meantime he gave instructions to the officers about the expedition and voyage, ordering those who were going on foot to be ready on the fourth day, and those who were going to sail with him to be ready to sail on the fifth day. From this place he was carried upon the couch to the river, where he embarked in a boat and sailed across the river to the park. There he again took a bath and went to rest.
>
> On the following day he took another bath and offered the customary sacrifices. He then entered a tester bed, lay down, and chatted with Medius. He also ordered his officers to meet him at daybreak. Having

102   The Last Will and Testament of Alexander the Great

> done this he ate a little supper and was again conveyed into the tester bed. The fever now raged the whole night without intermission. The next day he took a bath; after which he offered sacrifice, and gave orders to Nearchus and the other officers that the voyage should begin on the third day. The next day he bathed again and offered the prescribed sacrifices. After performing the sacred rites, he did not yet cease to suffer from the fever. Notwithstanding this, he summoned the officers and gave them instructions to have all things ready for the starting of the fleet. In the evening he took a bath, after which he was very ill. The next day he was transferred to the house near the swimming-bath, where he offered the prescribed sacrifices. Though he was now very dangerously ill, he summoned the most responsible of his officers and gave them fresh instructions about the voyage. On the following day he was with difficulty carried out to the sacrifices, which he offered; and nonetheless gave other orders to the officers about the voyage. The next day, though he was now very ill, he offered the prescribed sacrifices. He now gave orders that the generals should remain in attendance in the hall, and that the colonels and captains should remain before the gates. But being now altogether in a dangerous state, he was conveyed from the park into the palace. When his officers entered the room, he knew them indeed, but could no longer utter a word, being speechless. During the ensuing night and day and the next night and day he was in a very high fever. Such is the account given in the Royal Diary.[71]

Plutarch's *Journal* version was more specific on dates:

> Aristobulus says that he had a raging fever, and that when he got very thirsty he drank wine, whereupon he became delirious, and died on the 13th of the month Daisios. Moreover, in the court 'Journals' there are recorded the following particulars regarding his sickness. On the 18th of the month Daesius he slept in the bathing-room because he had a fever. On the following day, after his bath, he removed into his bedchamber, and spent the day at dice with Medius. Then, when it was late, he took a bath, performed his sacrifices to the gods, ate a little, and had a fever through the night. On the 20th, after bathing again, he performed his customary sacrifice; and lying in the bathing-room he devoted himself to Nearchus, listening to his story of his voyage and of the great sea. The twenty-first he spent in the same way and was still more inflamed, and during the night he was in a grievous plight, and all the following day his fever was very high. So he had his bed removed and lay by the side of the great bath, where he conversed with his officers about the

vacant posts in the army, and how they might be filled with experienced men. On the 24th his fever was violent and he had to be carried forth to perform his sacrifices; moreover, he ordered his principal officers to tarry in the court of the palace, and the commanders of divisions and companies to spend the night outside. He was carried to the palace on the other side of the river on the 25th, and got a little sleep, but his fever did not abate. And when his commanders came to his bedside, he was speechless, as he was also on the twenty-sixth; therefore the Macedonians made up their minds that he was dead, and came with loud shouts to the doors of the palace, and threatened his companions until all opposition was broken down; and when the doors had been thrown open to them, without cloak or armour, one by one, they all filed slowly past his couch. During this day, too, Python and Seleucus were sent to the temple of Serapis to enquire whether they should bring Alexander thither; and the god gave answer that they should leave him where he was. And on the 28th, towards evening, he died. Most of this account is word for word as written in the 'Journals'.[72]

These *Journal* entries present a dry and pedestrian account of Alexander's twelve-day illness at Babylon (a far longer journey to death than the five or so days suggested by the *Pamphlet* and Vulgate texts), and though short on detail and prosaic in style, the reporting is punctuated by references to the king's nightly drinking at the Macedonian-style symposia that preceded his decline.[73] These gatherings – like the final party at Medius' residence – more often than not degenerated into the drinking binges documented at both ends of Alexander's campaign, though his darkest moments in between were frequently accompanied by alcoholic excess.[74]

According to the *Journal*, at the conclusion of Medius' party, Alexander experienced a fever, after which he bathed and slept with no dramatic decline in health. Aristobulus, ever watchful over his dead king's reputation, justified the alcoholic consumption by claiming the raging fever moved him to quench a voracious thirst with more wine.[75] In fact the *Journal* depicts Alexander in firm organization mode for days thereafter, bathing and attending to religious rites (the Macedonian king's religious role was, we believe, to mediate between the men and their gods), fleet logistics and the continued organization of the army for the forthcoming Arabian campaign, all of it reported in an unemotional and almost sepulchral style.[76] Towards the end, the *Journal* entries become briefer still as Alexander slid into a coma and towards his speechless, silent death.

That silence remains deafening, and moreover, stylistically the *Journal* stands out like a torn sepia photo stapled unconvincingly to the end of a Technicolor film, a production that had paused for a moment and then resumed with a personality-changed cast that had been furnished with newly authored scripts.

The meek bedside Companions who acquiesced to Alexander's failure to nominate a successor became lions of ambition in the dangerous days that followed, when the monochrome entries attained their colour once again.

I contend that no matter how comprehensive a cover-up, clues always remain. The *Journal* entry, silent on the testament, with no succession instructions from the king, may nonetheless have unintentionally preserved the silhouette of a reading of the will, for the entry reads:

> On the next day, his condition now worsened, he [Alexander] just managed to make the required sacrifices, and then sent instructions to the generals to wait for him in the palace courtyard and the battalion and company commanders to wait outside his door.[77]

This correlates well with the lead-up to the reading of the will as outlined in the *Metz Epitome*. At this point, it is clear that Alexander was only just able to speak, making sacrifices with difficulty and finally commanding his chief officers (down to commanders of between 500 and 1,000 men) to be on close call. Consequently, he, and those closest to him, must have appreciated how gravely ill he was.[78] In these circumstances, the summons was unlikely to have been to provide them with further orders concerning the forthcoming expedition to Arabia. If, as the Vulgate texts claimed, Perdiccas – or Ptolemy – had to prise out of Alexander a decision on succession, and if, as the *Journal* claimed, he was speechless for his final two days, then here, with the commanders assembled immediately outside his bedchamber, something momentous was being written or being said inside.

The *Journal* entry appearing in Arrian and Plutarch included two further significant episodes that perhaps tell us, once again, more than the original author may have intended. The first concerns the Macedonian infantry contingent, which forced its way into the king's bedchamber where the Bodyguards and select Companions had their king closely quarantined. Fearing his death was being kept from them, the infantry officers smelled intrigue: '...others wished to see his body, for a report had gone around that he was already dead, and they suspected, I fancy, that his death was being concealed by his guards.'[79] The forced entry, or as Arrian more tactfully put it, 'insistence' on seeing the king, suggests there was a huge lack of trust in the senior command, whose cavalry status still resonated of the old aristocratic landowner–serf divide that underpinned the Macedonian tribal structure.

This episode of near mutiny became a permanent fixture in all accounts, and as it closely paralleled what was claimed in the *Pamphlet*, we would be justified in concluding that this was a genuine state of affairs no author could bypass. At this point, however, the king was still conscious, though conspicuously speechless, as the officers filed past him. According to the *Journal*, sometime after the intrusion and when all the soldiers had departed the bedchamber, Alexander was pronounced dead. Plutarch was clear that Aristobulus pinpointed that to the 30th of the Macedonian month of Daisios, which corresponded to the 'moon of May' (spanning May–June in the modern calendar), some two days after the *Journal* statement that it occurred on the 28th; the differing dates make it clear that Plutarch was drawing from both sources in parallel here.[80]

Daisios was what was known as a 'hollow' month of twenty-nine days, and any reference to 'month end', and whether that meant the 29th or 30th, could have caused additional slippage between accounts.[81] The latter date for the pronouncement of Alexander's death – which in this version was two full weeks after Medius' party on the 16th – may capture what Ptolemy's sanitary affair chose not to: two days of confusion as the tenuous life-signs ebbed and flowed, certainly not a fitting epitaph for the Macedonian king. The timing of Alexander's medical death has often been disputed, for his body professedly stayed fresh for days thereafter. If not more Vulgate 'wonderment', this hints at a huge blunder in the prognosis when a deep coma may indeed have fooled the audience for some time.[82]

Considering the common reporting of these episodes, I am not accusing Ptolemy of complete journalistic invention with what I propose was his brilliant example of fake-but-genuine-looking 'pseudo documentarism' (the creation of a genuine-looking record), for much we read in the *Journal* probably *did* take place. The nightly drinking and frequent celebrations that paint a month of irresponsibility may well be factual, even if such background detail was already a means of developing a rhetorical argument in Philip II's day: in Athens, the hostile Demosthenes, and Theopompus who spent time in Macedon, had certainly implicated the Argead court in bouts of extended insobriety.[83] Conversely, when upholding the historicity of the *Pamphlet* will, I am not claiming all the testament detail as genuine. Both authors needed to interweave their fictions with verisimilitude if they were to pass them off as genuine and have the desired effect, and so a rather appropriate symmetry existed in the ranks of this literary confrontation.

The second contentious episode which betrays the hand of the *Journal* author was a visit by other Bodyguards and court intimates to the Temple of Serapis to ask for divine guidance, and this does appear to be an overtly Ptolemaic device.

Hunting the Incomplete Month

Before I discuss Serapis (an episode already well autopsied), with its importance to Hellenistic Egypt and to this night in Babylon, we need to mention other briefer references to the royal diaries, the *Ephemerides*, that have survived, though they provide no additional detail and none of them contradicts the contention that only *one* event was being recorded. We find the first in Plutarch's moral essays (referred to as *Moralia*), in which a close friend of the Greek historian rebutted claims that Alexander drank moderately by citing the drink-laden entries from the *Ephemerides* as his witness to excess.[84] A second is an earlier reference in Plutarch's *Life of Alexander* detailing the king's daily routine of hunting, bathing and dining, but once more the emphasis is on frequent drinking sessions (Plutarch defended Alexander's excesses with 'but over the wine, as I have said, he would sit long, for conversation's sake'). Similar is another *Ephemerides* extract that can be found in Athenaeus' *Dinner Philosophers*, which additionally claimed Alexander slept two days and nights consecutively following a night of carousing.[85]

The water is supposedly muddied by another fragment found in the *Historical Miscellany* of Aelian (T5):

> The following behaviour of Alexander was not commendable. On the fifth of the month of Dios he was drinking with Eumaeus, they say; then on the sixth he slept because of the excesses. During the day he got up only long enough to discuss with his generals the following day's march, saying it would commence early. On the seventh he feasted with Perdiccas and drank freely again. On the eighth he slept. On the fifteenth of the same month he drank to excess once more, and on the following day he did what he would usually do after a party. On the twenty-seventh he dined with Bagoas – the distance from the palace to Bagoas' house was ten stades – and on the twenty-eighth he slept.[86]

This text is possibly incomplete, for though it is clear the *Ephemerides* was being referred to, the source was never formally introduced. Like much else in Aelian's compendium of historical titbits, the detail was tersely thrown in beside other non-relevant text. But here again, alcohol abuse served to illustrate the decline in Alexander's behaviour against a background of earlier finer Homeric qualities and restraint. However, Aelian's excerpt contained calendar references which contradicted Arrian and Plutarch, and thus, some scholars have argued, it was referring to a totally different event. One proposed date for that is Alexander's previous visit to Babylon in 331 BC, or his stay in Ecbatana, the summer residence of the Great Kings where Hephaestion died in the autumn of 324 BC.[87]

This last interpretation is linked to the decline in health of Hephaestion, the king's closest friend and first chiliarch, perhaps prompted by a fragment of scandalmongering from a historian named Ephippus in his book *On the Deaths of Alexander and Hephaestion* which claimed that this too was preceded by prodigious drinking bouts.[88] Moreover, an enmity had existed between the alleged *Ephemerides* author, Eumenes, and Hephaestion (whose above-reported slip of the tongue may be evidence of that),[89] so the alcoholic slant supposedly deflected blame away from Eumenes, for Alexander suspected his friend's death was due to deliberate poisoning. Attaching this *Ephemerides* extract to a different campaign episode would, of course, back up those scholars who contend various portions of the official campaign log were in circulation.[90] But that is a vexing conclusion, because Aelian's chapter is headed 'Of Alexander', and Hephaestion was never mentioned at all.[91] If taken together as two distinct episodes, these extracts would suspiciously confirm that any surviving *Ephemerides* fragments recorded little more than a string of decadent drinking bouts followed by fatal illnesses.

Aelian's text is deemed to conflict with that of Plutarch and Arrian because it commenced on the 5th of the Macedonian month of Dios, the month of Zeus linked to the moon of October, with the main narrative focusing on drinking bouts that followed on the 6th, 7th and 8th, then the 15th and 16th, after which it jumped to the king's dining on the 27th and sleeping on the 28th. Yet here there is no sign that illness or fever had taken hold of Alexander, and Medius' party is not mentioned at all.[92] But a little lateral thinking offers some reconciliation, and the clues lay in the opening statements of Plutarch and Arrian.

Plutarch told us that previously (that is before the commencement of Alexander's two-week decline), and upon hearing the news of Hephaestion's posthumous elevation to hero (or god) as approved by the oracle at Siwa, Alexander had allowed himself to indulge in a number of sacrifices and drinking bouts.[93] Arrian also mentioned that Alexander had previously celebrated the customary sacrificial rites with a view to his success. Diodorus commented on these earlier events too, claiming that following Hephaestion's funeral, the king turned to amusements and festivals.[94] How, then, can this help unite the texts?

The answer is to assume that Aelian's month of 'Dios' (Δίος in Greek) was a corruption of 'Daisios' (Δαίσιος), and then to insert Aelian's detail of banquets from the 5th to the 15th into the narrative before Medius' drinking party which took place on the 15th/16th, whence Plutarch and Arrian began their *Journal* entry (as implied by the date references in Plutarch's text). The result is a neatly dovetailed account of a full month's activity, including the 'previous' celebrations Plutarch and Arrian referred to, and this is where Plutarch's references to hunting would have originated. A corruption of names in Aelian's text appears an inherent part of the confusion, for we would expect his reference to Alexander's drinking at the residence of 'Eumaeus' (Eumaios in its Greek form) on the 5th to read either 'Eumenes' or perhaps 'Ptolemaios' – so Ptolemy.[95]

To finally resolve the conflict, the banquets described by Aelian on the 24th, 27th and 28th would have taken place at the end of the previous month, erroneously repositioned by a manuscript copyist trying to make chronological sense, possibly due to the lack of any introduction in Aelian's account; the extant manuscripts are, indeed, studded with scribal errors. Repositioning the activities of the 24th, 27th and 28th to the previous month makes better sense, considering the gathering took place at the residence of the prominent eunuch Bagoas some 10 stades (broadly equivalent to 1¼ miles) from the royal palace, an unlikely journey if Alexander was already at death's door. Considered this way, the middle-month date references finger-join too well for us to dismiss any coincidence out of hand.

Further evidence that Aelian's passage preceded the other *Journal* entries comes in the form of his statement that on the 6th of the month, Alexander discussed a 'march' with his generals, which was supposed to commence early the following morning. Alexander was preparing to follow the progress of the land army into Arabia with the fleet, so the army's departure was indeed due to commence in advance.[96] Arrian discussed how, in the days before his own *Journal* narrative commenced, fleet exercises were taking place 'constantly'; troop manoeuvres and army reorganization were well underway, and it seems this new campaign or 'voyage of discovery' was postponed because of the king's unrelenting fever.[97]

If I am correct, it appears that the archetypal *Journal* entry cited (a little over) a full month's activity. So why did the entries of Arrian and Plutarch not cover the whole period? The reason for their brevity is clear: the king's illness commenced halfway through, at Medius' party, and they were simply reporting on how Alexander died. This late start-point is supported by Plutarch writing that 'according to the *Journal* his *sickness* was as follows'.[98]

Aelian's agenda was different: for moralizing purposes, he was focusing on serial alcoholism and not the aftermath. He closed his entry with a revealing accusation:

> ...one of two alternatives follows: either Alexander damaged himself with wine by drinking so often within the month, or the authors of these stories are telling lies: from them one can infer that such writers, who include Eumenes of Cardia, tell similar tales on other occasions.[99]

The 'other occasions' could, of course, include Eumenes' aforementioned letter to Antipater concerning Hephaestion, or even later events which established Eumenes' reputation for brilliant documentary subterfuges in the Successor Wars.[100] Aelian's conclusion, which clearly referred to a *whole* month, was that 'a drinking marathon unique in history' was an impossibility, or suggestive of an author who wished the king's death to seem attributable to such.[101] Whilst it appears that Aelian believed he was reading a genuine fragment of the royal diaries, he was perhaps the first classical author to (obliquely) question the authenticity of its content. As we know, Athenaeus' *Dinner Philosophers* – written as a dialogue within a dialogue in the style of Plato – credited Eumenes with exactly the same secretarial role.[102] Athenaeus' work is uncertainly dated, but its contempt for the

Roman emperor Commodus (reigned AD 180–192) provides an indication, and from that we can conclude that he and Aelian were potentially contemporaries living in Rome.

Aelian's cynicism raises a fundamental question: could, or would, Eumenes or any other court secretary have been allowed the latitude to capture such degenerative behaviour in the real-time official *Ephemerides*? Surely not. Instead, I am proffering Ptolemy as the architect of this specific entry, and his penchant for subterfuge may have been more developed than we first suspected; he fabricated a sufficiently convincing extract from the official campaign diaries to wind up his authoritative history written perhaps twenty to thirty years after Alexander died, whilst heaping responsibility for its content on the royal secretaries. As Eumenes had died some years before Ptolemy came to publish, there was not much he could do about it. Additionally, Ptolemy's association with the *Journal* is completely plausible; he was, after all, behind the foundation of the Alexandrian Library that rapaciously collected documents of all kinds.

Certainly, his son Ptolemy II Philadelphus left extensive 'royal records' (referred to in ancient Greek texts as *basilikai anagraphai* and *hypomnemata*) which Diodorus was aware of, and which the later historian Appian of Alexandria drew from. An extract from a later royal journal appears in the 'propagandistic' *Gaurob Papyrus* describing events in the reign of Ptolemy III Euergetes ('the Benefactor'), whose twenty-four-volume collection of *hypomnemata* provided Athenaeus with material. So, it seems Arrian and Plutarch were satisfied that Ptolemy was guardian of Alexander's royal *Ephemerides* too.

To add muscle to our argument for a common *Journal* fragment for all the above extracts, we have a literary 'gene-marker' to guide us. Both Plutarch and Arrian noticeably sandwiched their extracts between remarks which inform us when they opened and closed their metaphrasing (T3, T4).[103] Uniquely for his final chapter, Plutarch employed the term 'almost word for word' to describe his entry, and Arrian added 'all these details are to be found in the Journals'.[104] This is rare evidence of an earlier historian's precise phraseology. So logic suggests their source: Ptolemy had also been quite precise on the *Journal* entry and exit points. The stress Arrian and Plutarch placed on informing us that this was uniquely sourced material rules out any speculation that other parts of their books were *Journal*-derived. Arrian conspicuously omitted any reference to it when detailing his sources on the opening page of his campaign account.[105]

Could Ptolemy have credibly accessed the original campaign diaries? It was first proposed that he did in 1894, since when other scholars have endorsed this.[106] A 1960 treatise on these non-surviving texts proposed an alternative explanation: the *Journal* entry was a fake, and yet because it corroborated Ptolemy's detail, its author was familiar with Ptolemy's book, and thus a look of authenticity was achieved. The study did not contemplate that the authors were one and the same, though it did conclude that its style was Alexandrian by comparison with a papyrus found there in the Roman era.[107]

If Ptolemy did have the complete campaign corpus, what happened to it and why did he not strengthen the veracity, authority and uniqueness of his history with more frequent references to the campaign logs, most relevantly for events he could not himself have witnessed? The answer is probably straightforward: if he did have the *Ephemerides*, it would have been foolhardy to broadcast its whereabouts to those who would undermine him by accessing it themselves, for it appears Ptolemy greatly inflated his own role in the Asian campaign. Like much else surrounding the death of Alexander, the official records, in whatever condition they survived, remained a closely guarded affair. If any campaign documentation did survive the Successor Wars, which eventually saw Antigonus plundering Babylon (310/309 BC), then Ptolemy would surely have coveted what remained. Writers in later antiquity suggested what survived was no longer accessible at Alexandria.[108]

It is not difficult to imagine how Ptolemy first came into possession of any archival material from Babylon following Alexander's death. War with Perdiccas commenced in earnest when Ptolemy hijacked or rescued (depending upon the interpretation) Alexander's funeral cortège somewhere near Damascus in Syria and 'escorted' it to Egypt, against Perdiccas' wishes.[109] Aelian provided a colourful addition to the episode, in which the bier carrying the coffin of hammered gold and pulled by sixty-four mules was simply a decoy that included a replica of the dead king's corpse; the real body was sped to Egypt by a different route.[110]

Aelian's account went on to report that Aristander of Termessus, the king's by-now famous seer, had predicted at Babylon that whichever land received the body would remain prosperous and forever unvanquished. Whilst this too has the air of a later Ptolemaic device, no one (after Perdiccas) demanded the return of Alexander's mummified remains, which suggests some legitimacy to Ptolemy's action, though it must be said that no one was ever able to cross the Nile to remove him from power. In the Vulgate texts, the final destination of the bier does appear to have been the oracular Ammonium at Siwa in the Egyptian desert, the home of the Zeus-Ammon and Alexander's 'immortality', and the extant wills additionally claim that Alexander chose to be entombed in Egypt, though this may have been politically opportune if Ptolemy was being courted.[111]

The Greek travel writer Pausanias concluded that Perdiccas planned to escort the bier to Aegae, the traditional burial ground of the Macedonian royalty. Whether endorsed by the Common Assembly at Babylon, or stemming from Perdiccas' later opportunism, Pausanias' interpretation is possibly supported by either of two noteworthy turns of events. The first is the Macedonian regent proffering his daughter (Nicaea) to Perdiccas, in which case he was probably on safe ground when taking the body 'home', for who except Ptolemy's supporters could object to its interment in Macedon? Aegae had been the spiritual home and necropolis of Argead kings some four centuries before. Moreover, King Perdiccas I had prophesized the end of the Argead line should any king be buried anywhere else.[112]

The second event that might have helped Pausanias reach his conclusion was the collapse of Perdiccas' planned marriage alliance with Antipater, following which we read Perdiccas and his generals voted in favour of defeating Ptolemy in Egypt 'in order that there might be no obstacle in the way of their Macedonian campaign'.[113] Perdiccas most likely planned to keep Alexander's funeral bier close (in Syria I propose) until events developed sufficiently to escort it to its permanent home in his bid for control of the Macedonian political capital at Pella.

So it is likely that royal archives and campaign correspondence departed Babylon with Perdiccas and remained with him as he planned his attack on the Nile.[114] Letters between him and Demades in Athens were reportedly retrieved from the archives immediately after his death, suggesting Perdiccas had indeed journeyed with the tools of bureaucracy about him.[115] His initial attack on the Ptolemaic defences at Pelusium, a necessary entry point into Egypt to avoid the marshes of the river delta, and again near Heliopolis further up the Nile, failed and cost him his life. Thereafter, deals were brokered and promises exchanged, and possibly court correspondence too. Ptolemy even acquired Perdiccas' surviving elephants – those his men had not managed to blind with pikes at the Battle of the Fort of Camels. Ptolemy was most likely already in league with Seleucus (possibly one of Perdiccas' assassins), who, I argue, had already inherited the governorship of Babylonia, in which case further exchanges of court correspondence would have taken place.[116]

Enter Serapis, the New God

Here I expand on the *Journal* references to the cult of Serapis, through which its author Ptolemy, I propose, might have made his biggest blunder. The topic has already been discussed, but not quite with the significance it might merit to the authenticity of Alexander's will. Arrian wrote:

> The Diaries [*Ephemerides*] say that Peithon, Attalus, Demophon and Peucestas, together with Cleomenes, Menidas and Seleucus spent the night in the temple of Serapis and asked the God if it would be better for Alexander to be carried into the temple himself, in order to pray there and perhaps recover; but the God forbade it, and declared it would be better for him if he stayed where he was. The God's command was made public, and soon afterwards Alexander died – this, after all, being the better thing.[117] (T3, T4 abbreviated)

The *Journal* unambiguously named the individuals who spent the night in the temple of the healing god to ask divine guidance on Alexander's worsening condition. The group appears to have included two of Alexander's leading seers, Demophon and Cleomenes; it was Demophon who had warned Alexander not to enter the Mallian city in India where he was nearly killed, so his words carried some gravitas.[118] More intriguing is the presence of Peithon, Peucestas and Seleucus, the men either complicit in Perdiccas' murder, or the most prominent of those named guilty at Medius' drinking party.[119] The list also looks to have included Attalus (initially hostile to Perdiccas, but who became his brother-in-law as part of the settlement at Babylon) and Menidas, who had recently arrived in Babylon from recruiting in Macedon, which suggests he could have arrived with Cassander, the scheming son of the allegedly scheming Macedonian regent.[120] It is a line-up which has the distinct air of a riposte to the accusations in the *Pamphlet*.

It is generally accepted by modern historians – a stance supported by a story in Plutarch's treatise titled *Isis and Osiris* – that the cult of Serapis was started in Egypt by Ptolemy I Soter at least a decade after Alexander's death, and probably later still.[121] Plutarch further asserted that Serapis was the Egyptian name for the equivalent of Pluto, either correctly or guided by this episode. All in all, some forty-two temples to the new god appeared across Egypt with the intention of uniting the Graeco–Macedonian ruling classes with their Egyptian subjects; the most prominent was perhaps in the Egyptian Quarter of Alexandria itself.[122] A reference to the Serapeum in Alexandria and to the 'great Serapis, ruler of all' appeared in the *Romance* version of the will (as well as other chapters), which does rather point to Egyptian influence in the book's provenance.[123]

The integrity of the *Journal* entry as an unedited source rests on the existence of a Serapis cult, and one that had arrived in Babylon, earlier than 323 BC.[124] This appears to counter the evidence (so some scholars believe), yet the notion may be challenged by the wording in what is known as the *Curse of Artemisia* which mentions an 'Oserapis' who was possibly worshipped at Memphis before Alexander's Egyptian invasion. But this deity, whilst similarly linked to death and the afterlife, was usually depicted as a mummified human male with the head of a bull, with a solar disk between its horns, which bears little resemblance to the statues and depictions of the familiar Ptolemaic Serapis.[125]

Egyptian residents of Babylonia could have twinned its temple of Bel-Marduk with that of Oserapis if they saw a religious overlap. Moreover, it was not uncommon for authors to employ contemporary names and terms to describe an earlier equivalent for the sake of clarity for the reader;[126] Herodotus equated Egyptian gods with Greek gods, and vice versa, long before Alexander's day.[127] We also know the new syncretized 'Serapis' was in effect the cult of the healing god Asclepius reinvented with a twist: it fused the Memphite cult of the bull Osiris-Apis with elements of Zeus and indeed Pluto.[128] Alexander is specifically

A bust of Serapis wearing a *kalathos*, a ceremonial basket used in religious processions and a symbol for the land of the dead. Statues of Serapis depicted a figure resembling Hades or Pluto, gods associated with the Underworld, often with a sceptre and the hellhound Cerberus at his feet along with a serpent. (Graeco–Roman Museum, Alexandria)

cited as having destroyed the temple of Asclepius in Ecbatana following Hephaestion's death, and so the healing god, at least, was an Eastern resident by then, if not another divine approximation.[129] As a further parallel, Zeus-Ammon is itself a Hellenization of Egypt's Ammon-Ra. Why then all the fuss?

The fuss over divine identification may be necessary because the reference to Serapis seems, nevertheless, self-damning if scholars upholding the 'late' emergence of the god in Egyptian are correct on the dating and naming conventions. The *Journal* may have been promoting a new anthropomorphic god,

114   The Last Will and Testament of Alexander the Great

but an original secretarial entry compiled in 323 BC must have used the Eastern title of the deity, or specifically 'Oserapis', if there were (against the evidence) 'striking similarities'. But after Ptolemy's reshaping of the god with elements of Greek religion, that identification no longer held. If it was the new Hellenistic god that was being referred to in the *Journal*, as the name we read implies, that would have been back-formation by the *Journal* author, and at best, the *Ephemerides* entry was edited, with Serapis' development in Egypt again pointing to Ptolemaic *Pamphlet* origins.[130]

There is a further reference to Serapis in Plutarch's narrative of Babylon, linked to an imposter who fatally adorned himself with the royal robes and irreverently took the throne while Alexander was exercising. When questioned on his treasonous behaviour, he claimed Serapis' divine will had unchained him and he blamed his otherwise inexplicable actions on the god's command (T21, see also T22).[131] This account was obviously compiled many years later, so the use of a familiar deity to approximate an Eastern god is less troubling. We know Arrian cited Aristobulus as his source on similar episodes such as the Chaldean prophecies, but not specifically for this event. So here the Serapic reference could be further evidence of Ptolemy's own strategic interweaving of 'his' god and the portentous into the end of his book to signal the king's imminent, inevitable and fate-determined end, though one clearly hastened by his unrelenting alcoholism, as the *Journal* made clear.[132]

If the cult of Serapis was connected to the snake, as some scholars suppose, then Ptolemy's claim that two talking serpents (Aristobulus mentioned ravens, Strabo stated crows) guided Alexander and his entourage to the Egyptian oracle at Siwa in the Libyan desert,[133] alongside Alexander's dream vision of an antidote-bearing serpent in India used to cure Ptolemy's own wound, suggest Ptolemy was introducing his new deity more insidiously through his work to highlight his importance and legitimacy as a successor.[134] The snake-god Glycon was, after all, the alleged reincarnation of the healing god Asclepius, Serapis' forerunner, and the *Romance* wove in the legend of the 'good fortunate' serpents (representing Agathos Daimon, the good fortune spirit) that appeared at the founding of Ptolemaic Alexandria.

Statuettes recovered from the city appear to show Alexander in a snake-fringed aegis (an animal-skin throw), and we should recall the claims that Olympias was seen with snakes in her bed; she was reportedly entwined by a huge serpent when she conceived her son, though this may be a product of Plutarch's hostility to her involvement in the Orphic rites and cults of 'magic'.[135] But in this tradition, Alexander's alleged father was Nectanebo II (ruled 360–342 BC) of the Thirtieth Dynasty, the last pharaoh of Egyptian stock. If Alexandria was the birthplace of this *Romance* claim, then the Ptolemies were truly immersing themselves in a realm of demi-gods. It was the perfect amalgam for a dynasty that had assisted Alexander in his deeds and which was nevertheless conscious of its 'new' ancient subject population.[136]

Demetrius of Phalerum, Ptolemy's learned court philosopher who had been expelled from Athens in 307 BC by Demetrius the Besieger, the son of Antigonus the One-Eyed, is said to have written five books focusing on 'true dreams' surrounding cures deriving from Serapis, composing paeans in the god's honour after his own blindness had been healed.[137] Demetrius appears to have been a major part of Ptolemy's fast-developing PR machine in the post-Ipsus years, which culminated in Alexander's prayer to Serapis, a section of which was discovered in fragmentary form on a papyrus dating to the first century BC.[138] Demetrius' treatise *On Fortune*, published around 310 BC, which gave fortune the lead role over virtue in Alexander's success, may well have stirred Ptolemy to remind the world of his *own* part in the campaign.[139]

Under the sanctuary of Ptolemy I Soter, after a term in Thebes (in Boeotia), Demetrius of Phalerum shepherded the expansion of the Alexandrian Library from the palaces in the Brucheion, otherwise referred to as the Royal Quarter and which would soon house the mausoleum where Alexander was buried. Demetrius' initial good fortune did not last forever; he was exiled once again by Soter's son, Ptolemy II Philadelphus, most likely for backing his half-brother, Ptolemy the Thunderbolt, upon his father's death. Demetrius' was an unsurprising stance, since the Thunderbolt was the son of Eurydice, the sister of Cassander who had initially installed Demetrius in Athens. The learned and experienced philosopher from Phalerum, who reportedly died of a snakebite in Upper Egypt, where he was continuing his literary pursuits,[140] is said to have once advised Ptolemy I 'to acquire the books dealing with kingship and leadership' and to read them, 'for the things their friends do not dare to offer to kings as advice, are written in these books'.[141] It seems that Ptolemy quickly learned his lessons on kingship and subterfuge. One of his finest outputs was the testament-killing *Journal*.

Politics of the Portentous

Serapic involvement with the *Journal* brought divine judgement into the picture, and this, in turn, worked well beside the biographical elements questioning Alexander's sanity, for the picture painted by Plutarch is one of a king losing his reason:

> His confidence now deserted him, he began to believe that he had lost the favour of the gods, and he became increasingly suspicious of his friends ... Meanwhile Alexander had become so obsessed by his fears of the supernatural and so overwrought and apprehensive in his own

mind, that he interpreted every strange or unusual occurrence, no matter how trivial, as a prodigy or a portent.[142] (T21)

The message is clear: the king had become 'a slave to his fears'. Did eyewitness historians dare to go this far, or was this 'fabulous' content scooped up later? Death-heralding omens proliferated Alexander's final chapter (T21, T22, T23, T24) in both the Vulgate accounts and the court genre represented by Arrian and Plutarch. Arrian's account is more sanitized, but we know he demonstrably 'whitewashed' Alexander where necessary to protect his reputation, such was his admiration.[143] Nevertheless, this suggests that a court source (or sources) may indeed have allowed this degenerate image of Alexander to creep in.

The Roman emperor Domitian (ruled AD 81–96) once quipped that no one believes there has been a conspiracy unless a ruler is actually killed.[144] But here we contend with the opposite, for Plutarch reported that no foul play was suspected in Babylon *at the time*. This is surprising in light of the regicidal history of the Argead kings, and something of a contradiction to his claim that Alexander feared assassination from the agents of Antipater, his Macedonian regent; this was an environment in which suspicion was unlikely to have *ever* been absent.[145]

The inclusion of portents – going back, in fact, to the death of the almost-naked Indian philosopher (a gymnosophist) Calanus a year before[146] – would, as one historian observed, 'certainly suggest that the king's death was due to natural or divine causes, rather than to human agency'.[147] And surely achieving that conclusion was the very purpose. Today, at least, this appears a rather obvious misdirection, but in Alexander's time the gods were not to be dismissed; the naming of Demophon and Cleomenes at the Serapic temple anchored the legitimacy of its reply: 'Leave Alexander where he is, for it would be the better thing.' This, and the collection of divinations that preceded the king's final decline, had the desired effect. The superstitious and stoical Arrian concluded: 'The truth was that divine power was leading him on to the point, which once reached, would seal his imminent death.'[148]

The Chaldean Magi had doubtlessly exploited the portent-gullible Macedonians to their advantage in Babylon when competing with Alexander's Greek 'philosophical corps' for control of his soul, and Diodorus captured something of the mystery that surrounded them: 'For they are reputed to possess a great deal of experience and to make most exact observations of the stars. Indeed they declare that for many myriads of years the study of these matters has been pursued among them.'[149] Herodotus had long before referred to the Magi as 'having performed magical rites'.[150]

Here, preceding Alexander's death in Babylon, superstition was being harnessed well. The Chaldeans had warned, the healing god had spoken and Asclepius had finally turned his back on the troubled Macedonian king.

The *Journal* recorded that Alexander was speechless for his final two days. If so, he had by definition spoken the day before. What orders did he give to the officers told to remain on call right outside his quarters?[151] What discussions took place with his intimates, his wife, secretary and Bodyguards? No doctor or physician is mentioned in the *Journal*, and not a purge, poultice or prayer. There is a troubling lack of zeal to save Alexander after Serapis had spoken. Whatever was said in the dying king's chamber was truly sanitized, muted and dried by Ptolemy to the brevity of a cuneiform tablet.

One final *Journal* detail is, however, noteworthy, because the author appears to have provided some valuable PR to both Nearchus and Medius. Alexander is portrayed listening to his admiral's account of his sea voyage and instructing him on the forthcoming campaign, presumably in a reconfirmed role as admiral of the fleet heading to Arabia, whilst Medius' intimacy with the king is highlighted by his playing private games of dice with the king (T3, T4). Both men had become valuable naval commanders, each supporting Antigonus in the Successor Wars at a time when Ptolemy needed as much sea power as he could muster. Moreover, the somewhat negative image of Alexander depicted in the *Journal* would have sat rather well with the *Pamphlet*-vilified Cassander, who was now Ptolemy's ally. Was the high profile of Nearchus and Medius an overture designed to swing their loyalty Ptolemy's way, in the same way that Eumenes was courting powerful men by naming them innocent of the plot in the *Pamphlet*?

With this in mind, the most relevant period for the *Journal*'s release would have been between late 313 and 307/306 BC, when both nautical men were known to be in active service: Nearchus advising Antigonus' son Demetrius at the battle at Gaza, and Medius seeing naval action at the battle off Salamis in Cyprus. This was a period in which Antigonus was threatening to invade Egypt itself (he tried unsuccessfully in 306 BC).[152] It raises the question whether Ptolemy might have commenced distributing the home-baked *Ephemerides* fragment – the *Journal* – to counter the claims in the *Pamphlet* (most likely issued by Eumenes and Olympias before their deaths sometime between 318 and the end of 316 BC) ahead of inserting it into the final pages of his book. Of course, the reverse may have occurred later: the uniqueness of the *Journal* entry may have led to it being extracted from Ptolemy's book and circulated independently some decades on.

So what do modern scholars conclude of the *Journal*? Generally, though not universally, it is branded a fraud. One theory concludes, ironically, that the *Journal* was a production of Eumenes and circulated within two years of Alexander's death, when Eumenes was supposedly under instruction from the Macedonian generals to squash any rumours of regicide. Interestingly, a 1986 study saw the hand of Ptolemy in its fabrication.[153] It is worth repeating one scholar's key contention 'that there is no evidence whatsoever that the *Journal* contained anything of a military or political nature'. This well-respected author followed by saying that 'given the suspicious nature of the portions cited, there is a strong possibility that the *Journal* is a fabrication, an attempt to disguise the truth about the king's last days, with the false claim that details given were extracted verbatim from an official journal'. Another commentator rather appropriately rounded-off an appraisal by stating that 'paradoxically' the Alexander *Romance* 'is nearer to the truth than the Royal *Ephemerides*'.[154] I wholeheartedly concur.

The Vulgate Genre

What is the relationship of the Vulgate portrayal of Alexander's death – represented by the accounts of Diodorus, Curtius and Justin (T6, T7, T8) – to the *Journal* and the *Pamphlet*, for the Vulgate stance on Alexander's last words – which left the kingdom 'to the strongest' – contradicts them both? As it has been neatly summed up for the *Journal*, if 'speechless for two days on his death bed, he can hardly have been so articulate in his utterances to his troops'.[155] Furthermore, the clarity of the *Pamphlet* will left no room for ambiguity: if the historian at the root of the Vulgate genre was aware of the claim of conspiracy, he was surely aware of Alexander's lucid testament that sat beside it. Assuming Cleitarchus was the source from which the Vulgate genre drew, as is widely accepted, the will's omission from his final pages was deliberate and clinical; it was an early literary keyhole-surgery that separated out the episodes to create the wrap to the genre once termed a 'muddy stream … full of flotsam'.[156]

Cleitarchus would have been on safe ground when dispensing with the will and probably the detail of the partition of the empire with it. When he came to publish (I suggest the late 280s through to the 270s BC),[157] the first generation of the Diadochi – the inheritors of the empire via Alexander's will, who fought for control of far larger domains than any granted to them by Alexander – were dead, and their offspring were embroiled in internecine strife. But to reinsure his position, I believe Cleitarchus highlighted Ptolemy's noteworthy grant of Egypt and provided an encomiastic description of his honouring Alexander's newly interred corpse at Memphis.[158]

The task facing Cleitarchus was daunting. The *Journal* and the *Pamphlet* were essentially the two outer-limit posts between which he could build his syncretic account of events at Babylon. He needed to accommodate 'silent' intestacy alongside rumours of a clearly vocal king, and then incorporate claims of conspiracy (aware it had exonerated Ptolemy) with reports of death-heralding portents and alcohol excess. Finally, Cleitarchus had to maintain the notion that it was Perdiccas who orchestrated the division of the empire, when the *Pamphlet* made it clear that the appointments came from Alexander's will (T1, T2).

All this had to be achieved from a desk in Ptolemaic Alexandria at a time when, if Cleitarchus published sufficiently late, competing claims from Hieronymus were entering circulation. Alexandria was full of veterans, or by now their offspring, and so Cleitarchus' final result needed to incorporate any additional detail he had garnered from them: the infighting, the challenge to Perdiccas, the executions and the proclamation of the new halfwit king, Arrhidaeus, who became Philip III Arrhidaeus. It was a construction that required deft hands, lateral thinking and the sacrifice and subordination of parts of one account to another. Out of this proto chaos emerged Alexander's famed final words.

'To the Strongest'

What specifically might have inspired Cleitarchus to equip Alexander with the Vulgate reply – 'to the strongest' – when questioned on succession (T6, T7, T8, T9)? And were the words pure fabrication?

Firstly, we should accommodate the possibility that they may indeed have actually been uttered, though in a very different context. Alexander was facing the deathbed prospect of leaving the Macedonian kingdom and Asian empire to two half-Asiatic sons (Heracles, his existing son by Barsine, and potentially a second son by Rhoxane, who was then pregnant). So the immortal Vulgate line 'to the strongest', or 'to the most worthy', if ever truly uttered, could have been to the question of which of the boys he wished to take the diadem when they reached throne age?

Justin concluded his narrative of the Babylon settlement with: 'A portion of the empire was reserved for Alexander's son, if a son should be born.' (T20) Though this clearly referred to Rhoxane's child, and supposedly to the compromise reached at Babylon, such a concession for two princes would not have been without precedent in Persia. For in his testament, Cyrus appointed one son, Cambyses, as king and granted the other a 'portion of the kingdom' to avoid an inevitable conflict. Insightfully, Xenophon's reinvented Cyrus predicted more happiness for the son without the crown – free from the 'plots and counter plots' that plagued Persian politics.[159]

If the campaign philosopher–historian Onesicritus had truly provided a fearful and guarded narrative on Alexander's passing, refusing to name those present as the *Pamphlet* detail claimed,[160] and if the title of his book, *On the Education of Alexander*, set out to emulate Xenophon's similarly titled biography of Cyrus (the *Cyropaedia*, literally *On the education of Cyrus*), then Cleitarchus might have been able to later extract useful reflections from there.[161] For Cyrus, on his deathbed, demanded that his sons throw 'entertainment that is fitting in honour of a man'. The narrative concluded: 'But no sooner was he dead than his sons were at strife, cities and nations revolted, and all things began to decay.'[162] It required but the lightest touch of the stylus by a historian schooled by the Cynics (as Onesicritus was) and with a good knowledge of Xenophon to conjure up the now-famous premonition of posthumous chaos and 'funeral games'.

Lucian claimed he found the following reflection from Alexander in Onesicritus' work:

> Dying, I should willingly come back to life again for a little while, Onesicritus, that I might learn how men read these things then. If they praise them and admire them now, you need not be surprised; each imagines 'he will gain our good will by great deceit'.[163]

This is perhaps a Homeric allusion to the brief return of Protesilaus from the dead of Troy in the *Iliad*, and it might have been another product of Lucian's satirical imagination.[164] But it hints that Onesicritus was somehow associated with the coverage of Alexander's death and perhaps truly did steer clear of revealing too much.

However, a more-obvious explanation, which has not been lost on modern historians, is that 'to the strongest' – *toi kratistoi* in Ancient Greek – is suspiciously close to *toi Krateroi*, 'to Craterus' (Greek form Krateros), Alexander's senior general who was entrusted to oversee the entire kingdom of Macedon in the will, along with the dowry of an Argead wife (T6, T7, T8, T9).[165] If genuinely uttered, then whoever overheard Alexander's last words at his bedside, and then manipulated them away from naming Craterus, was a Perdiccan (or Perdiccas himself). Otherwise, we would have expected a challenge at the time by those present. We cannot truly say there was no discord over this very issue, for infighting commenced almost immediately at Babylon.

But if Cleitarchus had been obliged to erase Alexander's last will and testament from his account, to confirm to Ptolemy's succession-less *Journal* ending, the vacuum at Babylon needed filling with another epitaphic construction. What other inspirations might Cleitarchus have had before him?

Onesicritus' sixth question to the wisdom-laden naked philosophers (gymnosophists) in India – how might a man most endear himself to mankind? – carried the reply, 'if he were the strongest, and yet an object of fear to no one'.[166] In addition, Cleitarchus had the immortal lines originating with Euripides, but possibly recirculating in Cleitarchus' day with a story now relating to Pyrrhus of Epirus, who was likened to Alexander in his warlike prowess. King Pyrrhus had three sons named Ptolemy, Alexander and Helenus, each by a different wife, and as a boy one of them is said to have asked his father which of them would eventually inherit his kingdom. Pyrrhus replied: 'To that one of you who keeps his sword the sharpest.' Plutarch revealed: 'This, however, meant nothing less than the famous curse of Oedipus in the tragedy: "with whetted sword", and not by lot, the brothers should divide the house. So savage and ferocious is the nature of rapacity.'[167]

The line came from *The Phoenician Women* of Euripides, the tragedian whom Alexander seems to have been most attached to. The play continued with: 'So they [his sons] were afraid that the gods might fulfil his prayers if they dwell together.' It is noteworthy that Cassander, at the centre of the conspiracy, and who *did* wipe out Alexander's Argead line by having his mother and sons executed, had offered a reward of 200 talents for the infant Pyrrhus so that he could terminate the royal line of Epirus too.[168] So, was Cleitarchus' syncretic conclusion to his book built on indirect inferences to already 'classic' but well-worn tragic endings, with an outcome that would have freed him from attempting to capture an unspeakable truth?

Like the fate of so many who came before him, Alexander's true final deathbed thoughts were stamped on by the jackboots of historical agenda. The poison, the intrigue and his famous last words were all stirred together in a rhetorical mortar and pestle, and ground into a textual epitaph that makes little sense today when he could have simply left a will.

Finally, what do scholars – old and new – make of the Vulgate claims? Arrian and Plutarch, adherents to the *Journal*, adopted a dismissive stance on the allegations of the conspiracy which led to Alexander's poisoning: 'I do not expect them to be believed' and they are 'pure fabrication'.[169] We do, however, have additional corroborating reports from Plutarch, Diodorus and Curtius that the detail of the *Pamphlet* conspiracy claims, lapped up by the Vulgate authors, hit Greece a few years after Alexander's death (T10, T6, T11).[170] The allegations, we are told, spurred Olympias into a bloody pogrom of revenge against the house of Antipater, the architect of the plot.

A further (though more dubious) corroboration is found in the *Lives of the Ten Orators*, erroneously once attributed to Plutarch but now considered pseudepigrapha (literally those 'inscribed with a lie');[171] it alleged that in the Lamian War which broke out in Greece soon after Alexander died, Hyperides, the Athenian speech writer, orated words which proposed honours to Antipater's son Iollas for his serving the poisoned wine. This was supposedly just a year after Alexander's death. The source of this detail is unreliable and seems to conflict with Plutarch's statement that it took five years for rumours of regicide to filter back to Olympias in Epirus. That would make it 318 BC, the year Eumenes was freed from captivity at Nora, though the allegations would have taken time to travel and percolate.[172] Moreover, Olympias' revenge killings (we believe of 317 BC) which targeted those accused of poisoning Alexander – principally against the family of Antipater in Macedon – do appear historical, even if the *Pamphlet* claims that justified them were not.

A fragment of Arrian's *Events After Alexander* somewhat dispels the earlier *Pamphlet* release date too, for it claimed that Iollas met with Perdiccas to broker the marriage to his sister, Nicaea. Perdiccas was not murdered until 321/320 BC, and if Iollas was already a publicized assassin (whether true or false), it seems unlikely that he would travel back to Asia to discuss a marriage because Perdiccas, like Eumenes, was a clear ally of Olympias.[173] Ominously, Iollas was said to have been accompanied by Archias; this may have been Antipater's 'unconvincing' actor-turned-assassin who became infamous for his hunting down of the vocally anti-Macedonian Hyperides, as well as Aristonicus, Himeraeus (the brother of Demetrius of Phalerum) and Demosthenes, who had made a career out of anti-Macedonian speeches.[174]

Conspiracy Within Conspiracy

Those who adhere to the tradition that Alexander died silent and intestate are surely correct on one point: the *Pamphlet*-based Will, in the form we have it today, was published by a person (or people) at the centre of the Successor Wars to further his, or their, political ends. However, it appears that all theorizing to date overlooked a very basic logic: recirculating a will that had never existed would have been dangerous and self-defeating for any one of the six innocents (or anyone in their employ), for all were notable figures. Even Holcias had a senior brigade command, and he may even have hailed from a prominent Illyrian family.[175] A reissued will would only have been an effective tool if it played on the knowledge, or the suspicion, that a genuine will had been read at Babylon. The author of the *Pamphlet* was appealing to those who knew full well what had taken place in mid-June 323 BC, and he, or they, positioned their reproduction with such effective verisimilitude that nothing short of a full-scale campaign to eradicate it had to be undertaken.

As we will soon discover, Eumenes' actions in the Successor Wars, and his alliance with Olympias, strengthen his candidacy for *Pamphlet* authorship, to the point where a partisan document of this nature appears an inevitable production from his campaign tent. Linking Ptolemy and Lysimachus to its genesis by proposing they witnessed the will's drafting was a stroke of genius that provoked an equally deceptive retort: Ptolemy's *Journal* extract, with its implication that Eumenes and Diodotus of Ethyrae were the royal secretaries who compiled it.

In 309 BC, fourteen years after the settlement at Babylon and when based on the island of Kos overseeing the birth of a son who would eventually be epitheted 'Philadelphus', Alexander's general and boyhood friend Ptolemy I – now satrap of Egypt and soon to name himself king (and gain the epithet 'Soter' for his part assisting the Rhodians under siege) – compelled Polemaeus, a talented though 'presumptuous' defecting nephew of Antigonus, to drink hemlock.[176] Following this, Cassander, with the complicity of Polyperchon, arranged for Alexander's oldest son, Heracles, to be executed, having already disposed of Rhoxane and the young Alexander IV, thereby exterminating Alexander's direct branch of the Argead line.[177] Diodorus reported that Ptolemy was 'relieved', as surely were Cassander, Lysimachus and Antigonus.[178] Ptolemy was now in league with Cassander, so rumours of the *Pamphlet*-based conspiracy were indeed 'extinguished by the power of the people defamed by the gossip', a comment no doubt recalling Olympias' execution by Cassander in 316/315 BC.[179] With allegations of treason at Babylon buried, the will soon succumbed to a similar acid bath in Ptolemy's book.

Although Alexander's will had been the legitimizing agent for kingdoms that emerged from the governorships of Antigonus, Ptolemy, Lysimachus and Seleucus – built around their 'rightfully' inherited satrapies and regional strategoi roles – once they had established themselves the will became redundant, and its memory fell into the hands of men who neither wanted it, nor could afford it, to resurface.

As for the reporting of Alexander's death, it seems that little, save Cleitarchus, squeezed in between the silent *Journal* on the one hand and the vociferous *Pamphlet* on the other, except perhaps the teenage Heracles himself for a moment, care of Polyperchon and probable silent backer Antigonus. Arrian cited an 'Ephippus of Chalcidice' as overseeing the garrisoning of Egypt; did he stay on and become a tool that Ptolemy put to work?[180]

'Absence of evidence is not evidence of absence' is an adage often applied when sources are thin, and it is particularly apt for the *Journal* and the *Pamphlet*, for their origins have stonewalled historians, the *Journal* dividing the community into believers and atheists, while the *Pamphlet* has no disciples at all. Fighting their cases in different arenas, they have done nothing but stare each other down since the Successor Wars, for the genesis of both lay there. As for the final outcome, Ptolemy's *Journal* entry became something of an impenetrable buttress at the foot of Alexander's intestate walls, and no subsequent historian's inquisitive scaling ladders have quite reached to the top.

Yet the testament was too tenacious a tradition to disappear completely. The *Pamphlet* resurrected it, Curtius claimed other historians had mentioned it, Diodorus clearly linked the testament to Rhodian guardianship, and the preservers of the *Metz Epitome* – along with the compiler of the *Kronika Alexandrina* – preferred it over Alexander's alleged silence and his incendiary last words. Nevertheless, Curtius branded the will nothing more than an imposter, and on the whole the Roman-era historians wrapped their cloaks against the uneasy breeze it arrived upon, deeming it mere romantic driftwood floating past. So it was boat-hooked aboard and into the safe haven of the *Greek Alexander Romance*, in whose final chapter still lay a welcoming and empty bed. Truth and romance make unlikely bedfellows, yet in Alexander's story they never slept apart.

7

ROYAL SECRETARY, ROYAL SEAL, ROYAL CHARADE

Did Eumenes of Cardia have the credentials to be the chief architect of the *Pamphlet*, and was it he who broadcast the existence of Alexander's will?

The first eight years of the Successor Wars in Asia were dominated by the rivalry between Eumenes of Cardia and Antigonus the One-Eyed. I review the unique, tragic and mercurial relationship between these former generals of Alexander and their respective patronage of the eyewitness historian who recorded their careers. For in these years emerged the tensions, battles, treacheries and alliances of desperation that led to the drafting of the *Pamphlet* and to its subsequent eradication.

But modern scholars are at odds on who issued the *Pamphlet*, with its accusations of conspiracy to poison Alexander and his last will and testament; attached to each candidate is that inexplicable 'conundrum'.

While fingers have been pointed at Perdiccas, Ptolemy and the elusive Holcias, no one has previously suggested Eumenes. I argue his credentials and why he was fit for purpose ahead of any other candidate.

> Antigonus paid no heed to the edicts of Perdiccas, being already lifted up in his ambitions and scorning all his associates.[1]
>
> Plutarch, *Life of Eumenes*

> If Eumenes could have contented himself with the second place, Antigonus, freed from his competition for the first, would have used him well, and shown him favour.[2]
>
> Plutarch, *The Comparison of Sertorius with Eumenes*

> I regard no man as my superior, so long as I am master of my sword.[3]
>
> Plutarch, *Life of Eumenes*

Whoever published the *Pamphlet* in the Successor Wars after Alexander's death was either one of those it named innocent of conspiracy at Medius' banquet – so Eumenes, Perdiccas, Ptolemy, Lysimachus, Asander or Holcias – or an agent acting on their behalf.[4] I have explained why Perdiccas and Ptolemy must be ruled out (they were at war with each other and neither would have salvaged the reputation of the other) and have highlighted why Lysimachus (now related to Antigonus and Ptolemy) and Asander (a likely relative of Antigonus) are poor candidates. Other contenders – Polyperchon (never mentioned in the *Pamphlet*) and Antigonus himself (not at Babylon and no ally of Ptolemy, Perdiccas nor Eumenes) – must logically be ruled out too. That leaves Eumenes and Holcias (or their agents) as the remaining authors. But only one of them truly had the pedigree and contacts to have articulated the *Pamphlet* content and capitalized upon its effect.

The Royal Secretary at War

Eumenes of Cardia was the unsung mediator of Alexander's generation, and here I explain his impact on the early Successor Wars when his coercive genius heralded a remarkable solo career. For an influential time, the son of a 'man whom poverty drove to be a waggoner', according to Duris of Samos – or the son of an impoverished funeral musician in Aelian's text – innovated something of a political sensation in his bid for survival in Alexander's fragmenting empire.[5]

Eumenes was first employed for seven years as secretary to Philip II at the royal court at Pella from the age of 20 (*ca*. 342 BC).[6] Long before Alexander set off on his Asian campaign, Eumenes had successfully straddled the growing divide between Alexander's parents, Philip and Olympias, as well as Alexander's own rift with his father.⁷ The decade-long Asian campaign saw Eumenes reconcile his additional administrative and secretarial duties under Alexander with a cavalry command, while integrating his Greek origins into the Macedonian war machine.⁸ And he remained a friend, confidante and, finally, an accomplice of Olympias until his death, a relationship, I argue, that played a significant factor in the birth of the *Pamphlet*.⁹

As his prominence grew, Eumenes engendered and then had to sidestep the jealousy that stemmed from his proximity to, and rapport with, Alexander; it was an intimacy that rankled with Hephaestion, the king's first chiliarch.¹⁰ After Hephaestion's death in Ecbatana in 324 BC, Eumenes was entrusted with Perdiccas' cavalry command once he in turn assumed Hephaestion's command (hipparchy) of the Companion Cavalry.¹¹ The increased responsibilities saw the Cardian royal secretary become a court Companion (*hetairas*, 'friend'), and the status brought him wealth. That qualified him as a trierarch (an officer commanding, and funding, a trireme ship) of the Hydaspes–Indus River fleet. A melted mass of gold and silver totalling 1,000 talents (a suspiciously high sum, almost as much as the total income of Athens for a year) was reportedly retrieved from his burned tent (imagine, rather, a multi-tented pavilion housing the secretariat) in India.¹² Moreover, Eumenes was one of the men Alexander selected to marry into the Persian nobility at Susa, where he, along with Ptolemy and Nearchus, became a relative of the king's mistress, Barsine, whose son Heracles was rejected by the Assembly at Babylon.¹³

Crucially, at Babylon in the days after Alexander's death, Eumenes managed to bridge the divide between the senior infantry officers and the aristocratic cavalry Companions when brokering a settlement which averted a Macedonian 'civil war'.¹⁴ At the opening of his account of the Successor Wars, Arrian gave a summary of the leading commanders at Babylon and it included all of the surviving Royal Bodyguards corps (the *Somatophylakes*):

> The most eminent of the cavalry and leaders were Perdiccas the son of Orontes, Leonnatus the son of Anteas, and Ptolemy, son of Lagus. The ones after them were Lysimachus the son of Agathocles, Aristonus the son of Peisaeus, Peithon the son of Crateuas, Seleucus the son of Antiochus, and Eumenes of Cardia. These were the leaders of the cavalry; Meleager led the infantry.¹⁵

As many as fourteen names have been associated with the position of the king's personal Royal Bodyguard corps in the campaign accounts. Some died and one was executed, whilst others were retired (those originally appointed by Philip II) or simply faded out of the story.¹⁶ After Hephaestion's death, a vacancy presented itself and Peucestas was already absent in the East. Possibly an established royal shield bearer (a *hypaspist* or *hyperaspisantes*), Peucestas had become an 'eighth' addition to a fellowship traditionally the auspicious number of seven. Peucestas had been appointed governor of Persis and the Bodyguard role was only bestowed on those operating in the king's immediate presence (as the title suggests).[17] In which case, and perhaps alongside a recently promoted Seleucus, Eumenes was being cited in his place, an elevation that might have come with the acquisition of Perdiccas' hipparchy.[18]

Eumenes' significance to Alexander and the campaign is unquestionable. Recalling the politics that shaped the early eyewitness accounts, we should not be alarmed or even surprised that neither Ptolemy, Aristobulus nor Cleitarchus mentioned Eumenes' military prominence more frequently. But it was in the Successor Wars that Eumenes demonstrated the abilities that argue so strongly for his candidacy as author (or co-author) of the *Pamphlet*. For we are presented with a string of brilliant intrigues borne out of his precarious position as a prominent Greek satrap in a Macedonian-controlled empire.

Eumenes Unpopular Inheritance

Eumenes' solo career commenced the minute he departed Babylon to take up his satrapal inheritance centred on Cappadocia. Hieronymus appears to have given the impression that Alexander bypassed much of Cappadocia, so leaving it wholly unconquered, due to his preoccupation with facing Darius III.[19] This was perhaps to emphasize the task Eumenes now faced, though clearly no Macedonian had since been governing the province. Eumenes' expansive grant included Paphlagonia as far eastwards as Trapezus (modern Trabzon in Turkey), the influential Black Sea port found by Milesians (T16, T17, T18, T19, T20). It was the city that Xenophon and his Greeks had finally reached eight years before on their strategic retreat from Persia and as somewhat unwelcome arrivals.[20]

Paphlagonia had previously been associated with the satrapy of Hellespontine Phrygia,[21] and according to Strabo, Cappadocia had since been divided into two: Cappadocia Pontica in the north and Cappadocia Proper (or Cappadocia near Taurus) in the south, where Sabictas was governor.[22] Under Persian rule, the northern region had extended to the Black Sea coast past Amisus and Trapezus, effectively absorbing the kingdom of Pontus. Lycaonia, too, had formerly been part of the southern Cappadocian satrapy.[23]

Ariarathes, the first 'king' (as opposed to a governor appointed by the Great King), had retained independence in the northern region, which was nominally under Achaemenid rule, and though he is not attested as fighting for Darius at Issus, he may have been present at Gaugamela. Alexander had annexed the south, but Ariarathes seems to have regained control of the southern region soon after, possibly through an accord struck with Antigonus for his neutrality in the interest of keeping the Royal Road open.[24] Ariarathes was 82, wealthy and a figure of much historical confusion, but he appears to have had at his disposal some 30,000 infantry (many of them mercenaries) and 15,000 cavalry to defend his still ungarrisoned kingdom.[25] Eumenes' expansive inheritance and the trust placed in him by Perdiccas in the First Successor War made it abundantly clear that he had already proven himself as a commander of men.

Perdiccas had ordered both Leonnatus, named as the new satrap of Hellespontine Phrygia (commonly shown as 'Mysia' on maps of the Achaemenid satrapies), and Antigonus, the pan-provincial governor of much of central Anatolia (spanning all of Phrygia), to assist Eumenes in subduing Cappadocia. They refused, and crossed to Greece to link up with the aged regent Antipater and the popular veteran Craterus to fight the Lamian War.[26] It was left to Perdiccas and the royal army in Asia to go to Eumenes' support, diverting him from more urgent matters of state.

After two decisive battles, the side-tracked Perdiccas was in no mood for leniency. Ariarathes was tortured and crucified, with all his followers impaled, or, according to Justin, Ariarathes killed his wife and children himself to stop them falling into Macedonian hands.[27] A rebellious Lycaonia and Pisidia soon felt Perdiccas' wrath; the city of Laranda was stormed, all men of fighting age put to the sword and the population sold into slavery. A defiant Isauria put up a fight and its defenders self-immolated in despair, though, tellingly, Antigonus' pan-provincial mandate in Phrygia was never touched at this time.[28] Perdiccas' iron fist set the tone for Diodorus' description of the next campaign against Egypt, led by a chiliarch now described (possibly following the sentiment in Cleitarchus' final pages) as a 'man of blood' and a 'usurper of power'.[29]

The rising tensions between Perdiccas and the 'anti-royalist' faction through the next two years saw him repudiate Antipater's daughter Nicaea (Perdiccas had recently married her, or was pledged in marriage; texts are ambiguous on whether the wedding actually took place) in favour of a union with Alexander's full sister Cleopatra, who probably arrived at the city of Sardis in Lydia from Macedon at about the same time.[30] Perdiccas had initially planned to 'work in harmony' with Antipater, but Eumenes' advocating of the marriage to Cleopatra put an end to that. The implication here is that only after success in Cappadocia (and the death of Leonnatus in the Lamian War), underpinned by Eumenes' friendship with Olympias, did Perdiccas seek what was reportedly an independent path to supreme power in Macedon, with Cleopatra buttressing its legitimacy.

Upon their return to Asia following eventual victory in the Lamian War, a war council (*synedrion*) was convened by Antipater and Craterus (Antigonus may have been present). It appears the former Perdiccan fleet commander, White Cleitus (distinguishing him from 'Black' Cleitus, whom Alexander ran through with a spear), was now supporting their cause. After naval victories off Greece, his newly expanded fleet had facilitated the regent's re-crossing to Hellespontine Phrygia in the spring of 320 BC.[31] The gathering of generals, which took place close by, signalled the opening of what is referred to as the 'First Successor War', and here it was decided that Craterus would confront Eumenes or turn him to their cause. The regent and Antigonus would journey south to face the remainder of the royal army under Perdiccas.

At an earlier Perdiccan war council convened after installing Eumenes in Cappadocia, and following further campaigning to install Perdiccas' younger brother Alcetas in Pisidia, it was decided that the bulk of the royal army would invade Egypt in response to Ptolemy's capture of Alexander's funeral bier, for that action (justified or otherwise) amounted to a 'declaration of independence' from the central authority the acting chiliarch now represented. Perdiccas additionally ordered the invasion of Cyprus; a fleet of merchant ships procured from Phoenicia set off from Cilicia, led by the Rhodian admiral Sosigenes, though the Royal Bodyguard Aristonus was in overall command.[32] Along with other Cypriot kings, Nicocles, who was already minting independent coinage, had recently aligned with Ptolemy, who needed the island's timber resources and strategic location for his own naval plans. Their pro-Ptolemaic fleet was now besieging the city of Marium with almost 200 ships, a state of affairs which suggest that a pro-Perdiccas initiative in Cypriot governance must have been in place.[33]

In response to the threat of hostile forces crossing to Asia from Macedon, Eumenes, along with Alcetas and Neoptolemus, were to delay for as long as possible any bridgehead being formed when the regent and Antigonus landed on Asian shores. If too late, they were to hinder the regent's southwards progress until the royal army could unite with them once more. Eumenes was now commander-in-chief of lands west of Mount Taurus, as well as 'commander of the forces in Armenia and Cappadocia with plenary powers'.[34] His military mandate now encompassed Paphlagonia, Caria, Lycia and Phrygia; in other words, Antigonus' abandoned satrapies, 'in addition to the provinces that he had already received'.[35] That amounted to the whole of Anatolia.

But it was here that Eumenes' ethnic dilemma as a Greek commanding Macedonians began to manifest itself: Perdiccas' brother Alcetas 'flatly refused to serve in the campaign on the ground that the Macedonians under him were ashamed to fight Antipater, and were so well disposed to Craterus that they were ready to receive him with open arms'. The rift with Alcetas had widened over Eumenes advising Perdiccas to seek Cleopatra's hand (Alcetas had urged his brother to marry Nicaea), and it was unlikely to heal now. In addition, Neoptolemus, the newly appointed governor of Armenia, was already hatching plans to undermine Eumenes' new command because it subordinated his own authority.[36] Eumenes summoned him on suspicion of treachery and drew up his forces for a confrontation.

Eumenes' cavalry routed Neoptolemus' infantry, though the latter managed to flee with 300 horsemen to the fast approaching Antipater and Craterus.[37]

Envy, it is said, slays itself by its own arrows. Neoptolemus, a notable commander of the mobile infantry and possibly a scion of the royal house of Epirus, had famously mocked the Cardian scribe after Alexander's death: he proposed that whereas 'he had followed the king with shield and spear, Eumenes had followed with stylus and tablet'.[38] But the pen he slighted was to become Eumenes' most effective weapon, and it helped him survive these few remarkable years in which the *Pamphlet* was launched.

A head-on clash with Craterus was now inevitable, and it came in May 320 BC (perhaps ten days after the initial confrontation with Neoptolemus) somewhere close to Cappadocia.[39] Prior to the battle, and to raise the spirits of his men, Eumenes exploited his former intimacy with Alexander; he described a portentous dream vision in which two images of the king had confronted one another, one helped by the Goddess Athena and the other by Demeter. Demeter prevailed, and 'culling ears of grain, she wove them into a victory wreath'. Having learned that the enemy's watchword was 'Athena and Alexander', and since they were fighting for grain-planted land, Eumenes spurred his army on towards a god-augured mission, ordering 'all his men to crown themselves and wreath their arms with ears of grain'.

It is probably no coincidence that this appears an emulation of a strategy once employed by Philip II, for he had played a similar laurel-wreathed card when 'marching his soldiers to battle as if under the leadership of a god' (Apollo) before the Battle of the Crocus Field in 353/352 BC in what is known as the Third Sacred War. Moreover, Alexander himself had also declared a 'victory dream' when besieging Tyre.[40] And here on the plains near Cappadocia that favoured cavalry manoeuvrability, and to guard against any drop in morale, Eumenes made sure his men were still unaware that it was the much-loved Craterus, now joined by Neoptolemus, whom his Macedonian contingent would be riding out to fight.

Neoptolemus and Eumenes spotted one another and 'their horses dashed together like colliding triremes'; 'carried away by their anger and their mutual hatred', they let the reins fall from their left hands and grappled each other to the ground.[41] Although he sustained wounds in his arms and a thigh, Eumenes dealt Neoptolemus a deathblow to the neck and reportedly stripped his dying opponent of his armour in the style of the Homeric heroes (Ptolemy appears to have provided himself similar *Iliadic* honours in India).[42]

Eumenes had wisely deployed his Asiatic squadrons against Craterus, who was dumbfounded as to why Eumenes' 'Macedonians' did not desert. Craterus and his purple Macedonian-style hat (known as a *kausia*) fell 'in the crowd' and his wounded body, trampled by his own horse, was not immediately recognized, though he ended up dying in Eumenes' arms.[43] Despite this resounding and unexpected victory, the Perdiccan alliance was fractured with the chiliarch's death in Egypt just a few days later when he tried to force a crossing of the Nile, following which the two reconciled Macedonian armies levied a death sentence on Eumenes as soon as they learned of Craterus' death.[44] It was alleged that in Egypt, some fifty of Perdiccas' supporters had been condemned to die.[45] The list included Perdiccas' sister, Atalante, fatally then in camp and by now married to the newly pro-Perdiccas Attalus, and Eumenes was on this extended proscriptions list.[46] It was a wholesale effort to wipe out any support for the royalist faction.

The next war council held by the anti-Perdiccan coalition, in the late summer of 320 BC (adhering to what is termed the 'low' chronology; the exact dating of this period was ambiguously reported), took place at Triparadeisus, a convergence of a trio of ancient game parks probably close to the source of the Orontes River in northern Syria. Old acquaintances were reunited, the most prominent being those of Peithon, Antigenes and Seleucus, who greeted Antipater for the first time in some fourteen years. Almost as many years had passed since Alexander's expeditionary force had marched south out of Anatolia, leaving Antigonus in command of a region centred on Phrygia. Some veterans of the united phalanx must have met young sons they had left behind in Macedon, but now grown men in arms.

Here Antipater, approaching 80 years old, appointed a younger generation of personal Bodyguards to the joint kings (the halfwit Arrhidaeus, now crowned Philip III, and Rhoxane's son, crowned Alexander IV at Babylon), who had been captured (or rescued, they would have argued) in Egypt. The new Bodyguards included Lysimachus' youngest brother, the brother of the absent Peucestas, Antigonus' nephew and Polyperchon's son.[47] The royal powers that had been vested in Perdiccas – chief guardian of the kings, overseer of the realm and commander-in-chief of the royal army in Asia – were now divided between Antipater and Antigonus. It was here that the one-eyed veteran was, in fact, provided with plenipotentiary powers that would result in him founding his own dynasty, a somewhat ironic outcome if the regent already suspected his expansionist ambition, as texts report:

> As general of the royal army he [Antipater] appointed Antigonus, assigning him the task of finishing the war against Eumenes and Alcetas; but he attached his own son Cassander to Antigonus as chiliarch, so that the latter might not be able to pursue his own ambitions undetected.[48]

Antigonus was, as Diodorus put it, 'chosen supreme commander of Asia ... and at the same time he had been appointed general of a great army'. In fact, Diodorus later referred back to this appointment as 'regent [*epimeletes*] of the kingdom'.[49] Antigonus assumed the role with enthusiasm, and there soon began a number of skirmishes and set-piece battles with Eumenes that extracted the best, and arguably the worst, from the former Pellan court associates. Our extant sources severely compressed the eyewitness testimony of Hieronymus of Cardia, who was by now serving Eumenes. Nonetheless, what we do read suggests Hieronymus must have originally given vivid descriptions of these complex battles, the detail and tactical observations perhaps only rivalled by the accounts of the Roman civil war of a later era between Caesar and Pompey.

The subtler part of their manoeuvring saw Eumenes and Antigonus searching for 'royal legitimacy', as well as military supremacy on the plains of Asia, as they employed magnanimous gestures that gave the illusion of official sanction to their respective campaigns; each was presenting himself as a constitutionalist legitimized by the kings.[50] Typifying the charade, Eumenes requisitioned new cavalry in the Troad region (where the ruins of Troy lay) to equip his cavalry officer Apollonides:

> When Eumenes fell in with the royal herds of horse that were pasturing about Mount Ida, he took as many horses as he wanted and sent a written statement of the number to the overseers; at this, we are told, Antipater laughed and said that he admired Eumenes for his forethought, since he evidently expected to give an account of the royal properties to them, or to receive one from them.[51]

Having narrowly avoided an earlier ambush by Antigonus, Eumenes journeyed once more to meet Alexander's sister, Cleopatra, still based at Sardis.[52] The meeting was brief. Cleopatra warned him off, fearing it would further antagonize the regent, who was fast approaching with his army on its way northward from Syria. A battle on the plains outside the city was averted, but she and Antipater, nevertheless, clashed, though she 'defended herself vigorously' and 'brought counter-charges against him'. He may have upbraided her for her attempted liaisons with Leonnatus and then Perdiccas; she would have reminded him that she was royalty whereas he was not. She would have likely said more besides: her wish to enter into a union with Alexander's chosen guardian of affairs, Perdiccas, and parley with her brother's former secretary, Eumenes – now unlawfully proscribed in her opinion – was her decision to make. Furthermore, Antipater's proffering of his daughters to the leading Diadochi was threatening her dead brother's wishes as well as his last instruction which had demanded Antipater step down as regent in Macedon in favour of Craterus.[53]

We may imagine them storming at one another about much else, and what was reportedly an amicable-enough parting would be their last ever meeting. Had the infantry not already revolted over the death of Philip's other daughter, Cynnane (killed recently by Perdiccas' brother Alcetas), and if the Perdiccans had already been fully rounded up, who knows what measures that Antipater might have taken right there to silence Cleopatra for good.[54]

With the newly united royal army seeking him out, Eumenes occupied Antigonus' winter base at Celaenae in Phrygia, 'a landscape more of villages than cities', in late 320 BC. The surrounding plains were fertile, and the city stood on the crossroads of the ancient highways to Ephesus in the west, to the narrow defile of the Cilician Gates in the east and to Synnada and Telmessus on the north–south route. Alexander had first taken Celaenae (broadly occupied by modern Dinar in southwest Turkey) in 333 BC after a sixty-day 'truce' in which the citizens put their faith in the strength of the walls and in military aid they were expecting.[55] The city was also renowned for its enormous game park fed by the River Meander (today's Buyuk Menderes) and the River Marsyas which flowed through the middle of its fortifications.[56] Antigonus was given 1,500 troops to see out the siege and the city had been a Macedonian stronghold, as well as his winter quarters, ever since.[57]

Eumenes' occupation of Celaenae was undoing a decade of Antigonid control. It was as symbolic a gain as it was practical, and he set about rewarding his troops with homesteads and castles (rather, rocky hilltop crag fortresses, many ruins of which are visible today) from the spoils and distributing 'purple caps [the Macedonian *kausiai*] and military cloaks'; these were 'a special gift of loyalty among Macedonians' which signified the bearers as court friends and Companions of the king or their commanders.[58]

To spike the gathering of 'outlaws', Antigonus is said to have smuggled letters into the camp offering 100 talents for Eumenes' death, though Plutarch is vague on exactly where this occurred. The move apparently backfired as spectacularly as if it had been a ruse of Eumenes himself: once the letters were found, 'his Macedonians were highly incensed and made a decree that a thousand of the leading soldiers should serve him continually as a bodyguard, watching over him when he went abroad and spending the night at his door'.[59] If the textual recovery of the manuscript known as the *Gothenburg Palimpsest* (a palimpsest is reused scroll, with texts overwritten) is correct, Antigonus, or perhaps Antipater, had good reason for the assassination attempt. Either en route from Lydian Sardis to Phrygia, or in the environs of Celaenae itself, Eumenes made a mockery of Antipater's forces (if this is not a misspelling of 'Antigonus'); his army was too fast and too mobile and it eluded the regent's greater numbers, taking 800 talents in booty, leaving Antipater as 'nothing but a spectator' to the suffering of his outmanoeuvred men.[60]

With success under his belt, Eumenes had called the scattered Perdiccan remnants to Celaenae: Alcetas, Perdiccas' brother-in-law Attalus (who had briefly held Tyre with the remnants of the Perdiccan fleet in the wake of Perdiccas' death), Attalus' brother Polemon and Docimus the deposed governor of Babylonia. They all either arrived in person or communicated through envoys.[61] Despite Alcetas' initial enthusiasm (which may simply have been a ruse to take command), the Perdiccan generals refused to unite under Eumenes and they moved southwest into Caria, leaving him without the benefit of their combined numbers. The chance for a unified front was gone, while closing in was Antigonus, now strengthened by a further 8,500 of Antipater's infantry (the regent himself was heading to Macedon with the kings) along with a mounted contingent. Eumenes had no choice but to head to the plains of Cappadocia, where his own superior cavalry could operate at full potential and perhaps exert what influence he wielded in his expansive 'home' satrapy.[62]

Eumenes' cavalry command in India and his acquisition of Perdiccas' hipparchy make it clear that he was obviously a seasoned campaigner on horseback who must have mastered the techniques of the flying wedge and the oblique order flank-guard introduced by Philip and Alexander.[63] Eumenes would now need to call on that experience. It was early 319 BC and he wisely prepared his forces on favourable Cappadocian ground, where his mounted brigades could be effectively deployed. It became clear that battle was inevitable once scouts confirmed Antigonus' approach, and Plutarch displayed his open admiration of, or sympathy for, Eumenes in what occurred next:

> Now, prosperity lifts even men of inferior natures to higher thoughts, so that they appear to be invested with a certain greatness and majesty as they look down from their lofty state; but the truly magnanimous and constant soul reveals itself rather in its behaviour under disasters and misfortunes. And so it was with Eumenes. For, to begin with, he was defeated by Antigonus at Orcynia in Cappadocia through treachery.[64]

That treachery, according to Justin, included more bribes for Eumenes' head. Finding the covert correspondence, Eumenes claimed these were *his* own forged tell-tales to gauge the strength of loyalty in the ranks, which somewhat casts suspicion on the veracity of the other reported rewards for his death.[65] Loyalty proved thin: shortly before battle, Eumenes witnessed the defection of an officer with 3,000 infantry and 500 mounted men, while Antigonus corrupted Eumenes' cavalry officer Apollonides with 'great promises' and 'secret persuasion' to defect once fighting had commenced.[66]

But before leaving the field in the face of these setbacks, Eumenes had the opportunity to seize the enemy baggage train. Knowing the booty would only slow down his own retreat, he sent a secret communication to its defender, Menander, a high-ranking Companion serving Antigonus, imploring him for the sake of 'old friendships' to move himself to higher ground to better defend it. The false magnanimity impressed the enemy troops, but Antigonus saw through the misdirection: 'Nay my good men, that fellow did not let them go out of regard for you, but because he was afraid to put such fetters on himself in his flight.'[67] Waggons full of booty and temptations would have encumbered the mobility of any army. This was vintage Eumenes playing vintage Alexander, who had in fact been following Xenophon when he burned the army's accumulated wealth before entering India: 'thus deprived of their treasures, [they] immediately became anxious for more; and, in order to obtain it, of course ready for new enterprises.' And that meant spoils from victory in future battles and meanwhile plundering the surrounding area.[68]

Eumenes reportedly 'lost' 8,000 men at Orcynia in spring 319 BC from a total of 20,000 infantry and 5,000 cavalry. It is a huge number that must have comprised the dead, wounded, captured and probably the deserters too, and he was left with no option but flight.[69] The flattering version of events painted his departure as a tactical feint, in this case to double-back to the battlefield to burn the dead on pyres made from wooden village doors – that is if Plutarch was not confusing the occasion with the 'magnificent burial' mentioned by Diodorus after the later clash at Paraetacene.[70] What is revealing for any analysis of camp practice and the distinctions of army hierarchy is the report that officers were burned on separate pyres from those of the common soldier.

A more sober narrative from Diodorus suggested Eumenes was overtaken in his flight and had little directional choice. The best hope of immediate survival lay in the mountain fortress of Nora, but before entering that 'lofty crag', Eumenes 'persuaded most of his soldiers to leave him, either out of regard for them, or because he was unwilling to trail after him a body of men too small to give battle, and too large to escape the enemy's notice'.[71] The First Successor War was all but over.

The Siege and the Siege Craft

Following Eumenes' incarceration at Nora, Antigonus found himself in a formidable position, potentially dominating the empire from the Mediterranean shores of Anatolia to the eastern borders of Armenia. He was, of course, still acting for the kings at Pella, or so his official dispatches would have claimed. But secretly he aspired to 'greater things ... and decided ... he would no longer take orders from Antipater, while maintaining the pretence of being well disposed to the aged regent'.[72]

Antigonus invested the stone stronghold with 'double walls, ditches and amazing palisades' so there was no hope of escape for Eumenes and his 600 loyal confederates. The fortress of Nora was termed 'impregnable' and 'marvellously fortified, partly by nature, partly by the work of men's hands'; presumably this explains why we read of no storming attempts.[73] The besieger instigated a hostage exchange and invited Eumenes to parley, sending in his own talented nephew, Polemaeus (who would later try to subdue Eumenes' satrapies), for goodwill. Eumenes exposed himself for negotiation and Hieronymus was offered in exchange; this achieved hostage symmetry for the historian was likely Eumenes' own nephew.[74]

According to Plutarch, 'Eumenes went out to meet him [Antigonus] and they embraced one another with greetings of friendship and affection, since they had formerly been close associates and intimate companions.'[75] The relationship between Eumenes and Antigonus is truly intriguing. The poignant moment highlighted here, which took place early in the siege at Nora, implied Antigonus felt some kind of 'guardianship' as well as affection for the gifted young former court secretary, a bond that must have been established during Eumenes' late-teenage years under Philip.[76]

The commencement of the siege was a fulcrum point for Hieronymus and his history. It was (we believe) the moment his two patrons – present and future – first met in his presence. Yet it was Plutarch, and not Diodorus (who appears to have more rigidly followed Hieronymus), who most effectively captured the poignancy of the face-off between the veteran general and his captive, who was now demanding full satrapal reinstatement and the return of his possessions:[77]

> ...the bystanders were amazed and they admired his [Eumenes'] lofty spirit and confidence. But meanwhile, many of the Macedonians came running together in their eagerness to see what sort of a man Eumenes was; for no one else had been so talked about in the army since the death of Craterus. Then Antigonus, afraid that Eumenes might suffer some violence, first loudly forbade the soldiers to approach, and pelted with stones those who were hurrying up, but finally threw his arms about Eumenes and, keeping off the throng with his bodyguards, with much ado removed him to a place of safety.[78]

Despite the alleged warmth, Antigonus demanded that Eumenes address him as 'his better', and received as a result the following alleged response: 'I regard no man as my superior, as long as I am master of my sword.'[79] That exchange was probably the end of any chance of progress through immediate negotiations.

Some six months or more into the siege, and soon after the death of the regent, Antipater, in Macedon in autumn 319 BC, Antigonus invited Eumenes to 'share in his own undertakings'.[80] According to Plutarch, before Eumenes was released in early 318 BC, Antigonus demanded he sign an oath of loyalty. Eumenes allegedly amended the wording, cunningly adding the words 'Olympias and the Kings' to those he pledged his fealty to. Both the original and the extended oaths were shown to the Macedonian siege captains, who agreed that Eumenes' version was the fairer, whereupon they let him loose.[81] The inference here is that the amendment embedded the latitude for Eumenes to oppose Antigonus if his actions were deemed hostile to the Argead royal house. If this episode genuinely took place, this oath taking was a strategic deception.

When he was eventually informed of Eumenes' deception, Antigonus ordered the siege to be reinstated, no doubt pondering the consequences of the amendment. It was too late; Eumenes had fled the vicinity and was heading to Cilicia. This episode is absent from Diodorus' text, either due to aggressive précising or because Hieronymus thought it cast a shadow on Eumenes' *volte-face*.[82] Of course, the re-rendering of the oath may simply be a device of a later historian, which might, nevertheless, be a subtle embellishment of a less attractive truth: Eumenes simply did not honour his word to Antigonus and claimed a higher loyalty when justifying it.[83]

What *does* appear clear is that once he departed Nora, Eumenes initially tarried in Cappadocia, apparently provisioning for campaigning and returning his Cappadocian hostages for 'horses, beasts of burden and tents'.[84] The delay, potentially of several months, suggests that Eumenes was either using the time he had to physically recover from the siege where he and his men reached near starvation point, or to raise troops before Antigonus' inevitably hostile reply came back to Nora. But in an oathless scenario, it suggests that Eumenes may not have immediately abandoned an alliance with Antigonus; he may have been waiting for word on affairs in Macedon or missives from former Perdiccans still on the loose before declaring his hand.[85] Eumenes was most likely rounding up any men he had dismissed before entering the fortress, and he managed to rather quickly assemble a corps of 1,000 cavalry and some 2,000 soldiers in total, including those who had been freed with him.[86] Having lost his waggons at Orcynia, the only way his supporters were going to retrieve their possessions would be to fight alongside him again, for defection to Antigonus was unlikely to yield the same tangible reward, his promises of rewards for desertion aside.[87]

With Menander hot on his heels once his direction was known, Eumenes traversed the Taurus Mountains and descended into Cilicia. His immediate goal was Cyinda, a fortified treasury in a still-debated location that held nearly 20,000 royal talents; it was possibly the ancient Kundi that served a similar purpose for the Assyrian kings.[88] The Second Successor War was about to begin.

En route, or in fact before his departure to Cappadocia (and perhaps precipitating it), Eumenes received two remarkable missives that regally empowered him once more.[89] They were, it is claimed, from Polyperchon, Antipater's successor as regent in Pella. The first offered him either co-guardianship of the kings in Macedon, or, should Eumenes prefer, money and an army to fight Antigonus in Asia. Polyperchon additionally offered to journey across the Hellespont himself if Eumenes needed further support, presumably with the war elephants Antipater had taken to Macedon.[90] The second letter compensated Eumenes with 500 talents for his personal losses, authorized further funds for the raising of an army and assured him that the crack Silver Shields brigade (the *Argyraspides*) had been summoned to operate under him.[91]

Eumenes was transformed from prisoner to royal commander-in-chief in a matter of weeks. Diodorus recorded the general dismay: 'All wondered at the fickleness of Fortune [Tyche] … for who, taking thought of the inconstancies of human life, would not be astonished at the alternating ebb and flow of fortune?'[92] In fact, we see a full page of moralistic and educational reflections on the 'sensational reversals'. Eumenes would now command the 3,000-strong Silver Shields, but we can only speculate if they constituted, or incorporated, some of the 3,000 'most rebellious Macedonians' (a description which recalls the notorious 'unruly' brigade) that Antigenes, now the satrap of Susiane as well as a Silver Shields commander, had been given when tasked with collecting treasure (or revenues) from Susa. Whether the Silver Shields were still on treasury duty there, or had already returned to Cyinda in Cilicia, remains debatable, but they reportedly journeyed a 'considerable distance to meet Eumenes and his friends', and fast approaching was the winter of 318 BC.[93]

The treasuries across the empire held immeasurable wealth and crack squads would have been required to defend them, overseen by a local trusted treasury officer. Located in natural fortresses, these treasuries had to be defensible; the 'lofty crag' of Nora itself later became a depository for Sisines (ruled 36 BC–AD 17), Rome's client king of Cappadocia in Strabo's day.[94] The consistent nature of the roles of the allegedly aged Silver Shields (though surely not as advanced in age as Diodorus claimed: the youngest was 60) raises the question of whether their role as roving treasury guards, or porters of treasure from one citadel to another, was the true inspiration behind the brigade's name.[95] It's possible that with this crucial 'state' duty came expensive silver adornment for their armour and shields, for heavy and soft semi-precious metal was not a practical accessory in battle; and yet what better way to recognize and secure the loyalty of the defenders of the royal deposits?

Although Eumenes had been provided with a suspicious-sounding carte blanche to dig into state funds and campaign against the extremely powerful Antigonus – who had in fact never directly challenged Polyperchon's authority in Pella (rather, he provisioned Cassander to do it) – Eumenes declined his new military mandate and the 'donation from the kings'. This was quite brilliant. He was shunning a royal promotion that he may (as I will argue) himself have birthed: …he said, it was not of his own will that he had yielded with respect to his present office, but he had been compelled by the kings to undertake this great task.'[96] The feigned reluctance was a showpiece designed to eventually bank the silver in a more loyal purse, for the Silver Shields were always unpredictable.[97] Appreciating that 'the fickleness of fortune tests the reliability of friends', Eumenes 'prudently made his own position secure':[98]

These men, on receiving their letters, ostensibly treated Eumenes with friendliness, but were plainly full of envy and contentiousness, disdaining to be second to him. Eumenes therefore allayed their envy by not taking the money, alleging that he had no need of it; while upon their love of contention and love of command, seeing that they were as unable to lead as they were unwilling to follow, he brought superstition to bear.[99]

That new play on superstition saw Eumenes declare another dream vision of Alexander; the Cardian commander was acting out the role of a divine man empowered by another portentous ghostly apparition.

Eumenes had certainly learned what moved and mystified soldiers through a decade on the march. Here, in the fragile and intriguing air of Eumenes' camp, the soldiers' natural superstition was being artfully employed once more. The campaign headquarters became a mobile prophecy place, with Eumenes a self-proclaimed sacred deputy. He required the troops and the officers who led them to 'make ready' a gold throne in a magnificent tent, and arranged alongside it the diadem, sceptre, crown and armour of Alexander, and here he would conduct his councils of war. This, we recall, is reminiscent of Perdiccas' actions at Babylon and of Ptolemy's speech that suggested 'group rule' by council in the presence of the symbols of royal office.[100] The rundown of insignia sounds familiar too: it is reminiscent (though not perfectly matching) of the finds in Tomb II at Vergina, ancient Aegae, discovered in 1977.[101]

What was transmitted as a 'tent' in Cilicia was more realistically a royal pavilion formed from multiple open canopies.[102] Incense was burned upon an altar to invoke the presence of 'Alexander the God' and to raise morale; it was a charade through which Eumenes reinforced his own unique relationship with their dead king and to the Argead house in the frequent councils of war that were to follow.[103]

In these convocations, Eumenes no doubt reminded his officers of Alexander's will, and of the rightful inheritances of his sons and mother whose legacy they were defending, for the Silver Shields – once destined for Macedon with Craterus – had not been present in Babylon when the king died. Somewhere in his speech, Eumenes would no doubt have slipped in his own rightful inheritance while pointing out to them that Antigonus' lands would be available for them as prizes of war. His thaumaturgy worked; the officers were 'filled with happy expectations, as if some god were leading them'. The dream vision produced the cult of Alexander and with it the acceptance of his supreme command. Curiously, a similar cult appeared on the island of Rhodes, which was so prominently favoured in the *Pamphlet* will and where Diodorus confirmed in his later chapters the testament was lodged for safekeeping.

The army wintered near Cyinda and Eumenes sent out recruitment agents who 'travelled through Cilicia, others through Coele-Syria ["Hollow" Syria, broadly thought to apply to Lebanon, so Phoenicia, and possibly the Beqaa Valley], and some through the cities in Cyprus'.[104] Eumenes was clearly blocked from mustering support from further north by Antigonus' dominance in Anatolia, and mustering in Cyprus must have been a calculated risk after the recent Perdiccan defeat there. But the initiative added 10,000 infantry and 2,000 cavalry to his ranks, though we may ask ourselves whether Eumenes concealed the identity of his opponent (like Cyrus did when recruiting the army that Xenophon served in two generations before), for facing Antigonus would have been a daunting prospect for any mercenary to contemplate.[105]

Having weathered new attempts to solicit the Silver Shields' defection, this time by Ptolemy – who had anchored at Zephyrium in Cilicia (modern Mersin, and surely with an eye on the riches at Cyinda) – and with Antigonus now fast on his heels and attempting to subvert the crack brigade again, Eumenes marched south with the new recruits to Phoenicia in early spring 317 BC.[106] He planned to 'assemble a considerable fleet, so that Polyperchon, by the addition of the Phoenician ships, might have control of the sea and be able to transport the Macedonian armies safely to Asia against Antigonus whenever he wished'. A new fleet could, vitally, oust Cassander's garrison from Piraeus, for by now Cassander was operating in league with Antigonus, who had provided him with troops and ships from Asia.

The outcome in Phoenicia was disastrous: laden with 'great sums of money', the ships' captains defected to Antigonus' approaching fleet, which was 'splendidly adorned' from its recent victory over White Cleitus, who, along with Arrhidaeus – the new satrap of Hellespontine Phrygia – had defected in the face of Antigonus' aggression – helped on (I suggest) by Olympias' pleas for support. Eumenes and the ill-fated Rhodian fleet admiral, Sosigenes, watched on powerless to intervene as his working capital (whether destined for Polyperchon or use in Asia) was rowed away.[107]

With the nucleus of a new land army still about him, but with his paths back to Cilicia and into Anatolia blocked, and with an Antigonid army of 20,000 infantry and 4,000 cavalrymen heading his way, Eumenes was once again left with little choice in the matter of direction. He headed east through Coele-Syria and into Mesopotamia on his way to the further eastern satrapies, for they held more promise and less prejudice against his own Greek origins. Eumenes must have already heard rumours of eastern satrapal unrest, and this was a situation he could potentially exploit.[108]

Taking the War East

Eumenes' army, still insufficiently large for a set-piece battle, arrived in Mesopotamia, or northern Babylonia, sometime in late 317 BC and wintered in the 'villages of the Carians'.[109] He sent embassies to Seleucus and Peithon asking them to aid the kings and to join him in the struggle against Antigonus. Peithon had been appointed satrap of Media and Seleucus named satrap of Babylonia when the second distribution of satrapies was made at the meeting of generals at Triparadeisus after Perdiccas' death.

While encamped there, yet more letters conveniently 'appeared' from the kings to assist Eumenes' passage:

> He [Polyperchon] had already sent to the commanders of the upper satrapies the letter from the kings in which it was written that they should obey Eumenes in every way; and at this time he again sent couriers bidding the satraps all to assemble in Susiane each with his own army ... for it was to him alone that the kings in their letter had ordered the treasurers to give whatever sum he should ask.[110]

The Mesopotamian governor, Amphimachus, must have joined Eumenes at this point for he is later found in the allied ranks.[111]

Eumenes narrowly avoided disaster when Seleucus diverted an old canal to inundate his camp some 300 stades (approximately 34 miles) from Babylon. Overtures to the prominent Royal Bodyguard, now the governor of Babylonia, had failed. Seleucus replied that he was 'willing to be of service to the kings, but that he would nevertheless never consent to carrying out the orders of Eumenes, whom the Macedonians in assembly had condemned to death'.[112] Rather predictably, Seleucus, along with the now-present Peithon, once more attempted to seduce the Silver Shields by reminding them that Eumenes was a 'foreigner' responsible for the deaths of many Macedonians. He and Peithon simultaneously sent dispatch riders to Antigonus to solicit his support in the East in a combined front.

It has been proposed that Eumenes may have initially managed to take the citadel in Babylon with his 15,000 infantry and royal squadron of 300 cavalry, but this seems unlikely, and he was harried further east into the Persian heartland when Seleucus, under truce, conceded Eumenes a river crossing, only too glad to see him head out of his province.[113] Nevertheless, with the Susa royal treasury now open to him under the 'kings' decree', and guided by Alexander's continually invoked spirit, Eumenes would soon be in command of a force to be reckoned with, and it would significantly include war elephants from India.[114]

The eastern satraps and some 18,700 infantry and 4,600 cavalrymen, with 120 elephants, had already assembled at Susiane (ancient Elam, the region centred on Susa and extending to the south) under the command of Peucestas, a fortuitous gathering if Eumenes could exploit it. The alliance was precipitated by the mutual threat from Peithon, who had killed the Parthian satrap and installed his own brother in his place, whereupon those fearing his further expansion combined to force him back to Media; this was the precursor to Peithon's presence with Seleucus in Babylonia.[115]

Antigonus' now-even-more-formidable army was advancing on the treasury at Susa after successfully concluding a self-serving alliance with Seleucus and Peithon along the way.[116] He attempted to force a river crossing to establish a bridgehead close to where the 4-plethra-wide (approximately 400ft) Coprates River flowed into the Pasitigris (the modern Karun), apparently unaware of the proximity of Eumenes, who, alone from the gathered commanders, led a repelling action that led to the capture of 4,000 of Antigonus' men.[117] This disaster forced Antigonus to march north into Media after reviewing local options. He made a similarly costly decision by taking the short route (nine days) through the mountainous territory of the never-subdued Cossaeans, the unruly tribe that guarded the passes. This was the same tribe that Alexander had butchered after the death of Hephaestion some seven years before. Their lingering hatred was poured down on the Macedonians in the form of rocks and arrows, Nearchus barely making it out alive with his advance brigade of lightly armed troops.[118]

While Antigonus retreated to Ecbatana, Eumenes and the Silver Shields commanders advocated returning westwards to the Mediterranean coast with the eastern army, no doubt to exploit the vacuum created by Antigonus' absence. The eastern satraps disagreed. Fearing a split in the new coalition, Eumenes led the gathered forces on a twenty-four-day march to Persepolis though arid valleys, elevated plains and finally hospitable parks in the densely populated country. When they arrived in the capital of Peucestas' sphere of influence, the army was fêted. The men were arranged in a remarkable series of concentric circles for a feast, which recalled the format of Alexander's Susa wedding celebrations, and Peucestas was no doubt playing on just that.

But this would be no marriage. At Persepolis, Peucestas prudently offered sacrifices to the memories of Alexander and his father, so perhaps more than scholars suppose of the royal palace, or surrounding buildings at least, must have survived Alexander's burning of the former Achaemenid capital thirteen years before. Eumenes, here termed Peucestas' former 'friend' (though 'colleague' may be implied), sensed the eastern satraps were attempting to beguile his men.[119] Plutarch captured the scene:

> Moreover, by flattering the Macedonian soldiery extravagantly and lavishing money upon them for banquets and sacrifices, in a short time they made the camp a hostelry of festal prodigality, and the army a mob to be cajoled into the election of its generals, as in a democracy.[120]

Uniquely popular with the Persians for his adoption of their language and customs, Peucestas controlled the wealth of Persis, Pasargadae and what remained of Persepolis itself, though much of the treasury had already been ferried to Susa, which would become a clear target for all.[121] The question of supreme command inevitably arose.

To counter the seduction, Eumenes crafted a document which makes his candidacy for the *Pamphlet* authorship so strong: he drafted a fake letter written in Assyrian and claimed it had arrived from Orontes, the Persian satrap of Armenia, a known friend of Peucestas and one who had previously fought for Darius at Gaugamela. Its contents falsely claimed the hostile Cassander was dead, Olympias was in control of Macedon and Polyperchon was making good on his earlier offer to march through Asia with the royal army from Macedon.[122] If true, it would have signified a tide turned, and Eumenes' influence as Pella's favourite son would have been unquestioned.

The gambit worked: Eumenes was voted in 'with the prospects that he would be able by help of the kings to promote whomever he wishes and exact punishment from those who had wronged him'. As part of his plan to further undermine his host, and using his new authority, Eumenes brought false charges against Sibyrtius, the Greek satrap of Arachosia (broadly today's southern Afghanistan) and another close friend of Peucestas. Eumenes seized his baggage 'to overawe those who did not obey him or who craved command', and Sibyrtius may have immediately fled to join Antigonus.[123]

There followed a financial manipulation intended as an insurance policy. Eumenes extorted 400 talents from those whose loyalty he questioned, calculating that they would prefer him alive to receive repayment in full.[124] According to Plutarch, 'The consequence was that the wealth of others was his bodyguard, and that, whereas men generally preserve their lives by giving, he alone won safety by receiving.'[125] The continued fragility of Eumenes' position was evident: his Macedonian campaign veterans were now serving an outlaw while being hounded around an empire they had themselves fought to secure. Furthermore, they were being hunted by the regional governors and Royal Bodyguards they had previously served under. The cost of fealty to the new kings in Pella was beginning to take its toll, and the promise of being paid in treasury silver was now haunted by uncertainty.

Eumenes' subterfuges, by now a wholly necessary and integral part of his war arsenal, could only have ever been short lived, and, somewhat suspiciously when considered beside the central allegations of regicide in the *Pamphlet*, Eumenes fell seriously ill a few days after the banquet that Peucestas and his friends had thrown.[126] We have no idea whether he took the precaution of employing a court food taster to guard against poisoning, but Eumenes was so weak that he had to be carried around in a litter 'outside the ranks where it was quiet and his sleep would not be broken'. Assassination was only ever a wine cup or bribed bodyguard away, so each of the Diadochi appears to have created a personal cavalry guard unit for protection. Eumenes and Antigonus, whose repaired army was heading his way, both retained a handpicked royal squadron (an *agema*) of some 300 mounted men in the style of the late Argead kings.[127]

When Antigonus' formation of 'golden flashing armour and purple-towered elephants' was spotted descending the nearby hills, the Macedonians called for Eumenes to lead them and refused to deploy without him, beating spear on shield in acknowledgement when he finally appeared. The description of him greeting his men from his litter recalls Alexander's plight in India when he too was recovering from the near-mortal wound suffered at Mallia.[128] Aware of his incapacity, Antigonus prepared to attack, but noting the impressive discipline and organized battle order that was deploying on the plain below, he hesitated and laughed off Eumenes' plight: 'This litter, it would seem, is what is arrayed against us.' Whereupon he retired his ranks and set about pitching camp.[129]

The two armies settled just 3 stades apart (approximately 660 yards) in the region of Paraetacene in Media (near modern Isfahan), with a river and ravines separating the two camps; the unsuitable terrain was likely the reason battle did not immediately commence. It was summer 316 BC, and the generals pondered their next move for a further four days whilst pillaging the countryside to keep the troops fed, so skirmishing likely took place between the foraging parties vying for precious provisions.[130] Once again, Antigonus sent envoys into Eumenes' ranks to solicit desertions from the eastern satraps and to lure the Silver Shields brigade commanders with promises of land grants, honours, gifts and employment within his army. Eumenes deflected the temptation with Aesop's fable of the lion and the maiden to illustrate the covert intent; it was a story that warned against succumbing to false promises.[131] Here the divergence between the accounts of Diodorus and Plutarch widens in both detail and chronology, and yet each captured something of the manoeuvring ahead of the approaching need to winter their forces in the well-provisioned town of Gabiene.

Well-paid 'deserters' were employed on both sides to carry disinformation to the enemy camp in attempts to steal a march. Eumenes sent his baggage train ahead during the night; Antigonus countered with a cavalry push. Spies were sent out, false battle lines were exposed and the opponents finally came to a halt and arrayed for a confrontation.[132] In Diodorus' words, 'The two armies each outwitted the other as if they were taking part in a preliminary contest of skill and showing that each placed his hope of victory in himself.'[133]

The 'baggage' is an insufficiently weighty and rather dismissive terminology for a waggon train housing 'wives, and children, mistresses, gold and silver'. When families, chattels and weapons were captured, it left veterans 'dismayed and despondent at the loss of their supplies'.[134] Plutarch's description of Antigonus' train at Orcynia included 'many freemen, many slaves, and wealth amassed from so many wars and plunderings'.[135] So the enemy baggage train was a military 'Achilles heel' when it became a strategic target to turn the tide of battle.

Baggage was booty for the victor, and it acted as hostage for the good behaviour of the vanquished, who, more often than not, were enrolled in the victor's ranks. Craterus had motivated his men before battle with the promise of Eumenes' possessions, just as Eumenes had coveted and exploited Neoptolemus' waggons some ten days or so before; his securing them had been instrumental in compelling the captives to enter his service, along with his threat to harry the leaderless forces to starvation should they not.[136] Clearly, the loyalty of an army of 'detainees' was questionable when its cause was muddied by deceits and bribes, and it helps explain the frequent turncoating and defections we read of in the Successor Wars. The lack of mobility of these heavily laden waggons explains why no mercenary squad, or private army, raided the treasuries scattered across the empire, for talents of gold and silver were not easily moved, minted or shipped, unless huge manpower was available.

The soldiers now risking their lives in the malaria-ridden regions of Anatolia, Mesopotamia and on the Iranian Plateau in freezing forced marches north of the Zagros Mountains, cannot by this stage have been fighting for a figurehead in Pella, despite Eumenes' ongoing dream visions of Alexander and the royal letters of empowerment that kept appearing at crucial moments.[137] The promises of land grants in Asia with cultivation leases and earnable tax immunity were now more valuable weapons, as Antigonus knew.

Diodorus' description of the battle that ensued at Paraetacene was remarkably detailed, obviously tapping into an ore-laden seam from Hieronymus' historical papyrus that captured a formative day of war.[138] He described the intricate battle lines, the manoeuvres and counter-manoeuvres, oblique fronts, wheeling tactics and flanking movements that pitted Antigonus' 28,000 infantry (including new reinforcements under Seleucus and Peithon), 8,500 cavalry and sixty-five elephants against Eumenes' allied total of 35,000 foot soldiers, 6,100 horsemen and 114 elephants.

These were by now diverse coalition armies: only 6,000 of the infantry that fought under Eumenes were specifically referred to as Macedonians, and the 8,000 provided to Antigonus by Antipater were probably a generation younger than the veteran campaigners.[139] This was highly developed, high-stakes warfare of calculation, and spearheading Eumenes' attack were the inimitable 3,000 Silver Shields, whose battle experience saw them smash through the opposing phalanx with few casualties. The result suggests their more-mobile-hoplite-style (*hypaspist*) training saw them either hit the opposing rigid sarissa phalanx in the vulnerable flanks, or they targeted other lighter troops. The crack brigade may have even rolled up the younger and inexperienced Macedonians provided by Antipater. It was a spectacular penetration that nevertheless left the units on their own left flanks exposed.

The light, manoeuvrable cavalry under Peithon facing Eumenes' right wing was pushed back to nearby foothills by a reinforcement of horsemen, backed up by the elephants Peithon had attempted to intimidate with spears and arrows. To counter the setback on his left, Antigonus' own cavalry unit charged through the gap in the phalanx, threatening Eumenes' left wing where Eudamus' mounted men were stationed. Both generals tried to rally their men and reorganize their ranks, and by lamp-lighting time the armies were still arrayed on the field for a new confrontation in what now appeared an eerie stalemate silhouetted by a full moon. By midnight, the armies retired to their camps bloodied, exhausted and no doubt dehydrated and famished. The result was inconclusive, and once again the defence of their respective baggage trains played a significant role in that outcome.

Antigonus reportedly lost 3,700 foot soldiers and fifty-four horsemen, with a further 4,000 men wounded, whereas Eumenes lost 540 infantry and 'very few cavalry', with some 900 injured.[140] The losses were to some extent irrelevant, for Antigonus managed to occupy the ground of the fallen and thus had first rights to the burial – a key component in claiming victory – when Eumenes' men refused to abandon their waggons.[141] There is no mention, however, of the symbolic victory 'tree' on which the panoply of the fallen was hung with shields about the base and erected at the spot at which the tide of the battle was turned.[142] This might suggest Antigonus knew his claim to the ground was dubious, considering his far greater losses. According to Polyaenus, Antigonus detained the herald Eumenes, sent to agree the terms of cremation and burial, until all his own dead had been burned on a pyre.[143] Eumenes countered with his own 'magnificent funeral' once the enemy had departed.

It was Eumenes' army which, nevertheless, managed to gain entry into the environs of Gabiene, while Antigonus, smarting from his deeper wounds, retired again to Gamarga in Peithon's home satrapy of the still-unplundered Media to re-provision as winter closed in. The armies were separated by a nine-day march through a bitterly cold and waterless desert 'that contained nothing but sulphur mines, and stinking bogs, barren and uninhabited'. The alternative route involved a twenty-five-day march through a more hospitable landscape.[144]

It was close to the winter solstice and Antigonus had his men prepare ten days' food that did not require cooking. Fearing he had spies in his camp, he let it be known that he was marching to Armenia. According to Polyaenus, 10,000 water casks had to be readied for Antigonus' ten-day march to confront Eumenes through a desert that provided 'neither water, nor grass, nor wood, nor plant'.[145] Antigonus struck out across the desert instead of for Armenia and issued orders that no fires were to be lit at night, a plan that was soon challenged by winds and bitter cold, forcing his men to heat themselves after five days on the march. The flames alerted local inhabitants to his presence; fast camels were sent to Peucestas, who, noting the abundance of the enemy lights, prepared to make off with his eastern command. Fearing a wholesale flight, Eumenes 'calmed their fears' by promising a delaying action, and he quickly roused his troops from their scattered billets. Riding to a position clearly visible to Antigonus' forces, he likewise ordered a string of fires to be lit as if a consolidated battlefront faced the advancing army. Antigonus abandoned his frontal assault and headed to provision.[146]

The one-eyed veteran general was initially 'filled with rage and mortification, imagining that the enemy must long ago have known his plans'. Realizing 'that he had been out-manoeuvred' by a ruse, Antigonus nevertheless determined to settle their disputes with an immediate pitched battle.[147] He was informed that Eumenes' forces were still strung out, with some detachments stationed a six-day march from others; Plutarch claimed Eumenes' unruly Macedonians had distributed themselves where they liked.[148] Keen to exploit the opportunity, Antigonus marched on Gabiene. Eumenes gathered his dispersed forces into a palisaded fort, but the elephant contingent was slow to arrive. A cavalry clash ensued that saw Eumenes narrowly avert the capture of his entire corps of Indian beasts.[149]

The pre-battle manoeuvres and continued chicanery, the double deceits and the realities of the brutal climate in this seasonal campaigning set the scene for the forthcoming final confrontation at Gabiene at the close of 316 BC. Eumenes had employed his Cappadocian levies effectively, and by now, Antigonus had also harnessed the skills of foreign auxiliaries: Lycian, Pamphylian, Phrygian and Lydian troops were supporting the Macedonian ranks, no doubt supplied by Nearchus and Menander, governors of these regions. Antigonus' long tenure of Anatolia was being well exploited.[150] They were supported by local Medians, care of Peithon, and alongside them Tarentine cavalry, local conscripts and mercenaries had been gathered from Alexander's settlements along the way. Apart from harnessing their unique skills, fresh recruits arrived with little or no accumulated baggage, reducing their weighty vulnerability.[151]

'Not out of goodwill or kindness, but to protect the money they had lent him [to Eumenes], Phaedimus and Eudamus the master of the elephants, brought word of the planned treachery of Teutamus, the Silver Shields commander.'[152] Eumenes may have already suspected intrigue; Teutamus had almost been turned by Antigonus' promises before they departed Cilicia. Before the final scene played out, however, Eumenes might have dealt one more effective theatrical card. Facing opponents a generation younger, Antigenes of the Silver Shields sent out a horseman to the opposing phalanx and proclaimed aloud: 'Oh wicked men, you are sinning against your fathers, who conquered the world under Philip and Alexander!' This recalls the vocal threats from Xennias 'in the Macedonian tongue' when he attempted to dissuade the opposing Macedonians from fighting Eumenes' veterans before the battle with Neoptolemus. And here, at Gabiene, it was a masterstroke of mental warfare.[153]

Antigonus had strengthened his right wing. Screened by the strongest elephants, Eumenes took position directly opposite on his own left as they prepared for the final confrontation. As trumpets blasted and ranks engaged once more, Antigonus' infantry again collapsed under the Silver Shields' charge. But the advancing elephants trampled dust from the uncultivated salt flat into a confusing haze, enabling the Median cavalry under Peithon and the Tarentines to seize Eumenes' baggage train, while father and son – Antigonus and the young Demetrius the Besieger – flanked the cavalry wing under Eudamus' command. Although the Silver Shields killed 5,000 of those facing them without a single casualty (or so propaganda claimed), the loss of the baggage train, along with Peucestas' 'lax and ignoble' withdrawal from the battlefield, handed the day to Antigonus.[154] It was Peucestas' non-performance that the Silver Shields ultimately blamed for their final defeat. Perhaps it was a bittersweet on-the-battlefield revenge that Peucestas coordinated with the one-eyed veteran for having been out-generalled by Eumenes *off t*he battlefield at Persepolis. Or Hieronymus, when penning his account, may have simply saddled Peucestas with a legacy of betrayal for his earlier attempt to wrest control from Eumenes.

Eumenes' repeated cavalry charges had not turned the tide. The now cut-off veteran infantry commanders were forced to form a defensive hollow square, retreating to safety by the bank of a river, spitting accusations at Peucestas as they went. Eumenes' Asian satraps advised flight, while he proposed fighting on because their overall casualties were few.[155] But the capture of their baggage, and the loss of '2,000 women and a few children', decided the outcome for the influential Silver Shields brigade, who now asked themselves why the 'best of the soldiers of Philip and Alexander, after all their toils, in their old age [should] be robbed of their rewards'.[156]

Their commander Teutamus soon opened covert negotiations with Antigonus. Promises were exchanged, Eumenes was seized and handed over, and Plutarch recorded a scathing speech in which Eumenes upbraided the traitors. He and Justin, possibly drawing from Duris of Samos – who may have displayed hostility towards the Cardian (that would be consistent with his apparent iconoclastic treatment of the reputations of other 'great men', especially those working on behalf of the Macedonian regime) – presented the allegation that Eumenes attempted to flee.[157] So, guarded as if he was 'a furious lion or a savage elephant', Eumenes was eventually executed when a war council of Antigonus' Macedonians voted for his death, despite the reported pleas from Demetrius and Nearchus for his life to be spared. Eumenes was aged 45.[158]

In Plutarch's expanded account of the aftermath of Gabiene, Antigonus 'could not endure to see Eumenes, by reason of their former intimate friendship'. After deliberating for some days on his dilemma, Eumenes was deprived of food before being dispatched.[159] Any hesitation Antigonus had shown to his men was surely contrived and politically expedient, for his army now swelled with ranks of angry captured soldiers, and this was most likely why Peucestas was not immediately executed, for his eastern coalition was significantly present.

Antigonus slew Eumenes' commander Eudamus. Antigenes, the long-time career soldier honoured by Alexander in a military contest some fifteen years before, and more recently rewarded for his part in slaying Perdiccas in Egypt, was reportedly thrown into a pit and burned alive. The earlier intrigues of his fellow Silver Shields commander, Teutamus, might have saved his life, though his fate is unattested. Amphimachus the governor of Mesopotamia, and Stasander, a supporting satrap from Areia-Drangiana, were most likely executed too as they disappear from texts thereafter. A further 1,000 of the Silver Shields were sent off to Arachosia. Diodorus claimed the region's satrap, the previously humiliated Sibyrtius, who subsequently enjoyed a long tenure there, was given orders to send them on dangerous missions to annihilate the unit. The rest were forced into garrison duty so 'that not a man of them might ever return to Macedon or behold the Grecian sea'.[160]

The Silver Shields brigade was never heard of again, though Seleucus might have later managed to recruit survivors into his ranks.[161] But who could blame the one-eyed general for Eumenes' final execution? The Cardian was simply too unpredictable an adversary to trust in any future coalition, as Antigonus' men appear to have vocally pointed out.

Meanwhile, in Macedon, the fate of Olympias, Rhoxane and her son Alexander IV, as well as his fiancée Deidameia the Epirote princess, and Alexander's half-sister Thessalonice with them, was in the balance as they were besieged by Cassander at Pydna (close to modern Makrygialos and Kitros).[162] Although the loyal Bodyguard Aristonus still held Amphipolis, and his ally Monimus controlled Pella, neither they nor Olympias' nephew, Aeacides of the Molossian royal house, nor Polyperchon – who was himself under siege by Cassander's army in Azorus in northern Thessaly – were able to come to her aid by land or sea. After holding out for months by eating the rotting flesh from the corpses, and while watching her followers (and elephants) die of starvation, Olympias' soldiers asked to be released from her service. Following a failed escape by ship, she sued for terms with Cassander, who agreed to nothing but her personal safety. She ordered Aristonus to submit and hand over Amphipolis on similar pledges of safety.

Cassander immediately had Aristonus murdered and called for a similar end to Olympias, who was condemned *in absentia* by a hastily convened Assembly, as any wider forum might have voted more sympathetically. After failing to lure her into a further sham escape attempt, some 200 of Cassander's best soldiers were sent in for the kill, but they were 'overawed by her exulted rank'. It was left to relatives of Olympias' victims (so, Cassander's family) to finally slay her. She was either run through with a blade or summarily stoned to death, though she 'uttered no ignoble or womanish plea' so that 'you might have perceived the soul of Alexander in his dying mother'. Clearly recalling her treatment of the grave of his brother Iollas, Olympias' body was left unburied by Cassander, though her clan, the Aeacids – possibly in Pyrrhus' reign (who named his daughter Olympias) – may have interred her nearby with honours some years later.[163] The 'royal alliance' perpetuated by Olympias and Eumenes, which saw them both under siege, had finally been wiped out.

Eumenes' portfolio of subterfuges had ensured his survival for a time, but there remains an inevitability to the fate of 'the pest from the Chersonese', as the Macedonians lately called him.[164] His credentials, though impressive, were ultimately non-Macedonian in origin. Despite his intimacy with Alexander and his last acting chiliarch Perdiccas, both of whom sheltered him from the full force of domestic prejudice, Eumenes remained an ineligible candidate for either the throne at Pella or as the overarching commander (*strategos*) of the Asian Empire. We recall that Eumenes had himself refrained from voting at the Common Assembly at Babylon (an enfranchisement only possible if he had been nationalized as a citizen by Philip or Alexander). He was ultimately impotent with anyone but his own Asian levies, a handicap he himself is said to have openly voiced.[165] It is a testament to Eumenes' charisma, powers of persuasion and cunning that he managed to hold the Macedonian core of his coalition together to fight three major pitched battles when veteran home-grown generals of repute lay across the plain.

Alexander's Companions and Royal Bodyguards appear to have discarded their Asiatic wives at, or soon after, his death, with the notable exception of Seleucus, who remained married to Apame, daughter of the troublesome warlord Spitamenes (of Bactria or Sogdia), and possibly with the exception of Eumenes too.[166] For his biographers, Plutarch and Nepos, reported that at his death, Eumenes' bones were conveyed to his mother, wife, and children in Cappadocia in a silver urn following a 'magnificent funeral'.[167] We have no evidence that Eumenes was married to anyone other than a daughter (or, as I have argued, granddaughter) of Artabazus, which explains the presence in his ranks of Artabazus' son, Pharnabazus.[168] This suggests that far from abandoning his wife, Eumenes saw the value in maintaining his marriage with Persian nobility.

'Children have to be deceived with knucklebones, men with oaths.' The aphorism has been variously attributed to Philip II and the Spartan general Lysander, but applies to Eumenes best.[169] The years 320 BC to the close of 316 BC are studded with military intrigues that appealed to Polyaenus (who claimed to be of Macedonian descent). They included doctored oaths, wills, royal mandates, faked letters, dream visions, guile and brilliant deceits. And I suggest the *Pamphlet* was part of Eumenes' military repertoire.

Aside from Alexander himself, no one of the age attracted more biographers than Eumenes. None of the long-lived dynasts – Antigonus, Ptolemy, Seleucus nor Lysimachus – merited Plutarch's biographical attention, and it has been insightfully suggested that as Macedonians who had oppressed Greeks, they presented negative models.[170] Unsurprisingly, the portrait of Eumenes embodied in the surviving texts is one of outright admiration.

Although Eumenes left us no history 'book', if he was indeed the keeper of the Royal Dairies, or *Ephemerides*, as Aelian and Athenaeus supposed, then his entries were a truly unimpeachable account of the campaign years.[171] Taking into account everything we know about Eumenes' brief career between his incarceration at Nora and his death after the Battle of Gabiene some three years later, he alone ought to be proposed as the architect of the 'partisan scrap' which combined the poisoning of Alexander with his written testament. It fits Eumenes' behavioural patterns perfectly: he was a born pamphleteer. From whatever angle we inspect the *Pamphlet* will alongside the conspiracy allegations, there was only ever one man and one woman who in those years had cause to line up the names with the peculiar associations we see them: Eumenes in league with Olympias.

8

HOW, WHY AND WHEN THE WILL EMERGED

Under what specific circumstances might the detail of Alexander's testament and the conspiracy to kill him have first been circulated, and for what specific purpose?

The tumultuous years between 320 and 315 BC revealed the true nature and subterfuges of the alliance between Eumenes, Polyperchon, Olympias and Cleopatra, and also the extent of the opposition arrayed against it.

I analyse the specific detail within the *Pamphlet* and argue why the will and the conspiracy were reconstructed as we read them from Alexander's original testament, and why the mysterious list of projects found at Babylon, known as his 'last plans', need to be factored in.

Finally, I attempt to pinpoint the timing of its release and why its incendiary claims never achieved their intended outcome.

> Shut up there [at the fortress of Nora] and surrounded by the enemy with a double wall, he [Eumenes] had no one to give him aid in his own misfortune. When the siege had lasted a year and hope of safety had been abandoned, there suddenly appeared an unexpected deliverance from his plight; for Antigonus who was besieging him and bent on destroying him, changed his plan, invited him to share in his own undertakings.[1]
>
> Diodorus, *Library of World History*
>
> Where the skin of the lion does not reach, it must be patched with the skin of a fox.[2]
>
> Plutarch, *Apophthegms* or *Sayings of Kings and Commanders*

The exact location of Nora remains unidentified. Plutarch described it as a 'small ... but wonderfully strong' grain-stocked stronghold with 'water in abundance' where Eumenes fled following the battle with Antigonus at Orcynia, another debated location and a name otherwise unknown.[3] Yet within that impregnable stone fortress in the Phrygian highlands or on the confines of Lycaonia and the Cappadocian Plateau, contemplating his fate and the permutations of the outcomes with the odds stacked against him, Eumenes may well have conceived of the content of the *Pamphlet*.[4]

The shockwaves from this precision-guided weapon targeted everyone then in power, with a range that reached from India to Epirus. Although its blast was short-lived, the fallout lingered on until it had been safely contained by Ptolemy's sanitising *Journal*. But its heat signature remained in what we have come to name *The Book of the Death and Testament of Alexander the Great*, most visible at the end of the *Greek Alexander Romance*.

If the months of the siege at Nora *did* inspire Eumenes to craft his path of retribution, just when – amongst his later invocations of the ghost of Alexander, the epistolary subterfuges, the forced campaign marches and the full-scale battles – did this unique propaganda cup appear? Two significant factors hamper attempts at an exact dating: our sources' methodologies and the corruption of the texts which house the *Pamphlet* remnants today.

Chronology Challenges

Diodorus' *Library of World History* remains the fullest coverage of events of the years 319–315 BC in which the siege and its aftermath fell, and he principally extracted its detail from Hieronymus' history, but in an extremely abbreviated form, with the compression of detail varying by chapters. This led to chronological slippage and some synthetic attempts to arrange years around non-concurrent episodes in Greece and Asia, which confuses events order. Plutarch was even less concerned about being clinical on the sequence of events, as long as the resulting narrative satisfied his character development and the thematic shape he sought.

Nevertheless, studies of the so-called *The Book of the Death and Testament of Alexander the Great*, which represents the *Pamphlet* in the form we inherit it today, have pinpointed two broad periods that best suit its original publication: 322–321 BC, or better still, 319–316 BC. The latter period commenced, significantly, with the siege of Nora and ended with Eumenes' death after the Battle of Gabiene (December 316 BC or early January 315 BC). Within these dates, broadly occupied by the Second Successor War, several windows of opportunity, or moments of desperation, manifested themselves, and each could have precipitated the *Pamphlet*'s release. If we systematically break down its content, we can certainly narrow down the moment at which Eumenes' strategic rehash of Alexander's will was broadcast to the fragmenting Macedonian-governed world.

Negotiations at Nora

Eumenes' early attempts at a negotiated settlement at Nora failed; it seems he had been 'asking for more than his hopeless position deserved'. Diodorus' text appears unequivocal on what happened next: Antigonus referred the matter back to Antipater, the aged regent in Pella. Eumenes also 'later sent envoys to Antipater to discuss the terms of surrender. Their leader was Hieronymus, who has written the history of the Successors.'[5] Although this sentence is written in the third person, it may be a direct quote from Hieronymus who declared his identity as the recorder of events. The reference to 'later' is vexing, but whenever Hieronymus undertook the journey as Eumenes' envoy, he would have needed his besieger's blessing and potentially his protection, for Hieronymus may have been on the proscription list (those to be hunted down and killed) of Perdiccans drawn up at Triparadeisus, assuming he was already operating with Eumenes when Craterus was killed.[6] So it is possible that Hieronymus departed Nora for Pella with Antigonus' own named envoy, Aristodemus of Miletus.[7]

More confusing still is the implication that Antigonus, in his position as the Macedonian regent's senior commander (*strategos*) of Asia, was obliged to seek the regent's advice on Eumenes' fate; his mandate had given him plenipotentiary powers to hunt down the Perdiccans and put them to the sword, as the fate of others made quite clear. One possible explanation for his hesitation is the fame of the siege, perhaps as notorious as Eumenes himself: 'No one else had been so much talked about in the army since the death of Craterus.'[8] If discussed from Pella to Persis, and with a situation so unique, then starving the occupants of Nora to submission, and executing the now powerless Eumenes without at least soliciting Antipater's blessing, might have broadcast ambition that Antigonus was not quite ready to unveil: the ambition and love of power that Antipater already suspected.[9]

If Eumenes *was* pressing for his claims to be heard in Pella, he was simply buying time. No doubt he planned to ask Antipater, perhaps already known to be ill, to extend a similar offer of reconciliation to that he proffered to Eumenes before his confrontation with Craterus, the terms Eumenes then rejected due to old enmities.[10] Although he had nothing to lose from diplomacy, Eumenes cannot have hoped for much: he had urged Perdiccas to repudiate Antipater's daughter, Nicaea, as a prelude to the invasion of Macedon, he had widowed another of the regent's daughters (married to Craterus) and had come close to a clash with Antipater himself at Sardis, a conflict saved only by a warning from Cleopatra's intelligence system. Moreover, he had bettered Antipater to an embarrassing extent in Lydia or Phrygia before taking Celaenae, if the content of manuscript known as the *Gothenburg Palimpsest* is reliable.[11] Any reply from Pella would likely be a death sentence, and perhaps Antigonus knew it, explaining why he sent the embassy. When considering that Eumenes remained incarcerated at Nora until after Antipater's death, we may conclude the answer from Pella was to continue the siege, assuming the embassy arrived before the regent expired.

When briefing Hieronymus for the journey, Eumenes would have tasked him with contacting Olympias, who was still based in the Molossian region of Epirus, and possibly also with getting word to Cleopatra, who was now alone as an 'unofficial' hostage of Antigonus in Sardis.[12] If Eumenes expected a death sentence from the regent, he also knew he had an ally in Alexander's mother. Diodorus reported that some Molossians joined the Greek alliance against Antipater in the Lamian War, though their initial support ended in treachery soon after.[13] There does exist a clear epistolary tradition that details Olympias' denigration of Antipater, and, in turn, it captures his complaints about her obduracy which had already prompted Alexander's famous quip: 'She was charging him a high rent for ten months' accommodation inside her womb.'[14]

Plutarch believed Alexander had even warned Antipater about a plot being laid against him, and if not specifically named, Olympias is a strong candidate as its architect, though this appears later embellishment to the tale that was possibly motivated (or supported) by the conspiracy detailed in the *Pamphlet*. Plutarch went as far as stating: 'Olympias and Cleopatra had raised a faction, Olympias taking Epirus, and Cleopatra Macedon.' When he heard of it, Alexander allegedly commented that his mother had made the better choice, for 'the Macedonians would not submit to be reigned over by a woman'. More plausible still is Antipater's deathbed caution: 'Never permit a woman to be protector [*prostates*] of a kingdom.'[15]

Antigonus must have been able to control the flow of information into Nora, but it would have benefited him to reveal to Eumenes the gravity of his position. The proscribed Perdiccan confederates under Docimus, Attalus and Polemon were in a siege that was to last sixteen months in Phrygia, which would end with their deaths or defections.[16] The necrology may have included Laomedon, the displaced satrap of Coele-Syria, care of Ptolemy's annexation, as he was never mentioned again. Alcetas, faced with an impossible situation, finally committed suicide at Termessus in Pisidia and his body was posthumously mutilated, whilst Holcias and his 3,000 renegades had been rounded up more locally and their fate was in the balance.[17] Moreover, Eumenes had himself been served a painful reminder of his non-Macedonian origins at Orcynia, with significant defections from his ranks before, during and after the battle. Enlisting and retaining Macedonians was becoming dangerous.

Antipater still dominated Pella and the dynastic stakes through a clutch of eligible daughters: the eldest, the twice-widowed Phila, with an infant son by Craterus who had amicably passed on his Persian wife Amastris to Dionysius of Heraclea, remarried Antigonus' son, Demetrius the Besieger. Another daughter, Nicaea, following her rejection by Perdiccas, was sought by Lysimachus (probably before Antipater died).[18] Ptolemy had married a third daughter, Eurydice, sometime in 321/320 BC. The defeated pro-Perdiccan Royal Bodyguard Aristonus had agreed to retire to Macedon under Antipater's watchful eye, and Polyperchon had crossed to Europe with Craterus and supported Antipater in the Lamian War. Its successful conclusion saw the regent maintaining his stranglehold over Greece through the oligarchies he had installed over the previous fifteen years.[19] Additionally, White Cleitus, the former Perdiccan fleet commander, had been confirmed as satrap of Lydia at Triparadeisus in return for naval assistance given to the regent.[20]

Now, months into the siege, Eumenes cannot have truly fancied his chances of exiting Nora alive as anything more than a captive in chains. Supplies were dwindling and despite his ingenious mechanical device for exercising his horses (their forelegs were hoisted by straps to make them kick furiously), the military mounts must have looked more like meals, even though Eumenes 'seasoned' what remained with 'charm and friendliness'.[21] 'Whatsoever friends asked to be dismissed because they could not endure the asperities of the place and the constraint in diet, all these he sent away, after bestowing upon them tokens of affection and kindness.' Underlining the plight of those who remained was the knowledge that Antigonus now commanded the most powerful force in Asia under a single Macedonian general: 60,000 infantry, 10,000 cavalry and thirty war elephants, with 'pay without end' from the treasuries if more were required.[22]

The biography from Cornelius Nepos, however, provided unique additional detail that might allow us to reconsider the true nature of Eumenes' plight. He claimed that: 'During that siege, as often as he desired, he [Eumenes] either set on fire or demolished the works and defences of Antigonus.' Nepos further implied that Eumenes could have broken out, but he was awaiting spring and meanwhile 'pretended to be desirous of surrendering' and treating for terms.[23] If Eumenes was indeed playing a delaying tactic, it was to exploit any one of several outcomes: a new offer from Antigonus, the appearance of Perdiccan renegades still operating in the region, the death of Antipater, or as Nepos suggested, better breakout weather, for the mountain passes may well have been snowbound. The friends whom Eumenes dismissed may have been able to slip away individually and get word to supporters, and an escape in the planning explains the need to keep horses in shape. Antipater died first, and with him any death sentence appears to have expired, as Antigonus' next move suggests.

Having dealt with Alcetas, who had been attempting to install himself in Pisidia – perhaps more legitimately than historians have assumed – Antigonus was now on his way to his customary winter quartering at Celaenae when Aristodemus arrived with news of the regent's death, which points to late 319 BC. Antigonus had reached Cretopolis ('city of the Cretans', most likely strategically located in Pisidia) and was reportedly 'delighted' at the turn of events, whereupon he prepared to make an offer to Eumenes, apparently prompted by the knowledge that Polyperchon had been appointed as the new Macedonian regent in Antipater's place. Support for Antigonus in Pella was thus now uncertain.[24]

Hieronymus had either recently returned from Macedon, perhaps in the company of Aristodemus once more, or he had already returned to Nora, when he was summoned to hear Antigonus' terms.[25] Before agreeing to Eumenes' freedom, Antigonus unsuccessfully invited Hieronymus to join him with the promise of 'great gifts'. This raises several questions. Was this offer independent of Eumenes' fate, or was Hieronymus being enrolled in order to turn Eumenes to Antigonus' cause? And had Hieronymus operated under the one-eyed general before in an otherwise undocumented career? We may never know, but Diodorus provided a typically stoic philosophical summation that was unlikely to have been wholly of his own design: 'For in the inconstancy and irregularity of events history furnishes a corrective for both the arrogance of the fortunate and the despair of the destitute.'[26]

With Antipater dead, Antigonus must have considered himself the foremost of all the surviving Macedonian generals, both in Europe and in Asia. Polyperchon, as events were to prove, was malleable, and Antigonus must have known it. Furthermore, Cassander, always suspicious of Antigonus' plans, had been subordinated in the process to a role he would not accept: Polyperchon's second-in-command.[27]

At the conclusion of negotiations, Antigonus invited Eumenes to 'share in his own undertakings', offering him a pardon, 'a greater satrapy besides' and 'gifts many times the value of what he had' before.[28] These are somewhat reminiscent of the terms Antipater had offered earlier.[29] Nepos claimed Eumenes only signed the (purportedly amended) oath of release at the approach of spring, thus early 318 BC. The release date is sound, as the likely distance from Nora to Celaenae (from summons to final agreement, a journey possibly made twice by Hieronymus) and the demands of winter travelling in the mountainous region speak of a deal being brokered for many weeks before Eumenes' final freedom.

Antigonus was now in his early sixties. The assimilation of an extended Anatolia, and even the whole Asian empire, must have seemed possible to him. As Diodorus put it:

> Antigonus made up his mind to maintain a firm grip upon the government of Asia and to yield the rule of that continent to no one ... Indeed he had in mind to go through Asia, remove the existing satraps, and reorganise the positions of command in favour of his friends.[30]

There was, however, much to marshal in Anatolia in the first step of assimilation, and between Antigonus and Macedon already stood an apparently accommodating Lysimachus in Thrace.[31] But there was one missing ingredient that would provide the approbation Antigonus' muscle-flexing needed: official support of the Argead house. The royal line now potentially had Olympias as its figurehead, and Antigonus knew full well that she would return to the centre of Pellan policy with Polyperchon holding the regency for two incapable kings (the halfwit Arrhidaeus, now King Philip II Arrhidaeus, and Rhoxane's young child, King Alexander IV).

Antigonus also knew that without the formalized approval of these 'kings' (through their regent-come-guardian), his men-at-arms did not constitute a royal army at all, for with the death of Antipater his own state mandate had lapsed. That meant royal treasuries were closed to him too, unless he went renegade. Eumenes must have positioned himself as the missing regal link in either scenario; had he maintained his support for Antigonus and not (allegedly) doctored the oath, the face of the Asian empire would have assumed a totally different complexion, as Plutarch pondered when comparing the fate of Eumenes with the parallel position of Roman renegade Quintus Sertorius with which he rounded off his biography.[32]

Polyperchon: The Unwitting Saviour

Polyperchon, the son of Simmias of the Macedonian Tymphaean aristocracy, was a notable and high-profile campaign veteran, yet he has been labelled 'a jackal among lions' for his performance and manoeuvrings in the Successor

Wars.[33] And he does fit somewhat uneasily into the general scheme of things, if the portrait we see in Diodorus is anywhere near accurate.

Curtius claimed Alexander had once vocally rejected Polyperchon's advice (termed a subterfuge), likening it to the counsel provided by 'brigands and thieves'. This hostile treatment extended into the texts of Aelian, who indeed termed him a brigand, and Athenaeus too, who (drawing from Duris) described him as like a 'dancer when drunk'. Curtius went as far as claiming that Alexander once threw him in prison after he mocked a Persian who was prostrating himself before the king in the oriental-style obeisance known as *proskynesis*.[34] This sounds like propaganda, for Alexander entrusted Polyperchon with significant responsibilities; he became a commander (*taxiarchos*) of some 1,500 elite infantrymen known as 'Foot Companions' (*pezhetairoi*) from 330–325 BC, operating alongside the likes of the prominent infantry commanders Coenus and Meleager. He was later designated second-in-command to Craterus when escorting some 10,000 veterans back to Macedon from Opis.[35] Polyperchon's own son, Alexander, had been appointed a personal bodyguard to the new kings at Triparadeisus after the death of Perdiccas. And now, likely well into his sixties, Polyperchon was at Antipater's bedside when the failing regent passed away.[36]

Antipater had retained his position in Macedon from an unforeseen chain reaction of events: the clamour for his continued regency by the infantry at Babylon, his eventual (though much assisted) victory in the Lamian War and the early deaths of Leonnatus, Perdiccas and then Craterus, any of whom could have challenged for the regency or even the throne. Though there had existed abrasive relations with Olympias, Antipater seems to have remained loyal to the Argead house until Alexander's death, despite the king ordering the execution of his son-in-law, Alexander Lyncestis. The *Pamphlet* allegations, along with the regent's reported fear of being summoned to execution in Babylon, have led some scholars to conclude he had actually rebelled against Alexander in 323 BC, but the evidence is scant and circumstantial.[37]

Antipater had been among the first of Philip's generals to acknowledge Alexander as king upon his father's death, though as it has been aptly put, there is a difference between loyal service and devotion to an individual. It was claimed that Alexander used the affectionate salutation 'greetings' (less formally, 'joy to you') exclusively with Phocion in Athens (the city's pragmatic and widely trusted military commander for many years), but also with Antipater.[38] Antipater, in turn, clearly had confidence in Polyperchon, entrusting him with the defence of the kingdom when campaigning in Greece in the Lamian War.[39] On his deathbed, to the disgust of his ambitious son, Cassander, Antipater passed the regency to Polyperchon, who then became the principal guardian of the kings and caretaker of the kingdom.[40] Antipater's appointment was unsurprising when reviewing his career, for 'Polyperchon, who was almost the oldest of those who had campaigned with Alexander, was held in honour by the Macedonians'.[41]

Unfortunately, this new arrangement in Pella both overestimated Polyperchon's ability at court and underestimated Cassander's drive for power, which would feed off his father's well-established network of agents. Moreover, Cassander was to prove remarkably good at operating with limited financial and manpower resources, a skill he must have learned from his father.[42] This potentially fractious state of affairs doubtless added to Antigonus' delight, plotting as he was his own independence in Asia. But understanding what took place next requires the unravelling of a severely knotted and tight-packed string of events that were formative to the shape, and the issue date, of the *Pamphlet*.

The disgruntled Cassander immediately aligned himself in Pella with the new queen, Eurydice, the daughter of Alexander's widowed and warlike half-sister Cyanne. Named at birth Adea, the now-teenage girl received the official court moniker 'Eurydice' by virtue of her marriage to the mentally deficient King Philip III Arrhidaeus (which, I argue, was in line with Alexander's succession instructions at Babylon). Eurydice was able to exert control over her half-witted husband despite Polyperchon's attempt to exploit Arrhidaeus himself.[43] Her strength and her pugnacious nature came from her mother Cynnane, who reportedly slew the Illyrian queen, Caeria, with her own hands when in her mid-teens; this was perhaps a clan revenge killing on behalf of her Illyrian grandmother, Audata, Philip's first or second wife who had also taken the regal title 'Eurydice'.

As far as we know, Cynnane had never been endowed with a state-celebrated marriage by her father like the wedding occasion Philip had given to Cleopatra and her uncle, Alexander Molossus, the new king of Epirus; it was during this public display of wealth and power when Philip was murdered at Aegae.[44] Cynanne's husband, Amyntas, the son of former King Perdiccas III (making Amyntas Philip's nephew), was executed by Alexander on accusations of treason at Philip's death, but Amyntas had left Cynnane with a child: Adea.[45] Alexander had attempted a useful new political match for Cynnane with Langarus, king of the Agrianians, before departing on campaign, but Langarus died before any official marriage ceremony took place.[46] The Agrianians, a Paeonian tribe to the north of Macedon, nevertheless became an indispensable part of Alexander's campaigning army in the wake of that match.

Sometime before Perdiccas' failed invasion of Egypt in 320 BC, Cynnane raised her own brigade of Macedonian soldiers (probably a modest bodyguard contingent, despite Polyaenus' inference of an 'army') and crossed the River Strymon, heading west into Thrace and then on to Asia with Adea (who was not older than 15), against Antipater's instructions.[47] Previously living in obscurity under Antipater's watchful eye, Cynnane clearly saw her chance to re-enter the dynastic game through her daughter who carried Philip's blood. As Polyaenus put it, 'upon Alexander's death, his generals parcelled out his dominions among themselves, in exclusion of the royal family', or so it must have appeared to the Roman historians who never contemplated the historicity of the will. Cynnane next demanded that Adea be presented as a bride to the newly elevated Arrhidaeus, and it was not the first time the hapless halfwit had been strategically targeted for marriage.[48]

Perdiccas, whose own authority would also be undermined by Cynnane's move, had equal reason to see the Argead women halted in their tracks, so he sent his brother, Alcetas, to intercept them. A defiant Cynnane was killed by Alcetas, whose men, however, were infuriated at this outcome and demanded Adea be duly presented to King Philip III Arrhidaeus; some of them, who 'at first paused at the sight of Philip's daughter', according to Polyaenus, could conceivably have seen Cynnane in action with her father in the Illyrian campaigns (mid-340s BC).[49] Perdiccas was forced to agree to the match and could not prevent Adea assuming the regal title 'Queen Eurydice'.[50] Unfortunately for all those with an eye on the throne and independent paths to power, the daughter of Alexander's half-sister was now married to Alexander's half-brother (an 'Amazon and an idiot') and Eurydice became the 'first true Macedonian queen in almost a generation'. Here the reference applies to her upbringing at Pella, for she clearly had part-Illyrian ancestry, though Illyria was not nominally subordinate to a 'greater Macedon'.[51]

With the new turn of events in Pella after Polyperchon assumed the regency, Eurydice, who seemingly harboured a hatred of Alexander's side of the Argead line (no doubt for his murder of her father; moreover, Alexander's former chiliarch Perdiccas was now responsible for the death of her mother), had her halfwit husband issue letters demanding Polyperchon deliver up his army to Cassander, who was obviously promoting himself in the parallel role of regent to the kings.[52] Justin recorded that a similar royal demand for submission was sent to Antigonus in Asia, which presumably meant she and Cassander required his military support.[53] 'When everything necessary for his departure was ready', Cassander journeyed to Celaenae with the kings' edict, whereupon he secured for himself 4,000 infantry (probably Greek mercenaries) and a useful fleet of thirty-five of Antigonus' ships with which to return to Greece and build an opposition bridgehead against Polyperchon.[54]

The assumption that Antigonus declared war on Polyperchon by agreeing to this requisition does not need to be made. He simply, though rather conveniently, complied with a royal directive from Pella. Cassander simultaneously reached out to Ptolemy (now his brother-in-law) in Egypt, and probably to Lysimachus as well (married to, or soon to wed, Cassander's sister Nicaea).[55] With an oathless Eumenes now on the loose, and with him and Polyperchon apparently corresponding with Olympias, Antigonus was only too happy to assist the old regent's son to embroil himself in a war with the new regent across the Aegean.[56] Antigonus' true intent was nevertheless clear:

> ...he pretended to be aiding him [Cassander] because of his own friendship for Antipater, but in truth it was because he wished Polyperchon to be surrounded by many great distractions, so that he himself might proceed against Asia without danger and secure the supreme power for himself.[57]

Polyperchon finally 'foresaw the serious character of the war that was to be fought with him'. According to Diodorus, he sought council approval before taking any actions and 'many shrewd suggestions' were made about the war. The council was presumably the veneer of an Assembly, but here, with the Pellan royalty being tugged at from both sides, it was more likely a council of war (*synedrion*) convened with court allies. 'But it was clear that Cassander, reinforced by Antigonus, would hold the Greek cities against them ... since some of the cities were guarded by his father's garrisons and others dominated by Antipater's friends and mercenaries.'[58]

Cassander must have promised his dying father he would serve Polyperchon well. He lied; as a direct result of his hostility, Polyperchon and his advisers 'decided to free the cities throughout Greece and to overthrow the oligarchies established in them by Antipater ... for in this way they would best decrease the influence of Cassander and also win for themselves great glory and many considerable allies'.[59] The Pro-Macedon Athenian orator Demades had pleaded with Antipater to take these steps himself, but his words had fallen on deaf ears. Cassander executed him in Pella after killing the orator's son who was standing at his father's side.[60]

'Many in fact obeyed' Polyperchon and 'there were massacres throughout the cities', whilst others 'were driven into exile; the friends of Antipater were destroyed, and the governments ... began to form alliances with him'. Although Polyperchon had clearly been 'forced into a political stance that was diametrically opposite' to the Antipatrid regime in Greece, at no time was a declaration of war against Antigonus in Asia mentioned, a contention backed up by the fact that they would join forces three years later.[61] Polyperchon had, nevertheless, been manoeuvred into a position not of his own choosing, and he would have surely avoided a confrontation in Asia when Greece itself was now in turmoil. In this light, the 'remarkable' missives he allegedly sent to Eumenes empowering him to wage war in the name of the kings look rather suspicious, especially so when recalling Eumenes' local deceits. Diodorus recorded the content of the avowed Pellan correspondence in the greater detail:

> He [Polyperchon] also sent to Eumenes, writing a letter in the name of the kings, urging him not to put an end to his enmity toward Antigonus, but turning from him to the kings, either to cross over to Macedon, if he wished, and become a guardian of the kings in co-operation with himself, or if he preferred, to remain in Asia and after receiving an army and money fight it out with Antigonus who had already clearly shown that he was a rebel against the kings. He said that the kings were restoring to him the satrapy that Antigonus had taken away and all the prerogatives that he had ever possessed in Asia. Finally, he set forth that it was especially fitting for Eumenes to be careful and solicitous for the royal house in conformity with his former public services in its interest. If he needed greater military power, Polyperchon promised that he himself and the kings would come from Macedon with the entire royal army.[62]

Polyperchon additionally compensated Eumenes for his losses, providing him with a useful war chest and the crack infantry brigade:

> Eumenes, just after he had made good his retreat from the fortress [Nora], received the letters that had been dispatched by Polyperchon. They contained … the statement that the kings were giving him a gift of 500 talents as recompense for the losses that he had experienced, and that to effect this they had written to the generals and treasurers in Cilicia directing them to give him … whatever additional money he requested for raising mercenaries and for other pressing needs. The letter also added that they were writing to the commanders of the 3,000 Macedonian Silver Shields ordering them to place themselves at the disposal of Eumenes and in general to co-operate wholeheartedly with him, since he had been appointed supreme commander of all Asia.[63]

Polyperchon, under whose higher command the Silver Shields had once operated, must have appeared an unexpected saviour to everyone but Eumenes, but I propose the true intervention was something less surprising. Diodorus obviously believed the correspondence to be genuine, and I suggest Hieronymus' pro-Eumenes hand was at work here.

Polyperchon could not have dispatched the letters in the format we read them; he would not have crossed to Asia from Macedon when Cassander was recruiting an army in Greece and with Adea on the loose in Pella issuing her own 'king's' edicts. If Eumenes had elected to return to Macedon, that would have meant Polyperchon had at once declared war on Antigonus through the missives and yet invited the only man capable of executing it away from the theatre of operations. It is a prospect rendered even more unlikely when considering the size of Antigonus' conglomerated army, and when factoring in the support the one-eyed veteran might receive from Ptolemy and Lysimachus, related as they now were.[64] And at none of the war councils Polyperchon held was there mention of open hostilities in Asia, or the inciting of other Asian satraps to rise against him, a wholly necessary step if he was to head an Asian counterchallenge. Polyperchon, the so-called jackal, would have indeed then become a lion among the predatory Diadochi. So, what was really couriered east from the beleaguered regent's desk?

First of all, the two missives were potentially one: a king's edict and a regent's covering letter, that is if Polyperchon sent anything at all, for at this point in his narrative, Nepos only mentioned correspondence and messengers from Olympias to Eumenes, which confirmed a dialogue both ways. In the accounts of Diodorus and Plutarch, these dispatches appeared to have arrived together, so we might credit Olympias with covertly 'assisting' Polyperchon with his 'royal' directives on behalf of Eumenes' cause.[65] Additionally, Polyperchon's communications and pledges need to be considered in light of what was clearly reported to be faked correspondence drafted by Eumenes in the camp of Peucestas at Persepolis some two years on:

> Eumenes had fabricated a false letter ... the purport of which was that ... Olympias, associating Alexander's son with herself, had recovered firm control of the kingdom of Macedon after slaying Cassander, and that Polyperchon had crossed into Asia against Antigonus with the strongest part of the royal army and the elephants and was already advancing in the neighbourhood of Cappadocia.[66]

As one scholar elegantly put it: 'In the murky world of Macedonian "constitutionalism" and legitimacy, a recent edict issued by the kings and their regent, and endorsed by Alexander's mother, carried more weight than a disinterred resolution of the Macedonian assembly sanctioned by the same kings.'[67] Realizing just that, it seems more likely that Eumenes and Olympias between them had fully concocted, or partly exploited, an original letter from the regent in Pella and turned it into a mandate for war in Asia. As Eumenes also knew, this was not an age of high literacy or readily available writing materials, so there was no widespread counterfeiting. The arrival of a state missive, penned in court officialese on fine parchment with an ornate Argead seal, and delivered by a suitably primed courier, would have carried the weight of unquestionable authenticity and an aura of royal gravitas for all but a court Companion of the inner sanctum more familiar with the royal secretariat.

Other deceits aside, fabricating court correspondence would have been too preposterously bold to contemplate, as would its repercussions, and those who knew how to carry it off were even rarer still. Anyone who might dare to challenge the veracity of a king's edict would be a brave man indeed, as the former king's secretary knew. It was a state of affairs Eumenes now exploited; after all, he may well have crafted the bogus letters Philip II send out for Athenian 'interception' twenty-odd years before in 340 BC during the siege of Byzantium.[68]

Olympias Enters the War

There can be no doubt that Olympias would have wanted Eumenes back in Pella to help face the threat from Cassander once Anatolia was secured, so the cry for help we read in the texts appears genuine at least. According to Nepos:

> Olympias ... sent letters and messengers into Asia to Eumenes, to consult him [on] whether she should proceed to re-possess herself of Macedon ... She then entreated Eumenes ... not to allow the bitterest enemies of Philip's house and family to extirpate his very race, but to give his support to the children of Alexander; adding that, if he would do her such a favour, he might raise troops as soon as possible, and bring them to her aid; and, in order that he might do so more easily, she had written to all the governors of the provinces that preserved their allegiance, to obey him, and follow his counsels.[69]

By now Olympias had already reached out from her base in Epirus to Polyperchon in Pella, or possibly he to her, beset as they were by a mutual enemy. Alexander's son by Rhoxane, King Alexander IV, was by now 4 years old. Olympias, with Eumenes' support, was clearly planning to back her grandson over her despised dead husband's idiot offspring, Arrhidaeus (now co-King Philip III Arrhidaeus), by another wife. We may question whether Olympias truly harboured grandmaternal feelings for Rhoxane's boy, but promoting him was her best route to survival. Strategically, that support made sense for Eumenes too: troops sent by Rhoxane's father, Oxyartes (appointed satrap of Bactria and/or the region of Paropanisadae), were in the ranks of those assembled at Persepolis and they remained with Eumenes through the battles at Paraetacene and (we may assume) Gabiene.[70] So it is unsurprising that Rhoxane featured prominently in the *Pamphlet* in a 'tender' death scene in which it was made clear that she was the foremost wife at the king's court; her restraining Alexander from disappearing into the Euphrates may have been crafted to showcase her loyalty to her husband *and* his men (if original detail and not later *Romance* colour).[71]

A blood feud was inevitable with Alexander's mother planning to return to Pella. It would have already taken place if Polyperchon's administration had any teeth. Nevertheless, after he once again 'had consulted with his friends', Polyperchon 'summoned Olympias, asking her to assume the care of Alexander's son'. She must have promised the desperate regent she would bring an Epirote army with her, and that is exactly what she did.

Nepos confirmed that 'Eumenes was moved with this communication', but not in the immediate direction Olympias might have hoped. Diodorus added that he 'at once replied to her advising her to remain in Epirus for the present until the war should come to some decision … he therefore assembled troops, and prepared for war against Antigonus' in Asia.[72] Olympias was, however, active in rallying assistance for him: Diodorus was clear that the support of the Silver Shields held firm in the face of Antigonus' subversion because 'Olympias, the mother of Alexander, had written to them that they should serve Eumenes in every way.'[73] She was also active in Greece; she sent instructions to Nicanor, Cassander's Macedonian garrison commander of Munychia, demanding he return the strategic district and adjacent harbour at Piraeus to the Athenians.[74] On good terms with Phocion, Nicanor (possibly Aristotle's nephew) had strengthened his numbers and soon controlled the Great Harbour and the adjacent Bay of Phalerum along with the harbour booms. Athens was now landlocked.

Control of the harbours had been an essential part of Cassander's return with his new ships provided by Antigonus in his recruiting mission in Asia. But the Athenian Assembly, backed by an army under Polyperchon's son, Alexander, and the anti-Macedonian agitator Hagnonides, who was once exiled by Antipater, now banished Phocion and prepared to oust the Macedonian garrison from Piraeus. This precipitated a chain of events that would result in the executions of both Phocion and Hagnonides, as well as the pro-Cassander Corinthian, Deinarchus, as the hopes of the city ascended to, and descended from, the high point of Polyperchon's promise of 'freedom', and then fell to a decade of 'tyranny' under the Cassander-installed philosopher-politician Demetrius of Phalerum.[75] Cassander, in the style of Eumenes' counterfeiting in Asia, used forged letters to rid himself of the by-now overly successful Nicanor who, it must have appeared to him (possibly with good cause), had been intriguing with Antigonus when on the Asian coast.[76]

Although Eumenes had cautioned Olympias to delay her return to Macedon and warned her against exacting revenge too soon, plans *were* clearly in place for retribution.[77] His advice, 'not to stir until Alexander's son should get the throne', anticipated the execution of Eurydice and King Philip III Arrhidaeus in the coming months, perhaps to be carried out by the agency of the newly repatriated Holcias and his men, the elusive sixth 'innocent' at Alexander's final banquet mentioned in the *Pamphlet*.[78] But it seems that Olympias *did* return against Eumenes' advice, and thus potentially earlier than he had expected.[79] She journeyed towards Pella – possibly with Polyperchon already at her side – with the help of her nephew, Aeacides of the Molossian house of Epirus (Pyrrhus' father), and in autumn 317 BC she defeated the army of Queen Adea-Eurydice which was attempting to block the path out of the Pindus Mountains that separated Macedon from the Molossian kingdom to the southwest.[80]

In the confrontation referred to by Duris of Samos as the 'first war between women', Eurydice the warrior (following the lead of her pugilistic mother) emblematically paraded herself in full battle armour, uniquely styled according to Duris, while Olympias marched out as a worshipper of Dionysus to the haunting beat of a drum. At this point, Eurydice's men, 'remembering the benefits that they had received from Alexander, changed their allegiance'.[81] The veterans were simply not ready to slay the mother of Alexander, who then captured Adea in attempted flight and rode into Pella and assumed her rightful place. Cassander was absent at the time in southern Greece. Olympias must have thought that her 'haste and timing' was justifiable after all; she may well have orchestrated trouble in the south to enable herself to strike.

Olympias immediately set about issuing orders to garrison commanders, directing generals and conducting personal vendettas.[82] The fate of Eurydice was forced suicide. Olympias gave her a sword, a noosed-rope and hemlock: three instruments of death to choose from. Shunning these tools, she is said to have hung herself with her own girdle, although she took the rope in another account. The half-witted King Philip III Arrhidaeus, presumably unable to decide for himself, was put to the Thracian dagger after wearing the crown for six years and four months; that chronologically useful statement by Diodorus places his death in October 317 BC, but possibly later if the *Babylonian Chronicle* can be relied on.

Alexander's mother and Eumenes were clearly working together on a bigger emerging picture, even if they did not concur on its timing. His experience at court and on campaign, and her role as head of the Argead house, formed a team with unique abilities, perhaps with Cleopatra facilitating their communication from Sardis; the new lower city lay astride the coast road (though not the Royal Road) to Ephesus some three days' travel away.[83] Thanks to the royal missives supposedly sent by Polyperchon, Eumenes had become the kings' commander-in-chief in Anatolia, a role Nepos suggested Perdiccas had granted him before, though this time it was either self-appointed or manipulated from missives with the help of Olympias' hand. At this point, again thanks to Olympias' groundwork, the prospect of other satraps joining him was real. It was Antigonus who now appeared the 'rebel of the monarchy'.[84]

Through missives and widely broadcast letters of correspondence (some not originating at Pella), the unwitting Polyperchon was embroiled in the intrigues and cunning of all those vying for control of the kings, the throne and Asian empire, and found himself in the crossfire of war between Cassander and Antigonus against Olympias and Eumenes. Although a decorated military veteran, it seems his political chess was simply one-dimensional in the face of more complex gambits. But with an Antigonus-backed Cassander making headway in Greece, and a Eumenes-supported Olympias now resident in Pella, what could Polyperchon possibly reverse?[85] Eumenes must have anticipated just that.

The Call to Arms to Defend Alexander's Will

It appears that two satraps in Antolia *were* activated by Olympias' call to arms, and their activity appears coordinated with a likely initial goal of facilitating Eumenes' eventual return to Macedon. Had he not been hounded east out of Phoenicia after wintering in Cilicia, Eumenes may have headed north through Anatolia and linked up with these newly defiant allies. The first was Arrhidaeus, the governor in Hellespontine Phrygia, who was probably the brother of Amphimachus the governor of Mesopotamia and would soon link up with Eumenes when he made his way east. Arrhidaeus moved to garrison the strategic cities of Cyzicus as a 'defensive measure'; he further dispatched a rescue force to free Eumenes from Nora.[86] These actions are more consistent with the trust Perdiccas placed in him when instructing him to oversee construction, and delivery, of Alexander's funeral bier at Babylon.

Basing their conclusions on the remnants of Photius' severe compression of Arrian's *Events After Alexander*, commentators generally accept that the bier's Syrian destination was a 'redirection' of its intended course, and so Arrhidaeus defied Perdiccas from the outset, as 'desertion' is mentioned. But this need not be so, and Hieronymus' rendering of the episode may well have made Arrhidaeus pay handsomely for his failure to assist Eumenes earlier, or to justify the Perdiccan loss of the corpse – or, perhaps, Arrhidaeus' help in its handing over to Ptolemy under a higher loyalty (thus, Alexander's testament). For I propose there are grounds to believe Perdiccas was himself based in Syria, so the cortege was being delivered to him as instructed, though no doubt Ptolemy's spies had advance knowledge of its route.[87] Besides, if Alexander had requested burial in Egypt in his will, its final destination was legitimate, the redirection aside. As previously noted, it is significant that no demands for the return of the body emerged. Arrhidaeus' elevation (alongside Peithon) to a guardian (*epimeletes*) at Triparadeisus suggests he was both held in high esteem and had not alienated either side of the previously feuding armies.[88] He was demonstrably no lover of Antigonus, which is perhaps why Antipater confirmed him in Hellespontine Phrygia, so that any 'rogue' crossing of the Hellespont could be monitored by him.

Presumably, with his territory bordering the narrow seaway that separated the former Persian Empire from Europe, Arrhidaeus was the first governor in Asia to receive messages and instructions from Pella or Epirus. An attempt to break Eumenes out of Nora would have been a hugely ambitious undertaking as a sole initiative, but it is conceivable as part of a bigger emerging plan. It was too late, that is if the relief force ever reached the fortress, for its fate is unattested. But the timing confirms that Olympias *was* corresponding with satraps to solicit support when Eumenes was still incarcerated; Hieronymus' mission to Pella may well have been part of that. Intimate with the defences, the siege guard strength and the locations of Antigonus' army billeting, Hieronymus could have provided the detail that would have made a breakout possible. Nepos' wording suggests the perimeter was far from watertight.

If Antigonus harboured the belief that he alone was the architect of events unfolding in Asia, and potentially now those evolving in Greece, he would have been completely wrong on both campaign fronts. When Arrhidaeus moved against him, the second satrap to declare for the pro-Eumenes alliance, White Cleitus, sailed to Macedon after garrisoning his principal cities, to inform Polyperchon of Antigonus' latest plans. Before returning to the Asian theatre of war, he briefly acted as general for the new regent and journeyed to Athens to oversee the execution of Phocion, who had submitted himself to Polyperchon when Hagnonides, his arch enemy, was reinstalled.[89]

In reply to these new threats, Antigonus dispatched 20,000 infantry and 3,000 cavalry to relieve Arrhidaeus' 'siege' of Cyzicus, and he journeyed himself with his remaining forces to take Ephesus in response to Cleitus' naval actions. Antigonus had opportunistically intercepted four ships under Rhodian captaincy carrying 600 talents of silver, ostensibly destined for Polyperchon in Macedon. This sounds suspiciously like the shipment Eumenes dispatched from Phoenicia with the treasury haul from Cynda. Was it in fact bound for the combined front of Cleitus and Arrhidaeus, rather than Macedon?[90] Antigonus refused to give up the captured funds, claiming they were needed for the payment of mercenaries (perhaps the 4,000 he 'officially' furnished Cassander with). That he provided an explanation *at all* reinforces the contention that no formal war had been declared between himself and the Pellan regime under Polyperchon. Cassander's execution of his naval commander Nicanor, who *had* returned from a coordinated action with Antigonus at the Hellespont, suggests there was little trust between the 'allies'; Antigonus was simply playing both sides of the discord.

The reprimand Antigonus next levied on the soon-defeated satrap of Hellespontine Phrygia evidenced the weight he still placed on his Triparadeisus-granted authority, despite Antipater's death: 'He sent envoys to Arrhidaeus, bringing against him these charges ... he ordered him to retire from his satrapy and, retaining a single city as a residence, to remain quiet.'[91] Ignoring the demand, Arrhidaeus took refuge in adjacent Bithynia and joined up with Cleitus' fleet upon its return from Macedon; their new instructions were to block the crossing of enemy troops expected from Europe.

This statement – the prospect of troops crossing *from* Europe – is curious, for Cassander needed all the men he could muster in Greece, and Antigonus, who furnished Cassander with men, was already funding an army of immense size in Anatolia. Was there the prospect of Lysimachus entering the frame?[92] After an early success, Cleitus' fleet was captured by Antigonus, who employed typical cunning in the face of initial defeat. Cleitus was on the run, though he was soon captured near the Bosphorus, where, revealingly, he was executed by men operating under Lysimachus.[93] Nothing more was heard of Arrhidaeus, who either heeded Antigonus' demands or was quietly dispatched. The Anatolia initiative had collapsed, and Eumenes and Olympias were left to face Antigonus and Cassander without the support they had hoped to muster from the governors in the region.

Matters were worse in Macedon. We are told that Olympias' immediate actions – the violent murder of the royals, Arrhidaeus and Adea, alongside the pogrom she launched against Cassander's family and supporters – caused a popular revulsion against her, something Eumenes may well have feared. Olympias would have justified her actions under a Macedonian law that demanded the death of all those related by blood to those deemed guilty of a crime against the crown.[94] But more than 100 of Cassander's supporters are said to have been hunted down, including his brother Nicanor; the grave of the already-deceased Iollas, implicated in Alexander's poisoning, was desecrated and his body mistreated in true Homeric style.[95] As a consequence, Olympias' ally, King Aeacides of Epirus, lost his support and was soon expelled. His daughter, Deidameia, once pledged in marriage to Alexander's son, would be later destined for Demetrius the Besieger instead.[96] The murdered Argeads, King Philip III Arrhidaeus and Queen Adea-Eurydice – son and granddaughter of the still revered Philip II – along with her previously murdered mother, Cynnane, were later honoured by Cassander, who held funeral games once he had disposed of Olympias and gained control of Macedon a year or so later.[97]

The Planned Alliance of the Innocents

In securing himself a release from Nora, Eumenes had given a masterclass in diplomatic chicanery which led to one of history's 'great reversals of fortune'. But now that the prospect of assistance from Cleitus and Arrhidaeus had evaporated, Eumenes and Olympias needed a more significant weapon that would galvanize other satraps into a coalition; a mechanism that would advance the status of supporters, while undermining satraps and generals in the service of the enemy. The two-part *Pamphlet*, with its conspiracy allegations and

Alexander's reissued will, was designed to achieve just that. Along with what were arguably Eumenes' 'self-issued' 'letters of marque and reprisal' that manoeuvred Polyperchon into the frame of war in Asia, it was a production only Eumenes and Olympias between them could pull off. If there was anyone in the empire who would have known the original uncorrupted content of Alexander's will – and, moreover, who additionally bore long-term grudges against the family of Antipater – it was the former king's secretary and the dead king's mother.

When developing the shape of the *Pamphlet* and its regicidal finger-pointing, Eumenes and Olympias simply played on several well-known facts: Alexander's planned retirement of Antipater in favour of Craterus, the regent's subsequent (alleged) summoning to Babylon (both moves could be interpreted as a suspicion of treason), the subsequent arrival of Cassander in his place, the previous execution of Alexander Lyncestis (Antipater's son-in-law) and that well-documented bitterness between the regent and the queen mother. All this was neatly enveloped in the rising tensions of the court in Babylon. One of Plutarch's sources claimed Alexander physically and verbally assaulted the newly arrived Cassander, contemptuous of his behaviour and his double-sided arguments. Plutarch additionally stated, in a seeming contradiction, that the king *was* now fearful of the threat posed by the presence of the regent's sons.[98]

Preceding the will in the *Pamphlet* was a list of those at Medius' banquet at which Alexander was professedly poisoned; the enemies were being sighted in the coalition crosshairs by implication in the crime.[99] We may recall that the *Pamphlet* also claimed: 'No one was unaware of what was afoot, with the exception of Eumenes, Perdiccas, Ptolemy, Lysimachus, Asander and Holcias.' The coalition of 'friends' being solicited by Eumenes and Olympias was clear.

The names of this select few are more valuable to us than the identities of the guilty, for they represent a narrower focus of intent that might point to the *Pamphlet*'s dating. Moreover, these names are less corrupted. The first two, Eumenes and Perdiccas, need no explanation as a product of the royal secretary's hands. Rather overtly, the *Pamphlet* beckoned Ptolemy and Lysimachus into the new order by stating they both were present at the drafting and the first private reading of the will. Ptolemy had the vast resources of a veteran-strewn Egypt, while Lysimachus could control the Hellespont and the route through Thrace to Macedon.

The *Pamphlet* will went on to grant them (or rather 'bribe' their support with) Argead wives: for Ptolemy it was Alexander's full-sister Cleopatra, with his half-sister Thessalonice going to Lysimachus.[100] Most likely in her mid-twenties when Alexander died, Thessalonice was the daughter of the Thessalian Nicesipolis of Pherae, one of Philip II's early brides who died soon after giving birth. Remarkably (in light of the court hostility and threat from other wives) Nicesipolis and Olympias seem to have struck up a lasting friendship.[101] Now a ward of Olympias, Thessalonice's Argead blood (and the Thessalian noble line) explains her continued spinsterhood in the campaign years, for she would have been a threat if powerfully wedded. But in these dangerous times, Olympias and Eumenes had good reason to use her to galvanize support. Furthermore, these will pairings were clearly designed to undermine the marriages that Antipater had contrived when proffering his own daughters to the most powerful generals.

By implication, the current plight of Cleopatra was being highlighted if she was now under 'house arrest' in an Antigonus-controlled Sardis. One modern historian has suggested that Cleopatra had come to an understanding with Antigonus: she would enter no foreign marriage negotiations as long as he and his son Demetrius did not themselves forcefully wed her.[102] Her attempt to unite with Perdiccas on Eumenes' urging suggests that it was certainly within Eumenes' power to broker a new marriage between her and Ptolemy using his influence with Olympias.[103]

If Olympias' vested interest in the *Pamphlet* is evident through its hostility to Antipater – though clearly both she and Eumenes shared that – the 'holy union' suggested by the will's opening claim that she sired Alexander with the god, if this is not later embellishment, points more firmly to her involvement. That in turn posed Alexander as a true reincarnation of Heracles, Theseus and Dionysus, each born of gods through mortal mothers. Alexander appears to have returned the favour in the hope for a 'consecration to immortality' for his mother.[104] Callisthenes had apparently claimed Olympias was already spreading 'lies' about Alexander's semi-divine status when the historian-philosopher was compiling his book on campaign.[105] Her rejection of Philip for a god was no doubt energized by her son's visit to the oracle of Zeus-Ammon at Siwa in Egypt (if not vice versa), where the propaganda for his own divinity was born. The search for that status was, in fact, inevitable and overdue: Lesbos had erected altars to his father, now Philippic Zeus, some years before.[106]

Furthermore, Plutarch recorded the tradition that Philip had been warned by the Delphic oracle to hold Zeus-Ammon (the god's Hellenized form) in special reverence, and that further, there was a tradition that Philip had lost his eye as punishment for spying upon Olympias' Orphic rituals. This story was bound up with Philip's dream in which he put a seal upon Olympias' womb with a lion device, where she herself dreamed a thunderbolt fell upon her as Alexander was conceived. That was no doubt inspired by Euripides' play *Bacchae*, written at the Pellan court some eighty years before, which claimed the same occurred at the birth of Dionysus. Philip's fate further recalls the punishment of the maenads on Pentheus for banning the worship of Dionysus.[107] No doubt divine titbits of this nature circulated most Hellenistic courts. But Ammon's attachment to the *Pamphlet* will was really something of a *fait accompli*. Of course, the well-documented commemoratives to Alexander's mortal father, rejected as part of the 'last plans' at Babylon, could not be fully dispensed with if a reissued will was to appear genuine.

Could Olympias have authored the *Pamphlet* independently? Its structure certainly did require her support to fully realize the plans it was ushering in, and she would have added her designs to its more malevolent intent; she surely became an aggressive distributor of copies. The proposal that it was a Pella-sanctioned document was probably part of its expected efficacy, and because of that its origins would have been fairly obvious at the time. But the *Pamphlet* needed a military focus and an execution of martial policy that only Eumenes could provide. In that respect, some calls for help were obvious steps to take, but the complex web of military intrigues needed the experience that only the campaigning Cardian and his satrapal intimacy could provide. The *Pamphlet*'s failure to feature Polyperchon, already bettered in Pella by Adea-Eurydice, reminds us that the new regent was neither the architect of nor party to its design.[108]

Also on the 'innocent's' list is Asander, and the *Pamphlet* will confirmed his inheritance of Caria. Named satrap of the region at Babylon, he received the Antipater–Craterus–Antigonus alliance that returned to Asia in 321/320 BC 'as a friend', though resistance was probably futile in the face of such a dominant force.[109] Asander's later confrontation with Perdiccas' brother Alcetas and Attalus, in which he came off worse, suggests he might have been a reluctant Antigonid ally from the outset. This is supported by his defection to Ptolemy in 315 BC.[110] Eumenes sensed Asander could be turned, and he was right, though his defection came too late. But we know little about his activity in the five or six years after Triparadeisus. He may well have withdrawn active support for Antigonus long before the final battle at Gabiene, as the war with Eumenes in the final two years was conducted far to the east of his own satrapy. The gifts of 150 talents of silver to Cnidus and Miletus provided by the will ought to be mentioned, as both cities resided in Caria. This looks like a promissory war chest with which Asander would conduct naval operations and incursions into Phrygia, or at least a bribe for neutrality.[111]

The final guest salvaged from guilt alongside Perdiccas, Asander, Ptolemy and Lysimachus was Holcias, whose fate must have been linked in some strategic way to the author's. His prominence in the *Pamphlet* reads:

> Over all the Illyrians, I appoint Holcias as governor and I award him a detachment of 500 requisitioned horses and 3,000 talents of silver coin, which he is to use for the making of statues of Alexander, Ammon, Athena, Heracles, Olympias and my father Philip. These he is to set up in the shrine of Olympia.[112]

Holcias commanded 3,000 'heavy' Macedonian infantry (Polyaenus termed them 'hoplites', so possibly hypaspists, shield-bearers equipped with the smaller, lighter shield – an *aspis* – thus more mobile infantrymen), and having defected from the ranks of Antigonus, he set about ravaging the Taurus Mountains bordering Lycaonia and Phrygia. That action in autumn 319 BC coincided with Eumenes' incarceration at Nora, which, recalling Plutarch's geographical description, must once again have been located nearby.[113]

Holcias' brigade of renegades was potentially among the captives rounded up by Antigonus after battle at Orcynia and included in those who pledged their loyalty to their captor in the absence of immediate options. In which case, their 'opportunistic defection' becomes more readily explainable. Alternatively, they may have been with the Macedonian 'friends' and soldiers Eumenes disbanded before entering the fortress, which does not discount their capture immediately after. Plutarch described the start of the siege as follows: 'As he wandered about and sought to elude his enemies, Eumenes persuaded most of his soldiers to leave him.'[114]

Now at large once again, and defying Antigonus' calls for their surrender, Holcias and his men may have been lingering in the vicinity, waiting for either an opportune moment to storm the Nora palisade (in spring) or for Eumenes to negotiate his own freedom in the meantime. Other allies had remained in the region, as Diodorus' coverage of Eumenes' release some months on confirmed: 'Thus unexpectedly saved after a considerable time, he stayed for the present in Cappadocia, where he gathered together his former friends and those who had once served under him and were now wandering about the country.'[115] Holcias may even have attempted to get word to the Perdiccan faction under Alcetas, who was himself either under siege at Cretopolis or meeting a bloody end at Termessus, where his tomb has now been identified.[116]

Antigonus hesitated to kill Holcias and his brigade when they were eventually lured out of the mountains and captured through a deception. He, along with two other 'leaders of the revolt', agreed to a forced repatriation to Macedon and to being chaperoned home by Leonidas, who, curiously, had been the commander of the 3,000-strong 'disciplinary unit' (known as the *ataktoi*) that Alexander had formed from unruly soldiers after Parmenio's execution when fearing an uprising in his ranks. Yet this seems a rather quixotic amnesty from Antigonus, and more so when we consider the eventual fate of the Silver Shields and their commanders who were executed at Gabiene.[117] Either Antigonus had his own plans for Holcias and his brigade back in Macedon, or they were freed as part of the bargaining between Eumenes and him at Nora, suggesting machinations yet to unfold.[118] It is not inconceivable that Antigonus envisaged Holcias and his men operating under Eumenes, who would then become his advocate with the royals at Pella.

From the perspective of the pamphleteers, however, once Holcias was back in Macedon, he could give Olympias the personal army she had begged Eumenes to provide. The actual fate of he and his men is unknown; she may even have employed them against the family of Cassander in her well-attested pogrom. In the *Pamphlet*, the will grant to Holcias included control of Illyria, and an additional 500 horses and 3,000 talents of silver, which was ostensibly a donation for the construction of statues, but presumably, like Asander's purse, actually a campaign fund for waging war.

But why place Holcias in Illyria? Well, the location was strategically opportune. The region did not encroach upon Lysimachus' satrapal grant or upon Macedon itself, and yet it provided a 'local' staging point for operations against Pella. Holcias' authority may have been specifically aimed at suppressing any trouble in the region that could be stirred up by Adea-Eurydice with her Illyrian roots and claims that stretched back to King Bardylis.[119] If Eumenes and Olympias planned to remove Philip III Arrhidaeus and his queen in favour of Alexander IV, they might have expected the Illyrian regime to mount a new challenge to the throne, as they had done for generations when Macedon was in turmoil. This could now be mitigated, and Illyrian support even harnessed; Holcias' own standing and legitimacy was being boosted by the will's pairing of his sister, Cleodice, to the now-dead but useful Leonnatus, the prominent Royal Bodyguard linked to the Lycestian royal house.[120]

Completing the rundown of those favourably dealt with by the *Pamphlet*, we have Craterus, the 'overseer of the whole Kingdom of Macedon', for the will granted him a wife of royal blood, suggesting posthumous respect. As he was not at Babylon when Alexander died, he did not need to be added to the list of conspiratorial 'innocents'. Eumenes may have genuinely offered to reconcile Perdiccas and Craterus before settling affairs in battle, and he certainly knew how important Craterus was to the veterans. As Plutarch put it, the death of 'Craterus ... of all the successors of Alexander, was most regretted by the Macedonians'.[121] He had after all rivalled the first chiliarch in importance to Alexander, whom Diodorus said had 'most affection for Hephaestion, most respect for Craterus'. His son of the same name went on to support his half-brother, Antigonus II Gonatas, and somewhat ironically, he may have later befriended Hieronymus at Gonatas' court.[122]

But it was not posthumous respect that was being displayed in the *Pamphlet*, and neither was Eumenes' post-battle contrition at Craterus' death anything more than contrived 'suffering togetherness', to defray immediate Macedonian anger. Eumenes cast the blame on Neoptolemus, who precipitated the clash, and he ensured Craterus' body was cremated, with his bones returned to his widow, Phila, Antipater's influential daughter.[123]

Alexander's original will most likely would have paired Craterus, the new regent-to-be, with an Argead woman, though it's questionable whether it was the choice proposed in the *Pamphlet*: Cynnane. But this was now a safe pairing to broadcast without repercussions, since both of them were dead. The match cast a shadow on both Antipater's extended regency and his offering Phila to Craterus, as it implied Cynnane had been displaced by the regent and rejected by Craterus too. The match would, nevertheless, provide an explanation for Cynnane's crossing to Asia with her daughter, for Craterus was then still based in Cilicia; if she *had* already been rejected, better prospects for their survival lay in Asia too in the form of the newly crowned King Philip III Arrhidaeus.[124] The *Pamphlet*'s promotion of Cynnane additionally damned her killer, Alcetas, for he had all but abandoned Eumenes when refusing to work under him at Celaenae.[125]

Craterus' appointment by Alexander to the regency of Macedon was clearly too well attested to doctor in the new *Pamphlet* will, but Eumenes may have found a subtler way to cast suspicion on the popular general he had recently killed in battle. For the *Pamphlet* claimed that the central plotters against Alexander's life, Cassander and his brother Iollas, had planned to meet up in Cilicia once the king was dead, and this was exactly where Craterus was still encamped with his 10,000 veterans. That smacked of complicity and even called into question the support Antipater had enjoyed from Polyperchon, for he too was in Cilicia with Craterus, as were the prominent commanders Polydamas (possibly a Thessalian noble and hence a close acquaintance of the 'guilty' Medius of Larissa), Gorgias and Antigenes, who might be openly accused if they failed to unite with Eumenes.[126]

The *Pamphlet* testament allocated Cilicia to a Nicanor. Eumenes must have been attempting to seduce him into the coalition; he was plausibly the officer who was allocated Cappadocia at Triparadeisus. Sensing he too could be turned (he was obviously not at Medius' banquet or he would have been named 'innocent'), Eumenes respectfully shunted him sideways to make way for his own reinstatement in the previously unconquered satrapy. The flattery didn't work. Nicanor appears to have served Antigonus well, possibly receiving Eumenes' final surrender at Gabiene, though a mutual respect does seem to have been in place: he is said to have allowed Eumenes his request to speak to his men before incarceration.[127] Nicanor may even have been subsequently elevated to pan-regional governor (*strategos*) of Media and the upper satrapies after Peithon's execution in 315 BC, though a dozen Nicanors are identified with Alexander's campaign.[128] Another credible alternative, in the context of the *Pamphlet*'s courting of useful allies, is Nicanor, the court friend (*philos*) of Ptolemy who captured Coele-Syria from Laomedon and then garrisoned Phoenicia. An allied presence in Cilicia would give the coalition powerful naval bases and wider shipbuilding capability.[129]

Before I similarly dissect the *Pamphlet*'s guilty list, Eumenes' release from Nora raises another fundamental question: could Antigonus the One-Eyed – who 'had in mind to go through Asia, remove the existing satraps, and reorganise the positions of command in favour of his friends' – have been involved in the *Pamphlet*'s birth, for much of its directed malice matched his aims?[130] Antigonus did go on to remove Peithon and Peucestas before targeting Seleucus, and he may well have agreed to wipe out the house of Antipater had events taken a different path; in fact, he did try, through Polyperchon, in a post-315 BC realignment. Ptolemy and Lysimachus were initially in league with Antigonus. So, the answer to involvement is 'yes', but not to the *Pamphlet* in the final format we see it, for too many of his friends (Nearchus, Medius and Menander, for example) were implicated in the treason. If it had been drafted independently, then Eumenes and Perdiccas would have fallen on the wrong side of conspiracy. But an 'early model' of the *Pamphlet* (like an early model of the amended oath) may well have been discussed as part of Eumenes' release mechanism at Nora, and had he chosen to join Antigonus then, the *Pamphlet*'s overall aims may well have become more fully realised.

If one of the central aims of the *Pamphlet* was to bring down Antigonus, why didn't Eumenes and Olympias implicate him in conspiratorial guilt? Simply put, it would not have been credible; Antigonus had not been at Babylon and neither had he been associated with the other accused high-ranking court friends in many years. Moreover, Antipater and Cassander maintained what appears to be a well-documented distrust towards Antigonus, who was, therefore, a hardly viable partner in their plot to murder the king.[131] Perhaps Eumenes was using the *Pamphlet* – potentially threatening to Antigonus through his associations but with no outright accusations yet made – to bring him to the bargaining table, and this time not as his 'better', but as an 'equal'.

The Damnation of the Guilty

The following, with conspicuous corruptions in place, remains the clearest list of those attending Medius' fatal banquet:

> Now, so not to appear evasive, I shall name those who were there, unlike Onesicritus who, in his desire to avoid controversy, refrained from telling. There was Perdiccas, Medius, Leonnatus, erat teon, Meleager, theoclus, Asander, Philip, Nearchus, Stasanor, Heracleides the Thracian, polydorus, Holcias, Menander … (Peithon, Peucestas, Ptolemy, Lysimachus … Europius, Ariston of Pharsalus, Philip the engineer, Philotas).[132]

We should first address the oft-cited reference to Onesicritus and his reported fear of retribution in the *Metz Epitome* version of the plot to kill Alexander (T1), whose text, however, has obviously suffered through time. Once again, we cannot be sure that the reference to Onesicritus is original content, though the same sentiment can be found in the Vulgate texts and so is potentially traceable back to Cleitarchus. That does suggest it could be *Pamphlet*-originating, as he templated the Vulgate conspiracy detail.[133] It is widely held that Onesicritus published a book covering major aspects of the campaign before the other eyewitness sources, and earlier than Nearchus, who, it seems, found fault with Onesicritus' claims on naval chains of command and who was subordinate to the other.[134] Not associated with the military strife of the early Successor Wars (that we know of), Onesicritus could have published an account – which touched upon Alexander's death (he may, or may not, have mentioned nameless rumours of foul play) – before the *Pamphlet* was released, a necessary conclusion if the extract with allegations of his fear is to be taken at face value.

The opening lines of this *Metz Epitome* allegation were written by someone who could only have been renowned as an eyewitness to events at Babylon. Here Eumenes may well have usefully contrived, and then attached, a fearful silence to the already famous court philosopher, in order to authenticate the *Pamphlet* allegations with a truly cynical and brilliant twist. This brings us to the men Onesicritus supposedly declined to name, and who were rather creatively represented (in what was most likely later embellishment) as the living parts of the gruesome creature brought to Alexander.[135]

The first of those named as guilty was Medius, who became a central cog in the *Pamphlet*'s wheel of misfortune when he was cited as the complicit organizer of Alexander's final banquet. He and Aristonus had initially operated under Perdiccas when tasked with the invasion of Cyprus.[136] Their quick defeat by Antigonus may perhaps have been 'easy capitulation', for they came to immediate terms; Aristonus retired to Macedon (though his allegiance to the 'royal cause' remained intact) and Medius joined Antigonus on the spot or sometime soon after.[137] Arrian believed that Iollas, the bearer of the poisoned cup, was Medius' younger lover (his *eromenos*). If there was any truth in the claim, then Medius' role in the treason was easily fabricated and probably an inevitable association for the pamphleteers to make.[138]

The prominent Leonnatus was next heaped on the guilty pyre, and it is not difficult to imagine why. Something resolved him to a course of action that was painted by Plutarch as underhanded: the abandoning of Eumenes in Anatolia as part of a covert bid to claim Cleopatra's hand and take the throne of Macedon. Olympias was no doubt proffering her daughter to powerful men to 'spike Antipater's dynastic guns', and in Plutarch's version the offer did originate with Cleopatra, who may then have enrolled Eumenes in the cause.[139]

Leonnatus did attempt to lure Eumenes into the scheme and promised to reconcile him with Hecataeus, the Cardian tyrant who was probably installed by Philip II when Alexander was a youth. The likelihood of Eumenes accepting the offer of reconciliation was slim, as 'hereditary distrust and political differences' existed, and Eumenes had repeatedly asked Alexander to remove Hecataeus.[140]

Although Leonnatus had travelled to Phrygia to meet Eumenes, Nepos claimed he attempted to kill the uncooperative Cardian, who immediately decamped in the night with 300 cavalry, 200 armed camp followers and the enormous sum of 5,000 talents, which, we assume, had been provided to Eumenes (from Cyinda?) by Perdiccas for the planned conquest of Cappadocia; that sum must have been a tempting target.[141] Withdrawing from the 'capricious man' of 'rash impulses', Eumenes reported Leonnatus' intentions to the chiliarch, gaining great influence with Perdiccas in the process. Diodorus' account was more compressed: Leonnatus' departure was in response to Antipater's request for assistance in the Lamian War, but this nevertheless defied Perdiccas' standing orders, that he assist Eumenes. Perdiccas, in fact, had everything to gain from seeing Antipater's regime defeated by the Greeks.

Moreover, Leonnatus had been promised another of Antipater's daughters, no doubt in return for that help. His early death in the marshes of Thessaly, however, was an outcome that apparently made Antipater 'rejoice', as it not only disabled Leonnatus' possible union with Cleopatra, but also saved the regent a useful daughter. All this made the deceased Leonnatus an easy target for Eumenes in the *Pamphlet*, and it opened up his satrapies (I argue that he inherited a region far greater than Hellespontine Phrygia) for coalition assimilation.[142]

Next on the guilty list is the vocal Meleager, the most important infantry officer at Babylon (and, briefly, Perdiccas' senior officer – *hyparchos*), who was then executed for insurrection. Long dead, Meleager could be safely incriminated by the *Pamphlet* to good effect. The will proposed he was the inheritor of Coele-Syria, rather than Laomedon of Mytilene, though this *Pamphlet* appointment was not philanthropy at work. Soon after Laomedon's reconfirmation to the region at Triparadeisus (surviving texts have Laomedon originally appointed at Babylon), Ptolemy had tried to buy him out of the province.[143] Ptolemy knew the strategic value of fortifying the route to Egypt, whose borders had been recently tested by Perdiccas' invasion. Laomedon, a high-ranking friend at the Pellan court and by now fluent in Persian, declined, and Ptolemy sent his general, Nicanor (referred to above), to commence military operations which resulted in his capture. Laomedon managed to bribe his guards and escape to join Alcetas and the Perdiccan remnants in Caria.[144] They were finally cornered at Cretopolis and captured after fierce resistance. Laomedon may well have perished there, for he was never mentioned again.

Branding the rebellious Meleager guilty, and yet posing him as the original satrap of Coele-Syria, justified both his execution by Perdiccas and Ptolemy's annexation of the region, for it emphasized that Laomedon had not been the king's choice. The olive branch being proffered to Ptolemy was more of an olive bough, for it is difficult to imagine that Meleager would have challenged Perdiccas at Babylon 'on behalf of the passed-over infantryman' had he genuinely inherited the governorship of the influential region.

The prominent Menander, based in Lydia, was named with the guilty. Menander's long and well-attested tenure of the province (since 331 BC) was dismantled when Perdiccas provided Cleopatra with a role in its governance at Sardis. He was sidelined again by Antipater at Triparadeisus, replaced by White Cleitus. As a result, the orphaned Menander became a useful Antigonid tool, and we might imagine with the promise of reinstatement.[145] He had been hot on Eumenes' heels in his flight from Nora to Cilicia, and the Orcynian baggage-train charade at Menander's expense had no doubt added impetus to the chase. Though referred to as an 'old friend' of Eumenes by Plutarch (which may again simply mean 'former colleague'), Menander's early support for Antigonus and his snitching on the plan to see Perdiccas wed to Cleopatra sealed his guilty-list fate.[146] With no prospect of turning him, Eumenes branded Menander a traitor and may also have scratched any reference to Lydia from the will, as the region does not appear in the extant will texts. Menander was never mentioned in action again, even though Lydian troops did feature in later battles. His more enduring legacy was a painting by the famed artist Apelles.[147]

Nearchus also suffered at the hands of the pamphleteers. He was sufficiently distinguished by his naval voyage and his latter-day friendship with Alexander to have featured prominently in empire governance, so it is unlikely he would have been bypassed in Alexander's original will.[148] Although the campaign governors were predominantly Macedonian, a few select Greeks had been chosen as satraps, though, notably, none of them originated from the mainland: Laomedon came from Mytilene on Lesbos, and Stasander along with Stasanor were both Cypriots by birth. Nearchus, born on Crete – though his later residence at Amphipolis was now situated in an expanded Macedon – had been appointed to Lycia and Pamphylia in the early campaign. Lycia would have been his most obvious satrapal inheritance, for it would explain his mission there in 319/318 BC to recover Telmessus, its largest city (modern Fethiye), though Polyaenus provided no date to this particular action.[149] Nearchus may additionally have been instrumental in establishing Cretopolis, the Cretan city in the strategic Telmessus passes linking Phrygia, Lycaonia and Cappadocia.[150]

What *is* beyond conjecture is his loyalty to Antigonus and his son Demetrius in campaigns, which suggest he was steadfastly hostile to Ptolemy; perhaps this stemmed from their alleged conflicting interests in the Assembly at Babylon.[151] Nearchus fell on the *Pamphlet*'s guilty list and was targeted for removal, and any satrapal inheritance was scrubbed from history too.

Stasanor of Soli was implicated in the conspiracy as part of Eumenes' attack on Peithon, under whose mandate I propose the upper satrapies fell, and so

182   The Last Will and Testament of Alexander the Great

Peithon's under-governors were fair game too. There does, however, seem to have been some confusion between Stasanor and his neighbour, Stasander. Both were Greek Cypriots who (confusingly or mistakenly) exchanged the satrapies granted them at Babylon and Triparadeisus. Though Stasander sent troops and supported Eumenes in person at Paraetacene, Stasanor's presence was not mentioned at all.[152] Antigonus allowed Stasanor to retain Bactria-Sogdia after Eumenes' death, though Diodorus suggested that was simply due to the region's remoteness.

That acquiescence by Antigonus seems unlikely if the satrap had openly opposed him from what was a region renowned for effective fighters. From there Spitamenes had, for example, been bitterly opposed to Alexander to the end, rejecting honourable defeat and causing significant trouble for the Macedonian forces. Diodorus reported that over 120,000 Sogdians were killed in three successive revolts; this was a dangerous part of the empire unless its satrap was benign, and Antigonus certainly had generals capable of removing Stasanor if a threat, once Eumenes' forces had been assimilated.[153] Stasanor's good conduct towards the inhabitants of his region was clearly stated, correlating with his successful governance under Alexander, and his distant neutrality seems to have allayed any fears Antigonus might have harboured.[154]

The most likely identification for the next plotter, Philotas (of the many so-named men associated with the campaign), is the Babylon-nominated satrap of Cilicia. Perdiccas had removed him in 320/321 BC due to his well-attested friendship with Craterus, and had then installed Philoxenus, his own man. That eviction would have sat uncomfortably with Antigenes, commander of the Silver Shields, and with the other remaining veterans whom Perdiccas had enrolled into the royal army on the way to attacking Egypt. Philotas was not reinstated at Triparadeisus (possibly due to his staunch support for the 'expansionist' Antigonus), where the apparently 'undistinguished' and no doubt compliant Philoxenus was reconfirmed to the province. Philotas was enrolled into Antigonus' ranks by 318 BC, probably due to his experience in the region, and once again with the likely prospect of reinstatement. Philotas attempted to lure the Silver Shields from Eumenes in Cilicia, which may well have sealed his fate in the *Pamphlet*.[155]

We are on softer ground with the identifications of the less prominent banqueters because we are dealing with textual corruptions alongside a dearth of career information, so focusing on them too sharply is problematic. But some names appear historical and broad deductions may be made.

If Polydorus can be identified as the physician from Teos, then it appears he was at some point a court guest of Antipater and thus was likely sympathetic (at that stage) to the Cassander-backing Antigonus. If this is a corruption of 'Polydamas', then he was possibly the prominent Thessalian court friend cited as being with Craterus in Cilicia.[156] As for Ariston, his Pharsalian origins were stated, and that makes him Thessalian with roots that might link him to

Medius of Larissa as well. If it was the same Ariston who eventually delivered Craterus' remains to Antipater's daughter Phila, then his allegiance may well have resided with the opposing faction.[157]

Two Philips (possibly an engineer and a physician) are referred to in corrupted texts. One obvious identification is the brother of Cassander and Iollas, thus he was another of the royal pages and central to the plot, a role that was supported by his mention in Justin's account.[158] The other Philip is potentially the satrap of Parthia who was later killed by Peithon, but then assumed by the pamphleteers to be under his sway as part of his upper satrapy governance. The origins of a 'Philip the physician' might have come about on the back of earlier allegations of poisoning linked to Alexander's trusted doctor. Little save conjecture is known of Heracleides the Thracian; he may even have operated in Greece under the command of Cassander, and that could point to his being added to the list by Olympias.[159]

Possible *Pamphlet* Publication Dates

A key reference in dating the *Pamphlet*'s emergence is Plutarch's claim that it was some five years after Alexander's death that the conspiracy allegations first hit Greece (T10).[160] Although this is a less than clinical chronological guide, Eumenes' presence in Cilicia throughout the winter of 318 BC becomes an attractive publication period when he was evidently corresponding with Olympias.

At this point, Seleucus' potential role in the emerging coalition needs explanation, because at first glance he does not appear in the list of Babylon banqueters. Diodorus never named him as one of Perdiccas' assassins in Egypt, nor is he amongst those Ptolemy felt indebted to after the event – the men then elevated to guardians of the kings.[161] In which case, we might suppose Eumenes had no cause to incriminate him; this would explain why he could have credibly solicited Seleucus' support when wintering in Babylonia in 317 BC, although Peithon's presence would have undermined the negotiations.[162]

Nepos' account, on the other hand, did cite Seleucus as present in Egypt, and in the ϒ recension of the *Romance* Seleucus does appear at Medius' party, though this text is derived from a far later (post-seventh-century) embellished manuscript. His attendance may also be supported by an otherwise unattested 'Europius' in the Armenian version of the *Romance*, as this could be a reference to Seleucus' ethnic, for he was most likely born in Europus near the Axius River in Macedon.[163] If Eumenes was implicating Seleucus in Alexander's death, a Cilicia-based early *Pamphlet* release date is unsupportable, because we cannot imagine Eumenes making overtures to him in 317 BC if the accusations were already out.

What confounds historians is the observation that the *Pamphlet* will bestowed Babylonia on Seleucus, which would suggest another olive branch was being proffered by the pamphelteers, because the mainstream texts (which I propose are Hieronymus-derived) claim Seleucus was only granted the province at Triparadeisus, some three years on, either for his part in Perdiccas' execution or for his defending Antipater against the angry mob being whipped up by Eurydice; that was the first of two 'mutinies' over back-pay Antipater would see before re-crossing the Hellespont.[164] Before that, ambiguously worded texts suggest Seleucus was simply Perdiccas' second-in-command – as hipparch of the Companion Cavalry – with absolutely no territory to govern.

One scholar has logically argued that the *Pamphlet* must therefore have a creation date after May 320 BC (thus Triparadeisus) for its author to have witnessed Seleucus' appointment to Babylon. To the contrary, I argue that Babylonia was part of Seleucus' original and genuine will-sanctioned pan-provincial governorship, and not a coalition 'gift', in which case such a prominent post could hardly be hidden by the architects of the *Pamphlet* now that Seleucus was back there governing.

Recalling Plutarch's chronology which suggested accusations made in the *Pamphlet* hit Greece five years after Alexander's death, we must consider how early Olympias could have 'glutted her rage with atrocities' from years of pent-up Antipatrid hatred,[165] because that was supposed to coincide: the *Pamphlet*'s accusation would vindicate Olympias' revenge killings, and no doubt the murders were supposed to imply that the *Pamphlet* content was genuine.[166]

This could have only taken place once Olympias had re-established herself in Pella after defeating and executing Eurydice and Philip III Arrhidaeus; so October 317 BC or later, if we adhere to Diodorus' statement on the length of the king's reign.[167] Release of the *Pamphlet* from Cilicia in late 318 BC is perhaps still supportable, as news took time to travel, but it appears to be dangerously early, that is unless Olympias *did* imprudently (and so against Eumenes' advice) spread allegations of regicide when she was still in Epirus.[168] But that would have been an unwise move, broadcasting her intent. Perhaps we should also ponder whether it was exactly these allegations that swayed the Cassander-backed army of Eurydice to Olympias' cause when she finally marched on Pella.

A more viable date for the *Pamphlet*'s release would be when, or shortly before, Eumenes arrived in Persepolis and attempted to wrest command of the eastern coalition from Peucestas in the winter of 317 BC, because by then Seleucus and Peithon had already united against him, and their *Pamphlet* incrimination (assuming Seleucus' name *was* present on the guilty list) would have logically followed.[169] Moreover, it was here that Eumenes' faked letter from Orontes 'arrived', and here that Eumenes brought false charges against Sibyrtius. Had the Persian satraps not already combined under Peucestas, and if they had not outnumbered Eumenes' own men, Eumenes may well have terminated the prominent Persian-speaking former Bodyguard right there.

This later release date would mean that Eumenes was still hoping Ptolemy and Lysimachus might join his cause; they had been meddlesome to his plans, but no open hostilities had taken place. Eumenes' attempt to include them in an anti-Antigonus coalition was not altogether unrealistic considering Antigonus' rising power, for he was by then a formidable threat to *any* Asian satrap. Some two years on, Ptolemy was indeed assisting Seleucus in his bid to oust Antigonus from Babylonia, for with Eumenes' death came the unsuccessful demands from Ptolemy, Lysimachus and Cassander for a share of Anatolia (the return of Babylon was also required for Seleucus) and, curiously, Syria (where I propose Perdiccas was based), along with the accumulated treasure seized in the war.[170]

If there still exist various other scenarios that suit the *Pamphlet*'s release, we do now at least have a broad date *after* which it must have emerged: Eumenes' departure from Nora in spring 318 BC, with a more obvious terminus *before* it must have appeared established by his death in early 315 BC, or at Olympias' execution later the same year.

The Complex Art of the *Pamphlet*

The *Pamphlet* fired warning shots across the bows of the remaining satraps and their prominent supporting officers, whose guilt in Alexander's death, if not specifically mentioned, could be brought into question by association: those in Cilicia with Craterus, for example. That was Eumenes' own silent siege craft, a clever intrigue that left doors open for future alliances, but with safety catches on.

If Olympias' hatred for her opponents is palpable, we should not underestimate Eumenes' own hunger for revenge, having been placed on a proscription list with fifty Perdiccan supporters. Now, through the shockwave of the *Pamphlet*, Eumenes and Olympias were effectively returning the compliment with its widespread accusations of treason.

The *Pamphlet* was clearly a one-time bid for a huge prize: the lion's share of Asia after Antigonus' fall, and complete control of Macedon if Cassander could be silenced. But its virulence would mean a death sentence for both of its architects should the gambit fail, so Eumenes and Olympias packed it with layers of purpose. The guilty and the innocent, and those wedded to Argead royalty, were just the more prominent front lines of deeper, subtler ranks. The *Pamphlet* was built on complex political substrates lying beneath, some probably still eluding us today. Others are more obvious, and they fit their joint predicament. The first was Perdiccas' position of authority in the will:

> As for the areas lying between the boundaries of Babylonia and Bactria, the satraps should retain what they variously govern, and as

commander-in-chief over them, I appoint Perdiccas, on whom I also bestow as a wife Rhoxane.[171]

From his reading of Hieronymus, Arrian interpreted that the outcome at Babylon entrusted Perdiccas with the 'care of the whole empire' in his capacity as the foremost of Alexander's Royal Bodyguards, acting chiliarch and the recipient of his ring.[172] But the compression of power suggested above sees him overseeing only what I propose were the regions inherited by Seleucus and Peithon (thus Babylonia east through Bactria), the most prominent of his murderers, if Nepos was correct.[173] And this *Pamphlet* ploy was to suggest a clear motive for his assassination in Egypt: they wished to rid themselves of Perdiccas' overarching authority of their regions.

A curious gift in the testament is 'Syria as far as the so-called Mesopotamian Line', for this went to a Peithon, clearly not the hostile son of Crateuas who held the upper satrapies. If this referred to the prominent Peithon son of Agenor, who governed regions bordering on (and in) India on campaign and certainly until 320 BC, then the pamphleteer had anticipated his return to Syria, which did take place in 314/313 BC.[174] Peithon's whereabouts from Triparadeisus in 320 BC to 315 BC, when he was installed by Antigonus in Babylonia once Seleucus fled to Ptolemy in Egypt, remain unknown. If this is indeed our man, he too was being courted away from the one-eyed general.

The only other so-named candidate would be Peithon son of Antigenes, whose importance is attested by the reference to his patronym.[175] If the 'Antigenes' referred to was the commander of the Silver Shields, Eumenes was granting his most important soldier honours and estates through his son; Antigenes himself now governed Susiane (though his service under Eumenes took him away from the province).[176] Events made it clear that Eumenes needed every coercive tool to keep the unruly Silver Shields brigade marching. Yet none of these identifications present ideal candidates.

A further possible identity – for what could have become corrupted to 'Peithon' – is Aristonus son of 'Peisaeus', though this would involve a gap in texts (a 'lacuna', and there are many, some chapters long, in the surviving sources) that lost the first name (*onoma*) and saved the patronymic, with a scribe reverting the name to the more familiar Royal Bodyguard. The loss of this type of detail must have occurred as patronyms would have been more widely employed, and they were certainly needed where first names were identical. Mistakes were often made: Arrian, for example, used varying patronyms for Leonnatus in four different passages.[177] Little is known of the campaign career of Aristonus, the seventh attested Bodyguard, apart from a reference to his trierarch role with the Hydaspes-Indus fleet, and a wound in the Mallian city. Curtius proposed he had spoken out for Perdiccas at Babylon,(T11) and we know he commanded his Cypriot invasion (the identity of the existing pro-Perdiccas governor remains unanswered), so he ought to have featured in governance in a meaningful way, either in Alexander's will or (for the adherents to the intestacy) by virtue of Perdiccas' self-interested division of empire.[178]

The relative obscurity of Aristonus in the Alexander biographies suggests his contribution to the campaign was deliberately sidelined. In Ptolemy's account that may have been due to these 'royalist' sympathies, and that stance may have influenced Cleitarchus. The unique references to him in Arrian's texts appear to come from Nearchus' *Indica*, and Aristonus is not mentioned by name (only inference) in the Susa honours list.[179] Aristonus was eventually murdered on Cassander's orders in 315 BC after a brief resurgence the previous year when Olympias was confined to Pydna and he controlled Amphipolis in her name.[180] References to him by Diodorus suggested he was popular and respected, in post-Alexander Macedon at least.[181] If 'Aristonus son of Peisaeus' was truly being referred to as the inheritor of a part of Syria in the *Pamphlet* will, it is not difficult to rationalize why. Either the pamphleteers were beckoning him out of forced retirement to operate for them in Macedon or Asia once more (in which case he cannot have been present at Medius' banquet in Babylon or he would have been cited as an 'innocent'), or Alexander's most obscure Royal Bodyguard did genuinely inherit a part of Syria (excluding the Coele-Syrian region) and the pamphleteers were conveniently returning it to him.

Bringing Rhodes into the Alliance

Strikingly prominent in the *Pamphlet* is the favourable treatment of Rhodes, both within the main will narrative and in Alexander's so-called 'Letter to the Rhodians' which preceded its bequests.[182] This letter, as we read it today in the extant will texts (T1, T2), could be the product of gradual embellishment. But to quote one scholar who focused on the issue: 'A single coherent document composed at a particular moment for a particular purpose is preferable to a composite production, growing layer by layer according to the interests of different groups at different times.'[183]

It would have benefitted Eumenes and Olympias to reach out to Rhodes, 'an aristocracy disguised as a democracy', to galvanize her naval resources to the planned alliance.[184] Rhodes was described by Diodorus as the 'best-governed city of the Greeks' and the island was strategically important: a seafaring power with a reputation for remaining politically neutral, with much of its wealth derived from tributes paid by those inclined for it to remain so. Additional income was earned from the renting out of Rhodian galleys (principally triremes) to clients lacking a fleet.[185] By now the smaller nearby islands and strategic mainland land tracts had become part of the Rhodian state. The Rhodian currency standard had eclipsed its Chian forerunner and was uniquely maintained in the face of Alexander's adoption of the Attic standard, probably due to long-standing trade and shipping contracts.[186]

It is unlikely that the dying Alexander gave complete autonomy to the major Greek islands, despite the earlier rhetoric surrounding the 'freedom of the Greeks', and if any of them in the eastern Aegean did consider themselves nominally independent, they were to soon lose their impartiality in the Successor Wars. Many examples survive of new law codes imposed by Antigonus, in particular on Kos, Chios and Lebedos, despite independent federations such as the Cycladic League of the Islanders which 'liberated' them in 313 BC.[187] Any reference to their future at Babylon appears absent from Hieronymus' satrapal rundown, and the fate of strategically important Cyprus remains vexing; the island saw little activity during Alexander's campaign and it was never formalized into the empire, though its fleet assisted with the siege of Tyre. When Ptolemy later gained possession of the island in 315 BC, he installed his brother, Menelaus, which perhaps suggests a gap in its governance still existed following the Perdiccan defeat.[188]

In contrast, the *Romance* bestowed Rhodes with authority over *all* other Greek islands (T2). If a relic of Alexander's original will, it was a sound step, for a carefully chosen Macedonian regional governor would have directed this greater Rhodian authority through the Aegean. Rhodes had already become directly answerable to Alexander and not to its ten former governors, and it had not been immune to Macedonian law, resulting in arrests in the campaign years.[189] If this is a design of the *Pamphlet*, then clearly a governor of some repute had held the island in Perdiccas' interest. Either way, Alexander's past attachment to Rhodes was being exploited by the pamphleteers.

Alexander had sported a belt of significance into battle taken from the Rhodian temple of Athena at Lindos, a relic no doubt ascribed to a suitable hero or king, for thanks to an inscription on a marble slab referred to as the *Lindian Chronicle* we know the temple was a depository of heroic significance. Heracles, Persian kings (through their generals and satraps) and the kings of Egypt had made votive offerings of weapons and armour at Rhodian shrines, and after the Battle of Gaugamela, Alexander is said to have made a gift of caltrops (iron spikes used against cavalry on a battlefield, here captured from Persians) and armour to the temple, just as he had at Troy. After all, Lindos, the daughter of Danaus (Alexander's ancestor, so the Argead PR machine claimed), was worshipped on the island that named its templed city after her.[190] The island had always been closely associated with Heracles, who visited it on his way from Egypt; Heracles' son, Tlepolemus, was the founding king of Rhodes. We also have evidence of a cult to Alexander, Heracles' alleged descendant (from similar court PR), appearing on the island after his death. An inscription titling Alexander 'Lord of Asia' was found in a Lindian temple,[191] so the Athena 'Guardian of the city' cult (Athena *Poliouchus*) might have resounded with a special significance.

The *Pamphlet* overtures to the powerful Rhodian confederation, made through the reworked will, included 300 talents of gold, forty triremes, and annual grain and wheat subsidies from Egypt and from the regions of Asia adjacent to Rhodes.[192] The island was promised its own 'freedom' with a pledge to have the garrison removed, a meaningless (yet symbolic) concession as it had already been expelled after Alexander's death, and it had more recently resisted Attalus' attempts to form a Perdiccan bridgehead there after the gathering of generals at Triparadeisus.[193]

Egypt's role in Rhodes' wellbeing was also being emphasized: through the *Pamphlet*, Eumenes bestowed Ptolemy the 'honour' of providing the island with grain, the most influential currency in the empire.[194] Rhodes *did* become Ptolemy's most faithful ally in the Aegean, with a relationship further strengthened by the enormous export, and to fund the grain subsidy the will granted Egyptian priests 2,000 talents from the public purse.[195]

As conspicuous in the reworked *Pamphlet* testament is Ptolemy's task of transporting Alexander's body to Egypt, for this justified his attack on the Perdiccan escort that was leading the bier elsewhere. A further 200 talents were to be used for the construction of the sarcophagus. The courting of Ptolemy continued; in the *Romance* text, the Rhodian letter closed with an emphasis on his role as the executor of the will.[196] It was a golden handcuff shackled on by Eumenes: now Ptolemy was not only present at the will's drafting, as were Holcias and Lysimachus, but he was now also responsible for its enactment.

Olympias was granted the right to live on Rhodes.[197] Linking Alexander's mother to residency implied a 'guardianship' of the island, and any hostile move against it could result in a legitimate military response, which rather underpins the story of the doctored oath Eumenes allegedly signed when exiting Nora, as Eumenes would have known Antigonus would court Rhodes as he lacked a significant navy.[198] With Rhodes on board, and with Ptolemy annexing Coele-Syria with the Phoenician ports, the Eastern Mediterranean seaboard would be theirs to control.[199]

Reaching out to Thebes

Another visitor to the pages of the *Pamphlet* testament is Ismenias, apparently a Theban to whom the will was entrusted for delivery to the city still in ruins.[200] An 'Ismenias' is mentioned earlier in verse in the *Romance* as the best of the Theban pipers, ordered to play his shrill instrument while the city burned.[201]

The name is demonstrably Theban in origin.[202] As for a possible historic identification, Alexander did free Thessalicus, a son of Ismenias, after capturing the Theban and Greek envoys to Darius following the Battle of Issus. Alexander's respect for Thessalicus' illustrious lineage was reportedly the reason for his release. Moreover, Pelopidas, the renowned general Philip II would have come to know well at Thebes, had been a member of the political party of Ismenias who was himself 'admired for valour' and for his ingenuity too, according to Aelian: he found a way to avoid the obsequious need for prostrating himself (*proskynesis*) when visiting the Persian Great King.[203] Could a grateful son of Ismenias have joined Alexander's entourage, or have become a well-known agent in the Boeotian city with whom a copy of the will was being entrusted?

Alexander is said to have regretted his destruction of Thebes, when children 'wailed piteously the names of their mothers', though Arrian gave his best shot at damning the city's past actions supporting Persia in the king's defence: he then claimed its Greek enemies inflicted more damage than the Macedonians in the attack.[204] Alexander apparently feared the wrath of Dionysus (whose favourite city was Thebes – despite Euripides' portrayal of his hostility towards it), though this story might have emanated from Ephippus, who claimed the god's anger was behind Alexander's death. The Theban ancestral oracle had nevertheless cryptically declared that 'the woven web is bane to one, to one a boon' before Alexander took the city.[205] Heracles himself was born there in legend, and so to hedge his bets on oracular fate, a donation of funds for the reconstruction of the ancient city (including the aforementioned temple) is not insupportable as one of Alexander's testament 'last wishes'.[206] The demand would have doubtless been cancelled by Perdiccas at Babylon, and surely with little objection.

But restoration of the city by the *Pamphlet* architects is also credible, as securing support of a renewed Boeotian confederacy headed by Thebes would turn central Greece against Cassander. Cassander knew it himself, and he embarked upon his own Theban rebuilding programme after the death of Eumenes. Many cities in Greece, Sicily and Italy pledged their support and 'played a part' in the city's rebuilding, despite Antigonus' objection, for he demanded it be reversed in a proclamation from Tyre.[207]

The Olive Branch to Argos

The *Pamphlet* will requested a significant votive to Argos: Alexander's arms, insignia plus 1,000 talents of silver.[208] Conflicting texts direct the donation either to the Temple of Hera or as 'first fruits of war for Heracles'.[209] The Argive Heraion (its temple to Hera) was destroyed in 423 BC, but had featured in the *Iliad*.[210] Alexander's lineage was traceable back to Argos and the returning Heraclidae (descendants of Heracles), and so a bequest of this nature may be original.[211] But, once again, there was more reason for the Eumenes–Olympias-led coalition to exploit Polyperchon's position in Greece. Cassander had garrisoned Argos, and yet the inhabitants offered to hand the city over to Polyperchon's son, Alexander, when its occupying general was campaigning elsewhere.[212] Although this was soon after Eumenes' death in Asia, it may have been the first opportunity the city had to show the support solicited by the promise of a significant financial gift.

Wooing Veterans of the Campaigns

The *Romance* text (T2) contains additional endowments not appearing in the *Metz Epitome* will (T1): three talents apiece for 'feeble' Macedonian and Thessalian veterans due for repatriation.[213] Again, if an original *Pamphlet* clause, Eumenes and Olympias were simply seeking to enrol the celebrated cavalry (whether in Thessaly or still in Asia) and other experienced Macedonian infantry into their ranks to help install Olympias in Pella, and potentially those resettled in Asia for Eumenes to muster. Antipater and Craterus must have destroyed much of Thessaly after the Battle of Crannon, which ended the Lamian War. This, along with much else in the document, only makes sense if Olympias and Eumenes were broadcasting their identity as the capable upholders of these *Pamphlet* pledges through their unique positions and mandates. Although three talents per veteran, which is equivalent to a total of almost fifty years' infantryman's pay, is clearly an excessive gift and looks embellished, the concept was nevertheless sound once Eumenes gained control of a major Asian treasury.

The Virulence of the *Pamphlet*

Authenticity would have demanded a reworked testament from Alexander that appeared complete. For that reason, the collaborating pamphleteers left untouched what they could and what had no value in changing. Eumenes also knew he could not manipulate beyond reason what was too widely known, indiscriminately elevating those who turned 'ally', for example, or downgrading those who opposed him, beyond a believable level. This is probably why the *Pamphlet* narrative appears to have referred to the suspicion that Alexander's death was being kept from the infantrymen who attempted to storm his bed chamber, for this likely correlated with what did take place at Babylon.[214]

The passing of the ring to Perdiccas was clearly broadcast too, for this justified Eumenes placing initial support in him, and it reinforced the heinous nature of Perdiccas' murder in Egypt (in which Ptolemy was not implicated).[215] Eumenes would not, however, have been motivated to restate the grander untenable last wishes that were absorbed into Diodorus' 'last plans', for they were irreverently cancelled by Perdiccas at Babylon. The reasonable scale of Alexander's commemoratives is the carefully edited result, though they have since been contaminated in the surviving texts.[216]

Alexander's secretary, in collusion with Alexander's mother, was reissuing the will as a genuine *Ephemerides*-recorded testament into a world in which knowledge of the original still carried dangerous connotations. Beside it they poured a toxic concoction of threat, bribery, exoneration and falsification into a deep propaganda cup, whose content was washed down with the fluid authenticity its compilers could uniquely provide.

Ironically, Aristotle was at some later point dragged into the frame, and not in a minor role: a Vulgate tradition embellishing the original conspiracy claims cited the great Peripatetic scholar in the role of providing the poison and encouragement to Antipater and his sons. When Aristotle agreed to be executor of Antipater's will (as is historically recorded), Alexander's teacher might have unwittingly laid himself open for posthumous propaganda, as it lent the plot to kill Alexander a weighty audacity and something of a philosophical gravitas (T9, T10).[217] Before the *Pamphlet* was published, Aristotle's student and successor, Theophrastus, may have already published his *Enquiry Into Plants*, in which he recommended disguising the bitter taste of the poison strychnine by serving it in undiluted wine, inspiring the *Pamphlet* authors' conspiratorial imaginations in the process.[218] After all, everyone knew that 'regicide was something of a Macedonian tradition'.[219]

The immediate effect of the publication was short-lived, despite its contents reaching Greece. Cornered on a Macedonian chessboard himself, Eumenes had castled himself out of trouble with a folio of fakes, but he sacrificed too many pieces in the process. Once Cassander had engineered a guilty verdict at a sham trial of Olympias and overseen her execution near the fortified town of Pydna, the *Pamphlet* became dangerous to quote.[220] Here, Curtius' contention – echoed in other Vulgate texts – that 'whatever credence such stories gained, they were soon suppressed by the power of the people implicated by the rumour', finally comes to life.[221] In the vacuum left behind, Antigonus expediently broadcast his new 'royalist' side by demanding Cassander restore the imprisoned Rhoxane and Alexander IV 'to the Macedones'.[222] This was the veneer of loyalty and court-sanctioned legitimacy he had once hoped to obtain from an alliance with Eumenes, and Alexander's sons now started to glow with a lustre that failed to shine at Babylon.

In response, Cassander had his henchman, Glaucias, murder mother and son. Soon after, the polemical noises from Greece started haranguing the behaviour of the conquering Alexander, possibly broadcast by the Peripatetic philosophers of Athens under Cassander's shield and protected by the new city tyrant, Demetrius of Phalerum.[223] It was now 310 BC, the 'seventh year of Alexander IV' according to the *Babylonian Chronicle* (here calculated from the death of Philip III Arrhidaeus, suggesting that had indeed been in 317 BC), the same year that Antigonus commenced a concerted campaign to remove Seleucus from Babylon.[224] Diodorus described the mood:

> When Glaucias had carried out the instructions [to kill Rhoxane and her son King Alexander IV], Cassander, Lysimachus and Ptolemy, and Antigonus as well, were relieved of their anticipated danger from the king, for henceforth, there being no longer anyone to inherit the realm, and each of those who had ruled over nations and cities entertained hopes of royal power.[225]

The short-lived 'Peace of the Dynasts' of 311 BC had in fact been 'a disguised invitation to the jailers to eliminate any members of the family they held', and by 309/308 BC, with the murder of Alexander's older son, Heracles – who was then approaching adulthood – and once Antigonus had executed Cleopatra when she attempted to depart Sardis in 308 BC to marry Ptolemy, the *Pamphlet* faded into romantic obscurity.[226] The original will had now outlived its useful sell-by date and the royal charade was gone; or almost, for Cassander had extracted the Argead Thessalonice (Alexander's half-sister) at the conclusion of the siege at Pydna and took her as his bride, forcefully according to Antigonus, a potentially valid accusation when recalling she was Olympias' ward.[227]

Cassander's treatment of Olympias (he refused her a proper state burial), Rhoxane and Alexander IV (imprisoned and then executed) suggests, as one scholar put it, that he tried to categorize Alexander's 'branch of the Argeads as illegitimate' while seeding his line.[228] Cassander did, in fact, clear the way for the rise of the Ptolemaic, Seleucid and Antigonid dynasties when weeding the path for his own. Soon, once Pyrrhus the Epirote royal had killed Cleopatra's son, who reigned as Neoptolemus II in Epirus for five years (to 297 BC, if that identification is correct), the only surviving males of any Argead blood were the next generation Philip, Antipater and Alexander, Cassander's sons by Thessalonice.[229]

In his biographical *Parallel Lives*, we recall that Plutarch rather fittingly paired Eumenes with the brilliant Roman outcast Quintus Sertorius, whose craft and ability was additionally compared to the achievements of Philip II, Antigonus the One-Eyed and even Hannibal. Plutarch's obituary to both men is a fitting way to close the chapter:

> With him [Sertorius] we may best compare, among the Greeks, Eumenes of Cardia. Both were born to command and given to wars of stratagem; both were exiled from their own countries, commanded foreign soldiers, and in their deaths experienced a fortune that was harsh and unjust; for both were the victims of plots, and were slain by the very men with whom they were conquering their foes.[230]

The final lines were of course referring to the Silver Shields' treachery at Gabiene, when Eumenes had been 'unable to fly before being taken prisoner'.[231] The influential biographer historian from Chaeronea gave us a vivid picture of a man contemplating his fate upon hearing of the fermenting treachery:[232]

> Eumenes ... went off to his tent, where he said to his friends that he was living in a great herd of wild beasts. Then made his Will, and tore up and destroyed his papers; he did not wish that after his death, in consequence of the secrets contained in these documents, accusations and calumnies should be brought against his correspondents.[233]

This rather contradicts the allegation that followed from Plutarch, who said that Eumenes 'neither took good precautions against death, nor faced it well', possibly echoing the continued hostility of Duris of Samos.[234]

What else did Eumenes have in the box of secret correspondence? The blueprint of the grand plan he was hatching with Olympias? Perhaps a copy of Alexander's original will as a template to draw from? Or, possibly, the first written copies of the *Pamphlet* and other homespun Pellan letters of empowerment that were supposedly signed by Polyperchon and the kings? We might guess who the counter-correspondents were, apart from Cleopatra in Sardis, Olympias in Epirus and perhaps Polyperchon Pella: other promising, but vacillating, satraps waiting to see which way to jump. And to whom would Eumenes have chosen to pass the incendiary folio and then appoint executor to his own will? Hieronymus must be the obvious choice on both accounts, in which case the Cardian historian became the guardian of the knowledge of two vanished wills.

Here it is tempting to pinpoint the third, and possibly the most poignant, date for the release of the *Pamphlet*: before, or immediately after, the final battle at Gabiene on the Iranian Plateau. Eumenes was not immediately seized and handed over to Antigonus, for when negotiating the return of their baggage, the Silver Shields complained 'that their wives should be spending the *third* night in a row in the arms of the enemy'.[235] During this time, and withdrawn in his tent, Eumenes had nothing to lose by drafting the toxic document while destroying the evidence behind it.

'Among the wounded there was also brought in as a captive the historian Hieronymus, who hitherto always had been held in honour by Eumenes, but after Eumenes' death enjoyed the favour and confidence of Antigonus.'[236] Did Hieronymus reveal the folio to his captor, Antigonus? Not burdened himself with guilt in the *Pamphlet* and with his satrapies still intact, and, moreover, intent on subduing those who were dammed by the publication and yet still in league with those who were not, how much would Antigonus have had to lose from letting the incendiary scrolls past his sentries, or in passing the garnishing detail to the named Hagnothemis (possibly Hagnon of Teos), who is said to have first broadcast it aloud?[237]

Following his victory at Gabiene, Antigonus must have heeded Lysander's Spartan advice: 'Where the skin of the lion does not reach, it must be patched with the skin of a fox', or perhaps in this case a jackal.[238] For upon Eumenes' death, he certainly patched up his differences with the now-bested 'jackal' Polyperchon and had him battling in his own interests against Cassander in Greece. This raises the question whether Antigonus himself was the source of the added slander against Aristotle, for the great scholar and Cassander's father had clearly been confidants.

'Politics is history on the wing', Cicero is portrayed as declaring, and although 'unable to fly' at Gabiene (Plutarch recorded), what Eumenes may have initially conceived at Nora and then sculpted into its final form sometime in the three following years, was indeed a masterstroke of political forgery that rivalled the best Macedonian art of war.[239]

9

THE OVERLOOKED EVIDENCE

We know the *Pamphlet* presented a manipulated version of Alexander's will. What might the original have contained, how would it have distributed the empire, and how much of its content might be retained in the testament we read today?

Guided by the settlements at Babylon and Triparadeisus, and by the behaviour of the Diadochi in the Successor Wars that followed, I attempt to rebuild the content of Alexander's genuine will.

I question whether the testament that appeared in the *Pamphlet* mirrored the true division of the empire and the intended roles of the royal women and Alexander's sons. Finally, I contemplate how the so-called 'last plans' might be reconciled with extant will texts and with an original.

> We can claim to have learnt reasonably well how to detect forgeries of ancient texts made either in the Middle Ages or in the Renaissance or later ... On the other hand, it would be fatuous to maintain that we can readily expose a forgery when the forgery was made in Antiquity ... What we are tempted to label as a forgery, may, on closer examination, be a perfectly honest work attributed to the wrong author.[1]
>
> Arnaldo Momigliano, *Studies in Historiography*

I have sought to explain the motive and mechanisms behind the origination of the *Pamphlet*. In doing so, I have argued why the re-emergence of a will could have been so potent. Yet any attempt to trace the outline of Alexander's actual succession instruction remains as precarious as profiling Alexander himself. Corruptions and later embellishment of the *Romance* and *Metz Epitome* wills over the 2,000 intervening years leave them laden with well-baited traps

The Shape of the Empire

When considering the distribution of Alexander's empire at his death, an impartial read of the list of appointed satraps, with its twenty-four-plus governors answering to no clear overarching hierarchy structure, transmits the inevitability of fragmentation. It was a fate underlined by Alexander's alleged prediction of posthumous 'funeral games'.[2]

Despite the superficial workability of such an arrangement, regional administration would have been complicated by the divided responsibilities of officials who feature in texts with their reporting lines to absent kings, a roving chiliarch, local satraps and, no doubt, local bureaucrats. We variously read the titles frequently attached to these posts: treasurers (*gazophylakes*), garrison commanders (*phrourarchoi*), jurors (*diskastai*), financial officials (*dioiketai*), stewards (*epitropoi*), some under the authority of an 'overseer' (*epistates*), superintendent (*epimeletes*), governor (*hyparchos*), military regional administrator (*stategos*) or commander-in-chief (*hegemon*). Frustratingly, these titles and their relative position in a hierarchy evolved through the Hellenistic era when the formative histories were being written. Even Rome was vexed at the old Greek and Macedonian terms associated with these chains of command and political–military structures.[3]

Unless there was some cohesive force holding these fragmentary appointments in place, loyalties would have crossed borders with bureaucratic bottlenecks, factions would have aggregated, garrisons would have walked out and locally recruited mercenaries could have poured in to plunder. Each satrap's own designs would have paid scant heed to the bigger picture, if it was indeed laid out this way.

Some further regional coherence was required: the centripetal strings that would hold these 'centrifugal forces' at bay that would spin the empire away from central authority.[4] And when considering the locations of royal treasuries and mints scattered unevenly across the empire, counterbalances must have been in place to ensure the accumulated wealth and incoming tribute, now nominally belonging to the kings in Pella, was not squandered by the local administration or appropriated by a local warlord. This required pan-provincial governance that prevented accounting anarchy, and which, for example, did keep the treasuries broadly intact until 316/315 BC when Eumenes accessed Cynda, explaining why he felt compelled to provide an account of his appropriating horses from the royal herds. Any financial extraction before that was officially mandated (genuinely or forged) by the chiliarch or the acting Macedonian regent on behalf of the kings.[5]

My explanation of this missing cohesive glue is relatively simple: Alexander appointed the Royal Bodyguards along with the most prominent of generals as empire overseers in his will. Ptolemy's proposal that a select few Bodyguards – those Alexander had customarily relied on for advice – should make crucial decisions on governance in his 'group rule' speech at Babylon, is a relic of just that.[6] These super-governors oversaw their surrounding satraps, so binding the empire together in perhaps nine or ten pan-provincial jurisdictions (if we include a 'greater' Macedon itself), under roles in which, according to Justin, they eventually 'became princes instead of prefects'.[7] And to head up this arrangement, Alexander nominated Perdiccas as the overseer of the new Asian empire, with Craterus in a similar position in Europe, their responsibilities overlapping in their guardianships of Alexander's sons.

The greater cohesion this implies would have ensured the borders of the Macedonian-governed empire, stretching from Scythia in the north to the Indus in the east, from Arabia and Ethiopia in the south to the Adriatic in the west, did not soften under incompetent or secession-inclined satraps. It is highly probable that the men selected had already been groomed for the roles, so that Alexander could venture westward from Babylon, leaving Asia distributed securely behind him. Perhaps the crowning of the unified body of Royal Bodyguards at Susa, with their new regal Persian wives, was a step towards (or undocumented fulfilment of) this public declaration of intent.[8]

Pan-provincial administrators had necessarily been installed throughout the Asian campaign. Philoxenus, who replaced the treasurer Harpalus after his first flight with royal funds, had an overarching authority west of the Taurus range as administrator of coastal forces and governor of the region; he potentially operated as the director of financial affairs as well.[9] Balacrus, a former Royal Bodyguard (*Somatophylax*), had enjoyed similar responsibilities stemming from his long tenure of Cilicia, and certainly Antigonus enjoyed a regional mandate in the hinterland of Anatolia from the Battle of Issus onwards (Curtius' Latin text termed him *praetor praerat* – broadly 'supreme commander').[10] Parmenio exercised similar power in all directions from Ecbatana when Alexander was further east, and Black Cleitus looks to have been appointed in a homogenous role in the upper satrapies shortly before his death at Alexander's hand. Craterus had operated in a regional capacity from Bactria/Sogdia when Alexander was absent on expeditions.[11] Moreover, we imagine that the Persian satraps – Mazaeus for example at Babylon, Abulites in Susiane, Phrasaortes in Persis and Phrataphernes in Parthia, as well as Artabazus and then Oxyartes (father of Rhoxane) in Bactria (later Parapamisadae) – must have always answered to the Macedonian regime through these regional overseers.[12]

Could such a fundamental command structure remain buried beneath the literary topsoil for so long? I propose the answer is 'yes', and the 'how' and 'why' these regional overarching roles were condensed to plainer governorships and core satrapies in texts is not difficult to explain. Hieronymus' original detail may have simply been compressed by Diodorus and epitomizers into what we have today, just as the patronyms attached to important individuals have been lost. But we must also factor in the possibility, or even the probability, that Hieronymus' Antigonid-sponsored book had no interest in reinforcing knowledge of the huge will-mandated remits of the territorial stakeholders who remained steadfastly opposed to his patrons. However, because today's 'standard model' of Alexander and his administration stands as intimidating as ever, proposing a radical overhaul sounds inevitably controversial.

If we take a closer look at the satrapal boundaries broadcast at Babylon, Ptolemy's grant *does* appear extended. It included 'all the Libyan peoples subject to Macedon' and 'part of Arabia bordering Egypt', presumably extending through Cyrenaica to the west and the Sinai east of Egypt. Similarly, Lysimachus received 'Thrace, the Chersonese and the peoples bordering Thrace as far as the sea at Salmydessus on the Euxine [Black Sea]' as well as 'the neighbouring tribes of the Pontic Sea', so north to the Danube. The only other mandate that looks pan-provincial, or at least as expansively well-defined, is Eumenes' Cappadocia, Paphlagonia and 'the country on the shore of the Euxine as far as Trapezus', alternatively transmitted as 'all the lands bordering these that Alexander did not invade'.[13] In other words, this far-reaching authority coincides with the three most prominent 'innocents' at Babylon, Perdiccas aside.

The original *Pamphlet* in its less abbreviated form (and recalling that names were corrupted) may have likewise expanded on these regions, for the correlation between these governors and the *Pamphlet*'s 'coalition team' should not be ignored. Antigonus' control of Lycia, Pamphylia and Greater Phrygia is significant too, but Hieronymus had every reason to broadcast it once in Antigonid employ. So, we may see in the Hieronymus-originating rundown of satrapies given at the Babylonian settlement (T16, T17, T18, T19, T20)

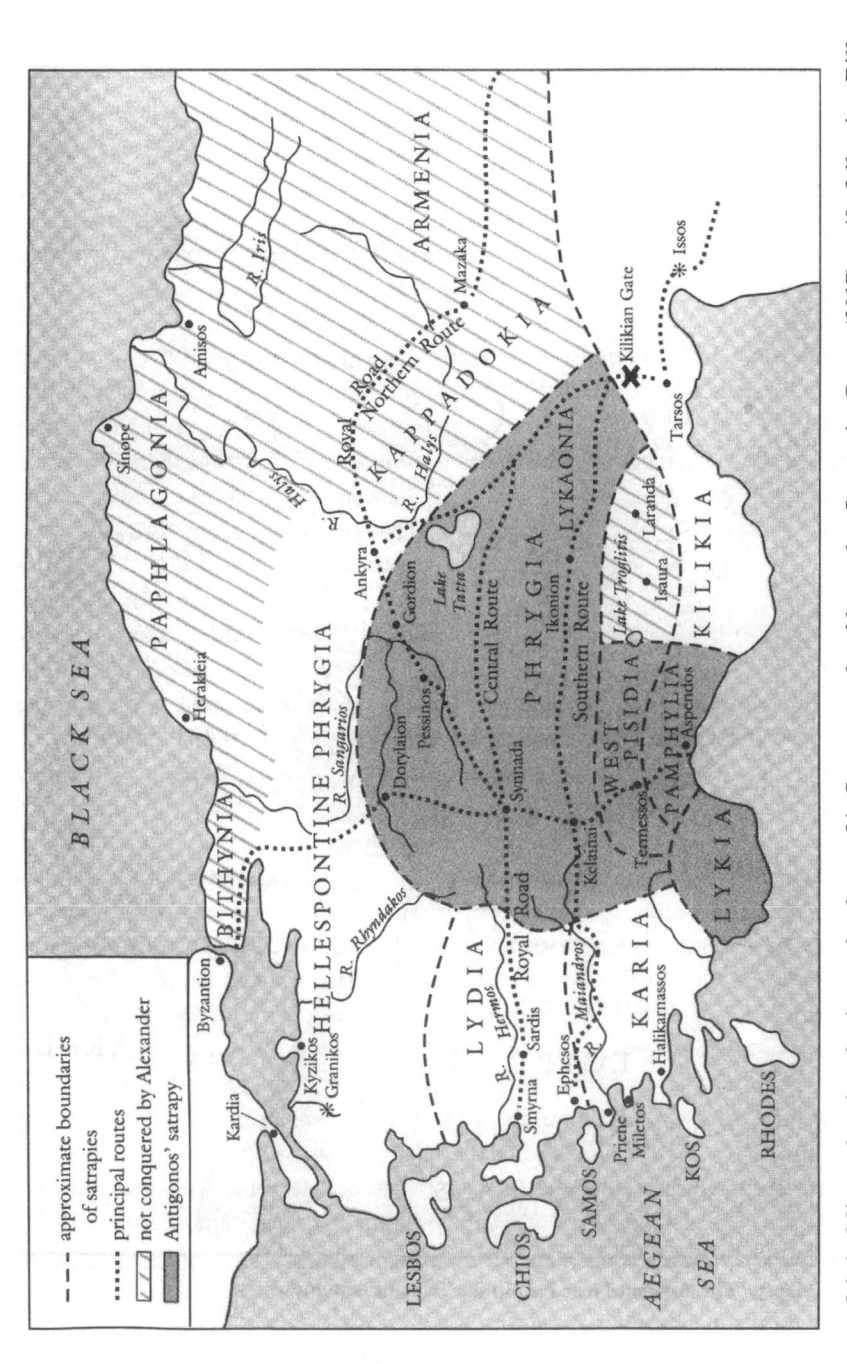

A map of Asia Minor showing Antigonus' sphere of influence under Alexander. Image in Grant (2017) p. 49, following Billows (1990), Maps. (Provided with the kind permission of The University of California Press)

something of the *original* will, something of the Eumenes-inspired *Pamphlet* and something of Hieronymus' duty to his two early patrons.

Ptolemy's authority in 'Libya' suggests his continued 'annexation' of Cyrene was possibly more legitimate (in the eyes of the Diadochi) than historians have assumed.[14] At Triparadeisus, Antipater did not demand Ptolemy's withdrawal from the region, rather 'Egypt and Libya and all the territory that had been conquered to the West went to Ptolemy'.[15] Cyrene had offered its supplication to Alexander on his way to the Siwa Oasis in 331 BC, and thereafter Cyrenaica enjoyed (almost) uninterrupted Ptolemaic rule for over two centuries until it passed to Rome.[16]

Under the terms of Alexander's original will, Craterus would have enjoyed authority over a Macedon that controlled its immediate Balkan neighbours (including Illyria, the Triballians, Paeonians and Agrianians), a domain that was referred to as 'the Kingdom of Arrhidaeus' (Philip III). The Epirus of Olympias and Cleopatra would have been dealt with respectfully, ruled as it was by the extended royal family, but Epirus was for all intents and purposes now a vassal state, while oligarchs and garrisons in Greece further extended Macedon's political arm, though an overhaul of the regime looked imminent with Craterus' return to take the regency.[17] His reported emulation of Alexander certainly suggests he felt endowed with an authority beyond a blunt caretaker role, which, due to unforeseen demands at Babylon, manifested itself as Antipater's second-in-command, a regent-in-waiting and joint guardian to the kings.[18]

Perhaps more appropriately, Photius' epitomes described Craterus' intended office as 'the highest honour'.[19] The new guardian of the kingdom even invited Diogenes the Cynic, based in Corinth, to dine with him. 'I would rather lick salt in Athens,' came the reply.[20] Craterus' monument crafted by the famous sculptors Lysippus and Leochares, which overlooked the terrace of the Temple of Apollo at Delphi, replete with a hunting scene bronze from Asia depicting him coming to the aid of Alexander who was attempting to down a lion (lion hunts had taken place in Syria and Sogdia) – the earliest and possibly the most significant of all the successor monuments (though likely completed by his son) – suggested the same. Its surviving stone niche is over 50ft long and 20ft wide.[21]

Peucestas was already administering what I argue were pan-provincial Persian provinces centred on the Achaemenid capitals of the now partly charred Persepolis (the palace complex at least) and Pasargadae before Alexander died.[22] I propose his regional authority extended over the bordering lands that stretched eastwards to the Indus; the universal sentiment that in the East the governors were to remain unchanged is no doubt accurate, for Peucestas was popular and he commanded widespread loyalty.

In the case of Peithon and Seleucus, the clues to their original expansive and pan-provincial grants lie in the Successor Wars.

Peithon the 'Revolutionary' and the Mercenary Revolt

> The Greeks who had been settled by Alexander in the upper satrapies, as they were called, although they longed for Greek customs and manner of life and were cast away in the most distant part of the kingdom, yet submitted while the king was alive through fear, but when he was dead they rose in revolt.[23]

Soon after news of Alexander's death reached the upper satrapies, 20,000 discontented Greek mercenary infantrymen and 3,000 allied cavalry, 'all of whom had many times been tried in the contests of war and were distinguished for their courage', were making their way through these upper satrapies (not Media) in a state of revolt under an Athenian general, Philon. This was the second mass defection of mercenary garrisoneers; the first wave had successfully returned to Greece from Bactria.[24] Peithon son of Crateuas, the prominent Royal Bodyguard who, we are told, was given Media to govern (T16, T17, T18, T19, T20) at Babylon, was charged with quelling the uprising.[25] He 'was a man of great ambition, [who] gladly accepted the expedition, intending to win the Greeks over through kindness, and, after making his army great through an alliance with them, to work in his own interests and become the ruler of the upper satrapies', so Diodorus concluded from his reading of Hieronymus.[26]

Upon departing Babylon, Peithon's troop numbers were insignificant. From the royal army he had been supplied with just 3,000 Macedonian infantry (of perhaps 13,000 then remaining in Babylon) and 800 Macedonian cavalry (of possibly some 2,000 left), all chosen by lot and many surely unwilling to head back to the East. Perdiccas provided Peithon with letters to the regional satraps ordering them to furnish him with a further 10,000 Asiatic foot soldiers and 8,000 cavalry.[27]

Firstly, the numbers are not credible. Alexander and his generals knew full well no Asiatic force, even with 3,000 Macedonian infantry at its heart, could take on 20,000 Greek mercenary hoplites. In disciplined phalanx formation, they would have pierced the more lightly armed Asiatic ranks and outflanked the opposing phalangites, assuming the Macedonian contingent were the sarissa-bearing pikemen unsupported by more mobile shield bearers. On the other hand, if the 3,000 Macedonians were in hoplite panoply themselves, and not the pike-bearers, then no 'first-strike' weapon had been provided to Peithon; there is no mention of a further 10,000 pikes being collected along the way with which to equip those local recruits, that is if they had even been trained in the use of the sarissa as the Asiatic cadets which arrived at Susa had presumably been.[28] Mounted troops would not have been able to charge a tight infantry formation with spears arrayed forward unless they were equipped as lance-wielding cavalry and accomplished in the flying wedge (and perhaps not even then), and if Peithon's mounted ranks simply acted as static cavalry guarding the infantry flanks, they would have been vulnerable themselves.[29]

Perdiccas' distrust of Peithon had led him to issue orders to the effect that all the renegades were to be slaughtered, suspecting he might indeed raise a private army from their ranks.[30] This raises the question: why task Peithon with the mission in the first place? Diodorus believed his personal ambition and intriguing were real, the 'revolutionary behaviour' Aelian picked up on.[31] But Diodorus' source, Hieronymus, may have swung the episode around a little unconvincingly, for Peithon quelled the uprising and managed to rejoin Perdiccas, either in time for the conquest of Cappadocia and Pisidia (if so, he was never mentioned) or before the ill-fated invasion of Egypt, where he took part in the murder of the chiliarch.[32]

Although 3,000 Greek infantry were reportedly persuaded by Peithon to betray their comrades, the mercenary numbers look grossly inflated, for it is difficult to imagine that the remaining 17,000 who were 'distinguished for their courage' – a formidable army in any circumstances – took flight in confusion, as the text claims. Peithon supposedly gained a victory over them (no detail of how he accomplished this is given) and sent a herald to the 'conquered' mass offering false terms of repatriation to their garrison towns if they laid down their arms. Diodorus claimed that Peithon's Macedonians, remembering Perdiccas' instructions, were able to 'shoot them all with javelins' after betraying the trust of the Greeks. This sounds dubious, despite Diodorus' claim that the Macedonians 'set upon them unexpectedly' (which would have been difficult to pull off as it was against Peithon's alleged objective) and caught them 'off their guard', because the text additionally stated that the unwitting Greeks 'were interspersed among the Macedonians', hardly a situation in which javelins could be hurled.[33]

We recall how reluctantly hoplites ever gave up their shields, especially to what must here have been a largely Asiatic force half the size of their own. If the Greeks were still equipped with their shields and grouped together, to quote one scholar on the issue, 'Missile weapons seem, in fact, to have been comparatively ineffective against the hoplite phalanx', and as has been pointed out, the day of the Persian archer had ended at Plataea.

We may imagine what was deemed a hostile mass of '20,000' was, in fact, made up from predominantly non-combatants – the families of the forced settlers and their baggage train – and they were the vulnerable target being threatened in the negotiations.[34] Their possessions *were* plundered; so more logically, what amounted to just a few thousand remaining infantry were set upon at Peithon's orders once they were isolated, and the 3,000 complicit hoplites were probably sent back to their satrapies (Peithon did not entirely lose the potential future army), with the surviving women and children left to march with them.

Peithon's mission becomes more credible and explicable if we accept that he had already become the overarching regional governor of the upper satrapies, with his authority centred on Media Major and extending to the Caspian Gates to the west and India to the east (authority in India is less clear; Peithon son of Agenor or Philip son of Machatas – thus Harpalus' brother – may have governed a region in a similar role).[35] So it was *his* 'upper satrapy' regional revolt to deal with, whether Perdiccas liked it or not.[36]

The contention that this authority was a genuine will inheritance, and not one of Perdiccas' designs, is strengthened when we recall that Atropates, Perdiccas' father-in-law since the Susa weddings, was only granted Lesser Media at Babylon when he appears to have previously governed Media complete, a more powerful mandate his new son-in-law could have readily reconfirmed (T16, T20).[37] A later statement by Diodorus seems to further support the expanded role: 'Peithon had been appointed satrap of Media, but when he became general of *all upper satrapies*, he put to death Philotas, the former general of Parthia, and set up his own brother Eudamus in his place.'[38] What is seen as Peithon's unbridled ambition by Diodorus may have had more legitimate origins.

It appears that Peithon was nevertheless testing the patience of his subordinate governors, and his arrogance soon backfired. But as has been pointed out, that Seleucus provided him sanctuary in Babylonia indicates he was not troubled by his colleague's cross-provincial meddling.[39] Although Diodorus explained the 'upper satraps had concentrated their armies in a single place' (in response to the threat from Peithon), the coalition that Eumenes met was principally conglomerated from the forces from what I argue was Peucestas' domain: in other words, those 'lower' eastern satrapies (as opposed to 'upper') comprising Peucestas' own Persian archers and slingers alongside troops from Susiane, Carmania, Arachosia, Areia, Drangiana and Paropanisadae.[40] An addition to their ranks was Eudamus (not Peithon's brother), who had taken control of the Paurava region in India.[41]

Diodorus employed the term 'upper' loosely when referring to the eastern provinces. But what does remain clear is a clinical regional divide: Peucestas' coalition did not, for example, feature Peithon son of Agenor, the satrap of the northern Indus region bordering Paropanisadae, who later joined Antigonus. Neither were troop contingents mentioned from Hyrcania or regions north of Bactria and Sogdia – under Stasanor, for example, who was vilified by the *Pamphlet* – for these were the regions that fell under Peithon's pan-provincial mandate.[42] Though some troops do appear to have originated from Bactria itself, these were raised by Stasander, the satrap of Areia-Drangiana, and he was probably able to achieve this because he had (curiously) previously governed Bactria and still had loyal contingents.

This geographical division of allies appears less than coincidental and falls neatly in line with the pan-regional mandates (*strategia*) I propose. In which case the two gold-crowned Royal Bodyguards, Peucestas and Peithon son of Crateuas, were the overseers of the further-eastern empire to India with its named satrapal governors under them, and there is much evidence that neither had plans to abandon their considerable inheritances.[43] Any confusion within these eastern subdivisions are understandable: Bactria and Media 'embraced many regions with distinctive names' and, moreover, they 'afforded an ejected commander many refuges and retreats'.[44] Atropates himself is one example in northwest or 'lesser' Media. He eventually declared himself king and his territory was thereafter referred to as Media Atropatene, and that came, significantly, after Peithon's execution by Antigonus in 315 BC.[45]

Following Peithon's removal, Antigonus granted Nicanor, potentially the general who received Eumenes' surrender at Gabiene, a pan-regional mandate to govern (as *strategos*) what Diodorus clearly stated as all the 'upper satrapies'.[46] More telling still was his failure to unite the remaining governors to the south, for Peucestas had by then also been removed. It appears the southern and central satraps of the East were reluctant to unite under a non-legitimate regional governor who had not adopted their customs. In this newly fragmenting environment, it was no surprise that Seleucus was able to inflict a crushing defeat on Antigonus' divided forces there when they put up a 'perfunctory and negligent guard'.[47]

Seleucus' Hidden Inheritance: Babylon and Beyond

There is scarcely a mention of Seleucus in the extant texts between Alexander's death and his re-emergence at Triparadeisus some three years later, when a 'new' satrapal role was supposedly conferred on him: the governorship of Babylon. I have already argued why Hieronymus had little interest in featuring his patrons' eastern opponent and his regional inheritance more prominently. But when Antigonus threatened Seleucus' tenure of the region after Eumenes' death in 315 BC, Diodorus stated that Seleucus claimed he had been given 'the country' (not just city) in 'recognition of his services rendered while Alexander was alive'.[48]

The reference to 'Macedonians' bestowing the role on him discounts it being the manipulative hand of Perdiccas alone. Superficially, at least, it is more representative of either the endorsement of Seleucus' inheritance at the original Assembly at Babylon, or his reconfirmation at Triparadeisus in 320 BC; in fact, reminding Antigonus of either of these events would have been a better riposte than 'as per the testament of Alexander', for Antigonus had already demonstrated by then that he completely ignored satrapal boundaries established by *any* regal authority.

Diodorus was under the impression that Seleucus had been granted the hipparchy (cavalry command role) of the Companion Cavalry by Perdiccas at Babylon in 323 BC, the prestigious command Perdiccas had himself inherited at Hephaestion's death (T16). This is supported by Justin, who more generally stated Seleucus received 'chief command of the camp' (T20), and it is perhaps strengthened by the fact that Seleucus had already led the Royal Hypaspists (Shieldbearers) after Hephaestion was promoted to hipparch, probably in 330 BC (when Philotas was executed).[49] That this post, previously held by the king's chiliarch, was separated out, clearly indicates that Perdiccas' own continued 'chiliarchy' is to be interpreted as the higher-functioning quasi-regent post, and not limited to the cavalry command. Like the authority it had vested in Hephaestion before him, the title equated to administrator of the kings and their realms and with no power above, save kingship itself.[50]

Diodorus further accepted that a more obscure figure named Archon was appointed as the principal Babylonian governor.[51] But giving Seleucus a token hipparchy command cannot be compared to Ptolemy's inheritance of the ancient land of Egypt, deemed 'the best' due to its revenues, a sentiment no doubt originating with the Alexandrian Cleitarchus. Neither was it equal to Peithon's governance of Media, also referred to as 'the greatest of all' due to its regional diversity.[52] It did not match Peucestas' control of the ancient Persian heartlands, or even, for that matter, Eumenes' grant centred on Cappadocia, which hosted the Royal Road on its northern route from Susa to Sardis.[53] Although Justin interpreted Seleucus' new post as 'second-in-command' (in Perdiccas' immediate camp), he would have been witnessing his colleagues exploit their new chunks of the empire when he had nothing but the prestige of serving Perdiccas on horseback. Named amongst the most eminent of cavalry leaders at Babylon, would Seleucus, the future builder of the most expansive of all the successor empires, have truly been excluded from the territorial honours list in Alexander's will?[54] Or could Perdiccas himself, in the accepted intestate scenario, have really orchestrated this estateless role?

In contrast, we know the *Pamphlet*-based will, which had every reason to pass Seleucus over (he was clearly not named 'innocent' of regicide, so was not on the coalition's target team of allies), appears to have unambiguously allocated him Babylonia – city, province and 'territory adjoining it'; and here the *Romance* and *Metz Epitome* texts are in clear accord (T1, T2). In which case Archon, and potentially Arcesilaus too – if Mesopotamia came under a Babylonia-centred expansive remit – were operating under Seleucus as subordinate governors.[55] Under-governors usually appeared in Diodorus' narrative when their overlords were on campaign; Seleucus appointed Patrocles to Babylon, for example, when campaigning in Media against Nicanor in 312 BC.[56] If Mesopotamia was a part of that territorial grant, then Amphimachus (appointed there at Triparadeisus and also over the Arbelitis region) and Blitor, who assumed a similar post after him, operated in similar subordinate roles later. Amphimachus appears to have joined Eumenes when he passed through the region in winter 317 BC, following which Seleucus replaced him with Blitor, who facilitated Seleucus' escape from Antigonus in 315 BC.[57]

So, who was this Archon? He had been named as a trierarch of the Hydaspes-Indus fleet, but he is otherwise unattested on campaign.[58] Perdiccas replaced him with Docimus, and Archon was supposed to retain the role as collector of revenues in the province, a demotion Perdiccas may have assumed (and wished) he would never accept. Archon may have colluded in the interception of Alexander's funeral hearse by Ptolemy, presumably with the blessing of Seleucus, thus prompting his removal. Enmity was clear; he and Docimus ended up fighting it out for control and Archon lost his life.[59] Reconfirmed at Triparadeisus, Seleucus entered the city unopposed when Docimus, now a proscribed Perdiccan, fled to join the 'royal rebel' cause.[60] None of this excludes Seleucus inheriting the honorific hipparch title of the First (Hephaestion's) Command (here *chiliarchia*) of the Companion Cavalry in Perdiccas' royal army, or attending to the administration of his wider region. This would explain why he was absent from Babylon when Docimus was installed, and, moreover, why he claimed the region was his 'by right' when confronting Antigonid expansion in 315 BC.

How could Diodorus have arrived at his conclusions about Seleucus' hipparchy post? The first explanation would once again be to assume Hieronymus omitted his regional mandate as payback for his long history of hostility; publishing his account some fifty years after events, Seleucus' demotion was easily made, though carefully reconstructed to rebroadcast that he had become Perdiccas' 'number two'. Yet we do have a contradiction, for in Photius' epitome (of Dexippus' summary) of Arrian's *Events After Alexander*, which is ultimately Hieronymus-sourced, we read that Seleucus *did* indeed receive control of Babylon from the outset (T18), though this may simply be an epitomized merging of the appointments at Babylon and Triparadeisus once more. Unfortunately, in Photius' own direct précis of Arrian a lacuna has swallowed this part of the satrapal list, robbing us of a useful comparison, whilst another lacuna (we imagine) resulted in the total loss of references to Babylonia in Curtius' run down, which is otherwise inexplicable when considering the space he dedicated to the infighting at Babylon (T17).[61]

We cannot discount a further – and perhaps the most obvious – explanation: Diodorus simply misunderstood Hieronymus' original wording, and it is not difficult to imagine a sufficiently ambiguous statement:

> Seleucus campaigned with Perdiccas in the role of hipparch of the Companion Cavalry, a prestigious role amounting to a second in command and formerly held by Perdiccas and Hephaestion before him, and in his absence, Archon was appointed governor of Babylon.[62]

Whatever the cause of the compression of Seleucus' role, Diodorus' explanation has been formative to interpretations ever since.

Leonnatus' Hidden Inheritance: Lands West of the Halys

The extant sources unanimously stated that Leonnatus was allocated Hellespontine Phrygia at Babylon (T16, T17, T18, T19, T20).[63] Leonnatus was raised with Alexander at the Pellan court and was a decorated Bodyguard credited with saving the king's life.[64] His father, Anteas, was a relative of Eurydice, the mother of Philip II; Leonnatus was therefore a member of the Lyncestian royal house and his correspondence with Alexander's sister Cleopatra hints that he felt every bit as regal as his heritage suggested.[65] Additionally, at Babylon, Leonnatus was clearly chosen beside Perdiccas to be a guardian of the unborn king by Rhoxane, and Curtius positioned him as the second most important of the king's Companions then present.[66]

In traditional interpretations, Leonnatus and Antigonus were tasked by Perdiccas with assisting Eumenes in his pacification of the geographically vast and important unconquered Cappadocia, when Leonnatus' own authority was restricted to the relatively diminutive (in size) Hellespont-bordering province once governed by a 'son of Harpalus', possibly a relative of the embezzling treasurer who fled to Greece. The region's principal importance lay in its bordering the narrow sea-crossing to Europe, though its boundaries are less than clinically outlined by our sources.[67] Once again we need to question whether Alexander would have really carved up the empire so disproportionately when considering the accepted territorial grants of Ptolemy, Peithon, Peucestas, Lysimachus, Antigonus and Eumenes. We need to similarly challenge the notion that Perdiccas could have attempted the same, for he and Leonnatus were in action together as far back as Philip II's death in Aegae some thirteen years before.[68]

Alexander would surely have bestowed a grander role on Leonnatus which recognized his prestige: logically this was authority over northwest Anatolia governed from Hellespontine Phrygia, just as Antigonus had initially operated in a wider role from his own early 'capital' at Celaenae in Phrygia. Anatolia had never been governed under a single mandate; with Alexander campaigning east, Antigonus was supplemented by Balacrus in Cilicia, Nearchus south of the Taurus (to the west of Cilicia), with Calas and Asander in the Hellespontine region and Lydia.[69] If the bulk of Anatolia was to be divided between them now, then Leonnatus' authority could have spanned the still nominally independent Bithynia (alongside Mysia and the Troad region), Lesser Phrygia, Lydia and Caria, with lesser governors under him.[70]

Antigonus would have then received the adjoining hinterland and much of the south: Greater Phrygia, Lycia, Pamphylia and Lycaonia.[71] Pisidia and Cilicia as far as the Cilician or Amanian Gate bordering Syria (so southeastern Anatolia) appear to have fallen outside his mandate, as they had before. This division of power explains why both Leonnatus and Antigonus were charged with helping Eumenes pacify Cappadocia and presumably Paphlagonia (separated from Bithynia by the Parthenius, the modern Bartin River). Quite credibly, Eumenes was also a pan-satrapal governor to the east of both, and whose own region would have stretched eastwards through Armenia.[72]

Armenia may have been bestowed upon Neoptolemus on similar conditions to Eumenes' region: the territory first needed subduing, and a similar reciprocal arrangement for assistance might have been demanded. As we read it, Perdiccas 'sent Eumenes back from Cilicia, ostensibly to his own satrapy [Cappadocia], but really to reduce to obedience the adjacent country of Armenia, which had been thrown into confusion by Neoptolemus'. So it is tempting to join Armenia to Eumenes' wider mandate, as this would explain Neoptolemus' resentment of the 'man who followed Alexander with a pen', as he stated at Babylon, suggesting jealousy. Peucestas' friend, Orontes, had either claimed the region or later been reinstated as satrap.[73] If Armenia was part of Eumenes' genuine inheritance, or even if it was a more-duplicitous *Pamphlet*-will grant, it would better explain why Eumenes' ruse involving the unwitting Orontes worked so convincingly at Persepolis, helping him wrest regional control from the equally unwitting Peucestas.[74] Eumenes' governance of Armenia would have then logically extended his authority towards the Caspian, whence Peithon's own governance commenced from Media and stretching eastward, and it would have been neatly bordered by Mesopotamia in the south.

In the aftermath of the Second Successor War, which ended in 315 BC, Lysimachus demanded Hellespontine Phrygia when he, Cassander and Ptolemy sent envoys to Antigonus. The satrapy was vacant following the defeat of its governor Arrhidaeus, and the same delegation of envoys demanded Lycia for Cassander along with Eumenes' Cappadocia.[75] 'Lycia' should surely read 'Lydia', the satrapy left ungoverned since the death of White Cleitus, because with Leonnatus dead, the region had become divisible at Triparadeisus.

At this point, 315 BC, Cassander was the *de facto* ruler of Macedon, for he had King Alexander IV and his mother Rhoxane under lock and key at Amphipolis. His role in the defeat of Eumenes had been restricted to distracting Polyperchon in Greece, and yet he seems to have already sent advanced forces into Cappadocia, besieging the city of Amisus (modern Samsun in northern Turkey), possibly to distract Antigonus from invading Macedon.[76] But why here specifically? As Cassander had no experience in Asia and no previous Asian claims, we might conclude it was the publication of the *Pamphlet*, with its obvious authorship, that incited him to occupy Eumenes' inherited region. Whether this led to the rift between him and Antigonus, who realigned with Polyperchon, or whether it followed it, is unclear, but Antigonus had no intention of letting Cassander stay on Asian soil.

Perdiccas' Inheritance: the Argument for Greater Syria

With Craterus appointed to govern the Macedonian kingdom as the principal resident guardian of the kings, and with Alexander's Royal Bodyguards spread through the vast provinces of the former Persian Empire they would now govern, tax and harvest, I pose a huge but as yet unarticulated question: where was Perdiccas, the supposedly itinerant overseer of the empire, supposed to base himself? The one hugely important region, greater in significance than those assigned to govern it and less than satisfactorily accounted for in the divisions listed at Babylon, is a 'Greater Syria' that would link Egypt, Arabia, Mesopotamia-Babylonia and Anatolia (through Cilicia and Pisidia) together. The only reference to Syria in the Babylonian settlement, or later at Triparadeisus, was a governorship linked to Laomedon, and that was more convincingly Coele-Syria, as Diodorus and other satrapy-citing texts later clarified. Arrian was clear that his territory bordered Egypt, and Justin additionally stated: 'Laomedon of Mytilene was allotted Syria, which bordered on Ptolemy's province.' (T17, T20)[77]

Coele-Syria was ambiguously referenced throughout history, though it was more specifically delineated in the *Pamphlet*-originating wills. In the *koine* or 'common' Greek which emerged in the Hellenistic period, Coele (*koile*) meant 'hollow', and this referred to the fertile Bequaa Valley in modern eastern Lebanon, and/or – as some scholars interpret it – Israel.[78] Diodorus' Hieronymus-inspired digression on the geography of the empire was clearer on the constituent Syrian parts:

> Next to Mesopotamia are Upper Syria, as it is called, and the countries adjacent thereto along the sea: Cilicia, Pamphylia, and Coele-Syria, which encloses Phoenicia. Along the frontiers of Coele-Syria and along the desert that lies next to it, through which the Nile makes its way and divides Syria and Egypt ...[79]

In previous times, Coele-Syria was annexed, along with Phoenicia, by the Egyptian pharaohs. Diodorus often referred to the region bordering Egypt as 'lower' Syria. So a 'Greater Syrian' governorship might have encompassed lower Syria, Coele-Syria (encompassing Phoenicia) and Upper Syria (in total, broadly modern Israel, Lebanon, Jordan and Syria) to the Mesopotamian Line (thus including 'Mesopotamian Syria'), which we assume was the River Euphrates, and it would have been a strategically sound base of operations, linking as it did the major Asian regions.[80] On this basis, the division of what we might term the 'Levant' today is clear-cut.

The extended domain, as far north as Cilicia and eastern Pisidia, operated as a buffer zone through which any army would need to pass if it were to invade another. Certainly Cilicia was carved out of Anatolia in texts: following battle at Gaugamela, Alexander appointed Menes in a role that was to govern from Babylon (probably again though Syria and Phoenicia) to the Taurus.[81] So the Taurus Mountain range was the natural cut-off of a cohesive region that was still in existence when Mark Antony and Cleopatra allocated it to their son, Ptolemy II Philadelphus, under the Donation of Alexandria in 34 BC.

It is generally supposed that Eumenes returned to Babylon to report on events to Perdiccas once Leonnatus and Antigonus refused to assist his pacification of Cappadocia.[82] Yet his and Perdiccas' whereabouts are not actually stated; the urgency of Antigonus' flight, and the speed with which a new campaign against Ariarathes was initiated – 'moreover, a little while after he [Eumenes] was conducted into Cappadocia with an army which Perdiccas commanded in person' – suggest the chiliarch might have been rather closer, and northern Syria is a strategically sound option. It does appear that Perdiccas was based just to the north of Syria, in Cilicia, when he ordered Eumenes to take control of Armenia with plenipotentiary powers, and this further explains Perdiccas' own hostile campaign in the region, and why his brother, Alcetas, was cited at Cretopolis and Termessus.[83]

Perdiccas' tasking of Arrhidaeus with the construction of the dead king's funeral bier indicates that he was not based at Babylon, otherwise he could have overseen it himself, and Arrhidaeus had no technical or engineering background that we know of. As its destination was Syria (it was hijacked by Ptolemy's men near Damascus), then, as I previously posed, Arrhidaeus did not 'redirect' its path at all. As has already been pointed out, the wording Diodorus used – 'return journey' and 'home' – clearly indicates that Perdiccas eventually planned to send the body to the royal necropolis at Aegae in Macedon.[84]

In summary, I propose that this Perdiccas-governed Syria was to be the temporary home of Alexander's embalmed corpse while the dust from the recent tensions settled and until Perdiccas himself could launch his own 'invasion' of Macedon. Routing the funeral cortège though Damascus conforms to no practical route to Macedon from Babylon; the more direct journey to the Dardanelles sea crossing and the one best served by established roads would have been to follow the Euphrates north, or better, the western bank of the Tigris, to connect with the Royal Road network in upper Mesopotamia, and then journey northwest through Cappadocia into western Anatolia.

It is possible that Alexander's throne, weapons and panoply (the 'set' of which later resurfaced with Eumenes) had originally travelled with it.[85] But loading an enormously weighty sarcophagus – housed in an ornate 'Ionic temple' that required sixty-four mules to pull it – on a ship would have been a tricky business for even the best of engineers in the most peaceful of times, and this suggests the funeral hearse was never constructed with a maritime voyage in mind, which argues for Egypt as its legitimate destination as per Alexander's will. Perdiccas was not deterred. The Macedonians had witnessed Alexander in action and they were now hardly deterred by such challenges: elephants were just as much of a transportation headache, and Antipater managed to take some seventy of them back with him across the Dardanelles.[86]

Further clues to Perdiccas' extended presence in a Greater Syria exist. He is recorded as having founded (or re-founded) the city of Samaria (now in northern Israel), probably during this period, and he launched his campaign against Ptolemy from Damascus. It was here that the ancient network of roads converged: the *Old Testament* 'way of the Philistines' (or the 'way of the sea') and 'way of the kings' which had an offshoot – the 'way of the wilderness' from Babylonia to Egypt and across the Sinai and Negev.[87] Damascus, Alexandria ad Issus (Roman Alexandretta, modern Iskenderun) and Beroia (today's Aleppo) to the north were similarly connected and therefore strategically sound choices as bases for empire administration. Diodorus described the location as 'naturally well adapted for watching over Babylon and the upper satrapies, and again for keeping an eye upon lower Syria and the satrapies near Egypt'.[88] Antigonus would later learn the strategic value of Syria when founding Antigonea-on-the-Orontes near Antioch, his residence from 306–302 BC.[89] Seleucus later positioned the city of Apamea in calculated fashion on the right bank of the Orontes as part of a Syrian tetrapolis of four regional cities.[90]

Following Perdiccas' death in Egypt, and as further evidence of his regional governance here, Archelaus, the garrison captain at Tyre, handed over the 800 talents to Attalus, which Perdiccas kept there for safekeeping. As one scholar noted, this was a transaction that appeared to take place independently of the local authority of Laomedon, suggesting an overarching authority at work.[91] We know Ptolemy offered to buy Laomedon out of Coele-Syria to better secure his border and for the proximity of the Phoenician ports.[92] Diodorus' account of the episode is brief; either a lacuna exists or Hieronymus oversimplified the rationale behind Ptolemy's move.[93]

If I am correct in identifying these wider roles for the Royal Bodyguards, a financial offer would have only been acceptable to the remaining Diadochi if it did not infringe upon a still-living pan-regional governor. That implies there was now an absence of that overarching authority in the Syrian region following Perdiccas' death. Unless we introduce a missing mechanism, Ptolemy's annexation would have appeared controversial and indeed expansionist, and yet no challenge emerged. The region was not contested until Eumenes 'thought to recover for the kings Phoenicia' in early 317 BC.[94] In 315 BC, after war with Eumenes was concluded, Ptolemy's envoy to Antigonus demanded 'all Syria' be granted for the part he played in the victory; once again this suggests there was no in-place governor of the Greater Syrian region.[95]

Perdiccas may well have initially succeeded in surrounding himself with trusted governors, potentially with Alexander's approval, in the interest of stability: Aristonus could have governed a northern part of Syria 'to the Mesopotamian Line' (therefore close to Cilicia, from where he set off on the failed Cypriot invasion), Arcesilaus in Mesopotamia itself, Laomedon in Coele-Syria, Philoxenus in Cilicia and his brother Alcetas in Pisidia. No doubt Docimus in Babylonia (to spy on Seleucus' movements), Cleomenes in Egypt (to keep an eye on Ptolemy) and Eumenes in eastern Anatolia were supposed to report on developments across the immediate borders.[96]

Why then was Hieronymus not more lucid on Perdiccas' Syrian mandate? Diodorus could have misunderstood the role of the roving chiliarch, as he did that of Seleucus, or, quite simply, it did not benefit Hieronymus to broadcast it, for once he had made it clear Perdiccas enjoyed foremost authority at Babylon, he had achieved all he needed to legitimize Eumenes' early career. Syria was after all raped and torn apart by Hieronymus' own patrons in their bid to secure Phoenician ports and a path south to Egypt.

Could the famous and still-debated coffin, the so-called 'Alexander Sarcophagus' that was discovered in Sidon in 1887, have actually been crafted for Perdiccas, perhaps after the conference at Triparadeisus, itself in Upper Syria? The spectacular sarcophagus now has pride of place in the Istanbul Archaeology Museum. One scholar commented: 'It is tempting to see its scaled roof, running vine garlands, guardian lions, and long narrative friezes, as an homage to Alexander's hearse, which must have passed close by the city in 321 BC, but nothing can be proved',[97] though the frieze clearly depicts the Macedonian king and Hephaestion. The sarcophagus is now popularly accredited to Abdalonymus, the 'rags to riches' King of Sidon (or as another scholar suggests, the prominent Persian satrap Mazaeus), but that has been recently challenged; Laomedon, the displaced satrap of Coele-Syria, has been proposed as its alternative inhabitant.[98]

Forensics now reveal that the Pentelic Marble sarcophagus was brightly painted in polychromatic style, with evidence of gold plating. This is not inconsistent with the 'hammered gold' in Diodorus' description of Alexander's hearse.[99] And so we might be forgiven for wondering whether Ptolemy left the ponderously heavy cask in Syria in his hurried flight back to Egypt after kidnapping Alexander's body. Perdiccas' brother-in-law, Attalus, was close by gathering up any soldiers who made it out of Egypt, and Eumenes could have even commissioned the 'highly conflicted' coffin when he passed through the region in early 317 BC with his pockets full from the Cyinda treasury. It is

A scene from the so-called Alexander Sarcophagus (short side 'A') which may depict the murder of the unarmed Perdiccas. (Istanbul Archaeology Museum)

noteworthy that carved on one pediment (the top of short side 'A') is a relief reckoned by some scholars to depict Perdiccas' murder; an unarmed man is being attacked by what appear to be three armed Macedonians (Antigenes, Peithon and Seleucus, Perdiccas' named assassins?). A second victim (perhaps his sister, Atalante) looks to be holding a shield for protection, and one attacker has fallen, implying a spirited defence. If that theory is correct, this would hardly be a fitting commemorative for anyone else but Perdiccas.[100]

Clues in the War Council at Triparadeisus

At the reconvening of generals at Triparadeisus in the late summer of 320 BC after Perdiccas' death, the discord from Babylon re-emerged, incited by the new teenage queen, Adea-Eurydice and stirred by 'accusations' delivered in her speech, though the unexpected presence of the Perdiccan naval commander, Attalus, and his fleet (perhaps moored nearby, but surely not at the convocation, where he would have been seized and executed), may have added to the tension. Adea-Eurydice was fanning a fire lit by grievances related to pay and promised bonuses (and probably more besides), a crisis finally defrayed by Antigonus and Seleucus.[101] With Perdiccas, Craterus and Leonnatus now dead, and with Eumenes along with the remaining Perdiccans scattered under sentence of death, and with Peithon, Antigenes and possibly Seleucus having recently shown their dissatisfaction with the state of Perdiccan affairs, the empire could have been completely redistributed.[102]

This was also the perfect opportunity to take a second and perhaps more legitimate vote on the accession of the kings. Antipater, we should recall, arrived with a Macedonian army not tainted by Babylonian assembly politics or by years of service under the Royal Bodyguards. Alexander's half-Asiatic son by Rhoxane (as well as his existing son, Heracles by Barsine) was almost rejected at the Assembly, and the principal backers of King Philip III Arrhidaeus – Meleager and his supporters – were dead or firmly outnumbered.[103] A completely new order could have emerged, and yet it did not.

The most significant of the territorial grants made by Antipater at Triparadeisus matched the original satrapal appointments supposedly orchestrated by Perdiccas at Babylon. The few changes that were made simply plugged the gaps left by the dead or by the clearly untrustworthy. Ptolemy, Laomedon, Lysimachus, Antigonus (though now with wider powers), Asander, Peithon, Peucestas and I also propose Seleucus all retained control of their original regions, as did the majority of the eastern satraps.[104] If Alexander had made no effort to formalize the governance of the empire and they were Perdiccas' own orchestrations (as texts uniformly tell us), this would be a vexing status quo, and it is far better explained as adherence to his will that no one dared reverse. Besides, the Royal Bodyguards did not yet wish to challenge their inheritances, for they had surely been discussed, shaped and agreed upon well before Alexander's death.

The Macedonian Women and their place in Alexander's Testament

> ...once the father is dead, heirs are for practical purposes (assuming they are well below the age of maturity) no man's sons, and can do no would-be-dynast any more than short-term good, whereas the king's sisters can be married and thus, legitimise the seizure of royal or quasi-royal power. Better yet, a king's sister may produce children of the blood of the royal house, as well as the new.[105]

This extract from a study of Argead women has particular relevance to the situation Alexander was faced with on his deathbed in Babylon, and to the struggles of ascendancy his successors were faced with after. The contribution of women in Macedonian dynasties is well-documented, and the Hellenistic period history was peppered with their typical Macedonian names: Stratonices,

Berenices, Laodices, Arsinoes and of course Cleopatras, all of whom played significant political roles at the royal courts of their day.[106]

There is evidence that Olympias and Cleopatra were executing Alexander's policy in their role as caretaker/protector (*prostates*) throughout his absence on campaign, an arrangement that frustrated and clashed with Antipater's authority. Alexander's mother and sister were listed as the recipients on desperately needed grain shipments from Cyrene (without patronymic, suggesting a head of state and probably in the famine years of 330–326 BC) alongside other dignitaries.[107] After the death of her husband Alexander Molossus, Cleopatra may have been acting protector of the Kingdom of Epirus, where women appear to have enjoyed a higher social status; here roles akin to 'presidents' were attested in the absence of a king. Cleopatra may well have held the position of the official who received sacred envoys (known as a *thearodochos*) for the Epirote League. It has been argued that the whole Argead clan possessed this sacral power, and Olympias had certainly taken over custody of the oracle of Dodona during her tenure of Epirus, warding off Greek interference in the process. She had also attempted to intervene in the Harpalus affair by demanding he be surrendered up when he fled to Athens in 324 BC, for she would surely have preferred to take control of the Asian treasury funds he absconded with rather than letting them be scooped up by Antipater.[108]

In the post-Alexander world, Phila the sagacious daughter of Antipater, Cynnane the daughter of Philip II with their daughter Adea, and Polyperchon's daughter-in-law Cratesipolis were all involved in military actions or state decision-making.[109] Stratonice the wife of Antigonus had a role in the conclusion of the siege of the Perdiccan rebels in Pisidia, and a generation on, the Successor Wars were permeated by intermarriages between more of these remarkable daughters of the Macedonian Diadochi – as families sought dynastic advancement and protection from rivals. And none of them 'could be reproached either for cowardice or for scrupulousness'.[110]

The will preserved in the *Romance* and *Metz Epitome* is Greek in style, an endogamous document that saw the pairing of the royal women and the king's leading men. But do any of these arrangements reflect Alexander's original wishes, or are they the political machinations of the pamphleteers? Alexander appears to have trusted two men above all: Craterus and Perdiccas. However, inconveniently, they mistrusted one another, and despite allegations to the opposite, Alexander relied upon two women to protect his interests: Olympias and Cleopatra.[111] Both men and women could presumably be counted as guardians of Alexander's sons. 'Macedonian kings arranged marriages for themselves and their offspring', and Alexander would have wanted to stage-manage exactly that through his will.[112]

Although overwhelmingly influential, Olympias was past childbearing age and she could not in any case produce an Argead heir, being Molossian in origin, now that there were no surviving or suitable Argead males. Cleopatra was in her early thirties when Alexander died, and sources suggest she was already the mother of two children; as the daughter of Philip II, she *could* still provide a half-Argead heir.[113] Contemplating their respective positions, Olympias saw the two obvious means to surviving the turmoil: find Cleopatra a powerful husband 'complete with a Macedonian army', and establish herself as principal guardian of the young Alexander IV.[114] It appears she attempted both.

With the strongest contenders – Perdiccas, Leonnatus and Craterus – dead by 320 BC, Cleopatra courted, or was variously courted by, Cassander, Ptolemy, Lysimachus and possibly even by Antigonus during her twelve years at Sardis.[115] If Perdiccas' approach to Cleopatra (brokered through Eumenes) had led to war with Antipater – suggesting this match was not endorsed or demanded by Alexander's will – and when considering that no other suitor appeared immediately after to claim the 'right' to Cleopatra's hand, then it follows that she was most likely paired with either the already dead Leonnatus or Craterus. This would further explain why Antipater was relieved when Leonnatus fell at Lamia. If Cleopatra had been paired with the fallen Royal Bodyguard, then her correspondence with Leonnatus carried a legitimacy that has been lost or deliberately camouflaged; her overtures to Perdiccas and her crossing to Asia did only take place once Leonnatus had fallen in Thessaly.

A pairing of Cleopatra with Craterus in Alexander's will is more troublesome, for we would have to assume that Craterus rejected Alexander's sister in favour of Phila after considering the permutations and after crossing to Greece to assist Antipater in the Lamian War. Although Craterus does seem to have initially delayed his departure and only journeyed upon realizing Leonnatus had not turned the tide,[116] Arrian's *Events After Alexander* makes it clear that once Menander revealed Perdiccas' designs on Alexander's sister, Craterus (and Antipater) was 'more than ever determined to make war on Perdiccas', hardly a position Craterus could adopt if he had himself rebuffed her, assuming our understanding of the order of these events is correct.

It seems even more unlikely that Cleopatra would have rejected Craterus, for his 'bride price' would have included his 10,000 veterans and an imminent Macedonian regency to underscore the guardianship of her and Alexander's children, though Perdiccas and his royal army was equally attractive. Logic demands, therefore, that we accept the (unlikely) possibility that Craterus' increased determination to meet Perdiccas in battle was because of his undermining of the union Craterus had yet to conclude.

What of Thessalonice, Alexander's half-sister who was paired with Lysimachus by the *Pamphlet* (T1, T2)? Cassander is said to have forced Thessalonice into marriage following her capture at Pydna, which clearly highlights the danger posed by the continued availability of an unmarried daughter of an Argead king. For exactly this reason, Olympias, most likely with Alexander's approval (despite reports of the contrary), had murdered Europa, a daughter from Philip's seventh marriage, upon Alexander taking the throne.[117] Antipater had probably kept Thessalonice carefully quarantined at Pella (as he attempted with Cynnane), just as Antigonus had attempted to keep Cleopatra 'safe' from marital intrigue at Sardis.[118] Alexander would have likewise been cautious and planned a 'safe' pairing for Thessalonice in his will. Lysimachus was a credible option, as were several prominent others. But then there is no evidence Lysimachus 'claimed' his inheritance-bride; he married another of Antipater's daughters, becoming Cassander's brother-in-law, and so this pairing does appear to be a *Pamphlet* overture to the satrap of Thrace and its bordering regions.

What the early years of the Successor Wars made abundantly clear is that Antipater's long control of Macedon and Greece made his daughters desirable currency, and especially so in the face of an Argead dynasty promising a half-Asiatic and only quarter-Argead princess (Alexander himself was half-Epirote) or a halfwit king, Philip III Arrhidaeus, married to a troublemaking queen, Adea-Eurydice, who had Illyrian roots. Antipater's daughters initially cemented a brief accord with Antigonus (via his son Demetrius the Besieger), Craterusm and Ptolemy, with Perdiccas and Leonnatus apparently being invited to join the fold to stave off immediate challenges. With the exception of Antigonus, these were effectively the surviving 'guardians' appointed at the Assembly at Babylon, or, in Ptolemy's case, the guardianship offered following Perdiccas' death in Egypt (T11, T12).[119] Clearly, Alexander would not have orchestrated, or condoned, this Antipatrid family dominance.

In contrast to this early nuptial nepotism, none of the Diadochi or their offspring intermarried until after the Battle of Ipsus in 301 BC, when in quick succession Lysimachus took Arsinoe, a daughter of Ptolemy, and another daughter Lysandra for his son Agathocles. Upon the death of his wife Deidameia (the sister of Pyrrhus) soon after, Demetrius was betrothed to a further daughter of the Egyptian dynast (though he only married her twelve years later), and Seleucus asked for the hand of Stratonice, Demetrius' own daughter by Phila (thus Antigonus' granddaughter and Cassander's niece). Cassander, in turn, later arranged for his young sons to marry daughters of both Ptolemy and Lysimachus; even the Epirote royal line was to marry into the ranks of the Macedonian Diadochi.[120] The royal women, then, were indispensable to the survival of dynasties, and they would not have been bypassed in Alexander's will.

The Role of the Halfwit King

The testaments found in the *Romance* and *Metz Epitome* positioned the newly elevated King Philip III Arrhidaeus as a 'caretaker king' to act in the name of the juvenile Alexander IV: 'In the *interim* Arrhidaeus, son of Philip, should lead the Macedonians.'[121] Why would the pamphleteers have thrown what amounted to an idiotic spanner into their artful works?

Bearing in mind Olympias' hostility to Philip III Arrhidaeus and his young wife Queen Adea-Eurydice, this must have been an original will edict that simply could not be hidden; a regal appointment already notorious for the conflict it caused in Babylon and further publicized by the antics of the new queen at Triparadeisus. Alexander had presumably designed his half-brother's role exactly as outlined in the extant wills: it was a temporary kingship to 'housesit' for his sons under the benign and trusted protectorship (*prostasia*) of Craterus to thwart any rivals coveting an empty throne. The office of *prostates* appears to be an extraordinary role only ever linked to the Macedonian court when the monarch was deemed incapable of immediate rule.[122] Perdiccas' charge of Rhoxane, whether their marriage was truly demanded by Alexander's will or not, represented a balance that provided Alexander's sons with a further guardian.

The mentally impaired Philip III Arrhidaeus was presumably physically developed and able to procreate (a fear that never materialized, as far as we know), so the pairing with Adea-Eurydice would be precipitous if they produced a son, and not much less dangerous if a daughter was born to them. So, it is unlikely that Alexander would have provided Arrhidaeus with a bride in his will, and certainly not an ambitious one who was hostile to his name. Adea-Eurydice was 'no cipher to be manipulated at will'; from her presence at Triparadeisus where her 'rabble-rousing' almost resulted in Antipater's death, to her final face-off against Olympias' army in 317 BC, demonstrated how dangerous she was.[123] Too young to be a threat when Alexander departed for Asia, she may well have been targeted for 'removal' in his private 'last wishes'.

The Precarious Position of Alexander's Persian Royal Family

Alexander would have additionally needed to provide for the welfare of his Asiatic wives and mistresses: Parysatis the daughter of Artaxerxes III Ochus, Stateira the daughter of Darius III, the already accounted for Rhoxane the daughter of Oxyartes, and Barsine, whom we are told was a daughter of Artabazus (I have argued she was a granddaughter).[124] The last two required special attention, as they were mothers of Alexander's children. The noise from Babylon suggests Rhoxane was placed under Perdiccas' protection (a contention reinforced by Meleager's speech), and she could have credibly been pledged to Perdiccas in marriage, as the extant wills suggest. Macedonian tradition was indeed to appoint a relative of an immature king as guardian-cum-regent.[125] If Alexander's mistress Barsine and their son Heracles were to remain in the region of Artabazus' family estates in Hellespontine Phrygia, then Leonnatus would have been expected to assume the role of guardian; if he was paired with Alexander's sister Cleopatra, then the 'relative' status held.

Assuming a prominent former Bodyguard was to safeguard the welfare of the remaining childless Achaemenid wives, that role would have likely fallen to the Persian-speaking Peucestas, controlling as he did the Achaemenid homelands.[126] Stateira and her younger sister Drypetis (Hephaestion's widow) were reportedly murdered in Babylon by Rhoxane, working in league with Perdiccas, possibly for that reason; their unfortunate fates had been determined by their recognition – so legitimization – in marriage at Susa. Parysatis may have been executed too, for she was never mentioned thereafter. The daughters of the last two Great Kings could have been influential Persian rallying points in the forthcoming uncertainty.[127]

If so, it suggests an attack on Darius' branch of the Achaemenid line had already commenced. Sisygambis, Alexander's 'second mother', passed away with grief-laden suicide, which raises the question: was it suicide at all?[128] Or did a quiet pogrom take place that has almost eluded history's pages? Had Sisygambis' dark reflections, fuelled by memories of the Great King Ochus (otherwise known as Artaxerxes III) and his onslaught of her eighty brothers a generation before, now anticipated a re-run at Macedonian hands?[129] Now, a generation on, another Ochus, Darius' own son, was never again mentioned,[130] and Darius' brother Oxyathres, who had been one of Alexander's court Companions, disappeared from the texts; he was likely Sisygambis' only remaining child.[131] Although the prominent Asiatic wives of the Diadochi did feature in the new order – Oxyathres' daughter Amastris, for example (she was briefly the wife of Craterus and later Lysimachus) – the women who were widowed or rejected faced far bleaker prospects with Alexander dead.

In this period, many attested children vanished with their parents: Eumenes' children were never referred to after his death, and the daughters of Attalus by Perdiccas' sister, Atalante, were captured with Thessalonice at Pydna and never reappeared.[132] We may wonder what became of the myriad half-Asiatic offspring sired by Alexander's soldiers and born in the wake of the decade-long campaign. They must have had an estate claim or two in the name of their fathers, and surely this is one of the reasons why Alexander forbade their repatriation to Macedon; the fear for their integration into families 'at home' was mentioned too. Although promises were provided by Alexander for their education and eventual return, it is difficult to imagine that such prejudice in Macedon would change, and it seems a rather hollow-sounding pledge bearing in mind these offspring (*epigonoi*) were the most likely descendants to accept Alexander's own half-caste sons as overlords in Asia.[133]

Alexander's Bypassed Son: Heracles

Heracles, by Alexander's part-Rhodian mistress Barsine, was 3 or 4 years old when Alexander died.[134] Barsine, who had a Greek education, was captured at Damascus in Syria following the Battle of Issus in 333 BC. Sources tell us she was a daughter of Artabazus (I argue she was a granddaughter), the 'chief of courtiers' and the former Persian satrap of Hellespontine Phrygia (and son of a king's daughter, added Plutarch) who was known at the Macedonian court where he had once taken refuge in Philip's day following an unsuccessful satrap revolt. So, Heracles was of royal Persian stock.[135] Plutarch's rundown of Barsine's qualities included her 'agreeable disposition', and thus 'Alexander determined [at the instigation of Parmenio, the senior veteran general on campaign, claimed Aristobulus] to attach himself to a woman of such high birth and beauty'.[136] Her status is further implied by the marriage of Eumenes, Ptolemy and Nearchus to Barsine's family at Susa.[137]

Unfortunately, as events made clear, they thought it of little significance. Nearchus' alleged speech at the Assembly in Babylon, in which he made a case for the boy, certainly supports the connection, if it was not a back-construct of Cleitarchus. Eumenes also appears to have gained family loyalty, for Artabazus' son Pharnabazus fought for him in 321/320 BC against Craterus.[138]

Heracles himself never featured in the *Pamphlet* will, and this would appear counterproductive to Eumenes in the circumstances, that is until we recall Antigonus was in control of the region where the boy resided, thus in control of the boy himself. In which case Heracles' absence from the testament was an attempt to neutralize exactly that, while it promoted the cause of Alexander IV, who was in Olympias' custody in Pella.

It is universally assumed that Alexander never married Barsine, so Heracles remained an unrecognized bastard son, which would of course go some way to explaining his rejection at Babylon. But at the mass weddings at Susa, Alexander was demonstrably 'marriage-minded' in the face of whatever objections Rhoxane may have thrown up or the fears she harboured, for there he took the hands of the Persian princesses Stateira and Parysatis.[139] If Heracles' mother was also descended from an Achaemenid line, there remains the question of why Alexander did not legitimize his (then) only son.[140] We cannot in fact be sure he did not, for a slight amendment to Arrian's statement (or Aristobulus' before him) changes the context of the marriages altogether, and I have already proposed an explanation for why Arrian also named Darius' daughter 'Barsine'.[141]

But what of Heracles' fate in Alexander's original will? As the outcome of Rhoxane's pregnancy was unknown in summer 323 BC, Alexander must have recognized his existing son (with a clause 'to the strongest or most worthy of them', when they reached throne age?). As with the historic 'oversupply' of Argead kings (until Philip and then Alexander had all potential claimants executed), two sons raised at Pella in Macedon would have been a recipe for court intrigue and yet more royal fratricide that would pit one guardian against another. Moreover, the sons each had family claims in different regions: Alexander IV with hereditary residencies in Bactria (or Sogdia) through Rhoxane, and Heracles in Hellespontine Phrygia via Artabazus' estates. But what testament strategy was not dangerous in Babylon, given one full-sister, two half-sisters, two sons, three or possibly four wives and at least seven ruthlessly ambitious Bodyguards overseeing even more regional satraps with discontented garrisoned veterans and mercenaries accumulating under them? And what alternatives existed?

In his heart, Alexander himself may have doubted whether his half-barbarian sons would ever be named as kings in conservative Macedon. But if he was to truly defy history, it would now take sons of royal blood from both sides of the Aegean to carry the title 'King of Kings'.

The Testamental Bequests

Can the references to temples, statues and the tombs Alexander demanded in the 'last plans' which were allegedly 'discovered' at Babylon be reconciled with the surviving will texts (T1, T2)? They can, but only if we accept corruption at the edges: *Romance* accretion and Roman-era contamination from one side, and deception in the *Pamphlet* on the other, for the pamphleteers had a clear agenda and it was not to bring attention to any will-demanded monuments that Perdiccas had cancelled.[142]

In return for their hardly unexpected 'gifts from the fates', the extant will texts demand that the most notable of the beneficiaries erect statues of Alexander, Heracles, Olympias, Ammon, Athena and Philip II in their respective territories, whilst offerings were to be sent to other notable religious sites such as Delphi and Olympia. Ambitious, but not unreasonable, this is the content we would have expected the pamphleteer(s) to preserve in a testament focusing on satraps and satrapies and not diversionary costly commemoratives. So, the temples we see in the 'last plans' to be built at Delos, Delphi, Dion (the most important centre of worship of Zeus at the foot of Mt Olympus), Dodona, Cyrnus (Thrace) and Amphipolis, with one to surpass them all at Troy, appear to have been expediently dumped by the *Pamphlet*, if they were indeed a part of Alexander's original will (T25).[143]

The testament may well have attempted a sound strategy for what were nevertheless fundamentally unsound circumstances. If our conclusions are valid, it featured the sensible deployment of the Royal Bodyguards and the leading generals as empire pan-provincial governors with multiple satraps under them, power counterbalanced by strategic Argead marriages at the top of the chain of command. On the other hand, those grandiose last plans – that conglomerate of untenable will demands and campaign projects – were the product of a deeply troubled man whose sense of scale had been corrupted by fortune's unswerving companionship and fawning courtiers, as well as the profound but not bottomless depths of the Great Kings' treasuries.

Why the *Pamphlet* Will Ever Existed

Here I reiterate my central contention when autopsying the veracity of the *Pamphlet* and its reason for being: rebroadcasting the existence of Alexander's testament in the early years of the Successor Wars would have only been a tenable strategy if knowledge of the original – or hearsay and rumour of its existence to those not at Babylon – was circulating in the Diadochi armies and their courts. And Alexander *was* ever Alexander; facing death at Babylon, a will by which his sons would rule under the protection of his few trusted men was the only route to immortality when requests for divinity had been so hard to come by in his lifetime.[144]

10

EPITAPH IN ROME, OBITUARY TODAY

Why was Alexander's last will and testament so thoroughly discounted by both the Roman-period historians and modern scholars?

Roman-era historians were no more forensic than their Greek counterparts when biographing Alexander and reporting on conflicting campaign episodes, especially his death. They were either ambivalent on the lack of succession instructions or downright hostile to his will.

I analyse why the Roman writers and antiquarians gave little credence to the reports and rumours that Alexander left clear succession instructions at Babylon, and why today, some 2,300 years later, we still adhere to the 'standard model' of intestacy.

> honouring Rhodes above all cities [Alexander] both deposited there the testament disposing of his whole realm and in other ways showed admiration.[1]
>
> Diodorus, *Library of World History*
>
> Some have believed that the distribution of the provinces was prescribed by Alexander's Will, but I have ascertained that this report, though transmitted by our sources, is without foundation.[2]
>
> Curtius, *The History of Alexander*
>
> Augustus heard Alexander at the age of thirty-two years had subdued the greatest part of the world and was at a loss what he should do with the rest of his time. But he wondered why Alexander should not think it a lesser labour to gain a great empire than to set in order what he had got.[3]
>
> Plutarch, *Sayings of Kings and Commanders*

Somewhere between his death in Babylon and Rome's domination of Macedon 150 years later, Alexander became 'the Great'. But this Hellenistic-era-originating epithet did not always hold good in Republican Rome. While its military men admired, learned from and adapted to the mighty Macedonian military machine, ultimately destroying it, the still-conservative conscience of the Republic vilified Alexander and his father as tyrants, partly because Republican Rome found monarchy abhorrent and so shuddered at the prospect of charismatic personalities who might one day revive it.

But as the Republic became 'Empire', and when its dictators and then emperors emulated Macedon's influence in the East, Alexander re-emerged into the sunlight of approbation, even if court philosophers still crafted their declamations around his character portrayals. In fact, the Roman emperors Pompey – who shared the epithet 'unconquered' (*invictus*) with Scipio and Alexander – and then Julius Caesar, Augustus, Caligula, Nero, Trajan, Marcus Aurelius, Caracalla and Septimus Severus, who locked up the Alexandrian tomb to deny anyone else a glimpse of Alexander's corpse, all felt the need to stylize themselves on the Macedonian conqueror in some way.[4] Even Crassus believed he was treading in his footsteps en route to his disastrous invasion of Parthia, and Mark Antony must have too, with similar calamitous results.

Septimus Severus is even reported (perhaps spuriously) to have reconstituted a Silver Shields brigade in emulation of the elite Macedonian infantry corps. Caracalla, who named his officers after Alexander's generals, demanded the title 'Great', and he even took the name 'Alexander' after inspecting his body in its tomb in Alexandria; he deposited his own cloak, belt and jewellery, we are told, in return for Alexander's drinking cups and weapons.[5] Caracalla is said to have persecuted philosophers of the Aristotelian school based on the lingering Vulgate claim that Aristotle had provided the poison that killed the Macedonian king (T9, T10).[6] The toxic territory was familiar, as the Roman emperors (or families of) Augustus, Caligula, Claudius, Nero, Vitellius, Domitian, Hadrian, Commodus, Caracalla, Elagabalus and Alexander Severus were all associated with some form of scandal involving poison. This helps explain why Alexander's conspiracy-ridden Vulgate death was ever topical in Rome and why Cleitarchus remained a popular read, even by the sapient no-nonsense Cicero.[7]

Most closely paralleling Alexander's death in the Roman world was the demise of Claudius, allegedly at Nero's hand. Suetonius recorded that 'most people thought he [Claudius] had been poisoned', by his official food taster no less.[8] Suetonius followed with 'an equal discrepancy exists between the accounts of what happened next. According to many, he lost his power of speech.'[9] Suetonius described a painful night and brief recovery, followed by a second dose of poison and then a coma. Tacitus reported that the second dose was administered to Claudius on a feather, a technique used to induce vomiting and a standard part of the physician's purge.[10]

Compare this to the *Metz Epitome* and the *Romance* texts (T1, T2), which extend the Vulgate recounting of the conspiracy in Babylon. Here we have the description of the second poisoning from a feather by Alexander's cupbearer, Iollas (Chares interestingly claimed Ptolemy had been Alexander's taster), along with the king's final night of agony and speechless condition, juxtaposed beside the *Journal*'s claim that Alexander was speechless for the final two days and nights (T3, T4):[11]

> In the meantime, Alexander was in a sorry state. He wanted to vomit and so asked for a feather: Iollas gave the king a feather smeared with poison. When he put this down his throat ... he was continuously racked with renewed and ever more excruciating pains. In this condition, he passed the night.[12]

Familiar territory indeed. But as for any forensic dissection of Alexander's death, there has always been an uneasy silence in Rome as if this was hallowed ground, like a dark and abandoned cemetery they dare not set foot in for fear of upsetting the pre-agreed order of the Underworld.

We can, however, be sure that apart from what was said of Alexander's silence in the *Journal* (most fully recounted by Arrian and Plutarch), the conspiracy claims of poison made in the *Pamphlet* with the attached description of the will (captured by the *Romance* and *Metz Epitome*) and the Vulgate hybrid with the poison conspiracy attached to Alexander's 'last words' (Cleitarchus' syncretic ending, adopted by Diodorus, Justin and Curtius, but mentioned by Arrian and Plutarch as well), there were *no other versions of his death in circulation*. We know this because Arrian, the last of all the surviving authors to biograph Alexander and report on his death (Justin lived later than Arrian, but was precising the far-earlier writing of Trogus), made this absolutely clear: 'no one had anything else to say about Alexander's death.' Nothing save the above versions emerged in the 500 years between Babylon and Arrian's own career fighting in Asia during the reign of the Roman emperor Trajan.

One of the reasons the Roman-era historians were forensically blunt in their autopsies may be down to the monopoly of information that emanated from Hellenistic Alexandria, as well as the prevailing philosophical doctrine in Rome. And those who did directly challenge the reporting may have had a very specific personal agenda, as I shall explain.

The Alexandrian Monopoly

The conflicts that frequently appear in the surviving accounts, many of them relating to names, numbers and relative chronology, suggest that neither Callisthenes' official account nor the Royal Diaries (the *Ephemerides*), from which the *Journal* was supposedly extracted, survived to the Roman period, except in isolated fragments of episodes and through second- or third-hand testimony. If they had survived in full, no contradictory reporting should ever have appeared, for together they would have provided a near-perfect campaign log, whilst any archetypal inaccuracies would have been uniformly carried forward.[13]

The conclusion to be drawn here is that the books of the Alexandrian-influenced historians – Ptolemy, Aristobulus (I argue he may have worked for Ptolemy and been influenced by his already-published book) and Cleitarchus – dominated the Roman-era perceptions of Alexander. And the surviving Roman-era derivative accounts are the basis of the interpretations we make today. One result is that modern scholars conclude: 'The history of events after his [Alexander's] death is intelligible only on the assumption that he made no Will.'[14] Yet that contention falls apart if we are prepared to accept that those blueprint histories were specifically fashioned to give credence to, or to serve obeisance to, the claims of intestacy and Alexander's failure to clarify his succession.

If Ptolemy and Aristobulus were at the foundation of Arrian's court-sourced biography (as Arrian himself stated on his opening page), and if Alexandria-based Cleitarchus' book substantially templated the Vulgate-genre accounts, my suggestion of an 'Alexandrian' monopoly seems to hold. The combined tradition carried forward by these three historians became a robust pesticide on the tenuous roots of any mention of a succession attempt by Alexander; it was a Hellenistic literary inheritance tax that foiled his estate planning. This is my suggested publication order for these three influential books: Ptolemy, who first set the intestate template, then Aristobulus, who followed his *Journal*-citing final pages – as Arrian confirmed – and lastly Cleitarchus, a discussion which is not without contention and discord itself.[15]

We know the author (or authors) of an original highly flamboyant biography of Alexander, which quickly metamorphosed into what became the quasi-mythical *Greek Alexander Romance*, unfortunately boat-hooked the *Pamphlet* detail aboard. And this surely killed any chance of Alexander's will being taken seriously. Arrian's had the following stern words for the other 'brazen' writers: 'I let these stories stand here simply to show that I am aware of their currency, and not to give them any credence.'[16] As for the lingering hearsay of the will, Cleitarchus' erasure of its presence, alongside his epitaphic 'to the strongest' and the reference to Homeric 'funeral games', was an early nail in the testate coffin for the Roman-era historians.[17] But there were other diversional influences, including Stoic philosophy, which was pre-eminent in the imperial halls of Rome.

Stoicism and the Acceptance of Alexander's Intestacy

Stoicism has been termed 'a system put together hastily, violently, to meet a bewildered world'. It was more of a therapy than a philosophy, and that was certainly needed, for following Alexander's death, the world was thrown into turmoil by the early unsettled Hellenistic monarchies, 'when political freedom became a simple political catchword, rather than a battle cry'. The Greek city-state became subordinated to new and revived leagues and kingdoms of Alexander's successors, and soon by the ever eastward-lengthening shadow of Rome.[18]

The Hellenistic era, which truly began at Alexander's death, had witnessed the emergence of the philosophical schools of the Cynics, Stoics and Sceptics, along with the happier followers of Epicurus, at the expense of the old doctrine of the Academy and Lyceum of Plato and Aristotle, as thinkers tried to rationalize the radically changing world – or, as Epicurus espoused it, 'withdraw' from it. Inevitably, Alexander became the perfect canvas on which to project their new ideas for Roman contemplation. The Macedonian king was used as a punchbag in a syllabus on morality which was testing Rome's own conscience as its empire expanded in the East. As one scholar put it, Alexander was 'both a positive paradigm of military success and a negative paradigm of immoral excess'.[19]

Zeno of Citium established the school of the Stoics in 301 BC from the painted arch in the Athenian Agora (known as the *Stoa Poikile*, from which

'Stoic' derives), directly after the Battle of Ipsus, where the arrayed forces of Lysimachus, Seleucus and Cassander, with the support in spirit of the cleverly absent Ptolemy, finally vanquished Antigonus the One-Eyed and his son Demetrius the Besieger. Thereafter, almost all of the successors of Alexander professed to be Stoics, who believed reasoned argument (encapsulated by the word *logos*) could explain the order and coherence of the universe in which a man could plan and rationalize against overwhelming odds.[20]

Stoicism became the dominant philosophy for the Roman-era literati once the Greek philosopher Panaetius arrived from Athens for a tour of indoctrination, despite the century-and-a-half of attempts by the Sceptics and more conservative aristocrats to combat the spreading doctrine. Panaetius befriended Scipio Aemilianus, whose 'Scipionic Circle' of intellectuals included poets and the once-hostaged Greek historian Polybius. Polybius' own outlook, and his frequent use of 'fortune' (expressed as *tyche*, after the Greek Goddess of fortune) to explain events, appears to have stemmed from here.[21] Panaetius' wisdom later found fertile ground in Cicero, in whose *Stoic Paradoxes* we find a plain-language explanation of the doctrine.[22] Cicero claimed 'some Stoics are practically Cynics', and this becomes important when considering their attitude to Alexander's alleged last words.[23] The schools had indeed been connected through Crates of Thebes, a follower of Diogenes the Cynic who famously met Alexander in Corinth and became a teacher to Zeno of Citium.[24]

Stoicism helped shape the instructional essays on ethics and conscience (referred to as *suasoria* in Latin) of Seneca, who used Cato the Younger and his 'heroic suicide' as a righteous example of the opposition to tyranny. The imperial tendrils of Stoic moral choices crept in through Augustus' teacher, Athenodorus of Tarsus, and ultimately it laid the foundations for the *Meditations* of Marcus Aurelius, the last of the 'five good emperors', nostalgically written in Greek and housing reflections on a life that witnessed an empire at its peak. Arrian himself was a student of the Stoic philosopher Epictetus, whose teachings he reverently preserved.

It is within this philosophical framework, which accepted Alexander's 'stoical' last words and his declining to appoint a successor, that Plutarch and Arrian lived and closed their biographies of Alexander with the *Journal* entry – what they believed to be an extract from the genuine royal diaries of *Ephemerides*.

Despite the philosophical background noise and their elitist pretensions, Plutarch and Arrian ought to have raised their heads above Alexander's almost stoical acceptance of his fate to question why, like Augustus had, the campaigning king made no attempt to formally arrange his far-reaching estate. Neither of them considered that the *Journal* entry they cited was by definition propaganda from a royal court. But Ptolemy's pedestrian treatise appealed to Arrian's military palate, so he mistook plodding competency for historical fidelity.

As has been neatly pointed out, what Ptolemy had not written, Arrian could not have read, so he and Plutarch fell into the same *Journal*-baited trap.[25]

Arrian's misplaced faith took the form of a liturgy to the honesty and fidelity brought by the office of kingship:

> ...but my view is that Ptolemy and Aristobulus are more trustworthy on their narrative. Aristobulus accompanied Alexander on his campaigns. Ptolemy not only campaigned with Alexander, but as a king himself, it would have been more dishonourable for him than for anyone else to provide untruths; moreover both wrote when Alexander was dead and so there was no compulsion nor anything to gain from writing anything but what actually happened.[26]

The sentiment from Arrian recurs in the speech given by Alexander to his untrusting and debt-burdened men after the mass weddings at Susa.[27] In his satirical treatise titled *How to Write History*, Lucian wryly noted: 'The impossible was believed of Achilles because Homer, preserving his deeds posthumously, would therefore have no motive for lying.'[28] Lucian had indeed identified an Achilles' heel in historical method, and it sounds remarkably similar to Arrian's introductory digression. Had Ptolemy himself opened with a similar self-declaration on his content? We might try and approximate it as follows:

> I write as a King whose word and honour counts above all things, and as a Companion and Bodyguard of King Alexander III of Macedon, privileged myself to be present at and a part of great events; and just as Homer recorded the deeds of Achilles with no agenda – for his subject was then long dead – I write an account only of things that truly took place, as I witnessed them, and as stated in the Royal Diaries.

Could Arrian's campaign account, the *Anabasis*, which ended with the notorious *Journal* extract (T3), have been mirroring Ptolemy's wording at both ends of the book?[29]

In stark contrast to the past Classical Age views of Plato and Pythagoras, the Stoics (and Epicureans) were tolerant of suicide in extreme circumstances, considering it an appropriate escape from the frustrations of the world.[30] Not only was suicide the man's right, it was also considered a rational means of freeing the soul from the suffering body if the Greek and Roman embodiments of 'inevitability' and the twist of fate (*moira* and *fatum*) had decreed an impossible position.[31] Although Tacitus, as one example, placed little value on 'self-murder', which he considered politically useless, he did incorporate its detail to add dramatic tones to his chapters. He also reported on more widespread suicides which were prompted by the fact that wills remained valid (and so their bequeathed assets too) for those who killed themselves, whereas those condemned to death by execution forfeited their estates if they did not commit suicide first.[32]

Pliny came to regard suicide as the greatest gift amid life's hardships.[33] Livy recorded that the residents of Marseilles (excluding soldiers and slaves, for whom suicide was illegal) had petitioned the Senate and were given permission to end their life by taking hemlock, which was provided to them by the state free of charge. At home, 'patriotic suicide' became widespread; a high proportion of well-known philosophers ended their lives this way (some forced to), including Seneca and Lucretius, whose poem *On the Nature of Things* introduced Epicureanism to Roman culture.

The Roman intellect was therefore receptive to what we might term Alexander's 'succession suicide' and his vision on posthumous chaos. His last words, more cynical than useful, somehow became a demonstration of moral duty, stoic behaviour espoused by Cicero in his posthumously published *On Duties* or *On Obligations* (*De Officiis*) encapsulating his own moral code. Moreover, Alexander's words suggested he was dying content, as Epictetus proposed everybody should.[34] Plato had proposed: 'If a man has trained himself throughout his life to live in a state as close as possible to death, would it not be ridiculous for him to be distressed when death comes to him?'[35] If Cleitarchus' intent when framing the Vulgate lines was to portray Alexander's death with undertones of selfishness in the face of impending chaos, then Stoicism simply re-rendered that as 'selflessness' and that interpretation stuck.

Alexander's death scene at Babylon houses elements of a moralizing pastiche, and yet Justin's summation provided a perfect example of the Stoic interpretation:

> While they [the soldiers] all wept, he not only did not shed a tear, but showed not the least token of sorrow; so that he even comforted some who grieved immoderately, and gave others messages to their parents; and his soul was as undaunted at meeting death, as it had formerly been at meeting an enemy.[36]

Alexander's end was ultimately chewed over with a removed dispassion (the stoic expression was *apatheia*) that would have made even Zeno proud. The Roman Republic had given way to a more contemplative mind of philosophical reflection which passed over unexplained and troubling events beneath, and inevitably Alexander's biography fell into its clutches.

The liberally sprinkled Hellenistic attributions to inner yearning that attached itself to Alexander (referred to as *pothos*), and to fate (*tyche*) that was first showcased in Demetrius of Phalerum's treatise *On Fortune* which so impressed

Polybius, took on the new mantle of stoic vocabulary and digressions on divine Fate, Providence and Destiny, uniting the various philosophical loose ends.[37] These stoical overtones seem to have side-tracked investigative minds, leaving Alexander with an unmarked grave and a makeshift headstone with the indelible intestate graffiti, 'to the strongest', scrawled awkwardly across it (T6, T7, T8, T9).

Curtius' Will Reference

Questioning the death of an emperor in the Julian-Claudian age was never a healthy business, especially if you were on the political stage or a writer under imperial patronage. There were too many intrigues, manipulation of wills and estates, as well as the formidable Pretorian Guard to contend with if anything was said in contravention to the prevailing political wind. This calls into question Curtius' direct attack on the veracity of Alexander's will, a strange forensic digression to make in a book which accepted far greater leaps of faith in his sources.

Curtius' short forensic speech (written mid-first century AD, I propose) is quite out of character with his final chapter narrative, and I have argued for its political significance to him at the political heart of Rome's imperium, most likely in Nero's reign.[38] Curtius' vocal assault on the will (T11) was quite specific in its wording and is worth repeating:

> ...some have believed that the provinces were distributed by Alexander's Will, but we have learned that the report of such action was false, although handed down by some authorities.[39]

The repeated plurality of the use of 'some' and 'sources' (both plurals have been challenged) suggest Curtius knew of more than one will-adhering account.[40] Although he would have been undermining his own credibility if he was referring above to the obviously fable-ridden *Romance* as historians read it today, we must again accommodate the possibility (or probability) that the lost archetypal *Romance* text we label 'α', once more-simply titled along the lines of *The Life of Alexander of Macedon*, had not yet become so blatantly 'romanced'. It remains highly unlikely that Curtius was echoing any testate denial that his principle source, Cleitarchus, had written, because we would expect to see it reappear in other Vulgate verdicts. Moreover, as Cleitarchus' book was so popular in Rome, Curtius' statement would have been a ridiculous plagiarism when he presented it, as he did, as his own investigative skill.

Apart from Curtius' will dismissal, we additionally have an earlier direct reference to Alexander's will from Diodorus (written before *ca*. 30 BC and certainly before Curtius' day) which appeared in the prelude to his account of the siege of Rhodes (his narrative of events in 305 BC). This confirmed

Alexander's testament had resided with the islanders: '...honouring Rhodes above all cities [Alexander] both deposited there the testament disposing of his whole realm and in other ways showed admiration.'[41] Once again, it is highly unlikely that Diodorus would have included this detail in his *Library of World History* if extracted from the *Romance* (recalling that the *Metz Epitome* will reference post-dated both Curtius and Diodorus). Arrian did refer to one 'brazen' writer who recorded that the dying Alexander attempted to throw himself into the Euphrates, and yet he stopped short of branding this source a book of ridiculous fables, so he, perhaps like Curtius and Diodorus before him, was either dealing with an early 'α' text *Romance* or the still free-floating *Pamphlet*.[42]

Diodorus statement was casual and matter of fact, and it is easy to dismiss it as a 'Homeric nod' (so-called because Homer contradicted himself at times). I contend that Diodorus, who certainly used the history of Hieronymus (as he himself stated) as the information backbone for the Successor War period, took this Rhodian guardianship of the will directly from Hieronymus, who therefore *must* have mentioned Alexander's testament when recounting the state of affairs at Babylon and beyond.

Diodorus faced a difficult task when dealing with Alexander's death. His attempt at conjoining what he saw in the scrolls of Cleitarchus and Hieronymus, whose accounts respectively ended and began at the point of Alexander's death, was not wholly successful, and it resulted in an untidy, inaccurate, hybrid abbreviation of affairs.[43] This stemmed in part from Cleitarchus' own earlier dilemma of blending the claims in the *Journal* and *Pamphlet* with non-corroborating eyewitness testimony from veterans in Alexandria, and now with potential contradictory claims of Alexander making succession instruction mentioned by Hieronymus as well.[44]

Diodorus additionally opened his follow-on (eighteenth) book with one hugely misleading statement: 'Alexander the king had died without issue, and a great contention arose over the leadership.' (T13)[45] Here he failed to mention the pregnancy of Rhoxane, though his later books featured her and her son who became King Alexander IV, and he also bypassed any mention of Heracles, Alexander's existing child when, once again, the boy appeared in his later chapters.[46]

The motivation for compression is only so strong and it is usually dispensed when momentous detail is afoot; events at Babylon *were* momentous. So we may conclude that, like Cleitarchus some two centuries before him, Diodorus was faced with the irreconcilable, though he chose to sidestep controversy and move speedily on. After all, unlike Cleitarchus' single biography (a monograph), his library of world history spanning 1,138 years still lacked the twenty-three books that would cover the next 280 years down to the Roman dictators. Fatally for the will, the common link preserved in all the conjoined accounts was the distribution of the empire by Perdiccas at the conclusion of the Babylonian settlement, for this suggested the action was necessary because Alexander had failed to transfer power and designate successors himself.

It is not impossible that other *bona fide* historians we are unaware of – or those we know of but whose accounts are lost – accepted the will as factual (like the later author of the *Metz Epitome*), although Arrian must have been unaware of them. But it is Curtius whose above-quoted treatment of the will looks to be the most blatantly political contrivance; his account is elsewhere full of exaggeration and rhetorical devices, and to be so clinically judgemental here on Alexander's succession instructions suggests another more-immediate agenda. What could that have been?

Curtius remains as anonymous as Justin. We simply don't know who he was, though it is generally agreed that the language and style of Curtius' prose places him in the first three centuries of the Roman Empire.[47] Studies have variously promoted publication dates as early as Augustus (ruled 27 BC–AD 14) and as late as Constantine (emperor AD 306–337), whilst more recent opinions incline to Claudius (emperor AD 41–54) and Vespasian (emperor AD 69–79).[48]

The most likely periods are the emperorships of Claudius, Vespasian and Nero, but I find the case for Nero's reign (AD 54–68) most compelling, and I have argued why at length.[49] Many scholars have dissected Curtius' laudation of his frustratingly anonymous emperor for clues, as it appears in the final chapter of his book on Alexander focusing on the infighting at Babylon, along with a digression on Alexander's character strengths and failings, which was a common method of wrapping up a biography. Curtius' obsequious imperial paragraph suggests an intimacy or acquaintance at least with his emperor, if not necessarily respect. This is consistent with the belief that he was a senator.[50]

This so-called 'Julio-Claudian Age' in Rome (spanning the dynasties of Augustus to Nero), the strongest contender for the publication date, arrived with additional historiographical challenges: as one scholar put it, 'the gradual concentration of political power within a smaller and smaller group, together with the secrecy and mystery which resulted, could not but affect the task of recording Roman history.'[51] His imperial encomium does suggest Curtius knew all too well the dangers of criticizing power if you were a loose-lipped writer: Seneca and his nephew Lucan found that out with some finality in Nero's reign.

But I believe Curtius' oddly vocal denial of Alexander's will is the divining rod back to the reign of the mercurial, thespian, musical and ultimately 'mad' Nero.[52] Curtius was attempting to suppress any further debate on the matter of Alexander's testament with his emphatic wording, and the relevance of this stems from the lingering rumour that Nero had recently poisoned Claudius, with Nero's mother Agrippina destroying the will that would have publicly reconfirmed Claudius' 14-year-old son Britannicus as his successor.[53] We may also recall that Curtius' portrayal of Arrhidaeus' behaviour at Babylon in the days immediately following Alexander's death recalls the supposedly pathetic Claudius who was discovered cowering behind curtains as the Praetorian Guard searched the imperial residence at Caligula's assassination.[54]

As has been pointed out, 'both Alexander and Nero had domineering mothers, both of whom were suspected of complicity in the deaths of the two fathers and accessions of the sons'.[55] Curtius' idiomatic will denial seems aggressively penned in the context of distant Alexander, when he could have simply stated he knew of the tradition of a succession document, just as Arrian had dismissively referenced the *Pamphlet* conspiracy. But it would have resonated loudly as a rumour-buster, or a suppressant at least, for allegations still pointing at Nero, and earned Curtius imperial points, which he had clearly set out to do.

Everyone, including Curtius, would have known of Nero's attachment to, and emulation of, Alexander, who also played the cithara (a stringed instrument similar to a lyre).[56] Nero even formed a bodyguard he named The Phalanx of Alexander (which became the First Italica Legion), so the obituary in Curtius' final chapter could have fed that nostalgia. Further, an 'Alexander of Aegae' was allegedly employed as one of Nero's tutors.[57] Curtius may even have written his history of Alexander specifically as a gift to an emperor so enamoured.

Alongside the adherence to the *Journal* by Arrian and Plutarch, and the final words 'to the strongest' which appear to have been first inserted into Alexander's deathbed scene by Cleitarchus, Curtius' will denial was another long nail in the testate coffin lid for Rome's contemplations on the conqueror's death.

Obituary Today: the Straight-Jackets of Intestacy

Modern biographies of Alexander have become preoccupied with unravelling the 'nature' of the man and, more recently, comparing him with his father, because the pool of source evidence is stagnant, with nothing new appearing. At the same time, hundreds of new books have appeared documenting Alexander's campaign, all adhering to the 'standard model'. Of course, summing him up against the backdrop of his thirteen-year kingship – a reign in which he conquered more, eye-witnessed more, slaughtered more and inherited more power than anyone in previous history – remains a precarious business. It has been said that these studies 'have both added to our understanding and multiplied uncertainties' attached to the Macedonian king.[58] And to sum up the thoughts of one formative scholar: we so risk being side-tracked in our excessive concentration on dissecting sources to find out 'what was said by whom' means we risk failing to focus on '*what in fact actually happened*'.[59]

Despite these many portrayals, none has attacked his intestacy. One modern scholar came as close as anyone to the genuine article when stating that 'the production of Wills, *post mortem*, was a feature of Attic Inheritance cases', and therefore, 'it would not have seemed beyond belief that the Will of Alexander had been suppressed'.[60] This is the closest I have ever seen to an acceptance of an original will by a modern scholar, and yet it was never followed up with the vigour this momentous episode of history deserves.

To reiterate my central contention when autopsying the *Pamphlet* and its will: rebroadcasting the existence of Alexander's testament in the early years of the Successor Wars and the deadly 'funeral games' being played out would have only been a tenable strategy if knowledge of the original – or hearsay and rumour to those not at Babylon – was circulating in the armies and the courts of Alexander's successors at war. Moreover, Alexander was ever 'Alexander'; facing death at Babylon, a will by which his sons would rule under the protection of his few trusted men was the only route to immortality when requests for divinity had been so hard to come by in his life.

So it is high time that the discredited document was de-accessorized of portents and accusations of conspiracy, and then extracted from the clutches of 'romance'. It could bring coherency to Alexander's 'last words' and his 'last plans', and it would explain the mechanism behind the division of the empire, as well as the references to the will made by Curtius and Diodorus. Finally, it would demystify the intent of the *Pamphlet* itself. Because the entertaining though implausible, corroborating though more often conflicted, the largely intact but irrevocably damaged, and inspiring yet troubling biographies of Alexander we gaze upon today, were framed by those extracting something useful from his life, whether for political, territorial or philosophical gain.

NOTES

Reference Notes

Reference notes provided are as brief as practically possible, to act as a guide to both ancient and modern commentary, rather than an exhaustive list of reading materials on any particular episode.

Author's Foreword

1. Referred to in the bibliography as Heckel (1988).

A Reader's Resource

1. In particular the fragments collected and translated in Robinson (1952) and Pearson (1960). Covered in some details in Grant (2017), chapters 3 and 5.

Chapter 1: Introducing Three Warring Witnesses

1. Green (1974), p. 479.
2. Following Hammond, *Journal* (1989), p. 158, for the singular use of 'Journal'.
3. Curtius 10.7.1–3 and 10.9.20 used the term *bellorum civilium Macedonibus* when describing the first at Babylon following Alexander's death.
4. For the importance of the symposia at the Macedonian court, see Thomas (2007), pp. 82, 87, 97, Borza (1995), pp. 159–69, and F. Pownall's discussion in Carney-Ogden (2010), pp. 55–63. Heckel (1988), p. 10, for the guest list. Full conspiracy text in the *Metz Epitome* 87–101 and *Romance* 31–32.
5. While the surviving will text references only one son, I argue in this book *both* would have been recognized in Alexander's original testament.
6. 'Argead' was the hereditary tribal name of the royal line dating to the seventh century BC Macedonian king, Perdiccas I. The Macedonian royal line retained its hereditary name, Temenid, allegedly stemming from Temenus of Argos, an alleged ancestor of Perdiccas I; Herodotus 8.137.
7. Fraser (1996), p. 206, for discussion on its title. The original name of the archetypal text is unknown. Pseudo-Callisthenes is the popular alternative name, though the work was attributed to other notable writers; also discussion in Fraser (1996), p. 206.

8. Textual similarities which argue for a common Vulgate source discussion in Bosworth (1983), p. 156, and in J.E. Atkinson (1994), p. 25, with a useful summary of earlier studies in Brown (1950) citing the works of Müller, Schwartz and Jacoby in particular.
9. Diodorus 17.117.4 and Arrian 7.26.3 for *toi kratistoi* from *kratistos*: 'the strongest or noblest'. Latin interpretation of that from Curtius 10.4.5 *qui esset optimus* (the 'best') and *dignissimus* (broadly the 'most worthy') from Justin 12.15.
10. For the funeral games or contests, see Curtius 10.5.5, Diodorus 17.117.4, Arrian 7.26.3 reporting 'other historians'. Justin (so we assume Trogus) 12.15.6–8 gave a darker more expansive account of the disputes and slaughter that the dying Alexander expected would follow.
11. *Iliad* 23. Some scholars believe the Homeric funeral games (pre-1200 BC) led directly to the founding of the Pan-Hellenic athletics contests, the Olympic, Pythian, Isthmian and Nemian Games. Roller (1981), pp. 107–19.
12. Quoting Justin 12.15, trans. Rev. J. Selby Watson, 1853; Curtius 10.6–10.10 and Justin 13.1 for the sentiment in Babylon.
13. Plutarch 77.2. Olympias' actions are detailed by other historians and discussed in later chapters.
14. For Onesicritus' fear, see *Metz Epitome* 97. The theme of 'fearful historians' is reiterated in the Vulgate texts at Curtius 10.10.18–19, Diodorus 17.118.2, Justin 12.13.10.
15. Grant (2017), p. 708.

Chapter 2: The Portentous Prelude to Death

1. Plutarch 75.1 and 74.1, trans. from the Loeb Classical Edition, 1919.
2. Arrian 7.26.2.
3. Quoting Hornblower (1981), p. 211.
4. Following the observation by Griffiths (1935), p. 39, for the nationalist spirit of Antipater's men.
5. Justin 13.1 for 30,000 talents annual income. For confirmation of Athens' annual income, see Athenaeus 12.542g where it was alleged Demetrius of Phalerum spent most of Athens' 1,200 talent income on parties rather than the army or city administration. Confirmed by Aelian 9.9. Adams (1996), p. 33, argues for 600 talents.
6. Following the discussion in Adams (1996), p. 33, and Tarn (1948), p. 131, for the sums spent in the last two campaign years. Arrian 7.5.3, Justin 12.11.1 for the 20,000 that went to settle debts, though this might be a combination of debt and veteran bonuses, each 10,000; Arrian 7.12.2 for the 1 talent bonus paid to each of the 10,000 retiring veterans. Curtius 10.2.10, Plutarch 70.3 stated that of the 10,000 talents laid out for debt repayment, only 130 remained. Diodorus 17.109.2 stated 'a little short of 10,000'. Athenaeus 9.398e for Aristotle's grant, though when this was made is uncertain. Chares claimed the crowns were valued at 15,000 talents but this appears scandal (Athenaeus 12.538a–539b). Athenaeus 9.398e for Aristotle's grant.

7. Blackwell (1999), pp. 13–14 footnote 13, for the relative weights of Harpalus' stolen talents. Curtius 8.12.16, Plutarch 59.5 for the gift to Taxiles (otherwise Omphis or Ambhi).
8. Arrian 7.14.8–10 and Plutarch 72.3 for the cost of Hephaestion's funeral, and Diodorus 17.115–116 for the 12,000-talent cost. Curtius 10.1.19 for warship numbers.
9. Plutarch 23.9–10 and Athenaeus 4.146c–d for the dining expenses of 100 minas; 1 mina was worth 100 drachmas according to Aristotle, *Constitution of the Athenians* 10.2. It has been calculated that a mina was equal to approximately 1/60 of a talent. Plutarch confirmed 10,000 drachmas. According to the *Persica* of Ctesias or Heracleides, the Great King's daily food supply could feed 15,000 people.
10. Justin 13.1. For the estimates of sums captured, see Lane Fox (1973), p. 437, and Cook (1983), p. 228. For the estimate of 180,000 talents, see Strabo 15.3.9. Green (2007), p. 62, for the modern (1970s/80s) value calculation, and Adams (1996), p. 33, for the two centuries of Athenian and Aegean income. Adams (1996), p. 33, for Athens' 600-talent annual income a century before. Engels (1978), p. 79, for the estimate of tonnage of bullion.
11. Pseudo-Aristotle, *Economics* 2.1352 for the 10 per cent import duty.
12. Tarn 1 (1948), p. 30, for the probable working basis of the tax collecting regime.
13. Discussed in Hatzopoulos (1996), p. 431 ff, and citing Arrian 7.9.9, Curtius 10.6.23, with other examples of the view that common Macedonians regarded wealth as a state commodity at Arrian 1.27.4, Diodorus 16.71.2. For the repayment of debt, see Curtius 10.2.8, Diodorus 17.109.2 and quoting Justin 12.11.1–4.
14. Archibald, Davies, Gabrielsen (2005), p. 59, for the new minting by Alexander, the tonnage of silver. Also Wheatley (1995), pp. 438–39, and following Wheatley on the 'unusually large issue' minted for 'grandiose plans'.
15. For the numbers of 'home-grown' Macedonians sent to Asia for Alexander's campaign, see discussion in Anson (2013), p. 160, and in Adams (1985), p. 79. Anson (2013), p. 70, for population discussion; some 250,000–375,000 Macedonians might have been eligible for service from a total population estimate of 1–1.5 million.
16. Following the observation in Briant (1974), p. 126, for the three remaining Persian governors.
17. Curtius 10.2.8.
18. For Philip's governorship and rapidly expanding provinces, Arrian 5.8.3, 5.20.7, 6.2.3, 6.4.1, 6.14.3 and Plutarch 60.16. For his death, Arrian 6.27.2 and Curtius 10.1.20. For the revolt of 3,000 mercenaries, Curtius 9.7.1–11.
19. Plutarch 68.3 stated the empire was in chaos. See Diodorus 17.106.2 and 17.111.1 for his decree that all satraps disband their mercenary forces as a result. Griffiths (1935), p. 39, for the 100,000 mercenary numbers.
20. For the timing of the drafting of the Exiles Decree, see Bosworth (1988), p. 221, and Blackwell (1999), pp. 14–15.
21. Diodorus 17.111.3 for Athens authorizing Leosthenes to recruit mercenaries and 18.9.1 for the sum of 50 talents he was provided with. Pausanias 1.25.5 for his appointment as commander-in-chief of Greek forces following Alexander's death. Diodorus 18.9.12 for the alliance with Locris, Phocis and Aetolia. Anson (2014), p.

29, for the amassed 18,000 talents at Athens. Harpalus left Asia with 5,000 talents and when turned away by Athens he re-entered the city a second time with 700 talents; Blackwell (1999), pp. 11–31 for sources and discussion.

22. Pausanias 8.52.5 gave 50,000 soldiers, but Diodorus 18.9.1 for 8,000 dismissed satrapal mercenaries, 18.9.5 for 7,000 Aetolians, 5,000 Athenian foot, 500 horse and 2,000 mercenaries.

23. The request for divine honours from Athens is most colourfully recorded in Aelian 2.19 and 5.12, Plutarch *Moralia* 804b and 842d, Polybius 12.12b.3, and Pausanias 8.32.1 mentions what is considered to be a shrine at Megalopolis dedicated to Alexander, housing a statue of Ammon. Tarn 1 (1948), p. 42, for discussion of the presence of a cult to Ammon in Athens before 371/370 BC. Discussed in full in Blackwell (2005). Hyperides, *Against Demosthenes* 31, and Deinarchus, *Against Demosthenes* 94, for Demosthenes proposing divine honours. Yet Timaeus (see Polybius 12.12b.3) suggested Demosthenes had voted against divine honours, though the timing is uncertain; see Blackwell (1999), p. 151 ff, for discussion.

24. Discussed in Worthington (2000), p. 105. Demades' quip is preserved in Valerius Maximus 7.2.13.

25. The doctor treating Alexander's closest companion, Hephaestion, had been executed for failing to cure him the previous year: see Heckel (2006) for sources. Arrian 7.14.4, Plutarch 72.3. Alexander executed the seer who predicted a propitious day when his father was murdered; Hammond (1994), p. 176, for discussion; a fragment of the report of the trial following Philip's death is preserved.

26. Quoting Plutarch 72 for Alexander's sacrifice to the shades of Hephaestion and 'blood-soaked hunt'. Plutarch, *Pelopidas* 34.2 for the shearing of horses and mules, Arrian 7.14.5 for the references to the temple of Asclepius in Ecbatana.

27. Diodorus 17.110.8 for Perdiccas being charged to take Hephaestion's body to Babylon.

28. Arrian 7.5.6 suggested the Bodyguards each received a gold crown, yet only the Bodyguards Leonnatus, Peucestas and Hephaestion were named. Nearchus and Onesicritus were also named in the honours list.

29. Arrian 7.14.10. The hipparchy retained Hephaestion's name out of respect.

30. Plutarch, *Moralia* 65c for Medius being a flatterer, and Arrian 7.27.2 for his relationship with Iollas.

31. See Grant, *Ancient Sources* (2021) for details of Onesicritus' career.

32. Justin 12.13.

33. See Grant (2017), p. 212, for the debate on visiting embassies.

34. Arrian 7.16–17 and 7.22.1 for the Chaldean warning to Alexander not to enter Babylon. Justin 12.13.3–7 for the Magi warning and Alexander's diversion past the 'uninhabited' Borsippa; the Babylonian surviving documents, however, suggest Borsippa was still a trade centre; see Bosworth (2000), p. 220, for detail. Also Arrian 7.16.5–7, Plutarch 73.1 and Diodorus 112.2–5, who terms them Chaldeans as opposed to Magi.

35. Arrian 7.17.1.2 for Alexander's plans to rebuild the temple on his return to Babylon. Diodorus 17.112.3 for the Chaldean terms.

36. Arrian 7.19.3–6 for Nearchus' warning and Justin 12.13.

37. Plutarch 73.1–3.
38. Arrian 7.18–7.19 and Plutarch 73.3 ff for the other prophesises and warnings, drawing from Aristobulus.
39. Arrian 7.19–22.
40. Arrian 7.22–23.
41. Arrian 7.23.1.
42. Curtius 10.2.8 ff for the remaining Macedonian troop numbers after the demobilization of the veterans at Opis.
43. Diodorus 17.115.1 for the gold and silver likenesses being prepared for the funeral of Hephaestion. Diodorus 17.115.5 for the covering of expenses. Nearby cities were to contribute too. Hammond (1998), p. 337, for *eidola* discussion.
44. Arrian 7.23.8 ff for the letter to Cleomenes. For Cleomenes' role as *Arabarchos* (a financial administrator), see Heckel (2006), p. 88; it was a financial administration position akin to revenue collector. For his death, see Pausanias 1.6.3.
45. Diodorus 17.115.1–5.
46. Diodorus 18.4.2 used pyre rather than a tomb or more permanent structure; McKechnie (1995), p. 421. Quoting Diodorus 17.114.1. Diodorus 17.114–116 for the full episode.
47. Plutarch 72.5 for the name Stasicrates. He is otherwise referred to as Deinochares, Diocles and Cheirocrates. He may have been in Babylon overseeing the city's reconstruction projects, or in Ephesus overseeing the reconstruction of the Temple of Artemis, for Plutarch's use of 'longing' suggests he was not immediately available.
48. Diodorus 15.115.6. Anson (2013), p. 114, for discussion of 'associate god' as indicated by Diodorus 17.115.2–116.1. Plutarch 72.1–3, Arrian 7.14.7, 7.23.6 for Hephaestion's elevation. Arrian claimed the oracle permitted 'hero' only. Discussed in McKechnie (1995), p. 420.
49. Plutarch 75.1 ff.
50. Atkinson (2009), pp. 35–36, for discussion of mind-altering drugs. For his paranoia and fears Plutarch 74.2–5, translation from the Loeb Classical Library edition, 1919, and Plutarch 73.7–9. Arrian 7.24–25 described that Alexander and his friend, whilst playing ball, beheld a man seated on the king's throne, in silence, wearing the royal diadem and robes. He claimed the god Serapis had come to him and bid him sit on the throne. Alexander had him 'put out of the way' as advised by his seers. The whole episode sounds remarkably like the Babylonian ritual of the substitute king; following Oates (1979), p. 140, and Green (1974), p. 472.
51. Arrian 7.24.4; Heckel (2006), p. 158, for other sources.
52. Alexander recited from the *Andromache* at Medius' banquet; see Athenaeus 12.537b, fragment on Robinson (1953), p. 89. The cup held 2 *choes*, which verged on a *krater*, so mixing-bowl-sized. Athenaeus 10.44p for the size of Alexander's drinking cup, and Iliad 11.632–637 for Nestor's cup; Diodorus 17.117.1 also terms the cup 'huge'. Discussed by F. Pownall in Carney-Ogden (2010), p. 64. The fragment is from Eubolos' *Semele of Dionysus*.
53. Justin 12.13.

244   *The Last Will and Testament of Alexander the Great*

54. Justin 12.13, Diodorus 17.117. There is a lacuna in Curtius' text but he would surely have closely followed Justin and Diodorus.
55. Justin 12.14, trans. by Rev. John Selby Watson, 1853.
56. Justin 12.15.
57. Justin 12.15.
58. Arrian 7.27–28.
59. Plutarch 75.5.
60. Arrian 7.25.1.
61. Quoting Griffith (1935), p. 38.
62. It was reckoned the Macedonians had walked 12,000 miles by the time they reached the Hyphasis River; discussion in Thomas (2007), p. 19. By their return to Babylon this has obviously increased by perhaps 9,000 miles to approximately 21,000 in total. T.A. Dodge, cited in Heckel-Jones (2006), p. 20, calculated the infantryman that had campaigned with Alexander in both Europe and Asia had marched some 20,870 miles. Engels (1978), p. 12, however, suggested waggons were not used and the sarissa would have been portered much of the way.

Chapter 3: The assassins' Assembly; Path to Civil War

1. Lucian, *Dialogues of the Dead* 13.
2. Justin 13.1, trans. by Rev. J.S. Watson, Henry G. Bohn, London, 1853.
3. Discussed at length in Grant (2017), p. 206 ff.
4. Billows (1990), p. 331, for discussion of the name of Hieronymus' book or books. It was epitomized by Photius the Patriarch of Constantinople (*ca.* AD 810–893) and in a parallel work by Dexippus (*ca.* AD 210–273), the Athenian historian and hero of the Gothic invasion of AD 262.
5. Greek historians of the age of Philip and Alexander were accustomed to opening their accounts with a geographical digression to establish the terrain for the reader; Thucydides had established the style for the later chroniclers, and evidence suggests the openings of Hecataeus, Timaeus and Ephorus followed suit. Hieronymus was not atypical; he explained the shape and extent of Asia, and this provided a framework on which he could pin his list of the newly appointed (and reconfirmed) provincial governors in what amounted to informal introductions to place characters in context.
6. As detailed at Arrian, *Events After Alexander* 1.2; Eumenes' role at Plutarch, *Eumenes* 3.1; discussed in more detail below.
7. Anson (1992), pp. 39–41, and Blackwell (1999), p. 88, for discussion of the various titles afforded to Perdiccas; Diodorus 18.23.2 and Appian, *Syrian Wars* 52 for *prostates*; Diodorus 18.2.4 for *epimeletes*; Arrian, *Events After Alexander* 1a.3 for *epitropos*, Plutarch *Eumenes* 3.6 for *strategos*. It was in this new post-Alexander world that the term 'chiliarch', used to denote the king's second-in-command (and possibly only meant for Hephaestion, initially), was contested and appears to have fallen out of use after the state regent, Antipater, died (late 319 BC), though others would certainly act as if they had inherited the title. Also Collins (2001) for

the development of the chiliarch role. Livy 40.6.3 for an example of *custodes corporis* being employed; Roisman-Worthington (2010), p. 459, for discussion. Full discussion of titles and relative authorities in Anson (1992) and Hammond (1985), p. 157, for the disappearance of *chiliarchos*. Cassander was appointed chiliarch by Antipater following Triparadeisus, Arrian, *Events After Alexander* 1.38, though this was arguably just command of the Companion Cavalry previously under Seleucus as suggested by the Heidelberg Epitome; see Collins (2001), p. 279. Cassander may have retained the position under Polyperchon, implied by his being second-in-command; Diodorus 18.48–4–5, Plutarch, *Phocion* 31.1; Collins (2001), p. 279.

8. Curtius 10.8.16 and 10.7.8 for Arrhidaeus' speech. Perdiccas and Leonnatus were appointed as joint guardians at the Assembly and the compromise included Antipater and Craterus; see Justin 13.2. Also Ptolemy supposedly proposed group rule; Curtius 10.6.15. Justin 13.2 captured the same undertones, suggesting the framework was indeed from Cleitarchus, unless we are prepared to accept Curtius was following Trogus' lead.
9. Lock (1977), p. 96, for discussion of the reconstructed constitutional procedures. And for Curtius' embellishment p. 104, referring to a law that demanded all relatives of those condemned to death were destined to die also. Baynham (1998), pp. 171–80, for Roman themes in Curtius' account of the Philotas affair.
10. Justin 13.1, trans. by Rev. J.S. Watson, Henry G. Bohn, London, 1853. Quoting Bevan (1902), p. 28, on ambition at Babylon.
11. Plutarch, *Galba* 1, trans. by J. Dryden, 1683; repeated at Plutarch, *Moralia* 336e–f.
12. *Romance* 3.32, *Metz Epitome* 103.
13. Arrian 7.25.6 for the officer waiting outside the door. Arrian 7.26.1, Justin 12.15.2–4, Plutarch 76–77 for the forced entry.
14. Trans. from Heckel-Yardley (2004), p. 285.
15. Curtius 10.5.9–10.6. For the mutiny at Opis and alleged rejection at (or derision of) his attachment to Zeus-Ammon; Plutarch 71.1, Diodorus 17.109.2. Requests for divinity aside, Arrian 7.29.4 confirmed Alexander saw himself as the son of Ammon, and 7.20.1 with Strabo 16.1.11 stated he planned to attack the Arabs to be worshipped as a third god. For the Athenian Assembly's refusal to grant Alexander's deification, see Polybius 12.12b.3 and Deinarchus, *Against Demosthenes* 1.94, and for the fine to Demades who proposed the bill, Athenaeus 6.251b, Aelian 5.12. Aelian 5.12 and Strabo 16.1.11 cited Aristobulus as confirming Alexander had laid claims to divinity. However, Flower (1994), pp. 259–60, points out that Theopompus seemed to have known of an Alexander cult in Anatolia worshipping him as Alexander-Zeus in his lifetime.
16. Justin 13.1, trans. based on Rev. J.S. Watson, published by Henry G. Bohn, London, 1853.
17. Quoting Bosworth (2002), p. 32.
18. Quoting Mitchell (2007) and discussed in Atkinson (2009), p. 181.
19. Following the discussion in Anson (1991), pp. 230–47, and quoting W.S. Greenwalt in Carney-Ogden (2010), p. 152.
20. A good summary of arguments in Lock (1977); Hammond (1991) for Herodotus' and Thucydides' confirmations.

21. Following the argument in Thomas (2007), p. 59. Amyntou, the son of Amyntas.
22. This explanation of the origins of the Assembly is supported by Lock (1977) and Anson (1991), and reproduces the earlier study of Granier (1931). See further discussions in Lock (1977), pp. 91–107. Also see Thomas (2007), p. 59, and citing Herodotus 9.44, who outlined the dual role of king and commander. Anson (2013), pp. 26–42, sees a less formal structure, suggesting there were no fixed rules for bringing the Assembly together. Quoting Hatzopoulos (1996), p. 267, for hardly 100 aristocratic families.
23. Anson (1991), pp 24–42, for discussion of the Assembly role.
24. Hammond (1994), pp. 38–39, for the naming convention. Flower (1994), pp. 110–11, for Theopompus' stating 800 Companions. For the theatre location, see discussion in E. Carney in Carney-Ogden (2010), p. 45.
25. For discussion on the religious position of the Macedonian king, see Roisman-Worthington (2010), p. 10.
26. First described in Herodotus 1.134.
27. Quoting Borza (1990), pp. 245–46. Hammond (1978), pp. 340–42 for Macedonian trial procedure. For the Assembly's role in treason, see the coverage of the Philotas affair, especially Curtius 6.7–11, which gave additional detail that all Macedonians present were invited to the trial. Also covered in Diodorus 17.79, Plutarch 49.3–12, Arrian 3.26.1, Justin 12.5.1–3 and the text that follows in each for his subsequent execution. Also Diodorus 19.12.2 made it clear that it was an Assembly decision that levied a death sentence on Eumenes; presumably his action against Craterus was deemed treasonous. For Olympias' death after an Assembly gathering, Diodorus 19.51.1–4 and Justin 14.6.6; both recorded a judicial proceeding in the form of an Assembly gathering. Arrian 7.8.3 provided the most negative coverage of the hasty execution of ringleaders at Opis.
28. Anson (1991) as an example of the interpretation of absolute power. Curtius 6.8.25 suggested in peacetime royal power was not effective in Assembly trials, 'except in as far as a king's personal prestige had been of influence before the verdict'; translation from Hammond (1978), p. 341.
29. Livy 40.9.8 for Perseus' claims to the right of primogeniture; though this is a later event, it is unlikely the rules of succession had changed.
30. Alexander I left five sons behind him who, in turn, produced ten (known) grandsons from five collateral branches of the royal line. The period 399–391 BC saw six kings in eight years from three competing lines, and six sons and a daughter were born to Amyntas III (died *ca*. 370 BC), including Philip II. Hammond (1991), pp. 34–35, for the equal rights of Macedonian princes. Justin 8.4.4–6 for the offspring of Amyntas III. 'Oversupply' quoting Bosworth (1992), p. 29.
31. See discussion in Lock (1977), p. 92, for the dominance of primogeniture. Hammond (1994), p. 18, for the joint rule discussion; this occurred after the death of Alexander I of Macedon.
32. Following and quoting Bosworth (1971), p. 128.
33. Schachermeyr (1970), pp. 81–84, cited in McKechnie (1999), p. 47; Justin 13.2 mentioned the meeting took place in the palace.
34. Curtius 10.6.2.

35. Curtius 10.10.5.
36. Curtius 10.6.1. Curtius 10.5 for his comments on the will.
37. Diodorus 18.4.1–4, based on the translation from the Loeb Classical Library edition, 1947.
38. Arrian 7.1.1–3 and Curtius 10.1.17 for the proposed voyages around Arabia, Africa and the conquest of Carthage and the Scythians via the Black Sea; Arrian 7.19.3–5 for the Babylonian projects.
39. Quoting Bosworth A to A (1988), p. 186. A good summary of the views up to his time can be found in Badian (1968), rejecting Tarn's cynicism and supporting Wilken and Schachermeyr in their belief in the detail.
40. Full discussion of views and Hellenistic and Roman contamination in Tarn (1948), pp. 378–99. Also Tarn (1939), pp. 124–35. 'Embroidery' quotes Badian (1968). See Tarn (1948), pp. 374–78, for discussion of the invented embassies.
41. Diodorus 18.4.4–6 based on the translation from the Loeb Classical Library edition, 1947. The footnote reads 'Cyrnus in Macedon is otherwise unknown, but the name is found elsewhere in Greece.' (Herodotus 9.105, Pliny 4.53).
42. Alexander had already constructed a large tumulus some 125ft high and 'great in circumference' for Demaratus of Corinth; Plutarch 56.2; a tumulus for Hephaestion; Plutarch 72.5; and a first modest tumulus for Philip upon his death; Justin 11.2.1. See Grant (2019) for full discussion of both tumuli.
43. See discussion in Behrwald (1999). The *Historica Hypomnemata* was used and quoted by Timagenes through Josephus 13.3.9. Strabo also associated the term *hypomnemata* with his *Geography*. Others such as Hegesippus titled their memoirs *hypomnemata*. Athenaeus 4.162a for reference to Hegesander's work. Plutarch 4.4 for Arostoxenus' title.
44. Curtius 10.10.1 for the re-entry into the city. Plutarch 77.5 for three days, Curtius 10.9.13 for six days, Aelian 12.64 for thirty days, following which Aristander the seer entered the Assembly.
45. Hatzopoulos (1996), p. 295, and Polybius 4.87.7–8 for Antigonus Doson's Will; trans. from Marasco (2011), p. 57, and following the observations of C. Bearzot in Marasco (2011), p. 58.
46. Arrian 7.12.3–4, Diodorus 18.4.1, Justin 12.12.7–9 for Craterus replacing Antipater.
47. For Meleager's career, see Heckel (2006), pp. 159–61; for his service with or under Craterus, see Arrian 3.18.4, 6.17.3 and Curtius 5.4.14. Heckel (1988), p. 20, sees Meleager as looking after Craterus' interests in Babylon. Curtius 10.2.8 ff for the remaining Macedonian troop numbers after the demobilization of the veterans at Opis.
48. Bosworth (1992), p. 32, for Craterus' resources.
49. Diodorus 18.12.1 for Antipater's call for help. Bosworth (1971), p. 125, and Atkinson (2009), pp. 238–39, for discussion on Craterus' delay in Cilicia and the rumours that Craterus had been sent to assassinate Antipater. Heckel (1988), p. 21 footnote 8, suggested Craterus' delay might have been due to unrest in Cilicia, where the Satrap, Balacrus, had been killed by the Pisidians. Anson (2014), p. 39, for the ten days of

travel from Babylon to Cilicia. Diodorus 18.25.3 for Antigonus reporting Perdiccas' design on the Macedonian throne.
50. Diodorus 18.4.1 based on the translation from the Loeb Classical Library edition, 1954.
51. Curtius 10.1.19 for the commodities requisitioned from Cyprus and Mount Lebanon. Meiggs (1982), p. 49, for the Epic of Gilgamesh and Diodorus 19.58.3.
52. Plutarch 68 and Curtius 10.1.19 for Thapsacus and the planned navigation of Africa. Morrison-Coates-Rankov (2000), pp. 109–11, for naval crews.
53. Murray (2012), pp. 96, 190, for discussion of the equipment needed to build and fit out a ship. For the implied journey west by Craterus and his veterans including Antigenes, the commander of the Silver Shields, see Justin 12.12.8, implied in Arrian 7.12.4, Curtius 10.10.15. As Antigenes was later found in Egypt, it is reasonable to assume he remained in Cilicia and was collected by Perdiccas on his journey to invade Egypt in 321/320 BC; Arrian, *Events After Alexander* 1.35 and Diodorus 18.39.6 for his part in Perdiccas' assassination.
54. Justin 12.12.9, Arrian 7.12.4 for confirmation that upon Alexander's death the replacement troops remained in Macedon.
55. 'White Cleitus': so named to distinguish him from 'Black' (*Melas*) Cleitus, son of Dropidas. Diodorus 18.15.8–9, Plutarch, *Moralia* 338a, Plutarch, *Demetrius* 11.3 for the actions off Amorgas. Diodorus 18.15.8 for 240 ships. The Parian Chronicle also referred to the battles. Heckel (2006), p. 88, for the 130 ships and Echinades; after victory Cleitus' fleet swelled. Cleitus was given charge of Perdiccas' fleet before his invasion of Egypt; Justin 13.6.16.
56. Diodorus 18.15.8–9 for the fleet assembled by White Cleitus, who accompanied Craterus as far as Cilicia; Arrian 7.12.4, Justin 12.12.8. This is a highly compressed account and possibly compresses two naval actions into one. See footnote 51 to the Loeb Classical Library edition, 1947, of Diodorus 18.15.8 for discussion. Bing (1973), p. 347, for discussion of Cilician natural resources including high-grade iron. Anson (2014) for the observation that Craterus might have been required to suppress a revolt in Greece.
57. Diodorus 18.3.4, with earlier confirmation in Diodorus 17.109.1 and Arrian 7.12–13.
58. Diodorus 18.3.5, Justin 13.4.6 for Arrhidaeus' instructions to build and deliver the funeral bier.
59. Diodorus 20.81.3, based on the translation from the Loeb Classical Library edition, 1954. See Tarn (1939), p. 132, for a discussion on whether Diodorus 20.81.3 drew from the *Romance* and Letter to the Rhodians, as proposed by Ausfeld. Heckel (1988), p. 2, suggested Hieronymus was the source.
60. Avramovic´ (2006), p. 4, for discussion of the Greek terms relating to wills. Also see discussion on the ancient Greek term *diatheke*, which was used for both lifetime covenants and wills.
61. Badian (1968), p. 203, agrees that Diodorus was unclear on the relationship of the orders of Craterus to the document produced by Perdiccas encapsulating the last plans. Also Hornblower (1981), pp. 94–95, for discussion on Diodorus' clumsiness with linking Craterus' instructions to the last plans.

62. See Grant (2019) for full discussion of the Vergina tombs.
63. Diodorus 18.4.2 and 18.4.4.
64. Badian (1968), p. 204, supports the case for Eumenes' hand in the extracting of the last plans from the campaign paperwork.
65. Dionysius of Halicarnassus suggested Hieronymus' style was boring, see Hornblower (1981), p. 1, and Bosworth-Baynham (2000), p. 304, the historian Psaon was also listed.
66. As proposed by Hornblower (1981), pp. 50–51, 94–97, for examples of wonders, *thauma*.
67. Curtius 10.1.16–19, Arrian 5.26.1–3, 5.27.7, 7.1–5. Also see discussion in Green (2007), pp. 6–7.
68. Quoting Hornblower (1981), p. 94.
69. Badian (1968), p. 204.
70. Curtius 10.6.4.
71. Tarn (1948), p. 148, for hypaspist discussion. There is some confusion as to whether *pezhetairoi* also referred to heavier infantry but not pike-bearers. See also Anson (1985) for further discussion of the origins of the *pezhetairoi*.
72. Following the mercenary comparison discussed by Anson (1991), pp. 230–47.
73. Curtius 10.6.4–10.9.21. See Atkinson (2009), p. 180, for discussion on the pregnancy; Rhoxane was either six months pregnant, according to Curtius 10.6.9, or eight months, according to Justin 13.2.5. See Errington (1970), p. 56, for discussion on Perdiccan hopes for Rhoxane and a son.
74. Justin 7.2.6–13. The Macedonians had carried the cradled Aeropus to the battle and positioned him behind their lines to spur them on against the Illyrians. The chronology of his reign is uncertain but *ca*. 602–576 BC.
75. Curtius 10.6.8.
76. See references to the 'Tiberian farce' below.
77. Curtius 10.6.10–11. Justin 13.2 attributed the same suggestion to Meleager, the notable infantry officer, who informed the Assembly that Heracles was then based at Pergamum. Further, Justin credited Meleager with reminding the gathering that Arrhidaeus was present in Babylon, and so immediately available. It appears that Justin carelessly, or even consciously, merged both speeches into one, something of an over 'efficiency' in his epitomizing efforts. Justin may in fact have merged three speeches together, for Meleager supposedly rounded off with a rejection of both of Alexander's Asiatic sons, a blatantly contradictory declaration.
78. If so, Nearchus' book must have been published before *ca*. 310 BC, when the boy was murdered on Cassander's instigation.
79. Curtius 10.6.13–16.
80. Curtius 8.4.30 for the Macedonian reaction to the marriage with Rhoxane.
81. Reiterated by Brunt (1975), p. 33.
82. Ptolemy's marriage policy discussed in Ellis (1994), pp. 41–43.
83. Curtius 10.6.15 for the group rule suggestion, reiterated at Justin 13.2.
84. Arrian 7.14.10.
85. Curtius 10.6.15–16. Following the observation of Stewart (1993), p. 214, for working together for the common good, *koinopragia*. Arrian, *Events After Alexander* 1.3, Perdiccas' chiliarchy.

250   The Last Will and Testament of Alexander the Great

86. Quoting Hammond-Walbank (1988), p. 145, on republicanism.
87. Curtius 10.6.16–18.
88. See Heckel (2006), p. 50, for discussion, and Diodorus 19.35.4 for Aristonus' role under Polyperchon, who was guardian to the kings, thus suggesting a real fealty to Alexander's wishes and sons.
89. Curtius 10.6.18–20, based on the translation in the Loeb Classical Library edition, 1946.
90. See Atkinson (2009), p. 179, for discussion of Perdiccas' returning of the ring at Curtius 10.6.5.1 and other Roman examples, most prominently Tiberius, described in Tacitus 1.11.1 and 12, Suetonius, *Tiberius* 24.1–2, Cassius Dio 57.2.3, Velleius Patreculus, *Compendium of Roman History* 2.124. Errington (1970), pp. 50–51, for comparisons between Arrhidaeus and Claudius. Suetonius, *Tiberius* 25.1 for the 'wolf by the ears'.
91. Suetonius Tiberius 23–25 for references to 'slavery' and his 'cruel fate'.
92. Curtius 10.7.7 for Meleager's hatred of Perdiccas. Curtius 10.6.20–24, based on the translation from the Loeb Classical Library edition, 1946.
93. Diodorus 17.117.4 and Arrian 7.26.3 for *toi kratistoi* from *kratistos*: 'the strongest or noblest'. Latin interpretation of that from Curtius 10.4.5, *qui esset optimus* (the 'best') and *dignissimus* (broadly the 'most worthy') from Justin 12.15.
94. Curtius 10.7.2, 10.7.10; reiterated in Hatzopoulos (1996), p. 270.
95. Justin 13.2. The broad term 'Persian' was being employed; Rhoxane was Bactrian or Sogdian. At Justin 13.4.6 he later proposed 'King Arrhidaeus' was charged with the task of conveying Alexander's body to Egypt. He also later termed Amphimachus, satrap of Mesopotamia, the 'brother of the kings' though again he was more likely the brother of the Arrhidaeus who later became the satrap of Hellespontine Phrygia.
96. Arrian 3.11.9 for the phalanx leaders, see discussion in Tarn (1948), p. 142.
97. See Curtius 8.12.17–18 for Meleager's dangerous quip at the banquet at which Alexander gave Omphis, dynast of Taxila, 1,000 talents; the same is suggested by Plutarch 59.5 in abbreviated form without names being mentioned. Alexander suppressed his anger recalling the Cleitus episode. Arrian, *Events After Alexander* 1.2 lists Meleager amongst the *megistoi* or most important men.
98. Curtius 10.7.7 for Meleager's proposal that Arrhidaeus be crowned King Philip III. Quoting Justin 13.3.
99. Curtius 10.7.1–3. Justin 13.2 credited this speech to Meleager. See discussion in Atkinson (2009) on Arrhidaeus' mental state. Rather than an affirmation that he was able to function in some titular capacity, the cited excerpt from Plutarch, *Phocion* 33.5–7 confirmed Arrhidaeus' retarded state and mental simplicity.
100. Diodorus 19.11.5 and Justin 14.5.10 for the regnal term. Discussed in Anson (2003), p. 377, and following the proposal of Bosworth (1992). Curtius 10.7.2 for Arrhidaeus becoming the king's associate in ceremonies and sacrifices.
101. See Grant (2019), chapter titled 'The First War of Women', for example of Olympias' treatment of royals from Philip's line and wives.
102. Athenaeus 13.557d, Justin 9.7.3, Plutarch 77.8.

103. Porphyry of Tyre FGrH 260 F2, Heidelberg Epitome 1 called him epileptic. Socrates' *daimonion* was described in Plato's *Apology* 31c–d, 40a, which has been postulated as epilepsy. Caesar's fits have likewise been posthumously attributed to epilepsy; see Plutarch, *Caesar* 17, 45, 60, and Suetonius, *Julius* 45. The symptoms exhibited by Caligula and described in Suetonius Gaius are likewise suggestive of epilepsy.
104. The qualifications for regent discussed in Miller (1991), p. 51, quoting Hammond-Griffiths (1979), p. 182. Hammond (1985), p. 157, and Justin 13.2.13 for the use of *tutores*. Justin 13.2 for Ptolemy's wording.
105. For Peithon's speech, see Curtius 10.7.8–9. Curtius himself stated Peithon was following Perdiccas' cause. Justin 13.13–14 for the guardian line-up.
106. Peithon was one of Perdiccas' assassins in Egypt; Diodorus 18.36.5. Perdiccas is said to have suspected intrigue immediately after Babylon when Peithon left to quell the mercenary revolt; Diodorus 18.7.4–6.
107. Curtius 10.7.8, 10.7.20, 10.8.4 and Justin 13.2 for Leonnatus' prominence. Curtius 10.7.8 for confirmation that Perdiccas and Leonnatus were of royal stock. Curtis 3.12.7 for *ex purpuratis*, thus wearing the purple, suggestive of a high-born courtier.
108. For the *prostasia* discussion, see Errington (1970), p. 56, and also Goralski (1989), p. 87. Heckel (2006), p. 96, for discussion of Craterus' supreme commands. He was clearly at that stage the second-in-command. Quoting and following Anson (1992), p. 39, for the 'honorific' role or a more powerful position. Hammond (1985), p. 156, for the relative roles of Craterus and Antipater. Arrian, *Events After Alexander* for Craterus as *prostates* of the kingdom of Arrhidaeus and Justin 13.4.5 for 'royal property'.
109. Alexander instructed Antipater to ensure the veterans were provided with garlands and front seats at performances – *prohedria*; Plutarch 71.8, Diodorus 18.18.7.
110. Arrian 7.4.8 for the 10,000 alleged marriages to Asian wives; each was given a wedding dowry. Billows (1990), p. 306, for the governing ethnicity.
111. Billows (1990), p. 355, for total Macedonian numbers in Asia up to 203 BC. Pliny 6.31.139 mentions a Pella in the district of Alexandria on Tigris. Anson (2013), pp. 138–39, for city-founding discussion. Billows (1990), p. 299, for 'Pella' being used as a name for new settlements, specifically what was to become Seleucid Apamea.
112. Justin 12.15, relating the activity to the last days of Alexander's illness.
113. Whilst Arrhidaeus was a son of Philip II, his mother was in fact Thessalian, though likely of aristocratic heritage; see Athenaeus 13.557c and Arrian, *Events After Alexander* 1.1. Discussion in Heckel (2006), p. 52.
114. Curtius 10.7.11–12, following Homer's *Iliad* 2.142–146.
115. Curtius 10.7.14–15.
116. Hammond (1991), p. 41 for Assembly protocol.
117. Curtius 10.7.16.
118. Aelian 12.64, referring to the *Iliad* 5.449.
119. Curtius 10.7.16–20.
120. For Ptolemy's treatment of Perdiccas in the campaign, see Errington (1969), pp. 238–39. For the publishing order of the eyewitness historians, see Grant, *Ancient Sources* (2021).

252   The Last Will and Testament of Alexander the Great

121. Curtius 10.8.1.
122. Justin 13.3.1–13.4.1.
123. Curtius 10.8.1-12 for the face-off, departure from the city and famine, and 5.1.27 for the cultivated areas to provide for the population in case of a siege. See below for Xerxes diverting the Euphrates when besieging the city.
124. Curtius 10.2.8 stated 13,000 Macedonian infantry and 2,000 cavalry. Bosworth (2002), pp. 64–97, for estimates of total troop numbers. Sprague de Camp (1972), p. 136, for the 300,000–400,000 estimate. A higher estimate of 600,000 is from Kloft (1992), p. 10, though no dating is specified and the number is likely based on the later population of Seleucia on Tigris. See population discussion in Boiy (2004), pp. 229–32. Further city size discussion in Archibald, Davies, Gabrielsen (2005), p. 29 ff.
125. Arrian 7.23.1, Curtius 8.5.1, Diodorus 17.108.1–2, Plutarch 47.3 and 71.1 for the arrival of new recruits. Diodorus 17.95.4 for the mercenary contingent that arrived in India before the voyage down the Hydaspes-Indus.
126. See Reade (2000), pp. 203, 215, for discussion of the Summer or Outer Palace and its military construction and purpose.
127. See Diodorus 18.2.2–4 and Justin 13.3.2 closely tracks. The same is implied, but not expressly stated in Arrian, *Events After Alexander* 1.2–4.
128. Heckel (2006), pp. 159–61, for Meleager's various commands. See below for Meleager's temporary elevation to third-in-command.
129. Curtius 10.8.8–11.
130. Plutarch Moralia 337d–e. See Heckel-Yardley (2004), p. 34, for translation.
131. As suggested at Curtius 10.5.12 (quoted) and 10.8.10. 10.8.7 for Meleager's three-day deliberations over uncertain plans.
132. Curtius 10.7.13.
133. Curtius 10.8.16–20.
134. Curtius 10.7.2 for Arrhidaeus taking part in sacrifices and ceremonies.
135. Diodorus 19.11.5 stated six years four months and Justin simply six years. However the date of the formal commencement of his reign is not specified. Arrhidaeus is later attested to have 'received Phocion', but this was in essence an embassy to Polyperchon, Arrhidaeus' regent and his *epimeletes*. In an outburst of anger he almost ran Hegemon through with a spear; again this suggests he was neither self-controlled nor predictable; Nepos, *Phocion* 3.3, Plutarch, *Phocion* 33.8–12.
136. McKechnie (1999), p. 59, and see full article for discussion on Roman themes in Curtius' portrayal of Arrhidaeus.
137. Following the observation in McKechnie (1999), p. 59, of the allusion to the Roman struggle of the common man and aristocrat.
138. Curtius 10.8.22–23; the infantry 'thought' the armies were reconciled. Arrian, *Events After Alexander* termed Meleager Perdiccas' *hyparchos*, whereas Justin 13.4–5 implied they were equals; see discussion by Heckel in *Quintus Curtius Rufus, The History of Alexander*, Penguin edition, 1984, p. 301 footnote 44.
139. Plutarch, *Eumenes* 3.1 for his neutrality and continued presence inside the city. Translations from the Loeb Classical Library edition, 1919.

140. Attalus, son of Andromenes, was probably enrolled by Perdiccas into his plan with the promise of marriage to his sister, Atalante; he had served with Meleager on campaign. Justin 13.3.2–7 has Attalus backing up Meleager at the Assembly; more below.
141. Anson (2013) suggests the lustration was linked to the death of the kings. Hammond (1991), p. 32, for more detail on weapons and insignia.
142. Curtius 10.9.12, Justin 13.4.7. See discussion on the chronology of the mutiny and lustration in Bosworth (2002), p. 55. Polybius 23.10.17 for the sacrifice to Xanthus in the eponymous month, though here horses are referred to, not dogs. Tarn (1948), p. 107, for Macedonian superstition related to fighting in Daisios, based upon Plutarch 16 claiming that Alexander doubled the length of April to justify the River Granicus battle.
143. Curtius 10.9.20 for the use of 'treachery' to describe Perdiccas' actions. Curtius 19.9.20–21, Justin 13.4.7–8, Arrian, *Events After Alexander* 1a.4, Diodorus 18.4.7 placed Meleager's death after the division of empire. Curtius' account suggests Perdiccas arranged the lustration with the unwitting Meleager himself; Justin claimed Perdiccas acted without the knowledge of his colleagues.
144. Aristotle, *Politics* 5.5, trans. by B. Jovett, published by The Internet Classic Archive.
145. See Anson (1988), p. 476, for discussion on the view of Briant and Errington that Perdiccas was acting in consultation with the other influential generals, as echoed by Diodorus 18.3.1, though these arguments exclude a will.
146. Plutarch 76.4.
147. Curtius 10.6.4.
148. Justin 13.4.4, trans. based on Rev. J.S. Watson, published by Henry G. Bohn, London, 1853.
149. Arrian, *Events After Alexander* 1.5 based on the translation in Goralsky (1989), p. 86.
150. *Metz Epitome* 123, trans. from Heckel-Yardley (2004), p. 289.
151. Curtius 10.6.1–4. Quoting Atkinson (2009), p. 26.
152. For their capture at Issus, see Curtius 3.11.25, Diodorus 17.36.2, Arrian 2.11.9, Justin 11.9.12, Plutarch 21.1. For their installation in Susa, Curtius 5.2.17 ff, Diodorus 17.67.1, and death at Babylon, see Plutarch 77.6.
153. Badian (1968), p. 203, suggested Eumenes did indeed have the king's papers or *hypomnemata* that outlined the last plans. I propose that position would have been used for faked correspondence too.
154. As suggested by Siebert (1969), pp. 27–28.
155. See discussion in Heckel (2006), p. 115. The final mention of Docimus is after Ipsus, at which he had defected to Lysimachus. He most likely betrayed the Perdiccans when besieged following the battle with Antigonus in Pisidia; see Simpson (1957), pp. 504–05. See Heckel, *A and A* (1978) for the argument for Attalus' marriage to Atalante after Babylon to secure his support. Justin 13.3.2–7 suggested Attalus had sided with Meleager and sent assassins to kill Perdiccas. Arrian, *Events after Alexander* 24.6 for Medius serving in the invasion of Cyprus in 321/210 BC.
156. Nearchus' initial whereabouts after Babylon are not recorded. He next emerged supporting Antigonus against Eumenes in 319/318 BC. As there was no initial hostility with Antigonus until Perdiccas' plans to repudiate Nicaea were revealed,

he may well have assumed the governorship of his satrapy or served the royal army until Perdiccas' death. For Nearchus' marriage at Susa, Arrian 7.4.6. Nearchus was married to the daughter of Barsine and Mentor.

157. See discussion of Ptolemy's ongoing communications with Antipater in Errington (1970), pp. 65–67. Leonnatus also defected to Greece, assisting Antipater in the Lamian War, and it appears he tried to turn Eumenes against Perdiccas too. Perdiccas' eventual murder by Peithon and the Silver Shield commanders (and possibly Seleucus) suggests a broad early coalition against him. Arrian, *Events after Alexander* 1.21 for Antipater's offer of Nicaea in marriage, Diodorus 18.23.1 for Perdiccas seeking her hand.

158. Perdiccas' dialogue with Demades discussed in Errington (1970), p. 62; Diodorus 18.48.2, Plutarch, *Phocion* 30.5–6, Plutarch, *Demosthenes* 31.4–6, Arrian, *Events After Alexander* 1.14–15 each described, with some variations, how letters from Demades to Perdiccas were later discovered, requesting Perdiccas' intervention in Greece. If genuine, their earlier concealment suggested to Antipater that Perdiccas was planning trouble. The correspondence may have been fabricated to enable Antipater to remove him; Goralski (1989), p. 106, for discussion. Arrian, *Events After Alexander* 1.14 for the 'rotten thread' analogy.

159. For Docimus' activity, see Arrian, *Events After Alexander* 24.3–5 and Plutarch, *Eumenes* 8.4. Pausanias 1.6.3 for Cleomenes' support from Perdiccas.

160. Antigonus was ordered by Perdiccas to support Eumenes' invasion of Cappadocia; he defected to Antipater and Craterus Macedon instead; Plutarch, *Eumenes* 3–4, Diodorus 18.23.3–4, Arrian, *Events After Alexander* 1.20.

161. For the failed invasion of Cyprus involving Medius and Aristonus, see Arrian, *Events After Alexander* 24.6. Quoting Roisman (2010), p. 118.

162. The date of Perdiccas' death, May/June 320 BC, is backed up by the Babylonian Chronicle extract BM 34, 660 Vs 4, though still disputed; see Anson (2003) for discussion on 'high' and 'low' chronologies.

163. For Perdiccas' murder, see Arrian, *Events After Alexander* 1.35, Diodorus 18.39.6, Nepos 5.1, Diodorus 18.36.5. For the canal project, Diodorus 18.33.2–3, possibly to allow Attalus to bring the fleet in tow as Perdiccas advanced. Detailed discussion of the attack in Roisman (2012), pp. 97–103. Diodorus 18.33.5 for Perdiccas' promises and gifts.

164. Arrian, *Events After Alexander* 1.28; this could be the epitomizer's confusion of Diodorus 18.36.6, a speech Ptolemy gave after Perdiccas' death. Diodorus 18.36.6 for Ptolemy addressing the Macedonians after Perdiccas' death.

165. Quoting Hornblower (1981), p. 103, on 'centrifugal forces'.

166. Augustus Roesiger in A.F. Roesiger, *De Duride Samio, Diodori Siculi et Plutarchi auctore*, Gottingen, 1874. See Justin 13.6 for his favourable treatment of Ptolemy. Trogus' treatment is epitomized at Justin 13.6 to 'Ptolemy, by his wise exertions in Egypt, was acquiring great power; he had secured the favour of the Egyptians by his extraordinary prudence.'

167. The Battle of Actium took place in 31 BC, probably when Diodorus finished his work, but Caesar had by then already caused damage in the city.

168. Diodorus 18.28.3, based on the translation from the Loeb Classical Library edition, 1954; also recorded by Strabo 17.8 and the *Romance* 3.34.6, though dates of the transfer from Memphis to Alexandria are not given. Pausanias 1.7.1 stated Ptolemy II Philadelphus brought the body to Alexandria from Memphis. Also see Aelian 12.64 for an alternative tradition.
169. Diodorus 18.28.3 and the earlier references to Alexandria at 17.52.1–6; Strabo 17.8 for his description of Alexandria.
170. Diodorus 18.28.5–6, based on the translation from the Loeb Classical Library edition, 1954.
171. Curtius 10.10.20, based on the translation from the Loeb Classical Library edition, 1946; Pausanias 1.7.1 stated Ptolemy II Philadelphus brought the body from Memphis to Alexandria.
172. Diodorus 18.33.3, based on the translation in the Loeb Classical Library edition, 1954, and reiterated at Justin 13.4.
173. Hornblower (1981) for discussion of Cleitarchus' extending of his account to the burial in Egypt. For a good discussion of Diodorus' change of source for these episodes, see Anson (2004), pp. 23–25.
174. Arrian 7.26.3 confirmed Aristobulus' account had nothing more to say on Alexander's death. It is possible Ptolemy said more about Alexander's corpse in a self-promoting way, but not about this death.
175. Arrian, *Events After Alexander* 1.25 for Arrhidaeus' complicity. Diodorus 18.3.5, Justin 13.4.6 for Arrhidaeus' instructions to build and deliver the funeral bier. Curtius 10.5.4, 18.3.5, Justin 12.15.7, Arrian, *Events After Alexander* 1.25, Pausanias 1.6.3, Strabo 17.8 for Alexander's desire to be buried at Ammon. Justin 13.4.6 reported the body was supposed to be destined for Egypt, as did Arrian, *Events After Alexander* 1.25; assuming this was Hieronymus-derived, then this argues strongly for Egypt as the legitimate destination. For accounts of the hearse's fate and Ptolemy's interception, see Diodorus 18.28.2, Strabo 17.8, Arrian, *Events After Alexander* 1.25, Pausanias 1.6.3, Aelian 12.64. Pausanias 1.6.3 stated Perdiccas planned to take the body to Aegae, and Arrian, *Events After Alexander* 1.25 suggested similar, both possibly following Antigonus' warning to Antipater, which may have been propaganda. No author linked its final destination to Alexander's own wishes, but rather to the opposing wishes of Perdiccas and Ptolemy. The will stated the destination was Egypt. Also Stewart (1993), p. 221, for discussion of Alexander's intent.
176. See discussion of the statues in Chugg (2009), p. 44, and Chugg (2002), p. 17.
177. Diodorus 18.28.3.
178. See full discussion and research in Chugg (2002), and for the location in Atkinson (2009), pp. 242–45. Strabo 17.8 for confirmation of the Sema being part of the royal palaces and housing the tombs of Alexander and the Ptolemies; also Erskine (2002) for discussion and p. 165 for the comment on inseparability. The *Proverbs of Zenobius* 3.94 (now available in the *Corpus paroemiographorum graecorum* I, p. 81) reported that Ptolemy IV Philopater built a burial complex, the Mnema, later called the Sema, to house all the royal corpses; discussed in Erskine (2002), pp. 165–66. The *Romance* 34.6 also confirmed the existence of the Sema (named the Soma of Alexander).

179. *Romance* 3.34.1–6 for the oracular predictions.
180. *Romance* 1.1–12.
181. Aelian 12.64 for the alternative version of the hijacking of Alexander's body.
182. Also known as Ptolemy '*kokkes*', or 'scarlet'; see Strabo 17.8, who also mentioned its location in the Sema, the burial place of kings.
183. Diodorus 18.26–28. For accounts of the hearse's fate, see Diodorus 18.28.2, Strabo 17.8, Arrian, *Events After Alexander* 1.25, Pausanias 1.6.3. For the dating, see discussion in Atkinson (2009), p. 242. Athenaeus 5.206e confirmed Hieronymus provided the funeral bier detail. Kebric (1977), p. 66, for its Durian style (i.e. taken from Duris of Samos).
184. 'Ionic temple on wheels' quoting Stewart (1993), p. 216.
185. Quoting Stewart (1993), p. 220, for the observation that 'no image of peace' was included in the description, and p. 221 for the absence of the phalanx.
186. Diodorus 18.26.1–3. The exact chronology according to the Roman consulships is open to debate; see discussion in Loeb edition, 1947, footnotes on pp. 86–87. However, Diodorus closed a previous paragraph with 'such then were the events of this year', generally attributable to 322 BC. And Diodorus stated at 18.28.2 that the engineer, Arrhidaeus, took almost two years completing his work.
187. For the timing of Eumenes' flight to Perdiccas in the face of Leonnatus' intriguing, see Anson (1986), p. 214. However, Perdiccas' whereabouts are not attested; the assumption that Eumenes returned to Babylon does not need to be made. Perdiccas might have been closer, in Syria for example, where he meant the hearse to reside.
188. 'Patchwork' quoting Hornblower (1981), p. 94.
189. A position supported by Hornblower (1981), p. 80. See Tarn (1948), pp. 6–7, for chronological arguments, and p. 33 for name-related arguments, and Hornblower (1981), pp. 80–82, for Tarn's dating of the satrapal list in Diodorus' geographical digression.
190. Quoting Bosworth (2002), p. 170, on Diodorus' preservation of Hieronymus' geographical digression.
191. Curtius 10.10.19.
192. Pearson (1960), p. 217, reinforced by M.C.J. Miller in Watson-Miller (1992), p. 108. Curtius' will dismissal could refer to Diodorus' later will reference at 20.81.3, but Diodorus never specifically linked the division of the empire to the will. And neither did Justin and so Trogus.
193. See Grant (2017), p. 465 ff, for full arguments. If we take each account up to this point, we see striking concord markers; any variation in expansiveness of some provincial detail would have occurred when the list was alternatively sourced from Hieronymus' original (Diodorus, for example, T16) or from epitomes (or summaries) of them (so Justin, Photius' précis of Arrian and Dexippus, T17, T18, T20). Clear stemma clues begin with a short digression mentioning Cleomenes in Egypt, thus linking Photius' précis with Justin's (T17, T18, T20). We have references to Antigonus almost identically transmitted in Curtius, Diodorus and Arrian's précis by Photius (T19, T16, T17) as far as the specificity of his domain: 'Pamphylia, Lycia, and what is called Great Phrygia', while the eastern border of Eumenes' territorial boundary

is uniformly marked with 'as far as Trapezus' in Curtius and Photius' epitomes. Diodorus additionally referred to Eumenes' task of pacifying his domain with 'all the lands bordering these, which Alexander did not invade'; this concurs (though less closely) with Curtius' reference to Eumenes 'conducting hostilities' with Ariarathes, king of the still-independent portion of Cappadocia. There are some discrepancies: in Curtius' account, the text dealing with Macedon failed to mention either Craterus or Antipater, and simply mentioned 'the king' holding supreme power: Curtius 10.10.1–5. Here Asander has been mistaken with, or corrupted to, Cassander. There is another lacuna in Photius' epitome of Arrian's *Events After Alexander* 1.7 dealing with the eastern provinces. And Justin's précis of Trogus work is corrupted the most, containing several otherwise unattested appointments, suggesting he clumsily merged the satrapal allocations at Babylon with those made later at Triparadeisus; Nearchus appeared in Lycia and Pamphylia, and Cassander was appointed to the king's guard, as he was at Triparadeisus.

194. Ptolemy, Laomedon and Philotas are the first three names in all versions. Antigonus, Asander, Menander and Leonnatus likewise appear in the same order in all. Eumenes and Peithon always appear side by side, although their relative positions in the overall list change. A reference to Illyria in Justin's epitome is a corruption of either Pamphylia or Lycia, each assigned to Antigonus.

195. See Grant (2017), p. 465 ff, for full arguments. There is, however, some divergence in the second part of the roll call of satraps in the eastern and upper provinces where governorships were to remain largely unchanged, and in particular with the roles linked to Seleucus, Craterus and Perdiccas. But these were the most difficult appointments to decipher due to what we propose were overarching authorities or pan-provincial mandates with regional satraps under them. The relative authorities of what were once the chiliarch of the empire, the guardians or caretakers to the new kings, and the protector roles assigned to the remaining regional governors, as well as Seleucus' first hipparchy cavalry command, were easily misinterpreted; Hieronymus himself may have transmitted them ambiguously or misrepresented them deliberately as a client of the Antigonids. The various terminologies associating satrap with satrapy should not necessarily be considered a source 'variance'; these are as much the product of modern translation as they were early scribal interpretation. To 'rule', to 'govern' and 'take charge of'; and 'received', 'fell to', or 'were allotted to', with the geographical tags 'adjacent', 'close to' and 'bordering', do not require more than a single source. What is surprising is the lack of bandwidth these early historians used in their regurgitations, for they must have been tempted to season the list with additional commentary. Yet they did not, and neither did they significantly rework the order of its presentation.

196. Arrian 7.27.1–3, Plutarch 77.5.

Chapter 4: Wills and Testaments in Classical Greece

1. An interpolated author translation.
2. A *medimnos* was about 11½ imperial gallons; from Hecke-Yardley (2004), p. 288 footnote 25.

3.   The text actually reads 'Craterus', which should be 'Peithon son of Crateuas'.
4.   Cicero *De Officiis* 3.8.36.
5.   Diogenes Laertius, *Aristotle* and *Theophrastus*.
6.   Chroust (1967), pp. 90–114, and Chroust (1970), p. 629.
7.   Davis (1914), Part 2, Ch. XI, *The Funerals*, section 69.
8.   Suetonius, *Nero* 17 for an example of the use of 'testator'.
9.   Davis (1914), Part 2, Ch. XI, *The Funerals*, section 69. How Solonian law translated into will structures is not fully clear as the speeches we draw inspiration from may be abiding by, challenging, reinterpreting or suggesting new avenues of law.
10. Keyser (2011), p. 111, for the Mesopotamian and neo-Babylonian wills.
11. Harris (1911), pp. 12–13, and Kenyon (1899), p. 58, for the mummy cases at Gurob.
12. Hesiod, *Theogonia* 22–34.
13. Plutarch, *Agis* 5.1–4, and for general attributions to the *rhetra* of Sparta, see Plutarch, *Lycurgus*. Detailed discussion of Spartan law and estate planning in Avramovic' (2006). Russell (1946), p. 99, for Spartan land law, and Aristotle, *Politics* 1270a ff.
14. Referred to as the *seisachtheia*, literally 'shaking off the burdens'.
15. Plutarch, *Solon* 2.1–3, trans. from the Loeb Classical Library edition, 1914.
16. In translation the 'Rock of Ares', the Areopagus, situated northwest of the Acropolis, functioned as Court of Appeal for criminal and civil cases in ancient times. Discussed in Arnaoutoglou (1998), pp. 1–5.
17. Callias was fined 50 talents upon his return, but seems to have brokered a peace known as the Peace of Callias, see Herodotus 7.151, Diodorus 12.4, Demosthenes, *On the False Embassy*, and in Shilleto (1874), p. 428. Neither Thucydides nor Herodotus mentioned the peace treaty.
18. Diogenes Laertius, *Solon* 1.62.
19. Chroust (1970), p. 635.
20. Plutarch, *Solon* 20.1–4 for the laws relating to women. Sparta had a similar rule. If a daughter, *epikleros*, was already married but childless, she might have been forced to divorce under this arrangement.
21. Chroust (1970), p. 635.
22. Chroust (1970), p. 629.
23. Diogenes Laertius, *Epicurus* 10.
24. Quoting Cicero, *Academica* 1.12.
25. Diogenes Laertius, *Arcesilaus* 4.19.
26. Arrian 7.28, Plutarch 77 for Aristotle's involvement.
27. Quoting Chroust (1973), p. 195, on 'ample correspondence'.
28. Diogenes Laertius, *Aristotle* 12 for the letters. Quoting Chroust (1970), p. 12, for the correspondence with Antipater, and pp. 9–11 for Aristotle's citizenship. At the time of Aristotle's death, Nicanor was said to be away on a 'dangerous mission', which further suggests a role under Cassander; discussed in Chroust (1970), p. 640; the known danger may explain why Theophrastus was named as 'interim heir designate' in Aristotle's will. Also Pausanias 6.4.8 for Aristotle's influence with Antipater; discussed in Bosworth (1971), p. 114.

29. Olympias and Antipater quarrelled and she departed Macedon for Epirus: Diodorus 18.49.4, Pausanias 1.11.3, Arrian 7.12.6–7, Plutarch 68.4–5, Justin 12.14.3.
30. Plutarch, *Demosthenes* 28.4 for the cutting out of Hyperides' tongue, and Plutarch, *Moralia* 849f (Life of Hyperides) for linking that to his proposing honours to Iollas.
31. See discussion in Barnes (1995), p. 6. Aristotle allegedly wrote to Antipater informing him the honours bestowed on him had been stripped. Marasco (2011), p. 45, for Aristotle's letter to Antipater concerning the withdrawn Delphic honours, cited in Aelian 14.1; an inscription by Aristotle was mentioned in Diogenes Laertius, *Aristotle* 5–6.
32. In the *Romance* 3.33 and *Metz Epitome* 122, Alexander requested gilded statues to be erected in Delphi and Athens; and statues of his mother, father and select gods in Egypt. See Heckel (1988), p. 17, for *Metz Epitome* translation, and Stoneman (1991), p. 155, for the *Romance*.
33. Chroust (1979), p. 637; Stagira was a colony of either Chalcis or Andros.
34. A visitor to the city would have had some days' exemption before taxes became payable ahead of becoming a metic.
35. Hansen (1999), p. 130, for the fifty grants of citizenship.
36. Finlay (1973), p. 116, for the breakdown of Demosthenes' father's estate. Aeschines, *On the False Embassy* 93 claimed Demosthenes was called the 'son of a sword-maker'.
37. Polybius 4.87.7–8; discussed in Marasco (2011), pp. 57–58, and following the observations of C Bearzot, p. 58.
38. See discussion of the importance of waggons and wealth in Billows (1990), pp. 102–03, citing Diodorus 19.42.4–43; and evidence of their vulnerability in battle in Plutarch, *Eumenes* 16.5–6, Polyaenus 4.6.13. Also Anson (2004), pp. 187–89.
39. Sophocles, *Ajax* lines 565–577.
40. Discussed in Keyser (2011), pp. 115–17. Details found in the *Iliad* 2.100–108, 6.476–481. Heracles' oral will as interpreted from lines 161–63 in Sophocles' *Women of Trachis*; discussion in Keyser (2011), pp. 117–18, also referring to Euripides, *Heracles* lines 460–73.
41. The *Metz Epitome* 120 and *Romance* 3.33 have Alexander leaving his arms and insignia to the temple of Hera at Argos.
42. For Alexander's financial position and borrowing of 800 talents, see Plutarch 15.1–3, Curtius 10.2.24 and Arrian 7.9.6.
43. Diodorus 17.16.2.
44. Curtius 9.6.6–14 and 9.6.15 for Craterus' and Ptolemy's speeches and concerns.
45. Aristotle, *Nicomachean Ethics* book 10 1177b32–1178a, but a theme recurring through books 9 and 10.
46. Arrian 1.12.1 and Aelian 12.7 confirmed Hephaestion crowned, or wreathed, Patroclus' tomb at Troy, whilst Alexander did the same to the tomb of Achilles, suggesting their parallel relationship.
47. Plutarch, *Eumenes* 16.2–4.
48. Plutarch 77.5, Curtius 10.9–13, Aelian 12.64.
49. See Grant (2017) for discussion of the tombs at Vergina and associated funerary rites.

260   *The Last Will and Testament of Alexander the Great*

50. Aristobulus' account of the sophists at Taxila captured by Arrian 6.22.4–8 included reference to Phoenicians 'who had been following the expedition in search of trade' collecting spikenard, myrrh, gum and other roots. Ada was reinstated as satrap of Caria and she adopted Alexander; see Arrian 1.23.8. Alexander addressed Sisygambis, Darius' mother, in terms that suggest he adopted her as his second mother; see Curtius 5.2.22. Plutarch 21.7–9. Rhoxane was Bactrian or Sogdian; the campaign and siege of the so-called Rock of Sogdia, the Rock of Sisimithres (Choriense) and the Rock of Ariamazes are confused; see Heckel (2006), pp. 241–42 and 187 for identifications, and Heckel (1987), p. 114, for discussion. Barsine and Parysatis were from Persian royal lines, see Arrian 7.4.4–7. The prominent non-Macedonian drinking partners mentioned at Alexander's final banquet were Medius from Thessaly, Heracleides the Thracian, Ariston of Pharsalus, Nearchus the Cretan and Stasanor, a Cypriot; Heckel (1988), p. 10, for a further list of those present. Holcias may have been Illyrian and Lysimachus was originally Thessalian but became a naturalized Macedonian; Heckel (2006), p. 153.
51. Full description of the funeral hearse in Diodorus 18.26–28.
52. The slip of the tongue was recorded in Plutarch 27, though this is hardly likely. Strabo 17.1.43 indicated Callisthenes stated the oracle's reply confirmed Alexander as the son of Zeus.
53. Justin 12.15.1–3 for his reflection that most of his line died before reaching 30.
54. Plutarch, *Themistocles* 29.3.

Chapter 5: Death and Poison: The Toxic Cup

1. Translation from Stoneman (1991), p. 33.
2. Xenophon, *Cyropaedia* Book 1.3.8–10, trans. by H.G. Dakyns, Project Gutenberg.
3. The list of assassinations discussed in Bosworth-Baynham (2000), p. 53; Anson (2013), pp. 80–81, for a list of the Argead kings who died in court intrigues.
4. Pausanias 9.7.2 for the allegation of poison at the death of Alexander IV and Heracles.
5. Ovid, *Metamorphoses* 7:404–424 where Medea attempted to poison Theseus with an aconite mix.
6. Homer, *Odyssey* 1.300–310. Helen's actions discussed in Collins (2008), p. 144, quoting Homer, *Odyssey* 4.230.
7. Mayor (2003), p. 72, for 'spear poison'. In Latin *strychnos* (the root of strychnine) – 'a kind of nightshade' – became the generic word for plants with similar effects. Pliny 21.177–182 and Celsus stated that what the Greeks knew as *strychnos* (acrid) was known as solanum by the Romans.
8. Hutchinson (1997), p. 314, Mayor (2003), p. 41, and Luch (2009), p. 2.
9. Collins (2008), p. 30, and Cilliers-Retief (2000), p. 90, for the root cutters, *rhizomotoi*.
10. Blyth (1906), p. 573.
11. Diodorus 17.5.6.
12. Hesiod, *Work and Days* 342, Photius, *Epitome* 72 of Ctesias' *Persica* 29; Plutarch, *Artaxerxes* 19 for Parysatis' poisoning of Stateira.

13. Diodorus 17.90.5–6 and 17.103.5 for the venomous snakes and the preparation of poison, and quoting 19.33.2–4.
14. Diodorus 17.103.7–8 and Curtius 9.8.22. Ptolemy suffered the consequences and allegedly nearly died before an antidote was found. Discussion of *the Laws of Manu* in Mayor (2003), p. 91. Strabo 15.2.5–7 for a description of the snakes and their effects in India.
15. Following Collins (2008), p. 43, using Plato, *Laws* 11.933a as examples.
16. Collins (2008), p. 134.
17. Strabo 10.5.6, see full discussion in Griffin (1986), p. 192.
18. Theophrastus, *Enquiry into Plants* 9.16.8.
19. Plutarch, *Phocion* 36.3–4. The executioner refused to 'bruise' more hemlock unless he paid 12 drachmas. Blackwell (1999), p. 63, for discussion of Phocion's career. Aelian 11.9 for Phocion's gift from Alexander.
20. Plutarch, *Demosthenes* 29.3, trans. from the Loeb Classical Library edition Vol. VII, 1919.
21. Diogenes Laertius, *Aristotle* 8, trans. from the Loeb Classical Library edition, 1925, and *Aristotle* 7 for his death by aconite. Chroust (1970), p. 650 footnote 90, for the alternative traditions. Eurymedon (or Demophilus) had tried to associate Aristotle's encomium (or hymn) to Hermias with impiety for casting Virtue as a goddess and for the inscription on his statue at Delphi; Diogenes Laertius, *Aristotle* 5–6.
22. Theophrastus, *Enquiry into Plants* 9.16.2 for aconite and 9.11.5–6 for strychnine, referenced in Engels (1978), pp. 224–28, although this apparently refers to the non-lethal and less bitter variety. See Kaufman (1932), p. 164, for discussion about masking poison in wine, and Juvenal 1.69–70 and 6.663.
23. Green (1970), p. 259.
24. Green (1970), p. 260.
25. See Atkinson-Yardley (2009), pp. 148–49, and Atkinson (2009), pp. 28–46, for a useful summary of the theories propounded to date on a natural death. Renault (1975), pp. 228–30.
26. A mule or ass's hoof according to Plutarch 77.4, Pliny 30.149, Vitruvius 8.3.16; Justin 12.14; Pausanias 8.17–18; the *Romance* 3.31 on the other hand claimed lead inside an iron container was used; it made no mention of Aristotle. The *Metz Epitome* stated that Antipater 'prepared some poison in a small iron box. This he locked within an ass's hoof with an iron clasp, that the virulence of the poison might be contained.'
27. For the punishment of the gods at the Styx, see Hesiod, *Theogonia* 775–819.
28. Pausanias 8.17–19 and quoting from Mayor (2010), p. 4.
29. Full discussion of the waters of the Styx at Nonacris in Mayor (2010), pp. 1–29. Modern theory suggests that if indeed this was its source, the effects came from naturally occurring corrosive acids, lethal minerals from (non-evident) ancient mining close by, toxic salts from the venting of a thermo-active fault-line or the seasonal flooding and washing-in of local toxic plants. A case has also been made for the presence of the killer bacteria Calicheamicin occurring in *Micromonospora echinospor* thought to be present in adjacent limestone and soils. Discussed in Mayor (2010), pp. 9–13.

262   The Last Will and Testament of Alexander the Great

30. Plutarch 77.5, Aelian 12.64 claimed thirty days unburied; Aelian 13.30 for Olympias' grief upon hearing it.
31. Curtius 10.9–13; Aelian 12.64.
32. Blyth (1906), p. 573.
33. Milne (1968), p. 256 argued for strychnine poisoning; Engels (1978), pp. 224–28. See Atkinson-Yardley (2009), pp. 232–33, and Atkinson (2009), p. 26, for the coma theory. Curtius 10.9.1, Plutarch 77.5 and Aelian 12.64 for references to the corpse remaining fresh for days (or a month – Aelian) after being pronounced dead. The clinicopathological protocol was established by Dr D.W. Oldach in the *New England Journal of Medicine* 338, no. 24 (11 June 1998), pp. 1764–69.
34. Schep-Slaughter-Vale-Wheatley (2013), p. 4.
35. Plutarch 41.7. For antimony use, see U Arndt, *The Philosopher's Magnet – Alchemic Transmutation of Antimony*, first published in the magazine *Paracelsus*, November 2005, pp. 12–17.
36. Schep-Slaughter-Vale-Wheatley (2013), p. 5.
37. Schep-Slaughter-Vale-Wheatley (2013), p. 4.

Chapter 6: Hunting the Architects of Deceipt

1. Arrian 7.25.6, trans. by A. de Selincourt, Penguin Classics edition, 1958.
2. Curtius 10.5.5–6, based on the translation in the Loeb Classical Library edition, 1946.
3. For what I term an 'Alexandrian monopoly', see Grant, *Ancient Sources* (2021).
4. For Diodotus, see Athenaeus 10.434b for Diodotus and Eumenes, and Aelian 3.23 additionally for Eumenes. *Archigrammateus*, chief clerk, may well be a Hellenistic term that would not have been used before; Sekunda (1984), p. 12.
5. Arrian, *Indica* 18.8 for Evagoras. But if Athenaeus' text came down to us from the single corrupted manuscript that was transferred from Constantinople to Vienna in 1423 by the Italian historian, Giovanni Aurispa, then rather than 'Diodotus', a 'Diognetus' of Ethyrae, one of the known *bematistes* (map makers) on campaign, may well be our man. The manuscript is referred to as the St Mark Codex A. Recently Chugg (2007), pp. 226–29, suggested Diodotus was a *bematistes* and thus, an author of the *Stathmoi*, the Stages correcting the name to Diognetus of Ethyrae mentioned as a bematist at Pliny 6.61. This has no bearing on our argument except to illustrate how misidentification has crept into extant texts. Further identification suggestions from Heckel (2006), p. 308 footnote 301.
6. Plutarch 77.3–4. By then Antigonus was referred to as 'king', but this does not necessarily mean the rumours circulated after 306 BC when he was formally crowned. Plutarch may well have not been clinical in the differentiation between when Antigonus was considered a dynast and king.
7. Holcias' role in the will reading and his satrapal inheritance of Illyria is mentioned at *Metz Epitome* 97–98, 103, 106, 109, 111–112, 114–116, 122, and also *Romance* 3.31–23. Heckel (2006), p. 314 footnote 373, for citations. Polyaenus 4.6.6 mentioned

he was pardoned for his opposition to Antigonus on the proviso that he retired to non-activity.
8. Fraser (1996), p. 41, for the correct title of what we now term the *Liber de Morte*. The oldest manuscript of recension A of the *Romance* is the MS Parisinus 1711, a descendant of the original *Romance* from some 700–800 years earlier.
9. The earlier work was the Greek *Kronika Alexandrina*. Discussion of the so-called *Excerpta Latina Barbari* in Fraser (1996), pp. 14–15. Other similarities with the *Romance* suggest this was its source.
10. See Grant (2017), p. 229 ff, for full detail of the emergence of the *Romance*. See discussion in Stoneman (1991), p. 14. The oldest fragment containing the will is considered to be Pap. Gr. Vindobonesis 31954, see Pearson (1960), p. 261 and footnote 96 for details.
11. For its preservation in other *Romance* recensions, see Bosworth-Baynham (2000), pp. 207–08; Heckel (1988), p. 1 footnote 1; Stoneman (1991), pp. 8–11. For further discussion on dating of the first Alexander *Romance* and *Metz Epitome*, see Stoneman (1991), pp. 8–9. Fraser (1996), pp. 41–46, for discussion of the *Liber de Urbibus Alexandri*.
12. Fraser (1996), p. 213, for discussion of the Egyptian papyrus containing a fragment of the will. Of course the will could have been extracted from the *Romance* and reproduced as a stand-alone document, but it remains more likely that it came from a stand-alone document.
13. *Romance* 3.30, *Metz Epitome* 90–94. Scylla was a part-human, part-beast monster from Greek mythology; here a baby born as a human boy from the belly up, below which it was part lion, panther, dog and boar. As Merkelbach and Heckel (1988), p. 9, agree, the beast represented Alexander's own men and their betrayal and not his subject nations as translations suggest. See 'A Baleful Birth in Babylon' by E.C. Carney in Bosworth-Baynham (2000), p. 242 ff, for the context of the Scylla and its possible historicity. Spargue de Camp (1972), p. 140, for the sirrush.
14. See Grant (2017), p. 346, for superstition in ancient Greece.
15. Following and quoting Heckel (1988), p. 10.
16. Antipater's fear of assassination by Alexander expressed or implied at Justin 12.14.3, Curtius 10.10.5, Arrian 7.12.4–7, who alone reported that Alexander had summoned Antipater to Babylon; this may well have been a hangover of the whole conspiracy rumour. Arrian nevertheless attempted to defend what he believed was an actual summons.
17. The florid letter, in 'clotted officialese' and supposedly written to the island's council and people, is widely considered a later interpolation, though adjoining references in the earliest surviving version of the *Romance* suggest that embellishment, not complete invention, gives us its now extended form. See Heckel (1988), pp. 12–13, for full translation of the Letter to the Rhodians. Quoting Stoneman (1991), Introduction p. 12, for 'clotted officialese'. *Metz Epitome* 110 for the roles of Perdiccas and Antipater. Heckel (1988), pp. 12–14 for full discussion referring to Recension A of Pseudo-Callisthenes, and Heckel-Yardley (2004), p. 285, for a full translation of the *Metz*

Epitome version of the Rhodian 'interpolation'. Bosworth-Baynham (2000), p. 213, agrees the Rhodian issue could have formed part of the original *Pamphlet* will. See Stoneman (1991), pp. 152–53, for a translation of the *Romance* version of the Letter to the Rhodians. The Letter to the Rhodians is concurrent in Pseudo-Callisthenes. A. Fraser (1996), p. 212, for the Boule and demos and discussion on the Latin manuscript in which the letter appeared separately.

18. Heckel (1988), p. 14, for translation and discussion. Atkinson (2009), p. 178, proposed chiliarch was the equivalent post of the Achaemenid *hazarapati*, the king's second in command. The term traditionally meant commander of a thousand men, but the Persian usage was adopted, meaning the king's second in command. Also Collins (2001) for the development of the chiliarch role.
19. For the five days citation, see discussion in Heckel (1988), p. 13.
20. *Metz Epitome* 118, *Romance* 32 for confirmation of Rhoxane's Bactrian (or Sogdian) father, whereas *Romance* 20; Stoneman (1991), pp. 110, 113–14 – she became the daughter of Darius. Discussed in Tarn (1948), p. 335 footnote 2, thus Tarn concluded the will is far older than the rest of the *Romance*.
21. Dubbed by Reinhold Merkelbach in 1954; he was an archaeologist and philologist and was following the title of a manuscript from the Escorial Monastery in Spain (*Codex Scorialensis* b III 14 E). Fellow philologist Adolf Ausfeld had already pointed this out sixty years before; (1894), pp. 357–66; discussed in Baynham (1998), p. 74. The detail describing pre-death portents was not part of the original *Pamphlet* but a later addition. Fraser (1996), p. 213, for the Escorial manuscript attachment.
22. Quoting Heckel (1988), p. 1.
23. Others, notably Siebert and Samuel, dismiss the idea of the *Pamphlet* altogether as a propaganda piece emanating from the Successor Wars; see Heckel (1988), pp. 4–5 and footnotes for full citations.
24. The original; separation by Ausfeld's 1894. As examples, Heckel (1988), pp. 1–5, Bosworth-Baynham (2000), pp. 207–41, Atkinson (2009), pp. 229–30. Ausfeld (1901) proposed a dating of 319 BC. He and later Merkelbach (1954) concluded Holcias might have been the self-promoting author. These first conclusions were clouded by the views of Wagner (1900), Reitzenstein (1904) and Nietzold (1904).
25. Quoting Bosworth-Baynham (2000), p. 241.
26. *Metz Epitome* 97–98 for the full list given in Heckel-Yardley (2004), p. 283.
27. Pausanias 1.6.3. Ptolemy murdered Cleomenes, whom Perdiccas had reappointed in Egypt, and Ptolemy's speech at Babylon in Curtius 10.6.13–16 clearly undermined Perdiccas' position. The date of Perdiccas' death, May/June 320 BC, is backed up by the *Babylonian Chronicle* extract BM 34, 660 Vs 4, also known as *The Diadochi Chronicle* or *Chronicle of the Successors*.
28. Citing Bosworth in Bosworth-Baynham (2000), p. 209.
29. Even Tarn's 1921 case for its possible dating, and which did hinge on Perdiccan origins, conceded that it may have been a somewhat later publication (specifically, from the years that saw the new regent, Polyperchon, in opposition to Cassander, commencing late 319 BC).

30. Bosworth (1971) noted this 'anomaly' and salvaged Ptolemaic authorship by suggesting the will be unyoked from the conspiracy detail in the *Pamphlet* (thus inconsistencies stemming from those named guilty and innocent in the plot disappear); he was alternatively proposing that there might be substance to the spurious story which appears to be a later *Romance* 3.32.9–10 addition. Here Perdiccas initially tried to share power with Ptolemy; a plan that backfired when he himself was unexpectedly passed the ring by the dying king. Yet this episode has been 'long recognized' as Ptolemy's own propaganda, and one that in fact reconfirmed Perdiccas' inheritance of power. Would it not have been far simpler for Ptolemy to simply claim Perdiccas was guilty?
31. Arrian's statement that 'neither Aristobulus nor Ptolemy had anything to add' is much debated and does not necessarily mean the book was ended here, only the account of Alexander's death did. There is equally no evidence that either extended their books past this point.
32. Quoting Carney (2006), p. 110, for 'scrap of partisan literature'.
33. The alliance of Olympias and Eumenes and the circumstances behind the *Pamphlet* discussed in later chapters.
34. Heckel (1988) with a good summary of previous work on pp. 1–5.
35. Following the reasoning in Bosworth-Baynham (2000), p. 212. If Polyperchon wished to damn Cassander, his new opponent, he could have achieved this without implicating Antipater.
36. Diodorus 20.20 for Polyperchon's return to affairs; 20.28.1–3 for his alliance with Cassander and troops and grants.
37. Hammond (1993), pp. 145–46. He suggested Antigonus shifted blame to Aristotle (implicated in the Vulgate tradition) to counter Olympias' accusations against Antipater and his sons, before providing Hagnothemis with the story. Quoting Heckel (1988), p. 5, on Antigonus' insignificance.
38. Quoting Bosworth in Bosworth-Baynham (2000), p. 210.
39. Diodorus 19.57.1–3 for the demands of Lysimachus, Ptolemy and Cassander for their role in Eumenes' defeat. Lysimachus' men had captured and executed White Cleitus on behalf of Antigonus; Justin 13.6.16 for Cleitus' operation under Perdiccan forces. For his operations under Polyperchon, see Plutarch, *Phocion* 34.2–4 and 35.2.
40. Arrian, *Events After Alexander* 25.1, and Bosworth-Baynham (2000), pp. 210–11, for Asander's relationship with Antigonus. Contra Heckel (2006), p. 57, there is actually little evidence Asander supported Perdiccas and then defected to Antigonus. His grant of Caria is, as we pose, an original will appointment and not a result of his pro-Perdiccan politics.
41. Heckel (1988), pp. 64–65, suggests Asander was opposed to Antigonus, yet Heckel (2006), p. 57, clarifies he was aligned with Antigonus at least until 315 BC, after Eumenes' death. Thus he opposed Eumenes before. For his defection to Antigonus, see Arrian, *Events After Alexander* 25.1, and Diodorus 19.62.2 for his later defection to Ptolemy.
42. Some argue that was 321 BC, following the 'high chronology', Eumenes and 50 Perdiccans were first outlawed and sentenced to death in Egypt by the troops upon

hearing of the death of Craterus: Diodorus 18.37.1–3, Plutarch, *Eumenes* 8.2, Arrian, *Events After Alexander* 1.39, Justin 13.8.10–13.8.14.1.1, Appian, *Syrian Wars* 53. For the dating of Triparadeisus and the 'high' and 'low' chronologies of the years 323/319 BC, see Wheatley (1995).
43. Tarn (1948), pp. 378–88. *Metz Epitome* 123 for the gods, and 97 for the reference to the 'senate' at Rhodes.
44. Following and quoting de Polignac (1999), p. 8; the emergence of Serapis discussed in detail below.
45. For the penning and private reading of the will by Holcias to Ptolemy, Lysimachus, Perdiccas and Rhoxane, see *Metz Epitome* 106, *Romance* 3.33.1.
46. Plutarch, *Eumenes* 1.2 for Neoptolemus deriding Eumenes' position as secretary. See below for Aelian linking the *Ephemerides* to Eumenes.
47. Polyaenus 4.6.6 for Holcias' defection, capture and repatriation to Macedon.
48. Despite Tarn's conclusion that Holcias was nothing but a 'ringleader of some mutinous soldiery'; but then Tarn also believed 'Alexander's fictitious Testament is not historical evidence for anything.' Quoting Tarn (1948), p. 317.
49. Taking the observation from Bosworth-Baynham (2000), p. 240.
50. For Hagnothemis, see Plutarch 77.3, and for Hagnon of Teos, see Plutarch 40.1.
51. Discussion of sources for Hagnon in Heckel (2006), p. 128, and also Billows (1990), pp. 386–88. For Hagnon's hostility to Callisthenes, see Plutarch 55.2.
52. Plutarch, *Moralia* 65d, or *How One May Discern A Flatterer from a Friend* 442.
53. Arrian, *Indica* 18.8 for Hagnon's trierarch role. Trierarchies were expensive and often didn't return capital to those obliged under the Athenian system of 'liturgy'. It came with the obligation to fit out and provision a naval ship.
54. Athenaeus 12.539c, Plutarch 40.1, Aelian 9.3 for his extravagance. Arrian, *Indica* 18.8 for example called the Tean 'Andron', suggesting how easily names can be eroded in transmission. Nepos additionally erroneously named Hagnonides as Hagnon; Heckel (2006), pp. 128–29, for references.
55. Heckel (2006), p. 310 footnote 300, for discussion of Hagnon's whereabouts in 315/314 BC. Plutarch 77.2–3 for Hagnothemis hearing of the plot from Antigonus, who here is called a 'king' but this does not suggest he had been formally crowned yet. It is more likely the title represented Antigonus' supremacy in Asia.
56. Plutarch 76–77; Arrian 7.25–26. The Greek translation of Arrian's claims that Aristobulus and Ptolemy had nothing more to say is much debated; see Arrian 7.26.3, *Alexander the Great, The Anabasis and the Indica*, Oxford World Classics 2013 edition, footnote to 7.26.3 on p. 324 for discussion.
57. Lucian, *Encomium of Demosthenes* 26 for reference to the *Makedonika hypomnemata tes basilikes oikias*, the Macedonian royal archives. Polyaenus 4.6.2 for the Antigonid *hypomnemata*. Discussed in Marasco (2011), p. 57.
58. Discussed in Marasco (2011), pp. 57–65.
59. Persian archive tradition suggested at Hellanicus fr. 178, Herodotus 1.99, 3.128, 8.85.4, 8.90.4, *Old Testament*, *Ezra* 4, *Old Testament*, *Esther* 6.1, 10.2; Anson (2013), p. 57, and Momigliano (1977), p. 31, for discussion. Hammond (1988), pp. 129–50, is the most vocal on the existence of a complete campaign journal. Also see Anson

60. Nepos, *Eumenes* 1.4–6 and 13.1 (aged 20), also Plutarch, *Eumenes* 1.1–3 for his background.
61. Lucian, *A Slip of the Tongue in Greeting* 8.
62. The *Journal* format in cuneiform tablets was proposed by Cartledge (2005), p. 278.
63. Citing Van der Spek (2003), pp. 289–346.
64. As pointed out by Casson (2001), p. 1.
65. An attested greater antiquity of the astronomical observations came from Porphyry through Simplicius, so may be an exaggeration; discussion in Neugebauer (1957), p. 151, and Robinson (1953), p. 45, for citation. Polcaro-Valsecchi-Verderame (2008), p. 5, for the oldest extant diary. For Berossus' claim of antiquity, see Drews (1975), p. 54.
66. Quoting Dalley (2013), p. 1, for the extent of Babylonian and Assyrian writings.
67. 'Nerve centre' following the comment by Anson (2004), p. 233.
68. Curtius 8.11.5 for Mullinas, but possibly identifiable with Myllenas son of Asander; see Bosworth, *A in the East* (1996), p. 51, for discussion on identity, and Heckel (2006), p. 120. He was placed in command of lightly armed troops.
69. See Grant, *Ancient Sources* (2021).
70. See discussion in Robinson (1953) *The Ephemerides* p. 69, in agreement with 'metaphrasing'. Not all historians agree with the similarity; see discussion in *Bosworth A to A* (1988), chapter 7, and Anson (1996), p. 503 footnote 6. Nevertheless, Bosworth p. 506 did concede that a single source was being followed.
71. Arrian 7.25–7.26, trans. by E.J. Chinook, 1854.
72. Plutarch 75–77.
73. See the version from Aelian below, which reported the binges leading up to Alexander's illness.
74. Baynham (1998), p. 96, for a list of tragic episodes linked to drinking binges or *komoi*. Borza (1995), pp. 159–69, for discussion on the Macedonian banquets and drinking parties. The most famous was given by Medius heralding in Alexander's death, and a nine-day festival was given on the eve of Alexander's departure for Asia; see Borza (1995), p. 160.
75. Plutarch 75.6.
76. Following the definition of Briant (1974), p. 138, for the king mediating between the gods and men.
77. Arrian 7.25.6.
78. The presence of these commanders discussed by B. Bosworth in Carney-Ogden (2010), p. 92.
79. Arrian 7.26.1; this is also related at Plutarch 76.8 and Justin 12.15. There is a lacuna in Curtius where we expect this to feature. Diodorus' brevity appears to have passed over this detail.
80. Plutarch 75.6 stated 30th and at 76.9 the 28th.
81. See Atkinson (2009), p. 148, for discussion of the hollow month of Daisios and possible confusion that it caused.

268 *The Last Will and Testament of Alexander the Great*

82. Curtius 10.10.9–14 stated seven days, and Aelian 12.64 referred to a thirty-day period; it is highly unlikely that a body could remain unattended that long in the climate of Babylon in June. Plutarch 77.5 follows the 'fresh corpse' tradition without being specific on duration, apart from 'many days'. Hammond and Engels argued that malaria brought on a deep coma that fooled the audience; see discussion in Atkinson (2009), p. 232.
83. Arthur-Montagne (2014), p. 3, for the explanation and origins of pseudo-documentarism. Discussion of the Macedonian symposia and its rhetorical treatment in Greece by F. Pownall in Carney-Ogden (2010), pp. 55–65.
84. See fragment in Robinson (1953), pp. 31–32, from Plutarch's *Moralia* 623e or *Quaestiones Conviviales* 1.6.1.
85. Plutarch 23–24 and Athenaeus 434b. Whilst Plutarch's earlier *Journal* reference does not mention Babylon, the grandeur of the dinner arrangements and the king's sleeping habits hardly suggest an 'on campaign' occasion. Athenaeus may have followed Plutarch's detail; we cannot in fact be sure where Plutarch's *Journal* detail begins and ends in this passage.
86. Aelian 3.23.
87. Bosworth A to A (1988), pp. 158–67, for these proposals, and Hammond (1988), pp. 170–71. Also Anson (1996), pp. 501–04, Robinson (1953), Preface p. x, suggested the *Journal* extract dealing with Alexander's death could be a surviving extract from Strattis' *On the Deaths of Alexander*. Discussion summarized well in Atkinson (2009), pp. 142–43.
88. Athenaeus 120c–d, 146c–d, 434a–b, each extracting from Ephippus' *On the Funerals of Alexander and Hephaestion* and each suggestive that drinking bouts took place before Hephaestion's death.
89. Hammond (1988), pp. 177–80, for the identification with Hephaestion. Athenaeus 120c–d for the fragment of Ephippus; full text in Robinson (1953), p. 86. That Eumenes reported Hephaestion's slip of the tongue, an embarrassment, suggests he might have been subtly undermining him; Lucian, *A Slip of the Tongue in Greeting* 8, and see above.
90. Hammond (1988), pp. 129–50, is the most vocal on the existence of a complete campaign journal. Also see Anson (1996), pp. 501–04, for discussion. Robinson (1953), Preface, believed the journals entered the 'general stream' of histories early on.
91. Aelian 3.23. It is quite clear that Alexander is being referred to, as the drinking bouts formed a part of Aelian's overall treatment of him.
92. The paralleled and columned comparisons of the *Journal* entries from Plutarch, Arrian and Aelian are provided in Robinson (1953) The Ephemerides, pp. 64–68. Some confusion still exists as to the modern month equivalent to the Macedonian calendar. Josephus' commentary in which he juxtaposed the Macedonian calendar against the Hebrew, Athenian and Roman months is useful though. Also details in Hannah (2005), p. 95, for reference to 29 Daisios.
93. Plutarch 75.3, Diodorus 17.115.6, Arrian 7.23.8 for Hephaestion's elevation. Diodorus claimed this was to a 'god', whilst Arrian claimed the oracle permitted 'hero' only.

94. Diodorus 17.116.1.
95. At Aelian 3.23 Alexander is cited as drinking with Eumaios (or Eumaeus) on the 5th and with Perdiccas on the 7th. See Heckel-Yardley (2004), p. 43 footnote 14, for detail of the possible mistransmission of the name.
96. Arrian 7.25.2.
97. Arrian 7.23–24. Tarn (1948), p. 395, questioned whether it was a military campaign, likening it to the crossing of the Gedrosian Desert.
98. Plutarch 76.1.
99. Aelian 3.23.
100. More on the subterfuges in the following chapters.
101. Quoting Bosworth (1971), p. 467, on the drinking marathon.
102. Athenaeus 10.434b.
103. Arrian 7.25–26.
104. Plutarch 77.1.
105. Arrian, Preface 1.1–4.
106. Well covered by Bosworth *A to A* (1988), chapter 7, and Pearson (1960), pp. 260–61.
107. Pearson (1960), p. 261.
108. The Roman geographer Strabo implied that he knew of Babylonian records from which he concluded the campaign historians had provided only cursory *geographic* detail compared to expert data he found. This material may have included the topographical records of Baeton and Diognetus (termed 'measurers of roads'), Philonides and Amyntas, whose names appeared in the texts of Athenaeus, Aelian and Pliny, though these eyewitness accounts seem, once again, to have included the marvels of India, thus we may question their intent. The polymath Eratosthenes (*ca.* 276–194 BC), however, who became chief librarian at the Library of Alexandria around a century later, stated that no copies of such records, referred to as the 'measurements' or 'stages' (in Greek *stathmoi*), were available for him to consult, and we would have expected Arrian to use them, or at least reference them, if only to follow the example set by Xenophon, who referred to these types of precise records in his Persian campaign account, the *Anabasis*. This upholds the contention that the campaign *Ephemerides*, Strabo's Babylon-originating data aside, disappeared in the Successor Wars.
109. Diodorus 18.3.5, Justin 13.4.6 for Arrhidaeus' instructions to build and deliver the funeral bier. No author linked its final destination to Alexander's own wishes, but rather to the opposing wishes of Perdiccas and Ptolemy. Also Stewart (1993), p. 221, for discussion of Alexander's intent. The suggestion that Ptolemy 'hijacked' the funeral bier is found in Arrian, *Events After Alexander* 1.25, Pausanias 1.6.3 (stated Perdiccas planned to take the body to Aegae), Strabo 17.8, Aelian 12.64. We propose this is Hieronymus-derived propaganda against Ptolemy. Diodorus 18.28.2 suggested its intended destination was the sanctuary of Ammon at Siwa, whilst Ptolemy decided to entomb it in the city Alexander had founded himself.
110. Aelian 12.64 for the alternative version of the hijacking of Alexander's body. Diodorus 26.2–28.2 for a description of the funeral bier.

270   *The Last Will and Testament of Alexander the Great*

111. Aelian 12.64 for Aristanders' prediction. *Romance* 3.32, *Metz Epitome* 119 for Alexander's wish to be entombed in Egypt. For Alexander's previous journey to Siwa, see Diodorus 17.49.2–52.7, Arrian 3.4–5, Curtius 4.7.8–4.89, Plutarch 26.3–27.11, Justin 11.11.1–13, Strabo 17.1.43, *Itinerarium Alexandri* 48–50.
112. Justin 7.1.7–10 for the etymology of Aegae, and Justin 7.2.4–6 for King Perdiccas I's prophecy.
113. Diodorus 18.25.2–3.
114. Arrian, *Events After Alexander* 24.1–8 for the statement that part of the motivation for Perdiccas' invasion of Egypt was to gain control of Alexander's body. Discussed in Erskine (2002), p. 171. For Typhon's Breathing Hole, see Plutarch, *Antony* 3. The Egyptians referred to the region inland of Pelusium at the Acregma and Serbonian marshes as Typhon's Breathing Hole. Perdiccas was in fact murdered further up the Nile near Heliopolis.
115. Diodorus 18.48.1–4, Plutarch, *Phocion* 30.5–6, Plutarch, *Demosthenes* 31.34–36, Arrian, *Events After Alexander* 1.13–15 for the tradition of letters between Perdiccas and Demades undermining Antipater.
116. Ptolemy's men used their pikes to blind Perdiccas' elephants in the battle on the Nile; Diodorus 18.34.2.
117. Arrian 7.26.2–3.
118. Following the identifications of Heckel (2006), pp. 109 and 89; for Demophon in Mallia, see Diodorus 17.98.3–4, Curtius 9.4.27–29.
119. Seleucus may have been mentioned as a guest: the corrupted 'Europios' was possibly a reference to Seleucus' ethnicity. Menidas had a history of serving alongside Ptolemy and Attalus; detail in Heckel (2006), p. 165. For his service with Ptolemy, see Arrian 4.7.2, Curtius 7.10.11. The identification of Attalus cannot be confirmed; the most prominent individual would have been the commander, who became Perdiccas' brother-in-law; Heckel (2006), pp. 62–63, for his career. For Peithon's prominence and standing at Perdiccas' death, Nepos 5.1, Diodorus 18.39.6, Arrian, *Events After Alexander* 1.35, *Heidelberg Epitome* 1.3.
120. Arrian 4.18.4 for Menidas' recruiting campaign in Macedon and 7.23.1 for his return. Attalus was never heard of after his capture from a siege of the last Perdiccans lasting sixteen months; see Diodorus 19.16.5. His death is not specifically attested. He had already married Perdiccas' sister Atalante; Diodorus 18.37.2. Asander was present in Babylon and at Medius' party according to the *Pamphlet*.
121. See Stoneman (1991), p. 12, for discussion, and *Romance* 1.32 for Alexander's relationship with Serapis. Also Atkinson (2009), p. 233, for a discussion and opinion on the dating and origination of Serapis. Diogenes Laertius, *Diogenes* 63 claimed that Diogenes the Cynic referred to Serapis, yet this is a late composition and does not prove the early use of the name or its existence in Babylonia. The earliest known cult statue in Alexandria was initially thought to have been sculpted by Bryaxis around 286–278 BC, but this appears to have been a colossal likeness of Pluto (evidenced by its inclusion of the Underworld dog Cerberus and a serpent) dating back to 350 BC that was later shipped to Alexandria from Sinope on the Black Sea to be renamed in its new home by Ptolemy I Soter. Plutarch, *Isis and*

Osiris 27–28 (361f–362e) for the shipping of the statue from Sinope to Alexandria, and footnote 7 from the Loeb Classical Library edition, 1940, for discussion on its origins. The sculptor *may* have been the celebrated Bryaxis of Athens. Ptolemy allegedly had a dream vision of the statue, which sounds like a veiled mandate for its theft.

122. Vrettos (2001), p. 34, for the temple in the Egyptian quarter.
123. *Romance* 3.32 for the reference to Great Serapis and its link with Alexandria. Also mentioned at 1.21; see Stoneman (1991), p. 110.
124. See Anson (1996), pp. 501–04, for discussion.
125. For Oserapis, see Bosworth *A to A* (1988), pp. 168–70, and Atkinson (2009) citing Goukowski (1978). Following the text in Eidinow-Kindt (2015), p. 319, for the description of Oserapis.
126. Following Bosworth (1971), p. 120, for 'strikingly similar' in resemblance. As an example of the use of contemporary terminology, Curtius used *testudo* for a Roman tortoise-shell-like shield formation the Greeks used at 5.3.9, and implied its shield formation again at 5.3.21 and 7.9.3.
127. See Plutarch's *Isis and Osiris* 27–28 for examples of other gods the Greeks claimed were identical to Egyptian deities. In fact, Serapis was claimed to be none other than Pluto.
128. Discussed in De Polignac (1999), p. 6. A tradition circulates that the Sumerian deity Enki (Babylonian Ea) was titled 'Serapsi' ('king of the deep'), but there is little, it seems, to substantiate this.
129. However, evidence has been found to prove that Ea, alternatively the Chaldean-named Sarm-Apsi, 'king of the deep (sea)', who was also great in learning and magic, had a temple in the city. For the Chaldean god, see Cumont (1911), p. 73. Also Bosworth (1971), pp. 120–21. Arrian 7.14.5 for the references to the temple of Asclepius in Ecbatana.
130. Following Bosworth (1971), p. 120, for the incorporation of elements of Greek religion and the argument that the new Serapis would have lost is resemblance to Bel-Marduk; Bosworth, however, sees this as an argument that the *Journal* entry is 'early' for any comparison to have been made.
131. Plutarch 73.8.
132. Plutarch 73.7–9 and more briefly Arrian 7.24–25 described that Alexander and his friend, whilst playing ball (possibly the game of *sphaira*), beheld a man seated on the king's throne, in silence, wearing the royal diadem and robes. He claimed the god Serapis had come to him and bid him sit on the throne. Alexander had him 'put out of the way' as advised by his seers. Arrian 7.17.5 and 7.18.1–3 for reference to Aristobulus' reporting of portents and seers.
133. Arrian 3.3.6 reported that Aristobulus claimed they were guided by two ravens; see discussion in Robinson (1953), Preface p. xiii. Strabo 17.1.43 for crows.
134. Diodorus 17.103.7–8 for Ptolemy's poisonous wound in India. Further discussion in Heckel (1992), p. 26.
135. Plutarch 2.5–6; Olympias' Bacchic behaviour also implied at Athenaeus 13.560 (from Duris); discussed in Carney (2006), p. 96 ff.

272   *The Last Will and Testament of Alexander the Great*

136. See the references to Glycon in Lucian's *Alexander or the False Prophet*, discussed in Costa (2005), p. 129. For the Alexandrian serpents, see Carney-Ogden (2010), p 126, and pp. 126–27 for the snake-fringed aegis. Plutarch 2.6 and Justin 12.16.1–4 for Olympias and the serpent and Alexander's more than human conception. Here the Pharaoh Nectanebo was the true father of Alexander and visited Olympias disguised as Ammon; *Romance* 1.1–12 for the full account of Nectanebo. Carney (2006), p. 97, for Plutarch's treatment of Olympias, though he himself was an initiate of the cult of Dionysus (*Moralia* 611d–e).

137. Diogenes Laertius, *Demetrius* 76 for the curing of Demetrius' blindness; the reference to five books comes from Artemidorus, *On the Interpretation of Dreams* 2.44.9, though these books are not mentioned by Diogenes Laertius. Harris (2009), p. 155 footnotes 186, for discussion on sources behind Demetrius of Phalerum's association with Serapis.

138. Demetrius of Phalerum was ousted from Athens in 307 BC by Demetrius the Besieger; he headed first to Thebes and around 297 BC to Egypt. Pearson (1960), p. 260, for discussion on the prayer to Serapis.

139. For the dating of Demetrius' *On Fortune*, see discussion in Bosworth-Baynham (2000), p. 299; Demetrius stated the fifty-year rise of Macedon, which would logically date from Philip II's reign from *ca* 360 BC, suggesting it was written around 310 BC. Polybius gave further guidance stating that Demetrius published some 150 years before the end of the Third Macedonian War culminating in the Battle of Pydna in 168 BC. It is a very loose triangulation but suggests Demetrius' work was one of the first treatises to deal with Alexander in a meaningful philosophic way.

140. For the fatal snakebite, see Diogenes Laertius, *Demetrius of Phalerum* 78, and Cicero, *In Defence of Rabirius Postumus* 9.23. Plutarch, *Moralia* 48e–74f (*How to tell a Flatterer from a Friend* 28 69c–d) for the reference to 'near Thebes'; full text in Fortenbaugh-Schütrumpf (2000), pp. 75–77.

141. Plutarch, *Sayings of Kings and Commanders* 189D, full text from Fortenbaugh-Schütrumpf (2000), pp. 81–82.

142. Plutarch 74.1–2 and 75.1, trans. by I. Scott-Kilvert, Penguin Classics edition, 1973. The portentous signs are scattered through Plutarch 73–76 and appear less vividly in the accounts of Arrian 7.16–17, Diodorus 17.116–117 and Justin 12.8.3–6. A lacuna in Curtius' final chapter has swallowed his detail.

143. 'Whitewashed' quoting Heckel-Yardley (2004), Introduction p. xxiii.

144. Suetonius, *Domitian* 21.1.

145. Plutarch 74.2 for the fear of assassination, 77.2 for the lack of suspicion at Babylon. The portentous signs are scattered through Plutarch 73–76 and appear less vividly in the accounts of Arrian 7.16–17, Diodorus 17.116–117 and Justin 12.8.3–6. A lacuna in Curtius' final chapter has swallowed any comparable detail.

146. Plutarch 69.7 reported that Calanus, before climbing onto his funeral pyre, told Alexander he would soon meet him again in Babylon.

147. Green (1970), p. 258.

148. The detail of pre-death portents straddles all traditions: Arrian 7.16.7 for the divine hand in Alexander's death, and 7.18.2 and 7.18.5 for Pythagoras' divining to reveal livers with no lobes. Also 7.24–25, and Aristobulus was mentioned five times as a

source for superstitious episodes. More portentous episodes at Diodorus 17.115.5, Plutarch 73–74, and Justin 12.13. Curtius' account surely contained the detail too, but a lacuna exists in the opening of his final chapter. The half-child, half-beast, Scylla-like creature appears at *Metz Epitome* 90–95 and the *Romance* 3.30; the seer Philip saw this as an ill omen for Alexander.

149. Diodorus 19.55.8, trans. from the Loeb Classical Library edition, 1947. Quoting McKechnie (1995), p. 418, on 'philosophical corps'. Diodorus 17.112.5 for allusions to his soul.
150. Citation from Ifrah (2000), pp. 158–61. Herodotus 7.113–114.
151. Arrian 7.25.6, Plutarch 76.
152. Nearchus was an advisor to the young Demetrius at Gaza in 312 BC according to Diodorus 19.69.1 and Medius served at Salamis in 307/306 BC; see Diodorus 20.50.3 and Plutarch, *Demetrius* 19.1–2.
153. Notable exceptions being Hammond (1988) and (1993), and Robinson (1953), Preface p. x, which ingeniously regarded the *Journal* extract as a surviving fragment of Strattis' *On the Deaths of Alexander*. Discussed in Bosworth (1971). A useful summary of arguments is given in Atkinson (2009), p. 143. The Ptolemaic link came from Wirth in 1986; see Atkinson (2009), p. 143, for detail.
154. Heckel (1993) summarizes the *Journal* arguments well and the quotations from Heckel are drawn from here. In this review of Hammond's work on sources, Heckel pointed out that the pre-eminent modern Alexander scholars – Badian, Bosworth, Samuel and Pearson – had discredited the *Journal* convincingly.
155. Lane Fox (1980), p. 410.
156. Tarn (1948), p. 43.
157. See Grant (2017), p. 200 ff.
158. The corpse was likely moved from Memphis to Alexandria in Cleitarchus' day once the Sema was built; Pausanias 1.7.1 claimed Ptolemy II Philadelphus brought the body from Memphis to Alexandria.
159. Xenophon, *Cyropaedia* 8.7.9–12.
160. *Metz Epitome* 97 for the allegation that Onesicritus avoided naming guests at Medius' party. This might be a later addition or it might have originated with the author of the *Pamphlet*.
161. Justin replaced the allusion to 'games' with a wholly darker premonition on the bloodshed and slaughter that would follow, but this could have originated with Trogus, not Cleitarchus.
162. Xenophon, *On the education of Cyrus*, trans. by H.G. Dakyns, Epilogue, section 2.
163. Lucian, *How to Write History* 40–41, trans. from Brown (1949), p. 5. See discussion of the authenticity of this extract in Brown (1949), p. 2.
164. Homer, *Iliad* 2.705 for his slaying by Hector. Protesilaus was Thessalian and the first Greek to step ashore at Troy. His wife negotiated his leave to visit her from Hades for a few hours. This was referred to in many later works, for example Lucian's *Charon of the Observers* 1 and Ovid's *Heroides* 13.
165. See discussion in Shipley (2000), p. 40. Quoting Atkinson (2009), p. 146, for an alternative transmission into *Kalistei*, a pun on the message on the Apple of Discord

274   The Last Will and Testament of Alexander the Great

from Homer, for Justin 12.15.11 suggested Alexander was tossing his men the Apple of Discord. Diodorus 17.117.4 and Arrian 7.26.3 for *kratistos*: 'the strongest or noblest'. Latin interpretation of that from Curtius 10.4.5 *qui esset optimus* (the 'best') and *dignissimus* (broadly the 'most worthy') from Justin 12.15.

166. Onesicritus' dialogue with the Indian sages preserved in Strabo 15.1.63–65; discussion of question six in Brown (1949), p. 47.
167. Plutarch, *Pyrrhus* 9–10 for the story of Oedipus and his advice to his sons. Taken from Euripides' *Phoenician Women*, line 68. Trans. from the Loeb Classical Library edition, 1920. Oedipus had invited his sons, unwittingly fathered with his own mother, to fight for the kingdom to the death, which they were to do.
168. Plutarch, *Pyrrhus* 3.3.
169. Arrian 7.27.3 and Plutarch 77.5 respectively.
170. For Olympias' pogrom, see Diodorus 19.11.8 and 19.35.1, Justin 14.6 (slaughter of nobility but no revenge for conspiracy mentioned); Curtius 10.10.18 suggested rumours were 'soon suppressed by the power of people implicated by the gossip'. Thus rumours abounded early and before Cassander had the last of Alexander's family murdered.
171. Plutarch, *Demosthenes* 28.4 and *Moralia* 849b (*Life of Hyperides*) for Hyperides having his tongue cut out, 849f for his proposing honours for Iollas. Some editions of the *Moralia* contained the spuriously assigned *Lives of the Ten Orators*.
172. Plutarch 77.1-2 and reinforced by Curtius 10.10.18–19. Olympias' pogrom is also recorded in detail by Diodorus 19.11.809 and 19.51.5. If we give six months either way in latitude to Plutarch's 'five years' from June 323 BC, then the whole of 318 BC becomes a candidate for rumours reaching Greece.
173. Arrian, *Events After Alexander* 1.21.
174. Demosthenes termed Archias' acting 'unconvincing' when confronted by him at his death. Plutarch, *Demosthenes* 29, Plutarch, *Moralia* 846f, 849d. Arrian, *Events After Alexander* 1.13–14 for his role hunting down 'exiles'.
175. Heckel (2006), p. 140, for Holcias' possible background.
176. Diodorus 20.27.3.
177. Diodorus 19.51; Justin 14.6.6–12.
178. Diodorus 20.27.1–20.28.29 and 19.105 for the relief.
179. Curtius 10.18–19, reiterated in Diodorus 17.118.2 and Justin 12.13.10.
180. Arrian 3.5.2–3 for the identification of Ephippus in Egypt, and Athenaeus 3.120c–d and 4.146c–d for the drinking references.

Chapter 7: Royal Secretary, Royal Seal, Royal Charade

1. Plutarch, *Eumenes* 3.3.
2. Plutarch, *Eumenes, The Comparison of Sertorius with Eumenes* 2, trans. by John Dryden, 1683.
3. Plutarch, *Eumenes* 10.2, trans. from the Loeb Classical Library edition, 1919.
4. *Metz Epitome* 97–98 for the full list given in Heckel-Yardley (2004), p. 283.

5. Plutarch, *Eumenes* 1.1. For other examples of Plutarch's use of Duris, see *Alcibiades* 32, *Demosthenes* 19.3. Anson (2004), p. 35, cites Aelian 12.43 for the alternative background of Eumenes' father.
6. Nepos 1.4–6 and 13.1 (aged 20), also Plutarch, *Eumenes* 1.1–3 for his background.
7. The most notable rift being the Pixodarus affair; see Plutarch 10.1–2 and Alexander's fleeing to Epirus following his outburst following Attalus' drunken toast; Plutarch 9.7.10, Athenaeus 13.557d, Justin 9.7.3–4.
8. *Metz Epitome* 116; see discussion in Heckel (1992), p. 346. The title 'archivist', *hypomnematographos*, is also discussed in Shipley (2000), p. 264. For Eumenes' first attested cavalry command, Arrian 5.24.6.
9. Diodorus 18.58.3, Plutarch, *Eumenes* 13.1, Nepos 6.3 for examples of the trust placed in Eumenes by Olympias.
10. Arrian 7.12.7 and 7.14.9–10 as an example of the tension that existed between Eumenes and Hephaestion.
11. Arrian 7.14.10. The hipparchy retained Hephaestion's name out of respect.
12. Plutarch, *Eumenes* 2.3 for the wealth found in Eumenes' tent. Discussed in Anson (2004), p. 42, and Berve (1926). He was awarded a golden crown at Susa, see Arrian 7.5.6. Arrian, *Indica* 18.7 for the trierarch role.
13. Plutarch, *Eumenes* 1.3 and Arrian 7.4.6 for Eumenes' bride; Ptolemy and Nearchus, along with Eumenes, allegedly married into the line of Artabazus; his daughter, Barsine, was the mother of Heracles, Alexander's older son.
14. Plutarch, *Eumenes* 3.2 for details of Eumenes' role in the Babylonian Settlement. Curtius 10.7.1–3 and 10.9.20 used the term *bellorum civilium Macedonibus* when describing the fighting at Babylon following Alexander's death.
15. Arrian, *Events After Alexander* 1.1–3 based on the translation in Goralski (1989), p. 84. Seleucus was not listed in Arrian's earlier list of the Royal Bodyguards (*Somatophylakes*) but he may well have been elevated by 323 BC. If the number had risen to eight, and considering Hephaestion had died and Peucestas was governing Persis and the surrounding regions, then both Seleucus and Eumenes might have been enrolled.
16. Full discussion of the *Somatophylakes*, their numbers and background in Heckel, *Somatophylakes* (1978). It was Berve who identified fourteen individuals who could have qualified for inclusion. Tarn 1 (1948, p. 12, identified thirteen individuals with the role.
17. Arrian 6.30.2 for Peucestas' governorship of Persis. Arrian 1.11.7–8 suggested the hypaspists carried the king's weapons, taken from Troy, into battle; as Peucestas allegedly carried the shield from Troy at Mallia, then he is credibly a former royal hypaspist of perhaps 200 elites.
18. Arrian 6.28.3–4 for the seven becoming eight. For 'auspicious': the Pythagoreans associated the number seven with 'opportunity', according to Aristotle, whose lost treatise on the Pythagoreans is preserved in fragments by Alexander of Aphrodisias. See discussion in Riedweg (2002), p. 194. The number seven was also associated with the wisdom of the Seven Sages of the *Epic of Gilgamesh* and Mesopotamian

and Assyrian Seven Gods (the Pleiades) as well as the seven heavens and earths; Dalley (2013), p. 6 for the associations of 'seven' in Mesopotamia. Arrian 6.28.4 did not include Seleucus in his line of Bodyguards, but this was referring to the *Somatophylakes* at Carmania in 325/324 BC. Seleucus was apparently later singled out for marriage honours at Susa; Arrian 7.4.6. Hephaestion died in 324 BC, requiring a further replacement. With Peucestas governing Persis, both Seleucus and Eumenes might have been enrolled as *Somatophylakes*. Further discussion earlier in the chapter.

19. Alexander's failure to conquer Cappadocia at Diodorus 18.3.1–2, 18.16.1 and implied at Curtius 10.10.3.
20. Dexippus FGrH 100 F8.6; Plutarch, *Eumenes* 3.2 for the extent of Eumenes' grant. Xenophon proposed the idea of founding a mercenary-based colony on the Black Sea coast but met with local opposition.
21. Arrian 2.4.2, Curtius 3.1.22–24 and 4.5.13 for the previous association of Paphlagonia with Hellespontine Phrygia.
22. Arrian 2.4.2 for Sabictas. Plutarch, *Eumenes* 3.6 for Ariarathes' control of all Cappadocia. See the discussion by Hornblower (1981), pp. 240–43. Arrian 2.4.1–2 suggested Alexander had conquered the whole region. However, Strabo 12.534 suggested there were two distinct Cappadocian satrapies.
23. Xenophon 7.8.25 for the inclusion of Lycaonia.
24. Ariarathes' position under Persian authority is discussed in Anson (1988), pp. 471–73 footnote 4. Anson noted that Curtius did not mention a Cappadocian contingent at Issus, citing Curtius 3.2.6. Also Anson noted that Bosworth concluded the Ariaces cited by Arrian 3.8.5 might have been a mistransmission of 'Ariarathes' at the Battle of Gaugamela.
25. As proposed in Anson (1988), p. 474. Diodorus 18.16.2 for the mercenary contingent.
26. Antigonus was ordered by Perdiccas to support Eumenes' invasion of Cappadocia; he defected to Antipater and Craterus Macedon instead; Plutarch, *Eumenes* 3–4, Diodorus 18.23.3–4, Arrian, *Events After Alexander* 1.20.
27. Lucian, *How to Write History* 2.13. Diodorus 18.16.2–4 and 18.22.1 and Appian, *Mithridatic Wars* 2.8 reported Ariarathes himself was tortured and impaled. Justin 13.6.1 agreed.
28. Diodorus 18.22.1–8 for Perdiccas' campaign in Pisidia.
29. Diodorus 18.33.3 for 'man of blood'.
30. Diodorus 18.23.1 for the arrival of both women. Diodorus 18.23.1, Arrian, *Events After Alexander* 1.21, Justin 13.6.4 for Perdiccas' seeking the hand of Cleopatra. Only the *Heidelberg Epitome* FGrH 155F-4 suggested the marriage took place.
31. Diodorus 18.29.6 for the convening of the council of war. Errington (1970), p. 61, for discussion of Cleitus' association with Craterus. He was victorious at sea assisting Antipater in the Lamian War, receiving Lydia at Triparadeisus as a result, Diodorus 18.39.6, Arrian, *Events After Alexander* 1.37. Yet Cleitus had assisted Perdiccas before his failed invasion of Egypt, see Justin 13.6.16. His new alignment with Craterus and Antipater is implied at Arrian, *Events After Alexander* 1.26 with their recrossing

the Hellespont, but a change of allegiance was never specifically stated. For Cleitus' behaviour following naval victories in the Lamian War, see Plutarch, *Moralia* 338a. For his victory in three naval battles, see Diodorus 18.15.8–9.
32. Arrian, *Events After Alexander* 24.6 for the Cyprus affair.
33. For Nicocles issuing his own coinage immediately after Alexander's death, see Bellinger (1979), p. 88.
34. West of the Taurus suggested by Nepos 3.2, Justin 13.6.14–15 and following the observation in Heckel (2006), p. 121. Plutarch, *Eumenes* 5.1 for Eumenes' wide-ranging powers.
35. Following Justin 13.6, who mentioned Antipater too, though it appears he headed south with Antigonus.
36. Arrian 2.27.6 for Neoptolemus' dissent; the havoc he caused in Armenia (Plutarch, *Eumenes* 4.1) suggests he was already disdainful of central authority. Plutarch, *Eumenes* 5.2–6, Diodorus 18.29.2–6, Justin 13.6.15–13.8.5, Arrian, *Events After Alexander* 1.27 for his subordination to Eumenes' command and intriguing with and defection to Craterus.
37. Plutarch, *Eumenes* 5.2–4, trans. from the Loeb Classical Library edition, 1919.
38. Plutarch, *Eumenes* 1.2.
39. Diodorus 18.29.4 and 37.1. Plutarch, *Eumenes* 8.1 for the timing: '10 days after the former'. Also see Billows (1990), p. 65, for the May dating.
40. Diodorus 16.35, Justin 8.2.3–5 for Philip leading a coalition of Macedonians, Thessalians and Thebans wreathed like gods. This was the so-called Battle of the Crocus Field in Thessaly. For Alexander at Tyre, see Curtius 4.2.17, Arrian 2.18.1–2, Plutarch 24.3.
41. Plutarch, *Eumenes* 7.4–6 for 'dashing together like triremes' and the fight, and Diodorus 18.31.1–5 for their grappling together. Also covered at Arrian, *Events After Alexander* 1.27 and Justin 13.8.4.
42. Arrian 4.24.3–5 for Ptolemy's slaying and stripping the Indian leader of his armour; presumably Ptolemy provided the detail.
43. Plutarch, *Eumenes* 6.3–6. For varying reports on how Craterus died, see Plutarch, *Eumenes* 7.5–6, Arrian, *Events After Alexander* 1.27, Nepos 4.3–4, Diodorus 18.30.5. Pharnabazus and Phoenix commanded the cavalry against Craterus' wing; Eumenes claimed they were facing Neoptolemus and Pigres.
44. Diodorus 18.37.1–3, Arrian, *Events After Alexander* 1.39, Justin 13.8.10–14.1.1, Appian, *Syrian Wars* 53 for the death sentence levied on Eumenes and his outlaw status. Plutarch, *Eumenes* 8.2, Diodorus 18.41.6–8 and 19.12.2 also made it clear that an assembly gathering in Egypt resulted in a death sentence.
45. For the sentence of death placed on Eumenes and fifty Perdiccans, see Diodorus 18.37.1–3, Plutarch, *Eumenes* 8.2, Arrian, *Events After Alexander* 1.39, Justin 13.8.10–14.1.1, Appian, *Syrian Wars* 53; Atalante's two daughters by Attalus apparently survived her and were later murdered with Olympias at Pydna.
46. Diodorus 18.37.2 for Attalus' marriage to Atalante; Heckel (2006), p. 62 (Attalus 2), for the underlying motives.

47. Arrian, *Events After Alexander* 1.38. This assumes that the Ptolemy being referenced should read 'Polemaeus', in which case he was the son of Ptolemy, Antigonus' brother; Billows agrees, see Heckel (2006), p. 224, for discussion.
48. Diodorus 18.39.6–7, derived from trans. from the Loeb Classical Library edition, 1947, and reiterated by Arrian, *Events After Alexander* 1.38.
49. Diodorus 18.50.1–2 for Antigonus' role as commander, *strategos*, of Anatolia. For his hegemon or supreme commander, Diodorus 18.39.7, Arrian, *Events After Alexander* 1.38. Diodorus 19.29.3 referred to Antigonus' role as 'regency'. Discussed in Anson (1992).
50. 'Constitutionalist', summarizing the comment and observation in Billows (1990), p. 316.
51. Plutarch, *Eumenes* 8.3, trans. from the Loeb Classical Library edition, 1919.
52. Arrian, *Events after Alexander* 24.8 for the narrowly avoided ambush.
53. Plutarch, *Eumenes* 8.4. Arrian, *Events After Alexander* 1.40 for the clash at Sardis; Justin 14.1.7 and Plutarch, *Eumenes* 8.6–7 for Eumenes' earlier visit to Sardis when brokering the marriage.
54. Following the observation in Carney (1988), p. 401, on Antipater's leniency; more on Cynnane's plight in Grant (2019).
55. Curtius 3.1.11 for a vivid description of Celaenae and the surrounding countryside. Arrian 1.29 for the truce.
56. Curtius 3.1.2–6 for a description of the River Marsyas and city walls.
57. Arrian 1.29.3 for Antigonus' 1,500 troops.
58. Plutarch, *Eumenes* 8.5–7 reported: 'Having promised to give his soldiers their pay within three days, he sold them the homesteads and castles about the country, which were full of slaves and flocks. Then every captain in the phalanx or commander of mercenaries who had bought a place was supplied by Eumenes with implements and engines of war and took it by siege; and thus every soldier received the pay that was due him.' From the Loeb Classical Library edition, 1919. Hatzopoulos (1996), p. 332, for the status and garb of *philoi* and h*etairoi*: *purpurati* – 'clothed in purple'.
59. Plutarch, *Eumenes* 8.6, trans. from the Loeb Classical Library edition, 1919.
60. A translation of the recovered *Gothenburg Palimpsest* text can be found at http://www.attalus.org/translate/fgh.html.
61. Plutarch, *Eumenes* 8.7–8, *Gothenburg Palimpsest* line 19 and Arrian, *Events After Alexander* F1 41–42 associates Attalus and (the latter) Alcetas in negotiations with Eumenes; there is possibly a lacuna in Diodorus that lost additional detail; Wheatley (1995), p. 435 and footnote 25. Diodorus 18.37.3–4, Arrian, *Events After Alexander* 1.39 for Attalus' occupation of Tyre. Whether Ptolemy's annexation precipitated Attalus' departure or whether that came first is debatable.
62. Diodorus 18.39.7, Arrian, *Events After Alexander* 1.43–44 and see discussion in Anson (2004), pp. 125–27 for events at Celaenae, the failure of forces to combine and Eumenes' departure from Celaenae for Cappadocia. *Gothenburg Palimpsest* for Alcetas' enthusiasm; the incomplete text leaves leeway for seeing this as a cynical ruse by Alcetas.

Notes   279

63. Arrian 7.14.10. The hipparchy retained Hephaestion's name out of respect. Devine, *Gabiene* (1985), p. 93, for Eumenes' use of Alexander's cavalry techniques.
64. Plutarch, *Eumenes* 9.1–2, trans. from the Loeb Classical Library edition, 1919.
65. Justin 14.1.
66. Diodorus 18.40.1–6 for the two distinct defections and for Perdiccas' defection and subsequent capture by Phoenix of Tenedus; also Plutarch, *Eumenes* 9.1–2.
67. Plutarch, *Eumenes* 9.6, trans. from the Loeb Classical Library edition, 1919; also Diodorus 18.40.8, Polyaenus 4.6.12.
68. Plutarch 57.1–3, Curtius 6.6.14–15, Polyaenus 4.30.10, Plutarch, *Aemilius* 12.11 for Alexander's burning of the baggage. Diodorus 17.94.4 for the permission to plunder in India. Xenophon 4.1.12–13 burned his waggons before entering the mountains of Kurdistan in winter
69. Diodorus 18.40.8 for Eumenes' losses. Anson (1977), p. 251 footnote 1, for a discussion of the date of the battle at Orcynia.
70. *Anaklesis* is a flight from the battlefield. This episode is once more Plutarch-derived and Diodorus 18.41.1–4 made no such reference, though an earlier confrontation is possibly being described here; as it has been noted, Orcynia might have been a Cappadocian district and not a specific battleground. Only Diodorus 18.40–41 mentioned Eumenes' lost baggage train. It looks suspiciously as if Plutarch compressed the three battles into two and placed the doubling-back and funeral rites at Orcynia erroneously; see Diodorus 19.32.3.
71. Plutarch, *Eumenes* 10.1, trans. from the Loeb Classical Library edition, 1919. Also Justin 14.2, Diodorus 18.41.1–4, Nepos, *Eumenes* 5 for Eumenes' entry into Nora. Anson (2004), p. 131, for the date the siege commenced. Diodorus 18.41.2 for 'lofty crag'.
72. Diodorus 18.41.4–6.
73. Diodorus 18.41.2–6 for the walls, ditch and pallisades; Plutarch, *Eumenes* 11.1 simply mentioned 'a wall' was built around Nora.
74. Plutarch, *Eumenes* 10.2–4. See Heckel (2006), p. 139, citing Hornblower (1981), p. 6, and Diodorus 18.50.4.
75. Plutarch, *Eumenes* 10.3, trans. from the Loeb Classical Library edition, 1919.
76. According to Nepos 1, Eumenes was secretary to Philip for seven years before the king's death. Alexander's campaign headed south after the Battle of Issus in 333 BC, leaving Antigonus to suppress remnants of Persian resistance. Nearchus headed to join Alexander in 331 BC and Antigonus assumed control of a larger region including Phrygia, Lycia and Pamphylia in-between. Thus Eumenes could have only had perhaps two years of contact with Antigonus in the early campaign. See Diodorus 18.3.1 for detail.
77. Eumenes' 'demands' are consistently reported in both Plutarch's and Diodorus' accounts, so possibly Diodorus 18.41.7 compressed the moment for we would imagine the description of friendly relations and mutual respect was Hieronymus-derived.
78. Plutarch, *Eumenes* 10.3–4, based on the trans. in the Loeb Classical Library edition, 1919.
79. Plutarch, *Eumenes* 10.2.

80. Diodorus 18.53.4–5 suggested the siege lasted a full year; Nepos 5.6–7 suggested six months. If both are approximations, the answer may lie in between; the dating of the battle at Orcynia is uncertain, but if in spring of 319 BC, after Eumenes had wintered in Celaenae, then Antipater's death came approximately six months later.
81. Plutarch, *Eumenes* 12–13 for the oath; Nepos claimed Eumenes eluded Antigonus' officers but whether this means physically or psychologically with the oaths is uncertain.
82. Plutarch, *Eumenes* 12.1–2, Nepos 5–7.
83. Anson (1977) questioned the validity of the reporting of the changed oath. Anson (2004), p. 136, considers it a fiction of Duris.
84. Plutarch, *Eumenes* 12.3 for the return of hostages after Eumenes' release.
85. Eumenes' delay discussed in Anson (1977), p. 253.
86. Plutarch, *Eumenes* 12.3 and Diodorus 18.53.6–7 for Eumenes' regathering of forces.
87. The focus on the reporting of the battle was Eumenes' opportunity to seize Antigonus' baggage train, but in flight there is little chance Eumenes could have salvaged his own. Plutarch, *Eumenes* 9.3 left it unclear whether Eumenes had the opportunity to take the enemy booty during battle or after he had doubled back from his flight to Armenia. The former is most logical when considering Menander's role.
88. Diodorus 18.59.1–2 for Menander's appointment to track down Eumenes. Strabo 14.5.10 described the location; for the Assyrian association, see discussion in Bing (1973), pp. 346–50. Modern excavations suggest a location on Mount Carasis high in the Taurus Mountains; discussed in Sayar (1995), pp. 279–82. For the estimate of 20,000 talents, see Roisman (2012), p. 181. Quoting G. Maspero's *History of Egypt, Chaldea, Syria, Babylonia, and Assyria*, The Grolier Society Publishers, Volume 8 part B, 1903, 'Some Assyriologists have proposed to locate these two towns in Cilicia; others place them in the Lebanon, Kundi being identified with the modern village of Ain-Kundiya.' The name of Kundu so nearly recalls that of Kuinda, the ancient fort mentioned by Strabo, to the north of Anchialê, between Tarsus and Anazarbus, that I do not hesitate to identify them, and to place Kundu in Cilicia.
89. Diodorus 18.57.3–18.58.4, Plutarch, *Eumenes* 13.1–3, Nepos 6.1–5, *Heidelberg Epitome* F 3.2 for the letters sent to Eumenes.
90. Diodorus 18.57.2–4 and 18.58.1–4. Arrian, *Events after Alexander* 1.43–45 for the seventy elephants left with Antigonus and Antipater keeping the remainder; also Diodorus 19.23.2.
91. Diodorus 18.58.1–3 for the second letter offering funding and the Silver Shields. Also detailed in Plutarch, *Eumenes* 13.1–2.
92. Diodorus 18.59.4–6 based on the trans. from the Loeb Classical Library edition, 1947.
93. Diodorus 18.59.3 and Plutarch, *Eumenes* 13.3–4. Roisman (2012), pp. 177–236, for a useful study of the Silver Shields under Eumenes. Arrian, *Events After Alexander* 1.38 for reference to Antipater giving Antigenes 3,000 of the most rebellious Macedonians to collect the treasure, or revenues, from Susa after Triparadeisus. Heckel (1988), p. 49, assumed the Silver Shields were already at Cyinda, and Bosworth (2002), p. 100 footnote 9, disputes this, suggesting Diodorus' reference to 'distance' placed them

in Susa. Diodorus 18.58.1, however, stated orders were issued to 'the generals and treasurers in Cilicia', which might suggest the Silver Shields were already billeted there. If so, the residue guard apparently feared for their safety after Eumenes departed; Diodorus 19.62.1–2. They were labelled 'troublemakers' here and it could be that the 'unruly brigade' (*ataktoi*) and Silver Shields (both 3,000) were mistaken for one another, though '3,000' appears a utility number used for a medium-sized body of men. It is likely the Silver Shields were stationed in Cilicia when Perdiccas invaded Egypt in 320 BC and enrolled them there; see Heckel (2006), p. 30, (Antigenes) for discussion.

94. Billows (1990), p. 277, for discussion of the treasury officer, *gazophylax*, role, and Strabo 12.2.6 for his reference to the treasury of Sisines.
95. The legendary age of this veteran regiment stemmed from Diodorus 19.41.2 and was reinforced by Plutarch, *Eumenes* 16.4, Justin 12.7.5 and the *Romance* 1.25.3–5, in which it was claimed the youngest of them was 60 and the oldest over 70. The claims were repeated in other works, possibly in the belief this stemmed from an impeccable source: Hieronymus. The source was more likely Cleitarchus, and as it has been pointed out, this is likely Hellenistic misinterpretation, or simple exaggeration. The *Romance* does suggest Alexander wanted to keep the elderly hypaspists as instructors, which makes more sense, and there is no reason to believe such elderly men still formed the active fighting ranks. Following the discussion by M.C.J. Miller in Watson-Miller (1992), pp. 107–08.
96. Diodorus 18.60.3, trans. from the Loeb Classical Library edition, 1947.
97. For the gift and refusal, see Diodorus 18.60.1–4.
98. Cicero, *Laelius De Amicitia* 17, quoting Ennius on the fickleness of fortune. Diodorus 18.60.1.
99. Plutarch, *Eumenes* 13.2, trans. from the Loeb Classical Library edition, 1919.
100. Diodorus 18.60.6 for the show of insignia. Curtius 10.6.15 for Ptolemy's suggestion at Babylon. It is unlikely Eumenes appealed to the soldiers themselves but the hierarchy above them; see discussion in Hornblower (1981), p. 205. Diodorus 18.26.4 claimed the king's armour at least left Babylon with the funeral bier. Plutarch, *Eumenes* 13.4–8, Polyaenus 4.8.2, Nepos 7.2–3, Diodorus 18.60.4–18.61.3, 19.15.3–4 for the dream vision and its employment.
101. See Grant (2019) for the finds at Vergina.
102. Diodorus 17.16.4 for a description, for example, of the Tent of a Hundred Couches, which was again more a pavilion enclosure. It was used to celebrate the departure from Macedon in 335 BC and taken on campaign; see Athenaeus 12.538c and 12.539d; Aelian 9.3 described it as being held up by fifty gold pillars; the golden chair might have meant a 'throne' or represented one. Curtius 6.8.23 for the tent that housed over 6,000 men at the trial of Philotas.
103. Diodorus 18.60.4–18; Plutarch, *Eumenes* 13.3–4.
104. Diodorus 18.61.4.
105. Diodorus 18.61.4–5 for the recruitment drive and numbers.
106. For Ptolemy's attempts to subvert the Silver Shields, see Diodorus 18.62.5. Diodorus 18.62.4 for Antigonus' attempt to turn the Silver Shields; he almost succeeded as

Teutamus had to be convinced by Antigenes to remain loyal to Eumenes. Diodorus 18.73.1 for Antigonus' departure for Cilicia.

107. Diodorus 18.63.6 suggested Eumenes was hoping to gather a fleet to send to Polyperchon; Polyaenus 4.6.9 reported that Phoenician crews were heading for a Cilician port laden with Eumenes' funds, presumably from Cyinda and perhaps to collect more, though we must question whether the ships were coming from Cilicia rather than heading to it. There is, in fact, a similarity here with Diodorus 18.52.7 describing Antigonus' assault of Ephesus, where Antigonus again intercepted ships from Cilicia; we might wonder if Eumenes had sent the funds to Cleitus and was attempting to send more to him or to Olympias, perhaps via Polyperchon. Further detail of the victory over Cleitus at Polyaenus 4.6.8–9

108. Diodorus 18.73.1 for the size of Antigonus' force. At that stage, word of Peithon's aggression in the eastern provinces and the planned repercussions may well have reached Eumenes.

109. Diodorus 19.12.1–2 for Eumenes wintering in the villages of the Carians. This could be a reference to Carrhae mentioned again at 19.91.1 where Seleucus later raised veteran troops and where Alexander had marched through on campaign; Diodorus 17.110.3.

110. Diodorus 19.13.7 and 19.15.5, trans. from the Loeb Classical Library edition, 1947. Roisman (2012), p. 193 footnote 40, for a discussion on the dating of this new letter; dispatch from Phoenicia seems a sound conclusion, before Eumenes headed east.

111. Amphimachus is an unsurprising realignment if he can be identified as the brother of Arrhidaeus the satrap of Hellespontine Phrygia, who had already turned against Antigonus. Heckel (2006), p. 22, for discussion on Amphimachus' identity; probably 'brother of Arrhidaeus' in original manuscripts though later confused with King Philip III (Arrhidaeus). He was rewarded with the governorship of Mesopotamia at Triparadeisus; Diodorus 18.39.6, Arrian, *Events After Alexander* 1.35. We argue he came under the authority of Seleucus (or Perdiccas at Syria), and yet was found operating under Eumenes at Paraetacene, Diodorus 19.27.4, so logically he defected at this point. Diodorus 18.51.1–2 and 18.72.2–3 for Arrhidaeus' activity in defiance of Antigonus.

112. Diodorus 19.12.1–3 for the failed overtures to Seleucus and Peithon, and 19.12.4–19.13 for the confrontation that followed.

113. Diodorus 18.73.4 for Eumenes' numbers soon after. A useful discussion of the campaigns in Cilicia, Mesopotamia and Iran, and events surrounding its build-up and aftermath, can be found in Bosworth (2002), pp. 98–167. Tarn proposed Eumenes held the Babylonian citadel in October 318 BC, see the Loeb Classical Library edition, 1919 (1968 reprint) of Diodorus 19.13.5 footnote 1 for detail.

114. Diodorus 19.15.4–6 for the continued invoking of Alexander's presence and the arrival of Eudamus with elephants.

115. For Peithon's installation of his brother, see Diodorus 19.14.1–2. Diodorus used the general term 'upper satrapies' for the Eastern Empire. No satraps from the upper provinces were aligned with Peucestas, though it was they who drove out Peithon.

116. For the departure of Antigonus' forces from Media, see Diodorus 19.24.4, and for his alliance with Peithon and Seleucus, see Diodorus 19.17.2.

117. Plutarch, *Eumenes* 14.2 (Pasitigris); Diodorus 19.18.3–8 (Coprates). The total number routed is closer to 10,000, but presumably many drowned in upturned boats and others escaped. Diodorus 19.18.3 for 4 plethra and 19.17.3 for 3–4 stades.
118. Plutarch 72 for the previous butchery of Cossaeans; Diodorus 19.19–20 for Antigonus' clash with the tribe.
119. Diodorus 19.21–22 for the geography of the journey to Persepolis and the festivities upon arrival.
120. Plutarch, *Eumenes* 13.5, trans. from the Loeb Classical Library edition, 1919.
121. Arrian 6.30.3 and 7.6.3 for Peucestas' adoption of the Persian language and Diodorus 19.48.5 for his popularity amongst the Persians. Strabo 15.3.9–10 confirmed Alexander ferried the wealth of Persis to Susa. Plutarch, *Eumenes* 13.4 for the reference to the former friendship between Eumenes and Peucestas; Nepos 7.1 for their intense rivalry. This may be a device of Duris, however, to emphasize his later betrayal of Eumenes, for the reference is immediately followed by a damning description of Peucestas' behaviour at 13.5–6. Heckel (1988), p. 75, for 'high handed' and who agrees at the time we propose the *Pamphlet* was drafted, Peucestas showed little or no support for Eumenes; for his performance at Gabiene, see Diodorus 19.42.4, Plutarch, *Eumenes* 16.
122. Diodorus 19.23.2, Polyaenus 4.8.3. For Polyperchon's earlier offer to bring the army from Macedon to support Eumenes should he need it, see Diodorus 18.57.4. Diodorus stated the letter was in 'Syrian', but this presumably means 'Assyrian'. Diodorus often interchanged the terms geographically too. Arrian 3.8.5, Curtius 4.12.12 for Orontes at Gaugamela.
123. Diodorus 19.23.1–4, trans. from the Loeb Classical Library edition, 1947. Diodorus 19.23.1–2 for the undermining of Sibyrtius. We might assume he fled to the enemy as Antigonus gave Sibyrtius the remnants of the Silver Shields after their capture at Gabiene; see below.
124. Diodorus 19.24.1–5.
125. Plutarch, *Eumenes* 13.6.
126. Diodorus 19.24.5–5 for Eumenes' illness. Plutarch, *Eumenes* 14.5–6 stated 'a few days' after the banquet, but Diodorus' account at 19.24.4–5 portrays the illness commencing once Eumenes heard of Antigonus breaking camp, so the actual timing is uncertain. Plutarch's coverage of the events that followed is far more detailed and colourful than Diodorus'.
127. Anson (2014), p. 67, for discussion of the personal guard units of Eumenes, Peucestas, Leonnatus and Alcetas. Diodorus 19.29.5 and 19.28.3–4 for the guards of Eumenes and Antigonus at Paraetacene.
128. As noted and discussed by Bosworth (2002), pp. 12–127, and J. Roisman in Carney-Ogden (2010), pp. 142–43. Arrian 6.12.1–6.13.3 for Alexander's behaviour after the Mallian battle.
129. Plutarch, *Eumenes* 14.4–15.3, Diodorus 19.24.5–6.
130. Diodorus 19.25.1–3 for the relative encampments. Full battle tactics discussion in Devine, *Paraetacene* (1985).
131. Diodorus 19.25.2–19.

132. Diodorus 19.26–27.
133. Diodorus 19.26.1–7.
134. *Aposkeue*, Greek for the baggage train; see discussion of its importance in Hornblower (1981), pp. 188–89. It was variously referred to as *skeue*, *aposkeue* or *paraskeue* by Polybius, Cassius Dio and Appian, for example. Polyaenus 4.6.13 for the run-down of the baggage. Diodorus 18.40.8.
135. Plutarch, *Eumenes* 9.3 for the description of Antigonus' baggage train. Polyaenus 4.2 for a description of the Macedonian soldier's individual load.
136. Diodorus 18.30.2 for Craterus' promise to distribute Eumenes' baggage train. Eumenes' threat to harry the troops came after the battle with Craterus and is recorded in papyrus PSI 12: 1284; see Goralski (1989), pp 95–96, for full transcription of the fragment and Bosworth (1978) for full discussion.
137. For discussion of possible malaria in Alexander's army and those of the Diadochi, see Borza (1987).
138. Diodorus 19.27–32.
139. Diodorus 19.29.3 for Antigonus' Macedonian numbers and 27–28 for Eumenes' numbers. Diodorus simply stated Antipater had given the 8,000 Macedonians to Antigonus 'when he made him regent of the kingdom', which translates as commander-in-chief in Asia, at Triparadeisus. Additional Macedonians would have been present in the Companion Cavalry but numbers were not specified.
140. Diodorus 19.31.5 for the death toll and wounded.
141. Diodorus 19.31.3–5. Eumenes' men would not occupy the battlefield to recover the dead due to their concern with the unguarded baggage train, leaving Antigonus able to do so and claim victory. But he himself was forced to send his baggage train on ahead to a neighbouring city for security; Diodorus 19.32.1–2.
142. Xenophon, *Anabasis* 4.7.25 ff and Plutarch, *Agesilaus* 19.2 and *Timoleon* 29.4 for examples of the victory memorial or *tropaion* being erected.
143. Polyaenus 4.6.10; the location of the battle is not specified but the circumstances sound like Paraetacene.
144. Polyaenus 4.6.11 for the description of the land separating the armies. Diodorus 19.37–38 for the full account of their wintering and the relative distances between them at 19.34.8. The Gadamala mentioned at Diodorus 19.37.1 may well be the same Gamarga mentioned at 19.32.2.
145. Polyaenus 4.6.11 for the desert description and water cask numbers; also Diodorus 19.37.1–6, Nepos 18.8.4–9, Plutarch, *Eumenes* 15.8–13.
146. Plutarch, *Eumenes* 15.4–7 and Diodorus 18.38.1–4 for the ruses involving fire.
147. Diodorus 19.38–39 and Nepos 8–9 for the manoeuvring in the region of Gabiene, and Plutarch, *Eumenes* 15.6–7.
148. Plutarch, *Eumenes* 15.3–4, Nepos 8.1–4 for the separation of Eumenes' troops. Eumenes claimed that he could gather his commanders in three to four days, suggesting as Roisman (2012), p. 27, noted that the bulk of the army was close to Gab.
149. Diodorus 19.39–40.
150. The roles of Nearchus and Menander discussed further in later chapters. Menander had been governor of Lydia since early in the campaign; see Arrian 3.6.7. He was

reconfirmed at Babylon: Diodorus 18.3.1, Justin 13.4.15, Curtius 10.10.2, Dexippus FGrH 100 F8.2, Arrian, *Events After Alexander* 1.6. Nearchus had likewise governed Lycia and Pamphylia early in the campaign, Arrian 3.6.6, Justin 13.4.15, whilst Nearchus' activity post-Babylon is unattested until he reappeared in the region of Telmessus in Lycia in 320/319 BC; Polyaenus 5.35. Justin 13.4.15 alone granted Nearchus Lycia and Pamphylia at Babylon, which might once again be compression with earlier detail.

151. Discussed in Anson (1988), p. 475; Diodorus 19.29.2–3 gave a description of the make up of Antigonus' mixed army. As pointed out by Roisman (2012), p. 25, fresh recruits did not have baggage waggons to lose.

152. Plutarch, *Eumenes* 16.1–3 for the planned and reported treachery at Gabiene; Antigenes was mentioned but his subsequent fate suggests Teutamus led the intrigue, see Heckel (2006), p. 262, for discussion of *ignaris ducibus* suggested Antigenes' ignorance. For the possible *strategos* role, see Heckel (1992), p. 333.

153. Plutarch, *Eumenes* 16.4–5; Diodorus 19.41.1–2, trans. from the Loeb Classical Library edition, 1947. Eumenes is not directly credited with the plan, however it seems highly likely he was its architect when considering his other psychological ruses. Xennias' role is captured in papyrus PSI 12: 1284. See Goralski (1989), pp. 95–96, for full transcription of the fragment and Bosworth (1978) for full discussion.

154. Diodorus 19.40–43 for the battle and 19.43.5 for the Silver Shields blaming Peucestas' performance for the defeat. Plutarch, *Eumenes* 16.5.5 for Peucestas' performance at Gabiene: 'lax and ignoble' trans. from the Loeb Classical Library edition, 1919.

155. Polyaenus 4.6.13 suggested 300 losses compared with 5,000 for Antigonus; in fact Polyaenus reported Eumenes' soldiers were in high spirits at the end of the first day of battle until they learned of the loss of their baggage.

156. Justin 14.3 for the '2,000 women and a few children'; Plutarch, *Eumenes* 18.1 for the Silver Shields' responses.

157. Kebric (1977), p. 22, in contrast, sees Duris as generally laudatory to Eumenes, regarding his claim that he was a poor waggoner's son as a means to emphasize his achievement. The use of Duris is somewhat backed up by Plutarch's *Comparison of Eumenes with Sertorius* 2.3–4 in which he alleged the same.

158. Nepos 11.1, Plutarch, *Eumenes* 18.2 for the instructions to guard Eumenes. Diodorus 19.42–44 and Plutarch, *Eumenes* 16–18 for the outcome of battle at Gabiene; the pleas to spare him at Plutarch, *Eumenes* 18.6, Nepos 10.3, Diodorus 19.44.2. Plutarch, *Eumenes* 18.2 and 18.3 for the Silver Shields' claims to their baggage. Justin 14.3, possibly drawing from Duris, claimed Eumenes attempted to flee and only when captured again did he demand the right to deliver his final scathing speech. There is some confusion again between the accounts of Diodorus and Plutarch. The 'surrounded Silver Shields' in Plutarch's account are in the camp of Eumenes, arguing the merits of fighting on. Additionally, the speech provided to them by Plutarch refers to the 'three nights' the captive wives with the baggage train had been 'sleeping with the enemy', which suggests a protracted period before Eumenes was finally given up to Antigonus. Nepos 13 for Eumenes' age. Anson (2004), p. 35 footnote 1, for age discussion.

286   *The Last Will and Testament of Alexander the Great*

159. Diodorus 19.48.5 for Peucestas' fate. Diodorus 19.22.2 stated Peucestas had chosen many Asiatic advisers.
160. Anson (2014), p. 125, for discussion on the fate of Amphimachus and Stasander. Quoting Plutarch, *Eumenes* 19.2, also Polyaenus 4.6.15, Diodorus 19.48.3–4; the remaining Silver Shields included those who betrayed Eumenes, so Teutamus might have been with them; Heckel (2006), p. 262. Arrian related that the historian Megasthenes spent time with Sibyrtius in Arachosia when visiting the court of Chandragupta.
161. Polyaenus 4.6.15, Diodorus 19.48.3, Plutarch, *Eumenes* 19.3 and Justin 14.3.3–4 and 18 for the various fates of the disbanded Silver Shields. Bosworth (2002), p. 235, theorized that the troops recruited from Carrhae, and with which Antigonus successfully stormed the citadel of Babylon in 311 BC, comprised brigade veterans. Roisman (2012), p. 16, believes that Antigonus sent the Silver Shields to aid Sibyrtius and counter the rising power of Chandragupta, the Indian ruler. Disputed by Roisman (2012), p. 237. But if they were that effective, why send them away?
162. Diodorus 19.35.5 for those under siege at Pydna.
163. Diodorus 19.49–52 for Olympias' end and quoting from the Loeb Classical Library edition, 1947, and from Justin 14.6, trans. by Rev. J.S. Watson, 1853. Justin 14.6.1–13, Polyaenus 4.11.3 for further detail. Carney (2006), pp. 104–05, for Olympias' burial and Aeacid reverence and Diodorus 17.118.2 for her corpse remaining unburied.
164. Plutarch, *Eumenes* 18.1 for the title given Eumenes: 'pest from the Chersonese'.
165. Following Anson (1980) for Alexander and Perdiccas shielding Eumenes from the full Macedonian prejudice. See Anson (2004), p. 233, for Eumenes' open admittance of his 'handicap', referencing Plutarch, *Eumenes* 1.3, Diodorus 18.60.3–4, Nepos 7.1–2.
166. Plutarch, *Demetrius* 31; we know that Craterus amicably passed on his Persian wife Amastris to Dionysius of Heraclea.
167. Nepos 13, Plutarch, *Eumenes* 19.1–2.
168. Plutarch, *Eumenes* 1.3 and Arrian 7.4.6 for references to Eumenes' marriage to a daughter of Artabazus. The sources conflict on her name. Plutarch, *Eumenes* 7.1 for Pharnabazus' support for Eumenes; he was the son of Artabazus.
169. For Philip II, see Aelian 7.12; for Lysander, see Diodorus 10.9.1 and Plutarch, *Lysander* 8.4.
170. It has been alternatively argued that the encomiastic treatment of Eumenes against a more neutral background in Diodorus' texts comes from Duris; namely Diodorus 18.57.3–4; 58.2–4; 59.3; 60.4–63.6; 58.1; Plutarch, *Eumenes*, 1.4–5; 12.2–4; 12.6–7. As identified in Hadley (2001), p. 32.
171. Aelian 3.23.

Chapter 8: How, Why and When the Will Emerged

1. Diodorus 18.53.4–6, trans. from the Loeb Classical Library edition, 1947.
2. Plutarch, *Apophthegms* or *Sayings of Kings and Commanders* 8860 (5), *Lysander*.
3. The terrain is described by Polyaenus 4.6.7 and Diodorus 18.44.2–4. For the battle at Orcynia, see Plutarch, *Eumenes* 18.9–10, Nepos 5 (battle name not mentioned)

and Diodorus 18.39.7–18.40.4. As it has been noted, Orcynia might have been a Cappadocian district and not a specific battleground. Who provisioned Nora, and why, has never been questioned, but if it guarded the pass leading to the Cilician Gates, then it is more explainable as a permanently stocked fortress. Antigonus could have maintained its strategic value by keeping it provisioned for just such a battle outcome; Eumenes could have likewise provisioned the fortress as a fallback option. Plutarch, *Eumenes* 11.1 and Diodorus 18.41.3 for the water, firewood, grain and salt in abundance but, according to Plutarch, no other edibles.

4. For the location, see Plutarch, *Eumenes* 10.1; Nepos 5 simply stated 'Phrygia'. Diodorus 18.41.1–3 did not state a specific location.
5. Diodorus 18.41.7–18.42.1.
6. Arrian, *Events After Alexander* 1.39, Diodorus 18.37.1–3, Justin 13.8.10–14.1.1, Appian, *Syrian Wars* 53 for the proscription of the Perdiccans. Hornblower (1981), p. 11, agreed that Hieronymus would have needed Antigonus' permission to leave the fortress.
7. Diodorus 18.47.4–5. It was Aristodemus who later brought news to Antigonus of Antipater's death. One modern interpretation assumed the journey to Macedon was in response to Eumenes' immediate demands, whilst another considers it took place late in the siege when Eumenes saw little hope with local negotiations. See Anson (2004), p. 137, and compare to Billows (1990), p. 77, accepting Diodorus' version at 18.41.7. Considering the distance to be covered, and the timing of Antipater's death, it seems the journey was more likely linked to the early demands. For the first offer, see Diodorus 18.41.5–7. Also Diodorus 18.53.2–7 for the bargaining and release. For the full year of the siege, Diodorus 18.53.4–5. For six months, Nepos 5.6–7; either scenario is possible, that is until news of Antipater's death in late 319 BC arrived in Phrygia.
8. Plutarch, *Eumenes* 10.4 for Eumenes' fame.
9. Literally translated as either 'the love of honour' or the 'urge to be thought superior' and 'love of power'. Aelian 12.16 and 14.47a suggested Alexander had also been alarmed at the extent of his *philotimia* and *philarchia* before Antipater was.
10. Plutarch, *Eumenes* 5.4–7 for Antipater's offer of an alliance with Eumenes in defeating Perdiccas. Eumenes rejected the offer, stating they were old enemies.
11. For Sardis, see Arrian, *Events After Alexander* 1.40 and 24.8, Plutarch, *Eumenes* 8.6–7. Justin 14.1.7–8 for the prestige hoped for. *Gothenburg Palimpsest* for detail of Eumenes bettering Antipater in Lydia or Phrygia.
12. Diodorus 20.37.5 confirmed Antigonus' governor of Sardis had been instructed not to let Cleopatra leave. Diodorus 18.49.4 for Olympias' fleeing Pella, and Blackwell (1999), p. 94, for its dating.
13. Diodorus 18.11.1 for Molossian support of Greeks in the Lamian War.
14. Arrian 7.12.5–6 and Curtius 10.4.3 for the correspondence from Olympias and Antipater and Alexander's quip about his mother. Other examples at Justin 12.14.3, Plutarch 39.7–14. Slanders from Olympias against Antipater were cited at Arrian 7.12.5, Justin 12.14.3, Plutarch 39.7–14. Diodorus 17.118.1. Diodorus 18.49.4 claimed she fled Pella because of her quarrel with Antipater.

15. Plutarch 39.11–13 for Alexander's warning to Antipater and quoting Plutarch 68.4–5. Diodorus 19.11.9 for Antipater's deathbed warning.
16. For the capture of Attalus, Polemon and Docimus, see Diodorus 18.44.1–18.45.3, Polyaenus 4.6.7 and 19.16–17 for Alcetas' siege. Its final location in Phrygia is likely as Antigonus' wife was in the vicinity, possibly at Celaenae. An escape was attempted 'when Antigonus was heading to the East' (Diodorus 19.16.1–5), which suggests Eumenes had already headed into the upper satrapies in 317 BC when it finished; this vouches for the year-plus siege of the Perdiccans and for a far shorter siege at Nora. Diodorus 19.16 for Docimus betraying his comrades.
17. For the mutilation of Alcetas' body, Diodorus 18.47.3. Antigonus did pardon Docimus, who had betrayed Alcetas and Polemon to him. Moreover, Docimus had also refused to serve under Eumenes. Plutarch, *Eumenes* 8.4. Also Heckel (2006), p. 115. Nothing more is heard of Polemon or Attalus, who were likely executed.
18. Diodorus 18.25.3 stated Antigonus reported Perdiccas' designs on the Macedonian throne. Phila had been married to Balacrus, who died in Pisidia; Photius 166. Diodorus 18.22.1 for his death; discussion in Heckel (2006), pp. 68–69.
19. Arrian, *Events After Alexander* 1.42; Anson (2004), p. 138, for discussion. Alexander crossed the Hellespont in 334 BC and Antipater had controlled Greece since then, thus fifteen years.
20. Justin 13.6.16 suggested Cleitus was cooperating with Alcetas, Perdiccas' brother, in 322/321 BC; see Heckel (1992), p. 186, for detail. Arrian, *Events After Alexander* 1.26 (implied) Cleitus' alignment with Craterus and Antipater, and 1.37 for his satrapy at Triparadeisus. For Aristonus' capitulation, see Arrian, *Events After Alexander* 24.6.
21. Diodorus 18.41.4–5 for confirmation of Antigonus' military strength. Plutarch, *Eumenes* 11.7–9 and Nepos 5.4–6 for the exercising contraption. For Eumenes' charm and friendliness that 'seasoned' the meals they had, Plutarch, *Eumenes* 11.1.
22. Plutarch, *Eumenes* 10.1–3 for the suffering of the men, trans. from Loeb Classical Library edition, 1919. Diodorus 18.50.1–3 for Antigonus' strength.
23. Nepos 5 for Eumenes' delaying and his sorties on the palisade.
24. Diodorus 18.47.4–5, 18.50.1 and Plutarch, *Eumenes* 12.1–2 for news of Antipater's death arriving. Cretopolis has never been formally identified. See discussion of its location in Sekunda (1997).
25. Billows (1990), p. 80; Anson (2004), p. 135. Billows and Anson have differing views on Hieronymus' whereabouts.
26. Diodorus 18.59.4–6, trans. from the Loeb Classical Library edition.
27. Antipater had appointed Cassander second-in-command or chiliarch to Antigonus 'so that the latter might not be able to pursue his own ambitions undetected'; Diodorus 18.39.7 and also Arrian, *Events After Alexander* 1.38. The *Heidelberg Epitome* 1.4 reported Cassander urged his father to remove the kings from Antigonus' custody, though this makes little sense when Antipater took the kings back to Pella and did not leave them in Asia. This might, however, be a reference to Heracles based in Pergamum.
28. Diodorus 18.53.5, Plutarch, *Eumenes* 12.2–3, Nepos 5.7 and Diodorus 18.50.4–5, trans. from the Loeb Classical Library edition, 1947, for the terms of Eumenes' release.

29. Plutarch, *Eumenes* 5.4–6 for Antipater's offer of an alliance with Eumenes in defeating Perdiccas.
30. Diodorus 18.47.5 and 18.50.5, based on the trans. from the Loeb Classical Library edition, 1947.
31. Lysimachus was to assist the Antigonid cause in 318 BC when capturing and killing White Cleitus, who had aligned with Arrhidaeus, satrap of Hellespontine Phrygia; Diodorus 18.72.5–9 for events leading up to Cleitus' capture. Lysimachus was satrap of Thrace, although Heckel suggested he had a wider *strategos* role. See Heckel (2006), p. 155, and Curtius 10.10.4, Diodorus 18.3.2, Arrian, *Events After Alexander* 1.7, Justin 13 4.16 and Dexippus F8.3. Lysimachus must have initially relied upon the network of 'agents' and tyrants Antipater had installed over the previous decade and he had his hands full with the rebellious Thracian king, Seuthes. For the first clash with Seuthes, see Diodorus 18.14.2–15 and for the second referenced battle 19.73.8. Also Arrian, *Events After Alexander* 1.10, yet here Lysimachus is incorrectly reported as slain in the battle.
32. Plutarch, *Eumenes, The Comparison of Sertorius with Eumenes* 2; 'If Eumenes could have contented himself with the second place, Antigonus, freed from his competition for the first, would have used him well.'
33. Heckel (1988), p. 48, and (2006), p. 226, for a summary of Polyperchon's lineage. Heckel (1992), p. 188, for the label 'jackal among lions'.
34. Curtius 4.13.7–10 for Alexander's vocal rejection of Polyperchon's advice. This appears a Cleitarchean device to denigrate an opponent of Ptolemy. Aelian 12.43 for his living as a brigand, Athenaeus 4.155c for Duris' claim that he danced when drunk; see Heckel (1992), p. 188, for citations. Curtius 8.5.22 for the *proskynesis* incident.
35. Polyperchon operated at Gaugamela as taxiarch of the Tymphaean battalion; Diodorus 17.57.2 and Arrian 3.11.9, Curtius 4.13.28. He was involved in various other missions with Meleager, Amyntas and Coenus, and later under Craterus in India; Heckel (2006), pp. 226–27, for a career summary. He was appointed second-in-command to Craterus at Opis, Diodorus 18.48.4, 47.4, Plutarch, *Phocion* 31.1, Plutarch, *Eumenes* 12.1. Arrian 7.12.1 stated there were about 10,000 veterans to return under Craterus, Diodorus 17.109.1, 18.4.1 and Diodorus 18.16.4 suggested the make-up of the 10,000 was 6,000 who originally crossed to Asia with Alexander and 4,000 enlisted on the march. Further, '1,000 Persian bowmen and slingers and 1,500 horsemen' are also mentioned although their role and destination is unclear.
36. Arrian, *Events After Alexander* 1.38 for the appointment of Polyperchon's son as a bodyguard to the new kings.
37. Plutarch 49.14–15 reported that Antipater had entered into secret negotiations with the Aetolians after Alexander's execution of Parmenio, fearing for his own life. Yet an alliance with Aetolians was unlikely to have offered much protection against the agents of Alexander. For Antipater's acknowledging Alexander, see Arrian, *Events After Alexander* 25.1, Curtius 3.1.6–7, Justin 11.1.8, 11.2.2, Diodorus 17.2.2. Quoting Blackwell (1999), p. 35, on devotion. Alexander Lyncestis was held in captivity for three years and executed; he was Antipater's son-in-law; Justin 11.2.1–2 and Curtius 7.1.6–7; Curtius 7.1.5–9, Diodorus 17.80.2, Justin 12.14.1 for his execution. Blackwell

(1999), p. 156, for discussion of Antipater's fear of Alexander; Bevan and Berve believe he rebelled in 323 BC.
38. Plutarch, *Phocion* 17.10.
39. For Polyperchon being entrusted with the defence of Macedon in the absence of Craterus and Antipater, see Justin 13.6.9 and Diodorus 18.25.4–5.
40. Translated in texts as *epimeletes kai strategos autokrator*; Anson (1992), p. 41, for detailed discussion of the title and its relative authority.
41. Arrian 7.12.4, Justin 12.12.8 for Polyperchon's role under Craterus' returning veterans. Diodorus 18.48.4 for his reputation and standing in Macedon.
42. Following the observation on their respective abilities in Roisman-Worthington (2010), p. 212. For Antipater's skill at operating on limited resources, and Cassander's after him, see Adams (1985).
43. Justin 14.5.2–4 for the alliance between Eurydice and Cassander.
44. Arrian, *Events After Alexander* 1.22. Also discussed in Carney (1987), pp. 497–98, referencing Adea's warlike upbringing; and Carney (1988), pp. 392–93, following Polyaenus 8.60. Musgrave-Prag-Neave-Lane Fox (2010), section 9.1.3, argue an undocumented wedding would have taken place in 337/336 BC. Further discussion of Cynnane's age in Grant (2019).
45. Polyaenus 8.60 suggested the marriage ended 'swiftly' to illustrate her independent spirit.
46. Arrian 1.5.2–3. The Agrianians were from the Paeonian region of Thrace bordering the Macedonian northern frontier.
47. Polyaenus 8.60 for the crossing of the Strymon in the face of Antipater's wishes. Musgrave-Prag-Neave-Lane Fox (2010), section 9.1.3, for arguments for Adea's age.
48. Philip had supposedly pledged him to the daughter of Pixodarus, the Carian dynast, some years before; see Plutarch 10.5.1; Alexander's intervention led to his exile.
49. Arrian, *Events After Alexander* 1.22, Polyaenus 8.60.
50. Arrian, *Events After Alexander* 1.23 suggested Perdiccas brought about the marriage but surely under duress; it was not by his design. See discussion in Anson (2004), p. 111. Adea's father was the son of King Perdiccas III (Philip II's older brother) of the Argead line, and her mother was the daughter of Philip II by Audata-Eurydice, thus she was three-quarters Argead. Arrian, *Events after Alexander* 1.22 for confirmation that Audata, Philip's Illyrian wife, was renamed Eurydice. Philip's mother had been named Eurydice too.
51. Quoting Bosworth (1993), p. 425, for 'Amazon and an idiot', and Heckel (1978), p. 157.
52. Arrian, *Events after Alexander* 1.43–45 for the seventy elephants left with Antigonus and Antipater keeping the remainder; also Diodorus 19.23.2.
53. Justin 14.5 for Eurydice's demands to Polyperchon and Antigonus, though in Justin's narrative this move appears to take place later; it makes more sense that Cassander had her draft the royal demands before he departed for Asia. Some commentary such as Heckel-Yardley-Wheatley (2011), footnotes to Justin 14.5, see this as being directed at Eumenes, providing Antigonus with authority to take over his royal army. But he had already achieved that before the siege at Nora. Rather than 'deliver up the army',

the letter might have simply demanded Antigonus' military backing for their regime. Justin appears to place Cassander's alliance with Eurydice far later in events, but it makes more sense that Cassander made the alliance *before* journeying to Antigonus at Celaenae. Diodorus made it clear that he was *looking back* to events in Europe, having progressed them to a far more advanced stage in Asia in his text. So the timing is typically out of sync.

54. Diodorus 18.54.3–4 for Antigonus provisioning Cassander, and Diodorus 18.54.3 for the pre-departure planning. Diodorus 18.68.1 for the size of Cassander's new force.
55. For Cassander's activity after the death of Antipater, Diodorus 18.49.1–2, Plutarch, *Eumenes* 12.1, Plutarch, *Phocion* 31.1 and 32.2. For the hostility between Cassander and Polyperchon, Plutarch, *Phocion* 31.1. Diodorus 18.49.3 for the attempts to renew an alliance with Ptolemy. Diodorus 18.58.1–2 for Cassander's expectations and the strength of his father's oligarchs in Greece.
56. Diodorus 18.57.2 and 18.49.4 appear to suggest Polyperchon invited Olympias twice to Macedon.
57. Diodorus 18.54.4 for Antigonus' covert intentions, trans. from the Loeb Classical Library edition, 1947.
58. Diodorus 18.49.4 and 18.55.1–2 for Polyperchon taking counsel before making policy decisions, and his appreciation of the gravity of what he had done.
59. Diodorus 18.55.2–4 and repeated at 18.57.1–2 and 18.64.3. Diodorus 18.69.4 for the consequences. Trans. from the Loeb Classical Library edition.
60. For Demades' execution, see Diodorus 18.48.1–4 (no mention of Cassander here, just 'men in charge of punishments' and a 'common prison'), Arrian, Eve*nts After Alexander* 1.14, Plutarch, *Phocion* 30.8–9, Plutarch, *Demosthenes* 31.4–6; Antipater was already ill and Cassander was, it appears, giving the orders.
61. For Polyperchon's later hostility to, and warring with, Cassander, see Diodorus 19.11–36, 19.49–75, 19.50–19.64. Following the discussion and observations in Heckel (1992), p. 194. The two war councils mentioned at Diodorus 18.49.4 and 18.55.1 focused on dealing with Cassander. Hostilities against Antigonus are not mentioned at either.
62. Diodorus 18.57.3–4, trans. from the Loeb Classical Library edition, 1947; also see Plutarch, *Eumenes* 13.1–3.
63. Diodorus 18.58.1–3, trans. from the Loeb Classical Library edition, 1947. Reiretated in Plutarch, *Eumenes* 12.1–3.
64. Ptolemy had married Antipater's daughter, Eurydice, and Lysimachus may have already concluded his marriage to Nicaea, Perdiccas' widow (if they ever married) and another of the regent's offspring. Antigonus' son Demetrius had recently married Phila, Craterus' widow and a further daughter of Antipater; Diodorus 19.59.3–6. Antipater's daughters were of course Cassander's sisters.
65. See Rozen (1967), pp. 29–32, for the order of the letters and the possibility of a single edict and a regent's covering letter. Nepos 6 for messengers and correspondence; also Diodorus 18.58.2–4, Plutarch, *Eumenes* 13.1–2.

292   The Last Will and Testament of Alexander the Great

66. Diodorus 19.23.2, trans. from the Loeb Classical Library edition, 1947. Also Polyaenus 4.8.3 for the later episode involving a faked letter from Pella. Discussion of the possibility that these were false letters in Roisman (2012), pp. 179–80.
67. Quoting Roisman (2012), p. 186.
68. Theopompus fragment 217 and Polyaenus 4.2.8: discussion in Gabriel (2010), pp. 198, 211. If Eumenes served Philip for seven years before his king's assassination, he was potentially acting as secretary on campaign.
69. Nepos 6–7, trans. by Rev. J.S. Watson, George Bell and Sons, London, 1886. This parallels the letter at Diodorus 18.58.2–4.
70. Diodorus 19.14.6 and 19.27.5 for the troops sent from Parapamisadae by Oxyartes. Curtius 9.8.9–10 referred to Oxyartes in Latin as *praetor Bactrianorum*. This in fact makes more sense than appointing him to a foreign province: Paropamisadae according to Arrian 6.15.3.
71. 'Tender' quoting Heckel (2006), p. 242. *Metz Epitome* 101–102, 100, 112, *Romance* 3.32.4–7, Arrian 7.27.3 for Rhoxane's role at Alexander's death. *Metz Epitome* 115 was clear that the son of Rhoxane 'before all others' was to be the king of Macedon; restated in the *Romance* 3.32. Her stopping Alexander throwing himself in the Euphrates reinforced that notion.
72. Nepos 7.1, trans. by Rev. J.S. Watson, George Bell and Sons, London, 1886; Diodorus 18.58.3–4.
73. Diodorus 18.62.2 for Olympias writing to the Silver Shields.
74. Diodorus 18.64–65 for Nicanor's receipt of Olympias' instructions and his response. Heckel (2007) for discussion of Nicanor's identity.
75. Plutarch, *Phocion* 29–38 for the chain of events; also Diodorus 18.65.6, Nepos, *Phocion* 3 ff. For Nicanor's execution by Cassander, see Diodorus 18.75.1–1, Polyaenus 4.11.2.
76. Polyaenus 4.11.2 for the forged letter. Nicanor had been involved in coordinated action with Antigonus at the Hellespont, see below.
77. Nepos 6, Diodorus 18.58.2–4 for Eumenes' advice to Olympias on her return to Macedon.
78. Diodorus 19.11.6–7, Aelian 13.36 for the capture and execution (forced sucide) of Eurydice and King Philip III (Arrhidaeus). More on Holcias' role below.
79. Nepos 6 for Olympias' failure to heed Eumenes' advice to wait until the situation was safer. Anson (2014), p. 129, for the treasury sum. As Olympias and Polyperchon combined forces at the battle, he may have journeyed to Epirus after failures in the Peloponnese.
80. Aeacides supported Olympias' return to Macedon, Diodorus 19.11.2, Justin 14.5.9.
81. Diodorus 19.11.2 for the victory of Olympia and Polyperchon over Eurydice. Carney (2006), pp. 79–80, for the chronology. A tympanum is a drum used in Dionysiac rites; Carney (2006), p. 97. Athenaeus 13.560f for Adea's battle dress.
82. Following the observation about Olympias' activity in Anson (1992), p. 40; examples of Olympias' political activity are found in Diodorus 18.49.4, 18.57.2, 18.65.1, 19.11.8–9, 19.35.3–5, 19.50.1, 19.50.8.

83. Herodotus 5.53 for the three days from Ephesus to Sardis on the Royal Road.
84. Diodorus 18.62.3–4 for 'rebel of the monarchy' and Nepos 3.1–2 for the suggestion that Perdiccas granted him authority from Mount Taurus to the Hellespont.
85. See Roisman (2012), p. 180 footnote 8, for discussion. Briant also believed the letters from Polyperchon were partially forged.
86. Diodorus 18.51.3 for the siege of Cyzicus and 18.52.4 for Arrhidaeus' rescue mission. Justin 14.2.4 reported an unlikely story that Antipater sent aid to Eumenes at Nora; it is more likely Justin confused 'Arrhidaeus' for 'Antipater', or confused references to the old and new 'regents', believing Polyperchon (probably under instruction from Olympias) sent the aid.
87. For Arrhidaeus' instructions at Babylon, Diodorus 18.3.5, Justin 13.4.6; for his collusion with Ptolemy, Arrian, *Events After Alexander* 1.25.
88. Diodorus 18.36.6–7 for Arrhidaeus' elevation to *epimeletes* following Perdiccas' death.
89. Diodorus 18.52.6–7 for Cleitus' preparations for an attack and his departure for Macedon and Antigonus' seizure of 600 talents. Plutarch, *Phocion* 34–37 for Phocion's execution; Diodorus 18.72.2–4 for Cleitus' naval action against Nicanor and 18.52.5–8 for his role in Greece.
90. Diodorus 18.63.6, Polyaenus 4.6.9 for Eumenes shipping funds from Cilicia. There is in fact a similarity here with Diodorus 18.52.7 describing Antigonus' assault of Ephesus where Antigonus again intercepted ships from Cilicia; we might wonder if Eumenes had sent the funds to Cleitus and was attempting to send more to him or to Olympias, perhaps via Polyperchon.
91. Diodorus 18.52.2–4 for Antigonus reprimanding Arrhidaeus, trans. from the Loeb Classical Library edition, 1947.
92. Diodorus 18.51–52 for Arrhidaeus' failure in Hellespontine Phrygia and 18.72.2–3 for his linking up with Cleitus. The origin of the troops they were instructed to block is not specified. Either Cassander was already pouring troops into Asia in support of Antigonus, or Antigonus had hired mercenaries, or this referred to Nicanor's fleet from Piraeus. Some three years on, an army of Cassander's was, however, besieging Amisus in Cappadocia against the forces of Antigonus; Diodorus 19.57.4. Antigonus had all the men he needed in Asia and was soon having to raid treasuries to pay them. It is unlikely he was recruiting in Europe when we consider that he had sent Cassander aid in Greece.
93. Diodorus 18.72.5–9 for Cleitus' defeat and execution.
94. Following Carney (2006), pp. 63, 77, for the Macedonian law recorded by Curtius 6.11.20 and 8.6.28 and the great 'lamentation' from the *Romance* 3.33.
95. Plutarch 77.1–2 linking Olympias' pogrom to the conspiracy rumours; also Diodorus 19.11.8–9. As Carney (2006), pp. 85–96, points out, the mistreatment of the bodies of the dead featured prominently in the *Iliad*; 22.395–404 for Achilles' maltreatment of Hector, 23.20–23 and 24.14.21 as the most notable examples.
96. Diodorus 19.11.9, Justin 14.6.1 for the hostility caused by Olympias' actions. Plutarch, *Pyrrhus* 2.1 for Aeacides' expulsion. Plutarch, *Demetrius* 25.2 for Demetrius' marriage to Deidameia.

97. Diodorus 19.49–52 for the fate of Olympias and Diodorus 19.11.1–9, Justin 14.5.8–10, Aelian 13.36 for the deaths of King Philip III and Eurydice. Diodorus 19.11.5 for the length of his reign; Justin 14.5.10 stated 'six years'. Aelian claimed Eurydice chose the rope. Diodorus 19.52.5, Athenaeus 4.155a (using Dyllus) for Cassander's burial honours. Alexander died 10/11 June 323 BC and Arrhidaeus was proclaimed king a week or so after, so a reign of six years and four months takes it to mid-October 317 BC.
98. Plutarch 74.2–6 and *Moralia* 180f for the hostility between Cassander and Alexander.
99. See Heckel (1988), p. 10, for a discussion of those at the banquet, and *Metz Epitome* 97–98 for the full list given in Heckel-Yardley (2004), p. 283.
100. *Romance* 3.32 and *Metz Epitome* 116–117 for the marriage pairings. *Romance* 3.32, *Metz Epitome* 111 and 103 for Alexander's instructions to Ptolemy and Lysimachus and their presence at the drafting and first reading of the will.
101. Athenaeus 11.784c, 13.557c for Thessalonice's maternal side. Plutarch, *Moralia* 141b–c for Olympias' admiration of Nicesipolis.
102. Diodorus 20.37.5 confirmed Antigonus' governor of Sardis had been instructed not to let Cleopatra leave; a state of affairs which most likely went back to Triparadeisus. This does suggest she was an unofficial hostage. Following Carney (1988), p. 402.
103. Diodorus 18.23.1, Arrian, *Events After Alexander* 1.21, Justin 13.6.4 for Perdiccas' courting of Cleopatra. Eumenes had journeyed to visit Cleopatra at Sardis with gifts from Perdiccas. Moreover, his close relationship to Olympias suggests Cleopatra had complete trust in him.
104. *Romance* 3.31.1, *Metz Epitome* 87 for Olympias' pleas. The will opens by confirming Alexander's parentage; *Metz Epitome* 113, *Romance* 3.32; reiterated at *Metz Epitome* 116 and in the *Romance*. Curtius 9.6.26 for Alexander requesting Olympias' consecration to immortality.
105. Arrian 4.10.2 and Plutarch 3.2–3, Justin 11.11.3–4 for Callisthenes' claim that Olympia was spreading 'lies' about Alexander's alleged immortal father.
106. Discussion of the cults to Philip and Alexander in Briant (1974), pp. 135–37.
107. Plutarch 2–3 for the dreams and oracles of Philip and Olympias. Euripides, *Bacchae* 1. In the play, Dionysus lured Pentheus to the forest where the maenads tore Pentheus apart limb from limb.
108. Diodorus 19.11.1 stated that Eurydice 'assumed the administration of the regency' from Polyperchon.
109. Diodorus 18.3.1, Curtius 10.10.2, Arrian, *Events After Alexander* 1.6, Dexippus FGrH 100 F8 §2, *Metz Epitome* 117 for Asander's satrapal grant. Arrian, *Events After Alexander* 25.1 for his possible family relations to Antigonus. For his defection to Perdiccas, see Arrian, *Events After Alexander* 25.1, where Photius' epitome stated 'Asander the satrap of Caria welcomed him as a friend.' Diodorus 19.62.2 for his subsequent defection to Ptolemy.
110. Arrian, *Events After Alexander* 1.41 for Asander's poor performance against the Perdiccans.
111. See Heckel (1988), p. 17, and Heckel-Yardley (2004), p. 288, for the *Metz Epitome* 120 will translation, and Stoneman (1991), p. 155, for the *Romance* translation.

112. *Metz Epitome* 122.
113. Polyaenus 4.6.6 confirmed this took place when Antigonus was wintering in Cappadocia but suggested there was campaigning earlier, before Holcias' capture. The same entry mentioned Holcias' subsequent repatriation to Macedon.
114. Plutarch, *Eumenes* 10.1. This detail is paralleled in Justin 14.2.1–3; also Diodorus 18.41.1–4 and Nepos 5 for Eumenes' entry into Nora.
115. Diodorus 18.53.6. The numbers do look suspiciously like the defectors (under a general named Perdiccas) before the battle at Orcynia that were rounded up by Eumenes' general, Phoenix of Tenedus.
116. Diodorus 18.45–46 for the fullest account of the fate of Alcetas and the Perdiccan remnants. Roisman (2012), p. 29 footnote 48, for identification of Alcetas' tomb. Polyaenus 4.6.6 did suggest Antigonus was worried they would link up with Alcetas. Diodorus 19.16.2 for Attalus, Polemon and Docimus hoping for Eumenes' support. Stewart (1993), p. 312, for Alcetas' tomb.
117. Polyaenus 4.6.6 for the capture of Holcias and his being escorted to Macedon by Leonidas.
118. The timing of Holcias' release and Eumenes' release bargaining is supported by reports that their winter campaigning was followed by a ruse to lure them from their stronghold, their subsequent capture and parole. Anson (2004), p. 121 footnote 21 and p. 124 for a discussion of the timing of Holcias' campaign and capture. If Leonidas can be identified as the commander of the *ataktoi*, the 'disciplinary unit' Alexander formed after Philotas' trial and execution, then his value with 'renegades' had again been appreciated. See Heckel (2006), p. 147, for discussion on Leonidas' identity.
119. Cynnane was the granddaughter of King Bardylis of Illyria (through her mother Audata-Eurydice), Athenaeus 13.557b–c, Arrian, *Events After Alexander* 1.22.
120. For Cleodice's marriage to Leonnatus in the will, see *Metz Epitome* 119, *Romance* 3.34.14, Julius Valerius 3.58, a Latin translation of the *Romance*. Heckel (2006), p. 146, for Leonnatus' royal links.
121. Plutarch, *Eumenes* 5.4–6 for Eumenes' offer to reconcile Perdiccas and Craterus. Plutarch, *Demetrius* 14.2, Plutarch, *Eumenes* 6.2, 6.7, 7.1 for Craterus' popularity.
122. Plutarch, *Moralia* 250f–253q, 486a, Polyaenus 2.29.1, Frontinus, *Stategemata* 3.6.7 for Craterus' son supporting Gonatas. Plutarch 47.10 for the quote on comparative affection and respect and for Alexander's statement that they were the two men most loved by Alexander. Diodorus 17.114.1–2 for Craterus rivalling Hephaestion for Alexander's affections.
123. For Eumenes' treatment of Craterus, see Plutarch, *Eumenes* 7.6–13, Nepos 4.4, Diodorus 19.59.3.
124. *Metz Epitome* 116, *Romance* 3.32 for Craterus' appointment in Macedon and his marriage pairing. Phila's husband Balacrus was killed in Pisidia; Diodorus 18.22.1. More detail on the fate of Cynnane at Arrian, *Events After Alexander* 1.22–23, Polyaenus 8.60.
125. Alcetas disregarded orders to serve under Eumenes: Diodorus 18.29.2, Justin 13.6.15; Plutarch, *Eumenes* 5.3.

126. *Metz Epitome* 100, *Romance* 2.32.3 for Cassander's plan to wait for Iollas in Cilicia. Heckel (1988), p. 10, discusses the later embellishments of Cassander's and Iollas' roles. Justin 12.12.8 for Polyperchon, Polydamas, Gorgias departing Opis with Craterus.
127. Plutarch, *Eumenes* 17.2 for Eumenes' speech when he was under the escort of Nicanor. He was unlikely to be the son of Balacrus, who had family ties with Antipater; Heckel (2006), pp. 68–69, for background.
128. Diodorus 18.39.6, Arrian, *Events After Alexander* 1.37, Appian, *Mithridatic Wars* 8 for Nicanor's grant of Cappadocia at Triparadeisus. Heckel (2006), p. 178, Nicanor (10) and (12) for possible identification. Plutarch, *Eumenes* 17.2 for Eumenes' surrender to Nicanor at Gabiene. For his possible role in the upper satrapies, see Diodorus 19.92.1–5, 100.3, Appian, *Syrian Wars* 55, 57. Heckel (2006), pp. 176–78, for the identifications of various Nicanors.
129. Diodorus 18.43.2 for Nicanor's operations in Coele-Syria and Phoenicia; see Heckel (2006), p. 178, Nicanor (11) for his career.
130. Diodorus 18.47.5 and 18.50.5 for the statements of Antigonus' intent.
131. Antipater had assigned Cassander to watch over Antigonus after Triparadeissus; Diodorus 18.39.7, Arrian, *Events after Alexander* 1.38. The *Heidelberg Epitome* 1.4 went further, stating Cassander urged his father to remove the kings from Antigonus' control.
132. *Metz Epitome* 97 provided eleven identifications as well as corrupted names; see Heckel (1988), pp. 34–35. The Armenian *Romance* version backs up the Greek *Romance* 3.31.8 though peripheral names vary in different recensions.
133. 'Fearful' historians are suggested at Curtius 10.10.18–19, Diodorus 17.118, Justin 12.13.
134. Pearson (1960), p. 83, for discussion on the nautical conflict with Onesicritus, and p. 15, for Nearchus' observations for crossing the tropics and equator. Other titles for his work are suggested by Pliny and Strabo; full discussion in Badian (1975), pp. 157–59. Arrian 6.2.3 suggested Onesicritus lied about his and Nearchus' relative authority and at 7.20.9 outlined a disagreement. There is evidence Nearchus slandered Onesicritus, as evidenced in Arrian's *Indica*. See discussion in Heckel (2006), p. 183. For discussion of *epiplous*, see Berthold (1984), p. 44.
135. The abominable Scylla appears at *Romance* 3.30 and *Metz Epitome* 90–94: Scylla was a part-human, part-beast monster from Greek mythology; here was a baby born as a human boy from the belly up, below which it was part-lion, panther, dog and boar. As Merkelbach and Heckel (1988), p. 9, agree, the beast represented Alexander's own men and their betrayal and not his subject nations as translations suggest.
136. Arrian, *Events After Alexander* 24.6.
137. Aristonus supported Polyperchon and the Olympias faction after Antipater's death; see Diodorus 19.35.4, 19.50.3–8, 19.51.1. Medius took part in Antigonid actions against Ptolemy both for Perdiccas and Antigonus.
138. Arrian 7.27.2 for Medius' relations with Iollas. For Medius' career under Antigonus, see Arrian, *Events After Alexander* 24.6, Diodorus 19.69.3, 19.75.3–4, 19.97.7–8, 19.77.2–5, 20.50.3, Plutarch, *Demetrius* 19.1–2.

139. Quoting Errington (1970), p. 60, and Plutarch, *Eumenes* 3.3–7 for Leonnatus' bid to unite with Cleopatra.
140. Diodorus 18.14.4–5 for Hecataeus' envoy role to Leonnatus, and Plutarch, *Eumenes* 3.3–7 for the whole episode including Eumenes' flight. Also see discussion in Anson (2004), p. 45. How long Hecataeus had governed Cardia is uncertain. Alexander sent a Hecataeus to Asia to murder Attalus soon after gaining the throne, see Diodorus 17.2.5–6 and implied by Curtius 7.1.38. They are likely one and the same man, and thus Hecataeus had been an agent of Alexander, and was likely a client of Philip II before. See discussion in Heckel (2006), p. 131. For Hecataeus' earlier attempt to reconcile Eumenes with Antipater, see Plutarch, *Eumenes* 5.4–5.
141. Nepos 2.4–5 and Plutarch, *Eumenes* 3.11 for Eumenes' troop numbers. Plutarch suggested Eumenes was either afraid of Antipater or 'despaired of Leonnatus as a capricious man' (trans. from the Loeb Classical Library edition, 1919) when explaining his decampment and his rejection of Leonnatus' offer to join his cause. Leonnatus must have coveted Eumenes' campaign funds too.
142. Justin 13.6 for Antipater rejoicing.
143. For Laomedon's grant of Coele-Syria, see Arrian, *Events After Alexander* 1.5, Diodorus 18.3.1, Curtius 10.10.2, Justin 13.4.12, Appian, *Syrian Wars* 52, Dexippus FGrH 100 F8 2. 'Coele' literally translated as 'Hollow', an association first made by Arrian 2.13.7, the region later disputed by the Ptolemaic and Seleucid dynasties. Appian, *Syrian Wars* 52 for reference to the 'buying' of the satrapy. Diodorus 18.43.1–2 and Pausanias 1.6.4 for Ptolemy's hostility.
144. Arrian 3.6.6 for Laomedon's language ability. Laomedon was banned by Philip from Macedon in spring 336 BC along with his brother Erygius, Ptolemy and Nearchus; see Arrian 3.6.5 and Plutarch 10.4. He was also appointed a trierarch on the Hydaspes; Arrian, *Indica* 18.4. For his flight to Alcetas, see Appian, *Syrian Wars* 52. Alcetas opposed Eumenes' suggestion of a marriage to Cleopatra, favouring Nicaea, Antipater's daughter. Arrian, *Events After Alexander* 1.21. He also killed Cynnane; Diodorus 19.52.5, Arrian, *Events After Alexander* 1.22–23; and disregarded orders to serve under Eumenes: Diodorus 18.29.2, Justin 13.6.15; Plutarch, *Eumenes* 5.3.
145. Arrian 3.6.7 and 7.23.1 for Menander's appointment to Lydia. Diodorus 18.59.1–2 for Menander's attempts to capture Eumenes. Arrian, *Events After Alexander* 25.2 suggested, but did not specifically state, that Perdiccas subordinated Menander to Cleopatra. For events at Sardis, see Arrian, *Events After Alexander* 1.26. A separate fragment of Arrian, *Events After Alexander* preserved in the *Vatican Codex* suggested a conflict between Menander, Cleopatra and Perdiccas, resulting in Eumenes' flight.
146. Diodorus 18.23.1, Arrian, *Events After Alexander* 1.21, Justin 13.6.4 for Perdiccas' seeking the hand of Cleopatra. Only the *Heidelberg Epitome* FGrH 155F-4 suggested the marriage took place. Plutarch, *Eumenes* 9.4 for the alleged former friendship with Menander. See discussion in Billows (1990), pp. 59, 63 for Menander's possible early collusion with Antigonus and 401–02 for his career; also Anson (2004), p. 91. Billows (1990), p. 77, for discussion of his role at the Battle of Orcynia as per Diodorus 18.59.1–2 and Plutarch, *Eumenes* 9.2–6. Menander had control of Antigonus' baggage

train that Eumenes almost captured. Plutarch, *Eumenes* 9.2–6 gave a very different account. Diodorus did not mention Menander at the battle.
147. See Heckel (2006), p. 163, for references citing Pliny 35.93; the identification may be incorrect. Lydia is not referenced in either the surviving *Metz Epitome* or *Romance* texts, though it is possible an early textual lacuna is responsible. Diodorus 19.29.2 for Lydian troops present at Paraetacene. Diodorus 19.60.3 brings Lydian operations into the narrative, but again Menander was not mentioned.
148. Nearchus' naval voyage and his reuniting with Alexander made him a prominent and celebrated commander during Alexander's lifetime. He was crowned for his services at Susa and was also illustriously paired in marriage to 'a daughter of Barsine'; Arrian 7.4.6 and also suggested by Arrian, *Indica*.
149. Arrian, *Indica* 18.4 cited Nearchus as coming from Amphipolis. Nearchus' whereabouts and affiliations from Babylon to his reappearance operating under Antigonus are unknown. He seems to have avoided the early conflict, perhaps as governor of Lydia or Pamphylia, or he was deliberately bypassed by Hieronymus' texts. For his undated mission to recover Telmessus, see Polyaenus 5.35. See Heckel (2006), p. 173, and (1988), p. 36, for discussion. Although supposedly an action carried out on Antigonus' orders, he may have been, with consent, reacquiring his nominated satrapy after activity elsewhere. Nearchus had governed satrapies bordering Antigonus' sphere of activity in 334 BC. Justin 13.4.15 did position Nearchus in both Lycia and Pamphylia after Babylon.
150. The founding of Cretopolis discussed in Sekunda (1997), though the suggestion is that this took place before Nearchus was recalled east by Alexander in 329/328 BC.
151. Diodorus 19.69.1 for Nearchus' later service under Demetrius. Nearchus fought against Ptolemy after his reappearance in 317/316 BC and is unlikely to have been pro-Ptolemy before.
152. Heckel (2006), p. 235, sees Stasanor as a supporter of Eumenes and supplying troops. However, there is considerable confusion between the switched roles and relationships of Stasander and Stasanor, both Greek Cypriots who alternatively governed Areia-Drangiana and Bactria-Sogdia between Babylon and Triparadeisus (Diodorus 18.39.6). We propose the troops came from Stasander, who either levied Bactria himself or Diodorus was again confused. If Stasanor was vilified in the *Pamphlet*, it would be surprising to see him and Eumenes join forces; though here that alliance was initially forged in the name of Peucestas. Diodorus 19.14.7 for Stasander's support for Peucestas' original alliance and 19.27.3 for his support for Eumenes.
153. Arrian 4.1.5. Spitamenes refused to attend a conference in Bactria. See Heckel (2006), p. 254, for discussion. Curtius, 7.6.14–15 for his continued resistance and for his siege of the Macedonian garrison, Arrian 4.3.6, 5.2.3. For his ambush of the Macedonian forces, see Arrian 4.5.4–9. Then he fled to Bactria; see Curtius 7.9.20. He attacked a Macedonian fort; see Curtius 8.1.3–5, Arrian 4.16.5. For his betrayal by the Massagetae, see Arrian 4.17.7, Curtius 8.3.1–16, Strabo 11.11.6. Diodorus, Introduction to book 17, contents part 2, for the 120,000 Sogdian casualties.
154. Diodorus 19.48.1–2 for Antigonus' decision not to remove Stasanor. For his career in the East under Alexander, Arrian 3.29.5, 4.18.1, 4.18.3, 6.27.3, 6.27.6, 7.6.1–3,

Diodorus 18.3.3, 18.39.6, Justin 13.4.22–23. The career of Spitamenes and Alexander's (and Persian) actions against the nomadic Massagetae suggested the region's (and bordering provinces') abilty to provide effective fighters.

155. For Philotas' appointment to Cilicia at Babylon, Diodorus 18.3.1, Justin 14.4.12, Arrian, *Events After Alexander* 1.5, Dexippus FGrH 100 F8 2. Photius' text uniquely placed Philoxenus in Cilicia, but this appears a corruption. See Heckel (1988), pp. 71–75, for discussion and suggestion that his Antigonid support might explain his being passed over at Triparadeisus. Also see Arrian, *Events After Alexander* 24.2; Justin 13.6.16 for references to Philotas' loyalty to Craterus. Cilicia went to Philoxenus: Arrian, *Events After Alexander* 1.34, Diodorus 18.39.6. For Philotas' attempt to lure the Silver Shields away from Eumenes, Diodorus 18.62.4, and for the outcome, 18.62.5–18.63.5. Arrian, *Events After Alexander* 24.2 termed Philoxenus 'undistinguished'.

156. Heckel (2006), pp. 225–26, for the carers of Polydorus and Polydamas; the latter had carried the orders for Parmenio's execution.

157. Athenaeus 12.548e for Polydorus' association with Antipater. Diodorus 19.59.3 for Ariston's actions after the death of Craterus (or even after the death of Eumenes). Heckel (2006), p. 213, for discussion of Philip (8).

158. Justin 12.14.1–3 for Philip's collusion with Iollas.

159. Philip (though Philotas in Diodorus 19.14.1, probably a corruption, see Heckel (2006), p. 214) had been satrap of Bactria and Sogdia and was moved to Parthia at Triparadeisus; Diodorus 18.3.3, Dexippus FGrH F8 6, Diodorus 17.31.5–6. For Philip the physician and the earlier accusations of poisoning, see Arrian 2.4.9–10, Plutarch 19.5–10, Curtius 3.6.4–17, Justin 11.8.5–8, Valerius Maximus 3.8 extract 6, *Seneca de Ira* 2.23.2. Following Heckel (2006), pp. 214–15, for the rationale for implicating Philip the physician. For Philip who became satrap of Parthia at Triparadeisus, see Heckel (2006), p. 214, and p. 215 for Philip the engineer. Heckel (1988), p. 44, and (2006), p. 137, and for a possible identification of Heracleides.

160. Plutarch 77.1–2. Plutarch 77.3–4. By then Antigonus was referred to as 'king', but this does not necessarily mean the rumours circulated after 306 BC when he was formally crowned. By Plutarch's day, the differentiation between when Antigonus was considered a dynast and king was probably blurred.

161. Only Nepos 5.1 cited Seleucus amongst Perdiccas' murderers, but Antigonus, clearly not present, was mentioned too. This could be a corruption of Antigenes, commander of the Silver Shields, or alternatively Nepos was summarizing events at Egypt with Triparadeisus where Seleucus did appear alongside Antigonus. Moreover, this was some weeks later and he could have journeyed west from Babylon upon hearing of the failed attack on Egypt. Arrian, *Events After Alexander* 1.33 for Seleucus' role in saving Antipater from the crowd at Triparadeisus. He is not mentioned alongside either Peithon or Arrhidaeus. In fact, Seleucus is not associated with Perdiccas' campaigning from Babylon to his death in 320 BC in any of the sources. Diodorus 18.36.6–7 for the aftermath of the battle with Perdiccas and the nomination of Peithon and Arrhidaeus as supreme commanders and guardians of the kings.

162. Diodorus 19.12.1 for Eumenes' overture to Seleucus in Babylonia.

163. Heckel (1988), Introduction p. 1 footnote 1, for a list of extant texts housing the *Liber de Morte* including the Armenian *Romance* text, and pp. 34–35, for a comparison list of conspirators. The possible attachment of Europius and Seleucus' ethnic discussed in Heckel (2006), p. 246, and (1988), pp. 40–41. Moreover, this reference sits amongst the named Royal Bodyguards in the list of attendees given in the *Metz Epitome*. In another recension of the *Romance*, Seleucus is indeed placed on the guilty roster; Stoneman (1991), pp. 29, 150 footnote 120, for explanation of the ' ' recension. Other examples of manuscript corruption would certainly accommodate the deterioration and loss of the *onoma*, the personal name, and *patronymikon* of the father. As an example, Arrian gave Leonnatus four different patronyms through his account; discussed in Heckel (1978), pp. 155–58.
164. Diodorus 18.39.3–4, Arrian, *Events after Alexander* 1.33, Polyaenus 4.6.4 for Seleucus' defence of Antipater at Triparadeisus. Heckel (1988), p. 41, for the post-320 BC terminus for events; a proposed date for Triparadeisus at which Seleucus was 'first' confirmed in Babylon, as the pamphleteer could not have anticipated the appointment before.
165. Diodorus 19.11.8–9 for Olympias' pogrom and Diodorus 19.51.5 where the pogrom is again referred to and it is implied that Olympias was 'revenging' Alexander's death thus suggesting the *Pamphlet* was by then possibly first circulating.
166. Plutarch 77.1–2 linking Olympias' pogrom to the conspiracy rumours; also Diodorus 19.11.8–9. As Carney (2006), pp. 85–96, points out, the mistreatment of the bodies of the dead featured prominently in the *Iliad*; 22.395–404 for Achilles' maltreatment of Hector, 23.20–23 and 24.14.21 as the most notable examples.
167. Diodorus 19.11.5 for the length of his reign; Justin 14.5.10 stated 'six years'. Aelian claimed Eurydice chose the rope. Diodorus 19.52.5, Athenaeus 4.155a (using Dyllus) for Cassander's burial honours. Alexander died 10/11 June 323 BC and Arrhidaeus was proclaimed king a week or so after, so a reign of six years and four months takes it to mid-October 317 BC.
168. Diodorus 18.58.3–4 for Eumenes' advice to Olympias not to make a move until the war in Asia had been decided.
169. Diodorus 19.12.1 for the envoys to Seleucus and Peithon and Seleucus' response.
170. Diodorus 19.57.1–3 for the envoys to Antigonus from Ptolemy and Lysimachus demanding their share of Anatolia and Syria. Also detailed at Justin 15.1.
171. *Metz Epitome* 118.
172. Arrian, *Events After Alexander* 1.3–4 for Arrian's interpretation of Perdiccas' role.
173. Nepos 5.1 alone included Seleucus in the list of Perdiccas' murderers. This section of the *Romance* will is corrupted, placing Perdiccas in Egypt and a Phanocrates as governor from Babylon to Bactria. We would imagine Phanocrates ought to be Perdiccas; a Persian would not have been granted such a pivotal role.
174. Peithon son of Agenor was appointed satrap of 'lower' India bordering the Indus; Arrian 6.15.4; reconfirmed by Justin 13.4.21 in his account of Babylon. Heckel (2006), p. 196, sees a move to the Cophen satrapy as per Diodorus 18.3.3, Dexippus FGrH 100 F8, a region reconfirmed as Triparadeisus in Diodorus 18.39.6, Arrian, *Events After Alexander* 1.36, Justin. Diodorus 18.3.3 for his installation in the region

between Parapamisus and the Indus. Peithon appeared in Syria in 314/313 BC advising Demetrius; Diodorus 19.69.1, 19.82.1.
175. *Metz Epitome* 117 for the grant of Syria to Peithon. The son of Antigenes was mentioned in Arrian's *Indica* 15.10; Heckel (2006), p. 194, for the possible identification (Peithon 1). Diodorus 19.56.4 for Antigonus installing Peithon son of Agenor in Babylonia.
176. Antigenes was granted Susiane at Triparadeisus (Diodorus 18.39.6, Arrian, *Events After Alexander* 1.34) and the will suggested all lands between Babylon and Bactria should retain the same governors.
177. Heckel (1978), p. 155, for Leonnatus' various patronyms at Arrian 3.5.5, 6.28.4, *Events After Alexander* 1a.2, *Indica* 18.3.
178. For Aristonus' identity and roles on campaign, Arrian 6.28.4; this may have come from Nearchus' list of trierarchs of the Hydaspes-Indus fleet; see the *Indica* 18.4 and Arrian, *Events After Alexander* 1.2–3. Curtius alone cited him protecting Alexander in the Mallian campaign at 9.5.15–18 and again at the assembly in Babylon at 10.6.16 ff. Heckel (2006), p. 50, for explanation of Ptolemy's omission and Errington (1969), pp. 233, 242, for a similar argument. For his Successor War roles, Arrian, *Events After Alexander* 24.6 (*Vatican Palimpsest/Codex* 6), for his leading the Perdiccan invasion force to Cyprus and for activity and support of Olympias, see Diodorus 19.35.4 and 19.50.3–19.51.1.
179. Arrian 7.5.6 suggested the Bodyguards each received a gold crown, yet only the Royal Bodyguards Leonnatus, Peucestas and Hephaestion were named. Nearchus and Onesicritus were also named in the honours list. See Heckel (1988), p. 50, for discussion of other possible corrupted references to Aristonus.
180. Aristonus supported Polyperchon and the Olympias faction after Antipater's death, see Diodorus 19.35.4, 19.50.3–8, 19.51.1, Diodorus 19.49–51.1 for Aristonus' murder and his control of Amphipolis.
181. Diodorus 19.51.1 for Aristonus' high standing amongst the Macedonians.
182. *Metz Epitome* 110 for the roles of Perdiccas and Antipater. Heckel (1988), pp. 12–14, for full discussion referring to Recension A of Pseudo-Callisthenes, and Heckel-Yardley (2004), p. 285, for a full translation of the *Metz Epitome* version of the Rhodian 'interpolation'. Bosworth-Baynham (2000), p. 213, agrees the Rhodian issue could have formed part of the original *Pamphlet* will. See Stoneman (1991), pp. 152–53, for a translation of the *Romance* version of the Letter to the Rhodians. The Letter to the Rhodians is concurrent in Pseudo-Callisthenes A. Fraser (1996), p. 212, for the boule and demos and discussion on the Latin manuscript in which the letter appeared separately.
183. Bosworth-Baynham (2000), p. 213.
184. Berthold (1984), p. 39, on Rhodian government.
185. Diodorus 20.81.2 and discussed in Berthold (1984), p. 38. Polybius 33.16.3 and Strabo 14.2.5 amongst others reiterated the same sentiment, though without stating the date or Hellenistic period they were referring to. Rodgers (1937), p. 262, for the renting out of Rhodian ships.
186. Berthold (1984), pp. 42–43, on Rhodes' expansion and state governance, and pp. 48–49, for the continuation of the Rhodian coinage weight after Alexander adopted

the Attic standard. Rhodes had seceded early from the Delian League controlled by Athens, remaining neutral for example in the Peloponnesian War.
187. O'Neil (2000), p. 425, for discussion of the law codes imposed, and Billows (1990), p. 220, for the League of the Islanders.
188. Arrian 2.20.2 for Cypriot assistance at Tyre. Diodorus 19.62.4, 20.47.3, Pausanias 1.6.6 for Menelaus' early role in Cyprus before his removal after the Battle of Salamis in 306 BC.
189. Berthold (1984), p. 34, for discussion of Rhodian independence from Caria. The arrests of the Rhodian brothers Demaratus and Sparton and Harpalus' treasurer, probably by Philoxenus, demonstrated the reach of Alexander's authority over Rhodes.
190. For a description of caltrops at the Battle of Gaugamela, see Curtius 4.13.36. Also see *Lindian Stele Votive* 38 and discussion in Higbie (2003), pp. 134–35; 234–35 for Persian votives. Spiked iron caltrops were used to maim horses and protect ground littered with them against cavalry charges. In legend, Danaus had fifty daughters, one of whom was Lindos and worshipped on Rhodes, taking her name for its city; Diodorus 5.38 and Strabo 14.2.6 for the legend that Danaus had founded the sanctuary of Athena Lindia on his way to Egypt.
191. Discussed in Stewart (1993), p. 220, and Lindian subtext at p. 237. More detail about the cult on Rhodes in Brandt-Iddeng (2012), p. 255. Lock (1977), p. 100, and Tarn 1 (1948), p. 59, for the Lindian inscription. Also Shipley (2000), p. 37, and Tarn 1 (1948), p. 59, for inscriptions on Rhodes.
192. *Metz Epitome* 118–119.
193. Arrian, *Events after Alexander* 1.39 for Attalus' attack on Cnidus, Caunus and Rhodes, where he was repulsed; Diodorus 18. 37.3–4 for his rounding up orphaned Perdiccans.
194. See Casson (2001), p. 32, for grain discussion and Egyptian supply.
195. Quoting Brandt-Iddeng (2012), p. 255, for Rhodes' long-standing alliance with Ptolemy.
196. *Romance* 3.33.9; see Stoneman (1991), p. 154, for translation and Heckel (1988), pp. 12–13, for discussion. Ptolemy's executor role reiterated in Lucian's *Dialogues of the Dead* 13.
197. *Metz Epitome* 116, *Romance* 3.23.
198. Diodorus 19.58.1–6 for the state of Antigonus' naval power.
199. Diodorus 18.43.1–2 for Ptolemy's annexation of Coele-Syria.
200. *Metz Epitome* 109.
201. *Romance* 1.46.
202. Ismenas the son of either Oceanus and Tethys or Asopus and Metope, and who settled on the banks of the River Ismenus in Boeotia. For examples, see Plutarch, *Demetrius* 1.6 for the musician of Thebes and for the fourth century BC statesman by the same name, and Xenophon, *Hellenica* 2.31 for another Ismenias; the name also appears in Plato, *Meno* 90a as well as Plato, *Republic* 336a. *Romance* 1.46, Pausanias 9.10.6, Ovid, *Metamorphoses* 3.169, Callimachus, *Hymn 4 to Delos* 77, Diodorus 4.72.1, 31.12.6. Aelian 12.57 for the portents at Thebes. In a surviving fragment of the third book of Callisthenes' *Hellenica* we have the reference 'that of Ismenas at Thebes: the

trophonian oracle at Levadia'. Its existence is confirmed by Herodotus, who claimed to have visited the sanctuary of Ismenias, or better, the Temple to 'Apollo Ismenias', and it is additionally referenced in a passage in the penultimate chapter of Plutarch's *Life of Lysander* Herodotus 5.58–61. Plutarch, *Lysander* 29

203. Arrian 2.15.2–5 for the reference to the son of Ismenias, an envoy from Thebes and his lineage. Plutarch, *Pelopidas* 5.1 for Pelopidas' membership of Ismenias' party. Ismenias was put to death at Sparta (*Pelopidas* 5.4), an outcome that possibly endeared him to Philip, if the same man. Also Diodorus 15.71.2–3 and Plutarch, *Pelopidas* 27.1, 27.5 for Ismenias' reputation and relations with Pelopidas. Aelian 1.21; Ismenias dropped a ring as his excuse for kneeling to the Persian king.

204. Plutarch 13.5, *Moralia* 181b, Justin 11.4.9 and Arrian 2.15.3–4 for Alexander's later regret for such harsh treatment of Thebes. Diodorus 17.13.3. Arrian 1.8.8 for his defence of Alexander's actions by outlining the list of Theban treachery when aligning with Persia.

205. Athenaeus 434 a–b for Ephippus' remark. Diodorus 17.10.3, trans. from the Loeb Classical Library edition, 1963.

206. Justin 10.4.5–6 for Heracles' birth in Thebes.

207. Diodorus 19.54.1 for the list of cities that pledged support for the rebuild. Diodorus 19.61.3 for Antigonus' demand that the reconstruction of Thebes be reversed. Diodorus 19.61.1–3 for Antigonus' proclamation.

208. *Metz Epitome* 120; the *Romance* 3.32 stated 50 talents of coined gold; that suggests a gold to silver ratio of 1:20 when the actual ratio was between 1:10 and 1:12 in the early Hellenistic period.

209. The *Metz Epitome* translation in Heckel (1988), p. 17, claimed 1,000 talents for the temple of Hera at Argos. The *Romance* has Alexander's armour plus 50 talents, see Stoneman (1991), p. 155, for translation. Bosworth-Baynham (2000), p. 221, cites 150 talents. Variations in the texts range from the 'Temple of Hera' to 'the first fruits of war for Heracles'.

210. Homer, *Iliad* 4.50–52.

211. Pausanias 10.10.5 for the proposed lineage of the Argives. The essence of the story was captured by Euripides in his *Heraclidae*. See Diodorus 12.75.5–6 for the significance of the legend to Argos. The Return of the Heraclidae is also known as the Dorian invasion, when the scattered sons of Heracles come home to claim their rightful ancestral lands, including Sparta; see Pausanias 4.30.1 and Herodotus 8.73.

212. Diodorus 19.63.1–5 for the confrontation at Argos.

213. *Romance* 3.32.

214. *Metz Epitome* 104–05, *Romance* 3.32.12–13 for the rumour of Alexander's death causing a troop uproar.

215. The discord at Babylon was captured; *Metz Epitome* 104–06 and 113, *Romance* 3.32. Cleitarchus could have of course embellished what they read in the *Pamphlet* when developing his book conclusion.

216. Roman contamination discussion in Tarn (1948), pp. 378–98.

217. Arrian 7.27, Plutarch 7.27 for Aristotle's involvement.

218. Theophrastus, *Enquiry into Plants* 9.16.2, and for hemlock 9.16.8.

219. Quoting Green (2007), p. 2. As Champion (2014), p. 4, noted of the last eleven Argeads, they were either assassinated or executed.
220. For Olympias' death on Cassander's orders, Diodorus 19.51.5, Justin 14.6.6–12, Pausanias 1.11.4, 25.6, 9.7.2 (for stoning to death); Carney (2006), pp. 81–85, for discussion of the various accounts of her death.
221. Quoting Curtius 10.10.18–19. The theme of 'fearful historians' is reiterated in the Vulgate texts by Diodorus 17.118.2, Justin 12.13.10.
222. Diodorus 19.61.1–4, Justin 15.1.
223. As suggested by Tarn (1948), p. 297.
224. Bosworth (2002), p. 217, for the dating discussion according to the *Babylonian Chronicle*.
225. Diodorus 19.105.3–5 for the extracting of Thesalonice and Justin 15.2.2-5. Pausanias 9.7.2 for the murder of Rhoxane and Alexander IV.
226. Quoting Grainger (2007), p. 116. For the death of Heracles, Diodorus 20.28, Justin 15.2.3, Pausanias 9.7.2, and for its dating, Carney-Ogden (2010), p. 118, and Wheatley (1998), p. 13 and footnotes; it may have been 308 BC. Diodorus 20.37.3 for Cleopatra's leaving Sardis to join Ptolemy and her execution.
227. For Heracles' death, Diodorus 20.28, Pausanias 9.7.2–3, Justin 15.2.3. Antigonus claimed Cassander forced Thessalonice into marriage, Diodorus 19.52.1 and 61.2, Pausanias 8.7.7, Justin 14.6.13. For the death of Cleopatra on Antigonus' orders, Diodorus 20.37.5–6.
228. Quoting Carney (2006), p. 84, on Cassander's attempt to delegitimize Alexander's Argead branch.
229. Plutarch, *Pyrrhus* for Neoptolemus' death, though his identity is challenged; see Heckel (2006), p. 175. Also see Carney (2006), pp. 67 and 169 footnote 25; whilst not specifically attested as her children, Neoptolemus is mentioned as their father, though as Carney argues, this could mean 'descendants' and thus grandchildren, for Neoptolemus was the father to Alexander of Epirus, Cleopatra's husband.
230. Plutarch, *Sertorius* 1.4, trans. from the Loeb Classical Library edition, 1919, for comparisons with Philip, Antigonus and Hannibal, and quoting 1.6.
231. Plutarch, *The Comparison of Sertorius with Eumenes* 2.3–4.
232. Whilst Plutarch painted a picture of Eumenes' pre-battle contemplations, this episode may well have taken place once he took council and the outcome of the battle looked doubtful once the Silver Shields had been surrounded, as Diodorus clarified that a council took place immediately before his arrest.
233. Plutarch, *Eumenes* 16.2.
234. Plutarch, *Comparison of Eumenes with Sertorius* 2.4.
235. Plutarch, *Eumenes* 18.2 for the Silver Shields' complaint and 16–18 for the outcome at Gabiene. Italics my own.
236. Diodorus 19.44.3 for Hieronymus' capture and new employment.
237. Obviously before Hagnon's squadron was captured in a naval battle off Cyprus. See Billows (1990), pp. 387–88, for Hagnon's final activity; the date of the battle off Cyprus is disputed; 315/314 BC is proposed, though this conflicts with Diodorus 19.58.1, which claimed Antigonus had no naval force then (also see 19.59.1 and 19.62.3–4

for the possible engagement). Hagnon had been granted citizenship of Ephesus in 321/320 BC.
238. Plutarch, *Apophthegms or Sayings of Kings and Commanders* 8860 (5), *Lysander*.
239. 'Unable to fly' quoting Plutarch, *Comparison of Eumenes and Sertorius* 2.4. Justin 14.3, possibly drawing from Duris, claimed Eumenes attempted to flee and only when captured again did he demand the right to deliver his final scathing speech. The use of Duris is somewhat backed up by Plutarch's *Comparison of Eumenes with Sertorius* 2.3–4 in which he alleged the same.

Chapter 9: The Overlooked Evidence

1. Momigliano (1954), p. 22.
2. *Heidelberg Epitome* 1.2 for twenty-four satrapies.
3. A good summary of the various satrapal lists can be found in Goralski (1989), pp. 104–05. Anson (2014), pp. 49, 189 for discussion on the division of responsibilities. Billows (1990), pp. 276, 278 for the various satrapal posts. Anson (2013), p. 65, for the *epistates* role and pp. 141–46, for the layers of administration; full discussion of titles in Anson (1992).
4. Quoting Hornblower (1981), p. 103, on 'centrifugal forces'.
5. Notably, some four or five years after Alexander's death, Eumenes was still able to access the treasury at Cyinda in western Cilicia. It remained intact, as did the treasury at Susa, which Eumenes planned to use to pay his troops when wintering in Babylonia in 317 BC with his mandate from the 'kings'. Hieronymus pointed out that Antigonus benefited from an annual income of 11,000 talents after his defeat of Eumenes and assuming control of Cilicia in 315 BC. Bellinger (1979), p. 83, for a list of mints across Anatolia.
6. Curtius 10.6.15 for Ptolemy's proposal of group rule. I propose Seleucus was included in this line-up. Whilst Arrian 6.28.4 did not list him amongst the Bodyguards, he was listed as amongst the most important of the generals in Arrian, *Events After Alexander* 1.2; it is not impossible he replaced Hephaestion, who died in 324 BC, as a new 'eighth'.
7. Justin 13.4 for 'princes to prefects'.
8. Arrian 7.5.4–6 for the crowning of the Bodyguards.
9. Arrian 3.5.4, Plutarch 22.1, Polyaenus 6.49, Plutarch, *Moralia* 333a for Philoxenus' role from 333 BC.
10. Curtius 4.1.34–35 for a description of Antigonus' role and task in Lydia, here referring to the old Lydian kingdom of Anatolia west of the Halys. Also Arrian 1.29.3, Justin 13.4.14 for Antigonus' previous regional command. crus' career, see Heckel (2006), pp. 68–69.
11. See Heckel (2006), pp. 96–97, for Craterus' roles in Alexander's absence.
12. Diodorus 17.80.3 confirmed Parmenio's administrative role and guardianship of the 180,000 talents at Ecbatana. Black Cleitus was to govern the upper satrapies of Bactria and Sogdia, Curtius 8.1.19–21. Mazaeus had played a valuable role in Darius'

battles, especially Gaugamela; he was made satrap of Babylon soon after Gaugamela until his death in 328 BC; Arrian 3.16.4, Curtius 5.1.44, Diodorus 17.64.5–6; he surely reported to a Macedonian general: Parmenio, once installed. Phrataphernes was possibly reinstated in Parthia and possibly Hyrcania by Alexander after Darius' death; Arrian 3.23.4, 3.28.2. At Babylon he was reconfirmed; Diodorus 18.3.3, Justin 13.4.23, a position implied in the *Pamphlet* will, *Metz Epitome* 121. Arrian 3.16.9 and 3.18.11 for Abulites and Phrasaortes; Anson (2013), pp. 141–42, for discussion of the layers of satrapal government.

13. Curtius 10.10.1–5 and Dexippus FGrH 100 F8 for Ptolemy's regional grant. Curtius 10.10.1–5, Dexippus FGrH 100 F8, Justin 13.4–5 and Diodorus 18.3.1–3 for Lysimachus' territories.
14. The grain trade from Cyrene discussed in Carney (1995), p. 386. Justin 13.7 for the history of Cyrene. Bagnall-Derow (2004), pp. 3–4, for the list of grain shipments from Cyrene.
15. Arrian, *Events After Alexander* 1.34.
16. Diodorus 17.49.2–4 for the embassies from Cyrene that met Alexander on his way to the oasis at Siwa. For detail of Ptolemy's annexation of Cyrene, see Diodorus 18.21.7 and Arrian, *Events After Alexander* 1.17. This is following Harpalus' unsuccessful flight to Athens as Alexander re-emerged from Gedrosia. Thibron, leader of his mercenary force, fled from Cyprus to Cyrene. After initial defeats, the population was divided on how to deal with him and Ptolemy sent his general Ophellas of Pella, a former trierarch of Alexander's Hydaspes-Indus fleet, to restore order. Thibron was eventually captured and handed over to the populace for execution and Ophellas continued to govern the region until his misadventure with Agathocles, tyrant of Syracuse (361–289 BC) in 309/308 BC. Ophellas was fatally betrayed and his wife Eurydice returned to Athens, marrying Demetrius Poliorketes. For his death, see Diodorus 20.42.3–5, Justin 22.7.5–6, *Suda* O994. Cyrene was for a time ruled by Demetrius the Fair, youngest son of Demetrius the Besieger, yet he was related to the Ptolemaic regime through his maternal grandfather, Ptolemy Soter.
17. Arrian, *Events After Alexander* 1.3–4 for the 'kingdom of Arrhidaeus' and reiterated in Dexippus FGrH 100 F8 4. For Craterus being charged with safeguarding the freedom of the Greeks and thus a regime change was suggested, cosmetic or otherwise, Arrian 7.12.4.
18. Bosworth (2002), pp. 10–11, for discussion of Craterus' emulation of Alexander. Also see the full text of Demetrius of Phalerum, *On Style* 289 in Fortenbaugh-Schütrumpf (2000), p. 43. Craterus apparently received Greek emissaries on a raised golden couch dressed in purple robes.
19. Arrian, *Events After Alexander* 1a.3, Dexippus FGrH 100 F 8.4 for 'the highest honour'; discussed in Anson (1992), p. 39.
20. Diogenes Laertius, *Diogenes* 6.57 for Diogenes' reply to Craterus. The episode is not dated, but the only period Craterus was back in Greece or Macedon was either side of the Lamian War.
21. Plutarch 40.5 reported that a hunting scene in which Alexander fought a lion was represented on Craterus' monument at Delphi. Also Pliny 34.64 for the monument;

Borza-Palagia (2007), p. 97, for its significance, and pp. 90–103, for lion hunts and their representation; pp. 101–02 for Craterus' monument and dedication. Curtius 8.1.11–18, 8.1.14–18, 8.6.7, 8.8.3, Arrian 4.13–14, Plutarch 55 for additional hunting incidents involving Alexander. See discussion and measurements in Stewart (1993), p. 270, and descriptions on p. 390.
22. Diodorus 18.3.3, Justin 13.3.23, Dexippus FGrH 100 F8 6.
23. Diodorus 18.7.1–3, trans. from the Loeb Classical Library edition, 1947.
24. Diodorus 18.4.8, 18.7.1–9 and the new revolt and Curtius 9.7.1–12 for the previous uprising.
25. For T20, so Justin 13.4, there appears a lacuna that swallowed Peithon's name, for Perdiccas' father-in-law, Atropates, is clearly given Lesser Media.
26. Diodorus 18.7.4, trans. from the Loeb Classical Library edition, 1947, for the mercenary revolt.
27. Diodorus 18.7.3–18.8 for the troop numbers and outcome.
28. Numbers were often misrepresented. For example, it remains just as unlikely to interpret from Arrian 1.16.2–3 and Plutarch 16.12–15 that 18,000 mercenaries were slaughtered at the Granicus River. Arrian 1.14.4 suggested a similar number ('little less') of mercenaries to the Persian cavalry stated at 20,000, and that all died bar 2,000 prisoners; 1.16.2. The Macedonians allegedly lost only eighty-five cavalry and thirty infantry (less according to Aristobulus, so claimed Plutarch). Modern interpretations suggest more like 5,000 mercenaries were present. Discussion in Parke (1933), p. 180.
29. Discussed in Gabriel (2006), p. 114.
30. Diodorus 18.7.4–9.
31. Aelian 14.47a.
32. Diodorus 18.4.8, 18.7–8 for Peithon's actions quelling the revolt.
33. Diodorus 18.7.5–9 for the battle and its outcome.
34. Diodorus 18.7.8. Quoting J.K. Anderson in Hanson (1991), p. 21, and Tarn 1 (1948), p. 15 footnote 1.
35. Heckel (2006), p. 196 (Peithon 4), for the governorship of the Indus region and to the sea, and p. 212 (Philip 5).
36. See discussion of Peithon's role in Heckel (1988), p. 61 footnote 8, citing the *Metz Epitome* 118 and *Romance* 3.33.15. Heckel (2006), p. 195, concedes that 'special powers' were provided to Peithon to carry out this task. Heckel (2006), p. 195. Arrian, *Events After Alexander* 1.35 mentioned the Caspian Gates as the boundary of Media in the west.
37. Justin 13.4.13, for Atropates' grant of Lesser Media; implied at Diodorus 18.2.3 here Peithon is mentioned in Media first; see Strabo 11.13.1 for confirmation. Arrian 3.8.4, 4.18.3, 7.4.1 for his previous governance and Arrian 7.4.5, Justin 13.4.13 for Perdiccas' marriage to his unnamed daughter.
38. Diodorus 19.14.1, trans. from the Loeb Classical Library edition, 1947. Italics my own. Diodorus 18.39.6 named the governor of Parthia 'Philip' yet he referred to him as 'Philotas' at 19.14.1; Heckel (2006), p. 214, for the identity discussion.
39. Anson (2014), p. 101, for the observation on Seleucus' acceptance of Peithon.

308 The Last Will and Testament of Alexander the Great

40. Quoting Diodorus 19.14.4. See Heckel (1988), pp. 60–61, and Goralski (1989), pp. 104–05, for a useful full list and comparison of satraps and *Pamphlet*-nominated names.
41. Diodorus 19.14.8. Compare this to Diodorus' description of Triparadeisus at 18.39.6, where Porus and Taxiles are left unmoved solely because it would have required a royal army to do so. This suggests Eudamus might have been encouraged to kill Porus. Arrian 6.2 1 for Porus' extended territory.
42. Diodorus 19.14.1–2. For Peithon son of Agenor's appointment to the northern Indus bordering region, see Diodorus 18.3.3, Dexippus FGrH 100 F8, and for reconfirmation at Triparadeisus, Diodorus 18.39.6, Arrian, *Events After Alexander* 1.36, Justin 13.4.21. Forces from Bactria are also mentioned at Diodorus 19.14.7.
43. Arrian 7.5.6. Peucestas is mentioned by name but Arrian suggested *all* of the Bodyguards received gold crowns.
44. Quoting Diodorus 18.5.4 and Plutarch, *Demetrius* 46.4.
45. For Atropates' appointment to Lesser Media, see Justin 13.4.13, Diodorus 18.3.3. Arrian 7.13.2 and 6 for the 'Amazon' episode. Discussion in Heckel (2006), pp. 61–62, and Bosworth-Baynham (2000), p. 300. Diodorus 19.46.1–6 for events surrounding the removal of Peithon. Heckel (2006), p. 62, for discussion and Strabo 11.13.1 for Atropates' kingship and new title. Polybius 5.55.9–10 for Media Atropatene being always independent.
46. Diodorus 19.92.1–5 and 100.3–4, Appian, *Syrian Wars* 55 and 57 for Nicanor's installation as strategos of Media and the upper satrapies, Peithon's previous domain. See identification discussion in Heckel (2006), p. 178 (Nicanor 12), and Billows (1990), pp. 409–10. Anson (2014), p. 125, following Billows (1990), p. 393, suggested Hippostratus assumed this role first, though Diodorus 19.46.5 seems to have suggested that role (*strategos*) applied to Media only. Hippostratus may have replaced him due to his poor performance when attacked; Diodorus 19.47.1–3.
47. Diodorus 19.92.3 for the negligent guard and 19.100.3 for Antigonus giving up hope of gaining income from the lands east of Babylon.
48. Diodorus 19.55.3 for Seleucus rebutting Antigonus' demands. Diodorus referred to Babylon but nevertheless termed it the 'country', suggesting Seleucus governed the whole province not the city.
49. Following Heckel (2006), p. 247.
50. Collins (2001), pp. 270–73, for discussion of the chiliarch's peripheral roles.
51. Diodorus 18.3-4, Justin 13.4.17 and 13.4.23 for Seleucus' appointment and Archon's role.
52. Diodorus 18.6.3 described Egypt as the 'best due to its revenues' and Diodorus 18.5.4 described Media as the 'greatest of all the satrapies'; the importance of the treasury at Susa and Persepolis, coming under Peucestas' authority, made them desirable.
53. Justin 13.4.17; Diodorus 18.3.4 terms Peucestas' appointment 'a most distinguished office'.
54. Arrian, *Events After Alexander* 1 for 'second-in-command'.
55. For Arcesilaus' role (a probable Perdiccan), see Diodorus 18.3.3, Justin 13.4.23; Dexippus FGrH 100 F8 6 called him Archelaus.

56. Diodorus 19.100.5 for Patrocles and 19.99.3–4 for Seleucus' campaign into Media.
57. Appian, *Syrian Wars* 53.269 for Blitor and Seleucus' escape. Nothing else is known about him. For Amphimachus' appointment, see Arrian, *Events After Alexander* 1.35, Diodorus 18.39.6. Heckel (2006), pp. 22, 53, and Bosworth (2002), p. 113, for discussion on Amphimachus' identity; probably 'brother of Arrhidaeus' in original manuscripts though later confused with King Philip III (Arrhidaeus). He was awarded the governorship of Mesopotamia at Triparadeisus; Diodorus 18.39.6, Arrian, *Events After Alexander* 1.35. He was unlikely to have been the brother to the new King Philip III and was more likely brother of Arrhidaeus who became satrap of Hellespontine Phrygia and sources (Justin in particular) confused the identity of 'Arrhidaeus'. Amphimachus' later support for Eumenes at Gabiene suggests the latter too. As a governor of Mesopotamia, Amphimachus would have nevertheless been subordinate to Seleucus the regional *strategos* (or to Perdiccas in Syria), and yet was found operating under Eumenes at Paraetacene, Diodorus 19.27.4, so logically he defected at this point if not under Perdiccas' authority.
58. Arrian, *Indica* 18.3.
59. The conflict between Docimus and Archon covered at Arrian, *Events After Alexander* 24.3–5.
60. Diodorus 18.39.6 for Seleucus' 'reconfirmation' as satrap of Babylonia. Diodorus 18.37.1–3, Arrian, *Events After Alexander* 1.39, Justin 13.8.10–14.1.1, Appian, *Syrian Wars* 53 for the sentence on the Perdiccans.
61. The lacuna would follow Arrian, *Events After Alexander* 1.8 and before the reference to Rhoxane. Goralski (1989), pp. 10–15, and Heckel (1988), p. 61, for the relative satrapal references to Babylon; Photius' epitomes of Arrian suggest these three sources clearly stated Seleucus inherited the governorship of Babylon at least. The confusion with detail from Triparadeisus is supported in Photius' positioning Arrhidaeus in Hellespontine Phrygia.
62. Compare this reconstruction with Diodorus 18.3.3–4, where Archon and Seleucus are mentioned in bordering sentences.
63. Diodorus 18.3.1 and 18.14.4. At 18.12.1, Diodorus mistakenly named 'Philotas' as satrap of the region, but this is usually corrected to 'Leonnatus'. Also *Arrian*, Events After Alexander 1.6, Dexippus 82,62B, Curtius 10.10.2, Justin 13.4.16. Photius' epitome of *Arrian*, Events After Alexander has Arrhidaeus in the region but presumably this is again mistaking or compressing the detail of his appointment at Triparadeisus.
64. For Leonnatus' decoration for saving Alexander's life, see Arrian 7.5.4–5.
65. Leonnatus' heritage discussed in Heckel (2006), p. 147. Plutarch, *Eumenes* 3.5 for Leonnatus' bid to take the throne.
66. Curtius 10.7.8 for recognition of Leonnatus' royal stock and guardianship role, 10.7.20 for his cavalry command and 10.8.23 for a reiteration of the 'two' guardians of the king then in Babylon, the third being Meleager, by negotiation.
67. Heckel (2006), p. 150, suggests Leonnatus would have been 'disappointed' but goes no further. Many modern historians believe it was a manipulation by Perdiccas. Arrian 1.17.1–2, 1.25.2 for its governance by a son of Harpalus, Calas; Heckel (2006), pp. 74–75 and footnote 163, for identity discussion.

68. Leonnatus and Perdiccas are attested together in chasing Pausanias, Philip's assassin; Diodorus 16.94.
69. Arrian 2.12.2 for Balacrus, Arrian 1.17.1, 2.4.1, Curtius 4.5.13 for Calas, Arrian 3.6.6 for Nearchus, Arrian 1.17.7 for Asander.
70. Bithynia was ruled by Zipoetes, who formally became king in 297 BC; no conflict between him and the Macedonians is recorded. The Hellespontine Phrygia region may have still encompassed Bithynia, the Troad and Mysia, as it did after the conquests of Cyrus the Great, when Hellespontine Phrygia controlled the Asian shores of the Propontis from its capital at Dascylium.
71. Bithynia is not mentioned as a separate territory at this point by the sources. Arrian, *Events After Alexander* 1.37 for confirmation that Lycaonia fell within Antigonus' mandate from the outset.
72. Plutarch, *Eumenes* 3.3 for Antigonus' rejection of Perdiccas' orders. More below on how far east Eumenes' governance might have reached.
73. For Neoptolemus' opposition, see Plutarch, *Eumenes* 5.4, Diodorus 18.29.4–5 and Arrian, *Events After Alexander* 1.27. Quoting Plutarch, *Eumenes* 4.1–2 for reference to Neoptolemus' presence in Armenia and for his career, see discussion in Heckel (2006), p. 174, and for Orontes, Heckel (2006), p. 185, citing Dexippus' corrupt epitome FGrH 100 F8 6 which stated Neoptolemus inherited Armenia. Heckel (1988), pp. 61–63, for corruptions in satrapal and governor names. It remains unclear whether Orontes, the Armenian satrap under Darius III, ever made terms with Alexander, or whether the province remained unconquered. Orontes fought for Darius III at Gaugamela, see Arrian, *Anabasis* 3.8.5. He escaped and is heard of next in 317 BC back in Armenia as a friend of Peucestas, whom he may have met in Macedon originally. See Diodorus 19.23.3. Armenia had not been conquered despite Alexander attempting to install Mithrines after the Battle of Gaugamela; Diodorus 17.64.6, Curtius 5.1.44, Arrian 3.16.5. Neoptolemus' appointment, however, in 323 BC suggests plans were afoot for just that, as in Cappadocia. For later references to Orontes, see Diodorus 19.23.3, Polyaenus 4.8.3. See Plutarch, *Eumenes* 7.5–8, Diodorus 18.29.4 for the battle with Neoptolemus.
74. Diodorus 19.23.1–4 for details of the ruse.
75. Diodorus 19.57.1–3 for the envoys to Antigonus, also Justin 15.1.
76. Diodorus 19.57.4 for Cassander's incursion into Cappadocia.
77. Diodorus 18.43.1–2 clearly stated that Laomedon was removed from Coele-Syria, thus enabling Ptolemy to acquire Phoenicia too; reiterated at Justin 13.4. The will references reinforce it. The *Metz Epitome* 117 and *Romance* 3.32 both have Meleager in Coele-Syria rather than 'all Syria'.
78. McGing (2010), p. 98, for an example of Israel being cited as Coele-Syria.
79. Diodorus 18.6.3 for the geographical digression referring to Syria. That Coele-Syria included Phoenicia is reiterated by Diodorus at 18.43.2.
80. Arrian 3.8.6 and 5.25.5 as an example of 'Mesopotamian Syria' being referred to. The 'Mesopotamian Line' is also referred to in the *Metz Epitome* 117; Arrian, *Events After Alexander* 24.6.
81. Diodorus 17.64.5 for Menes' appointment.

82. Plutarch, *Eumenes* 3.6 stated Eumenes fled to Perdiccas but no location was given.
83. Diodorus 18.23.4 for Antigonus' flight; Plutarch, *Eumenes* 4.1 for the suggestion that both he and Eumenes were together in Cilicia. Diodorus 18.44–45, 50.1 and 18.45.2–47.3 for Alcetas' actions at Cretopolis and Termessus.
84. Atkinson (2009), p. 40 footnote 61, for Diodorus' wording concerning the fate of the funeral bier.
85. Diodorus 18.60.6 for Eumenes' possession of Alexander's throne, sceptre, weapons and insignia.
86. Arrian, *Events after Alexander* 1.43–45 for the seventy elephants left with Antigonus and Antipater keeping the remainder.
87. Arrian, *Events After Alexander* 1.28 for Perdiccas launching his campaign against Ptolemy from Damascus. Hill-Walton (1991), p. 49, for description of the ancient network of roads converging on Damascus. Samaria was garrisoned or settled by Alexander after the siege of Gaza; Curtius 4.8.10. St Jerome, *Kronographia* 1685 for its founding by Alexander and 1721 suggesting Perdiccas refounded it.
88. Diodorus 20.47.5, trans. from the Loeb Classical Library edition, 1954.
89. Billows (1990), p. 297, for Antigonus' tenure.
90. Strabo 12.8.15 and Livy 38.13.5 for the founding of Apamea. Appian, *Syrian Wars* 57 stated Seleucus Nikator named three cities after her; also Strabo 16.2.4. The Syrian tetrapolis consisted of Antioch, Apamea, Seleucia in Pieria and Laodicea.
91. Diodorus 18.37.3–4 for Alcetas' recovery of money from Tyre. Bellinger (1979), p. 84, for the observation on Laomedon's non-involvement.
92. For Laomedon's grant of Coele-Syria, see Arrian, *Events After Alexander* 1.5, Diodorus 18.3.1, Curtius 10.10.2, Justin 13.4.12, Appian, *Syrian Wars* 52, Dexippus FGrH 100 F8 2. Appian, *Syrian Wars* 52 for reference to the 'buying' of the satrapy. Diodorus 18.43.1–2 and Pausanias 1.6.4 for Ptolemy's hostility. See temporal discussion in Wheatley (1995), pp. 433–40. The likely date of Ptolemy's annexation was 321 BC and very shortly after the conference at Triparadeisus; Wheatley (1995) for dating discussion.
93. See Wheatley (1995), p. 437, for discussion of the lacuna after Diodorus 18.39.
94. Diodorus 18.73–74 for Eumenes entering Phoenicia.
95. Diodorus 19.57.1–2 for Ptolemy's and Cassander's envoy and demands to Antigonus.
96. Arrian, *Events After Alexander* 24.2, Justin 13.6.16 for Philoxenus' installation by Perdiccas. He was reconfirmed at Triparadeisus: Diodorus 18.39.6, Arrian, *Events After Alexander* 1.34. The 'Mesopotamian Line' is referred to in the *Metz Epitome* 117 and Arrian, *Events After Alexander* 24.6 for the Cyprus affair.
97. Stewart (1993), p. 294.
98. See Heckel (2006), p. 315 and text note 383, for Judeich's view that Laomedon was the original occupant. K. Schefeld convincingly made a case that the coffin was constructed before Abdalonymus' reign; see his review of Brunilde Sismondo Ridgway in the *American Journal of Archaeology* 73.4, October 1969, p. 482. Anson suggested Alexander's original sarcophagus would have been shipped up the Euphrates to Thapsacus and overland from there to Alexandria; see Anson (1986), p. 213. Anson (2013), p. 150, for the background to Abdalonymus; Curtius 4.1.16–26, Diodorus 17.47.1, Justin 11.10.7–9 for the Vulgate story.

99. Diodorus 18.26–28.
100. Stewart (1993), pp. 294–95, 297, 301, for analysis of the sarcophagus and description of the unarmed man being murdered, thought to be Perdiccas. For the panel on the Alexander Sarcophagus, and Arrhidaeus' possible portrayal, see discussion by V.A. Troncoso in Carney-Ogden (2010), p. 21 and footnote 53, and doubted in Heckel, *Sarcophagus* (2006), pp. 386–88.
101. Arrian, *Events After Alexander* 1.33 and Polyaenus 4.6.4 focused on money being the central grievance. Arrian, *Events After Alexander* 1.33, 1.39 for Attalus' presence at Triparadeisus. Many scholars accept Attalus, the Perdiccan general that commanded the fleet supporting the Egyptian invasion, was present; he later failed to unite with Eumenes. That seems unlikely. He may have managed to send communications to Eurydice, but as Alcetas had killed her mother, any Perdiccan support seems unlikely, especially with Peithon and Antigenes present, the murderers of Perdiccas.
102. The dissatisfaction of Peithon, Seleucus and Antigenes refers to their murder of Perdiccas.
103. Antipater would have benefited from the remnants of Leonnatus' troops and those of Craterus that had either crossed from Cilicia to Thessaly, or remained in Cilicia.
104. The similarity between Peithon and the 'son of Agenor' seems to have confused Diodorus, or a translator, when referencing Media. If Stasander and Stasanor were similarly confused, rather than strangely 'swapping' satrapies, they remained in place too.
105. Quoting Carney (1988), p. 385.
106. Quoting Green (2007), p. 11. Blackwell (1999) for further discussion of their roles.
107. The significance of the lack of patronymic observed and commented on in Carney-Ogden (2010), p. 44; Finlay (1973) for the specific grain deliveries of 76,000 Attic *medimni* (compared to a bushel) to Olympias and 50,000 to Cleopatra. Hammond (1985), p. 160, for Olympias' *prostates* role. Bagnall-Derow (2004), pp. 3–4, for the translated list of the grain shipments. Full discussion of the role of *prostasia* in Anson (1992).
108. Discussion on the roles of Olympias and Cleopatra in Epirus and Macedon in Alexander's final years in Carney (1988), pp. 396–97, Blackwell (1999), pp. 81–105, Anson (2013), p. 35. Plutarch 68.11 went as far as stating Olympias and Cleopatra planned to take over Epirus and Macedon from Antipater's control. Diodorus 17.108.7 for Olympias' involvement in the Harpalus affair. Blackwell (1999), p. 86, for Cleopatra's *prostasia*, pp. 81–105 for full discussion on Olympias' role and p. 88 for the status of women in Epirus. Blackwell (1999), pp. 89–91, for the grain shipments. For the death of Alexander Molossus, see Justin 12.2.4 and Blackwell (1999), p. 90, for Cleopatra's office as thearodoch. Blackwell (1999), p. 103, for the possible greater autonomy of the Epirote League states. Anson (2013), p. 21, for discussion on the sacral power vested in the Argead clan. Flower (1994), p. 190, for evidence of the higher social status of Etruscan women. Carney (2006), pp. 91–92, for Olympias' stance on Dodona. Hammond (1985), p. 156, and Thucydides 2.80.5 and the presidential role in Epirus.

109. Diodorus 19.59.4 reported that Antipater valued Phila's wisdom and consulted her on policy; she was charged with the defence of Cyprus late in Demetrius' reign, Diodorus 19.67.1, and she acted as a diplomat for Demetrius to Cassander, Plutarch, *Demetrius* 32.4. For Cratesipolis' actions at Sicyon, see Diodorus 19.67 and 20.37, Polyaenus 8, Plutarch, *Demetrius* 9. The roles of Phila, Cratesipolis, Cynnane and Olympias are discussed in Carney (1995), p. 389. Diodorus 19.16.4–5 for Stratonice's role in the sixteen-month siege that saw Docimus and Attalus finally captured, probably in Pisidia, though the location is not stated.
110. Quoting from Bury-Barber-Bevan-Tarn (1923), p. 11.
111. Plutarch 39.11 implied Alexander warned Antipater that Olympias might be planning to kill him and that Alexander kept her away from state affairs.
112. Quoting S. Ruzicka in Carney-Ogden (2005), p. 9.
113. See Heckel (2006), p. 90, for discussion of Cleopatra's age. See Carney (1988), p. 398, for Olympias and Cleopatra's ability to provide offspring. She had two children by Alexander of Epirus according to Plutarch, *Pyrrhus* 5.11: Cadmea and Neoptolemus.
114. Following the logic of, and quoting, Carney (1988), p. 399.
115. Diodorus 20.37.3–4 for confirmation of her suitors. As Anson (2014), p. 153, noted, any approach by Cassander must have been before he murdered Olympias in 315 BC and thus before he married Thessalonice soon after.
116. For Craterus' delay in crossing to Greece, see Heckel (2006), p. 98 and footnote 258.
117. Europa (or Caranus) was born just days before Philip died according to Athenaeus 13.557e, in mid-summer 336 BC according to Diodorus 17.2.3. According to Justin 9.7.12, she (or he) was murdered in her mother's arms by Olympias, who forced her mother to commit suicide by hanging, whilst Pausanias 8.7.5–7 claimed mother and daughter were burned in an oven or dragged over a brazier without Alexander's approval; Plutarch 10.8 confirmed Alexander's anger at treating her 'savagely'. The sex of the baby and whether there was more than one is debated: see Musgrave (1991), p. 7 footnote 23, for details, and Lane Fox (2011), p. 385. A full discussion on the significance of Alexander's sisters is given in Heckel (1988), pp. 55–59.
118. Diodorus 20.37.5 confirmed Antigonus governor of Sardis had been instructed not to let Cleopatra leave.
119. Diodorus 18.36.6 for Ptolemy being chosen as a guardian to the kings.
120. Plutarch, *Demetrius* 31.3–32.3 for a concise picture of the various intermarriages post-Ipsus. Ptolemy married Ptolemais to Demetrius the Besieger (Plutarch, *Demetrius* 32), Lysandra to Alexander V of Macedon (Cassander's youngest son by Thessalonice; Porphyry FGrH 695), Eirene to Eunostus king of Soli on Cyprus (Athenaeus 13.576e) and Arsinoe to Lysimachus (Pausanias 1.10.3); Carney-Ogden (2010), p. 131 and footnote 63, for detail. Pyrrhus married Antigone, a daughter of Ptolemy, and Demetrius married Deidameia, a daughter of Aeacides, so Pyrrhus' sister.
121. Quoting *Metz Epitome* 115, also *Romance* 3.32. Italics my own.
122. Following the argument of Anson (1992), p. 39; this is contra Hammond (1985), p. 158, who believed Olympias carried the title in Alexander's absence. Full discussion of the role of *prostasia* in Anson (1992).

123. Quoting Bosworth A to A (1988), p. 12. Diodorus 18.39.2; Arrian, *Events After Alexander* 1.30–31 for Eurydice's behaviour at Triparadeisus.
124. See Grant (2017), p. 733 ff.
125. Full discussion of the role of *prostasia* in Anson (1992).
126. Arrian 6.30.3 for Peucestas' ability to speak Persian.
127. Plutarch 77.6–7 for the death of Stateira and Drypetis.
128. Sisygambis allegedly died from self-imposed starvation five days after hearing of Alexander's death, see Curtius 10.5.19–25, Diodorus 17.118.3, Justin 13.1.5; for the Vulgate depiction as Alexander's second mother, Curtius 3.12.17, 5.2.22, Justin 13.1.5.
129. Curtius 10.5.23 for Sisygambis' reflections on the previous pogrom. For Ochus' pogroms, see Justin 10.1–10.3, Valerius Maximus 9.2.7.
130. See Heckel (2006), p. 181, for discussion. Ochus was left at Susa with Sisygambis and his sisters were never heard of again; see Curtius 5.2.17, Diodorus 17.67.1.
131. Curtius 10.5.23 suggested Sisygambis lamented that she had only one remaining child alive.
132. Plutarch, *Eumenes* 19.1–2 for Eumenes' children. Diodorus 19.35.5 for the daughters of Attalus; Heckel (2006), pp. 276–77, for discussion (F38–39).
133. Arrian 7.12.2 for Alexander's refusal to let the Asiatic children be repatriated to Macedon. This is reinforced by Diodorus 17.110.3 detailing the fund Alexander left for their upbringing and schooling.
134. Diodorus 20.20.1 for Heracles' being aged 17 when he was murdered by Cassander, and Justin 15.2.3 has Heracles in his fifteenth year. See discussion in Heckel (2006), p. 138. Brunt (1975), p. 28, suggests Heracles could have been born as early as 328 BC. Considering Justin's poor track record with identities, aged 17 is more convincing than 14; Justin's confusion (see 14.6.2 and 14.6.13), in which he claimed Heracles and his mother were murdered together, was actually a reference to Rhoxane and her son Alexander IV who, in 310 BC, would have been close to his thirteenth year; see Wheatley (1998), p. 19, for discussion.
135. Grant (2017), p. 733 ff, for arguments on Barsine' family. For her capture, see Curtius 3.13.12–17 for the captive list. Curtius 5.9.1 and 6.5.2 for Artabazus taking refuge in Macedon. The date of the arrival at Pella is uncertain; see Heckel (1987), p. 116 footnote 4. Alexander would have still been young (perhaps 8) when Artabazus and family departed *ca.* 348 BC, as suggested at Diodorus 16.52.1–4; the archonship of Callimachus is referred to 349/348 BC though communications, pleas and exonerations would have taken time, so we may add a year or so to the departure of Artabazus from Macedon. Heckel (2006), p. 275 (F12), for discussion of the wife captured at Damascus.
136. Curtius 3.12.21–23 for Barsine's descriptions and Arrian 4.19 for similar descriptions of both Rhoxane and Darius' wife. Discussed at Tarn (1948), p. 333, Plutarch 21.6.
137. See Arrian 7.4.6, trans. from the Oxford World Classics edition, 2013, and Plutarch, *Eumenes* 1.3, trans. from the Loeb Classical Library edition, 1919, for the marriages. See Grant (2017), p. 733 ff, for full discussion.
138. Plutarch, *Eumenes* 7.1 for Pharnabazus' support for Eumenes.

139. Arrian 7.4.4 and Curtius 10.3.11–13 for Alexander's additional marriages to Parysatis and the daughter of Darius III.
140. See Heckel (2006), p. 379, for the stemma of Artabazus.
141. See Grant (2017), p. 737 ff.
142. Tarn (1948), pp. 378–99, clearly demonstrated later Roman corruptions of the so-called last plans.
143. For the importance of the lesser-known Dion, see Arrian 1.11.1–2 and Diodorus 17.16.3–4. For Heracles' former possession of Amphipolis and Olynthus, see Carney-Ogden (2010), p. 74.
144. Requests for divinity aside, Arrian 7.29.4 confirmed Alexander saw himself as the son of Ammon, and 7.20.1 with Strabo 16.1.11 stated he planned to attack the Arabs to be worshipped as a third god. For the Athenian Assembly's refusal to grant Alexander's deification, see Polybius 12.12b.3, Deinarchus, *Against Demosthenes* 1.94, and for the fine to Demades who proposed the bill, Athenaeus 6.251b, Aelian 5.12. Aelian 5.12 and Strabo 16.1.11 cited Aristobulus as confirming Alexander had laid claims to divinity. However, Flower (1994), pp. 259–60, points out that Theopompus seemed to have known of an Alexander cult in Anatolia worshiping him as Alexander-Zeus in his lifetime.

Chapter 10: Epitaph in Rome, Obituary Today

1. Diodorus 20.81.3 based on the trans. from the Loeb Classical Library edition, 1954. See Tarn (1939), p. 132, for a discussion on whether Diodorus 20.81.3 drew from the *Romance* and Letter to the Rhodians, as proposed by Ausfeld. Heckel (1988), p. 2, suggested Hieronymus was the source.
2. Curtius 10.10.5.
3. Plutarch, *Apophthegms* or *Sayings of Kings and Commanders* 207D8, based on the trans. by E. Hinton, William W. Goodwin, Little Brown and Co., Boston, 1878.
4. For the use of *inuictus*, see Spencer (2002), p. 168. Atkinson (2009), p. 245, for discussion on the last sighting of Alexander's body in Alexandria. Septimus Severus had the tomb locked according to Cassius Dio 7513.2, but Caracalla, who saw himself as a reincarnation of Alexander, allegedly saw the tomb in AD 215. De Polignac (1999), p. 8, for discussion of the emperors emulating Alexander. For Crassus thinking he was following in Alexander's footsteps, see Cassius Dio 40.17 and 68.29.1, 68.30–31 for Trajanus' emulation.
5. *Historia Augusta, Alexander Severus* 50 for the Silver Shields. Further discussion in Roisman (2012), p. 243. Stewart (1993), p. 348, for Caracalla's title from the anonymous *Epitome de Caesaribus Sexti Aurelia Victoris* 21.4. Herodian 4.8.9 for Caracalla's deposits and Cassius Dio 78.7.1 for his withdrawals.
6. *Historia Augusta, Antoninus Caracalla* 2.1–3.
7. However, Cicero thought that at times he entertained with 'pretty fictions' and was a 'better orator than historian'; Cicero, *Brutus* 43. Cleitarchus was popular in Romae and he was cited as a source by Diodorus, Plutarch, Strabo, Athenaeus and Diogenes Laertius, to name a few.

8. Suetonius, *Claudius* 44.
9. Suetonius, *Claudius* 44.3.
10. Tacitus 12.66–67.
11. For Iollas as official cupbearer, see *Romance* 3.31.4, *Metz Epitome* 96, Arrian, 7.27.2 and Plutarch 74.2. For Ptolemy's role as 'taster', see Robinson (1953), p. 78, for full citation from Chares.
12. *Metz Epitome* 99, trans. from Heckel-Yardley (2004), pp. 218–89; also *Romance* 3.32.
13. Robinson (1953) believed Callisthenes himself drew from the Royal Diaries, as did later historians, yet paradoxically he believed the 'thin sources' in 327–326 BC were due to Eumenes' loss of the documents in a tent fire rather than Callisthenes' death. This is paradoxical, for while Callisthenes is mentioned as a source in later works, the *Journal* is never mentioned aside from the fragment dealing with Alexander's death.
14. Quoting Pearson (1960), p. 261.
15. For full arguments on the 'Alexandrian monopoly', see Grant (2017), p. 206 ff.
16. Arrian 7.27.3
17. Curtius 10.5.5, Arrian 7.26.3, Diodorus 17.117.4.
18. Bevan (1913), p. 32, and quoting Adams (1996), p. 33, on 'political freedom'.
19. Quoting Whitmarsh (2002), p. 175, on paradigms.
20. See discussion in Bury-Barber-Bevan-Tarn (1923), p. 26. The name Stoicism comes from the *Stoa Poikile* or 'painted arch' from where Zeno commenced teaching in the Agora at Athens. That the early successors declared themselves Stoics was observed by Murray (1915), p. 47. Long (1986), p. 18, for explanation of *logos*.
21. See discussion on Polybius' use of *tyche* in Brouwer (2011), pp. 111–32, and McGing (2010), pp. 195–201.
22. Cicero's references to Panaetius can be found in his *De Finibus* 4.9 in the *De Officiis* 1.26, *Laelius De Amicitia* 27; *Pro Murena* 31; *De Natura Deorum-Velleius* 1.13.3.
23. Cicero, *De Officiis* 1.35 for his thoughts on moral duty.
24. Brown (1949) for the career of Crates and his links to both philosophical schools.
25. Pitcher (2009), p. vii.
26. Arrian excerpts from 1.1.1–3. Here *basileia* meaning 'kingship' not queen, differentiated in Greek by a diacritic (not used here).
27. Arrian 7.5.2–3.
28. Lucian, *How to Write History* 2.40–41, noted that many people believed Homer's account of Achilles' deeds as he wrote long after the hero's death and hence had no agenda as a historian. Arrian stated something similar in his opening page of his Alexander biography.
29. Lucian and Arrian were broadly contemporaries. However, Lucian outlived him and made reference to Arrian's works with which he was undoubtedly familiar. We propose Arrian's opening statement about Ptolemy's may in fact mirror Ptolemy's opening, which Lucian may also have read.
30. Both Plato and Pythagoras objected to suicide except in exceptional circumstances. See Plato, *Phaedo* 61d–e; Pythagoras prohibited suicide; see discussion in Riedweg (2005), p. 110.

31. Discussed in Long (1986), p. 206. Also see Cicero, *On the ends of good and evil* (*De Finibus*) 3.60–61. The Moirae were the three parthenogenous daughters of the Goddess of Necessity: Clotho, Lacheis and Atropus. Under the Roman Stoic doctrine, the meanings of fate and fortune became hardly discernible. See discussion in Levene (1993), p. 13.
32. Tacitus 6.29; see Griffin (1986), p. 193, for full discussion on Tiberian treatment of suicide.
33. Following Griffin (1986), p. 193, and Pliny 2.5.27 and 7.5.190.
34. Discussed in Magee (1998), p. 45.
35. Plato, *Phaedo* 67a–68b.
36. Justin 12.15–16.
37. See Baynham (1995), p. 105, for a discussion of *tyche* being important in Hellenistic biography. Demetrius of Phalerum, *On Fortune* 29.21.1–7 discussed in Bosworth-Baynham (2000), p. 295. Also Billows' discussion on Polybius and *tyche* referenced in Bosworth-Baynham (2000), pp. 294–95.
38. See Grant (2017), chapter titled 'Comets, Colophons and Curtius Rufus'.
39. Curtius 10.10.5–6.
40. Chugg (2009), p. 5, refutes the use of the first person singular in favour of the first person plural, and in other translations 'we' is used; as an example the translation by John C. Rolfe of 1946 published by the University of Michigan. Nevertheless, it was not unusual for an author to use the plural 'we' when referring to his own efforts and this does not convincingly argue that Curtius was paraphrasing Cleitarchus, for example. Polybius switched between singular and plural where emphasis demanded it, and in particular to stress the veracity of either eyewitness reporting or personal vouching for facts; discussion in Marmodoro-Hill (2013), pp. 199–204.
41. Diodorus 20.81.3, based on the trans. from the Loeb Classical Library edition, 1954. See Tarn (1939), p. 132, for a discussion on whether Diodorus 20.81.3 drew from the *Romance* and Letter to the Rhodians, as proposed by Ausfeld. Heckel (1988), p. 2, suggested Hieronymus was the source.
42. *Romance* 3.32.5–7 and *Metz Epitome* 101–102. Arrian 7.27.3 for his recounting the tradition of Alexander's attempt to disappear into the Euphrates.
43. See Hornblower (1981), pp. 90–96, for full discussion on Diodorus' sources and use of Cleitarchus and Hieronymus.
44. I argue Hieronymus published before Cleitarchus; see Grant (2017), p. 206 ff.
45. Diodorus 18.2.1, trans. from the Loeb Classical Library edition, 1947.
46. Diodorus 20.20.1, 20.28.1 for later reference of Heracles.
47. Quoting Steel (1905), pp. 402–23, and following Hamilton (1988), p. 445, for the dating.
48. Dating arguments well summed up by Atkinson (2009), pp. 3–9, and Baynham (1998), p. 206, especially for Claudian supporters. Also see Tarn (1948), pp. 111–16, for late dating arguments.
49. See Grant (2017), p. 668 ff.
50. See Grant (2017), p. 671 ff.
51. Quoting Wilkes (1972), p. 178.

52. See Grant (2017), p. 68 ff.
53. See Suetonius, *Claudius* 43–46, trans. from the Loeb Classical Library edition, 1914. Britannicus had become the heir designate of Claudius under the name Tiberius Claudius Germanicus.
54. Discussed in chapter titled 'The Assassin's Assembly'.
55. Milns (1966), p. 502.
56. Aelian 3.32 for Alexander playing the cithara, like Nero.
57. Suetonius, *Nero* 19 for the phalanx. *Suda* α 1128= FGrH 618 T2 for Alexander of Aegae.
58. Atkinson (1996), pp. xvi, 218, and Atkinson (1963), p. 125. He was specifically referring to the studies of Droysen, Berve, Tarn, Schachermeyr and Badian.
59. Expanding upon the wording of Badian (1968), p. 189. Author italics.
60. Quoting Bosworth-Baynham (2000), p. 240.

BIBLIOGRAPHY

The English titles of ancient works are often the result of a very liberal translation process. I have used the most popular and accepted names.

Abbreviations – Ancient Authors

Aelian: *Historical Miscellany*
Arrian: *The Campaign of Alexander*
Athenaeus: *The Dinner Philosophers*
Cassius Dio: *Roman History*
Curtius: *History of Alexander the Great*
Dexippus: précis by Photius of Dexippus' epitome of Arrian's *Events After Alexander*
Diodorus: *Library of World History*
Diogenes Laertius: *Lives and Opinions of Eminent Philosophers*
Herodian: *History of the Empire From the Death of Marcus Aurelius*
Herodotus: *The Histories*
Josephus: *Jewish Antiquities*
Justin: *Epitome of the Philippic History of Pompeius Trogus*
Juvenal: *Satires*
Livy: *The Early History of Rome*
Nepos: *Eumenes; Lives of Eminent Commanders*
Pausanias: *Guide to Ancient Greece*
Pliny: *Natural History*
Plutarch: *The Life of Alexander from his Parallel Lives*
Plutarch: *On the Fortune or the Virtue of Alexander The Great*
Polyaenus: *Stratagems of War*
Polybius: *Histories*
Romance: *The Greek Alexander Romance*
Strabo: *Geography*
Suetonius: *About the Life of the Caesars*
Tacitus: *Annals*
Thucydides: *History of The Peloponnesian War*
Valerius Maximus: *Nine Books of Memorable Deeds and Sayings*
Xenophon: *The Education of Cyrus*

Modern Abbreviations

FGrH: *Fragmente der griechischen Historiker*, F. Jacoby (1926–58) Leiden.

Modern Bibliography

For clarity, only the publication being referred to in the book is italicized, though convention would also italicise the journal or publication in which the article appeared.

W.L. Adams, '*Antipater and Cassander, Generalship on Restricted Resources in the Fourth Century*', The Ancient World 10 (1985), pp.79–88.

W.L. Adams, '*Cassander, Alexander IV and the Tombs at Vergina*', The Ancient World 22, no. 2 (1991), pp.27–33.

W.L. Adams, '*In the wake of Alexander the Great: the impact of conquest on the Aegean world*', The Ancient World 27, no, 1 (1996), pp.29–37.

J.K. Anderson, *Ancient Greek Horsemanship* (University of California Press, 1961).

J.K. Anderson, *Military Theory and Practice in the Age of Xenophon* (University of California Press, 1970).

E.M. Anson, '*The Siege of Nora: A Source Conflict*', Greek, Roman and Byzantine Studies, 18 (1977), pp.251–56.

E.M. Anson, '*Discrimination and Eumenes of Cardia*', The Ancient World 3 (1980), pp.55–59.

E.M. Anson, '*The Hypaspists: Macedonia's Professional Citizen-Soldiers*', Historia 34 (1985), pp.246–48.

E.M. Anson, '*Diodorus and the Dating of Triparadeisus*', The American Journal of Philology 107, no. 2 (1986), pp.208–17.

E.M. Anson, '*Antigonus, the Satrap of Phrygia*', Historia: Zeitschrift für Alte Geschichte 37, no. 4 (1988), pp.471–77.

E.M. Anson, '*The Evolution of the Macedonian Army Assembly (330–315 BC)*', Historia: Zeitschrift für Alte Geschichte 40, no. 2 (1991), pp.230–47.

E.M. Anson, '*Craterus and the Prostasia*', Classical Philology 87 (January 1992), pp.38–43.

E.M. Anson, '*The "Ephemerides" of Alexander the Great*', Historia: Zeitschrift für Alte Geschichte 45, no. 4 (1996), pp.501–04.

E.M. Anson, '*The Dating of Perdiccas' Death and the Assembly at Triparadeisus*', Greek, Roman and Byzantine Studies 43 (2003), pp.373–90.

E.M. Anson, *Eumenes of Cardia: A Greek amongst Macedonians* (Brill, 2004).

E.M. Anson, *Alexander the Great, Themes and Issues* (Bloomsbury, 2013).

E.M. Anson, *Alexander's Heirs, the Age of the Successors* (Wiley Blackwell, 2014).

I. Arnaoutoglou, *Ancient Greek Laws* (Routledge, 1998).

Z. Archibald, J. Davies and V. Gabrielsen (eds), *Making, Moving and Managing, The New World of Ancient Economies 323–31 BC* (Oxbow, 2005).

J. Arthur-Montagne, '*Persuasion, Emotion, and the Letters of the Alexander Romance*', Ancient Narrative 11 (2014), pp.159–89.

J.E. Atkinson, '*Primary Sources and the Alexanderreich*', Acta Classica 6 (1963), pp.125–37.

J.E. Atkinson, '*A Commentary on Q. Curtius Rufus' Historiae Alexandri Magni, Books 5 to 7.2*', Acta Classica, Supplementum 1 (1994).

J.E. Atkinson, review of A.B. Bosworth, *Alexander and the East: the Tragedy of Triumph* (Clarendon Press, (1996).

J.E. Atkinson, '*Q Curtius Rufus' Historiae Alexandri Magni*', Aufstieg und Niedergang der römischen Welt II, no. 34.4 (1997), pp.3447–83.

J.E. Atkinson, '*Alexander's Last Days: Malaria and Mind Games*', Acta Classica 52 (2009), pp.23–46.

J.E. Atkinson and J.C. Yardley (trans.), *Curtius Rufus, Histories of Alexander the Great, Book 10* (Oxford University Press, (2009).

A. Ausfeld, '*Das angebliche testament Alexanders des Grossen*', Rheinisches Museum Für Philologie 50 (1895), pp.357–66.

S. Avramović, *The Rhetra of Epithadeus and Testament in Spartan Law* (University of Belgrade School of Law, Alan Watson Foundation, 2006).

E. Badian, '*A King's Notebooks*', Harvard Studies in Classical Philology 72 (1968), pp.183–204.

E. Badian, '*Nearchus the Cretan*', Yale Classical Studies 24 (1975), pp.147–87).

R.S. Bagnall and P. Derow (eds), *The Hellenistic Period, Historical Sources in Translation* (Blackwell, 2004).

J. Barnes, *The Cambridge Companion to Aristotle* (Cambridge University Press, 1995).

E.J. Baynham, '*An Introduction to the Metz Epitome: its Tradition and Value*', Antichthon 29 (1995), pp.60–77.

E.J. Baynham, *Alexander the Great, The Unique History of Quintus Curtius* (University of Michigan Press, 1998; 2004 edition).

A.R. Bellinger, *Essays on the Coinage of Alexander the Great* (Sanford J. Durst Numismatic Publications, 1979).

R. Behrwald, '*Review of J. Engels Augusteische Oikumenegeographie und Universalhistorie im Werk Strabons von Amaseia*', Geographica Historica 12 (1999), p.464.

R.M. Berthold, *Rhodes in the Hellenistic Age* (Cornell University Press, 1984).

H. Berve, *Das Alexandererreich auf prosopographischer Grundlage* (C.H. Beck, 1926).

E.R. Bevan, *The House of Seleucus* (Ares Publishers, 1902; 1985 edition).

E.R. Bevan, *Stoics and Sceptics* (Clarendon Press, 1913).

E.R. Bevan, *The House of Ptolemy: A History of Egypt under the Ptolemaic Dynasty* (Ares Publishers, 1927; 1968 edition).

R.A. Billows, *Antigonos the One-Eyed and the Creation of the Hellenistic State* (University of California Press, 1990; 1997 edition).

J.D. Bing, '*A Further Note on Cyinda / "Kundi"*', Historia: Zeitschrift für Alte Geschichte 22, no. 2, 2nd qtr (1973), pp.346–50.

C.W. Blackwell, *In the Absence of Alexander, Harpalus and the Failure of Macedonian Authority* (Peter Lang Publishing, 1999).

C.W. Blackwell, '*Athens and Macedonia, in the Absence of Alexander*', in C.W. Blackwell (ed.), Dēmos: Classical Athenian Democracy, July 1 (2005).

A.W. Blyth, *Poisons: Their Effects and Detection* (Charles Griffin and Company, 1906).

T. Boiy, *Late Achaemenid and Hellenistic Babylon* (Peeters Publishers and Department of Oriental Studies, 2004).

E.N. Borza, *In the Shadow of Olympus, The Emergence of Macedon* (Princeton University Press, 1990).

E.N. Borza, *Makedonika*, Essays by Eugene N. Borza (Regina Books, 1995).

E.N. Borza and O. Palagia, '*The Chronology of the Macedonian Royal Tombs at Vergina*', Jahrbuch des Deutschen Archäologisches Instituts 122 (2007), pp.81–125.

A.B. Bosworth and E.J. Baynham, *Alexander the Great in Fact and Fiction* (Oxford University Press, 2000).

A.B. Bosworth, '*History and Rhetoric in Curtius Rufus, A Commentary on Q. Curtius Rufus' "Historiae Alexandri Magni", Books 3 and 4*' by J.E. Atkinson, review in Classical Philology 78, no. 2 (April 1983), pp.150–61.

A.B. Bosworth, *From Arrian to Alexander: Studies in Historical Interpretation* (Clarendon Press, 1988).

A.B. Bosworth, *Conquest and Empire, The Reign of Alexander The Great* (Cambridge University Press, 1988).

A.B. Bosworth, '*Philip III Arrhidaeus and the Chronology of the Successors*', Chiron 22 (1992), pp.55–81.

A.B. Bosworth, '*Perdiccas and the Kings*', Classical Quarterly 63 (1993), pp.420–27.

A.B. Bosworth, '*In Search of Cleitarchus: Review-discussion of Luisa Prandi: Fortuna è Realtà dell' Opera di Clitarco*', Historia Einzelschriften 104 (1996), p.203.

A.B. Bosworth, *Alexander in the East, The Tragedy of Triumph* (Oxford University Press, 1996).

A.B. Bosworth, *The Legacy of Alexander, Politics, Warfare and Propaganda under the Successors* (Oxford University Press, 2002).

A.B. Bosworth, '*Mountain and Molehill? Cornelius Tacitus and Quintus Curtius*', Classical Quarterly (December 2004), pp.551–67.

J.R. Brandt and J.W. Iddeng, *Greek and Roman Festivals, Content, Meaning and Practice* (Oxford University Press, 2012).

P. Briant, '*Antigone le Borgne*', Annales littéraires de l'Université de Besançon 152 (1973), pp.366–68.

P. Briant, *Alexander the Great and his Empire, A Short Introduction* (Princeton University Press, 1974; 2012 edition).

T.C. Brickhouse and N.D. Smith, *The Trial and Execution of Socrates* (Oxford University Press, 2001).

R. Brouwer, '*Polybius and Stoic Tyche*', Greek, Roman and Byzantine Studies 51 (2011), pp.111–32.

T.S. Brown, '*Hieronymus of Cardia*', The American Historical Review 52, no. 4 (1947), pp.684–96.

T.S. Brown, *Onesicritus: A Study in Hellenistic Historiography* (Ares Publishers, 1949; 1981 edition).

T.S. Brown, '*Clitarchus*', The American Journal of Philology 71, no. 2 (1950), pp.134–55.

P.A. Brunt, '*Alexander, Barsine and Heracles*', Rivista di Filologia di Instruzione Classica 103 (1975), pp.22–34.

J.B. Bury, E.A. Barber, E. Bevan and W.W. Tarn, *The Hellenistic Age: Aspects of Hellenistic Civilization* (Cambridge University Press, 1923).

E.D. Carney, '*The Career of Adea-Eurydike*', Historia 36 (1987), pp.496–502.
E.D. Carney, '*The Sisters of Alexander the Great: Royal Relicts*', Historia: Zeitschrift für Alte Geschichte 37, no. 4 (1988), pp.385–404.
E.D. Carney, '*Women and Basileia: Legitimacy and Female Political Action in Macedonia*', The Classical Journal 90, no. 4 (1995), pp.367–91.
E.D. Carney, *Olympias, Mother of Alexander the Great* (Routledge, 2006).
E.D. Carney and D. Ogden (eds), *Philip II and Alexander the Great, Father and Son, Lives and Afterlives* (Oxford University Press, 2010).
P. Cartledge, *Alexander the Great: The Hunt for a New Past* (Pan Macmillan, 2005).
L. Casson, *Everyday Life in Ancient Egypt* (The John Hopkins University Press, 2001; expanded edition from the original published in 1975 as *The Horizon Book of Daily Life in Egypt*).
J. Champion, *Antigonus the One-Eyed, Greatest of the Successors* (Pen & Sword Military, 2014).
A.H. Chroust, '*Aristotle's Last Will and Testament*', Wiener Studien 80 (1967), pp.90–114.
A.H. Chroust, '*Estate Planning in Hellenic Antiquity: Aristotle's Last Will and Testament*', Notre Dame Lawyer 45 (1970), pp.629–62.
A.H. Chroust, *Aristotle: New Light on his Life and on Some of his Lost Works, Volume 1, some novel interpretations of the man and his life* (Routledge, 1973; 2016 edition).
A.M. Chugg, '*The Sarcophagus of Alexander the Great?*', Greece and Rome 49, no.1 (2002), pp.8–26.
A.M. Chugg, *The Quest for the Tomb of Alexander the Great* (Lulu.Com, 2007).
A.M. Chugg, *The Death of Alexander the Great, a Reconstruction of Cleitarchus* (AMC Publications, 2009; 2010 edition).
L. Cilliers and F.P. Retief, '*Poisons, Poisoning and the Drug Trade in Ancient Rome*', Akroterion 45 (2000), pp.88–100.
A.W. Collins, '*The office of Chiliarch under Alexander and the Successors*', Phoenix 22 (2001), pp.259–83.
D. Collins, *Magic in the Ancient Greek World* (Blackwell Publishing, 2008).
J.M. Cook, *The Persian Empire* (Schochen Books, 1983).
C.N.D. Costa, *Lucian Selected Dialogues* (Oxford University Press, 2005).
F. Cumont, *The Oriental Religions in Roman Paganism* (The Open Court Publishing Company, 1911).
W.S. Davis, *A Day in Old Athens* (IndyPublish.com, 1914).
F. de Polignac, '*From the Mediterranean to Universality? The Myth of Alexander, Yesterday and Today*', Mediterranean Historical Review 14, no. 1 (1999), pp.1–17.
A.M. Devine, '*Diodorus' Account of the Battle of Paraitacene (317 BCE)*', The Ancient World 12, nos 3–4 (1985), pp.75–86.
A.M. Devine, '*Diodorus' Account of the Battle of Gabiene*', The Ancient World 12, nos 3–4 (1985), pp.87–96.
R. Drews, '*The Babylonian Chronicles and Berossus*', Iraq 37, no. 1 (spring 1975), pp,39–55.
J.G. Droysen, *Geschichte des Hellenismus I, Geschichte Alexanders des Grossen* (Gotha, 1877).
W.M. Ellis, *Ptolemy of Egypt* (Routledge, 1994).
D.W. Engels, '*A Note on Alexander's Death*', Classical Philology 73, no. 3 (1978), pp.224–28.

D.W. Engels, *Alexander the Great and the Logistics of the Macedonian Army* (University of California Press, 1978).

R.M. Errington, '*Bias in Ptolemy's History of Alexander*', Classical Quarterly, New Series 19 (1969), pp.233–42.

R.M. Errington, '*From Babylon to Triparadeisus: 323–320 BC*', Journal of Hellenic Studies 90 (1970), pp.49–77.

A. Erskine, '*Life After Death: Alexandria and the Body of Alexander*', Greece and Rome 49, no. 2 (October 2002), pp.163–79.

M.I. Finlay, *The Ancient Economy* (University of California Press, 1973; second edition, 1985).

M.A. Flower, *Theopompus of Chios, History and Rhetoric in the Fourth Century BC* (Clarendon Press, 1994).

W. Fortenbaugh and E. Schütrumpf (eds), *Demetrius of Phalerum* (Transaction Publishers, 2000).

P.M. Fraser, *Cities of Alexander the Great* (Clarendon Press, 1996).

R.A. Gabriel, *Soldiers' Lives through History – The Ancient World* (Greenwood, 2006).

R.A. Gabriel, *Philip II of Macedonia, Greater than Alexander*, (Potomac Books Inc., 2010).

M.J. Geller, '*Astronomical Diaries and Corrections of Diodorus*', Bulletin of the School of Oriental and African Studies, University of London 53, no. 1 (1990), pp.1–7.

J. Goralski, '*Arrian's Events after Alexander, Summary of Photius and Selected Fragments*', The Ancient World 19, nos 3–4 (1989), pp.81–108.

H.B. Gottschalk, *Heraclitus of Pontus* (Oxford University Press, 1980).

P. Goukowski, *Essai sur les origins du mythe d'Alexandre, vol 1* (Publications de l'Universite de Nancy, 1978).

J.D. Granger, *Alexander the Great Failure* (Continuum Books, 2007).

F. Granier, *Die makedonische Heeresversammlung: Ein Beitrag zum antiken Staatsrecht* (Munchener Beitrage zur Papyrusforchung) (Munich, C.H. Beck, 1931).

D. Grant, *In Search of the Lost Testament of Alexander the Great* (Matador Press, 2017).

D. Grant, *Unearthing the Family of Alexander the Great, the Remarkable Discovery of the Royal Tombs of Macedon* (Pen & Sword History, 2019).

D. Grant, *Alexander the Great, A Battle for Truth and Fiction: the ancient sources and why they can't be trusted* (2022).

P.M. Green, *Alexander the Great* (Book Club Associates, 1970; 1973 edition).

P.M. Green, *Alexander of Macedon, 356–323 BC: A Historical Biography* (University of California Press, 1974; 1991 edition).

P.M. Green, *The Hellenistic Age: A Short History* (Random House, London, 2007).

M. Griffin, '*Philosophy, Cato and Roman Suicide*', Greece and Rome 33, no. 2 (October 1986), pp.192–202.

G.T. Griffiths, *The Mercenaries of the Hellenistic World* (Ares Publishers, 1935; 1984 edition).

M.D. Grmek, *Diseases in the Ancient Greek World* (The Johns Hopkins University Press, 1989).

R.A. Hadley, '*A Possible Lost Source for the Career of Eumenes of Kardia*', Historia: Zeitschrift für Alte Geschichte 50, no. 1, 1st quarter (2001), pp.3–33.

J.R. Hamilton, '*The Date of Quintus Curtius Rufus*', Historia: Zeitschrift für Alte Geschichte 37 (1988).
N.G.L. Hammond, '*Philip's Tomb in Historical Context*', Greek, Roman and Byzantine Studies 19, no.4, (1978), pp.331–50.
N.G.L. Hammond, '*Some Macedonian Offices: c. 336–309 BC*', Journal of Hellenic Studies 105 (1985), pp.156–60.
N.G.L. Hammond, '*The Royal Journal of Alexander*', Historia 37 (1988), pp.129–50.
N.G.L. Hammond, '*Aspects of Alexander's Journal and Ring in His Last Days*', The American Journal of Philology 110, no. 1, (spring 1989), pp.155–60.
N.G.L. Hammond, *The Miracle that was Macedonia* (Sidgwick & Jackson, 1991).
N.G.L. Hammond, *Sources for Alexander the Great: An Analysis of Plutarch's Life and Arrian's Anabasis Alexandrou* (Cambridge University Press, 1993).
N.G.L. Hammond, *Collected Studies III, Alexander and his Successors in Macedonia* (Adolf M. Hakkert, 1994).
N.G.L. Hammond, '*Portents, Prophesies and Dreams in Diodorus books 14–17*', Roman and Byzantine Studies 39, no. 4 (1998), pp.407–28.
N.G.L. Hammond and G.T. Griffith, *A History of Macedonia: Volume II: 550–336 B.C.* (Oxford University Press, 1979).
N.G.L. Hammond and F.W. Walbank, *A History of Macedonia* (Oxford University Press, 1988).
R. Hannah, *Greek and Roman Calendars, Constructions of Time on the Classical World* (Gerald Duckworth and Company, 2005).
M.H. Hansen, *The Athenian Democracy in the Age of Demosthenes, Structure, Principles and Ideology* (University of Oklahoma Press, 1999).
V.D. Hanson (ed.), *Hoplites, The Classical Greek Battle Experience* (Routledge, 1991).
V.M. Harris, *Ancient Curious and Famous Wills* (Little Brown and Company, 1911).
W.V. Harris, *Dreams and Experience in Classical Antiquity* (Harvard University Press, 2009).
M.B. Hatzopoulos, *Macedonian Institutions under the Kings 1, A Historical and Epigraphic Study* (Meletemata 22, 1996).
H. Hauben, '*The First War of the Successors (321BC): Chronological and Historical Problems*', Ancient Society 8 (1977), pp.85–120.
W. Heckel, '*The "Somatophylakes" of Alexander the Great: Some Thoughts*', Historia: Zeitschrift für Alte Geschichte 28, no. 1, 1st quarter (1978), pp.224–28.
W. Heckel, '*On Attalus and Atalante*', Classical Quarterly 28, no. 2, (1978), pp.377–82.
W Heckel, *Introduction to Quintus Curtius Rufus, The History of Alexander* (Penguin, 1984).
W. Heckel, '*Fifty-Two Anonymae in the History of Alexander*', Historia: Zeitschrift für Alte Geschichte 36, no. 1, 1st quarter (1987), pp.114–19.
W. Heckel, *The Last Days and Testament of Alexander the Great* (Franz Steiner Verlag GMBH, 1988).
W. Heckel, *The Marshals of Alexander's Empire* (Routledge, 1992).
W. Heckel, review of N.G.L. Hammond, *Sources for Alexander the Great: An Analysis of Plutarch's Life and Arrian's Anabasis Alexandrou* (Cambridge University Press, 1993; in the Bryn Mawr Classical Review 97.4.8).

W. Heckel, '*Mazaeus, Callisthenes and the Alexander Sarcophagus*', Historia: Zeitschrift für Alte Geschichte 55, no. 4 (2006), pp.385–96.
W. Heckel, *Who's Who in the Age of Alexander the Great* (Blackwell Publishing, 2006).
W. Heckel, '*Nicanor son of Balacrus*', Greek, Roman and Byzantine Studies 47 (2007), pp.401–12.
W. Heckel and R. Jones, *Macedonian Warrior, Alexander's elite infantryman* (Osprey Publishing, 2006).
W. Heckel and J.C. Yardley, *Alexander the Great: Historical Sources in Translation* (Blackwell Publishing, 2004).
W. Heckel, J.C. Yardley and P. Wheatley, *Justin: Epitome of the Philippic History of Pompeius Trogus, Volume II: Books 13–15: The Successors to Alexander the Great* (Clarendon Press, 2011).
C. Higbie, *The Lindian Chronicle and the Greek Creation of Their Past* (Oxford University Press, 2003).
J. Hornblower, *Hieronymus of Cardia* (Oxford University Press, 1981).
C. Huffman, *Philolaus of Croton: Pythagorean and Presocratic: A Commentary on the Fragments and Testimonia with Interpretive Essays* (Cambridge University Press).
G. Hutchinson, '*Poison Arrows*', British Medical Journal (8 March 1997).
G. Ifrah, *The Universal History of Numbers, from Prehistory to the Invention of the Computer* (John Wiley and Sons, 2000).
F. Jacoby, *Die Fragmente der griechischen Historiker I–II* (FGrHist) (Berlin, 1923–1958).
W.H.S. Jones, *Hippocrates Collected Works I* (Harvard University Press, 1868).
D.B. Kaufman, '*Poisons and Poisoning Among the Romans*', Classical Philology 27, no. 2, (April 1932), pp.156–67.
R.B. Kebric, *In the Shadow of Macedon: Duris of Samos* (Franz Steiner Verlag GMBH, 1977).
G. Kenyon, *The Paleography of Greek Papyri* (Ares Publishers, 1899; 1998 edition).
P.T. Keyser, '*The Last Will and Testament of Ajax*', Illinois Classical Studies 33–34, (2011), pp.109–26.
R. Lane Fox, *Alexander the Great* (Penguin, 1973; 1986 edition).
R. Lane Fox, *The Search for Alexander* (Little Brown and Company, 1980).
R. Lane Fox (ed.), *Brill's Companion to Ancient Macedon, Studies in the Archaeology and History of Macedon, 650 BC–300 AD* (Brill, 2011).
D.S. Levene, *Religion in Livy* (Brill, 1993).
R. Lock, '*The Macedonian Army Assembly in the Time of Alexander the Great*', Classical Philology 72, no. 2 (1977), pp.91–107.
A.A. Long, *Hellenistic Philosophy: Stoics, Epicureans, Sceptics* (University of California Press, 1986).
A. Luch (ed.), *Molecular, Clinical and Environmental Toxicology, Volume 1: Molecular Toxicology* (Birkhäuser Verlag AG, 2009).
B. Magee, *The Story of Philosophy* (Dorling Kindersley Ltd, 1998).
G. Marasco (ed.), *Autobiographies and Memoirs in Antiquity* (Brill, 2011).
R. Margotta, *The Story of Medicine* (Golden Press, 1968).
A. Marmodoro and J. Hill (eds), *The Author's Voice in Classical and Late Antiquity* (Oxford University Press, 2013).

A. Mayor, *Greek Fire, Poison Arrows and Scorpion Bombs, Biological and Chemical Warfare in the Ancient World* (Overlook Duckworth, 2003).
A. Mayor, '*The Deadly River Styx and the Death of Alexander*', Princeton/Stanford Working Papers in Classics, version 1.2 (September 2010).
B. McGing, *Polybius' Histories* (Oxford University Press, 2010).
P. McKechnie, '*Diodorus Siculus and Hephaestion's Pyre*', Classical Quarterly, New Series 45, no. 2 (1995), pp. 418–32.
P. McKechnie, '*Manipulation of Themes in Quintus Curtius Rufus Book 10*', Historia Zeitschrift für Alte Geschichte 48, no. 1 (1999), pp.44–60.
R. Meiggs, *Trees and Timber in the Ancient Mediterranean World* (Clarendon Press, 1982).
R. Merkelback, *Die Quellen des griechischen Alexanderromans* (C.H. Beck, 1954; second edition 1977).
M.C.J. Miller, '*The Regal Coinage of Kassander*', The Ancient World 22, no. 2 (1991), pp.49–55.
R.D. Milns, '*The Date of Curtius Rufus and the "Historiae Alexandri"*', Latomus 25, no. 3 (July–Sept 1966), pp.490–507.
L. Mitchell, '*Born to rule? Succession in the Argead royal house*', in W. Heckel, L. Tritle and P. Wheatley, *Alexander's Empire: Formulation to Decay* (Claremont, 2007), pp.61–74.
A.D. Momigliano, '*An Unsolved Problem of Historical Forgery: The Scriptores Historiae Augustae*', Journal of the Warburg and Courtauld Institutes 17, nos 1–2 (1954), pp.22–46.
A.D. Momigliano, *Essays in Ancient and Modern Historiography* (Blackwell, 1977).
J.S. Morrison, J.E. Coates and N.B. Rankov, *The Athenian Trireme, The History and Reconstruction of an Ancient Greek Warship* (Cambridge University Press, 2000).
G. Murray, '*Stoic Philosophy*', Conway Memorial Lecture delivered 16 March 1915 (G.P. Putnams and Sons, 1915).
W.M. Murray, *The Age of Titans, The Rise and Fall of the Hellenistic Navies* (Oxford University Press, 2012).
J.H. Musgrave, '*The Human Remains from Vergina Tombs I, II and III: An Overview*', The Ancient World 22, no. 2 (1991), pp.3–9.
J.H. Musgrave, A.J.N.W. Prag, R. Neave and R. Lane Fox, '*The Occupants of Tomb II at Vergina. Why Arrhidaios and Eurydice must be excluded*', International Journal of Medical Science 7, no. 6 (2010), pp,1–15.
O. Neugebauer, *The Exact Sciences in Antiquity* (Dover Publications, 1957; 1969 edition).
J. Oates, *Babylon* (Thames & Hudson, 1979).
J.L. O'Neil, '*Royal Authority and City Law Under Alexander and his Hellenistic* Successors', Classical Quarterly 50, no. 2 (2000), pp.424–31.
H.W. Parke, *Greek Mercenary Soldiers* (Ares Publishers, 1933).
L. Pearson, *The Lost Histories of Alexander the Great* (The American Philological Association, 1960).
L. Pitcher, *Writing Ancient History* (I.B. Tauris, 2009).
V.F. Polcaro, G.B. Valsecchi and L. Verderame, '*The Gaugamela Battle Eclipse, An Archeoastronomical Anaylsis*', Mediterranean Archeology and Archeometry 8, no. 2 (2008), pp.55–64.

F.P. Polo, *The Consul at Rome, The Civil Functions of the Consuls in the Roman Republic* (Cambridge University Press, 2011).

J. Reade, *Alexander the Great and the Hanging Gardens of Babylon*, Iraq 62 (2000), pp.195–217.

M. Renault, *The Nature of Alexander* (Pantheon Books, 1975).

C. Riedweg, *Pythagoras, His Life, Teachings and Influence* (Cornell University Press, 2002).

C.A. Robinson, *The History of Alexander the Great: a Translation of the Extant Fragments and the Ephemerides of Alexander's Expedition* (Ares Publishers, 1953).

W.L. Rodgers, *Greek and Roman Naval Warfare, A Study of Strategy and Ship Design from Salamis (480 BC) to Actium (31 BC)* (Naval Institute Press, 1937; 1977 edition).

J. Roisman, *Alexander's Veterans and the Early Wars of the Successors* (University of Texas Press, 2012).

J. Roisman and I. Worthington (eds), *A Companion to Ancient Macedonia* (Wiley-Blackwell, 2010).

L.E. Roller, '*Funeral Games in Greek Art*', American Journal of Archaeology 85, no. 2 (1981), pp.107–19.

K. Rozen, '*Political Documents on Hieronymus of Cardia (323–302 BC)*', Acta Classica 10 (1967), pp.41–94.

B. Russell, *History of Western Philosophy* (Routledge, 1946; 2004 edition).

A.E. Samuel, '*The Earliest Elements in the Alexander Romance*', Historia: Zeitschrift für Alte Geschichte 35, no. 4, 4th quarter (1986), pp.427–37.

F. Schachermeyr, *Alexander in Babylon und die reichsordnung nach seinem Tode* (Verlag der Osterreichischen Akademie der Wissenschaften, 1970).

R.L. Schep, R.J. Slaughter, A.A. Vale and P. Wheatley, '*Was the Death of Alexander the Great due to poisoning? Was it Veratrum album?*', Clinical Toxology 52, no. 1 (2013), pp.72–77.

N.V. Sekunda, *The Army of Alexander the Great* (Osprey Publishing, 1984; 2008 edition).

N.V. Sekunda, '*Nearchus the Cretan and the Foundation of Cretopolis*', Anatolian studies 47 (1997), pp.217–22.

C.T. Seltman, '*Diogenes of Sinope, Son of the Banker Hikesias*', in Transactions of the International Numismatic Congress 1936, London (1938).

R Shilleto, *Demosthenis De Falsa Legatione* (Deighton, Bell and Company, 1874).

G. Shipley, *The Greek World After Alexander 323–30BC* (Routledge, 2000).

J. Siebert, '*Untersuchungen zur Geschichte Ptolemaios' I*', Munchener Beitrage zur Papyrusforchung und antiken Rechtgeschichte 56 (1969).

R.H. Simpson, '*A Possible Case of Misrepresentation in Diodorus XIX*', Historia: Zeitschrift für Alte geschichte 6, no. 4 (1957), pp.504–05.

R.H. Simpson, '*Abbreviation of Hieronymus in Diodorus*', The American Journal of Philology 80, no. 4 (1959), pp.370–79.

L.C. Smith, '*The Chronology of Books XVIII–XX of Diodorus Siculus*', American Journal of Philology 32 (1981), pp.283–90.

D. Spencer, *The Roman Alexander* (University of Exeter Press, 2002).

L. Sprague de Camp, *Great Cities of the Ancient World* (Dorset Press, 1972).

A. Stewart, *Faces of Power, Alexander's Image and Hellenistic Politics* (University of California Press, 1993).

R. Stoneman, *The Greek Alexander Romance* (Penguin, 1991).

W.W. Tarn, '*Heracles Son of Barsine*', Journal of Hellenic Studies 41 (1921), pp.18–28.
W.W. Tarn, *The Hellenistic Age. Aspects of Hellenistic Civilisation, The Social Questions in the 3rd Century* (Norton & Comp., 1923).
W.W. Tarn, *Hellenistic Civilisation* (The New American Library, 1927, 1961 edition).
W.W. Tarn, '*Alexander's Plans*', Journal of Hellenic Studies 59, no. 1 (1939), pp.125–35.
W.W. Tarn, *Alexander the Great 1, Narrative* (Cambridge University Press, 1948; 1979 edition).
W.W. Tarn, *Alexander The Great, Volume II, Sources and Studies* (Cambridge University Press, 1948; 1979 edition).
W.W. Tarn, '*A King's Notebooks*', Harvard Studies in Classical Philology 72 (1968), pp.183–204.
C.G. Thomas, *Alexander the Great in his World* (Blackwell Publishing, 2007).
R.J. van der Spek, '*Darius III, Alexander the Great and Babylonian Scholarship*', Achaemenid History 13 (2003), pp.289–346.
T. Vrettos, *Alexandria, City of the Western Mind* (The Free Press, 2001).
R. Warner (trans.), *Xenophon, A History of My Times* (Penguin, 1996).
J.S. Watson and M.C.J. Miller (eds), *M. Junianus Justinus, Epitoma Historiarum Philippicarum, Books VII–XII Excerpta de Historia Macedonia* (Ares Publishers, 1992).
P.V. Wheatley, '*Ptolemy Soter's Annexation of Syria 320 B.C.*', Classical Quarterly, New Series 45, no. 2 (1995), pp.433–40.
P.V. Wheatley, '*The Date of Polyperchon's Invasion of Macedonia and Murder of Heracles*', Antichthon 32 (1998), pp.12–23.
T. Whitmarsh, '*Alexander's Hellenism and Plutarch's Textualism*', Classical Quarterly 52, no. 1 (2002), pp.174–92.
J. Wilkes, '*The Julio-Claudian Historians*', The Classical World 65, no. 6 (1972), pp.177–92, 197–203.
I. Worthington (ed.), *Demosthenes: Statesman and Orator* (Routledge, 2000).

Index

The Index relates to names appearing in the main chapter text only, not the footnotes, book titles, image captions, or the bibliography.

Abdalonymus, 214
Abulites, 200
Academy, Athens, 229
Achaemenids, 2, 8, 10–11, 31, 128–9, 143, 202, 221–2
Achilles, 4, 78–9, 146, 231
Aconite, wolfsbane, 82
Acropolis, 12
Adea Eurydice, 161–2, 164, 167–8, 171, 174, 176, 184, 215, 217, 219–20
Adriatic, 199
Aeacides, 150, 168, 171
Aegae, vii, viii, 9, 34, 38, 78, 110–11, 140, 161, 209, 212, 236
Aegean, 10, 35, 84, 163, 188–9, 223
Aelian, xii, 3, 47, 59, 78, 86, 98, 106–10, 126, 152, 160, 190, 204
Aeneas, 47
Aeropus I, 40
Aesop, 145
Afghanistan, 9, 144
Africa, 14, 36
Agamemnon, 76
Agathocles, father of Lysimachus, 127
Agathocles, son of Lysimachus, 219
Agathos Daimon, 114
Agenor, father of Peithon, 186, 205
Agnon, *see* Hagnon
Agora, Athens, 229

Agrianians, 161, 202
Ajax, 76
Alcetas, brother of Perdiccas, 54, 130, 132–4, 157–8, 162, 174–5, 177, 180, 212, 214
Aleppo, 213
Alexander III, the Great, 2, 6, 24, 82, 231
Alexander IV, 82, 123, 132, 150, 159, 166, 176, 192–3, 210, 218–19, 222, 234
Alexander Lyncestis, 160, 172
Alexander Molossus, 161, 217
Alexander, son of Polyperchon, 132, 160, 167, 191
Alexander Severus, 227
Alexandretta/Alexandria ad Issus, 213
Alexandria, Egypt, 4, 11, 16–17, 26, 41, 57–9, 64, 79, 91, 98, 109–10, 112–15, 119, 207, 212, 226–9, 234
Alexandrias, other cities found by Alexander, 12, 212–13
Amastris, 157, 221
Amazons, 162
Amisus, 128, 210
Ammon, Zeus-Ammon, Jupiter Ammon, Temple of, Ammonium, 20, 28, 37, 58, 68, 69, 79, 110, 113, 173–4, 223
Amphimachus, 142, 150, 169, 207

Amphipolis, 33, 150, 181, 187, 210, 223
Amyntas, general Gaugamela, 43
Amyntas Perdicca, 11, 32, 161
Anatolia, 9, 32, 35, 45, 52, 62, 77, 95, 129, 130, 132, 136, 141, 146, 148, 159, 166, 168–9, 171, 179, 185, 199, 209–12, 214
Anaxarchus, 15, 79
Andromeda, Euripides tragedy, 18
Andron, *see* Hagnon
Antony, Mark, 212, 226
Antigenes, 35, 55, 132, 139, 148, 150, 177, 182, 186, 215–16
Antigonus II Gonatas, 176
Antigonus III Doson, 75
Antigonus the One-Eyed, 9, 32, 35, 41, 54–5, 62, 68, 96–9, 110, 115, 117, 122–3, 125–6, 128–30, 132–3, 135–52, 154–74, 176–95, 199–201, 206–11, 213–19, 222, 230
Antioch, 213
Antiochus, father of Seleucus, 127
Antimenes, 10
Antipater, regent, 9–13, 18–19, 32, 34–6, 45, 51, 54–5, 62, 66–8, 74–5, 77, 85, 87, 93–4, 96–7, 100, 108, 111, 116, 121–2, 129–38, 146–7, 155–63, 167, 169–70, 172–84, 191–4, 202, 213, 216–20
Apame, daughter of Spitamenes, 151
Apamea, 213
Apelles, 181
Apis, 112
Apollo, 47, 82, 131
Apollo, Temple of at Delphi, 69, 202
Apollonides, 133, 135
Appian of Alexandria, 109
Arabia, Arabs, Arabian Peninsula, 15–16, 33, 36, 50, 103–104, 108, 117, 199–200, 211

Arachosia, Arachosians, 69, 144, 150, 205
Arbela, *see* Gaugamela
Arcesilaus, governor of Mesopotamia, 207, 214
Arcesilaus, philosopher, 73
Archaic period, 79
Archelaus, garrison commander at Tyre, 213
Archias, 85, 122
Archon, governor of Babylon, 55, 207–208
Areia/Areia-Drangiana, 69, 150, 205
Areopagus, 72
Ares, 69, 97
Argead, Argead line, vii, 3, 11, 32, 43–4, 47, 62, 76, 78–9, 105, 111, 116, 120, 123, 138, 140, 145, 159–60, 162, 165, 168, 171–3, 176, 185, 188, 193, 216–19, 222–3
Argaeus, 69
Argos/Argives, 69, 190, 191
Argive Heraion, 190
Argyraspides, see Silver Shields
Ariarathes, 128–9, 212
Aristander of Termessus, 34, 110
Aristodemus of Miletus, 155, 158
Ariston of Kea, 73
Ariston of Pharsalus, 178, 182–3
Aristonicus, 122
Aristonus, 9, 42, 45, 54–5, 73, 127, 130, 150, 157, 179, 186–7, 214
Aristotle, 5, 10, 13, 37, 52, 70–1, 73–7, 84–6, 91, 99, 167, 192, 195, 227, 229
Aristoxenus of Tarentum, 34
Armenia/Armenian, 130, 136, 144, 147, 183, 210, 212
Arrhidaeus, *see* Philip III Arrhidaeus
Arrhidaeus, satrap of Hellespontine Phrygia, 141, 169–70

Index

Arrian, xi-xiv, 3, 5, 8, 15, 20, 25–7, 38–9, 41, 43, 46, 53, 56, 58, 62–3, 85–6, 90, 94–5, 99, 101, 104, 106–11, 114, 116, 121–3, 127, 169, 179, 186–7, 190, 208, 211, 218, 222, 227–31, 234–6
Arsinoe, daughter of Ptolemy I Soter, 219
Artabazus, 151, 200, 220–2
Artaxerxes II, 83
Artaxerxes III Ochus, 24, 220–1
Artemis, temple at Tauropolis, 33
Artemisia, curse of, 112
Asander, 68, 93, 95–7, 126, 172, 174, 176, 178, 209, 216
Asclepius, 13–14, 24, 79, 82, 113–14, 116
Asclepius, temple of at Ecbatana, 13, 113
Assembly of Macedones, Common Assembly, 11, 27, 29–34, 37–63, 72, 75–6, 78, 97, 110, 127, 150–1, 163, 167, 181, 206, 216, 219, 222
Assyria, Assyrians, 15, 100, 138, 144
astronomical diaries, Babylon, viii, 100
Atalante, 132, 215, 221
Athena, 67, 69, 75, 97, 131, 174, 223
Athena, temple of in Athens, 69
Athena, temple of at Cyrnus, 33
Athena, Lindian, Rhodes, 188
Athena *Poliouchus*, 189
Athenaeus, 18, 61, 91, 99, 106, 108–109, 152, 160
Athenodorus of Tarsus, 230
Athens, 10, 16, 28, 35, 36, 69, 70–5, 82, 84–5, 105, 111, 115, 127, 160, 167, 170, 192, 202, 217, 230
Atropates, 205–206
Attalus, son of Andromenes, 8, 48, 51, 54, 111–12, 132, 134, 157, 174, 189, 213–15, 221

Attarin Mosque, 58
Attica, 71, 75
Audata, 161
Augustus, Octavian, 42, 226–7, 230, 235
Autumn crocus, 87
Avenue of Sphinxes, 58
Axius River, 183
Azorus, 150

Babylon, Babylonia, Babylonian, *passim*
Babylonian Chronicle, 44, 168, 192
Babylonian settlement, 25, 27, 29, 45, 51–2, 56, 63, 95, 112, 119, 122, 127, 197, 200, 211, 234
Bacche, Euripides play, 173
Bactra/Balkh, 9
Bactria, 9, 24, 41, 68–9, 94, 151, 166, 182, 185–6, 200, 203, 205–206, 222
baggage train, 135, 144–9, 181, 194, 204
Bagoas, vizier, 83
Bagoas, eunuch of Darius III, 106, 108
Balacrus, 199, 209
Balkans, 2, 202
Banks, banking, 72
Barbarians, 27, 40, 56, 223
Bardylis, 176
Basileus, basileia, 29
Battle of the Kings, *see* Ipsus
Bel-Marduk, 100
Bequaa Valley, 141, 211
Berenice, 217
Bergama, *see* Pergamum
Beroia, *see* Aleppo
Berossus, 100
Bithynia, 170, 209–10
Bitumen, 14, 36
Black Sea, 128, 200
Bodrum, *see* Halicarnassus

Bodyguards, 32, 34, 39, 42, 44, 46–7, 52–4, 56, 62, 77, 80, 87, 93, 104–105, 117, 127, 132, 144, 151, 186, 199, 206, 211, 213, 216, 223
Boeotia, Boeotians, League, confederacy, 69, 115, 190
Borsippa, 15
Bosphorus, 171
Brahmins, 84
British Museum, 59
Britannicus, 235
Bronze Age, 71, 82
Brucheion, 115
Bucephalus, 4
Byzantium, 166

Caeria, 161
Caesar, Julius, 44, 133, 226
Calanus, 116
Calas, 209
Calauria, 85
Caligula, 44, 50, 226–7, 236
Callias of Athens, 72
Callisthenes, 4, 14, 79, 92, 99–100, 173, 228
Cambyses, son of Cyrus, 119
Camels, 55, 111
Canaanites, *see* Phoenicians
Canopic jars, 64
cantons, Macedonia, 9, 30
Cappadocia, 54–5, 61, 68, 98, 128–31, 135, 138–9, 151, 154, 165, 175, 177, 180–1, 200, 204, 207, 209–10, 212
Cappadocia Pontica, 128
Cappadocia near Taurus, 128
Caracalla, 226–7
Caria, Carians, 49, 68, 79, 99, 130, 135, 141, 174, 180, 209
Carmania, 69, 205
Carthage, Carthaginians, 14
Caspian Gates, 205

Caspian Sea, 210
Cassander, 19, 31, 50, 54, 62, 74, 82, 87, 96, 99, 112, 115, 117, 121, 123, 132, 139, 141, 144, 150–1, 158, 160–72, 176–8, 182–7, 190–5, 210, 211, 218–19, 230
Cato the Younger, 230
Celaenae, 134, 156, 158–9, 162, 177, 209
Chaeronea, 194
Chalcis, Chalcidians, 74–5, 85
Chalcidice, 123
Chaldeans, 14–15, 24, 78–9, 100, 114, 116
Chiliarch, *chiliarchos, chiliarchia*, 26, 29, 32, 39–45, 48, 54, 77, 94–5, 97, 106, 127, 129, 130, 132, 151, 162, 176, 180, 186, 198–9, 204, 207–208, 212, 214
Chios/Chians, 188
Cicero, 70, 195, 227, 230, 232
Cilicia, 32, 34–6, 68, 130, 134, 138–41, 148, 164, 169, 177, 181–5, 199, 209–14
Cilician Gates, 134, 210
Claudius, 50, 227, 235–6
Cleisthenes, 72
Cleitus, Black, 9, 41, 77, 129, 200
Cleitus, White, 35–6, 129, 141, 157, 170–1, 181, 210
Cleodice, 176
Cleomenes, administrator in Egypt, 18, 55, 214
Cleomenes, at Babylon, 8, 111, 112, 116
Cleonice, 68
Cleopatra, daughter of Philip II, 55, 68, 95, 129–30, 133, 153, 156, 161, 168, 172–3, 179–81, 193–4, 202, 212, 217–20
cleruchy system, land grants, 46, 76–7, 145–6

Cnidus, 174
Coele-Syria, 68, 140–1, 157, 177, 180, 187, 189, 211, 213–14
Coenus, 43, 69, 160
Coinage, 11, 130
Colophon, Lydia, 73
Common Assembly, see Assembly of Macedones
Companions, Alexander's high-ranking courtiers, 99, 104, 127, 134–5, 151, 165, 209, 221, 231
Companion Cavalry, 127, 184, 206, 208
Companions, foot, *pezhetairoi*, 160
Coprates, river, 143
Corinth, Corinthians, 167, 202, 230
Cossaeans, 49, 143
Crannon, 191
Crates of Thebes, 230
Cratesipolis, 217
Craterus, 9, 12, 32, 34–8, 43, 45, 47, 49–51, 54, 62, 68, 77, 87, 99, 120, 129–33, 137, 140, 146, 155–7, 160, 172, 174, 176–7, 182–3, 191, 199–200, 202, 211, 216–22
Crete, Cretans, 79, 158, 181
Cretopolis, 158, 175, 180–1, 212
Croesus, 79
Crucifixion, 129
Ctesias, 83
Cuneiform tablets, 44, 100, 117
Curtius, xi, xii, xiii, xiv, 4, 5, 11, 18, 20, 25–8, 31, 32, 39–45, 47–53, 56–7, 62–3, 78, 86, 90, 94, 101, 118, 121, 123, 160, 186, 192, 199, 208–209, 226, 228, 233–7
Cyinda, 36, 138–41, 170, 180, 199, 214
Cynics, 14
Cynnane, 68, 133, 161–2, 171, 177, 219
Cyprus, Cypriots, 36, 55, 79, 117, 130, 141, 179, 181–2, 187–8, 214
Cyrene, Cyrenaica, 200, 202, 217

Cyrnus, 223
Cyrus the Great, 77, 82–3, 119
Cyrus the Younger, 141
Cyzicus, 169–70

Daisios, 52, 102, 105, 107
Damascus, 110, 212–13, 221
Danube, 200
Dardanelles, 212–13
Darius I, 82
Darius III, 12, 24, 43, 53, 83, 94, 128, 144, 190, 220–2
Deidameia, 150, 171
Deidameia, sister of Pyrrhus, 219
Deinarchus, 167
Deinochares, 243
Deinocrates, 17
Delian League, 75
Delos, 33, 223
Delphi, Oracle, Pythia, 33, 69, 173, 202, 223
Deme, demos, 70
Demeter, 131
Demetrius the Besieger, 75, 115, 117, 149, 157, 167, 171, 173, 181, 219, 230
Demetrius of Phalerum, 115, 122, 192, 232
democracy, 30, 56, 84, 143, 187
Demosthenes, 13, 75, 85, 105, 122
Dexippus, xiii, xiv, 208
Diadem, 15, 50, 119, 140
Diadochi, 25, 41, 46, 48, 96, 118, 133, 144, 165, 197, 202, 213, 217, 219, 221, 224
Diocles, see Stasicrates
Diodorus, xi–xv, 4–5, 15–20, 25–6, 33, 35–9, 44, 52, 56–63, 83, 94, 107, 109, 116, 118, 121, 123, 129, 132, 136–40, 145, 150, 154–60, 163–8, 175–6, 180, 182–5, 187, 191,

193, 200, 203–209, 211–14, 226, 228, 233–4, 237
Diodotus of Erythrae, 91, 101
Diogenes the Cynic, 24, 202, 230
Diogenes Laertius, 37, 72–4
Diognetus, 101
Dionysius of Heraclea, 157
Dionysus, 168, 173, 190
Dios, Macedonian month, 106–107
Docimus, 54, 134, 157, 208, 214
Dodona, 33, 217, 223
Domitian, 116, 227
Donation of Alexandria, 212
Drangiana, Zarangiana, 69, 150, 205
Drypetis, 53, 221
Duris of Samos, 126, 149, 160, 168, 194

Ecbatana, 9, 13–14, 77, 106, 113, 127, 143, 200
Egypt, Egyptian, *passim*
Elagalibus, 227
Elam, 142
Elephants, 16, 52, 78, 111, 138, 142, 145–50, 157, 165, 213
Elysium, Elysian Fields, 78
Ennea-Hodoi, *see* Amphipolis
Ephemerides, *see* Royal Diaries
Ephesus, 99, 134, 168, 170
Ephippus, 18, 106, 123, 190
Epigonoi, 49, 221
Epilepsy, 44
Epimeletes, 132, 169, 198
Epirus, Epirotes, 9, 11, 39, 76, 120–1, 131, 150, 154, 156, 161, 166–71, 184, 193–4, 202, 217, 219
Epirote League, 217
Eretria, 73
Esagila Temple, 15, 80
Ethiopia, 199

Eudamus, general of Antigonus, 147, 149, 205
Eudamus brother of Peithon, 205
Eudamas, master of elephants, 148, 150
Eumaeus, 106–107
Eumenes of Cardia, *passim*
Euphrates, 15–16, 24, 36, 86, 93, 166, 211–12, 234
Europius, 178, 183
Euripides, 18, 80, 120–1, 173, 190
Europa, daughter of Philip II, 219
Eursaces, 76
Eurydice, mother of Philip II, 209
Eurydice, daughter of Antipater, 115, 157
Eurydice, daughter of Cynnane, *see* Adea Eurydice
Eurymedon, 85
Evagoras, secretary, 91

funeral bier/hearse/cortège, 37–8, 55, 57, 61, 79, 110–11, 130, 169, 208, 212–13
funeral games, 4, 47, 90, 94, 120, 171, 198, 237
funeral masks, 78
funeral pyre, Hephaestion's, 16–17, 33, 38, 61, 77, 107

Gabiene, 94, 145, 147–52, 155, 166, 174–5, 177, 194–5, 206
Gaugamela, 43, 128, 144, 188, 212
Gaul, 14
Gaurob Papyrus, 109
Gaza, 117
Gedrosia, 49
Glaucias, 192–3
Glycon, 114
Gorgias, 35, 177
Gothenburg Palimpsest, 134, 156
Great Tumulus, Aegae, 34

Greek Alexander Romance, vii, xii, 4, 66, 82, 92, 123, 154, 229
Greek Dark Ages, 72
Gymnosophists, 14, 78, 116

Hades, 78
Hadrian, 227
Hagnon of Teos, Agnon, Hagnonides, 99, 167, 170, 195
Hagnothemis, 91, 98–9, 195
Halicarnassus, 77
Halys river, 68, 209
Hannibal, 193
Harpalus, 10, 12–13, 199, 205, 209, 217
Hecataeus, 179–80
Hegesander, 34
Heidelberg Epitome, 44
Heliopolis, 55, 111
Hellas, Hellenes, 35, 79, 87
Hellebore, 87
Hellenic world, Hellenization, 2, 12, 71, 113, 173
Hellenistic era/Age/world/period, 26, 33, 39, 65, 80, 99, 105, 114, 173, 198, 211, 216, 226, 228–9, 232
Hellespont, 35–6, 56, 68, 138, 169–70, 172, 184, 209
Hellespontine Phrygia, 128–30, 141, 169–70, 180, 209–10, 220, 222
Hemlock, 84–5, 87, 122, 168, 232
Henbane, 87
Hera, Temple of, 190
Heraclea, city, 157
Heracleidae, 190
Heracleides the Thracian, 178
Heracles, hero, 20, 66–7, 69, 76, 83, 97, 173–4, 188, 190
Heracles, Alexander's son by Barsine, 32, 40, 43, 52, 54, 82, 96, 119, 123, 127, 193, 216, 220–3, 234

Hercules, 97
Hermes, 78
Hermogenes, 98
Herodotus, 29, 112, 116
Hephaestion, 13–14, 16–17, 38, 41, 43, 53, 54, 61, 77, 79, 100, 106–108, 113, 127, 143, 176, 207–208, 214, 221
Hesiod, 71
Hieronymus of Cardia, 25–6, 37–9, 41, 48–53, 56, 58, 61–3, 77, 97, 100, 119, 128, 133, 136–8, 146, 149, 154–9, 164, 169–70, 176, 184, 186, 188, 194, 200, 202–204, 206, 208, 211, 213–14, 234
Himeraeus, 122
Hipparchy, 127–8, 135, 184, 206–208
Hippocrates of Kos, Oath, 82, 84
Hipponax, 70
Holcias, 66–9, 91, 93, 95–9, 122, 125–6, 157, 167, 172, 174–8, 189
Homer, 76, 82, 231
Homeric, 2, 4–5, 13, 18, 30, 47, 74, 76, 78, 106, 120, 131, 171, 229
Homeric nod, 234
Hoplites, 175, 203–204
Hydaspes river, 69, 91, 99, 127, 186, 208
Hydaspes-Indus fleet, 91, 99, 186, 208
Hygeia, 82
Hyparchos, 51, 180, 198
Hypaspists, 128, 146, 175
Hyperaspisantes, 128
Hypomnemata, 33–5, 38–9, 100, 109
Hyrcania, 69, 205

Ichor, 5
Iliad, 5, 18, 47, 58, 76, 120, 131, 190
Illium, *see* Troy
Illyria, Illyrian, 9, 69, 91, 122, 161, 162, 174, 176, 202, 219

India, 10–16, 24, 40, 45, 52, 69, 76–8, 83–4, 112, 114, 116, 120, 127, 131, 135–6, 142, 145, 148, 154, 186, 205–206
Indus river, valley, 12, 69, 91, 99, 127, 186, 199, 202, 205, 208
Iollas, 19, 66, 75, 87, 93, 121–2, 151, 171, 177, 179, 183, 227
Ipsus, 54, 58, 115, 219, 230
Iran, Iranian, 56, 146, 194
Ishtar Gate, 49
Isis, 112
Ismenias, Ismenas, 67, 189–90
Issus, 53, 100, 190, 199, 221

Journal, xii, 3, 5, 8, 18, 20, 23, 28, 41, 53, 56, 58, 63, 79, 85, 89–91, 94–5, 98–17, 120–3, 154, 227–31, 234, 236
Julio-Claudians age, era, 233
Jupiter, 20, 97
Justin, xi, xiii, xiv, 4–5, 10, 14, 18–20, 24, 26–8, 43–8, 51, 53–4, 56, 58, 79, 94, 118, 129, 135, 149, 162, 183, 199, 207, 211, 228, 232, 235

Karun river, *see* Pasitigris
koine Greek, 211
komos, 93
Kos, 82, 122, 188
Kundi, Kundu, Kuinda, *see* Cynida

Lacedaemon, 71
Lamian War, 12, 35–6, 46, 55–6, 121, 129, 156–7, 160, 180, 191, 218
Lampsacus, 73
Langarus, 161
Laodice, 217
Laomedon, 62, 157, 177, 180–1, 211, 213–14, 216
Laranda, 129

Last Plans, 23, 33–8, 77, 153, 174, 191, 197, 223, 237
Lebanon, 36, 141
Lebedos, 188
Leochares, 202
Leonidas, *ataktoi* commander, 175
Leonnatus, 9, 39, 44–5, 48, 51, 55–6, 62, 68, 93, 127, 129, 133, 160, 176, 178–80, 186, 209–10, 212, 216, 218–20
Leosthenes, 12
Lernean Hydra, 83
Lesbos, 173, 181
Lesser Media, 205
Letter to the Rhodians, 93, 187
Levant, 212
Liber de Morte, 94
Library, Alexandria, 109, 115
Libya, 38, 114, 200, 202
Lindian Chronicle, 188
Lindos, daughter of Danaus, 188
Lindos, Rhodes, 188
Livy, 31, 232
Lucan, 235
Lucian, 24, 100, 120, 231
Lycaonia, 128–9, 154, 175, 181, 209
Lyceum, 70, 84, 229
Lycia, Lycians, 68, 130, 148, 181, 200, 209–10
Lycophron, testator, 70
Lycurgan law, 71
Lydia, Lydians, 49, 129, 134, 148, 156–7, 181, 209–10
Lysimachus, 9, 46, 54, 56, 62, 66–8, 73, 93, 95–8, 122–3, 126–7, 132, 151–2, 157, 159, 162, 165, 171–2, 174, 176, 178, 185, 189, 193, 195, 200, 202, 209–10, 216, 218–21, 230
Lysippus, 202

Macedon, Macedonians, *passim*
Maenads, *see* Mimallones

Malaria, 85–6, 146
Mallia, Mallians, 112, 145, 186
Marduk, see Bel-Marduk
Marsyas river, 134
Mausoleum, Halicarnassus, 77
Mavroneri River, 86
Mazaeus, 200, 214
Meander river, 134
Medea, 82
Medes, 69
Media, 9, 142–3, 145, 147–9, 177, 203, 205–207, 210
Media Major, 205
Media Atropatene, 206
Meleager, 35, 42–4, 47–52, 55, 68, 93, 127, 160, 178, 180–1, 216, 220
Memphis, Egypt, 55, 57–8, 112, 118
Menander, Companion, 49, 93, 135, 138, 148, 178, 181, 218
Menelaus, king of Sparta, 83
Menelaus, brother of Ptolemy, 188
Menes, 212
Menidas, 8, 111–12
Mercenaries, 2, 11–12, 15, 36, 40, 46, 49, 51, 129, 141, 146, 148, 162–4, 170, 198, 203–204, 223
Mersin, Zephyrium, 141
Mesopotamia, 71, 141–2, 146, 169, 207, 210–12
Mesopotamian Line, 68, 186, 214
Metz Epitome, xi, 27–8, 34, 47, 53–4, 63, 66, 71, 75, 92–4, 97, 104, 123, 178–9, 191, 198, 207, 217, 219, 227–8, 234–5
Middle Academy, 73
Middle Ages, 4, 198
Miletus, 155, 174
Mints, minting, 11, 29, 130, 146, 199
Mount Ida, 133
Mount Lebanon, 36
Mount Taurus, 130

Mycenaen Greece, 72
Myllenas, 101
Myriobiblion, xiii–xiv

Nearchus, 14–15, 25, 40–1, 43, 54, 93, 102, 117, 127, 143, 148–9, 178–9, 181, 187, 209, 222
Nebuchadnezzar II, 24, 32, 49, 79
Nectanebo II, 58–9, 114
Negev, 213
Neoptolemus, Molossian noble, 98, 130–1, 146, 149, 176, 210
Neoptolemus II, son of Cleopatra, 193
Nepos, 77, 151, 157–9, 165–8, 170, 180, 183, 186
Nero, 226–7, 233, 235–6
Nestor, 18
Nicaea, daughter of Antipater, 55, 110, 122, 129–30, 156–7, 163
Nicanor of Stagira, 13
Nicanor, governor of Cilicia, 68, 177
Nicanor, son of Parmenio, 171
Nicanor, garrison commander Athens, 74, 167, 170
Nicanor, general of Ptolemy, 180
Nicanor, *strategos* of Media, 177
Nicanor, general of Antigonus, 206–207
Nicesipolis of Pherae, 172
Nicocles, 130
Nicomachean Ethics, 77
Nile/Delta/valley/Upper, 55–6, 58, 85, 110–11, 132, 211
Nonacris, 86
Nora, 97–8, 121, 136–9, 152, 154–9, 164, 169–71, 175, 177–8, 181, 185, 189, 195

Ochus, son of Darius III, 221
Odrysian Kingdom, 56
Odysseus, 83

Odyssey, 58, 82
Oedipus, 120
Old Testament, 213
Olympia, 12, 69
Olympia, Athenian festival, 85
Olympias, 5, 11–13, 19, 31, 44, 53, 55, 58, 62, 68–9, 74–5, 95–8, 114, 117, 121–3, 126–7, 129, 137, 141, 144, 150–3, 156, 159–60, 163, 165–74, 176, 178–9, 183–95, 190–4, 202, 217–18, 220, 222–3
Olympian Zeus, 97
Olympic Games, 12
Onesicritus, 5, 14, 25, 119–20, 178–9
Opis, 12, 28, 31, 34, 36, 40, 411, 160
Orcynia, 135–8, 145, 154, 157, 175, 181
Orestis, canton, 39
Orontes river, 132, 213
Orontes, father of Perdiccas, 127
Orontes, satrap of Armenia, 144, 184, 210
Orphic rites, 114, 173
Osiris, Osiris-Apis, 112
Ovid, 82
Oxyartes, father of Roxane, 68–9, 166, 200, 220
Oxyathres, 221

Paeonia, Paeonians, 161, 202
Pakistan, 9
Pamphlet, viii, xi–xii, 3–5, 18, 23, 27, 40, 53–6, 63, 71, 74–5, 77, 81, 85–7, 89–99, 103–105, 112, 114, 118–23, 125–8, 131, 140, 144, 152–6, 160–1, 166–7, 171–202, 205, 207, 210–11, 218–19, 222–4, 228–9, 234–7
Pamphylia, 68, 148, 181, 200, 209, 211
Panacea, 82
Panaetius, 230
Paphlagonia, 68, 98, 128, 130, 200, 210

Papyrus, 2, 36, 92, 98, 100, 110, 115, 146
Paraetacenae, 136, 145–6, 166, 182
Parian Chronicle, Marble, 57
Parmenio, 9, 19, 27, 31, 77, 175, 200, 222
Paropanisadae, 69, 166, 205
Parthenius river, 210
Parthia, Parthians, 69, 142, 183, 200, 205, 226
Parysatis, 83, 220–2
Pasargadae, 143, 202
Pasitigris river, 143
Patrocles, 207
Patroclus, 5, 78
Pausanias, travelographer, 82, 86, 110–11
Pausanias, physician, 87
Peace of the Dynasts, 95, 193
Peisaeus, father of Aristonus, 127, 186–7
Peithon son of Agenor, 186, 205
Peithon son of Crateuas, 8, 9, 44–6, 54–5, 62, 68–9, 93, 111–12, 127, 132, 141–9, 169, 177–8, 181–6, 202–207, 210, 215–16
Pella, 9, 34–5, 45–6, 50, 54, 76, 78–9, 100–11, 126, 133, 136, 138–9, 144, 146, 150–1, 155–70, 173–6, 180, 184, 191, 194, 199, 209, 219, 222
Pelopidas, 190
Peloponnese, 12, 86
Pelusium, 55, 111
Pentheus, 173
Perdiccas, Bodyguard, *passim*
Perdiccas I, 111
Perdiccas III, 161
Parchment, 38, 165
Pergamum, 43, 52
Peripatetics, 70, 73, 75, 192

Persepolis, 143–4, 149, 165–6, 184, 202, 210
Persia, Persians, 5, 41, 69, 142–3, 160, 180, 184, 188, 202, 207, 221–2
Persian army, 48, 204–205
Persian Empire, 2, 9, 26, 61, 169, 202, 211
Persian Gulf, 15
Persian nobility, 10–11, 32, 79, 127, 144, 151, 199
Persian politics, 119
Persian royals, Achaemenids, viii, 5, 8–9, 13, 24, 53–4, 79, 127, 157, 188, 190, 199, 220, 222
Persian rule, 128
Persian satraps, 144, 184, 200, 214, 222
Persian texts, 83, 100
Persian treasuries, 10–11
Peucestas, 8, 13, 46, 48, 54, 56, 62, 69, 93, 111–12, 127–128, 132, 142–4, 148–50, 165, 178, 184, 202, 205–10, 216, 221
Phaedimus, 148
Phalangites, 203
Phalanx, 43, 47–9, 52, 61, 76, 132, 146–8, 203–204
Phalerum, *see* Demetrius of Phalerum
Pharnabazus, 151, 222
Pharos, 16
Phila, daughter of Antipater, 157, 176–7, 183, 217–19
Philip II, father of Alexander, 8–9, 12, 30–1, 34, 43, 74, 82, 85, 100, 105, 126–7, 131, 135, 149, 151, 161, 166, 171–2, 179, 190, 193, 209, 218, 222–3
Philip III Arrhidaeus, 43–4, 49, 52–5, 119, 132, 159, 161–2, 167–8, 171, 176–7, 184, 192, 202, 216–17, 219–20
Philip, at Medius' banquet, 178, 183

Philip, son of Antipater, 19
Philip, satrap of Bactria, 69
Philip son of Machatas, 205
Philip, satrap of Parthia, 183
Philip the engineer, 178, 183
Philip the physician, 183
Philistines, 213
Philon, Athenian general, 203
Philotas, at Medius' banquet, 178
Philotas, son of Parmenio, 19, 27, 31, 207
Philotas, general in Parthia, 205
Philotas, satrap of Cilicia, 182
Philoxenus, *strategos* and treasurer, 49, 182, 199, 214
Phocion, 85, 160, 167, 170
Phoenicia, Phoenicians, 68, 72, 78, 130, 141, 169, 170, 177, 189, 211–12, 214
Photius, xiii, xiv, 53, 56, 62, 169, 202, 208
Phrasaortes, 200
Phrataphernes, 69, 200
Phrygia, Phrygians, 35, 129–30, 132, 134, 148, 154, 156–7, 170, 174–5, 180–1, 209
Phrygia, Greater, 68, 200, 209
Phrygia, Lesser, 209
Hellespontine Phrygia, 128–30, 141, 169, 180, 209–10, 220, 222
pike-bearers, 30, 203
Piraeus, 141, 167
Pisidia, Pisidians, 129–30, 157–8, 204, 209, 211–12, 214, 217
Plataea, Plataeans, battle at, 115, 204
Plato, Platonist doctrine, 34, 84–5, 108, 229, 231–2
Pliny the Elder, 83, 86, 232
Plutarch, xi–xiv, 3, 5, 8, 13, 17, 20, 26–7, 38, 50–3, 58, 62–3, 71–2, 77–8, 83, 85–7, 91, 94, 99–109, 112–16, 120–1, 126, 134–7, 143–52,

154–6, 159, 165, 172–3, 175–6, 179, 181, 183–4, 193–5, 222, 226–8, 230–1, 236
Poison, poisoning, viii, 3–5, 10, 13, 18–20, 54, 66, 70, 74, 81–7, 90–1, 93–4, 107, 121, 125, 144, 152, 171–2, 179, 183, 192, 227–8, 235
Polemaeus, nephew of Antigonus, 122, 136
Polemon, 54, 134, 157
Polyaenus, 98, 147, 151, 161–2, 175, 181
Polybius, 75, 100, 230, 233
Polydamas, 177, 182
Polydorus, 182
Polyperchon, 35, 43, 96–8, 123, 126, 132, 138–9, 141–2, 144, 150, 153, 157–70, 172, 174, 177–8, 191, 194–5, 210–11, 217
Pompey the Great, 133, 226
Portents, 3, 8, 14, 18, 24–5, 58, 68, 93, 114, 116, 118, 131, 140, 237
Porus, 69
Poseidon, 13
Poseidon, Temple, Calauria, 85
Pothos, 232
Primogeniture, 31
Proskynesis, 160, 190
Prostates, prostasia, 45, 156, 217, 220
Pseudepigrapha, 121
Ptolemies, Dynasty, Egypt, 26, 58, 92, 98, 114, 119, 202
Ptolemy, son of Pyrrhus, 388
Ptolemy I Soter, 9, 20, 25, 40–51, 54–63, 66–9, 75, 77, 84, 93, 95, 97–9, 104, 109–12, 117–20, 122–3, 125–31, 140–1, 152, 154, 157, 162, 165, 169, 172–4, 177–8, 180, 183, 185–91, 193, 199–200, 202, 207–11, 213–14, 216, 218, 218, 222, 227–31

Ptolemy II Philadelphus, 58, 109, 115, 122, 212
Ptolemy III Euergetes, 109
Ptolemy IV Philopater, 58
Ptolemy XI, 59
Pydna, 150, 187, 192–3, 218, 221
Pyrrhus of Epirus, 100, 120–1, 151, 168, 193, 219
Pythagoras, 79, 231
Pythia, 80

Quintas Sertorius, 159, 193

Rhetoric, 2, 4–5, 19, 26–8, 38, 48–9, 61, 63, 70, 75, 92, 105, 121, 188, 235
Rhodes, 37, 66–9, 93, 97, 140, 187–9, 226, 233–4
Roman-era authors, xi–xv, 3–4, 14, 20, 25–8, 33, 39, 43, 50, 63, 66, 91, 98, 139, 162, 225–37
Roman army, legions, 39, 41, 57, 100
Roman Gods, 97
Roman Republic, 226, 232
Roman senate, 97
Rome, Roman era, 14, 25, 42–3, 50, 57, 72, 74, 98, 109, 126, 198, 202, 223, 226–37
royal pages, 24, 28, 48, 183
Royal Diaries, 18, 20, 38, 90, 93, 111, 228, 231
Royal Road, 129, 168, 207, 212

Sabictas, 128
Salamis, island, 72
Salamis, Cyprus, 117
Salmydessus, 200
Samaria, city, 123
Samos, 73, 126, 149, 168, 194
Samsun, 210
Saqqara, 58

Sardis, 129, 133–4, 156, 168, 173, 181, 193–4, 207, 218–19
Sarissa 146, 203
Sceptics, 73, 229–30
Sceptre, 140
Scipio Aemelianus, Africanus the Younger, 230
Scipio Africanus, 226
Scipionic Circle, 230
Scylla, 92
Scythia, Scythians, 83, 199
Second Successor War, viii, 97, 138, 155, 210
Seleucid Empire, 15, 123
Seleucus I Nicator, Bodyguard, 8, 9, 15, 46, 54–5, 68, 103, 111–12, 123, 127–8, 132, 141, 143, 146, 150–2, 178, 183–6, 193, 202, 205–10, 213–16, 219, 230
Sema, Alexandria, 58
Seneca the Younger, 230, 232, 235
Serapis, Serapeum, 8, 14, 98, 103, 105, 111–17
serpents, *see* snakes
Seuthes III, 56
Severus, Septimus, 226
Shiraz, Iran, 56
Sibyrtius, 69, 144, 150, 184
Sicily, 14, 57, 190
Sidon, 214
Silver Shields, 55, 139–41, 143, 145–50, 164, 167, 175, 186, 194, 226
Simmias, father of Polyperchon, 159
Sinai, 200, 213
Sirrush, *see* Scylla
Sisines, client king of Cappadocia, 139
Sisygambis, 221
Siwa, 17, 20, 79, 107, 110, 114, 173, 202
Snakes, serpents, 69, 76, 83, 114–15
Socrates, 44, 84

Sogdia, Sogdiana, Sogdian Rock, 9, 12, 151, 182, 200, 202, 205, 222
Somatophylakes, *see* Bodyguards
Sophocles, 76
Sosigenes, 130, 141
Sparta, Spartans, 12, 30, 71, 151, 195
Sphinxes, Avenue of, 58
Spitamenes, 151, 182
Stagira, 13, 74–5
Stasander, 150, 181–2, 205
Stasanor of Soli, 69, 178, 181–2, 205
Stasicrates, 17
Stateira, 53, 220, 222
Stoics, stoicism, 73, 229–32
Strabo, 34, 57, 59, 84, 86, 114, 128, 139
Strategos, *strategia*, 151, 155, 177, 205–206
Strato of Lampsacus, 73,
Stratonice, wife of Antigonus, 217
Stratonice, daughter of Demetrius the Besieger, 219
Stream of Ocean, *see* Oceanus
Strychnine, 83, 85–6, 192
Strymon river, 161
Styx, 78, 86
Successor Wars, 3, 26, 31, 52, 56–8, 62, 73–4, 87, 91–2, 94, 96–7, 99, 101, 108, 110, 117, 122–3, 125–9, 146, 179, 188, 197, 202, 217, 219, 224, 237
Suicide, 76, 157, 168, 221, 230–2
Sulla, dictator, 59
Superstition, 14–15, 52, 84, 87, 93, 116, 140
Susa, 10, 12–13, 40–1, 46, 49, 52–3, 72, 77, 80, 127, 139, 142–4, 187, 199, 203, 205, 207, 221–2, 231
Susiane, 139, 142, 186, 200, 205
symposia, 79, 93, 103
synedrion, 129, 163
Synnada, 134

Syria, Syrians, 57, 59, 61, 68, 110–11, 132–3, 169, 185–7, 202, 210, 213–14, 221
Syria, Coele, 68, 140–1, 157, 177, 180, 187, 189, 211, 213–14
Syria, Upper Syria, 211, 214
Syria, lower, 211, 213
Syria, Greater, 211, 213–14
Syria, Mesopotamian, 211
Syrian tetropolis, 213

Tacitus, 227, 231
Taenarum, Cape, 12, 36
Tajikistan, 9
Tapurians, 49
Tarentum, Tarentines, 34, 148–9
Taurus ranges, 36, 128, 138, 175, 199, 209, 212
Taxation, 10, 75, 146, 211
Taxiarch, 43, 160
Taxila, 10
Tean Curses, 84
Telemachus, 83
Telmessus, 134, 181
Ten Attic Orators, 112
Teos, 99, 182, 195
Termessus, 110, 157, 175, 212
Teutamus, 148–50
Thapsacus, 36
Thaumasias, 73
Thebes, Boeotia, 19, 115, 189–90, 230
Themistocles, 79
Theophrastus, 70, 73, 84–5, 105, 192
Theopompus, 105
Theseus, 82, 173
Thessaly, Thessalians, 9, 14, 19, 79, 150, 172–3, 180, 182, 191, 218
Thessalicus, 189–90
Thessalonice, 68, 150, 172–3, 193, 218–19, 221
Third Sacred War, 131

Thrace, Thracians, 56, 62, 67–8, 73, 159, 161, 168, 172, 178, 183, 200, 219, 223
Thucydides, 29
Tiberius, 42
Tigris, 212
Tlepolemus, satrap of Carmania, 69
Tlepolemus, son of Heracles, 188
Toxicology, 81–7
Trabzon, *see* Trapezus
Trapezus, 128, 200
Treasurers, treasuries, 8, 10, 12, 51, 136, 139, 142, 164, 185, 198–9, 209
Triballians, 202
Trierarchs, trierarchies, 36, 99, 127, 186, 208
Triparadeisus, 97, 132, 142, 155, 157, 160, 169–70, 174, 177, 180–6, 189, 197, 202, 206–11, 214–16, 220
Triremes, 38, 68, 127, 131, 187, 189
Troad, 209
Trogus, Gnaeus Pompeius, xii–xiv, 4, 24, 56, 62–3, 228
Troy, Trojans, Trojan War, 5, 24, 47, 78, 120, 133, 188, 223
Tyche, 24, 79, 139
Tymphaea, Tymphaeans, 159
Tyre, Tyrians, 131, 134, 188, 190, 213

Uzbekistan, 9

Vergina, ancient Aegae, vii, 34, 38, 78, 140
Vespasian, 235
Vitellius, 227
Vulgate genre, xii, 4–5, 18–19, 23, 26, 28–9, 39, 43, 47, 58, 61–2, 74, 78–9, 84, 86, 89–90, 94, 103–105,

110, 116, 118–19, 121, 179, 192, 227–8, 232–3

wedge formations, 135, 204
Wills, development of, 65 ff
Wolfsbane, *see* aconite
Wormwood, 87

Xanthikos, 51
Xenophon, 30, 82–3, 119–20, 128, 136, 141
Xennias, 149
Xerxes, 15, 48

Zagros Mountains, 146
Zarangiana, *see* Drangiana
Zeno of Citium, 229–30, 232
Zenobius, 58
Zephyrium, 141
Zeus, 13, 69, 75, 79, 86, 97, 107, 112, 173, 223
Zeus-Ammon, oracle at Siwa, 28, 79, 110, 113, 173
Zeus, temple of at Dium, 33
Zeus, Philippic, 173